I0824114

1–3 John

BAKER EXEGETICAL COMMENTARY ON THE NEW TESTAMENT

ROBERT W. YARBROUGH and JOSHUA W. JIPP, EDITORS

Volumes now available:

Matthew *David L. Turner*
Mark *Robert H. Stein*
Luke *Darrell L. Bock*
Acts *Darrell L. Bock*
Romans, 2nd ed. *Thomas R. Schreiner*
1 Corinthians *David E. Garland*
2 Corinthians *George H. Guthrie*
Galatians *Douglas J. Moo*
Ephesians *Frank Thielman*
Philippians *Moisés Silva*
Colossians and Philemon *G. K. Beale*
1–2 Thessalonians *Jeffrey A. D. Weima*
James *Dan G. McCartney*
1 Peter *Karen H. Jobes*
1–3 John *Robert W. Yarbrough*
Jude and 2 Peter *Gene L. Green*
Revelation *Grant R. Osborne*

Robert W. Yarbrough (PhD, University of Aberdeen) is professor of New Testament at Covenant Theological Seminary. He has authored, coauthored, or translated numerous books.

1–3 John

Robert W. Yarbrough

BAKER EXEGETICAL COMMENTARY
ON THE NEW TESTAMENT

a division of Baker Publishing Group
Grand Rapids, Michigan

Published by Baker Academic
a division of Baker Publishing Group
PO Box 6287, Grand Rapids, MI 49516-6287
www.bakeracademic.com

Printed in the United States of America

Library of Congress Cataloging-in-Publication Data
Yarbrough, Robert W.
1–3 John / Robert W. Yarbrough.
p. cm. — (Baker exegetical commentary on the New Testament)
Includes bibliographical references and indexes.
ISBN 978-0-8010-2687-4 (cloth)
1. Bible. N.T. Epistles of John—Commentaries. I. Title. II. Title: One–three John.
BS2803.53.Y37 2008
227′.94077—dc22 2008016049

Baker Publishing Group publications use paper produced from sustainable forestry practices and post-consumer waste whenever possible.

24 25 26 27 12 11 10 9 8 7

Contents

Series Preface

The chief concern of the Baker Exegetical Commentary on the New Testament (BECNT) is to provide, within the framework of informed evangelical thought, commentaries that blend scholarly depth with readability, exegetical detail with sensitivity to the whole, and attention to critical problems with theological awareness. We hope thereby to attract the interest of a fairly wide audience, from the scholar who is looking for a thoughtful and independent examination of the text to the motivated lay Christian who craves a solid but accessible exposition.

Nevertheless, a major purpose is to address the needs of pastors and others involved in the preaching and exposition of the Scriptures as the uniquely inspired Word of God. This consideration directly affects the parameters of the series. For example, serious biblical expositors cannot afford to depend on a superficial treatment that avoids the difficult questions, but neither are they interested in encyclopedic commentaries that seek to cover every conceivable issue that may arise. Our aim therefore is to focus on problems that have a direct bearing on the meaning of the text (although selected technical details are treated in the additional notes).

Similarly, a special effort is made to avoid treating exegetical questions for their own sake, that is, in relative isolation from the thrust of the argument as a whole. This effort may involve (at the discretion of the individual contributors) abandoning the verse-by-verse approach in favor of an exposition that focuses on the paragraph as the main unit of thought. In all cases, however, the commentaries will stress the development of the argument and explicitly relate each passage to what precedes and follows it so as to identify its function in context as clearly as possible.

We believe, moreover, that a responsible exegetical commentary must take fully into account the latest scholarly research, regardless of its source. The attempt to do this in the context of a conservative theological tradition presents certain challenges, and in the past the results have not always been commendable. In some cases, evangelicals appear to make use of critical scholarship not for the purpose of genuine interaction but only to dismiss it. In other cases, the interaction glides over into assimilation, theological distinctives are ignored or suppressed, and the end product cannot be differentiated from works that arise from a fundamentally different starting point.

The contributors to this series attempt to avoid these pitfalls. On the one hand, they do not consider traditional opinions to be sacrosanct, and they are certainly committed to doing justice to the biblical text whether or not it supports such opinions. On the other hand, they will not quickly abandon a long-standing view, if there is persuasive evidence in its favor, for the sake of fashionable theories. What is more important, the contributors share a belief in the trustworthiness and essential unity of Scripture. They also consider that the historic formulations of Christian doctrine, such as the ecumenical creeds and many of the documents originating in the sixteenth-century Reformation, arose from a legitimate reading of Scripture, thus providing a proper framework for its further interpretation. No doubt, the use of such a starting point sometimes results in the imposition of a foreign construct on the text, but we deny that it must necessarily do so or that the writers who claim to approach the text without prejudices are invulnerable to the same danger.

Accordingly, we do not consider theological assumptions—from which, in any case, no commentator is free—to be obstacles to biblical interpretation. On the contrary, an exegete who hopes to understand the apostle Paul in a theological vacuum might just as easily try to interpret Aristotle without regard for the philosophical framework of his whole work or without having recourse to the subsequent philosophical categories that make possible a meaningful contextualization of his thought. It must be emphasized, however, that the contributors to the present series come from a variety of theological traditions and that they do not all have identical views with regard to the proper implementation of these general principles. In the end, all that really matters is whether the series succeeds in representing the original text accurately, clearly, and meaningfully to the contemporary reader.

Shading has been used to assist the reader in locating salient sections of the treatment of each passage: introductory comments and concluding summaries. Textual variants in the Greek text are signaled in the author's translation by means of half-brackets around the relevant word or phrase (e.g., ⌜Gerasenes⌝), thereby alerting the reader to turn to the additional notes at the end of each exegetical unit for a discussion of the textual problem. The documentation uses the author-date method, in which the basic reference consists of author's surname + year + page number(s): Fitzmyer 1992: 58. The only exceptions to this system are well-known reference works (e.g., BDAG, LSJ, *TDNT*). Full publication data and a complete set of indexes can be found at the end of the volume.

Robert W. Yarbrough
Robert H. Stein

Author's Preface

It is customary for commentary writers to muse aloud to try to justify yet another painstaking study of biblical books that have already been treated repeatedly. Nearly one hundred commentaries were written on the Johannine Epistles from patristic times to the early 1980s (for a listing see Schnackenburg 1992: 306–9); that number has grown by a dozen or more since. I offer no defense for this commentary if the requirement is earthshaking novelty, unprecedented profundity, or unrivaled comprehensiveness. Life is not long enough to do justice to even epistle-length snippets of Christian Scripture, and publishers are not going to wait a lifetime for the manuscript anyway (although Baker Academic has rivaled Job in waiting for this one). What I have written is limited in scope, incomplete in breadth, and restricted in insight. Nearing retirement Adolf Schlatter (1852–1938) took stock of his voluminous writings and pronounced them something of a crime scene (Neuer 1995: 126). Experts should prepare to encounter any number of limitations, serious even if not criminal, in the present work.

Since a commentary is supposed to be explication rather than creative or even historical fiction, its redeeming value, if any, will lie in communication of any truths observed and articulated. Here I may express more optimism, for even a modest witness to gospel verities carries divine promise. Oden (2003: 82–96; cf. Maier 1994: xiv) underscores this persuasively. Meteoric growth in what often looks like a fairly bibliocentric global Christian population echoes that notion (Jenkins 2002; 2006; for the continuing demise of popular support for the post-Christian ideologies that inform much Western biblical scholarship and church life, see Shiflett 2005). Like the exegetical labors of many interpreters through the ages, my work on the biblical text has grown out of a sense of conviction of sin, seizure by divine grace, and fascination with biblical wisdom as I sometimes think I understand it. I have yet to see Jesus with my eyes, but that was true of his followers long before the first century ended (cf. 1 Pet. 1:8), and they somehow managed a compelling affirmation of living faith in their benighted setting. Readers must judge whether here or there I have replicated their precedent in ours.

A few distinctive emphases in what follows are worth mentioning.

1. I have often related what John writes to aspects of Jesus's work or teaching. In other words, I have treated the history of Jesus's earthly ministry, as presented by the canonical Gospels and particularly the Fourth Gospel,

as if it really happened and carried a force that might well have left a fairly direct imprint in the Johannine Letters decades later. More commonly these letters are viewed as extrusions of a "Johannine theology" or community with minimal rootage in any particular historical chain of events. This becomes clear, for example, precisely in a study of the theology of John's Epistles that focuses on "Jesus in tradition and faith."[1] More convincing is the thesis that behind John's Gospel and John's Letters stands the voice of one or more eyewitnesses, a view that has recently received weighty and welcome support from Bauckham (2006).

2. I have used computer aids extensively to explore linguistic ties between John's Epistles and the LXX. More could have been done, but this commentary makes more extensive and explicit reference to LXX parallels than was feasible until very recently.
3. In the additional notes, which appear at the end of each exegetical unit, this commentary offers remarks on every textual variant in John's Epistles found in NA^{27}.[2] There were several motivations for this: (a) To my knowledge it had never been done before. (b) Students often cut their exegetical teeth on 1 John, scratch their heads over the critical apparatus, and are urged by professors to pay attention to the variants, but there is seldom much help with this in commentaries except where major variants are concerned. And there is too little classroom time for variants to be explained systematically. This commentary hopes to confirm even beginning students in the value of an attention to detail that extends to the variants. (c) For some time my interest has been piqued by the claim seemingly gaining traction of late that widespread scribal corruption and cross-fertilization among textual groups makes the text of much of the NT (never mind its message) suspect. Having gone through every variant of John's Letters, most of them (as it turns out) manifestly minor, I have found no reasonable grounds for suspicion of the soundness of our knowledge of what the author of these epistles wrote. Doubts cast on the integrity of the NT text and commended to undergraduates in a widely used NT introduction (Ehrman 1997: 414–21; 2004: 479–89) are, if 1–3 John are a fair indication, considerably overstated (see also Ehrman 2005 and the reply of Wallace 2006).

1. Lieu 1991: 71–79: Jesus's "coming, death, and continuing presence are not past events to be looked back and reflected on" (75); Jesus's "present meaning for believers" pales beside "the relationship with God which really defines the continuing existence of the community and its members" (78). In my view, for the author of the Johannine Epistles the past manifestation of Jesus is normative for present affirmations about him and for relationships to God claiming fidelity to him. Moreover, this is due in large measure to his eyewitness connection to Jesus and many events of his life, as the opening verses of 1 John claim. On this matter generally see Bauckham 2003.

2. In the course of research for this commentary, massively detailed text-critical analyses of all three Johannine Epistles appeared (Aland et al. 2003a; 2003b; 2005a; 2005b). I draw on these resources at points below, but in discussing variants this commentary limits itself primarily to the NA^{27} apparatus and witnesses cited there.

4. The last couple of decades have seen a burst of commentaries on John's Letters that is numerically unparalleled in the history of commentary writing on this corpus. Some of these (Marshall 1978; R. Brown 1982; Schnackenburg 1992; Strecker 1996; Painter 2002; Witherington 2006) are truly distinguished in various ways; others have notable strengths (Smalley 1984; 2007;[3] Stott 1988; Loader 1992; Sloyan 1995; Burge 1996; Rensberger 1997; 2001; Kruse 2002; 2003a; Akin 2001); and numerous others make contributions worthy of attention. I hope that by riding on the crest of this wave of sustained reflection I can pass on some of the learning that has recently emerged in astonishing quantity, though it was impossible to incorporate or even interact with it all within the guidelines of this particular commentary series. Nor was I able to incorporate as fully as I would have liked the epochal studies of Bauckham (2006) and Caragounis (2006), both of which became available only in the late stages of this commentary's production.
5. While academic protocol moves perhaps most commentators to take their primary discussion partners from among current doyens of the discipline, I have (without ignoring our day's intellects and critical industries) tried to draw on a range of thinkers from across temporal and cultural boundaries. In part with the help of the Ancient Christian Commentary on Scripture (Bray 2000), but also from my own independent reading, I have drawn on various ante-Nicene fathers as well as Augustine (who has left us sermons on much of 1 John). Luther (1967) and Calvin (1988) have been close at hand as I wrote. I have pored over the classic liberal lines of Holtzmann (1908) and studied the contrasting exposition of Schlatter (1950). As a result, this commentary seeks to cash in not only on the wealth of newer scholarship (see previous point) but also on an admittedly eclectic selection of other commentaries and studies—like that of Neander (1852), born with the Jewish name of David Mendel but a convert to Christian faith, who wrote with power and insight in the crucible of a Germany wracked with division over the rise of the Tübingen School and other challenges to Christian thought and confession. For better or worse this may give my commentary a sense of addressing classic Christian concerns and not only current technical and postmodern ones. I confess that Ericson's lines ring true: "The more closely we correlate our theology with the currently popular views, the more quickly they will become irrelevant, especially with the accelerating rate of cultural and intellectual change" (2003: 26). In my choice of discussion partners, I have sought to assure that the way I have approached John's Letters and the things I have found in them are not unduly confined to my short lifetime's frequently quirky agenda. To put it another way, to a modest extent this commentary is a step in the direction of attention to *Wirkungsgeschichte*, as this is being increasingly

3. The 2007 revision of Smalley's 1984 commentary appeared too late for consideration here.

acknowledged to be fundamental to constructive biblical exposition (cf. Bockmuehl 2006).

6. Readers may detect something of a divided loyalty in this exposition. My primary frame of reference, as the footnotes will indicate, is the North American and British (i.e., Western) academy within which I received my university training beginning in the early 1970s and where I have plied my vocation since 1985. Yet for nearly two decades now I have learned from colleagues and students in places like Muslim Africa and Eastern Europe. In the North American setting, I have been privileged to study with international colleagues and students from dozens of other countries, particularly from Asia. An outcome of this is that in reading John's Letters, I confess as much interest in how they look to followers of the prophet Muhammad or to citizens of a post-Marxist country trying to rebuild after decades of political assault on Christianity or to a pastor in Singapore, as to the direct heirs of Dodd and Bultmann. How should John's counsel be regarded in a country dominated by an Eastern Orthodox, Roman Catholic, neo-Marxist, Islamic, or Asian traditionalist hierarchy? What does John have to say to Christians who are dying for the faith they profess, in part because of the trust they have based in writings like the Johannine Epistles? These are questions typically untouched in the Western professional guilds where what used to be the study of "divinity" has become the pursuit of rarified "biblical studies" or even bloodless "religions." To all of the above should be added that in recent years, despite my ordination in the Presbyterian Church in America, a confessional body with a high view of Scripture, I have been laboring pastorally in a church belonging to a mainline denomination that is selective about which parts of the Bible it thinks are still true. And so it is not only for global reasons but also for local ones that I have been forced to consider carefully the question of the enduring truth (if any) of John's message and not devote myself primarily to testing and implementing theories about possible construals of historical documents (or are they rather literary? or theological? or none of the preceding?) based on various unprovable critical hypotheses.

The six distinctives listed above are at the same time deficiencies. To strike out in some directions is to leave others unexplored. I have been consoled by Schweizer's statement (1989: 7) in another setting: "The older I get, the clearer it becomes how much we do not know. That is, by the way, a liberating insight, one that has become evident in many discussions with my wife and continually recurs to me." He concludes: "And so I become ever more thankful for those who do what I cannot, and I am learning also to accept peacefully the limits of my own gifts."

My thanks are due to student assistants who have aided me on this project at various stages over the years, among them John Vonder Bruegge, Jeff Dryden, Roy Christians, Jonathan Davis, Dong-Wong Han, Ling Luo, Mark

Birkholz, Carl Park, and Andy Naselli. I am also grateful to Baker Academic, both former editor there Jim Weaver, who invited me to contribute to this series, and present editors Jim Kinney and Wells Turner, who held open the invitation. I am particularly grateful for Wells's careful scrutiny of all aspects of the manuscript and his many suggestions for improvements. For the mistakes from which he spared me and the material improvement he has made to my formulations, I am in debt to Moisés Silva. I retain full responsibility for failures that the best efforts of many failed to root out.

Thanks are also in order to the administrations of Covenant Theological Seminary and Trinity Evangelical Divinity School for their generous sabbatical provisions that made research for this study possible.

I dedicate this work to Walter A. Elwell and J. Julius Scott Jr., both emeritus professors at Wheaton College (Illinois), who, valiantly overlooking my blue-collar limitations, managed to move me forward decisively toward critical study of the NT writings about a quarter century ago. Their dedication (in the train of Merrill C. Tenney, whom I served as graduate assistant in autumn 1980) to teaching and scholarship and their exemplification of Christian graces in often costly fashion enriched the lives of a generation of Wheaton College Graduate School students. May something here and there in these pages serve to express my thanks.

Robert W. Yarbrough
February 2008

Abbreviations

Bibliographic and General

ABD	*The Anchor Bible Dictionary*, edited by D. N. Freedman et al., 6 vols. (New York: Doubleday, 1992)
BDAG	*A Greek-English Lexicon of the New Testament and Other Early Christian Literature*, by W. Bauer, F. W. Danker, W. F. Arndt, and F. W. Gingrich, 3rd edition (Chicago: University of Chicago Press, 2000)
BDB	*A Hebrew and English Lexicon of the Old Testament*, edited by F. Brown, S. R. Driver, and C. A. Briggs (Oxford: Oxford University Press, 1966)
BDF	*A Greek Grammar of the New Testament and Other Early Christian Literature*, by F. Blass, A. Debrunner, and R. W. Funk (Chicago/London: University of Chicago Press, 1961)
CCC	*Catechism of the Catholic Church* (Liguori, MO: Liguori, 1994)
CEV	Contemporary English Version
DPL	*Dictionary of Paul and His Letters*, edited by G. F. Hawthorne and R. P. Martin (Downers Grove, IL: InterVarsity, 1993)
ESV	English Standard Version
HCSB	Holman Christian Standard Bible
ISBE	*The International Standard Bible Encyclopedia*, edited by J. Orr (Chicago: Howard-Severance, 1925)
JB	Jerusalem Bible
KJV	King James Version
LB	Living Bible
LEH	*Greek-English Lexicon of the Septuagint*, edited by J. Lust, E. Eynikel, and K. Hauspie, rev. ed. (Stuttgart: Deutsche Bibelgesellschaft, 2003)
LN	*Greek-English Lexicon of the New Testament Based on Semantic Domains*, edited by J. P. Louw and E. A. Nida, 2 vols., 2nd edition (New York: United Bible Societies, 1988–89)
LSJ	*A Greek-English Lexicon*, compiled by H. G. Liddell and R. Scott, revised by H. S. Jones (Oxford: Oxford University Press, 1968)
LXX	Septuagint
𝔐	the reading of the majority of the Byzantine textual witnesses
MM	*The Vocabulary of the Greek Testament: Illustrated from the Papyri and Other Non-literary Sources*, by J. H. Moulton and G. Milligan (1930; reprinted Grand Rapids: Eerdmans, 1980)
MT	Masoretic Text
NA^{25}	*Novum Testamentum Graece*, edited by E. Nestle, E. Nestle, and K. Aland, 25th revised edition (Stuttgart: Württembergische Bibelanstalt, 1963)

NA[27]	*Novum Testamentum Graece*, edited by [E. Nestle and E. Nestle], B. Aland, K. Aland, J. Karavidopoulos, C. M. Martini, and B. M. Metzger, 27th revised edition (Stuttgart: Deutsche Bibelgesellschaft, 1993)
NASB	New American Standard Bible (1977 edition)
NEB	New English Bible
NIDNTT	*The New International Dictionary of New Testament Theology*, edited by L. Coenen, E. Beyreuther, and H. Bietenhard; English translation edited by C. Brown, 3 vols. (Grand Rapids: Zondervan, 1975–78)
NIDOTTE	*New International Dictionary of Old Testament Theology and Exegesis*, edited by W. A. VanGemeren, 5 vols. (Grand Rapids: Zondervan, 1997)
NIV	New International Version
NLT	New Living Translation
NRSV	New Revised Standard Version
NT	New Testament
OT	Old Testament
OTP	*The Old Testament Pseudepigrapha*, edited by J. H. Charlesworth, 2 vols. (Garden City, NY: Doubleday, 1983–85)
Phillips	*The New Testament in Modern English* (trans. J. B. Phillips)
RSV	Revised Standard Version
SHNT	*Scholia Hellenistica in Novum Testamentum* (London: Pickering, 1848)
TDNT	*Theological Dictionary of the New Testament*, edited by G. Kittel and G. Friedrich; translated and edited by G. W. Bromiley, 10 vols. (Grand Rapids: Eerdmans, 1964–76)
TEV	Today's English Version
TNIV	Today's New International Version
TWOT	*Theological Wordbook of the Old Testament*, edited by R. L. Harris, 2 vols. (Chicago: Moody, 1980)
UBS[4]	*The Greek New Testament*, edited by B. Aland, K. Aland, J. Karavidopoulos, C. M. Martini, and B. M. Metzger, 4th revised edition (Stuttgart: Deutsche Bibelgesellschaft/United Bible Societies, 1993)

Hebrew Bible

Gen.	Genesis	2 Chron.	2 Chronicles	Dan.	Daniel
Exod.	Exodus	Ezra	Ezra	Hos.	Hosea
Lev.	Leviticus	Neh.	Nehemiah	Joel	Joel
Num.	Numbers	Esth.	Esther	Amos	Amos
Deut.	Deuteronomy	Job	Job	Obad.	Obadiah
Josh.	Joshua	Ps(s).	Psalms	Jon.	Jonah
Judg.	Judges	Prov.	Proverbs	Mic.	Micah
Ruth	Ruth	Eccles.	Ecclesiastes	Nah.	Nahum
1 Sam.	1 Samuel	Song	Song of Songs	Hab.	Habakkuk
2 Sam.	2 Samuel	Isa.	Isaiah	Zeph.	Zephaniah
1 Kings	1 Kings	Jer.	Jeremiah	Hag.	Haggai
2 Kings	2 Kings	Lam.	Lamentations	Zech.	Zechariah
1 Chron.	1 Chronicles	Ezek.	Ezekiel	Mal.	Malachi

Greek Testament

Matt.	Matthew	Eph.	Ephesians	Heb.	Hebrews
Mark	Mark	Phil.	Philippians	James	James
Luke	Luke	Col.	Colossians	1 Pet.	1 Peter
John	John	1 Thess.	1 Thessalonians	2 Pet.	2 Peter
Acts	Acts	2 Thess.	2 Thessalonians	1 John	1 John
Rom.	Romans	1 Tim.	1 Timothy	2 John	2 John
1 Cor.	1 Corinthians	2 Tim.	2 Timothy	3 John	3 John
2 Cor.	2 Corinthians	Titus	Titus	Jude	Jude
Gal.	Galatians	Philem.	Philemon	Rev.	Revelation

Josephus

Ant.	*Jewish Antiquities*
J.W.	*Jewish War*
Life	*Life of Josephus*

Philo

Creation	*On the Creation of the World*
Decalogue	*On the Decalogue*
Flaccus	*Against Flaccus*
Moses	*On the Life of Moses*
QE	*Questions and Answers on Exodus*
QG	*Questions and Answers on Genesis*
Spec. Laws	*On the Special Laws*
Unchangeable	*That God Is Unchangeable*

Other Jewish and Christian Writings

Ag. Her.	Irenaeus, *Against Heresies*
1 Clem.	1 Clement
2 Clem.	2 Clement
1 Macc.	1 Maccabees
2 Macc.	2 Maccabees
3 Macc.	3 Maccabees
4 Macc.	4 Maccabees
Did.	Didache
Eccl. Hist.	Eusebius, *Ecclesiastical History*
Herm. *Sim.*	Shepherd of Hermas, *Similitude*
Hom. 1 John	Augustine, *Homilies on the First Epistle of John*
Ign. *Eph.*	Ignatius, *To the Ephesians*
Ign. *Pol.*	Ignatius, *To Polycarp*
Ign. *Smyrn.*	Ignatius, *To the Smyrnaeans*
Ign. *Trall.*	Ignatius, *To the Trallians*
Jud.	Judith
Pol. *Phil.*	Polycarp, *Letter to the Philippians*
Sir.	Sirach (Ecclesiasticus)
Tob.	Tobit
Wis.	Wisdom of Solomon

Qumran / Dead Sea Scrolls

1QS	Manual of Discipline (*Serek Hayaḥad*, Rule of the Community)

Transliteration

Greek

α	*a*	ζ	*z*	λ	*l*	π	*p*	φ	*ph*
β	*b*	η	*ē*	μ	*m*	ρ	*r*	χ	*ch*
γ	*g/n*	θ	*th*	ν	*n*	σ/ς	*s*	ψ	*ps*
δ	*d*	ι	*i*	ξ	*x*	τ	*t*	ω	*ō*
ε	*e*	κ	*k*	ο	*o*	υ	*y/u*	῾	*h*

Notes on the Transliteration of Greek

1. Accents, lenis (smooth breathing), and *iota* subscript are not shown in transliteration.
2. The transliteration of asper (rough breathing) precedes a vowel or diphthong (e.g., ἁ = *ha*; αἱ = *hai*) and follows ρ (i.e., ῥ = *rh*).
3. *Gamma* is transliterated *n* only when it precedes γ, κ, ξ, or χ.
4. *Upsilon* is transliterated *u* only when it is part of a diphthong (i.e., αυ, ευ, ου, υι).

Hebrew

א	*ʾ*	בָ	*ā*	*qāmeṣ*
ב	*b*	בַ	*a*	*pataḥ*
ג	*g*	חַ	*a*	furtive *pataḥ*
ד	*d*	בֶ	*e*	*sĕgôl*
ה	*h*	בֵ	*ē*	*ṣērê*
ו	*w*	בִ	*i*	short *ḥîreq*
ז	*z*	בִ	*ī*	long *ḥîreq* written defectively
ח	*ḥ*	בָ	*o*	*qāmeṣ ḥāṭûp*
ט	*ṭ*	בוֹ	*ô*	*ḥôlem* written fully
י	*y*	בֹ	*ō*	*ḥôlem* written defectively
כ/ך	*k*	בוּ	*û*	*šûreq*
ל	*l*	בֻ	*u*	short *qibbûṣ*
מ/ם	*m*	בֻ	*ū*	long *qibbûṣ* written defectively
נ/ן	*n*	בָה	*â*	final *qāmeṣ hēʾ* (בָה = *āh*)
ס	*s*	בֶי	*ê*	*sĕgôl yôd* (בֶי = *êy*)
ע	*ʿ*	בֵי	*ê*	*ṣērê yôd* (בֵי = *êy*)
פ/ף	*p*	בִי	*î*	*ḥîreq yôd* (בִי = *îy*)
צ/ץ	*ṣ*	בֲ	*ă*	*ḥāṭēp pataḥ*
ק	*q*	בֱ	*ĕ*	*ḥāṭēp sĕgôl*
ר	*r*	בֳ	*ŏ*	*ḥāṭēp qāmeṣ*
שׂ	*ś*	בְ	*ĕ*	vocal *šĕwāʾ*
שׁ	*š*			
ת	*t*			

Notes on the Transliteration of Hebrew

1. Accents are not shown in transliteration.
2. Silent *šĕwāʾ* is not indicated in transliteration.
3. The spirant forms ת פ כ ד ג ב are usually not specially indicated in transliteration.
4. *Dāgeš forte* is indicated by doubling the consonant. Euphonic *dāgeš* and *dāgeš lene* are not indicated in transliteration.
5. *Maqqēp* is represented by a hyphen.

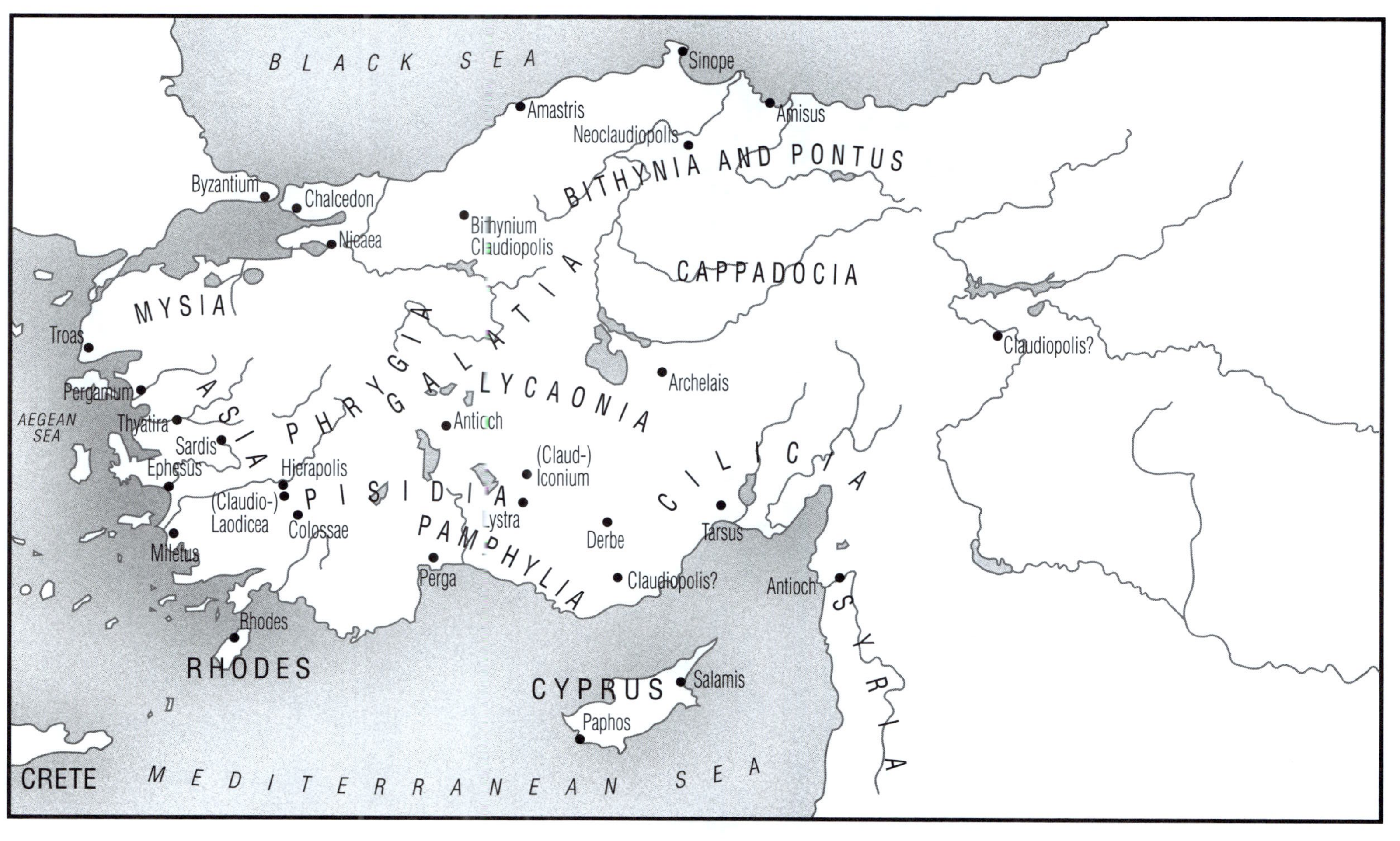
BLACK SEA
Sinope
Amastris
Amisus
Neoclaudiopolis
BITHYNIA AND PONTUS
Byzantium
Chalcedon
Nicaea
Bithynium
Claudiopolis
CAPPADOCIA
GALATIA
MYSIA
Claudiopolis?
Troas
Archelais
Pergamum
ASIA
PHRYGIA
LYCAONIA
AEGEAN SEA
Thyatira
Antioch
Sardis
(Claud-)
Iconium
Ephesus
Hierapolis
CILICIA
PISIDIA
(Claudio-)
Laodicea
Colossae
Lystra
Derbe
Tarsus
PAMPHYLIA
Miletus
Perga
Claudiopolis?
Antioch
SYRIA
Rhodes
RHODES
CYPRUS
Salamis
Paphos
CRETE
MEDITERRANEAN SEA

1 John

Introduction to the Johannine Letters

This introduction will focus primarily on 1 John. Because 2 John and 3 John left a much smaller footprint in patristic annals, there is little to discuss by way of specific evidence for matters like their date, provenance, audience, and reception history until more than a century after their putative composition. What can be said is that the language and substance of 2 John and 3 John, like that of 1 John, relate them to the Gospel of John (demonstrated concisely long ago by Weiss 1887–88: 2.186–87, 198; see also Holtzmann 1908: 362).[1] And as Hill (2004: 450) shows, knowledge of John's Gospel and at least two of his letters is probably attested in half a dozen writers prior to Irenaeus, perhaps as early as the late first century.[2] This would be within scant years of the epistles' composition and not long after the Fourth Gospel's first appearance. The Johannine tradition inscripturated in the extant canonical writings takes us back to within living memory of what the writer of John's Letters seeks to describe and apply to his readers' situation.[3]

Text

It would be frustrating, if not futile, to interpret ancient texts whose original wording is uncertain. The Johannine Epistles, in part or as a whole, have been preserved in about six hundred manuscripts, including two papyri (Klauck 1991: 4). They offer "relatively few text-critical problems," and no proposed emendation has found wide assent (1991: 5, 8).

Metzger's *Textual Commentary on the Greek New Testament* (Metzger 1994: 639–51) discusses variants at some thirty-nine junctures:

1. Note Bauckham's observation: "It is in any case generally recognized that" John's Gospel and three letters "share characteristic linguistic usages, whether these belong to the 'idiolect' of one author or to the 'sociolect' of a school of Johannine writers" (2006: 371).

2. For an index of patristic references and quotations of 1 John, see B. Aland et al. 2003b: B98–B104; for similar references to 2 John and 3 John, see B. Aland et al. 2005b: B133–35.

3. For fuller discussion of the interrelation between John's writings, see works cited below and junctures in this commentary where the language of John's Epistles is shown to resonate with that of the Fourth Gospel (on the language of John's Gospel itself, see Lieu 2005). For extended discussion of the full range of critical issues pertaining to 1–3 John, see the commentaries (Marshall 1978; R. Brown 1982; Smalley 1984; 2007; Schnackenburg 1992; Strecker 1996; and Kruse 2000) and standard NT introductions (R. Brown 1997; Schnelle 1998; L. Johnson 1999; and Carson and Moo 2005).

1:4 (2x)	2:20	3:14	5:1	5:18 (2x)
2:4	2:23	3:19 (2x)	5:2	5:20 (2x)
2:6	2:25	3:21	5:6 (2x)	5:21
2:7 (2x)	2:27	4:3 (2x)	5:7–8	
2:14	3:1	4:10	5:10 (2x)	
2:17	3:5	4:19	5:13	
2:18	3:13	4:20	5:17	

The variants listed are significant, first, in the sense that the Editorial Committee of the United Bible Societies deemed them important for Bible translators to be aware of in their work of rendering the NT into vernacular languages around the world. These variants have also been at the center of discussion in establishing what remains today's standard critical Greek text for scholarly research (NA^{27} = UBS^{4}).[4] As this commentary will demonstrate in detailed consideration of variants, no major doctrines or points of interpretation are seriously affected by manuscript deviation. The wealth of witnesses allows, if not definitive clarification, then at least well-informed conjecture, wherever ambiguities exist.

Work on the text of John's Letters has not stood still since the labors of the UBS Editorial Committee several decades ago. The Institute for New Testament Textual Research at the University of Münster in Germany conducted its own investigations and published its impressive findings on 1 John (B. Aland et al. 2003a; 2003b) and 2–3 John (B. Aland et al. 2005a; 2005b). Their selection of significant manuscript witnesses stands at 143 (not all of the six hundred extant witnesses noted above are significant for text-critical purposes): 2 papyri ($\mathfrak{P}^{9}$ [third century, containing several verses of 1 John 4] and $\mathfrak{P}^{74}$ [seventh century, containing much of 1–3 John]), 13 uncials, 117 minuscules, and 11 lectionaries (B. Aland et al. 2003b: B91). In addition, 37 other witnesses are excluded "because they are of minor importance for the history of the text" (2003b: B91), meaning that the selection of witnesses is actually about 180. There are said to be 761 "passages with variants in 1 John," most of which are scribal miscues of no significance (B. Aland et al. 2003a: 28*), like spelling or word order or inadvertent errors. In the end, "due to the simple style of 1 John there are very few passages where difficulties lead to major variants."

Like the UBS Editorial Committee, the Münster Institute scholars find that about forty 1 John passages require discussion. In a striking confirmation of the UBS committee's earlier work, as well as of the stability of the textual witness, the Institute after years of work and thousands of hours of labor concluded that it would correct the current NA^{27}/UBS^{4} Greek text at only three junctures in 1 John: (1) in 1:7 δέ (*de*, but) should be omitted; (2) in 5:10 ἐν ἑαυτῷ (*en*

4. As Moisés Silva (private correspondence) points out, some variation (e.g., Jesus Christ/ Christ Jesus) probably means little for exegesis or theology, though it will affect translation. Yet some variants that cannot be reproduced in translation may be important for exegesis or theology.

heautō, in himself) should be ἐν αὐτῷ (*en autō*, in him); and (3) in 5:18 αὐτόν (*auton*, him) should be ἑαυτόν (*heauton*, himself). In the world of scholarship, this counts as valuable corroboration of academic work old and new.

Our state of textual certainty for 1 John is very high. The numerous variants inherent in the manual copying process offer rich potential for reflection on lexical possibility and semantic nuance, but they offer no room for pessimism regarding whether we know almost exactly what the original text contained.

There are discussable variants in John's second epistle at 2 John 1, 3, 5, 8 (2x), 9, 11, 12, and 13 (Metzger 1994: 652–54). All are interesting but none critical for interpretation. The same can be said of 3 John, for which Metzger (1994: 655) discusses variants at 3 John 4, 9, and 15. These variants, plus about thirty more in 2 John and some three dozen more in 3 John, will be listed and discussed in the commentary.

Author

If the first concern of a commentary is the integrity of the text to be interpreted, the second is the identity of the writer, if this can be determined. The position taken in this commentary concurs with that expressed by Carson (2000: 132): "In line with the majority view among Christian students during the past two thousand years (though out of step with today's majority), I think it highly probable that John the apostle wrote the Fourth Gospel and the three letters that traditionally bear his name."

Extended technical justifications for this position—that John's Letters have the same author as John's Gospel and that all were written by Jesus's disciple John son of Zebedee—are accessible in NT introductions like that of Carson and Moo (2005: 229–54), in newer commentaries like those of Köstenberger (2004: 6–8) and Keener (2003: 81–114),[5] and in monographs like Blomberg's (2001: 22–41). The emerging work of Hill (2004) appears to be tending in this direction as well. Yarid (2003) makes a detailed comparison between 1 John and the Upper Room Discourse (John 13–17). Scholtissek (2004) writes of the close relationship between John's Gospel and 1 John seen in recent German scholarship, though his view that 1 John is simply an ad hoc epistolary rewrite of elements taken from the Fourth Gospel is unconvincing. Each of these studies cites corroborating sources. Finally, Bauckham (2006: 358–411) argues convincingly for the eyewitness origin of John's Gospel and John's Letters, though he thinks John is the Beloved Disciple mentioned in the Gospel, who was in turn the Elder who wrote the epistles. Bauckham's view concurs with that of this commentary that the Johannine corpus is not a literary contrivance or spiritual meditation but grows out of personal historical reminiscence of the life, teaching, and abiding will of Jesus.

5. Other commentators of the last generation or so to affirm Johannine authorship in this sense include Robinson 1985; Ridderbos 1997; and Kruse 2003a. For older commentators upholding this view (B. F. Westcott, E. Abbott, A. P. Peabody, J. B. Lightfoot, W. Sanday, H. P. V. Nunn) see Bauckham 2006: 413n2.

The Disputed Nature of the Authorship Question

It would be possible to leave the matter there. But as the series preface indicates, this commentary targets people who are "involved in the preaching and exposition of the Scriptures as the uniquely inspired Word of God." Such readers typically want to know whether what the text says is true. Some may be reading and teaching John's Letters in parts of the world where Christians face ostracism and even persecution for the faith they profess. No responsible teacher wants to be sending people into danger and perhaps death based on old writings that lack veracity. The opening verses of 1 John claim that the author was an eyewitness of Jesus's life. If this was really the case, the credibility of the letter is considerably enhanced. And since 2 John and 3 John stand in close conceptual relation—to each other and to 1 John—the gravity of their admittedly sketchy content is maximized. The Jesus Christ presupposed and presented in John's Letters takes the shape of a savior and master worthy of serious consideration and perhaps personal devotion. Luther (1967: 219) grasped this regarding 1 John: "This is an outstanding epistle. It can buoy up afflicted hearts. Furthermore, it has John's style and manner of expression, so beautifully and gently does it picture Christ to us."

D. F. Strauss (1808–74) is commonly credited with being among the first of an illustrious line of scholars who worked hard to destroy the status of the canonical Gospels as possible sources of firsthand information regarding the things they report.[6] In the judgment of many, he largely succeeded, as the generations of Gospels criticism since then attest. Grant and Tracy (1984: 12) observe that "more than a century of modern critical study make[s] it impossible for us to employ the Gospel of John in interpreting the thought of Jesus himself." But Strauss (1972: 69) also stated, "It would most unquestionably be an argument of decisive weight in favour of the credibility of the biblical history, could it indeed be shown that it was written by eye-witnesses, or even by persons nearly contemporaneous with the events narrated." I believe it can be and has been shown on cogent grounds that John's Gospel, and following from that John's Letters, are rightly understood as authored by an eyewitness to Jesus's ministry. The classic treatment, never really refuted, is Westcott (1881: v–xxxv; 1908: ix–lxvii), whose findings on this point are substantially confirmed and extended more recently by Blomberg (2001) as well as in commentaries and other works already cited above. Reim (2005: 101n15) states: "As far as I can see, in the Johannine Jesus-discourses there are virtually no words of serious substance not contained in the Synoptic words of Jesus and in Old Testament words of God or of the Messiah." The distance between John's writings and the Jesus of which they speak may be less vast and total than commonly supposed.

Nevertheless, it will not escape the notice of many conscientious preachers, students, and other thinking persons that a considerable mass of scholarly

6. For primary sources that help sketch the story, see Dawes 1999. More specifically on Strauss, see C. Brown 1985: esp. 183–87. For a lighthearted but piercing gibe at the loss of conviction of John's truth even among contemporary Christians, see Trueman 2005.

literature weighs heavily against the notion of the possibility of the Johannine tradition's close proximity to Jesus and his actual times. And so I offer a short characterization of Johannine studies in recent decades to help explain why I do not view the current majority consensus as compelling. I want readers to see why the consensus rejecting Johannine and eyewitness authorship commands respect but not necessarily obeisance. This is in no way to detract from the hard empirical work (which I do not intend to recount or extend here) that scholars like Carson, Köstenberger, Keener, Blomberg, Hill, Bauckham, and others have done, from several important vantage points, to call the consensus into question and establish the plausibility of a more credible historical account. It is enough to provide a larger context for viewing some currently dominant opinions that leave no room for dissent and a different conclusion. The point is to provide soft justification (harder justification is found in the works of the scholars referred to above) for the starting point of this commentary's reading of the texts before us.

John Son of Zebedee: Banished from the Canon

From early times and through most of the history of the church, 1 John, like the Gospel of John, was generally thought to have been written by the disciple of Jesus who bore that name (so also Witherington 2006: 394, 396). (Due probably to their brevity and limited horizon, 2 John and 3 John were much slower to receive widespread circulation and approbation in the early Christian centuries. To this day, most churches could function a whole lifetime without 2 John or 3 John in their Bibles and never miss their absence.) Rensberger (2001: 2) notes that "early on, by the second century in fact, Christian tradition identified their author as John son of Zebedee, one of the twelve apostles."[7] In the first Christian centuries, until Eusebius, there is scant record of anyone *but* this John being associated with the five books of the NT with which he is traditionally associated.[8] Witherington's peculiar claim (2006: 395n5) that "from a very early date . . . there was doubt that the Fourth Gospel, at least in its final form, was written by the same person who wrote these Epistles" is unconvincing and seems to be based solely on a statement by Isho'dad of Merv (ninth century). Similarly, Perkins (2004: 19) makes it sound like the identification of the Gospel writer with the author of one or more Johannine Letters was a post-fourth-century development. But the historical evidence runs in the exact opposite direction. Behind this encroachment of misinformation in some circles lies a fascinating story.

At the time of the Enlightenment (eighteenth century), a revolutionary approach to biblical study began to establish itself, particularly in Germany,

7. Rensberger, however, rejects Johannine authorship of these writings. R. Brown 1982: 14n26 writes that Eusebius rejects the common authorship of John's three letters, but on p. 11 he cites Eusebius's claim that the apostle John wrote all three (*Demonstration of the Gospel* 3.5.88).

8. Dionysius of Alexandria raises the question of the author of Revelation, whom he suggests could be some other John, but he underscores his conviction that the Gospel and the epistles come from the same hand (Eusebius, *Eccl. Hist.* 7.24.7; 7.25.6–8).

where Lutheran and Reformed scholars excelled in scholarly attention to the Bible. "In nineteenth-century Germany the critical movement reached its peak" (Grant and Tracy 1984: 5). It was revolutionary foremost in the success it met, not in its genius, for doubt, skepticism, and hostility toward the message and person of Jesus as his followers understood him were virulent already in Jesus's lifetime. The treasured hallmarks of (post)modern Western intellectual belief—doubt, skepticism, and in the end indifference if not hostility toward the message of the cross—can be reconstructed in considerable detail from the NT and extra-NT sources.[9] Hill (2004: 204–93) shows how second-century gnostics reacted to John and responded to his ideas in either an adversarial or supersessionary way. Biting skepticism of Christian claims can be studied in fairly full dress in the form of Celsus's powerful "intellectual" attacks on Christians (and Jews) around 180 (Hoffman 1987). So in a fundamental sense the Enlightenment *in biblical studies* marks a political victory as much as an intellectual one,[10] as it did not really arrive at new objections to Christian faith so much as it set in motion dynamics that gradually enshrined repristinated versions of ancient disbelief of historic Christianity in European Protestant universities that trained pastors. For example, when Adolf Schlatter enrolled in theological college in Switzerland in 1871, taking classes to prepare him for parish ministry, his philosophy professor was Friedrich Nietzsche. Two generations earlier, D. F. Strauss was taught NT by a professor (F. C. Baur) who rejected the historic Christianity he had embraced as a youth in favor of the Hegelian panentheism eventually immortalized as a central plank in the platform of the Tübingen School (Harris 1975). Handing over theological education to people with waning or no appetite for creedal Christian belief had the trickle-down effect of schooling generations of parishioners in post-Christian convictions, even though broadly speaking the gradually spreading consensus offered few critical insights that were not at least latent in ancient objections to Christian truth claims.

To sum up, at the Enlightenment the theological synthesis of historic Christianity (see Oden 2003) was rejected by influential individuals who were often not very sympathetic to it in the first place. To justify this, and to extend alternate syntheses like Continental rationalism (growing out of English Deism),

9. Given the considerable continuity between the saving message of the OT, understood as part of the Christian Scriptures, and the NT, many of the dynamics of modern/postmodern disbelief in God's saving but also damning self-disclosure are already discernible in the critiques of misguided Hebrew and Jewish belief and behavior found in the OT prophets.

10. The Enlightenment's greatest intellectual achievement in biblical studies was to have used historical interpretation to show how ecclesial hermeneutics were sometimes disloyal to the Bible they claimed to interpret. Theological systems were brought under scrutiny of biblical passages seen in their historical settings and thus freed from dogma to speak afresh and to correct the systems. But it was not long before the servant became the master. For some generations now the dogma—the theological or philosophical systems—informing historical interpretation has stood in need of hearing a fresh theological voice (see Yarbrough 2004b). This explains in part the recent rise of "theological interpretation of Scripture"; see, e.g., Cummins 2004 and Vanhoozer et al. 2005.

Hegelian philosophy of religion, Ritschlian liberalism, and the dogmatics, as it were, of the so-called history of religions school, the foundational historical bases of Christian doctrine were increasingly assaulted.[11] Within a few generations leading universities and theological schools were increasingly teaching the Christian Scriptures from the basis of post-Christian construals of them. Today, while attempts are continually made to argue that the effects of historical criticism (a convenient term for the hermeneutical approach that the Enlightenment championed and that is still dominant among many biblical scholars) are or by rights should be irrelevant for faith (e.g., Culpepper 1998: 37; Schnelle 1998: 14; Ehrman 2004: 14), this could be true only of a faith foreign to biblical writers. For they predicated their confessional claims on a God who created the world, superintended history, and revealed himself definitively and knowably within that material-temporal nexus through divinely appointed spokespersons and ultimately writers who bequeathed the Scriptures to God's people and thereby to the world (cf. Grant and Tracy 1984: 3–4). First John speaks much of just such faith. It is inconceivable that the author would assent to the proposition that the historical basis of 1 John 1:1–3 is irrelevant to his subsequent expressions of and calls for faith in the crucified and risen Jesus.

Today, after over two centuries of development of what has by now become a fairly predictable, traditional, and professionally obligatory outlook[12] in many centers of learning, it has become customary for scholars to disconnect the author John from the apostle John son of Zebedee (Schnelle 1998: 456; Ehrman 2004: 174; Witherington 2006: 395). Moreover, "1 John was not composed by the evangelist" who wrote the Fourth Gospel (Perkins 2004: 21). Further, the Letters of John (which themselves may come from different hands, so Holladay 2005: 521) were produced by a community rather than an individual (Schnelle 1998: 436–38; Rensberger 2001: 3). For that matter, even the Fourth Gospel does not go back to a follower of Jesus; it was rather produced by "a theologian of the later period who, on the basis of comprehensive traditions, rethought the meaning of Jesus' life, and interpreted and presented it in his own way" (Schnelle 1998: 474; cf. Lincoln 2002). This view tends to be presented as some daring and avant-garde find of cutting-edge scholarship, but a century ago Wrede (1907: 230) stated this outlook with admirable frankness:

> If one views [John's] chief intention as the transmission of actual history, many features of the narrative become practically grotesque and ridiculous. Historically speaking, the following features, and many others, are simply pure impossibilities: that Jesus interacted with the Jews regarding his execution or the Last Supper; that he discussed Johannine theology with the Roman procurator;

11. For details on this process in the field of NT theology, along with literature from other areas, see Yarbrough 2004b.

12. Cf. Grant and Tracy 1984: 5: "The historical method still lives. . . . By its most ardent defenders its methods are set forth with a rigidity unequalled by scholastic theologians."

> that his simplest words met with the most massive misunderstanding; that in prayers to God he used dogmatic formulations or reflections on the working of prayer on those who listened to him. However, whoever recognizes that the author is led by intentions entirely different than historical ones, that it is his ideas and biases which reshape and idealize [*beseelen*] the received material [i.e., the oral tradition] and add numerous traditions to it—that person learns to understand why so much must strike us as strange and odd, so delusional and removed from reality.

As for the epistles, the verdict on 1 John is held as true for all three: "Unquestionably 1 John, like the Qumrân literature and even [the Gospel of John], is a community document" (Sloyan 1995: 44; cf. Callahan 2005: 1–5).

The upshot of this conviction is that between the earthly Jesus and the God he somehow embodied—whom the Johannine Letters call readers to trust, love, and heed—and the claims of the Johannine writings lies an impermeable barrier. We need to be "delivered" from supposing that the Johannine tradition (including John's Gospel) tells us anything about Christianity (much less Jesus himself) in the first half of the first century (Callahan 2005: ix). Even though recent decades have witnessed a renewed quest for the historical Jesus, this has done little to rehabilitate the reputation of these writings as conveying the convictions of a personal acquaintance of Jesus and "the disciple whom Jesus loved" (John 13:23; 19:26; 21:7, 20). All of "John's" writings are viewed as late, reflective at best of historical conditions several generations after Jesus's death.

It is even possible to represent John's writings as originating in the mid- or late second century. In the interest of such a thesis, Strecker (1996: xli–xlii n79) casts doubt on our knowledge of the textual tradition. Along this same line, Schmithals (1992: 290–91) explains how, in the wake of Marcion and his canon, various Christian subgroups responded with their own canons. These subgroups favored three-document collections due to Philo's influence,[13] for whom three was the number of perfection. And so were born, it is theorized, various mini-proto-Bibles in the form of (1) Ephesians, Colossians, and Philemon; (2) 1 Timothy, 2 Timothy, and Titus; (3) the short recensions of Ignatius to the Ephesians and the Romans along with Polycarp's epistle; and (4) the Johannine Letters. Klauck (1998: 261) extends this charge of a sort of Christian gematria: for a while the writings of 1 Peter, 1 John, and James were widely accepted on their own. Then 2 Peter, 2 John, 3 John, and Jude were added, and the result was "not accidentally the number seven." Added to a fourteen-letter Pauline corpus (with Hebrews being regarded as Pauline), the mysterious plotters of the NT canon "arrived at 3 x 7 letters in the New Testament." Having attributed this transparent contrivance to second-century Christians, Klauck then condemns them for it: "This only underscores the artificiality of the whole construction."

Works advancing anonymous, pseudonymous, or community authorship of John's Letters, or some variation thereof, dominate the discussion today

13. Philo does not seem to be alluded to, much less quoted, in any NT writing.

(e.g., R. Brown 1982: 30n71 [four authors at work in composition, though his views fluctuated over the years]; Schnackenburg 1992: 41; Sloyan 1995: 3; Strecker 1996: xxxv–xliv; Culpepper 1998: 29–37; C. Black 2000: 386n3; Ehrman 2004: 164–65). Witherington (2006: 403) thinks that the author may have been the Beloved Disciple and possibly Lazarus. Or the authorship question may be largely skirted (Griffith 2002; T. Brown 2003). Reflecting a postmodern hermeneutic in its prime, Callahan states, "The 'relationship among texts' that we now call the Johannine Epistles . . . is not and cannot be a property of 'Johannine authorship'" (2005: 2). There are only texts, and therefore at some point and in some manner writers. But there were no authors.

The doctrine of a nonapostolic, noneyewitness authorship of the Johannine writings and therefore letters may be regarded as firmly established. Ancient tradition and in fact Scripture itself (Rev. 1:9) says that John was banished from the mainland to the island of Patmos. Today he is banished from connection with all the writings that people once thought he composed.

His exile is of little concern if the gospel he upheld is not true and binding on today's world and readers. If exegesis of 1–3 John is literally an academic exercise, then we can leave these authorless lines to whatever fate befalls them. Life goes on, however ir/religiously an interpreter cares to construe it. The paychecks, pensions, and (if one is lucky) royalties of tenured professors setting forth startling new ideas about discredited old traditions will continue.

The Vantage Point of This Commentary

Johannine studies has arrived at the place it is through the labors of generations of dedicated scholars. Even where the approach has been largely negative from the standpoint of John's claims as I would understand them, there is typically much to learn from the exegesis of any trained and thoughtful reader of the NT text. For that reason, this commentary will interact freely with a full range of interpreters who have assayed to interpret the Johannine Letters. Having said that, I also feel it legitimate to invite John back off his island and welcome him into the apostolic circle, where historical sources place him.

It is likely that first-century Christians, taught by both Judaism and Jesus (Wenham 1994) to acknowledge in the Hebrew Scripture and its Greek counterpart (the LXX) "oracles of God" of priceless worth (cf. Rom. 3:1–2), quickly treasured the writings of their own spiritual leaders as God inspired (cf. Holladay 2005: 575). The magisterial tone of NT epistles assumes this; if we were to write thus to one another today, it would strike us as parody. The writers wrote and were evidently read as possessing a certain authority (challenged by many, as the writings make clear, as was the Jesus they served). Why would they not be so regarded when they cast out demons and healed the sick (John and other disciples in Mark 6:13), caused the lame to walk (John and Peter in Acts 3:1–10), and raised the dead (Peter in Acts 9:36–43)? There is formal indication of their authority from before the end of the first century (1 Tim. 5:18b [if Paul is citing a written source]; 2 Pet. 3:15–17; 1 Clem. 47.1–3; 53.1). The phenomenon of inspiration of both OT and NT writings is a primitive Christian belief

(Westcott 1888: 417–56), rooted in Jewish belief preceding it: "Jewish exegetes believed that every word of Scripture had been spoken by God. There could be no question of its inspiration or authenticity" (Grant and Tracy 1984: 8). It would not be surprising if the writings of John son of Zebedee were regarded highly. And this is not merely the result of a theological conviction regarding inspired Scripture: it is also a historical conviction visible in the canonical Gospels, which "explicitly acknowledged their sources in the eyewitnesses and the authority of the eyewitnesses for their reliability" (Bauckham 2006: 292).

Moreover, Papias is said to have made use of 1 John (as well as 1 Peter; Eusebius, *Eccl. Hist.* 3.39.17), and Papias can be regarded as active in the 95–110 era along with Ignatius and Polycarp (Yarbrough 1983). I am unaware of good reason to doubt the claim that Eusebius, as he perused Papias's *Expositions of the Oracles of the Lord*, saw 1 John quoted or at least alluded to recognizably.[14]

It is worth noting that no ancient manuscripts of John's Epistles do not bear his name. True, it is commonly stated that early manuscripts circulated without indication of their author (R. Brown 1982: 5; Heckel 2004: 433), but in the absence of proof and perhaps even compelling evidence, this is a theory to be treated with caution regarding John's Letters. (For a similar argument regarding the four Gospels, see Bauckham 2006: 111, 302–4.) If for some considerable period of time no one knew, really, who wrote these letters as they circulated, and John represents a later guess, how likely is it that the hundreds of copies, or at least the numerous lines of manuscript transmission that are reflected in extant copies, all guessed the same person for just these three particular documents? Here the work of the Institute for New Testament Textual Research again deserves notice (B. Aland et al. 2003a: 263, 368), which lists (in Greek without accents or breathing marks) about fifty different titles given for 1 John (whether at the beginning as superscriptions or at the end as subscriptions). The following selection (from uncials, whose titles are picked up by minuscules) gives the flavor of ancient scribal convention:[15]

Uncials	Superscription or Subscription	Translation
01C2, 044	ιωαννου επιστολη πρωτη	John's First Epistle
01, 02, 03	ιωαννου πρωτη (03 has ιωανου)	John's First [Epistle]

14. See also Hill's conclusion (2004: 444–45), though he tends to date Papias ten to twenty years later than I would. The year 100 is exactly where Papias is placed in Eusebius's chronicle, which forms the backbone of his history (we have the chronicle courtesy of Jerome's translation of it; see Helm 1913: 193–94). Papias, Polycarp, and Ignatius are said to be "hearers of the apostle John" in the early years of Trajan, specifically at the year 100. This may seem to be very late for John to have been lucid. Yet John could have been born in 10–15, begun following Jesus at age fifteen to twenty, written 1–3 John anytime after 70 at the age of sixty or so, and even by 100, aged eighty-five or ninety, still have had plenty of life left.

15. The papyrus witnesses are fragmentary: $\mathfrak{P}^9$ contains only 1 John 4:11–12, 14–17, so what it contained fore and aft cannot be determined; $\mathfrak{P}^{74}$ is fragmentary in the first chapter and breaks off after 1 John 5:17.

Uncials	Superscription or Subscription	Translation
049 (superscription)	του αγιου αποστολου ιωαννου επιστολη πρωτη	First Epistle of the Holy Apostle John
0142	του αγιου ιωαννου του αποστολου επιστολη πρωτη	Saint John the Apostle's First Epistle
020	επιστολη καθολικη του αγιου αποστολου ιωαννου	Catholic Epistle of the Holy Apostle John
025V	ιωαννου του ευαγγελιστου και αποστολου επιστολη πρωτη	First Epistle of the Evangelist and Apostle John
025	επιστολη ιωαννου πρωτη	First Epistle of John
049 (subscription)	του αγιου ιωαννου επιστολη πρωτη	Saint John's First Epistle
018	επληρωθη συν θεω αδελφοι η πρωτη επιστολη ιωαννου του θεολογου	Completed with God, Brothers: The First Epistle of John the Theologian[16]

Of the 143 witnesses cited in B. Aland et al. 2003a (representing 180 total manuscripts), only two lack the name "John" in either the superscription or subscription. Minuscule 1751 contains the subscription τελος της πρωτης επιστολης ητις εγραφη απο εφεσου (End of the First Epistle, Which Was Written from Ephesus). Minuscules 607 and 1838 have the subscription εγραφη απο εφεσου (Written from Ephesus). These subscriptional clues, even without John's name, were surely adequate to imply it for Byzantine copyists and users of the manuscripts they produced. (Since 1838 is from the eleventh century and contained all the Catholic Letters, the placement of 1 John after 2 Peter would have betrayed its identity to any Byzantine scribe.) The textual witness for John's authorship of 1 John is uniform and pervasive. This does not prove that the name "John" was affixed to the very earliest copies (at which time it would perhaps not have needed to be: at the outset of the tradition process, it would be self-evident). But it is consonant with the theory that it may have been and the supposition that in any case these writings never circulated without being closely associated with John.

Finally, it is alleged that many NT writings owe their titles not to anonymity but to pseudonymity: the putative authorship was assigned by perhaps a community that knew full well that the named author was not the actual one. This theory has received recent careful scrutiny and can with good reason be viewed with skepticism (Wilder 2004; cf. Baum 2001; more broadly Carson and Moo 2005: 337–50). There is no compelling reason to doubt that the only known prominent John associated with the first-century church wrote John.[17] This is attested too early to be otherwise; as Heckel (2005: 1323) in

16. Evidently this scribe rejoiced to have his arduous copying work behind him. As for John being termed "the theologian," Turretin (1992–97: 1.2 §1.1.8) points out that the church "fathers designate particularly that part of the Christian science which treats of the divinity of Christ by the word 'theology.' In this sense, John is with emphasis styled 'Theologian' because he boldly asserted the deity of the Word."

17. Cf. L. Johnson 1999: 525: "Since nothing is ever said in this Gospel about a John, and the Synoptic Sons of Zebedee are mentioned only incidentally (21:2), it is not unreasonable to

reviewing Hill states: "The extant sources from Ignatius, Papias, Polycarp, and Justin to Irenaeus either explicitly presuppose John's Gospel or show absolutely no inclination to shy away from related ideas that were with considerable probability drawn from John's Gospel." If this has validity, it has implications for viewing the NT letters attributed to John as coming from his own hand.

What about John the Elder? No patristic writer prior to Eusebius (writing ca. 300) proposed the existence of such a person (for arguments that some second-century sources may support the theory of this person's existence, see Bauckham 2006: 438–71). I argue elsewhere (1983) that Eusebius interpreted Papias tendentiously to tease out an Elder John who was separate from the apostle (*Eccl. Hist.* 3.39.2–9). He needed someone named John to whom he could attribute the book of Revelation, since Eusebius under Origen's influence had embraced amillenarianism, whereas the ante-Nicene church generally and Eusebius in his younger years understood Revelation in millenarian terms (Grant 1980: 131). For polemical purposes,[18] then, Eusebius saw fit to invent the nonapostolic Elder John and then impute Revelation to him. Chapman (1911: 33) noted long ago: "It is certain that Eusebius was the first to discover two Johns in Papias, and he is proud of his discovery." It is telling that Eusebius elsewhere rejoins the consensus of his era, speaking of but one John and even linking him to the writing of the Apocalypse (*Eccl. Hist.* 3.18.1; 3.20.9; 3.23.1, 6). It is also significant that in his *Chronicon* (the framework for his history) Eusebius lists Papias, along with Ignatius and Polycarp, as hearers of "the apostle John" (Helm 1913: 193–94). To my mind this is a nagging weakness in Bauckham's impressive arguments for the existence of an Elder John separate from the apostle (2006: 412–37): they force a highly contestable reading on Papias's fragments, fragments carefully selected by Eusebius to furnish a basis for his unprecedented claim that there were two Johns.

But even these fragments can be understood to speak of only one John, the apostle and the son of Zebedee. It is significant that Eusebius himself admits that the word "elder" can for Papias designate an apostle: "Papias . . . confesses that he had received the words of the *Apostles* from their followers" (*Eccl. Hist.* 3.39.7 [Loeb translation, emphasis added]). In the quotation given by Eusebius from Papias's writings, Papias never uses the word "apostle." He speaks only of "elders" who were Jesus's "disciples": Andrew, Peter, Philip, Thomas, James, John, Matthew, "or any other of the disciples of the Lord" (3.39.4). Papias says that he had access to these elders as well as to others who had been their followers (such as Polycarp and Ignatius?). But Eusebius identifies those whom Papias terms "elders" as "apostles" (3.39.7). "Thus on his own showing this passage contradicts the thesis of Eusebius . . . that Papias was not a hearer of

identify the beloved disciple with John son of Zebedee (cf. Matt. 10:2; Mark 3:17; Luke 6:14; Acts 1:13), who was a 'pillar' of the first Jerusalem church (Acts 3:1; 4:13; 8:14; Gal. 2:9)."

18. Cf. Cross 1960: 61: "Eusebius was prejudiced against Papias on account of his Chiliasm."

the apostles" (Lawlor and Oulten 1954: 2.112; so also Lawlor 1922: 212). It seems that Eusebius exploits a linguistic ambiguity that had arisen between the respective apostolic and Nicene eras: Papias reflecting first-century usage could use "elder" to be inclusive of "apostle," as is occasionally the case in the NT (Acts 11:30; 21:18; 1 Pet. 5:1; possibly 2 John 1; 3 John 1). For Eusebius, however, it is feasible through selective quotation and tendentious exegesis to force on the word "elder" the connotation of a *follower* of an apostle or some other later Christian leader. Many are not convinced that Papias himself ever intended to refer to two different Johns (Lawlor and Oulten 1954: 2.114; R. Brown 1966: lxxxviii–xcii; Morris 1969: 278–79; Smalley 1978: 73–78). "The quotation from Papias *can* be understood to mean that Papias was a hearer of the apostle John" (Grant 1974: 210, emphasis original)—as Eusebius himself states in his *Chronicon*.

Yet even if there was an Elder John separate from the apostle, it seems that their views were so inseparable that we can interpret them as from a single body of recollection and conviction. Dodd's view is not atypical: "I conceive the First Epistle of John, then, to have been written by an author who was quite possibly a disciple of the Fourth Evangelist, and certainly a diligent student of his work. He has soaked himself in the Gospel, assimilating its ideas and forming his style upon its model" (1937: 156). Many agree that 2 John and 3 John resemble 1 John in language and style (e.g., L. Johnson 1999: 559–71).

When one combines these insights with the widely conceded fact that the vocabulary of John's Gospel and at least his first letter appear to point in the direction of common authorship (noted long ago and at length by Dionysius of Alexandria; see Eusebius, *Eccl. Hist.* 7.25.17–21), it is not unreasonable to adopt the interpretive assumption that the John of the Gospel also stands behind the Johannine Epistles. Neufeld (1994: 1–36) demonstrates that theories rejecting John's authorship have arrived at little *positive* consensus regarding the historical, social, and cultural settings or occasions that gave rise to 1 John (to say nothing of 2 John and 3 John). Neufeld concludes that "the almost complete lack of clues about [1 John's] historical genesis suggests that the historical critical method," which tends to interpret John's Letters as if an eyewitness of Jesus *cannot* have been the author, "can at best have a secondary claim only" (1994: 2). For that reason he opts for ahistorical speech-act theory as the hermeneutical key to 1 John's interpretation.[19] But since I do not understand John to be an anonymous document completely lacking in historical location, I have found it plausible to interpret his letters within the general time and setting ascribed to him by biblical and patristic sources. Further possible justification for this, and interaction with objections to it, will emerge in the course of exegesis below.

19. For similar reasons Schmid (2002: 291) opts for a reader-response approach, with most historical questions and particularly the views of the opponents in 1 John left up to the discernment of each successive set of new readers.

Genre

While 2 John and 3 John bear the earmarks of Hellenistic letters, modified to be sure by Christian sentiments and language, 1 John lacks classic epistolary elements in its opening and closing. Yet ancient writers much closer to literary forms of their time than we are felt it to be epistolary. Irenaeus (*Ag. Her.* 3.16.8), Dionysius of Alexandria (in Eusebius, *Eccl. Hist.* 7.25.8), and Eusebius (3.39.17) all call 1 John a letter without any expressed second thought about the matter. In the exegesis of 2:12–14 I point out that John does have direct address, as befits an epistle; he just defers it and omits mention of personal names, including his own. This could be because it is a circular letter (Kruse 2000: 28). But that it should be understood as a letter of some kind can hardly be doubted (contra Witherington 2006: 424, 436n25). Klauck (1998: 258–59) notes three possible indices for 1 John's epistolary identity: (1) the expressed motive of shared joy (1:4), (2) repeated mention of the act and purpose of writing to his recipients (thirteen uses of γράφω [*graphō*, to write] scattered throughout the letter), and (3) repeated instances of direct address of his readers.

Even the somewhat precipitous ending fails to erase this impression, for it does contain personal address (5:21: τεκνία, *teknia*, dear children; Ellis 2000: 220 thinks there could be indication here of the author's own hand) and a prescription for well-being for the recipients, just not in a conventional form. The most important interpretive questions pertain to 1 John's content, not its genre (Culy 2004: xiii).

Setting and Date

It is probably not possible to mount a convincing case for the order in which the Johannine Epistles were written. They reflect a milieu in which the writer presumes to exercise ecclesial, indeed apostolic, oversight, for he speaks as an eyewitness to Jesus's life and import (1 John 1:1–3). And even in the very brief letters of 2–3 John, he writes with a magisterial tone that comports with, though it does not in itself establish, apostolic self-consciousness.

The readers are regarded by the author as having believed on Jesus Christ for the salvation of their souls and the transformation of their lives (on the importance of "the genuinely past history" and "the really past story of Jesus" to the early Christian movement, see Bauckham 2006: 277). By all indications this is a Jesus conceived very much along the lines of the individual presented in the canonical Gospels. He was a human being (1 John 4:2) but also somehow deserving of the appellation "God" (5:20) despite God's indubitable transcendence (1:5; 4:12). By connection with him, people can receive the Holy Spirit (3:24). Jesus was preexistent, with the Father in the beginning (1:1–2). He lived a life worthy of emulation (2:6). He died as a sacrifice for sins (2:2; 4:10). He must have been raised, for he is the source of eternal life (5:11), and he is going to return (2:28). In the meantime he is at the Father's right hand in a mediatorial role (2:1). At the end of all things, Jesus will bring his followers to eternal life (5:11, 20), which is already inaugurated but has yet to be consummated in the current age.

The readers of the epistles are apparently living in fellowship with each other, albeit not a perfect fellowship, for there has been schism in 1 John 2:19, there is talk of deceivers in 2 John 7, and there is discord behind the scenes of 3 John 9. Most treatments of the epistles seek to reconstruct the respective settings based on a "mirror reading" of internal evidence regarding these problems. But there are severe limits to our knowledge here. "Almost all we know specifically" about the setting(s) "is drawn from the Johannine writings" (Painter 2002: 79; similarly L. Johnson 1999: 559: "The best one can hope for is to find traces of an internal development within the group," this group being the church or churches to whom the letters are addressed). I will comment on these matters as they pertain to 2 John and 3 John at appropriate junctures in the exegesis below.

As for 1 John, no explicit geographical or temporal indicators are given. Uebele (2001: 163) concludes, however, that the opponents whom 1 John addresses are very possibly the direct forerunners of the adversaries denounced by Ignatius in the following generation. Patristic sources plausibly affirm that in roughly 70–100 John was resident in Ephesus and ministered there. Reports to this effect come from Irenaeus and Clement of Alexandria, as Eusebius (*Eccl. Hist.* 3.23.1–2) observes:

> At this time [i.e., the beginning of Trajan's reign, ca. 98] that very disciple whom Jesus loved, John, at once Apostle and Evangelist, still remained alive in Asia and administered the churches there, for after the death of Domitian, he had returned from his banishment on the island. And that he remained alive until this time may fully be confirmed by two witnesses, and these ought to be trustworthy for they represent the orthodoxy of the church, no less persons than Irenaeus and Clement of Alexandria. (Loeb Classical Library)

Eusebius then cites supporting passages from Irenaeus's *Against Heresies* (2.22.5; 3.3.4) and Clement's *Salvation of the Rich* (42), the latter of which notes activity by John not only in Ephesus but also in its sister city Smyrna to the north.

Given this information, if we care to assign John's Letters to a particular historical milieu at all, it seems warranted to think of them as reflecting conditions in the region of Ephesus in the closing decades of the first century (Witherington 2006: 427 suggests the 80s). Information of some historical significance can be inferred from Rev. 2–3 regarding this era and locale in the form of short letters from the exalted Jesus to the seven churches of the Roman province of Asia, of which Ephesus was the leading city.

John's Epistles and the Seven Churches of Asia

The church at Ephesus (Rev. 2:1–7; for detailed treatment see Trebilco 2004: 293–350; Schnabel 2004: 1.819–20) receives praise for its works, toil, and perseverance, as well as its unwillingness to abide evildoers. These are individuals who make false apostolic claims. The Ephesians have exposed them as bogus. This is all praiseworthy. Yet their love is flagging. So they must repent and be renewed in good works[20] lest they be put to shame at Jesus's return. They receive a last word of approval for their rejection of the works of the Nicolaitans (about whom there are several theories but little definite knowledge beyond what John writes here; Trebilco 2004: 335). Greek words in this section that are reminiscent of John's Letters are the following:

Rev. 2	Greek Text	Translation	Johannine Parallels
2:1	ὁ περιπατῶν (*ho peripatōn*)	the one who walks	1 John 1:6, 7; 2:6 (2x), 11; 2 John 4, 6 (2x); 3 John 3, 4
2:2	οἶδα (*oida*)	I know	1 John (15x); 3 John 12
2:2, 5	ἔργα (*erga*)	works	1 John 3:8, 12, 18; 2 John 11; 3 John 10
2:2	ψευδεῖς (*pseudeis*)	liars	1 John 1:10; 2:4, 22; 4:20; 5:10[21]
2:3	τὸ ὄνομά μου (*to onoma mou*)	my name	1 John 2:12; 3:23; 5:13; 3 John 7
2:4	ἀγάπη (*agapē*)	love	1 John (18x); 2 John 3, 6; 3 John 6
2:5	ποιέω (*poieō*)	do (i.e., perform)	1 John 1:6, 10; 2:17, 29; 3:4 (2x), 7, 8, 9, 10, 22; 5:2, 10; 3 John 5, 6, 10
2:5	ἔρχομαι (*erchomai*)	I [Christ] come	1 John 4:2; 5:6; 2 John 7
2:6	μισεῖς/μισῶ (*miseis/misō*)	you/I hate [evil works]	1 John 2:9, 11; 3:13, 15; 4:20
2:7	ὁ νικῶν (*ho nikōn*)	the one who conquers	1 John 2:13, 14; 4:4; 5:4 (2x), 5

The situation presupposed by Rev. 2:1–7 conceivably resonates with John's Letters in several ways. Jesus praises the church for the diligence of its members (2:2–3); John commends his readers for their expressions of loyalty and faith (1 John 2:12–14; cf. 2 John 4; 3 John 3, 5–6). Jesus chides the Ephesians for lovelessness (Rev. 2:4); 1 John camps on this theme repeatedly from several angles, as do 2 John and 3 John (2 John 3, 6; 3 John 6). Both Rev. 2:5 and 1 John 2:28 use Christ's return as a spur to moral urgency. There are deceivers and spiritual

20. Throughout this section of Revelation, Schnabel's comment bears notice: "The 'works' (τὰ ἔργα, *ta erga*) do not describe 'services' generally but seem to stand particularly for missionary activity in the pagan world. When John uses the terms 'love,' 'faith' and 'patience,' particularly 'faith' and 'patience,' he nearly always describes continuous witness for Jesus Christ" (2004: 1.832).

21. The root of ψευδεῖς in Rev. 2:2 is ψευδής (*pseudēs*, lying); the word in the 1 John passages is ψεύστης (*pseustēs*, liar).

knaves at work in Ephesus (Rev. 2:2, 6); a subtheme of each of John's Letters is analogous individuals or groups. Through it all, Christ will reward those who prevail with the resources he provides (Rev. 2:7; cf. 1 John 5:4–5; 2 John 8).

The church in Smyrna (Rev. 2:8–11; cf. Schnabel 2004: 1.820–23) faces tribulation, poverty, and slander from people called false Jews and a synagogue of the devil. More suffering lies ahead, but believers should not fear despite imprisonment and persecution. After death they will receive "the crown of life"; the "second death" will not touch them.

Parallels between this counsel and John's Letters are less abundant than with Ephesus. Verbally, we find in Rev. 2:9 the expression οἶδα (*oida*, to know) and in 2:11 ὁ νικῶν (*ho nikōn*, the one who conquers), terms with Johannine parallels (see table above). At Smyrna, "Satan" and "the devil" are a factor; in 1 John it is not only "the devil" (3:8, 10) but also "the evil one" (2:13, 14; 3:12; 5:18, 19) and "antichrist" (2:18, 22; 4:3; 2 John 7). In general we may say that opposition from the world presupposed at Smyrna is very much a concern in John's Letters (e.g., 1 John 2:15–17; 5:19; 2 John 7–11; 3 John 9–11). So is the ultimate promise of eternal life (Rev. 2:11; 1 John 1:2; 2:25; 3:15; 5:11, 13, 20) from the conquering Jesus.

The church in Pergamum (Rev. 2:12–17; cf. Schnabel 2004: 1.823–31) faces dangers more dire and imminent than the settings addressed by 1–3 John. But there are false teachers who aid and abet behavior that is inexpedient and even immoral. There are points of contact here with ubiquitous calls for moral reform and forsaking of sin in John's Letters. As John adduces Cain as a role model to eschew (1 John 3:12), Jesus holds up Balaam as a negative example (Rev. 2:14). The Jesus who addresses Pergamum projects his coming in judgment (2:16), a feature of 1 John as well (2:28; 3:2–3). Jesus extols his name (see table above) and faith in him (Rev. 2:13), just as John makes much of faith (1 John 5:5) and the act of exercising it (πιστεύω [*pisteuō*, to believe] in 1 John 3:23; 4:1, 16; 5:1, 5, 10 [3x], 13). Idolatry is a concern in both Rev. 2:14 and 1 John 5:21.

The church in Thyatira (Rev. 2:18–29; cf. Schnabel 2004: 1.831–32) hears the words of "the Son of God," as John's Letters make him a major theme (cf. ca. two dozen occurrences in 1 John; 2 John 3, 9). The Thyatiran church is commended for its works (Rev. 2:19), as John commends his readers in all three epistles. But as Cain's example threatened to characterize the behavior of the readers of 1 John, Jezebel's misdeeds are to be avoided at Thyatira (Rev. 2:20). She heads up a wing of rebels guilty of false teaching, immorality, and idolatrous acts. Their sins "probably are connected with membership in or the activities of the trade guilds of Thyatira at their banquets" (Schnabel 2004: 1.832). They delight in "the deep things of Satan" (Rev. 2:24). John's Letters, in contrast, call readers to true teaching, moral probity, and a break with all that is less or other than God. The deepest thing people can entertain is the "understanding" that makes it possible "to know the one who is true" (1 John 5:20), not satanic esoterica or the lure of the antichrist (2:18, 22; 4:3; 2 John 7). John's readers have resources to circumvent deceptive teaching (1 John 2:26–27). As with previous Asian cities, so to Thyatira the Son of

God promises his return in judgment and reward (Rev. 2:25–28), themes we have already seen in John's Letters. The Son will also strike the "children" of Jezebel dead, as John warns his "children" (cf. "children of God" in 1 John 3:1, 2, 10; 5:2; "children" in the sense of "Christian believers" in 2 John 1, 4, 13; 3 John 4) against sin resulting in death (1 John 5:16). There is victory over sin, deception, and death for those who keep Jesus's commands to the Thyatirans (Rev. 2:26), just as eternal life (1 John 2:25) and communion in prayer (3:22; 5:14) should inspire the readers of 1 John to do likewise (2:3–6).

The Jesus who addresses Sardis (Rev. 3:1–6; cf. Schnabel 2004: 1.833–36) knows the works of his followers, as God knows all things (1 John 3:20). The Sardis believers are deficient in works, a concern of all three Johannine Letters (see table above). They should "remember what they received" (Rev. 3:3) as John's readers are told to actualize their anointing and their knowledge (1 John 2:20), to dwell on the nature of God (1:5), and to recall the eternal life that was made manifest in the incarnation (1:1–3). "The one who conquers" will never lose eternal life—themes and a promise that figure prominently in 1 John.

The church at Philadelphia (Rev. 3:7–13; cf. Schnabel 2004: 1.836–38) is addressed by "the Holy One" (ὁ ἅγιος, *ho hagios*) and "the True One" (ὁ ἀληθινός, *ho alēthinos*), expressions with parallels in 1 John 2:20 ("the Holy One") and 2:8 (Jesus is the "true" light) and 5:20 (his followers know and are in "the True One," who is also "the true God"). Jesus has "the key of David" (Rev. 3:7); he is the (Davidic) Christ in John's Letters (1 John 1:3; 2:1, 22; 3:23; 4:2, 15; 5:1, 6, 20; 2 John 3, 7, 9).[22] He knows their works, as he did the works of those at Sardis and Ephesus. They have not "denied" (from ἀρνέομαι, *arneomai*, to deny) his name (Rev. 3:8), an urgent concern in 1 John (2:22, 23) because it is vital to confess Christ aright (4:2–3; 2 John 7). They have rather kept (τηρέω, *tēreō*, to keep) Jesus's words (Rev. 3:8, 10), as John's readers are urged to keep them (1 John 2:5) along with his commandments (2:3, 4; 3:22, 24; 5:3).

The Philadelphians join other Asian churches addressed by Jesus in either being called to steadfastness or commended for it: Ephesus (Rev. 2:2–3), Smyrna (2:10: "faithful unto death"), Thyatira (2:19, 25–26), Sardis (3:3), Philadelphia (3:10–11). All these references beg to be compared with the Johannine teaching regarding "abiding" in Christ, a notion that carries with it all the rich associations of the Revelation passages, almost like musical refrains, that speak of "patient endurance," faithfulness, holding fast, bearing up, and remaining steadfast. Philadelphia in particular seems to have taken the message to heart: Schnabel (2004: 1.838, quoting Olshausen) notes that it was "'the last bridgehead of Christianity in Asia Minor,' which was overpowered not before AD 1391, when Sultan Bajesid I conquered the city."

The church at Laodicea (Rev. 3:14–22) is addressed by Jesus, who is a witness "faithful and true," words applied to divinity in 1 John (1:9; 2:8; 5:20). Concern for the tepid zeal and lackluster "works" (ἔργα, *erga*) of the Laodiceans

22. Cf. John's Gospel, in which "the Davidic Messiah, the King of Israel, is none other than the eternal Son of God" (Pryor 1992: 135).

is prominent because of their apparent smugness. They are a picture of people without a sense of sin or any need to repent—the very self-delusion that 1 John (1:6, 8, 10) condemns. The Laodicean Christ is full of love for the readers (Rev. 3:19) but will settle for nothing less than their victory in the spiritual and moral battles they face: he grants benefit to "the one who conquers" (3:21), a theme already noted repeatedly in 1 John.

In sum, there may be a need to rethink the consensus that there is no historical setting for John's Letters, that all we can do is infer a community of internecine strife from words in the letters themselves. Of course strife is reflected in the letters; but there is a known world around the Christian community of John's place and time, attested by sources of some historical credibility, and it is not a world on all counts friendly to Christian presence and witness. Seen in this light, John's Letters are not obscure brittle condemnations of personal enemies; Rusam's conclusion (1993: 232) seems overstated that the Johannine congregations "fought for their convictions and their entire existence in polemical demarcation against their hostile surroundings." These letters are not defensive expedients to salvage a few followers in the wake of John's previous failed leadership; in fact, "the remarkable thing about 1 John is that it does not consist of a bitter polemic against those who departed or a sustained refutation of their claims. The focus . . . is not on the outsiders but on those who remain" (L. Johnson 1999: 566). The same could be said of the other two letters. All three are frank, realistic, but positive pastoral missives (not congregational creations) seeking to affirm and reinvigorate doctrinal direction, ethical urgency, relational integrity, and a forward-looking faith in God, generally in a geographical setting and temporal era in which relatively young churches were facing the challenges of longer term existence.

Literary Structure of 1 John

There is no agreement on the organization of 1 John (for helpful discussion of various recent proposals, see Culy 2004: xiii–xvi).[23] Twofold, threefold (Witherington 2006: 436), fourfold, fivefold, sixfold, sevenfold, and tenfold divisions have been proposed (Klauck 1991: 62–63; 1998: 259; cf. R. Brown 1982: 764). Schmid (2002: 305) proposes an elevenfold organization. The table below (adapted from Yarbrough 2002: 182) simply follows the inner marginal numbers of NA^{27}, which in turn reflect the divisions that came to be standard among scribal copyists through the centuries, particularly in Byzantium, which reproduced and preserved the greatest share of the extant Greek manuscript tradition:

1 John	Opening Words	Theme
1:1–2:6	"that which was from the beginning"	Central burden: God is light
2:7–17	"my dear children"	Primary commandment: Embody the age-old message

Continued

23. Outlines of 2 John and 3 John will be provided in the introductions to these books.

1 John	Opening Words	Theme
2:18–3:8	"dear children"	Key counsel: Abide in his anointing and receive eternal life
3:9–4:6	"no one who is born of God will continue to sin"	Core teaching: Beware Cain's error and false prophets
4:7–14	"dear friends"	Foundational imperative: God's love
4:15–5:15	"if anyone acknowledges that Jesus is the Son of God"	Illustrative appeal: Believing in Jesus the Christ, the Son of God
5:16–21	"if anyone sees a brother commit a sin"	Concluding admonition: The true God and the threat of imposters

Detailed Outline of 1 John

I. Central burden: God is light (1:1–2:6)
  A. Announcement of authority and purpose (1:1–4)
    1. Eyewitness privilege and proclamation (1:1–3)
      a. The fact of the incarnation (1:1)
      b. The validity of eyewitness testimony (1:1–3)
      c. What the incarnation manifested (1:1–2)
      d. The truth and import of the incarnation (1:1–3)
      e. The goal of the proclamation (1:3)
    2. Pastoral desire: Shared joy (1:4)
  B. Main burden of the epistle: The character of God (1:5)
  C. Implications of God's character for the Christian life (1:6–10)
    1. Implications for fellowship (1:6–7)
      a. In the case of transgression (1:6)
      b. In the case of obedience (1:7)
    2. Implications for integrity (1:8–10)
      a. In the case of denial of sinfulness: Misrepresentation of the self (1:8)
      b. In the case of consciousness of sin (1:9)
      c. In the case of denial of sinful acts: Misrepresentation of God (1:10)
  D. Appeal to readers in the light of God's character (2:1–6)
    1. Author's hope: Readers' deliverance from sin via knowing God (2:1a)
    2. Author's promise: Christ's twofold ministry (2:1b–2)
      a. Intercessor (2:1b)
      b. Expiatory propitiation (2:2)
    3. Author's assurance: Chastened Christian confidence (2:3–6)
      a. Basis for assurance: Compliance with Christ's commandments (2:3)
      b. Disqualification from assurance (2:4)
      c. Expansion of the basis for assurance: The perfection of Christian love (2:5)
      d. Ethical obligation of the professing Christian (2:6)

- II. Primary commandment: Embody the age-old message (2:7–17)
  - A. The nature and implications of the message (2:7–11)
    - 1. The message old yet current (2:7)
    - 2. The message new yet true (2:8)
    - 3. Implications for the misanthrope (2:9, 11)
      - a. The futility of mere confession (2:9)
      - b. The darkness of lovelessness (2:11)
    - 4. Implications for the philanthrope (2:10)
  - B. Pastoral appeal in view of the message (2:12–17)
    - 1. De facto greeting: Reflexive appeal (2:12–13)
    - 2. De facto greeting continued: Reflective appeal (2:14)
    - 3. Imperatival appeal in view of the message (2:15–17)
      - a. Heart of the imperative: Warning against world-love (2:15a)
      - b. Warning regarding absence of love for God (2:15b)
      - c. Explication of warning (2:16–17)
        - i. The origin of world-love (2:16)
        - ii. The bane of world-love and the promise of doing the will of God (2:17)
- III. Key counsel: Abide in his anointing (truth) and receive eternal life (2:18–3:8)
  - A. Three considerations informing the counsel to abide (2:18–21)
    - 1. Eschatological consideration in view of antichrist (2:18)
    - 2. Ecclesiastical consideration in view of schism (2:19)
    - 3. Charismatic consideration in view of anointing (2:20–21)
  - B. The truth that abides (2:22–26)
    - 1. Who the liar is (2:22)
    - 2. Who is on the side of the truth (2:23)
    - 3. Who will abide in the truth and their reward (2:24–25)
    - 4. Who imperils those seeking to abide (2:26)
  - C. The imperative to abide (2:27–29)
    - 1. The basis for the imperative: Anointing and instruction (2:27)
    - 2. The imperative and its incentive: The parousia (2:28)
    - 3. The basis for heeding the imperative: Christ the Righteous One (2:29)
  - D. The glory of abiding (3:1–8)
    - 1. The marvel of the Father's love (3:1)
    - 2. The promise of divine transformation (3:2–3)
      - a. Future transformation (3:2)
      - b. Present ethical urgency (3:3)
    - 3. The ethics of Christ's presence (3:4–8)
      - a. Defiance of Christ's presence (3:4, 6)
      - b. Purpose of Christ's presence (3:5)
      - c. Victory of Christ's presence (3:7–8)
- IV. Core teaching: Love, works, trust (3:9–4:6)
  - A. Summons to love (3:9–18)

1. Two paternities: Divine versus devilish origins (3:9–10)
2. Two options: Love or hate (3:11–12)
3. Two paths: Life or death (3:13–18)
   a. The world's hostility and believers' charity (3:13–14)
   b. Cain's progeny and Christ's precedent (3:15–16)
   c. Love's practicality (3:17–18)

B. Confirmation of love (3:19–24)
1. Assurance of the heart (3:19)
2. God's sway over the heart (3:20)
3. Assurance of confidence (3:21–22)
4. Assurance of valid faith (3:23)
5. Assurance of abiding (3:24)

C. Summons to choose (4:1–3)
1. Admonition and basis (4:1)
2. Identification of the Spirit of Christ and the spirit of antichrist (4:2–3)

D. Confirmation of choice (4:4–6)
1. God's victory in his people (4:4)
2. The world's self-fixation (4:5)
3. The apostolic testimony (4:6)

V. Foundational imperative: God's love (4:7–14)

A. First exhortation to love (4:7–10)
1. Origin and effect of God's love (4:7)
2. Status of the one who does not love (4:8)
3. God's goal in revealing his love (4:9)
4. God's means of revealing his love (4:10)

B. Second exhortation to love (4:11–14)
1. Effect of God's love (4:11)
2. Importance of expressing God's love (4:12)
3. Assurance of God's love (4:13)
4. Apostolic confirmation that the Father sent the Son (4:14)

VI. Illustrative appeal: Renewed and expanded invitation to love (4:15–5:15)

A. Declarative invitation with supporting warrant (4:15–16)

B. Commendation of love (4:17–21)
1. Triumph of divine love (4:17–19)
2. Necessity of human love (4:20–21)

C. Commendation of faith as *fides qua creditur* (5:1–5)
1. Believing as entrée into free love of God (5:1–3)
2. Personal faith victorious over (the lovelessness of) the world (5:4–5)

D. Commendation of faith as *fides quae creditur* (5:6–12)
1. God's testimony to Jesus Christ, the object of saving faith (5:6–9)
2. Human reception of God's testimony (5:10–12)

E. Commendation of the full assurance of eternal life: Confident prayer (5:13–15)

VII. Concluding admonition: Pastoral counsel, assurance, and warning (5:16–21)
   A. Counsel regarding sinners and sin (5:16–17)
   B. The tie that binds: Shared certainties (5:18–20)
   C. Final pastoral appeal (5:21)

The Significance of John's Letters

A commentary introduction cannot compete with, say, the synthetic exposition of biblical books found in proper NT theologies. Three recent studies explore the wealth of teaching in the Johannine letter corpus and the interrelationships among the books in a complete and formal way (Marshall 2004: 529–47, 567–74; Thielman 2005: 536–68; Matera 2007: 318–34). It is my intention here merely to preview selected highlights of John's Letters. More detailed discussion and numerous additional important insights will emerge in the exegesis.

Bray (2000: xxi–xxv) comments helpfully on the importance of the Catholic Epistles generally ("Catholic" in his usage referring to the NT letters from James to Jude). First, they present a non-Pauline depiction of early Christian belief. Even if we welcome every line of Paul's writings, we can be grateful for alternate ways of construing the gospel message and for additional examples of how apostolic leaders (or their close associates) responded to the challenges of their day. Both the historical and the doctrinal contributions of this corpus of writings are vital.

Therein lies a second realm of their importance. John's Letters document the existence of aberrant Christian belief and behavior systems within or in close proximity to the church from early times. Christians in subsequent periods need not be demoralized when deception, corruption, or falsehood arise. There are resources for offsetting these ills, because they are precisely the things that Christ came to challenge and vanquish and then to give his followers victory over as they respond to him in faith. Many become disillusioned at wrongdoing in the church. First John reminds readers that the first problem to confront is the person in the mirror. The daily lot of every Christian is to confess his or her sins (1 John 1:9). From that point, but only from that point, John's Letters go on to commend a God of light, truth, love, hope, and life who through his Son and Spirit works renewal where darkness once lay deep and constantly threatens to reemerge.

A third area of the epistles' importance lies in their implicit trisection of authentic Christian experience. Life in the Son grows out of right belief, but not right belief alone. It extends to obedient behavior too. But correct behavior, even combined with high orthodoxy, can be overrated. Who has not encountered the doctrinaire, morally scrupulous, but hate-filled self-confessed follower of Jesus? Something is missing. First John in particular puts a finger on it (see also 2 John 1, 5–6; 3 John 1, 6). True godliness in John's conception consists of a third integral element: deep-rooted devotion of the heart to God. This is love. It changes not only our regard for God but also for people. Recent research shows this to be rooted in doctrine and directed toward action, but still a richly and deeply felt conviction and emotion: "When believers are to feel joy, hope and love, . . . these are not cold and dry exhortations to be analyzed and broken down into theological constructs. Instead, they are meant to foster a healthy and vibrant emotional life in what were often difficult situations" (Elliott 2005: 260).

The understanding, experience, and expression of love, so much an emphasis for John, are perhaps the major disconnect between what he writes and what many of his readers grasp, feel, and live. This is possibly due to true love being so close to the essence of the true God—"God is love" (1 John 4:8). Sinful persons will naturally be foreign to the purity, beauty, and transformative force of what is most essential to the God from whom our souls are by nature estranged (a signature Johannine conviction; John 3:19). There are also impediments from the human side due to any number of conditioning factors. To take but one example, if the findings of Baron-Cohen (2003) are valid, many men tend to excel at abstract understanding and building systems, but they struggle with interpersonal relations. Sinful males often cannot relate very well with the emotional needs and lives of others. It can be easy for them to suppress, deny, and in the end never discover the reality of love worthy of the name. For their part, most women, according to Baron-Cohen, are superior to most men when it comes to communicating and empathizing. But there are pitfalls and downsides here when love is defined, as it is for John, not merely as sinful woman's natural feeling and reflexive action but as doctrinally driven and ethically regulated in very rigorous ways. Heartfelt empathy, whether in a woman or a man, can blur the unwelcome rough edges of truth. Women and men alike face a lifetime of challenge in coming to grips with the implications of John's deceptively simple, but in reality sophisticated and elegant, religious psychology with its tripartite interplay of sublime elements (doctrine, ethics, relationality), for each in itself is, finally, beyond full human grasp. Yet John enjoins all three on Christ's followers, just as he vests the gospel message with the capacity to produce them.

A fourth area of these epistles' importance lies in their reminder of the nature of pastoral ministry: it is inherently and irreducibly microcosmic in focus, though it may well be macrocosmic in vision and effect. If Jesus Christ is the cosmic deliverer, the divinely anointed Christ presupposed by John's language, then surely the proper place for one of his handpicked followers and historic witnesses would be a high office from which to multiply his gifts through the mobilization of innumerable underlings. And no doubt John did mobilize many coworkers (hinted at, e.g., in 3 John 4). But the "co" is the point: John remained primary (because he was an apostle) among equals (because he too was a sinner and a servant of the gospel). This may help explain why he styled himself "elder" in 2–3 John, not insisting on the honorific "apostle" or "original disciple" that were his historical and ecclesial due (cf. Bauckham 2006: 172 on Peter's reserved personal reminiscences).

The default first-person tone of 1 John (note the numerous "we" passages) shows John often addressing his readers as one of them (some "we" statements could connote apostolic authority). Rusam (1993: 227–28) could be correct in his view that the congregation or congregations involved here are house churches, though their size and exact constitution are not vital for interpretation of the letters. Second John depicts a wizened spiritual leader delighting over a (probably small) congregation and every single one of its members (cf. 2 John 4: "your children"). He expresses concern for what comes through the front door of every family's house (2 John 10). He passes on greetings from every single "child" of his congregation to the children of the congregation he addresses (2 John 13). This is not the remote vantage point of a detached intellectual or political policy maker; it is rather the self-involved language of a player-coach. Third John is almost painfully intimate; if it were an e-mail on the screen of someone else's laptop, we would feel embarrassed to be reading it without the owner's permission. John does not write with clinical detachment but with unabashed interpersonal engagement: "The elder to Gaius whom I truly love" (3 John 1). Three times John uses the singular vocative "beloved" (ἀγαπητέ, *agapēte*; 3 John 2, 5, 11). He concludes by asking Gaius to greet his congregation by name (3 John 15 [14b NIV]), or one by one like a shepherd would account for sheep.

To the extent that John's Letters contribute to a template for Christian ministry and, in particular, leadership as part of that ministry, they model an influence that is simultaneously top-down and side-by-side. It is not as if ecclesiastical oversight were unimportant; various markers in 2–3 John indicate "that matters of authority and church order were growing concerns" (Hultgren 1994: 77). Yet in military terms, John is an officer alongside other grunts in the trenches or on patrol, not a smooth-shaven colonel warm and safe in some command post miles away. The ministry of Christ that John's Letters commends is truly a ministry, a service, down to the personal level of where each individual lives. In its macrocosmic implications and effects, if God should so grant, this ministry is constantly informed, steered, and infused with integrity through the minister's (in this case John's) constant full engagement in the truth, commands, and love he ardently commends in face-to-face interchange with fellow believers. This kind of hands-on personal service is also precisely what John commends in Gaius (3 John 3, 5).

Finally, if 1–3 John leave the disciple who studies them with any single lasting impression, it is the grandeur and centrality of God (here linking John's thought with Paul's, if Schreiner 2001 is correct). Part of this is the sheer volume of references to him. There is hardly a verse or even clause anywhere that does not name a person of the Godhead (Trinity), a divine attribute, or a divine work (like a command that has come from God). These letters are not simply theological, as one might say ale is alcoholic: they are rather theology distillate, analogous to highest-proof grain alcohol that is highly flammable and intoxicating in even small amounts. God—mainly Father and Son, but occasionally also Holy Spirit—suffuses every situation John envisions, each piece of counsel he issues, every sentiment he conveys, each affirmation he sets forth. No OT psalmist is any more God saturated in awareness than the writer of these letters.

It would be misguided to try to mimic John's consciousness by our own language, talking only of God or Jesus or the Spirit at every turn, as if the heart were transformed and the world redeemed by adopting hyperspiritual verbal affectation. Rather, the point here is to discern where John projects himself and his readers to be headed. Jesus's vision in the prayer of John's Gospel was for all his followers to "be one, just as you, Father, are in me, and I in you, that they may also be in us" (17:21). Paul envisioned a juncture where all things (this includes humans) will be subjected to God, and "then the Son himself will also be subjected to him who put all things in subjection under him, that God may be all in all" (1 Cor. 15:28). God is the grand *telos*, the goal and outcome, of the fallen creation that Christ came to restore. John's Letters foreshadow this by modeling awareness of God's pervasive goodness and of his people's mandate and privilege to progress in it even and especially as the Lord's return approaches.

One reason that determining the authorship of these letters is such a sticky question is that the writer's visceral urge is to witness to God, into whose truth and love he has ventured far, not to present a profile of his personal identity and petty human expectations. His own personality is obscured by the divine person to whom he has so thoroughly subordinated his thoughts, actions, and affection. He writes like someone well might whom perhaps sixty years earlier Jesus taught to pray, "Your will be done," and in composing these letters as a very old man has become an instrument of answer to his own daily petition.

I. Central Burden: God Is Light (1:1–2:6)
II. Primary Commandment: Embody the Age-Old Message (2:7–17)
III. Key Counsel: Abide in His Anointing (Truth) and Receive Eternal Life (2:18–3:8)
IV. Core Teaching: Love, Works, Trust (3:9–4:6)
V. Foundational Imperative: God's Love (4:7–14)
VI. Illustrative Appeal: Renewed and Expanded Invitation to Love (4:15–5:15)
VII. Concluding Admonition: Pastoral Counsel, Assurance, and Warning (5:16–21)

I. Central Burden: God Is Light (1:1–2:6)

First John opens with a calculated flourish (cf. Rensberger 1997: 45: "quite deliberate") that bristles with words, concepts, and doctrinal allusions. Most if not all of these will gradually emerge as central themes of the letter (Schnackenburg 1992: 48). Not until later does it become clear that the epistle has a polemical edge:[1] it is written to a believing community that is dealing with fallout from the departure (2:19) of persons with beliefs and practices the author cannot endorse. But for now, the opening verses angle toward addressing a bedrock truth that for John rules out the legitimacy of these persons and their ways: the character of God (1:5). In that sense the epistle has a point of contact with a celebrated Pauline epistolary trait: establish a doctrinal foundation and framework (e.g., Rom. 1–11; cf. Eph. 1–3), then based on this make inferences yielding ethical imperatives (Rom. 12–16; Eph. 4–6). John's approach is, finally, more complex than that, but that is the essential starting point.

The truths for which John stands, though simple to affirm, are easy to dispute, as allusions to the implied adversaries of the faith will keep reminding the reader throughout the epistle. First John accordingly begins by affirming the author's credentials to speak with that calm authority that marks the entire discourse (1:1–4). Like certain others specially chosen by Jesus (Mark 1:16–20; 3:13–19), John heard and saw and touched the deceptively mundane stuff of eternal redemption. He saw life—eternal life—embodied like no other human had embodied it before (despite the unquestioned greatness of towering figures like Abraham and Moses for John's teacher Jesus; cf. John 5:46; 8:56) or would ever embody it again. No wonder John's rhetoric, elsewhere so choppy that a flow of argument can be difficult to detect, here rings poetic and even borders on epic. He wants to assert the transcendent excellence, the purity, the perfection of the one whom Jesus Christ revealed. He wants God's people who hear or read his letter to be reminded of who God is and what it means to rest in the sure knowledge that he bestows. And he probably seeks to plant warning flags lest readers violate the ethical ways that are appropriate to God's sanctifying presence.

Yet despite the grandeur of the opening verses (Schnackenburg 1992: 52 speaks of "massive" phrases) and the searing brightness of transforming divine light (1:5), John writes not as a man of letters (like, say, Seneca) or a philosopher (like Epictetus) or an ideologue (like Juvenal). He writes rather as a pastoral counselor and practical theologian. "This is not an exercise in

1. But R. Brown 1982: 175 risks overreading when he concludes, "The crescendo of references to sensory experience in 1:1 reflects defiant exasperation provoked by opposition over the thrust of the Johannine Gospel."

abstract speculation; it is engaged pastoral care" (Loader 1992: 3). Griffiths's comprehensive study (2002: 1) serves to "demonstrate that 1 John has primarily pastoral, rather than polemical, aims."

John wastes no time with rhetoric[2] or even with dogmatics per se. As the outline above shows, he rather moves quickly to the import of God and his character for daily Christian living (1:6–10). Nor is he content merely to air practical truths as thoughts to treasure: he just as quickly urges them on the believing community as edicts to heed (2:1–6). And he does so, not from a learned or lofty distance, but with repeated avowal of his deep feelings for fellow believers (e.g., 2:1: "my children"). A threefold emphasis emerges from the start: historico-theological truth (or doctrine), ethical integrity, and relational warmth. In the exegesis of 2:1, I will explore the three corresponding dimensions of saving knowledge of God in Christ that John seems concerned to set forth. These three emphases, it will be seen, comprise rubrics under which many of the epistle's various sections and discussions take on their full contextual meaning.

2. Cf. Edwards 1996: 38, who is responding to Watson 1989: "Classical rhetoric hardly seems to be the key to 1 John's style." But see Painter 2002: 87 and Witherington 2006: 409–12.

I. Central Burden: God Is Light (1:1–2:6)
➤ A. Announcement of Authority and Purpose (1:1–4)
B. Main Burden of the Epistle: The Character of God (1:5)
C. Implications of God's Character for the Christian Life (1:6–10)
D. Appeal to Readers in the Light of God's Character (2:1–6)

A. Announcement of Authority and Purpose (1:1–4)

The discourse in the first section is syntactically convoluted[1] but fairly clear in referring to three temporal junctures. The earliest juncture is "the beginning" (1:1)—the time of Christ's incarnate existence (so Sloyan 1995: 10) or perhaps even preexistence—leading up to a second juncture: the era when witnesses, like the writer of 1 John, came into physical contact with him. The third temporal juncture is the time of John's composing this letter. One could even speak of a fourth moment: the time when the letter is read and responded to (1:4).

John lays out this scenario, however, not in neat linear sequential fashion but in a halting style that is more allusive than declarative and that interrupts itself, backtracks, then leaps ahead again. For the sake of clarity, my translation below seeks to follow a less labyrinthine logical course. Superscript numbers show that verses have been reordered, the only time this will occur in this commentary. What is lost is the meandering unfolding of John's meaning that the original somewhat laboriously conveys. What is gained is a more directly stated understanding of what John seeks to communicate.

Jesus Christ is the slightly veiled primary subject of this section. The first word ὅ (*ho*) is neuter, not masculine, and includes Jesus in its scope[2] but extends beyond him to encompass a more expansive horizon (cf. Loader 1992: 5; Caragounis 2006: 236–37). John begins on a solid christological[3] and by implication theological note. This is important, because the epistle's abundance of practical asides and its seemingly pedestrian and repetitious focus on elementary Christian graces like love and faith can lull the reader into

1. As observed by commentators across the centuries: Calvin 1988: 233 calls the passage "abrupt and confused." Haupt 1879: 2 writes that the opening words are sufficiently complex to furnish "some difficulties to the grammatical interpretation." Holtzmann 1908: 327 speaks of "thoughts that become opaque due to their complicated interweaving." R. Brown 1982: x (cf. 24) refers to sentences that are "infuriatingly obscure." And Rensberger 1997: 45 mentions "nearly impossible grammar." See also Thompson 1992: 35. Strecker 1996: 7 posits "the interweaving of the results" of discussions in a Johannine school; so also R. Brown 1982: 152.

2. Cf. BDF §138.1: "The neuter is sometimes used with reference to persons if it is not the individuals but a general quality that is to be emphasized." Akin 2001: 51n13 suggests "a neuter of abstraction, conceiving of the pre-incarnate Christ as 'abstract deity.'" Witherington's suggestion (2006: 440) that ὅ refers to God's wisdom is unconvincing.

3. Cf. Haupt 1879: 1: "No author in the New Testament canon has to the same extent as the Apostle John impressed upon the very introductory words of his writings a Christological stamp."

forgetting that the epistle's counsel flows, not from a simplistic religiosity,[4] but out of an epoch-making and life-transforming encounter with the Lord Jesus Christ: "We have seen his glory, the glory of the one and only, who came from the Father, full of grace and truth" (John 1:14).

The exposure to Christ that John sets forth, while it no doubt had its individual dimensions for John, was of a corporate nature (note the repeated "we"). John is not alone in the claims he advances. He is one member of a larger group whose combined testimony is far stronger than it could have been if it were isolated and solitary.[5] John's "we" makes it clear that the ground he occupies, while distinct from the location of his readers because he is an apostle and they are not (on John's "we of authoritative testimony," see Bauckham 2006: 370–83), is no desert island. The spirituality of this epistle is ecclesial.

Renowned for having written a "spiritual gospel,"[6] John in this epistle is nonetheless hardheadedly historical (cf. Alexander 1901: 88–98) in his foundational starting point. Christ came, and he somehow brought eternity ("eternal life") more clearly into view[7] within earth's historical vicissitudes. Precisely what Christ did was vouchsafed to witnesses to be passed along, and just what confessing Christians ought to do about it is the focus of the opening three sentences. They form the necessary prelude to the central claim of the section regarding God's character and its implications (1:5–2:6).

The section can be outlined as follows:

1. Eyewitness privilege and proclamation (1:1–3)
   a. The fact of the incarnation (1:1)
   b. The validity of eyewitness testimony (1:1–3)
   c. What the incarnation manifested (1:1–2)
   d. The truth and import of the incarnation (1:1–3)
   e. The goal of the proclamation (1:3)
2. Pastoral desire: Shared joy (1:4)

Exegesis and Exposition

[3][With this letter] we report to you, ⌜too⌝, what we have seen and heard, so that you may have fellowship with us—⌜and⌝ indeed our fellowship is with the Father and with his Son Jesus Christ. [1][We report] what was from the beginning—something we

4. Hofmann 1886: 317 (cf. 327–28) flirts with conveying this misconception in repeatedly stressing that 1 John is "the apostolic teaching brought down to its most elementary expression." See also Witherington 2006: 424, who subordinates John's doctrine to ethical behavior.

5. On the unified nature of the apostolic understanding of Jesus, see Bauckham 1998.

6. This phrase is from Clement of Alexandria, quoted in Eusebius, *Eccl. Hist.* 6.14.7. Schlatter 1999: 124 calls attention to the "spiritual" (and not merely moral) ethic that the letter contains.

7. Here and later when John speaks of Christ's destruction of the devil's work (e.g., 3:8), he sounds notes reminiscent of Paul's description of Christ's ministry to Timothy at Ephesus: "Christ Jesus, who has destroyed death and has brought life and immortality to light through the gospel" (2 Tim. 1:10).

heard and saw with our eyes, something we beheld and our hands felt concerning the word that bestows life. [2]This life was revealed, and ⌜ ⌝ we have seen and testify and report to you the eternal life that was with the Father and revealed to us. [4]These things we write ⌜to you⌝ so that ⌜your⌝ joy may be complete.

1. Eyewitness Privilege and Proclamation (1:1–3)

In 1:1–3 the focus is on what the author, together with others of a group that comprise a "we" (in these three verses as translated above, the words "we," "our," or "us" occur eleven times), has personally encountered and even physically contacted. This encounter has mediated an assurance of "eternal life" (1:2) to the author that he now seeks to share with his readers. The immediate goal is clear: to facilitate fellowship between the writer and the group he represents, on the one hand, and the readers, on the other. But this fellowship is not merely person to person; it also extends heavenward to God the Father and the Son (D. Smith 1991: 37). The grandeur of the claim may help account for the rhetorical complexity with which the author makes it; Candlish (1866: 9) exclaims, "It is a great [i.e., lofty] idea. Who can grasp it?"

The epistle lacks the mention of its author's name that is typical in a Hellenistic letter (R. Brown 1982: 788–89; Stowers 1986). But he must have been known to his readers by reputation. There is ample reason to suppose that he was John son of Zebedee (see introduction).

The writer speaks in the first-person plural (see additional note on 1:1–3). The most obvious possible reference here is to those members of Jesus's inner circle during his earthly days who were eyewitnesses of his remarkable life, death, and resurrection (Marshall 1978: 106).[8] The four Gospels and Acts present them as the church's foundation, Christ being the chief cornerstone (Eph. 2:20).[9] John was among their number. According to his Gospel, they received explicit commissioning on the night Jesus was betrayed (John 13–17; see Ridderbos 1988). When John speaks of "we," "our," or "us," he most likely has in mind particularly those who, along with him, were eyewitnesses of Jesus's earthly ministry.[10] This is perhaps not so much a regal plural of

8. The Johannine Epistles do not explicitly mention Jesus's resurrection (noted by Smalley 1984: 8), but they presuppose it with the ubiquitous assumption that Jesus Christ is still alive and offers those who believe in him eternal hope. The resurrection looms large in the Gospel of John, which prefers the verb ἀνίστημι (*anistēmi*) to the noun (ἀνάστασις, *anastasis*): the verb occurs eight times, the noun four times.

9. Cf. the understanding reflected in Heb. 2:3–4: the saving message was "first spoken through the Lord," then "confirmed to us by those who heard, God also bearing witness with them" (NASB).

10. For full discussion of whether the author of 1 John was a historical witness, see Schnackenburg 1992: 51–56; cf. Bauckham 2006: 358–411. Schnackenburg's claim (1992: 52) that John's interest was not historical but religious projects a Kantian dichotomy back onto John that is foreign to his thought. R. Brown 1982: 158 dismisses the view offered above in favor of reference to a Johannine school; against this may be urged the apparent uniformity of the epistle's style, the univocal ring of the implied author's voice, and the uniform patristic testimony that John son of Zebedee was the author. Kruse 2000: 53–56 decisively refutes Brown's appeal to

apostolic privilege as a plural of "*modesty*, when we share our privilege and dignity with others" (Grotius, cited in Alexander 1901: 98). John as member of this at least informal apostolate makes some five points in the opening three verses.

a. The Fact of the Incarnation (1:1)

The first point is that in Jesus Christ what is eternal and transcendent has become palpably immanent. In other words, John affirms the incarnation. Transcendence or eternality is implied by the words "what was from the beginning" (1:1).[11] Ἀπ' ἀρχῆς (*ap' archēs*) occurs frequently in the LXX to refer to what extends back to the dawn or even predawn of time (Wis. 6:22; 9:8; Sir. 16:26; Isa. 43:13). Habakkuk 1:12 LXX asks, "O Lord, are you not from everlasting [ἀπ' ἀρχῆς]?" Regarding idols, Wis. 14:13 says, "Neither have they existed from the beginning [ἀπ' ἀρχῆς] nor will they exist forever." In contrast, God *has* existed ἀπ' ἀρχῆς; his existence transcends creation's temporal boundaries. Old Testament messianic prophecy says that the origins of the Promised One will be "from the beginning [ἀπ' ἀρχῆς], from days of eternity" (Mic. 5:2 [5:1 LXX]). Without minimizing the historicality of Jesus's existence,[12] John evokes the horizon of eternity past as he opens his epistle (Akin 2001: 52n16; Witherington 2006: 442). "The fulness of the divine essence, leading back to the Eternal Source in the invisible God himself, and the human manifestation,—all this he contemplated inseparably and as one" (Neander 1852: 21).

But the eternal has somehow materialized in the carnal, for John limns the transcendent with overtly sensory language. It is clear that he is not speaking metaphorically or spiritually (contra Origen, *Against Celsus* 1.48) but literally as he enlarges on "what was from the beginning" with verbs of hearing, seeing, and touching.[13] He underscores the material reality of the eternal-made-flesh by noting that the seeing was "with our eyes," the touching performed with "our hands" (1 John 1:1). In every way possible, John stresses that the eternal and heavenly, in a word the divine, has made himself corporeal and historical

various ancient texts alleged to support the "Johannine school" theory. Painter 2002: 129–30 (cf. Rensberger 1997: 47) states that "neither the Fourth Gospel nor 1 John shows any real interest in establishing the facts based on eyewitnesses," but this is an argument from silence and does not account adequately either for the plain claims of 1 John's prologue or for Fourth Gospel verses like 1:14; 19:35; 21:24.

11. Calvin's view (1988: 233) that John refers to Christ's divinity is too restrictive. Mian 1988 explains "what was from the beginning" with respect to the whole of 1:1–5.

12. R. Brown 1982: 158 (cf. 167) thinks that "what was from the beginning" must mean Jesus's "person, words, and deeds" as these reflect "his self-revelation . . . to his disciples after his baptism." In arriving at this conclusion, however, he gives short shrift to OT convictions that likely informed both Jesus's and John's theological consciousness. Many commentators take "from the beginning" as referring to the incarnation but not the time before the world's creation; it is not easy to see why John should not be allowed to evoke thoughts of both.

13. Tertullian (*On the Soul* 17) points out that the Platonists disparage sense perception. In contrast, he argues against Plato's irrationality on this point and cites numerous NT passages that testify to sense cognition of Jesus Christ. He climaxes his citations with 1 John 1:1.

in a definitive way in the proximity of John and others with him. Whatever John's message in this epistle, his basis for writing clearly lies in the same conviction that he voiced in his gospel: "The Word became flesh and made his dwelling among us" (John 1:14).[14]

Only later in the epistle does the reader learn that John's addressees were facing blatant challenges to the doctrine of the incarnation. Those who denied that "Jesus is the Christ" (1 John 2:22) were denying that "Jesus Christ has come in the flesh" (4:2). Second John 7 broaches a similar theme: "Many deceivers, who do not acknowledge Jesus Christ as coming in the flesh, have gone out into the world." Second-century church leader Irenaeus (*Ag. Her.* 1.26.1) spoke of a teacher named Cerinthus, whose views answer to those John rejected. We cannot say for sure that John's epistle takes on Cerinthus explicitly. But his opening stress on the eternal being essentially present in humanity and corporeality points to a misrepresentation of Jesus Christ's identity that Cerinthus and others embraced.

b. The Validity of Eyewitness Testimony (1:1–3)

While 1 John's opening verses point, first, to the incarnation, a second emphasis is closely related: people, John among them, can bear and are bearing eyewitness testimony to the incarnation. Schnackenburg (1992: 53–54) rightly notes that the wording of the verses backs the claim that the viewpoint is one of "people who have had a historical experience of the great event of salvation." The importance of this claim is easily lost on modern readers accustomed to truth in public and empirical matters being established, as it commonly is in the popular mind, by science. While in many ways science's achievements are obviously impressive and welcome, they have unfortunately enthroned a metaphysic of naturalism in influential circles.[15] For naturalism, eyewitness testimony, especially of former times and of non-Western cultures, means little if it runs counter to the convictions of reigning naturalistic certainties.[16]

14. For further points of comparison between 1:1–3 and the prologue to John's Gospel, see, e.g., Gryclewicz 1958 (not accessible to me). More comprehensively see R. Brown 1982: 176–80; more succinct is Westcott 1883: 3, who notes that parallels between the prologues of 1 John and the Gospel of John were already discussed by Dionysius of Alexandria.

15. P. Johnson 1995: 7–8 notes, "In our greatest universities, naturalism—the doctrine that nature is 'all there is'—is the virtually unquestioned assumption that underlies not only natural science but intellectual work of all kinds." He continues: "If naturalism is true, then humankind created God—not the other way around. In that case rationality requires that we recognize the Creator as the imaginary being he has always been, and that we rely on things that are real, such as ourselves and the material world of nature. Reliance on the guidance of an imaginary supernatural being is called superstition." For trenchant observations on science's limits (often not acknowledged by scientists), see Maki 1999 and Collins 2006.

16. In mainstream views of science, it seems that "naturalistic certainties" are actually an oxymoron: even on the basis of scientific method, "everything we 'know' is taken to be, as it were, a temporary acquisition based on information at present available and a useful basis for speculation and analysis, but by no means absolute truth" (McLeish 1995: 663).

Though from John's point of view truth would by no means be antithetical to much of what naturalistic science affirms today, it would be markedly less reductionist. Truth is as much a matter of what God, by word or deed, in creation or redemption, has revealed as it is of what humans observe and infer. Ideally, divine revelation and humble human inference work together, and when they do, truth in a full sense can emerge. Precisely this concurrence of divine self-disclosure and human reception is what John writes about here as he "testifies" or "bears witness."

Solemn testimony following an event witnessed by two or more persons was the mechanism God ordained in OT times for the establishment of facts (Num. 35:30; Deut. 17:6; 19:15). Jesus (quoting Deut. 19:15) counseled observance of this protocol among his followers: "But if he will not listen, take one or two others along, so that 'every matter may be established by the testimony of two or three witnesses'" (Matt. 18:16). Jesus commissioned his handpicked followers to serve as his "witnesses" (Luke 21:13; Acts 1:8; 2:32; 3:15). A jurisprudence of multiple witnesses was maintained in the early decades of the fledgling church, whether at Corinth (2 Cor. 13:1) or at Ephesus in times prior to John's residence there: "Do not entertain an accusation against an elder unless it is brought by two or three witnesses" (1 Tim. 5:19).

As a result, when John writes "we have seen and testify" (1 John 1:2), he is not making conversation but virtually swearing a deposition (Thompson 1992: 34). While in the modern setting matters of faith like the incarnation and matters of fact or truth cannot be equated (see the classic statement by Pfeiffer 1951; also Gilkey 1961), and while in postmodern thought even the knowable existence of truth of any stripe is disputed (Vanhoozer 1998), for John the multiple attestation of witnesses grounds the reality of admittedly surprising human perception and gives it binding force, as seen in the following list of verbs of perception in 1:1–3:[17]

Verb (1 John)	Translation	NT and LXX Parallels
ἀκηκόαμεν (*akēkoamen*; 1:1, 3)	we heard/have heard	John 4:42; Josh. 2:10; 9:9; Zech. 8:23
ἑωράκαμεν (*heōrakamen*; 1:1, 2, 3)	we saw/have seen	John 3:11; 20:25; Gen. 26:28; Num. 13:28, 32, 33; Deut. 1:28; Judg. 13:22; Sir. 43:32
ἐθεασάμεθα (*etheasametha*; 1:1)	we beheld	John 1:14, 32; 1 John 4:14; 2 Macc. 3:36; 3 Macc. 5:47
ἐψηλάφησαν (*epsēlaphēsan*; 1:1)	[our hands] felt	Luke 24:39; Acts 17:27

Hearing (ἀκηκόαμεν) is the most easily discounted perception that John cites, even from the standpoint of ancient sensibilities. Philo writes that some throw out evidence based on hearing alone "on the ground that what is believed through the eyes is true but through hearing is false" (*QE* 2, fragment;

17. Louw 1975, followed by R. Brown 1982: 161, argues that all the perfects and aorists in the following list have the semantic value of the perfect tense.

see Yonge 1993: 884). Seneca calls for something more than hearsay, since "credulity is a source of very great mischief. . . . We should believe only what is thrust under our eyes and becomes unmistakable, . . . and develop the habit of being slow to believe" (*On Anger* 2.24). Yet hearing, while disputable, is apparently sufficient to mediate redeeming awareness of God, as the parallels in the table above variously show.[18] John 4:42, for example, has the Samaritans stating after hearing the testimony of the woman at the well, "We no longer believe just because of what you said; now we have heard for ourselves, and we know that this man really is the Savior of the world" (NIV). The LXX parallels are instructive, in that each depicts people hearing reports about God that compel acknowledgment of him. Hearing by itself may not be decisive, but in conjunction with other indicators, it may prove convincing. Paul's affirmation comes to mind: "Consequently, faith comes from hearing the message, and the message is heard through the word of Christ" (Rom. 10:17).

John also speaks of seeing (ἑωράκαμεν). The first-person plural form that appears here occurs only five times in the NT: three times in this context and twice more in the Gospel of John. In the Gospel occurrences, what has been seen is the core of God's messianic ministry through Christ (John 3:11) or his resurrection (20:25). Septuagint usage is similarly restricted and suggestive: of seven occurrences, four relate to what the spies saw in Canaan, while Gen. 26:28 is Abimelech's testimony that he and those with him "have seen that the Lord was with" Isaac. Judges 13:22 has Samson's parents shrieking in terror because, as they exclaim, "We have seen God [θεὸν ἑωράκαμεν]." It can be concluded that a possible function of this expression in biblical usage is to testify solemnly, particularly regarding God's presence or work. Porter (1989: 249; cf. Painter 2002: 121–22) suggests that the "firsthand witness" implied by ἑωράκαμεν in 1 John 1:2 forms "the basis for subsequent attestation" by the present-tense verbs μαρτυροῦμεν (*martyroumen*, we testify) and ἀπαγγέλλομεν (*apangellomen*, we report). John's "with our eyes" in 1:1 underscores "the personal nature of the witness," and what was seen was literal and historical, not merely a vision "of the soul within" (Westcott 1883: 6).

The verb ἐθεασάμεθα is rendered weakly in NIV/TNIV as "looked at." But "looked at" in vernacular American English narrative often[19] connotes an act that is incidental, subsidiary, or prefatory to a subsequent act or occurrence ("We looked at cars for days before we finally bought one"). But the meaning of ἐθεασάμεθα often appears to be something like fully seeing, contemplating, and drawing a particular inference from, witnessing, beholding. The two NT references in the table above certainly carry this more intensive sense. While the LXX references are not first-person plural, they show that the verbal root

18. BDF §342.2 suggests that the perfect tense of both "hearing" and "seeing" in the context underscores "the effect on the subject." What happened formerly constitutes John's witness now.

19. Doubtless there are exceptions. Moisés Silva (private correspondence) points out that in an imperative setting this might not hold true, as when a parent corrects a child by saying, "Look at me when I speak to you!" But that is not the semantic situation of this passage.

may incline more toward the connotation of solemn witness than casual observation (the same can be said of at least two NT references: Matt. 28:1; John 4:35). In 2 Macc. 3:36 the pagan ruler Heliodorus "bore testimony to all men of the deeds of the supreme God, which he had seen [τεθεαμένος] with his own eyes" (RSV). In 3 Macc. 5:47 Ptolemy IV "rushed out, . . . wishing to witness [βουλόμενος . . . θεάσασθαι] . . . with his own eyes" (RSV). Ample lexical evidence exists to support the prima facie contextual claim that John is talking about something more than perfunctory "looking at" the circumstances and evidences surrounding Jesus Christ's first coming.[20]

As for what John says his and others' hands "felt" (ἐψηλάφησαν),[21] the word connotes physical contact, especially tactile (Judg. 16:26; Ps. 115:7 [113:14 LXX]), sometimes of great significance: "Touch me [ψηλαφήσατέ με, *psēlaphēsate me*] and see; a ghost does not have flesh and bones, as you see I have" (Luke 24:39). This may be the most telling illuminatory reference to what John wished to express in 1 John 1:1: he was among those who had physical contact with Jesus Christ both before and after his resurrection—and in both modes, John insists, Christ combined the divine and human presence.[22] This would be an overt preemptive refutation of those who wanted to separate the earthly Jesus from the heavenly Christ, which, according to Cerinthus, animated Jesus but was not essential to his human identity. The word can also mean to grope for (Acts 17:27; Deut. 28:29) or touch awkwardly (Isa. 59:10), not fully cognizant of the thing touched. It is not impossible that John is expressing this nuance here: he and others rubbed shoulders with Jesus Christ, but not until later did they realize the glory of God's presence in and with him.[23]

c. What the Incarnation Manifested (1:1–2)

John's third point in this passage is that via the incarnation "life" was manifest (1:2), borne witness to by "the word that bestows life" (1:1).[24] The word "life" (ζωή, *zōē*) occurs three times in this brief section and is a signature Johannine term: of its 135 NT occurrences, a total of 66 (49 percent of total occurrences) are found in writings traditionally ascribed to John: 36 in John's Gospel, 13 in

20. R. Brown 1982: 162 attributes the word choice to imitation of John 1:14 and to the Johannine school's decision to use an aorist, which limited the usable range of verbs of seeing.

21. Greek verbs of touching usually take genitive direct objects, but ψηλαφάω is followed by an accusative (Turner 1963: 232).

22. The attempt of Schnackenburg 1992: 52 to drive a wedge between the touching of Luke 24:39 and that of 1 John 1:1 seems arbitrary.

23. Tertullian (*On Patience* 3) may allude to 1 John 1:1 in speaking of Christ who "has been grasped by hand among men openly on earth." His point would be to link Jesus's palpable corporeality with the patience of the divine condescension.

24. This translation takes "life" in τοῦ λόγου τῆς ζωῆς as a "genitive of product"; cf. Wallace 1996: 106. In this genitive construction it makes sense to replace "of" with "which produces." Whether "word" is to be taken as announcement or as the incarnate "Word" of the early verses of John's Gospel may be left open. Double entendre cannot be ruled out. Edwards 1996: 70 suggests the rendering "life-giving message."

John's Epistles, 17 in Revelation. The word can refer to life as opposed to death (Phil. 1:20) or to our present mode of earthly human existence in general (1 Cor. 15:19; 1 Tim. 4:8). But more commonly it denotes not only the fact but also a particular quality of vital existence (R. Brown 1982: 168). To underscore this the adjective "eternal" often precedes it (and may be implied when it does not).

Jesus frequently used the terminology of "eternal life" (esp. as John's Gospel presents him), and given his use of the OT (Wenham 1994), it is hard to avoid the impression that there is a close connection between what he had in mind by the expression and what key sections of the OT express (on 1 John's ties with the OT generally, see Lieu 1993). Deuteronomy is particularly suggestive. The words "live" and "life" there reverberate with the promise of "eternal life" sounded in 1 John (suggestive passages include Deut. 4:1, 9, 10, 40; 5:16, 33; 8:1, 3; 11:9; 12:1, 10; 16:20; 17:19; 25:15; 30:15, 16, 19, 20; 32:39, 47). Most telling perhaps is Deut. 30:6: "The LORD your God will circumcise your hearts and the hearts of your descendants, so that you may love him with all your heart and with all your soul, and *live*" (NIV, emphasis added). Talk of circumcised hearts and of loving God with all one's heart and soul is certainly language familiar to NT believers. It is the language not merely of biological life in an enhanced or extended sense but also of eternal life, the enjoyment of God's covenant blessing, in the here and now, with a view (at least for NT writers) to the age to come as well.[25]

The significance of life here could be twofold.[26] First, it was an emphasis of Jesus himself, a rubric under which he instructed his disciples to understand his identity (John 11:25) and his mission (3:16). As a faithful witness, John is voicing and applying what he learned in Jesus's earthly days. Second, it is a preoccupation of all reflective humans, for they and their loved ones face death. Is there any alternative? Is there any deliverance? Early Christian preaching, with its eschatological stress on coming judgment (implying earthly death and destruction) and its conviction of Jesus's resurrection from the dead, took the bull of death by the horns and wrestled it to submission with the doctrine of eternal life in Christ. First John opens with a focus on the life, in a very full sense, that in Christ was made known. Calvin (1988: 233) does not go astray in imputing doxological overtones to life in this context: "But if we consider how miserable and horrible is the state of death and also what is the kingdom and immortal glory of God, we shall see that there is something here more magnificent than can be expressed in words."

d. The Truth and Import of the Incarnation (1:1–3)

The epistle's fourth opening point is that with the incarnation there is something both true and momentous to report:

25. For a summary of biblical data, see Yarbrough 1996: 209–12. Still provocative in identifying awareness of eternity in OT writings is Calvin 1960: §2.10.7–23.

26. Tertullian (*On the Flesh of Christ* 12) finds another significance: an application against gnostics who argue that Jesus came to reveal the soul. Tertullian counters that when Jesus manifested life, he did so to save the soul, not reveal or explain it.

1. As for the truth of what John writes, he is obviously concerned to affirm that the things he writes grow inexorably out of the way that Jesus actually lived, taught, died, and rose. John shares the concern of other ancient writers that his claims be taken seriously as factual statements (cf. Philo, *Moses* 1.4). The Letter of Aristeas is emphatic: "To tell lies concerning matters which are being chronicled would be inappropriate: If I were to make a single error, it would be impious in these matters. On the contrary, we narrate things as they happened, eschewing any error" (297). Social stability was threatened when people no longer told the truth (Josephus, *Ant.* 16.376). Those claiming to relate historical matters must adhere to the facts upon which knowledge of history is based (Josephus, *Life* 336–39; cf. Josephus's concern for fact in *Life* 363–66). The historian Plutarch (ca. AD 100) distinguished between "conjecture" and "definite historical evidence" (*Parallel Lives*, Marius 11.7; translations from Warner 1972). What John reported was no less informed by concern faithfully to represent the facts.
2. The momentousness of what John relates is implicit in his claim that he testifies and reports "the eternal life that[27] was with the Father" (1:2). In the religious tradition of both OT and NT peoples, a key assertion is the transcendence of God (affirmed, e.g., in John 1:18; 1 John 4:12). But with God's loftiness, separateness, and uniqueness, the problem arises as to how sinful humans may connect with him. Schnackenburg (1992: 64–65) notes, "Jewish piety was . . . inclined to emphasize the majesty and transcendence of God. . . . It therefore hardly offers any point of contact" with him. This is largely the case, for example, at Qumran (1992: 66). But 1 John's opening verses declare that the "life"—Jesus Christ—who is the substance of his discourse has an origin "with the Father." Given the historical appearance of Christ, John sees the transcendence problem as overcome and Jesus set off as unique among humans. John thereby also sets the stage for subsequent lofty claims about Christ throughout his epistle. These claims to mediate the transcendent God grow out of affirmations made by Jesus, as affirmed in John's Gospel, all of which furnish background for John's counsel in this epistle:

John 6:46	"only he [Jesus] has seen the Father"
John 7:17	Jesus's "teaching comes from God"
John 8:40	Jesus tells "the truth that [he] heard from God"
John 8:42 (cf. 16:27, 30)	Jesus "came from God"
John 13:3	Jesus is "returning to God"

e. The Goal of the Proclamation (1:3)

A fifth and final point of the opening verses of John's epistle is that what he reports is intended to nurture fellowship: he writes so that his readers "may

27. R. Brown 1982: 168–69 calls attention to the pronoun ἥτις (*hētis*, which, that) as referring to the "specific quality" of life as it exists in the Father's presence.

have fellowship with us"—that is, the apostolic "we" who testify of Jesus's earthly and heavenly life.[28] And, John continues, this is not just any fellowship at all, but that fellowship shared peculiarly[29] by those who know God the Father in his Son Jesus Christ.[30] The word "fellowship" (κοινωνία, *koinōnia*) is not particularly common in the NT (nineteen times total) and never occurs in the Gospels (for thorough discussion, see Panikulam 1994). The LXX contains only three occurrences, none very informative for NT usage. In Johannine literature it is found in only 1 John 1:3 (2x), 6, 7. But the thing denoted by the word[31]—sharing, the experience of a common yet transcendent bond and especially the bond of trust in the crucified and resurrected Christ—is ubiquitous in the NT, whether as a state of relationship between human(s) and God or a state of relationship between or among humans. Among the numerous possible intents, functions, and applications of John's letter, a central one is the relational commonality that Jesus established among his first followers, like John, and that John now seeks to pass along to his readers.[32] Lyonnet (1957) makes the important point that this is the means whereby sinners become children of God; otherwise they are children of the devil, a state of affairs that Christ has come to undo.

John writes, then, to promote unity and harmony, what the Apostles' Creed calls "the communion of saints," both with God and with one another. He writes in order to stabilize and enhance the existence of "church" in the locale he addresses: "The term 'church' is not used, but *koinōnia* meaningfully interprets the reality of the believing community" (Painter 2002: 128).[33] This will be worth keeping in mind in later passages where it is easy to lose sight of John's ecclesial focus because of the intensity of his analysis of individual matters. It is also a fitting prelude to John's concluding statement of this opening paragraph in the next verse.

28. So Calvin 1988: 236: "In short, John says that, as the apostles were adopted by Christ as brethren who were gathered into one body to cleave to God, so he does the same with the other disciples (*collegis*). The many are made partakers of this holy and blessed unity." On the first-person plural by apostolic writers, see Turner 1963: 28.

29. The use of the less common possessive adjective ἡμέτερος (*hēmeteros*, our; see BDF §285.1), when the prosaic ἡμῶν (*hēmōn*, our) would have sufficed semantically, could have been encouraged by the sonorous audial effect of ἡμετέρα μετὰ τοῦ (*hēmetera meta tou*). Culy 2004: 8 views it as stylistic.

30. Tertullian (*Against Praxeas* 28) uses this verse to argue that the Father and Son are distinct. On Jesus as God's Son, see exegesis of 3:7–8.

31. The definition of R. Brown 1982: 170 seems limited to what humans bring to their relationships and share. Gehring 2004: 80–81 affirms that "it includes spiritual as well as material considerations."

32. Calvin 1988: 237 lays the stress too exclusively on the individual's communion with God. The social dimension is of comparable importance.

33. This does not, however, justify a dichotomized understanding that would have John asserting that "fellowship with God can really only be gained, not by an independent and individual religious life, but by joining this tradition and its adherents" (Rensberger 1997: 49). John calls for a full measure of both personal pursuit of God and corporate involvement with God's people.

2. Pastoral Desire: Shared Joy (1:4)

John has already expressed one reason for his letter: to promote fellowship (1:3). Now he adds a further consideration: that the readers' joy may increase and be sustained. John's purpose goes beyond religious instruction in a purely cognitive or even "spiritual" sense. He does not write as an austere pedagogue or mystical counselor. Nor does he indulge in political maneuvering or demagoguery. Rather, he seeks his readers' elevation as followers of Jesus. "He has the heart of a pastor which cannot be completely happy so long as some of those for whom he feels responsible are not experiencing the full blessings of the gospel" (Marshall 1978: 105; cf. Kruse 2000: 59). Human life, a dour and dreary thing when dissension and confusion wrack a community of faith, can be transformed by Christ. Jesus spoke to his disciples about this on the black night he was betrayed (John 16:20–24; cf. Yarid 2003: 66). In 1 John 1:4 John treads a similar path.

One could always read NT epistles a little deconstructively and construe such earnest, artless relational appeal as cant. And it cannot be denied that "joy in Jesus" might in fact be pure affectation for readers in a post-Christian age where cynicism is chic.[34] But granting John and his readers the close ties and quaint (in the eyes of some) convictions they appear to have harbored and that John wants his epistle to enhance, John merely confirms the same pastoral solicitude toward them that is amply attested in Paul (1 Thess. 3:9; 2 Cor. 2:3; Phil. 1:4). For that matter, joy was a prominent feature of the relationship that Jesus and his disciples shared if the Gospels are to be trusted (Matt. 13:20, 44; 28:8; Luke 10:17; 24:52). Jesus himself expressed "joy through the Holy Spirit" in response to God's wisdom and largesse (10:21). Perhaps in this same vein, John now writes to those whose lives have been redeemed by the gospel: "All the redeemed are brought into a close union with Christ, where they experience great joy" (C. E. Arnold, *ABD* 3:1023).

Joy is mentioned somewhat programmatically in all three of John's Epistles (see also 2 John 12 and 3 John 4; for full discussion, see Ferraro 1988). The Greek word χαρά (*chara*) is found fifty-nine times in the NT, nine of them in John's Gospel. In the Fourth Gospel it always bears an eschatological ring (noted also by R. Brown 1982: 173–74): John the Baptist expresses joy akin to that of the bridegroom's friend on his wedding day (John 3:29); Jesus promises a time when the disciples' joy will be unshakable (16:22) and prays for "the full measure" of his own joy to be within his followers (17:13); and his resurrection (not only a historical but also an eschatological event) will change the sadness and confusion prominent in John 13–17 to joy.

More broadly, joy is often associated with Jesus in NT writings. There was joy at his birth (Luke 1:14; 2:10); there was joy among his disciples as they ministered (10:17); there was joy in the presence of the Lord after his resurrection (24:41). "Joy" in American parlance can connote carefree celebration,

34. For sometimes sarcastic debunking of faith in a crucified and risen Jesus, see Funk 1996.

but in biblical annals there is a caution: "Even in laughter the heart may ache, and joy may end in grief" (Prov. 14:13 NIV). True joy comes from participation in the kingdom of God, and that is not a matter of partying (see third additional note on 1:4), "of eating and drinking, but of righteousness, peace and joy in the Holy Spirit" (Rom. 14:17 NIV). There is no reason to think that John would quarrel with this Pauline assertion.

The joy that John expresses is probably to be linked with the love he has for his readers (so Augustine, *Hom. 1 John* 1.3, who relates joy to both love and unity). After all, the word underlying John's "so that your joy may be complete" is πληρόω (*plēroō*, to fill or complete; see additional note). It occurs elsewhere in his epistles only once (2 John 12), but its meaning can be close to that of τελειόω (*teleioō*, to complete, perfect)—a word frequently associated with love in 1 John (2:5; 4:12, 17, 18; Smalley 1984: 14–15 brings out an eschatological dimension as well). The fellowship of 1:3 grows out of and ought to translate into a certain buoyant affection for others and praise for the Lord because of the community participation in forgiveness of sins, transformed lives, and ennobling labor to bring about kingdom ends.[35] This is a description of joy, a profound, heartening, and infectious[36] sense of how great the message of the cross is and what a privilege it is to share in gospel benefits, ministry, and challenges. Further, hard to quantify and difficult to speak of, but no less real, is the joy of the presence of Christ himself through his Spirit within believers' religious awareness; the joy found in prayer and worship, whether private or corporate; the joy of conviction of God's goodness and love through his gift of eternal life in his Son.[37]

John's mention of joy as a goal of writing, then, is eminently appropriate in the context of the shared Christian commitment that his epistle calls for. It is a reminder that John writes (not just these opening verses but also the whole of his epistle; cf. Smalley 1984: 14) with a personal and pastoral intent, one seeking the highest happiness of his readers, comparable perhaps to the pure hopes for bright, cheerful, and productive lives that parents bear for their children.

Stress on joy also constitutes a certain sober foreshadowing, like sunshine bathing a picnic while thunderheads boil up on the horizon. John speaks of joy. But he speaks to a community on the verge of losing it, if in fact joy has not already been put to flight, because of threats to the integrity of their Christian confession and praxis.

35. For a twentieth-century delineation of fellowship in such terms, see Bonhoeffer 1954.

36. CCC §425 notes in connection with 1:1–4 that the first disciples "invite people of every era to enter into the joy of their communion with Christ."

37. Nineteenth-century Scottish minister Alexander Moody Stuart tells of weekly meetings with a parishioner for prayer. One week the prayer time was cut short as the parishioner left abruptly in apparent distress. Later Stuart asked the man why he was so shaken. The response: "When we were on our knees I was so filled with a sense of the love of God, that the joy was too much for me; it was all that I was able to bear, and it was with a struggle that I did not sink under it" (Murray 1998: 97). More discursively, see Candlish 1866: 18–36.

Additional Notes

1:1–3. BDF §280 suggests that the first-person plural in these verses is equivalent to the first-person singular, which the author uses of himself a total of twelve times in this epistle (also 2:1, 7, 8, 12 [2x], 14 [3x], 21, 26; 5:13, 16). But there is no reason to force a uniform referent on plural and singular verbs. In the opening verses John uses the plural to include himself among a wider circle. On the basis of what membership in this group confers on him, he writes thereafter with personal authority in the singular. For a possible similar alternation, see John 21:24 (first-person plural) and 21:25 (first-person singular). Taking a different tack is Lillie 1967; see also Curtis 1992.

1:2. Codex B and a few other witnesses repeat the initial ὅ of 1:1 before ἑωράκαμεν in 1:2. This appears to be an isolated attempt to conform the diction of 1:2 to ὃ ἑωράκαμεν, found in 1:1 and 1:3.

1:3. Καί has superior external attestation. Also, it is the harder reading (since there is no obvious reason for scribes to have added it, and since καὶ ὑμεῖς in the next clause renders it somewhat superfluous). It may be a small historical indicator that John at the time was composing or dispatching other similar appeals.

1:3. External support for δέ is weighty. Scribal omission is understandable due to its slight semantic value and its unusual placement—but the analogous Johannine locutions listed below render δέ stylistically plausible in this verse (it is therefore hardly "odd" in 2:2, as claimed by Marshall 1978: 119n30). Δέ occurs 11 times in 11 verses in 1 John and 213 times in 204 verses in the Gospel of John (the consistency of occurrence is notable). Of these 224 Johannine occurrences, δέ (which usually occurs as the second word in its clause) occurs 8 times as the third, fourth, or fifth word. If δέ in 1 John 1:3 is genuine, it becomes the ninth occurrence in the Johannine literature of δέ in a position other than second (cf. 3 John 12 and 4 Macc. 2:15). Note how often καί occurs among the words preceding δέ:

John 5:7	ἐν ᾧ δὲ ἔρχομαι ἐγώ, ἄλλος πρὸ ἐμοῦ καταβαίνει
John 6:51	καὶ ὁ ἄρτος δὲ ὃν ἐγὼ δώσω ἡ σάρξ μού ἐστιν ὑπὲρ τῆς τοῦ κόσμου ζωῆς
John 7:31	ἐκ τοῦ ὄχλου δὲ πολλοὶ ἐπίστευσαν εἰς αὐτὸν καὶ ἔλεγον
John 8:16	καὶ ἐὰν κρίνω δὲ ἐγώ, ἡ κρίσις ἡ ἐμὴ ἀληθινή ἐστιν
John 8:17	καὶ ἐν τῷ νόμῳ δὲ τῷ ὑμετέρῳ γέγραπται ὅτι δύο ἀνθρώπων ἡ μαρτυρία ἀληθής ἐστιν
John 15:27	καὶ ὑμεῖς δὲ μαρτυρεῖτε, ὅτι ἀπ᾽ ἀρχῆς μετ᾽ ἐμοῦ ἐστε
John 17:20	οὐ περὶ τούτων δὲ ἐρωτῶ μόνον, ἀλλὰ καὶ περὶ τῶν πιστευόντων διὰ τοῦ λόγου αὐτῶν εἰς ἐμέ
1 John 2:2	καὶ αὐτὸς ἱλασμός ἐστιν περὶ τῶν ἁμαρτιῶν ἡμῶν, οὐ περὶ τῶν ἡμετέρων δὲ μόνον ἀλλὰ καὶ περὶ ὅλου τοῦ κόσμου

1:4. Did John furnish the personal pronoun ἡμεῖς after the verb γράφομεν? ℵ, B, and A*vid are among manuscripts that include ἡμεῖς. C, 1739, 𝔐, and early versions read ὑμῖν instead: "We write *to you*." Caragounis 2006: 530–32 argues convincingly that the latter reading is to be preferred. Hence my translation above. To Caragounis's comments these may be added: since the verb form implies the personal pronoun ἡμεῖς and since it is clear that John writes to the recipients of the letter whether he uses ὑμῖν or not, the net effect for interpretation is the same. It is, however, worth noting that in the nine other times ἡμεῖς occurs in 1 John, it never follows but always precedes the main verb. Of the eighteen times that ἡμεῖς is used in John's Gospel, only at 8:48 does it follow the verb (11:16 and 21:3 may not be true parallels due to desired emphasis). In terms of usage, this tips the scales away from ἡμεῖς being original. In the only other occurrence of γράφομεν in the NT (1 Cor. 1:13), Paul writes γράφομεν ὑμῖν.

1:4. Did John write ἡ χαρὰ ἡμῶν (our joy) or ἡ χαρὰ ὑμῶν (your joy)? The problem here involves itacism, a scribal error arising from seven different vowels or diphthongs that might have been pronounced the same in Greek, resulting in mistakes when scribes copied by dictation (Metzger 1992: 191). Once again, the difference is not great for interpretive purposes. External evidence is somewhat in favor of ἡμῶν (our). Within the Johannine corpus, John 16:24 has Jesus urging his disciples to make petition so that ἡ χαρὰ ὑμῶν ᾖ πεπληρωμένη. But in 2 John 12 we find the phrase ἵνα ἡ χαρὰ ἡμῶν πεπληρωμένη ᾖ (where, however, there is also textual divergence; see additional note on 2 John 12). So on internal grounds, too, no definite Johannine trend can be discerned. The writer identifies so fully with his readers and shares what he has come to know with them so completely that he could clearly have wished his apostolic joy to be theirs (and thus write ἡμῶν; cf. Metzger 1994: 639). But he sees his addressees as being sufficiently separate from the apostolic circle and sufficiently beset by the distinctive challenges they face that it is also not hard to imagine that he might have written ὑμῶν (so Dobson 1971, arguing on the basis of John's use of emphatic personal pronouns).

1:4. On the meaning of χαρά (joy), the word ἡδονή (*hēdonē*, pleasure) should also be mentioned. Strecker 1996: 21 notes that the word is sometimes used synonymously with χαρά, but this is never the case in the NT, where ἡδονή always carries a pejorative sense (Luke 8:14; Titus 3:3; James 4:1, 3; 2 Pet. 2:13). Christian joy has points of contact but should not be confused with pleasure in the sense of rollicking good times or self-indulgent gratification.

1:4. The verbal construction πεπληρωμένη (may be complete) should be understood as a periphrastic perfect with no force beyond the normal perfect (Turner 1963: 88–89).

B. Main Burden of the Epistle: The Character of God (1:5)

Optimal interpretation of a letter involves determining, if possible, the purpose(s) for which the author wrote it.[1] John explicitly states four (italicized below):

1:3 We proclaim to you what we have seen and heard, *so that you also may have fellowship with us.*

1:4 We write this *to make our joy complete.*

2:1 My dear children, I write this to you *so that you will not sin.*

5:13 I write these things to you who believe in the name of the Son of God *so that you may know that you have eternal life.*

In addition to such statements, the epistle contains ten imperatives (2:15, 24, 27, 28; 3:1, 7, 13; 4:1 [2x]; 5:21). In theory any of these might prove to furnish John's main purpose for writing. Or the last verse of the epistle might be taken as implying John's main intention: "Dear children, keep yourselves from idols" (5:21; cf. Alexander 1901: 3–20; Griffith 2002). Thüsing (1965) highlights another possible central purpose by bringing out the points at which "the greatness of God" is key to Johannine thought. And Lloyd-Jones (1993: 9–19) relates the epistle's overall message to 5:19: "We know that we are children of God, and that the whole world is under the control of the evil one."

But these are, in the end, secondary purposes for the letter. They are all part of the writer's aim and are therefore of obvious importance. But they are not the underlying foundation but part of the exposed edifice of John's instruction and exhortation. That is, they point to visible, attitudinal, or behavioral stances that he wants his readers to adopt, maintain, or guard against. But beneath John's stated aims and imperatives lies an indicative that is the basis for what he urges his readers to do and why he urges them to do it (D. Smith 1991: 55). It can be argued that 1:5, a statement of God's nature, is that basis.[2] "In many ways the statement that *God is light* is the

1. For defense of authorial intent as a legitimate concern of interpretation, see Vanhoozer 1998.

2. Schnackenburg 1992: 72–73 sees "God is light" as "the core and keynote" of the beginning sections of John. But the affirmation retains at least residual importance throughout the epistle. *CCC* §214 sees "the riches of the divine name" comprehended in the two terms "truth" and "love" and associates the light of 1:5 with truth. Hiebert 1988 sees God's nature as light as the basis for tests of fellowship in the immediate context.

thesis of the epistle" (Thompson 1992: 40). John's message "is essentially one about the character of God" (Kruse 2000: 62; cf. C. Black 2000: 391).

Three preliminary reasons for this assertion may be advanced: (1) the very words "this is the message we have heard from him and declare to you" have the ring of a summary declaration of the epistle's most fundamental assertion, the truth on which all assertions and exhortations and statements of purpose turn; (2) the verse is the first statement after the four introductory verses and seems to function as a head verse for what follows,[3] so by virtue of positioning it carries particular weight; and (3) although Jesus Christ is the formal content of John's message (1:1–4), the unseen Father who is revealed in the Son is the material content (a fact implied by the bracketing of Father and Son in 1:3, corroborated by 1:5, and suggested by the Fourth Gospel passages that speak of the Son revealing the Father). In other words, at all times when John speaks of the Son, he is at the same time, without pedantic reiteration of the fact, making a statement about the Father.

A fourth and perhaps decisive reason for viewing 1 John 1:5 as John's primary burden in writing[4] is its profound rootage in OT theology. Nothing is more fundamental to the OT taken as a whole than God's existence (or person) and his creative and redemptive activity (or work). This OT substructure forms the ultimate logical, theological, and historical background for Jesus's ministry, John's Gospel (see particularly Reim 2005: 101n15), and this epistle, because without this substructure the message of Jesus Christ's coming and ministry would be either an irrational assertion on John's part or an incongruous historico-religious intrusion out of nowhere into the first-century Roman world and Judaism. While there is interesting discussion about illuminatory ties between light in 1 John and in documents from Qumran (Schnackenburg 1992: 75) or various post-NT syncretistic texts (Strecker 1996: 26–28), far more obvious are ties between God and light (and by extension "darkness") in the OT.[5] This background will be sketched below.

Exegesis and Exposition

5 And this is the ⌜message⌝ that we have heard from him and report to you: God is light, and in him there is no darkness whatsoever.

John begins with the transitional words καὶ ἔστιν αὕτη (*kai estin hautē*, and this is). Here as often elsewhere (1 John 2:25; 3:11, 23; 5:3, 4, 11a, 14) they refer to what follows rather than to what precedes. The word translated "message" (ἀγγελία, *angelia*) occurs only twice in the NT, here and in 3:11. It seems to

3. R. Brown 1982: 192 agrees that the opening words of 1:5 point ahead to the ὅτι clause.

4. Antoniotti 1988 sees it as central for 1:5–3:10 but suggests other centers for later sections.

5. Few have followed Westcott's claim (1883: 17) that John was engaging "Zoroastrian speculations."

have no particular significance when compared to other Greek words translated "message" in the NIV: for example, λόγος (*logos*; Matt. 13:19; Luke 4:32), ἀκοή (*akoē*; John 12:38; Rom. 10:16), and κήρυγμα (*kērygma*; 2 Tim. 4:17). In the context of 1 John 1:5, in close proximity to a form of ἀκούω (*akouō*, to hear), it is related to the cognate word ἀπαγγέλλω (*apangellō*, to report) in 1:3, which was also associated with a form of ἀκούω. John speaks of the message that he and other apostles were commissioned to convey to those who did not have the direct experience of Christ that the Twelve did. They heard something from Jesus, and John now passes it along as the central assertion of his epistle. He does this by using ὅτι (*hoti*, that) to join the two halves of the sentences as "equivalent expressions" (BDF §397.3; cf. 1 John 5:11; Painter 2002: 124 calls this "epexegetical" and lists over two dozen examples in 1 John).

What they heard and saw and touched and so on (1:1, 3) pertains directly to God. This is in keeping with the assertion of John 1:18 that God is both invisible and revealed: "No one has ever seen God, but God the One and Only, who is at the Father's side, has made him known" (NIV; cf. 1 John 4:12). Christian belief, though centered on Jesus Christ as the visible pole of God's personal self-disclosure, extends to the invisible end of that same pole, God the Father (cf. John 14:9).[6] Scripture is a treasure trove of names and metaphors for God,[7] and one of these metaphors is light.

John's "God is light" stands in contrast to pagan religious systems whose gods or goddesses were associated with the heavenly bodies (Origen, *Against Celsus* 5.10–11, citing 1 John 1:5). Under Roman rule the Syrian Baal, for example, was associated with the sun; his female consort was the moon (Ferguson 1987: 222). Well after NT times a cult arose that worshiped the sun (1987: 252–53). But the true God is spirit and personal, not the material and impersonal fire of daytime sun or the pale gleam of heavenly bodies by night. He creates the natural light but is in no way to be identified with it: "Because he is called light, shall he be supposed to have any resemblance to the light of the sun?" (Origen, *First Principles* 1.1.1). In contrast to pagan gods of light, God's light furnishes ethical direction (implied by Isa. 8:20; 51:4; cf. Prov. 6:23: "For these commands are a lamp, this teaching is a light" [NIV]) and shows harmful or lawless acts to be darkness.

The connection between God and light has little to do with either gnostic or Qumran thought,[8] although formal parallels are obviously present. It is

6. Tertullian traffics in this truth extensively in *Against Praxeas* 15.

7. For God the Father, Elwell 1991: 10–34 tabulates 16 single names and expressions, 24 compound names, 119 descriptive names, and 152 designations, descriptive titles, and figures of speech. In addition, he catalogs 184 metaphors, titles, or names for Christ and 8 for the Spirit.

8. Similarities between Qumran documents and John are "concerns common to all great religions" (Hoffman 1978: 122; cf. Loader 1992: 10) and hardly necessitate an assumption of either literary dependence or direct social contact between Qumran and Johannine communities. Formal parallels are adduced in Schnackenburg 1992: 75, who also cites important differences (1992: 76). More positive toward Qumran parallels is R. Brown 1982: 242–45. Klauck 1991: 133, however, is much more cautious and concludes, "Existing similarities are due to a combination of common traditional background and an analogous contemporary situation."

rather from the OT (where "light" appears 139 times in the NIV), first of all, that John's Jewish religious heritage would have acquired associations between God and light.[9] God made the light of the physical world (Gen. 1:3). God gave his people visual light (fire by night) during their escape from Egypt (Exod. 13:21). In prayer, David extolled God's spiritual light, which dispels darkness (2 Sam. 22:29). With his last words he praised the derivative radiance of one who rules in righteousness and fear of God: that person "is like the light of morning at sunrise on a cloudless morning" (23:4 NIV). This implies that God's light has a communicable dimension (Origen, *Against Celsus* 2.71).

Ezra confirms this by praising God in prayer for the light he granted: "But now, for a brief moment, the LORD our God has been gracious in leaving us a remnant and giving us a firm place in his sanctuary, and so our God gives light to our eyes and a little relief in our bondage" (9:8 NIV). The book of Job has frequent references to God's light (and its antithesis, darkness); one example reveals God alone as the one who can answer the questions, "What is the way to the abode of light? And where does darkness reside?" (38:19 NIV). Micah proclaimed, "Though I have fallen, I will rise. Though I sit in darkness, the LORD will be my light" (7:8 NIV). Similarly both Psalms and Proverbs have frequent reference to light, often in contradistinction to darkness. Isaiah has the most occurrences (29) of "light" of any OT book, and many of these are in Isa. 40–66, chapters regarded by NT writers as redolent with typology and prophecies relating to Christ.

Like scores of OT passages likely familiar to him, John underscores God's light. He recognizes that in the church age, as at times in former redemptive history, there are "those who call evil good and good evil, who put darkness for light and light for darkness" (Isa. 5:20 NIV). Their ways are not illumined by God and his light, apparently a metaphor for his purity and moral excellence. Light is surely also to be associated with God's holiness, since the OT often represents God's holy presence as fire, which in turn radiates light (cf. Moses's face aglow with light following intimate communion with God; Exod. 34:29–35).

Not only God but also Jesus is light in John's writings (John 8:12; 9:5). Jesus said, "I have come into the world as a light, so that no one who believes in me should stay in darkness" (12:46 NIV). He urged, "Put your trust in the light while you have it, so that you may become sons of light" (12:36 NIV). While John's Gospel has twenty-four occurrences of "light" in the NIV, Matthew has eleven and Luke nine. It appears to be something to which Jesus made repeated reference.

9. Cf. Malatesta 1978: 99–102 and Marshall 1978: 109. Strecker 1996: 26 rightly asserts that with respect to John's light-darkness dualism, "derivation from the OT appears probable." But then he writes that in the OT, God is not "personally identified with light" and that the OT does not evince "a dualistic contrast of light and darkness." The OT does indeed identify God very closely with light (Pss. 27:1; 36:9 [36:10 MT]; 43:3; 44:3 [44:4 MT]), and a light-darkness dualism (ethical or eschatological, not ontological) is frequently in view.

In view of OT precedent and Jesus's usage, John's reference to light in 1 John 1:5 may be taken to have programmatic significance for the epistle as a whole.[10] It eventually becomes clear that the community he addresses is beset by darkness of a doctrinal, ethical, or relational nature, or some combination of the three. This marks a *theo*logical lapse—an inadequate response to God. Doctrinal error calls for corrective teaching, and John will offer it. Ethical negligence calls for fresh imperatives, and John will issue them. Relational breakdown (absence of compassion, presence of hate) calls for reinvigorated love for God and persons, and John will admonish readers in these directions.

But John's frame of reference in the epistle is not dominated first of all by his teaching, his commands, or his encouragement to love, or even the occasions that call all these forth. It is dominated rather by his vision of God—God's light, his moral excellence and efficacious purity.[11] These render the error and confusion that his epistle addresses quite inappropriate and in fact eminently correctable. God's light furnishes the standard and means by which John will be able to diagnose error and propound corrective measures. Because it is embodied in the crucified and risen Christ, it furnishes the transforming[12] dynamic that makes truth and love possible for sinners in a world and local setting beset by deception and apparent animosity.

"In him there is no darkness whatsoever" (1 John 1:5; on the meaning of οὐδεμία [*oudemia*, no], whose root form is οὐδείς [*oudeis*], see the second additional note). "John very often uses this way of speaking to amplify by a contrary negation what he has affirmed" (Calvin 1988: 237; cf. Nauck 1957: 4; other verses of this nature in 1 John: 2:7, 21, 27; 3:18; 4:10; 5:2; cf. 2 John 5). The meaning of darkness is obvious (and in any case made more explicit later in the epistle) in a canonical context where so much is made of God and light. At the very least it means that shadowy Christian belief, behavior, or devotion is revealed as sham when exposed to the divine radiance. "Draw whatever (veil of) darkness you please over your deeds, 'God is light'" (Tertullian, *On Repentance* 6). "It is the character of God, revealed by God, that norms the church's self-understanding and conduct" (C. Black 2000: 392).

In conclusion, the core of John's epistle is the conviction that there is a light, peculiar to God the Father though shared with Christ the Son, which those who know God recognize. Those who do not know God will not recognize,

10. Strecker 1996: 33 concedes that "God is light" is "the content of the author's proclamation" but asserts that this "is founded on the event of the cross." This seems to ignore important precedents of the claim in the OT and Jesus's teaching. It also subordinates the doctrine of God to Jesus's death when biblical writers overall seem to do the opposite.

11. This is to agree, then, with Akin 2001: 71 that light refers here most directly to who God is "by his very nature."

12. Augustine (*Hom. 1 John* 1.4) points to a notable effect that divine light has: it enlightens (similarly Origen, *First Principles* 1.1.1). Therefore words like "efficacious" and "transformative" are apt when characterizing it. So also Schlatter 1950: 7: "God is light; that tells us not merely who he is in himself but also how he is disposed toward us and how he acts upon us. . . . Like a bright sunlight his working and gift come to us and plant the truth in our understanding and righteousness in our will and in this way enlighten us."

much less honor, this intimate Father-Son connection but will define one apart from the other. From this verse on, much of 1 John addresses the evils that arise when this occurs. Schnackenburg (1992: 74) asserts ominously, "When the author wrote v. 5 he already had in mind the pernicious morality of the heretics which he is going to attack in the ensuing verses." The word "attack" connotes perhaps action too vicious to use fairly of a pastoral leader whose warnings are as measured and nonvituperative as those found in 1 John.[13] But Schnackenburg is correct that after 1:5 the writer shifts to the offensive.

Additional Notes

1:5. Some manuscripts and a very few versions (Bohairic, one Sahidic manuscript) read ἐπαγγελία (promise), instead of ἀγγελία (message). The external attestation is too weak for the reading possibly to be considered original. Further, John's statement in the verse as a whole comprises a declaration, not a promise; the errant manuscripts introduce a logical problem where originally there was none. On the other hand, "announcement" or "declaration" is a lexical meaning of the word outside the NT; see additional note on 3:11. Other variants noted in NA[27] involve negligible differences in word order. The variant ἀγάπη τῆς ἐπαγγελίας (love of the promise), only in ℵ[2] and Ψ, is an anomaly.

1:5. The adjective οὐδεμία and related forms appear 227 times in the NT (53 times in John, 2 times in John's Epistles, 12 times in Revelation). Roughly 90 percent of the time it is substantival and translated "no one" or "nothing."[14] When used attributively, as here, it almost always precedes the word it modifies in the Synoptics (Mark 6:5; Luke 4:24; 16:13; 23:4, 22, 41) and Acts (17:21; 20:24; 23:9; 25:18; the exceptions are Acts 4:12; 27:22) and always precedes it in Paul (Rom. 8:1; 1 Cor. 8:4 [2x]; 2 Cor. 7:5; Gal. 5:10; Phil. 1:20; 2 Tim. 2:4, 14). John is slightly more inclined to let the adjectival form trail behind the noun it modifies (as in John 10:41; 16:29; 19:11; the exceptions are 15:24; 18:38), and this is what happens in 1 John 1:5, where the reader must persevere five words beyond "darkness" to find its negation. Usage is perhaps too scant in John to establish firm conclusions, but a case could be made that whether the adjective follows or precedes the noun, when it is separated from the noun by one or more intervening words, a dramatic or emphatic nuance is intended (see Culy 2004: 13 for a slightly different explanation). This is confirmed contextually in the Johannine occurrences, in which, when these conditions obtain, οὐδείς used attributively appears to carry the weight of "none at all" or "none whatsoever."[15] Hence my translation "no darkness whatsoever."

13. One finds none of the vitriol, scorn, and contempt, for example, that drip from the poorly informed pen of the anti-Christian polemicist Celsus in 178.

14. More than forty times it is used as part of a double negative construction, as is the case in 1:5. The double negative is not uncommon in Hellenistic Greek; see Turner 1963: 286 and BDF §431.

15. In John 10:41 the sense is "John performed no miraculous sign *whatsoever*." In 18:38 it is "I find no ground for accusation *whatsoever*." In 19:11 Jesus tells Pilate, "You would have no authority over me *whatsoever*." This pattern is confirmed in Luke 23:4; Acts 27:22; Rom. 8:1; 2 Cor. 7:5; possibly Phil. 4:15.

C. Implications of God's Character for the Christian Life (1:6–10)

The thematic assertion of God's holy character in 1 John 1:5 precipitates a hail of five quick if-clauses (for the importance to daily Christian living of 1:5 and 1:6–10 taken as a single unified whole, see Hodges 1972). Each juxtaposes to God's light a hypothetical but plausible human verbal response along with a stated or implied mode of living. The first, third, and fifth if-clauses are negative,[1] while the second and fourth are positive. John elaborates on themes that he has already touched on earlier: fellowship, darkness, light, God's Son, God's Word. But he introduces new ones as well: "walking" as a metaphor for living (cf. Isa. 2:5), truth and "doing" the truth, Christ's blood, cleansing, sin and confessing sin, being deceived, righteousness and unrighteousness. Whereas in previous verses he laid a foundation of divine self-disclosure, apostolic testimony, and pastoral concern that his readers know true fellowship as they bear in mind the character of God (light, not darkness), he now moves abruptly to contrasting God's character with character traits of some people who claim to have fellowship with God. Schlatter (1950: 4–5) proposes that the text here reflects the situation in Asia Minor that Paul feared and projected might arise (Acts 20:30), with treacherous leaders betraying apostolic teaching and leading Christians astray. This cannot be proved, though Ignatius, addressing churches in the same geographical locale in the generation after John, considered that "false teachers within posed a greater threat than the pagan society without" (Holmes 1997: 532). In any case John is addressing issues of direct relevance to the church or churches receiving this epistle (Houlden 1982).

In a sense these verses are simply a logical extension of the pastoral concern found in 1:4 combined with the theological bedrock laid bare in 1:5. But John takes a surprising rhetorical tack, shifting the reader's gaze from the panoramic horizon of apostolic testimony regarding Father and Son to the contrasting harsh reality of just how far removed from divine blessing people resident in the community of faith can be. He does this by using a series of terse conditional clauses with diatribe-like features. Several of the formal elements of diatribe listed by R. N. Soulen and R. K. Soulen (2001: 48) are present: simple, paratactic style; parallelism and antithesis; rich vocabulary (for John); imperatives or warnings (implied). This is not

1. The theory of Wennemer 1960 that John has in mind gnostic errors that minimize sin correctly diagnoses a cavalier attitude toward transgression. But a definite gnostic connection remains historically unverifiable.

to say that the section should be labeled "diatribe" in terms of the author's conscious method, for it falls short on too many counts. But in terms of style there are diatribal features, particularly if one envisions John addressing hypothetical sloganeering troublemakers in the first, third, and fifth if-clauses (the negative ones in 1:6, 8, 10). Then it is as if, for example, John takes up in 1:6 (without quoting directly) the audacious claim, "We have fellowship with God, yet we walk in what John and his lot call 'darkness'!" Had John employed such explicit dialogical form, these verses would surely be added to the list of NT diatribe passages (see S. K. Stowers, *ABD* 2:190–93). That the passage can be likened to diatribe at all indicates the animated, even confrontational feel of the section, which may be outlined as follows:

1. Implications for fellowship (1:6–7)
   a. In the case of transgression (1:6)
   b. In the case of obedience (1:7)
2. Implications for integrity (1:8–10)
   a. In the case of denial of sinfulness: Misrepresentation of the self (1:8)
   b. In the case of consciousness of sin (1:9)
   c. In the case of denial of sinful acts: Misrepresentation of God (1:10)

Exegesis and Exposition

6If we say that we have fellowship with him, yet walk in the darkness, we lie and
do not do what truth calls for. 7⌜But⌝ if we walk in the light, as he is in the light, we
have fellowship ⌜with each other⌝, and the blood of ⌜Jesus his Son⌝ ⌜cleanses⌝ us from
all sin. 8If we say that we do not have sin, we deceive ourselves and the truth ⌜ ⌝ ⌜is
not in us⌝. 9If we confess our sins, he is faithful and just to forgive us ⌜our⌝ sins and
⌜cleanse⌝ us from all wrongdoing. 10If we say that ⌜we have not sinned⌝, we make him
a liar and his word ⌜is not in us⌝.

1. Implications for Fellowship (1:6–7)

John has already made clear that one of his intentions in writing was to facilitate fellowship in two connections (1:3). The first is between readers and the "we" among whom John situates himself. The second is between readers and both God the Father and God the Son, since it is with Father and Son, John insists, that the "we" group enjoys close bonds. (There is a third connection: believers with believers; but John has not yet broached this explicitly.) If the primary burden animating John in 1:1–2:6 is, as I am proposing, that God is light, a direct and immediate corollary is the imperative that believers have fellowship with him.

In 1:6–7 readers are instructed in what will cut them off from fellowship (1:6) and then what makes fellowship possible (1:7).

a. In the Case of Transgression (1:6)

While "mirror reading"—extrapolating from what a writer says to situational details that his remarks may seem to imply—is always risky, it often cannot be avoided. This is one of those times (cf. Culpepper 1998: 257). Having spoken of the high priority of fellowship and the loftiness of God's character in prior verses, in 1:6 John now seems to envision persons claiming a closeness with God while at the same time living contrary to what his character calls for. This is to live in darkness, because it is not living in God.

John starts with ἐάν (*ean*, if). All of the ἐάν clauses in 1 John 1 are so-called third-class conditional (Wallace 1996: 689, 696–99). The construction itself may be used in a wide range of semantic situations, the meaning of which must be inferred from the context. Here, given that the community has actually suffered open division among its members (2:19), John seems to envision a setting where the risk is high of people violating Christian protocol in a grave way.[2] The sense is "when" or "in the likely event that." Perhaps the horse is already out of the barn, and John moves too late to bar the door, but more likely he sees continuing evidence of the same moral volatility that earlier erupted in an at least small-scale schism. He seeks to enlighten those who remain and for whom there is still hope. There is danger unless they turn their backs on behavior that has already been modeled in their midst with unhappy consequences.

Some people say one thing ("we have fellowship with God"), yet do another ("walk in darkness"). In my translation I take καί (*kai*) after "fellowship with him" as "yet," an accepted rendering (BDAG 495; LEH 298; LSJ 857; cf. Hebrew ו [*wāw*, and] in BDB 252) and appropriate if the phrase following it expresses something surprising or unexpected. John juxtaposes the reasonable confession of closeness with God with the scandalous action of defying his will.[3] Baylis (1992) advances the reasonable theory that to "walk in darkness" means not so much sinning in the generic sense as rejecting the message of eternal life in Christ. Yet a rigid separation between the two is not envisioned in 1 John.

In the sadly likely event that persons live[4] this way, they are lying (ψεύδομαι, *pseudomai*, to lie), not merely in the verbal sense of propagating falsehood (though "walking in darkness" may include this) but in the larger sense of living outside the zone sanctioned by the God whose light ought to define the path believers follow. Believers who lie in this way are not "doing the truth,"

2. Washburn 1990 sees the construction pointing to a present state of affairs and not merely future possibilities.

3. For fuller discussion of John's use of καί as "yet/and yet," see Abbott 1906: §§2141–45. He makes the general observation that John often uses "the Greek additive conjunction in a non-Greek adversative fashion to introduce adversative clauses with a suddenness that heightens the sense of paradox" (§2145). This is contra Akin 2001: 77n142, who argues that "John never uses καί to connect opposing thoughts in 1 John."

4. Literally, the word is "walk," a Semitism (see Isa. 2:5) "for pursuing a way of life and action" (R. Brown 1982: 197; cf. Witherington 2006: 451). For more detailed comments on "walk," see the exegesis of 2:6.

a phrase that makes for awkward Greek and is probably indebted to Hebraic idiom, whether because of LXX influence or the effect of spoken Semitic language (whether Aramaic or Hebrew) on John's Greek. The LXX speaks of "doing the truth" (Gen. 47:29; Josh. 2:14; 2 Sam. 2:6; 15:20; Tob. 4:6; 13:6). In John 3:21 Jesus speaks of "the one who does the truth" (NIV has "lives by the truth"); Jesus says that person "comes into the light." He thereby makes the same connection between "light" and "doing the truth" that John does in 1 John 1:5–6. First John makes repeated use of the verb "do" with certain nouns in a fashion uncommon elsewhere in the New Testament:

1 John	Greek	Literal Translation	NIV
1:6	οὐ ποιοῦμεν τὴν ἀλήθειαν	we do not do the truth	we . . . do not live by the truth
2:29 (cf. 3:7, 10)	πᾶς ὁ ποιῶν τὴν δικαιοσύνην	everyone who does righteousness	everyone who does what is right
3:4 (cf. 3:8, 9)	πᾶς ὁ ποιῶν τὴν ἁμαρτίαν	everyone who does sin	everyone who sins
3:4	τὴν ἀνομίαν ποιεῖ	does lawlessness	breaks the law

While John's usage is awkward, his meaning is by no means opaque. In his Son, God has poignantly and clearly revealed the Word that bestows life (1:1). This life in Christ is meant to produce fellowship and joy, consistent with a God who is light and who in his Son has given light. But some prefer darkness (cf. John 3:19–21). They embrace error and reject the transforming rays of God's holy nature. What is dark and false and cannot stand before God has replaced true fellowship, and they have fallen into the trap of not living out the bright implications of the gospel ("what truth calls for"; see translation above). Positively, to do the truth would mean, at the very least, to live "in the simplicity of a life in conformity with the Lord's example" (CCC §2470, citing 1 John 1:6; cf. 2:6). Yet John seems to envision the operation of a dynamic more profound than human imitation of Jesus's example.

John puts his finger on perhaps the oldest syndrome of human fallenness in all of Scripture, and certainly one of the grimmest: claiming spiritual or moral high ground when from God's viewpoint we languish in some pit. Adam and Eve try to shift blame, evading their own guilt (Gen. 3:12–13). Cain does not give the impression of being smitten with a sense of remorse when queried regarding his brother's murder (4:9); in fact, he lies that he does not know where his brother is. (Recurrent mention of lying and liars in 1 John 1:6, 10; 2:4, 22 effectively foreshadows the appearance of Cain in 3:12.) When Noah awakened from shameful drunken stupor, he had the effrontery to curse his grandson (Gen. 9:25). Joseph's brothers seem generally agreed that selling him into slavery is a justified course of action (Gen. 37). Aaron blames the people when confronted for leading them into idolatry (Exod. 32:22). In the era covered by the book of Judges, people spurned God's counsel and enthroned their own as if it were God's, with disastrous results. Right down through and past the time of the captivity, God's general assessment of his own people's status could be stated in the words he gave through Jeremiah, "The prophets prophesy lies, the priests rule by their own authority, and my people love it this way" (Jer. 5:31 NIV).

The situation improves little with the onset of NT times. Both John the Baptist and Jesus confront case-hardened hypocrisy, not just darkness but people who call their darkness light. Jesus forecasts more of the same for his followers: "A time is coming when anyone who kills you will think he is offering a service to God" (John 16:2 NIV).

It could be protested that some of these examples relate to people outside the pale of redeemed gospel believers proper. This would be to assume that rebellion against God was somehow somewhat consonant with OT religion, an assumption that NT writers reject. Moreover, the admittedly often lamentable spiritual condition of OT "saints" turns out to be replicated many times in the Christian fellowships to which NT epistles are addressed. Both Corinthian letters take up the problem of a high-handed pseudospirituality that is so noxious that Paul tells his readers that some of them "have no knowledge of God" (1 Cor. 15:34). They are being hijacked by false apostles who, however sincere and zealous, are in fact Satan's servants (2 Cor. 11:13–15). Galatians consigns its first readers to the status of apostates unless they abandon a doctrine that some are apparently finding amenable (Gal. 5:4). Hebrews tackles different particulars in a different community, but the point is very much the same (esp. 10:26–31). Colossians warns of beliefs and practices that nullify the grace of the cross (Col. 2:4–23). The ills addressed by Jude and 2 Peter are gross and unsettling. The authors of most if not all NT epistles betray knowledge that churches are beset by profoundly sub-Christian undercurrents that threaten believers with shipwreck (note the litany pronounced by Darby 1907: 30). And a common denominator in these situations is an avowed rightness with God coupled with a defiance of his will as revealed in his Son and mediated through those whom Christ chose to organize and give leadership to the first generations of churches.

In light of this, John's jab at complacent talkers whose lives do not reflect divine light is not anomalous. But it has its distinct features. One of these is the way John moves immediately from the dark diagnosis of 1 John 1:6 to the cheering prospects of a contrasting scenario in the next verse.

b. In the Case of Obedience (1:7)

John contrasts the cheap talk of 1:6 with authentic living (walking "in the light") in 1:7. "As he is in the light" points back to 1:5 and God's character. Obviously the analogy between believers' living and God's character has limits—believers are not being told to reside in heaven (yet), exercise sovereignty, solicit eternal praise, and so forth. But the analogy is still telling. Even if the single point of real comparison between God and his people were God's communicable moral excellence (and it is in fact more extensive than this), that alone would mean revolutionary change in normal human life.

John continues: to live life in the light of God's light means that believers "have fellowship with each other." This is a momentous assertion. The fall ushered in social hostility (Gen. 3:15: LXX ἔχθρα, *echthra*; MT אֵיבָה, *ʾêbâ*, enmity, hatred) that only God's promise itself through his Promised One could vanquish and replace with love. The prospect of disparate peoples (early Christian churches were often multiethnic) upholding a true *koinōnia* (κοινωνία, fellowship) of humanness across ethnic and cultural lines would have been exceedingly rare in the ancient world (and is still far from universal). In fact, it might have been viewed by the shrewd, biblically informed observer as an eschatological harbinger. This is exactly how, for example, Paul interpreted it in Eph. 2:16 as he explained that God's eternal purpose lay in bringing Jew and gentile together as "one new man" in Christ, the cross putting to death their former hostility (ἔχθρα). Paul elaborates on this by spelling out the core of "the mystery" he proclaimed: "This mystery is that through the gospel the Gentiles are heirs together with Israel, members together of one body, and sharers together in the promise in Christ Jesus" (3:6 NIV). The significance of Jew-gentile rapprochement via common devotion to a single messianic deliverer seems also to have been a conviction of Jesus as presented in John's Gospel, for the precross climax—the arrival of the much-heralded but repeatedly delayed "hour" in that gospel—occurs when non-Jews seek an audience with Jesus (John 12:20–21). To this Jesus exclaims, "The hour has come for the Son of Man to be glorified" (12:23 NIV). As the Prince of Peace gets his due homage from Jew and gentile alike, fellowship among all who acknowledge his lordship will be among the richest of the benefits of God's light they enjoy.

The dynamic that dispels the darkness of social dislocation and makes the light of fellowship possible[5] is "the blood of Jesus his Son" (1 John 1:7; on Jesus as God's Son, see the exegesis of 3:7–8). This refers to his atoning death and not to some magical quality of his blood per se (Neander 1852: 34–35; Marshall 1978: 112; Smalley 1984: 24; Carson 1996a: 34–35; Akin 2001: 73n128). Since the saving efficacy of Jesus's blood in the NT "derives its meaning particularly from the sacrifices of the Day of Atonement" in the OT (F. Laubach, *NIDNTT* 1:223; cf. Lev. 16), John's assertion is a reminder of the OT substructure of his theology and his understanding of Christ's ministry (cf. Kim 2001–5, who finds disparities between John's atonement language and the use of ἱλασμός [*hilasmos*, atoning sacrifice] in Hellenistic thought). Jesus's death cleanses from the sin that is frankly depicted and thereby explicitly defined in much OT narrative, law, prophecy, and wisdom. While walking in the dark makes a mockery of fellowship (1 John 1:6), walking in the light facilitates fellowship and preserves believers from the ravaging effects of sin (1:7), from which no one in this life can claim to be completely immune (1:8, 10; 2:1).

5. Witherington 2006: 454 suggests that "it is only after sharing in common is mentioned that we hear about the blood of Jesus." This may be the literary sequence, but for John, Jesus's transforming death long predates the experience of any of his readers, and if they walk in the light, it is because of his prior provision for them. It is not the human act that procures the blessing of Christ's death.

The word for "cleanses" (καθαρίζω, *katharizō*) is found only here and in 1:9 in all the Johannine writings. By contrast, it is common in the Synoptics (eighteen occurrences), expressing the outcome of Jesus's healing and saving touch and word (e.g., Matt. 8:3). It also refers to what some Jewish theology sought to attain via ceremonial observances but could not bring about insofar as the observances in themselves failed to transform the heart (23:25). Paul uses the word three times, once to exhort believers in their duty (2 Cor. 7:1) and twice to describe the saving work of God's Word (Eph. 5:26) or God's Son (Titus 2:14). Hebrews uses the word to denote both what Christ achieved and what the OT sacrifices regarded in isolation from Christ could not accomplish (9:14, 22, 23; 10:2). John's use of this word shows that his doctrine of Christ's work is well within the flow of what is claimed for Jesus in his earthly life by Gospel writers and what was taught about the power of his death in a wide range of early churches.

Christ's blood cleanses "from all [πάσης, *pasēs*] sin" (NIV). This could also be "from every sin" (Wallace 1996: 253). The issue is whether, as in the NIV, "all" is taken to denote sinful acts as a class or whether the sense is distributive, "every" sin being singled out separately. At least once in 1 John a similar construction demands to be translated in the latter sense (2:21). But Wallace shows that ample precedent exists for "all" as well. Turner (1963: 199–200) brings out the challenge of sorting through the nuances of πᾶς (*pas*, every, all; see also Moule 1994: 93–95). Perhaps whichever rendering be followed, it cannot rule out all aspects of the sense of the other rendering. Choosing "all" does not necessarily rule out a nuance of "each and every," or in Turner's phrase "any you please." Conversely, translating "every" cannot be used to negate the comprehensive scope of Christ's atoning work—as if "every" might somehow fail to add up to "all" in the end—that John appears at such pains to stress.

2. Implications for Integrity (1:8–10)

"God is light" (1:5) has implications for fellowship, both between John's readers and his "we" group, on the one hand, and between his readers and God, whether Father or Son, on the other (1:6–7). But it also has implications for the integrity (or lack thereof) of those who would claim to have fellowship in either of these senses. First John 1:8–10 takes up key character issues that come to the fore when either the bogus claims (1:8, 10) or commendable piety (1:9) of Christians is seen in the light of God's superlative moral excellence—his light.

The major character issue pertains to the confession of the mouth as it reveals two things: (1) how the speaker assesses behavior that God finds reprehensible and (2) the condition of the speaker's heart. Jesus had taught that speech ultimately reflects the soul: "For out of the overflow of the heart the mouth speaks" (Matt. 12:34 NIV; cf. 1 Sam. 24:13 [24:14 MT]). A person's words will condemn or acquit him or her on the last day (Matt. 12:37), not because words alone save or damn, but because in God's wisdom they suffice to demonstrate the true inclination of the inner person, godward or elsewhere. From human words God can and someday will assay the state of each human heart. Has the integrity of God's own presence been established there in place of innate and willful guilt? Is there evidence of the God-wrought transformation without which entrance into the kingdom of God remains a mere postulate and not an appropriated personal destination (see John 3:1–21)? John is concerned to alert his readers to approaches to human wrong and wrongdoing that are—or are not—commensurate with God's brilliant character as revealed in his Son.

a. In the Case of Denial of Sinfulness: Misrepresentation of the Self (1:8)

In 1:8 John envisions someone claiming "not to have sin." The expression "to have sin" does not occur at all in the LXX. In the NT it is unique to John, who quotes Jesus's use of the expression four times in the Fourth Gospel:

John 9:41	If you were blind, you would not have sin [οὐκ ἂν εἴχετε ἁμαρτίαν]; but now that you claim you can see, your guilt remains.
John 15:22	If I had not come and spoken to them, they would not have sin [ἁμαρτίαν οὐκ εἴχοσαν]. Now, however, they have no excuse for their sin.
John 15:24	If I had not done among them what no one else did, they would not have sin [ἁμαρτίαν οὐκ εἴχοσαν]. But now they have seen these miracles, and yet they have hated both me and my Father.
John 19:11	You would have no power over me if it were not given to you from above. Therefore the one who handed me over to you has a greater sin [μείζονα ἁμαρτίαν ἔχει].

These samples are hardly adequate to propound a general doctrine of the meaning of "to have sin." Modern translations opt for various renderings of the phrase (taking John 9:41 as an example):

NIV/TNIV	"would not be guilty of sin"
NLT	"wouldn't be guilty"
RSV, ESV	"would have no guilt"
NRSV	"would not have sin"
JB, NEB	"would not be guilty"

We can observe that John uses the expression, only on Jesus's lips, in contexts predicating unforgiven guilt of individuals who fail to give Christ his due. In John 9:41 the Jerusalem religious authorities are culpable because they fail to draw the proper conclusions from Jesus's healing of the man born blind. In 15:22 and 15:24 Jesus speaks of "the world" (15:18–19) that does not know the one who sent him; because members of this world are those who have the law (15:25), he appears to be describing again the religious authorities of Judea. Since they have rejected Jesus, and will reject his followers too, they languish under sin's condemnation. In 19:11 Jesus addresses Pilate, who has just threatened him with crucifixion (19:10). Jesus's reply implies that Pilate, while not innocent, is not as guilty as those who handed him over to be arrested and tried. It is notable that each of these four examples pertains to what might be called christological error—failure to acknowledge Jesus's status and authority.[6]

These examples do not prove that "to have sin" can refer only to christological miscues. They do, however, show how fitting the expression is in an epistle associated with Jesus's disciple John and in a situation where the necessity or perhaps sufficiency of Jesus's death for sins is apparently being underrated. To say, "We have no sin" (1 John 1:8), is to conceive oneself as at least somewhat free from transgression and its penalty despite failure to give full acknowledgment to Jesus. Obviously John disputes such a self-justifying confession.

To claim to be without sin, or to be exempt from its consequences, may be repugnant to John for two reasons. First, looking ahead a few verses, 2:2 speaks of the universal implications of Jesus's death for sins. Anyone claiming not to have sin is in effect saying no thanks to the Father's offer of forgiveness of sin through the death of his Son (cf. Strecker 1996: 31).

Second, there is the consistent OT testimony to the radical fallenness of all humans. Numerous passages insist that everyone has sinned (Gen. 8:21; 1 Kings 8:46; Job 4:17; 9:2; 14:4; 25:4–6; Ps. 14:1–3; Prov. 20:9; Eccles. 7:20). The precepts of such passages are simply a crystallization of the whole OT corpus as grounded in the fall of Gen. 3. An original pristine creation has been marred by sin. The primary theme of the OT is God delivering persons, and in particular his chosen people, from their sin, personal and corporate. They may protest their innocence, but they "are not right in this, for God is greater than man" (Job 33:12 NASB; cf. 33:8–11). The final goal is world redemption, but central to the goal is people pursuing and receiving forgiveness of sin.[7] This conviction is reflected not only in NT writers like John (and for that matter, Paul)[8] but also other Jewish writers of the NT era. Philo states that awareness and admission of personal transgression are of the essence of godliness: "To be aware of what one has done amiss, and to blame one's self, is the part of a righteous man" (Yonge 1993: 885). More broadly, Philo writes, "Perfection and an absence of deficiency are found in God alone. But deficiency and imperfection exist in every man" (1993: 890). Philo concludes

6. The problem here was not that Jesus's detractors did not become "Christians," something that in a sense was impossible until after the resurrection. It was rather that they did not allow Jesus's words and deeds to check their hostility toward him and their confidence in inherited religious (or, for Pilate, political) certainties that Jesus, like John the Baptist before him, called into serious question.

7. Calvin 1960: §3.4.24 notes that "there is no function more proper to God than the forgiveness of sins, wherein our salvation rests."

8. D. Smith 1991: 46 notes that "there is a remarkable similarity between the Pauline and Johannine views of sin." Their shared rootedness in the OT probably goes far to explain it.

that "there is no man who self-sustained has run the course of life from birth to death without stumbling, but in every case his footsteps have slipped through errors, some voluntary, some involuntary" (*Unchangeable* 75). Pagan thinking on the subject was of a different order, but the consciousness of sin was still present (see third additional note on 1:8).

Sin was an acknowledged reality in both Jewish and non-Jewish circles, but Jewish writers show a greater concern to deal with it, although some of them give the impression that being an observant Jew exempts one from being a sinner.[9] John writes to sharpen awareness that humans too easily digress from divine standards—and then deceive themselves into protesting their innocence. The situation presupposed in 1 John 1:8 seems analogous to the scenario envisioned by Philo: "There are some persons who exult in the offences which they have committed as if they had done good actions, though they are in reality afflicted with a disease difficult to be cured, or I should rather say incurable" (Yonge 1993: 884). But what Philo considers irremediable, John prescribes a cure for in 1:9.

To claim to be exempt from sin or sinning, asserts John in 1:8, is to be self-deceived. The word πλανάω (*planaō*, to deceive, lead astray) is prominent (more than 120 times) in the LXX. It can mean to wander, as when a person walks aimlessly (Gen. 21:14; Sir. 9:7) or an animal strays (Deut. 22:1; Job 38:41). It then can have the metaphorical meaning of going or leading astray intellectually (Sir. 3:24) or morally (Tob. 10:7), a connotation found over a dozen times in Psalms and Proverbs. But in the LXX the πλαν- word group "is used generally for transgression of the revealed will of God and more specifically for instigation to idolatry" (H. Braun, *TDNT* 6:233). Idolatry (in the sense of faithlessness toward God, regardless of whether physical idols per se are constructed and worshiped) is, of course, the subject of John's parting word of the epistle (1 John 5:21; cf. πλανάω in Deut. 4:19; 11:28; 13:5; 30:17; 2 Kings 21:9; 2 Chron. 33:9; Isa. 41:29; 44:20; 46:5, 8; Ezek. 44:10, 13; Hos. 4:12; 8:6; Amos 2:4; Wis. 11:15; 12:24; 13:6; 14:22; 15:4; 17:1). Third Maccabees 4:16 and Wis. 5:6 bracket forms of the verb πλανάω with the noun ἀλήθεια (*alētheia*, truth) in a fashion similar to 1 John 1:8 (cf. James 5:19). The Gospels portray Jesus as echoing LXX usage of πλανάω when he warns against straying after "false Christs and false prophets" (Matt. 24:24; cf. 24:5, 11).

It can be concluded that John in 1 John 1:8 is affirming that readers stand in danger of an age-old human proclivity. He warns of the result of living in denial of sin when God's very being (1:5, 7) casts a shadow over the moral status of every human and calls for a response more morally discerning than simply saying "we do not have sin" (for additional discussion on sin in 1 John, see R. Brown 1982: 204–5).

9. For example, in Wis. 15:3 the impression is given that idolaters sin but "the righteous man" does not. Similarly, Sir. 13:13–17 implies that obedience to God's commands, which only the Jews achieve, is simply a matter of human inclination and right human choice, not radical divine deliverance and transformation of the heart.

By "the truth is not in us" (1:8), John may be using synonymous parallelism to restate the preceding words "we deceive ourselves." In John's writings "truth" is associated with the Father (John 15:26), the Son (1:14, 17; 14:6; 18:37), the Holy Spirit (14:17; 15:26; 16:13; 1 John 4:6; 5:6), and the divine word (associated with Father, Son, and Spirit alike) that sanctifies believers (John 17:17). Since thus far in his epistle, John has had Father and Son primarily in view, it is unlikely that here he is referring explicitly to the Spirit.[10] He rather means simply that something is fundamentally awry (for fuller discussion of "truth" here, see Schnackenburg 1992: 80–81). "The truth is not in us" underscores the bitter irony of claiming to be free from sin when in fact one is self-deceived and thus doubly damned—guilty before God objectively and sinning again by being oblivious to the fact. A vintage late-1990s American women's magazine beauty advertisement purred that "looking beautiful is one thing, feeling beautiful is everything." This will strike some who are not esthetic solipsists as smacking of self-delusion. In 1 John 1:8 John rejects an analogous moral delusion. What matters is how one looks (to God), not how one feels (to oneself). God's eye beholds sin when he looks on humans. "All members of the Church, including her ministers, must acknowledge that they are sinners" (*CCC* §827).

b. In the Case of Consciousness of Sin (1:9)

Instead of denying sin, John commends owning up to it (1:9). Old Testament passages clearly prescribe this practice:[11] "He who conceals his sins does not prosper, but whoever confesses and renounces them finds mercy" (Prov. 28:13 NIV). "Then I acknowledged my sin to you and did not cover up my iniquity. I said, 'I will confess my transgressions to the LORD'—and you forgave the guilt of my sin" (Ps. 32:5 NIV). Memorable personal enactments of redemptive confession include David's (Ps. 51; 2 Sam. 12:13), Hezekiah's (2 Chron. 32:26), Job's (Job 42:6), Ezra's (Ezra 9:6–15), and Nehemiah's (Neh. 1:6). A high point of the OT Apocrypha is the Prayer of Manasseh (cf. 2 Chron. 33:12–13, 18–19), in which acknowledgment of sin is prominent. Confession of his own and the people's sin was part of Daniel's prayer life (Dan. 9:4, 20) and can be inferred to have been a feature of the spiritual life of other OT figures like Abraham, Moses, Samuel, Isaiah, and Jeremiah. Bogus and ineffective "confession" is in evidence, too (Deut. 1:41–43; 1 Sam. 15:24–25). Old Testament writers seem to have confession of sin to God foremost in mind, though the fruit of that confession can hardly be confined to the purely private sphere (Ps. 51:13, 15 [51:15, 17 MT]).[12] James is among NT writers who explicitly commend

10. *CCC* §1108, under the heading "The Communion of the Holy Spirit," invokes 1:3–7 in support of the Spirit's activity "in every liturgical action." This seems to be freighting the passage beyond its intent.

11. Lieu 1993 points out that John's reasoning here is not merely traditional-Jewish but has ties with long-standing attempts to interpret and apply the OT. See also Schnackenburg 1992: 82.

12. Calvin 1960: §3.4.10 infers, mainly from OT writers, that "a willing confession among men follows that secret confession which is made to God, as often as either divine glory or our humiliation demands it."

confession of sin among Christians (5:16, using ἐξομολογέω [*exomologeō*] instead of ὁμολογέω [*homologeō*] as in 1 John 1:9—a negligible lexical difference in their respective contexts). Among NT writers more generally, the verb ὁμολογέω can mean to affirm plainly and honestly (Matt. 7:23), to promise or fulfill a promise (Matt. 14:7; Acts 7:17), to admit or concede (Acts 24:14), and to acknowledge (Matt. 10:32; Acts 23:8).[13]

First John 1:9 indicates that for John confession of sin is fundamental to proper acknowledgment of God.[14] "He meets frank confession with free blessing" (Westcott 1883: 23). Part of the reason for this likely lies in the precedent of OT practice. But it also lies in the precedent of the ministries of John the Baptist and Jesus. The proper response to their preaching was confession of sins or repentance (which presupposes confession of sin) and then baptism (Mark 1:4–5, 15; cf. John 3:22). Acknowledgment of sin, then, was required for status as a follower of Jesus or his kingdom movement from the beginning. It is in fact part of the Lord's Prayer ("forgive us our debts" uses the same verb, ἀφίημι [*aphiēmi*, to forgive], that John uses in 1 John 1:9) both in its canonical form and in Did. 8.2. John wants to affirm that in this respect nothing about following Jesus has changed now. It still entails acknowledgment of personal (and by extension societal) transgression before God and of the need for his forgiveness and restoration.

A third reason for the importance of confession of sin for John lies in the view of God that he established in 1 John 1:5. God is light. Humans are beset with darkness. The only way for those in the dark to come to the light and meet with acceptance rather than rejection is to come in the state of contrition that confession presupposes. Confession of sins is a necessary preliminary to receiving the healing touch of God's forgiveness. "To receive his mercy, we must admit our faults" (*CCC* §452). R. Brown (1982: 208; cf. Loader 1992: 12) argues that John had in mind public confession, and while this must remain a hypothesis (Kruse 2000: 68), Hiebert (1991: 66) helpfully suggests that "the confession of any act of sin should be as wide as the knowledge of the sin."

One might well expect John to situate the efficacy of confession in the virtue of the act itself. But he grounds it rather in the nature of God, who "is faithful and just to forgive" and to effect the cleansing previously spoken of in 1 John 1:7 and now essentially repeated in 1:9. Given God's status as light—moral excellence and justice that utterly abhors injustice and sin—it

13. The oft-heard claim that it means "to say the same thing as" (Hiebert 1991: 66), while technically true in some Classical Greek passages (LSJ 1226), lacks lexical backing in NT usage. The claim owes its existence to a semantic root fallacy (cf. Carson 1996a: 28–33). In few if any NT passages where ὁμολογέω appears can one make sense of a text by using the translation "to say the same thing as." The word λογέω (presumably the theoretical basis for deriving "say" from ὁμολογέω) does not exist in Classical or Hellenistic Greek.

14. Cf. the comment of *CCC* §2631 on 1:7–2:2: "Asking forgiveness is the prerequisite for both the Eucharistic liturgy and personal prayer." Martino 1979 calls attention to links between the action described in 1:9 and fellowship with God and the church. But Neander's synergistic representation of confession and forgiveness (1852: 40) as a quid pro quo transaction is foreign to John's reasoning.

seems contradictory to affirm that that very justice is a ground for forgiveness. God's being δίκαιος (*dikaios*, just; for more on this word see exegesis of 2:1b) would seem to mandate only punishment for all flesh. Yet God's sternness is permeated by mercy (Deut. 5:9–10; Rom. 11:22; cf. Rom. 3:26). God is just in the sense that he sheds his largesse presently and provisionally on those who will face only his displeasure eschatologically (Matt. 9:13). Δίκαιος can also be translated "righteous"; it is the adjective that Jesus used of the Father in prayer (John 17:25) and is not necessarily tantamount to cold aloofness or bloodless judgmentalness.

Moreover, God is πιστός (*pistos*, faithful). God's reputation for being faithful to his word or promise is a commonplace in the OT. He is termed πιστός in numerous passages (e.g., Deut. 7:9; 32:4; Ps. 145:13 [144:13 LXX]; Isa. 49:7). Noncanonical Jewish sources express the same conviction (Odes of Solomon 2.4; Psalms of Solomon 14.1; 17.10). It is not a word that could be used of pagan gods with their notorious, almost subhuman fickleness (decried even by the ancients; see, e.g., Cicero, *Nature of the Gods* 2.70–71). It is, however, a fitting adjective for a God who makes his will known and stands behind what he says. One of the things he says most emphatically is that he will show mercy on those who fear and seek him. It is this conviction that John traffics in here as he commends confession of sin.

John's optimism about such confession is based on conviction regarding God's magnanimous character, not a facile theory of sin management.[15] He "will not turn His face away from you if you return to Him" (2 Chron. 30:9 NASB). The word "if" is significant. Uses of 1 John 1:9 in the Christian community as a sort of palliative for chronic premeditated sin are misguided. Not only John (e.g., 3:9) but also Jewish literature of John's day condemned the presumptuous attitude that indulges in willful sin, then supposes that acknowledgment of it will make amends (Wis. 5:4–7; Sir. 5:4; 7:8–9; note also the disastrous consequences of presumptuous confession recounted in Deut. 1:41–45). Christ's cleansing tends toward eradication of sin, not dismissal of it in the sense that the sinner is exonerated in the very thing he or she claims to be acknowledging as wrong but at heart refuses to forsake. God's righteousness, when accessed by human contrition, is transformative: "Because [God] loves justice, he puts an end to our unrighteousness and invests his righteousness with the victorious power that makes righteousness dwell in us and that transforms our conduct toward God and others" (Schlatter 2005: 48).

God is, then, "faithful and just" to forgive. The conjunction ἵνα (*hina*, to, in order to) poses a challenge in John's Letters (where it appears twenty-six times) in that it can connote several senses: purpose (= final, telic), result (= consecutive, ecbatic), purpose-result, substantival. In occurrences of ἵνα prior

15. Cf. Augustine (*Hom. 1 John* 1.6): "A man, so long as he bears the flesh, cannot but have some at any rate light sins. But these which we call light, do not make light of." Calvin 1988: 241 writes: "Therefore, confession includes true repentance. God certainly forgives freely, but in such a way that the easiness of mercy does not become an enticement to sin."

to this point, the meaning is clearly purpose (1:3: "we make known also to you *in order that* you may have fellowship"; 1:4: "we write *in order that* your joy"). But it is unlikely that in 1:9 John is affirming that God is faithful and just *for the purpose of* forgiving humans their sins. The fact of God's existence and his raison d'être transcend human need as creator transcends creation. He is faithful and just inherently and not out of pragmatic considerations. Rather, God is faithful and just, and *as a result* he is in a position to forgive those who come to him contritely (cf. Moulton 1908: 210; BDF §391.5; an analogous wording with an infinitive of result instead of a ἵνα clause occurs in Heb. 6:10). It is not certain, therefore, that we need to follow Wallace (1996: 474n74) in declaring the verse "a theological conundrum" whose use of ἵνα could fit in any of the first three categories mentioned above.[16]

Confession leads to cleansing (on καθαρίζω [*katharizō*] see the exegesis of 1:7) "from all wrongdoing [ἀδικία, *adikia*]." The expression is parallel to "cleanse us from all sin" in 1:7, and it would be hazardous to seek too nuanced a meaning for ἀδικία, a word with wide-ranging semantic possibilities. Yet it can be argued that ἁμαρτία (*hamartia*) in 1:7 is a more generic term for failure to comply with God's will, while ἀδικία in 1:9 connotes specific acts of wickedness or wrongdoing. Support for this is found in 5:17, the only other place where ἀδικία occurs in John's Epistles: πᾶσα ἀδικία ἁμαρτία ἐστίν (all wrongdoing is sin). It would make little sense in the context to say "all [generic] wrongdoing is a [particular] sinful act"; John must be affirming that all (specific) evil deeds are to be understood as ἁμαρτία (sin). The understanding of ἀδικία as tending to point more toward specific evil deeds finds ample support in LXX usage (228 occurrences). "Wrongdoing, injustice, wrongful act, offence" are the primary glosses for ἀδικία offered by recent LXX lexicographers (LEH 10). By comparison, the primary glosses for ἁμαρτία are "guilt, sin" (LEH 31).

To sum up the message of 1:9, John is indicating that via confession there can be (1) absolution that removes guilt via forgiveness and (2) transformation that frees from wrongdoing via cleansing. The notion of freedom from wrongdoing will be important in subsequent (and difficult) passages (3:6, 9) that stress the incompatibility of sinful behavior with Christian confession.[17]

c. In the Case of Denial of Sinful Acts: Misrepresentation of God (1:10)

First John 1:10 marks the final of five ἐάν clauses. It begins with the familiar "if we say" (cf. 1:6, 8), again likely envisioning the kind of things that those among John's readership have said in recent times or may be tempted to say. John warns against asserting, "We have not sinned" (οὐχ ἡμαρτήκαμεν, *ouch*

16. Wallace 1996: 476 classifies ἵνα as epexegetical. But note the argument for a consecutive sense in Caragounis 2006: 196 (who, however, misquotes 1:9 in note 204).

17. Kotzé 1979 attributes the contrasting stresses of 1:9 vis-à-vis 3:6, 9 to Johannine eschatology, which furnishes grounds for both security and insecurity. Cf. Hays 1996: 153.

hēmartēkamen). In one sense, this is simply a restatement of 1:8's "we have no sin." But the perfect tense of 1:10 may call special attention to the stative aspect of the verbal action, "grammaticaliz[ing] the speaker's conception of the verbal process as a state or condition" (Porter 1989: 257; cf. corroborative findings in Hatina 1999). In view of the literary structure of 1:6–10, in this case 1:10 functions as a summary (although Schlatter 1950: 15 sees rather a progression from 1:8). This fits well with the observation that the final apodosis of this section's five ἐάν clauses would then be parallel (with a few notable differences) with the apodosis of the initial ἐάν clause in 1:6:

1 John 1:6	1 John 1:10
ἐὰν εἴπωμεν . . . ψευδόμεθα καὶ οὐ ποιοῦμεν τὴν ἀλήθειαν	ἐὰν εἴπωμεν . . . ψεύστην ποιοῦμεν αὐτὸν καὶ ὁ λόγος αὐτοῦ οὐκ ἔστιν ἐν ἡμῖν
if we say . . . we lie and do not do what truth dictates	if we say . . . we make him a liar and his word is not in us

To claim a state of sinlessness has an ill effect and a grave implication.

The ill effect is that those who speak this way make "him" (αὐτόν, *auton*) a liar. The antecedent of αὐτόν must be either God or Christ, and God is more likely since he is both the assumed subject of the main clause in 1:9 (the one who forgives and is "faithful and just") and the referent of αὐτοῦ in the phrase "Jesus his Son" in 1:7. From a first-century Jewish point of view, there could hardly be greater sacrilege than predicating untruth of God. Better to regard all humans as liars (Rom. 3:4), which the psalmist says they are anyway (Ps. 116:11 [115:2 LXX]). Lying was clearly forbidden in the Torah (Lev. 19:11). Second Temple Jewish conviction in Alexandria agreed that "the lie brings terrible disgrace upon every man" because "God loves the truth" (Letter of Aristeas 206). In the early church lying about property proved fatal (Acts 5:3–4), and the same type of lying was severely punished in the Qumran community (1QS 6.24–25). If lying was such a grave offense for humans, how much graver to make a claim that was tantamount to calling God a liar?

From the Johannine standpoint, lies and lying (like murder) are the special province of the devil (John 8:44). Liars are singled out alongside "the cowardly, the unbelieving, the vile, the murderers, the sexually immoral, those who practice magic arts, the idolaters" who will undergo the second death in the lake of burning sulfur (Rev. 21:8). Once again, to do or say anything that would place God in such a classification is clearly heinous. For a writer who is proceeding from the bedrock assertion that God is light (1 John 1:5), John is leveling a very serious charge indeed at those who say they are free from sin. They are committing "a crime against God" (Schnackenburg 1992: 84).

The grave implication of claiming sinlessness is that God's Word is thereby shown to be absent—in John's words, "His word is not in us" (1:10). If this refers to the individual human heart, it would suggest that the regenerating word of the gospel has yet to do its work. People who talk like this are not Christians, whatever they say. Paul made the same insinuation of certain Corinthians (1 Cor. 15:34). But ἐν ἡμῖν (*en hēmin*, in us) can have a distributive/corporate as well as locative/personal sense (Moule 1994: 75). When this is the case, the translation can be "among us" or "in our midst" (e.g., Luke 1:1; 7:16; John 1:14; Acts 1:17; 2:29; Eph. 3:20; Heb. 13:21). In the eight occurrences of ἐν ἡμῖν in 1 John, the NIV takes the locative/personal tack in each case (1:8, 10; 3:24; 4:9, 12 [2x], 13, 16; cf. 2 John 2). In 1:8 and 1:10, there is reason to suspect that both senses are in view. There is corporate self-deception because God's Word (or in 1:8, God's truth) is absent from the group mentality or identity of those who claim sinlessness. At the same time, in those who see fit to adopt this social consciousness, there is evident failure to receive individually and personally what James calls "the word implanted, which is able to save your souls" (1:21 NASB). Full reception of God's Word, a basic assumption of which is the need of every human for cleansing from both inherent and ongoing guilt (implied in the footwashing of John 13), is not compatible with belief in personal sinlessness. In a Western individualist climate, it is wise to keep squarely in view the social connotation of words from John's more communitarian social setting. For early church leaders like John, the authenticity of reception of God's Word had both personal and social criteria. This helps to account for John's concern, expressed later in the epistle, about those who fail to care for others.

Additional Notes

1:7. A single uncial, several minuscules, and a smattering of other witnesses omit δέ after ἐάν. External attestation for this is weak, and the context viewed *ad sensum* permits an adversative to be understood even if δέ were not original.

1:7. Hardly better attested is μετ' αὐτοῦ instead of μετ' ἀλλήλων, and the latter reading is surely original.

1:7. The words ἰησοῦ τοῦ υἱοῦ αὐτοῦ are found in various configurations (ἰησοῦ omitted; χριστοῦ added after ἰησοῦ; χριστοῦ added after ἰησοῦ but τοῦ υἱοῦ αὐτοῦ omitted), none of which cast doubt on the sense. Ehrman (1993: 152–53) suggests that additions of "Christ" were polemical "corruptions" by "orthodox polemicists" (see 1997: 414–21 on his general view that "scribes who copied texts changed them" [415]). The addition was meant to assert Jesus's divine-human unity, which the gnostics denied, and which Ehrman apparently feels the orthodox had no grounds to affirm against the gnostics. If Ehrman is correct, several questions are raised. (1) Why do א and B, which read ἰησοῦ τοῦ υἱοῦ αὐτοῦ and were likely copied in the time of Nicene controversy, fail to reflect the polemic? If, as Ehrman claims (1993: 164 [1 John 1:17 on the last line of this page is a typo for 1 John 1:7]), this is a case where "orthodox scribes . . . affirmed their belief in *Christ*'s death and resurrection by inserting the title 'Christ' into relevant passages that otherwise lacked it" (emphasis original), it should also be conceded that other orthodox scribes, faithful to their exemplars, did not take this step. (2) Should the possibility not be raised that "Christ" was interpolated into 1:7 as a result of reference to the blood of Christ, or of Jesus Christ, in other NT passages (Eph. 2:13; 1 Pet. 1:2, 19; 1 John 5:6; Rev. 1:5; cf. Rom. 3:25; 5:9; 1 Cor. 10:16; 11:27; Eph. 1:7; Col. 1:20)? This seems to be a simpler and more demonstrable theory. (3) Why were other NT passages that mention the blood of Jesus *not* interpolated with the word "Christ" (e.g., Heb. 10:19; 13:12)? Were the interpolators of 1 John 1:7 not only duplicitous but also dumb, or at least dumbly forgetful? (4) Is so much gained by pointing to the (presumably gnostic-friendly) readings of ℵ and B when those same manuscripts speak of the blood of Jesus Christ in 1 John 5:6? To conclude: since claims made by and about Jesus in NT documents (cf. gospel references by a clearly "divine" Jesus to his "human" blood of the covenant) so clearly affirm his status as both human and divine, if the addition of "Christ" in 1 John 1:7 needs to be called a "corruption," caution may be advised in casting it in an overly sinister light.

1:7. A few minuscules give καθαρίζει in its future form καθαριεῖ; too many manuscripts do this for it to be accidental, and Byzantine copyists may have wished to guard readers or listeners from complacency by making sure they understood their cleansing not yet to be a fait accompli.

1:8. A few minuscules and one Syriac version add τοῦ θεοῦ (*tou theou*, of God) after "truth." This is perhaps to underscore that by truth John has in mind particularly redemptive truth flowing forth from Christ and not simply valid knowledge from any quarter whatsoever.

1:8. Many manuscripts, including four uncials (A, C, K, P), rearrange οὐκ ἔστιν ἐν ἡμῖν as ἐν ἡμῖν οὐκ ἔστιν. Rhetorically this might have the effect of stressing *where* truth is not found—namely, in us if we talk this way—rather than truth not being found in us. The external evidence is too strong to rule out ἐν ἡμῖν οὐκ ἔστιν as possibly original. The same wording is proposed in 1:10, albeit by a weaker selection of witnesses.

1:8. Regarding sin outside Jewish and Christian circles: pagan thinking lacked definite, universal, and clear moral standards associated directly with religion. "In general the standard was public opinion and not a code of conduct," religious or otherwise (Ferguson 1987: 118). It was a culture more concerned about shame than guilt. The important question for them was, What will people think? not, What is right or wrong according to a revealed transcendent standard? "Cultus had little to do with morality except in cases of grave offence, and priests did not function as moral guides" (1987: 53). Part of the reason for this lay in the Greek belief that reason, not revelation, was the sole foundation for knowing how to live; Xenophanes (ca. 570–488 BC) wrote: "Truly the gods have not revealed to mortals all things from the beginning, but mortals by long seeking discover what is better" (Finegan 1989: 166). From a Christian point of view, no mortally devised scheme of reason or ethics yet has proved equal to the task of taming the downward proclivities of the human heart. But there could still be an awareness of sin. For example, in the ancient Greek religion Orphism, one could receive punishment for sins in the afterlife (Ferguson 1987: 124). The Latin poet Horace (65–8 BC) decries the sins of individuals and society at some length (*Odes* 3.6).

1:9. Several manuscripts, among them ℵ, C, and Ψ, include ἡμῶν (*hēmōn*, our) after the second occurrence of the word "sins." This serves to make explicit what is already implicit in ἵνα ἀφῇ ἡμῖν <u>τὰς ἁμαρτίας</u> (the underlined words can be rendered in English as "the sins" but are translated "our sins" in, e.g., KJV [with "our" italicized to show that it is technically not in the original], Phillips, RSV/NRSV, TEV, NIV/TNIV, JB, NEB). Who else's sins would be forgiven us (ἡμῖν) but "our" own? Taken in conjunction with the external evidence, the internal evidence suggests that this is a case where the longer reading is rightly rejected. English tends to feel the need for the explicit personal pronoun here, whereas Greek (like many modern European languages; e.g., Spanish, German, Romanian) does not. On the other hand, scribes might wish to include it for the sake of symmetry with the first clause of the verse. (It should also be noted that the definite article τὰς in ἵνα ἀφῇ ἡμῖν τὰς ἁμαρτίας could be felt as possessive by virtue of pointing back to the first clause; cf. Wallace 1996: 215–16. This would render ἡμῶν redundant.)

1:9. Codex A joins a smattering of minuscules in rendering καθαρίσῃ as καθαρίσει, that is, as a future indicative instead of an aorist subjunctive. The change makes little semantic difference, and the attestation of the reading is too weak to be original, particularly when the indicative would disturb the parallelism with the subjunctive ἀφῇ and when the variant could easily be explained in some cases by copyists' error of hearing.

1:10. Too weakly attested to be original is the aorist ἡμάρτομεν instead of the perfect ἡμαρτήκαμεν. Since the perfect form of ἁμαρτάνω is attested nowhere else in the NT (and is not present in the Apostolic Fathers either; Goodspeed 1960: 12), it might have been regarded as an unusual form in need of plainer dress.

1:10. On the word order οὐκ ἔστιν ἐν ἡμῖν, see second additional note on 1:8.

D. Appeal to Readers in the Light of God's Character (2:1–6)

Thus far John's epistle has announced its purpose (1:1–4), affirmed God's character as light (1:5), and explored implications of God's character for life in the Christian community (1:6–10), focusing on appropriate and inappropriate responses of the mouth and heart. In the present section John turns directly to his readers with the first of numerous poignant appeals growing out of the broad yet surprisingly deep foundation he has laid in such short compass. In 2:1a he restates his purpose in writing, relating it to the hope that his readers might transcend sin and its consequences.[1] Is this hopeless idealism or perhaps utopian cant? Not in John's view, as 2:1b–2 makes clear. The ministry of Christ to sinners renders John's high hopes plausible. Because of his sacrifice and its ongoing implications, sin need not be seen as the victor in either personal, ecclesiastical, or cosmic spheres. John follows with a combination of affirmations, instructions, and caveats that hold out the promise of assurance for his readers (2:3–6). He affirms (2:3) and then expands on (2:5) the basis for Christian assurance, warns of what will disqualify from that assurance (2:4), and lays down the ethical obligation that confession of Christ entails (2:6). The verses may be outlined as follows:

1. Author's hope: Readers' deliverance from sin via knowing God (2:1a)
2. Author's promise: Christ's twofold ministry (2:1b–2)
   a. Intercessor (2:1b)
   b. Expiatory propitiation (2:2)
3. Author's assurance: Chastened Christian confidence (2:3–6)
   a. Basis for assurance: Compliance with Christ's commandments (2:3)
   b. Disqualification from assurance (2:4)
   c. Expansion of the basis for assurance: The perfection of Christian love (2:5)
   d. Ethical obligation of the professing Christian (2:6)

1. Rensberger 1997: 50 notes that "2:1a should be taken as parenthetical rather than as introducing a new section." In other words, it links 2:1b–6 with the final verses of 1 John 1. Kruse 2000: 71–72 likewise treats 2:1a separately.

Exegesis and Exposition

1My children, the reason I am writing these things to you is so that you may not
⌜sin⌝. But if anyone does sin, we have a righteous intercessor who is with the Father:
Jesus Christ. 2He is the propitiation for our sins—and not ⌜only⌝ for ours but also for
those of the whole world. 3This is how we know that we truly know him: we ⌜keep⌝
his commandments. 4The one who says, ⌜"I truly know him,"⌝ but who does not keep
his commandments, is a liar; ⌜the⌝ truth is not ⌜in him⌝. 5On the other hand, whoever
keeps Christ's word, ⌜most certainly⌝ God has perfected his love in that person—this
is how we know that we are ⌜in him⌝. 6The one who claims to abide in Christ ought
to live the whole of life ⌜in the manner⌝ he did.

1. Author's Hope: Readers' Deliverance from Sin via Knowing God (2:1a)

If God is light, and if he desires the worshipful fellowship (1:3–7) of humans (cf. John 4:23), then those humans must somehow be delivered from darkness—that is, from sin, whether conceived of as so-called sin nature or as particular wrongful acts. To this end, their privilege is to embrace a saving knowledge of God, who is light. In popular Christian religion of modern times, the impression is sometimes given that sin is in the end not intrinsic to the person ("God hates the sin but loves the sinner"), or that sin is compulsory by God's design ("that's just the way God made me"), or that salvation alters the destiny of the soul *someday* but not necessarily the behavior of the body *today* ("Christians aren't perfect, just forgiven"; "I'm just a sinner, saved by grace"),[2] or that tolerance mandated by Scripture forbids ethical distinctions of any kind ("judge not lest you be judged"). While John would no doubt recognize the element of truth in some of these slogans in appropriate contexts, he would also decry their misuse. He writes to commend a higher road: liberation from the compulsion to believe, behave, and love in ways that fall short of God's glorious and transforming light. He writes to commend a full, satisfying, and efficacious knowledge of God.

"My children" (τεκνία μου, *teknia mou*) in 2:1a is the first of several apparent endearments in the epistle using either τεκνία as here (also 2:12 [see exegesis of 2:12–13], 28; 3:7, 18; 4:4; 5:21) or the equally common ἀγαπητοί (*agapētoi*, beloved; see 2:7; 3:2, 21; 4:1, 7, 11). As with John's invitation to joy (see exegesis of 1:4), one can suspect affectation on the writer's part; Strecker (1996: 35n2) sees further evidence here of "the (fictitious) apostolic claim already raised in 1:1–4." But if he has the integrity and affection to be sincere, then he is not being obsequious but rather expressive of the same love that he will repeatedly commend in the course of coming verses. If the tradition that John writes at an advanced age is correct, then fondly terming a community of normal-aged people "children" would be all the more understandable. Based on extensive research into child-parent relations and language in both pagan

2. Schlatter 1950: 17 takes issue with just such pseudospiritual resignation.

and Jewish antiquity, Balla (2006: 221) concludes, "By this way of addressing his recipients, the author implies that he has a loving relationship to them, and also that he writes with the expectation that they will obey him."

The significance of apostolic writing ("I am writing . . . to you") was discussed in the introduction. John now states straightforwardly what previous verses have implied rhetorically: his personal and pastoral wish for readers is that they not sin. In 1 John (where ἁμαρτία [*hamartia*, sin] occurs 17 times), as elsewhere in the biblical corpus (ἁμαρτία occurs in the NT an additional 156 times, in the LXX 545 times), sin is a central issue.[3] In order to grasp John's message, it is important to understand why sin is such an important matter for him. In many cases the discussion below anticipates exegesis that must await passages later in the epistle.

Viewing 1 John as a whole, it is clear that sin is understood along at least two lines, or axes. The first is unbelief, as contrasted with believing in Christ. Belief in the sense of personal trust resulting in reciprocal love is the key to knowing God in a saving way. Passages like 5:10, 13 underscore the black-white distinction that John makes between faith in Christ (which results in knowing God, a recurrent issue and theme in 1 John) and the absence of that faith (Greek πίστις, *pistis*, hence "pistic"). Appropriate response to a God who is light (1:5) and who forgives confessing sinners through the saving death of Jesus Christ (1:9) can be depicted anywhere on a line to the right of a hypothetical midpoint separating rejection of the gospel from commitment to it (see figure 1). When 2:1 says that John writes so that readers may not sin, he has in mind at least the pistic (belief-unbelief) issue.[4] To sin in this respect would be to not believe in the way that God calls for through the good news about his Son.

FIGURE 1

The Pistic Trajectory of Johannine Salvation: Knowing God

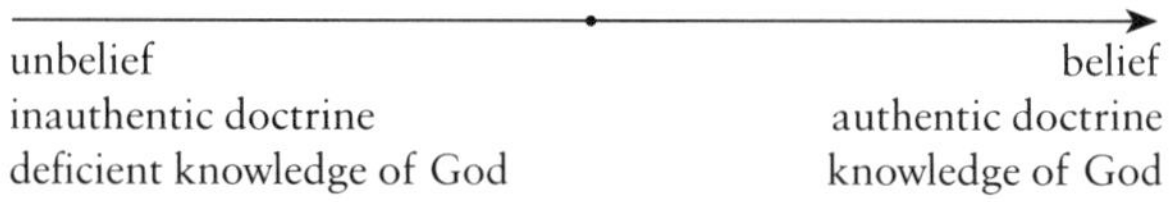

unbelief	belief
inauthentic doctrine	authentic doctrine
deficient knowledge of God	knowledge of God

But if a certain orthodoxy, so to speak, is for John integral to Christian redemption, so a certain orthopraxy (always bearing in mind that John concedes that it is delusion to claim absolute freedom from sin; recall 1:8, 10) provides the second axis. Passages like 2:3–5 tie blessedness in God's sight to

3. The NIV has about one thousand occurrences of the word "sin" or its cognates. And, of course, there are many other words used to denote sin. In a postmodern setting where sin has lost meaning (Henderson 1998: 156–66), biblical writers' belief in and attention to sin requires full acknowledgment if sympathetic interpretation is to occur.

4. It could also be termed a gnostic issue to the extent that for John knowing God and believing God are often near synonyms (e.g., 4:16). But the term "gnostic" is historically descriptive of a set of beliefs quite different from John's.

a particular ethical pattern—obedience to his commands. Redemption could be depicted anywhere on a line above the hypothetical midpoint separating violation of God's commands from compliance with them (see figure 2). Thus, when John says in 2:1a that he writes so that readers may not sin, he has in mind not only the (pistic) belief-unbelief issue but also the (ethical) obedience-disobedience issue. To sin in this respect would be to not obey in the way that God calls for through his Son.[5]

FIGURE 2

The Ethical Trajectory of Johannine Salvation: Knowing God

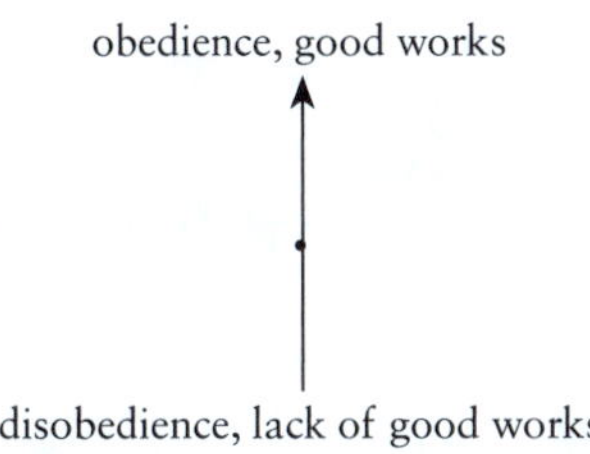

But the very structure of John, intertwined as it is, makes it obvious that John does not see these two dimensions separately but rather integratedly. Accordingly, the Johannine view of sin can be depicted as any mode of existence lying outside quadrant 1 in figure 3 (below). From 1 John one can reasonably surmise that John would commend the person living in quadrant 1, which represents both full faith and growing obedience. At least these are two areas in which he continually calls for diligence. Therefore, when John says in 2:1a that he writes so that readers may not sin, he is urging them to a knowledge involving true faith and diligent obedience, each conditioned by and symbiotic with the other. (See figure 3 on next page.)

But the matter does not quite end there. A third area of focus for John is love (already implied by references to eternal life, the Father, fellowship, truth, light, cleansing, and "my children")—not merely believing (or knowing) certain things (though this is imperative) and not merely obeying certain commands (though this is requisite), but also having a heart characterized by certain affections, both toward God and toward others (4:20). There turn out, then, to be three axes (not merely two) that for John locate knowing God in the full sense. The one who knows him walks in the *fullness* of his light through his Son: the pistic, the ethical, and the agapic (from Greek ἀγάπη, *agapē*, love). Figure 4 depicts eight different sectors (octants), in just one of which the three requisite characteristics of the redemption that John administers is present. In the other seven octants, one or more of the fruits of heavenly light are lacking, as the verbal descriptions of each octant at the bottom of figure 4 indicate.

5. I leave until the exegesis of 3:4, 6 the common view that aorist ἁμαρτάνω in 2:1 means to commit a particular sin, while the present in 3:9 refers to an ongoing and characteristic dwelling in sin. See also p. 75n7 below.

FIGURE 3

The Pistic-Ethical Profile of Johannine Salvation: Knowing God

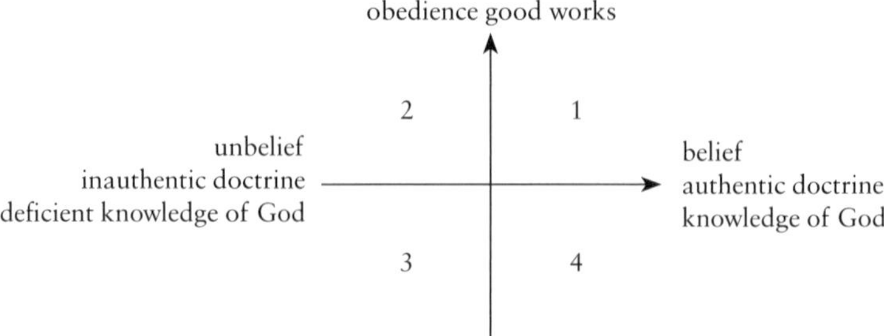

Quadrant 1 = acceptable belief and obedience
Quadrant 2 = unacceptable belief though some semblance of obedience
Quadrant 3 = neither acceptable belief nor obedience
Quadrant 4 = some semblance of belief but unacceptable obedience

FIGURE 4

The Pistic-Ethical-Agapic Dimensions of Johannine Salvation: Knowing God

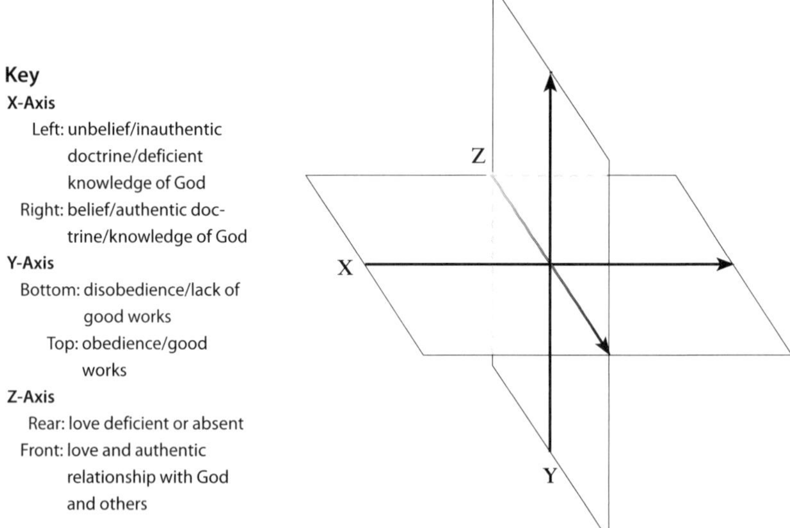

Octant 1 = authentic belief, appropriate obedience, authentic relationship (love)
Octant 2 = inauthentic belief, despite a semblance of obedience and love
Octant 3 = authentic(-sounding) belief and a semblance of obedience, but deficient love
Octant 4 = authentic(-sounding) belief and a semblance of love, but deficient obedience
Octant 5 = authentic(-appearing) love, but inauthentic belief and deficient obedience
Octant 6 = authentic(-appearing) obedience and love, but inauthentic belief
Octant 7 = authentic(-appearing) obedience, but inauthentic belief and deficient love
Octant 8 = absence of appropriate belief, obedience, and love

Fuller explication of details clarifying figure 4 must follow in the course of various Johannine passages that relate to it. But if there is validity to the illustration, John's call for avoidance of sin in 2:1a takes on new depth, for sin is not merely a superficial violation of a set of rules, whether folk-traditional, biblical, ecclesiastical, or otherwise. It is not failure to live up to the arbitrary expectations of a crotchety old apostle. Rather, it is deficiency in any of numerous and possibly complex senses that can be overcome only through robust response to the God of light (1:5), who has sent his Son.[6] The antithesis of sin is not simply the absence of unacceptable behavior or conviction at discrete forbidden points but the knowledge of God in a fullness that betokens the active presence of his saving grace. This is the subject of the following verses.

2. Author's Promise: Christ's Twofold Ministry (2:1b–2)

The heart of John's appeal to those prone to sin, and their ticket to rising above sin's ravages, is Jesus Christ the intercessor. Although John writes to move readers away from sinning (2:1a), he assumes that they will struggle in the process (2:1b). In due course he will state and imply several explicit commands; for now he does not rest his counsel on imperatives but on the indicative of Christ's finished work as set forth in this section. That work has a past aspect, implicit in the much-debated term ἱλασμός (*hilasmos*, expiation or propitiation), and a present aspect, as the Son has a continuing effective presence with the Father. His work has implications not only for God's people but also for the whole of humanity.

a. Intercessor (2:1b)

Καί (*kai*, and) joining 2:1a and 2:1b is often adversative and may be rendered "yet" or "but" (see exegesis of 1:6). John assumes that there will be sin among Christ's followers;[7] ἐάν (*ean*, if) does not rule out that John views this eventuality as probable (Zerwick 1994: §320). In view of 1:8, 10 it would be folly to view oneself outside the pale of John's "anyone" here. But despite John's possibly enervating assumption, he sounds an immediate note of deliverance and promise.

Hope lies in the existence of a παράκλητος (*paraklētos*, helper, intercessor). This word is unique to John in the NT and does not appear in the LXX, though it is found in pre-NT Greek to denote a legal assistant or advocate as well as someone who intercedes (LSJ 1313; cf. Deissmann 1911: 338–40).[8]

6. Thus Augustine (*Hom. 1 John* 1.6) stresses the positive exercise of love, and not just the defensive measure of confession, as integral to "extinguish[ing] sins."

7. Cf. Tertullian (*On Modesty* 19): "There are some sins of daily committal, to which we are all liable. . . . If there were no pardon for such sins as these, salvation would be unattainable to any." Note the fascinating confirmation of this understanding of John's use of the aorist subjunctives in this verse in Caragounis 2006: 90.

8. A related word, παρακλήτωρ (*paraklētōr*, one who encourages), is a hapax legomenon in the LXX; in Job 16:2 Job refers to his "friends" as παρακλήτορες κακῶν (terrible comforters).

More significant are references in Philo, where the word is used to describe the "helper" that God did not need in order to bless the world richly in creation (*Creation* 23), the son of an OT priestly figure who is an "advocate" assisting in forgiveness of sins and bringing blessing to the world (*Moses* 2.134), a "mediator" who assists a sinner seeking remission of penalty at the temple under Levitical law (*Spec. Laws* 1.237), and an "advocate" who might help Flaccus gain a hearing from Emperor Gaius (*Flaccus* 22–23).

Such passages furnish a semantic grid for understanding John's use of the word in his Gospel. Jesus promises that "another advocate" (ἄλλον παράκλητον, *allon paraklēton*) will be given to the Eleven by the Father (John 14:16). John names this advocate and describes his brief: "The Holy Spirit, whom the Father will send in my name, will teach you all things and will remind you of everything I have said to you" (14:26 NIV). He is "the Spirit of truth" (15:26). And ὁ παράκλητος will not come unless Jesus departs (16:7). Where Philo and John intersect in their usage is at the point of understanding that a παράκλητος is a party who represents the interests of a second party so they might be furthered with some third party. "Advocate" in the legal sense or "intercessor" or "mediator" are therefore apt translations of the word (cf. R. Brown 1982: 217, who sees Jesus here "both as intercessor and defending advocate"). Irenaeus applies these and broader insights in a powerful way (see second additional note on 2:1).

John's readers have such an advocate, mediator, or intercessor with the Father in the event that they sin (1 John 2:1). Whereas John's Gospel speaks of the Holy Spirit as the advocate, 1 John 2:1 applies the term to Christ. In Paul's theology, this figure serves in the same capacity as the one who "is at the right hand of God and is also interceding" for believers (Rom. 8:34 NIV). Hebrews is rich with similar imagery (7:25; cf. 4:14–15; 9:24). Once again John's theology proves to be in some measure common to that spread by other apostolic or subapostolic leaders to other churches.[9]

This intercessor is in the Father's presence (indirect evidence for John's belief in Jesus's resurrection). This is proof that his voice will be heard and carries weight, as well it must if sinners are somehow to pass muster before a righteous God.

But happily the intercessor possesses that same quality; he too is δίκαιος (*dikaios*, righteous). Old Testament background for this word is extensive and rich: in the LXX it is frequent, occurring well over four hundred times. It most often translates a form of Hebrew צדק (*ṣdq*), an adjective that occurs about 150 times in the MT. The word group "refers to an ethical, moral standard" that in the OT relates closely to "the nature and will of God" (H. G. Stigers, *TWOT* 2:752). The noun "righteousness" is perhaps the primary quality of God that gives definition to the light metaphor when applied to him.

Δίκαιος is infrequent in John's Gospel (only three times), where it refers (1) to Jesus's judgment being δίκαιος because it is actually not his own but the

9. Additionally, Jesus was termed "the Righteous One" in early Christian preaching (Acts 3:14; 7:52; 22:14; cf. 1 Pet. 3:18).

Father's (5:30), (2) to the quality of wise and measured judgment that ought to have characterized human assessment of Jesus's ministry but usually did not (7:24), and (3) to the nature of the Father as Jesus addressed him intimately in prayer (17:25). In John's Letters it occurs only in 1 John, where it refers to God (1:9), Christ (2:29; 3:7b), the person who does righteousness (3:7a), and the works of Abel (3:12).

John's point in 2:1b seems to be twofold. First, not only is Christ a heavenly intercessor, already a remarkable and encouraging assertion to those who have placed their life's trust in him. He is also righteous (δίκαιος) as God is righteous. There is no chance that what he urges in God's presence will be rejected because it fails to measure up to the standard of "the righteous judge" (2 Tim. 4:8), because the intercessor is of the same sterling character. "The Christ never steps out of his unity with the divine will" (Schlatter 2005: 365). Anything less than a righteous intercessor would leave sinners without the sure access to the God of mercy that their confession (1 John 1:9) seeks and their sin requires; "only a righteous person can pray effectually for the unrighteous" (Holtzmann 1908: 331; cf. Schlatter 1950: 18). Second, since Christ is δίκαιος, those who look to him for advocacy can be assured that he will do the right thing, fulfilling the daily prayer of Jesus's disciples: "Your will be done." John's confidence in the intercessor's high standing here is the basis of later affirmations of confidence in prayer (5:14–15).

b. Expiatory Propitiation (2:2)

Christ's intercession is dynamic and ongoing. It is made possible, not only by the resurrection and ascension, which lifted him into the Father's presence, but even more fundamentally by his sacrifice, which did something about human sin.[10] This is a primary ground and means for worshiping God the Father through him (Origen, *Against Celsus* 8.13). What he did was to serve as ἱλασμός (*hilasmos*) "for our sins" (2:2; cf. Clavier 1968). Words associated with ἱλασμός have been the focus of spirited debate for decades. The central question is whether here and in other NT passages containing the ἱλασ- word group (Luke 18:13; Rom. 3:25; Heb. 2:17; 9:5; 1 John 4:10) biblical writers are talking about "expiation" or "propitiation" (the question is aired fully in R. Brown 1982: 217–22; cf. Akin 2001: 82–84). The two "are to be differentiated . . . , and their categorical distinction is of considerable importance" (Alsup 1996: 319).

It has long been argued by some that atonement should be understood as expiation for sin, not propitiation.[11] "Expiation" (cf. 1 John 2:2 RSV) in

10. Calvin 1988: 243 shrewdly notes the link between "advocate" and his role as ἱλασμός: "Christ's intercession is the continual application of His death to our salvation." Cf. Schlatter 1950: 18: "His death and his [present] life serve the same grace."

11. Cf. Bloesch 1978: 172: "In modern theology, with few exceptions, the traditional meaning of the sacrifice of Christ on the cross has been drastically altered. . . . It is customary in modern theology to deprecate the concept of propitiation on the grounds that God's holiness does not need to be propitiated." A similar complaint about Johannine scholarship was voiced earlier

this sense means cancellation or dismissal. God simply waives the threatened penalty for transgressions. Alsup (1996: 320) grounds his contention to this effect in the conviction that God is characterized primarily by "mercy, love, and grace." But there are also linguistic grounds to consider. Underlying some ἱλασ- words in the LXX are various forms of Hebrew כפר (*kpr*), often translated "atone" or "atonement." R. E. Averbeck argues that there is good reason to understand the meaning of *kpr* as "to wipe away, wipe clean, purge" (e.g., Lev. 16:20, 33; Deut. 32:43; Dan. 9:24; Isa. 47:11); he suggests that "the underlying rationale of OT *kpr* was wipe away, not ransom" (*NIDOTTE* 2:708). Averbeck's lengthy discussion makes little mention of either divine wrath or human sinfulness, though these comprise a prominent background factor in OT atonement passages.

A variation of this view was developed by Westcott (1883: 34–37), who claimed that the OT imagery of sacrifice involved not only the death of the victim to whom sin was imputed but also life liberated from the victim in the form of the shed blood, whose "atoning virtue lies . . . in the life of which it is the 'vehicle'" (1883: 34). Marshall (1978: 112n8) rightly terms this an "extraordinary thesis" that "undoubtedly misrepresents biblical teaching." But it has found supporters over the years and has been used to uphold the expiation view of Jesus's death.

Others point out that atonement seems also to involve propitiation, the turning away of wrath by an acceptable offering. It does not merely expiate in the sense of dismiss; it propitiates in the sense of averting God's punishment in a substitutionary way. Smalley (1984: 40) underscores that "in 1 John 2:2 (cf. 4:10) both senses of ἱλασμός also seem to be present" (likewise Witherington 2006: 461–65). One strand of current LXX lexicography points in this direction (LEH 287). Alsup (1996: 320) concedes that in many OT passages a "propitiatory notion is likely," citing Gen. 32:20 (32:21 MT); Num. 16:47–48 (17:12–13 MT); 25:11; 1 Sam. 26:19; 2 Sam. 21:3–4; 24:25; Prov. 16:14. Nothing in the Johannine corpus prohibits attaching this connotation to ἱλασμός in 1 John (so Strecker 1996: 39 with n17), and the awareness of God's wrath (John 3:16, 36; cf. 8:24; 1 John 3:14; 5:16)[12] and of Jesus's suffering of it in place of sinners (John 3:14; 10:11; 11:51; 1 John 3:16) makes that connotation plausible if indeed not likely. While Jesus's death certainly has the effect of expiating sin (wiping away its penalty), it is difficult to avoid the impression that it also propitiates (turns away the wrath of) God's promised punishment of sin and sinners whose transgressions are not atoned for on the last day—a day of condemnation spoken of by Jesus in John 12:48.[13]

---

by Law 1909: 156. On current demotion of biblical atonement teaching to mere metaphor, see Blocher 2004. For recent support of the expiation option, see Sloyan 1995: 15; Rensberger 1997: 56; Culpepper 1998: 258; Painter 2002: 146–47, 153, 158–59.

12. Cf. Neander 1852: 66: John "beholds in man a being estranged from God; over whom impends the divine wrath."

13. Evidence adduced by Schnackenburg 1992: 88 (cf. Loader 1992: 15) for background in Second Temple Jewish martyr theology is unconvincing. Jesus's sacrifice for John was primarily

Some contemporary translations of 1 John 2:2 (perhaps to avoid theological jargon) have sought to transcend the debate by simpler terms:

NIV/TNIV, NRSV	"the atoning sacrifice for our sins"
JB (cf. CEV, NLT)	"the sacrifice that takes our sins away"
NEB[14]	"the remedy for the defilement of our sins"

The Greek text reminds the careful reader that while such renderings may attain a certain simplicity, they run the risk of downplaying the magnitude of what Christ did in propitiating wrath that humans must otherwise surely face (translations retaining "propitiation" include ESV and HCSB). (On Jesus's view of hell, see Yarbrough 2004a.)

Jesus's ministry as ἱλασμός, 1 John 2:2 goes on to say, extends beyond the sins of the "we" of John and his readers to "those of the whole world." Such a reference should not be surprising given John's stress on Christ's ministry to the world at large in the Fourth Gospel (e.g., John 1:9, 10, 29; 3:16, 17, 19; 4:42; 6:14, 33, 51). There is a universal dimension to Christ's death for sins (Segalla 1993), in the same sense that God's promise to Abraham has a universal horizon: "All peoples on earth will be blessed through you" (Gen. 12:3 NIV). Old Testament sacrifices were offered "for all Israel" (LXX περὶ παντὸς Ισραηλ, *peri pantos Israēl*; Ezra 8:35; 2 Chron. 29:24) even though by no means all of the people received the personal saving grace symbolized by the sacrifices.

This expansive application of the benefit of the atonement is fitting given that Christ is co-creator of the world (John 1:10). He was gracious in creation; he continues to be generous in redemption. It is not warranted to conclude from this, however, that all individuals in the world will be redeemed by Christ's death for sin—that is, that no one will suffer eschatological judgment or hell (cf. John 3:36; Kruse 2000: 75). His death should rather be seen as for "the whole world" in the sense that it provides the basis throughout all human history for God the Father to extend patience and forbearance to those who merit his rejection (i.e., every person since the fall) until the day Christ reappears.[15] The reason God can temporarily overlook human sin (cf. Acts 17:30), so to speak, not judging it eschatologically on the spot, is that the cross carves out a place for the exercise of divine longsuffering, with not only the already saved but also those yet to be saved in view (Turretin 1992–97: 2.459 §14.14.11). Christ "has laid down a sufficient price for all, and to this degree he has procured God's patience to forbear them, and his bounty to lead them to repentance" (Cotton 1962: 84–85; cf. Origen, *Against Celsus* 4.28). Paul preached that God

substitutionary, not exemplary. "There is . . . a great difference between the death of the martyrs (who though godly were yet sinners themselves) and the death of Christ (who is described as the righteous one)" (Kruse 2000: 74n35).

14. R. Brown 1982: 221 calls NEB's rendering "bland modernizing."

15. This goes beyond the view of Augustine (*Hom. 1 John* 1.8), who thinks that reference is to those from "the church throughout the whole world" who are saved. Similarly Calvin 1988: 244.

showed himself merciful to idolatrous nations who in no way deserved mercy (Acts 14:15–17; cf. Rom. 3:25). Was God being inconsistent or unjust in this? It is hard to separate God's stay of execution on the nations (and at times on his own wayward people; cf. 10:21) from the rich store of mercy accruing from Christ's death, even if that death is clearly not ultimately redemptive for those who reject the gospel call based on it.

At the Reformation the question of the extent of the atonement became acute.[16] The issue remains alive today for many.[17] Did Christ die for all or only for the elect? In light of the variegated biblical data,[18] the question so formulated begs the question. First John 2:2 indicates that there is a sense in which he did both.[19] The question should be sharpened: Is the full eschatological benefit of the cross applied to all equally or only to those who in God's design (election) receive the gift of grace by faith? For John, the answer to that question is surely the latter. In this sense, Jesus did not suffer for every individual indiscriminately but particularly for those whom God knew he would save (on election in John's Gospel, see Yarbrough 1995). The Johannine Jesus prays to the Father, "I am not praying for the world, but for those you have given me, for they are yours" (John 17:9 NIV). If the Son does not mind specifying that he prays for only a certain group given to him by the Father, it is not hard to imagine that in the same sense his cleansing blood is applied in its fullest sense only to that group.[20] In the same vein the redactional comment of 11:51–52 may be noted, where Jesus is said to die "for the Jewish nation" and "for the scattered children of God, to bring them together and make them one" (NIV). Amid the wideness of the atonement's scope—Jesus "suffered death, so that by the grace of God he might taste death for everyone" (Heb. 2:9 NIV)—there is at the same time an undeniable particularity. To this extent the interpretation of Turretin (1992–97: 2.474 §14.14.40, following Calvin) is correct: "the whole world" refers to believers scattered everywhere and in all times.

16. For references extending back to the patristic era, see Turretin 1992–97: 2.455–58 §14.14.1–6. Turretin's own discussion (2.458–82 §14.14.7–17) illustrates the complexity and seriousness of the dispute in the heyday of Protestant Scholasticism. For mainly post-Reformation discussion, see Hagenbach 1862: 268, 275–77.

17. It is very close to the surface throughout Murray 1995: 69–80, who discusses disputes related to the doctrine among Baptists in Victorian England. On the other hand, Thompson 1992: 48–51 does not even mention the issue. Marshall's discussion (1978: 119) limited to citation of a Charles Wesley hymn probably obscures the real tension between two important Johannine insistences: there is *both* universality *and* particularity in Christ's atoning work.

18. Bloesch 1978: 165 cites John 3:16; 1 Tim. 2:4; 1 John 2:2; and Titus 2:11 as supporting universal atonement. Yet he concedes "the truth in the doctrine of limited or definite atonement," which in his view is that "its efficacy does not extend to all persons," at least not in the same sense.

19. Turretin 1992–97: 2.474 §14.14.40 is too intent on refuting his opponents (and supporting Calvin?) to give sufficient weight to this possibility when discussing 2:2.

20. This is not to impute Amyraldianism as a system to John. It is only to suggest that John's frame of reference here seems less rigorously and explicitly decree regulated than those like Hodge, Shedd, and Warfield, who opposed Amyraut (see Demarest 1984: 41–42).

And yet none of this rules out certain positive benefits—God's common grace to humans generally (cf. Matt. 5:45; Origen, *Against Celsus* 3.49)—that are spin-offs of the central redeeming benefit proper of the cross.[21] "The Father has sent his Son to be the Savior of the world" (1 John 4:14 NIV). This does not rule out his being judge of those in the world to which the atonement does not apply. Nor does it justify, in practical theological terms, any attenuation of gospel proclamation on the grounds that the gospel cannot in good faith be offered to those who are not destined to accept it. A preacher of another time voiced the Christian interpreter's pathos here. Expressing not anger but the desire to do justice to the full range of biblical statements that make ostensibly contrasting claims, C. H. Spurgeon noted: God "has an infinite benevolence which, nevertheless, is not in all points worked out by his infinite omnipotence; and if anybody asked me why it is not, I cannot tell" (cited in Murray 1995: 152).

3. Author's Assurance: Chastened Christian Confidence (2:3–6)

The grounds for confidence described in 2:1–2 lead to immediate clarification and application (Strecker 1996: 40n21). So Christians have an intercessor, Christ is the propitiation for sin, his death's cleansing effects have a comprehensive scope. What does this mean for the business of everyday life, which John knows has become shaky in some respects among those he addresses? John's reply to this question is fourfold. (1) He lays out a basis for Christian assurance (compliance with Christ's commands) that corresponds to and is called forth by Christ's faithfulness in his own ministry (2:3). "There is a kind of existential reassurance that comes only when the testimony believed is acted upon" (D. Smith 1991: 53). (2) He speaks of disqualification from assurance (2:4). (3) He expands the basis for assurance so as to embrace, or be embraced by, divine love (2:5). (4) He makes explicit the ethical dimension that is essential to Christian identity (2:6).

First John 1:6–10 has already had the effect of making any reader with a conscience leery of claiming freedom from sin. Yet despite the necessity of a healthy measure of self-skepticism when it comes to ethical probity, confidence is still called for because of the sheer scope, grandeur, and power of Christ's sacrifice. But the confidence must be chastened and not brash, and it cannot be enjoyed at all if ethical tendencies are seriously out of sync with the exemplary life pattern and didactic guidance of the one claimed as Lord.

a. Basis for Assurance: Compliance with Christ's Commandments (2:3)

While previous verses were not without strong notes of assurance (1:7, 9; 2:1–2), they also contained unmistakable shots across the bow for some whose words,

21. In keeping with the universal scale of Christ's blessing, not many years after John's death Ignatius writes to Christians in Asia Minor: "Pray continually for the rest of mankind as well, that they may find God, for there is in them a hope of repentance" (*Eph.* 10.1).

walk, or both were out of line (1:6, 8, 10). John now continues the cadence of alternating encouragement with grave admonition.

Encouragement comes first in 2:3. The ἐν τούτῳ (*en toutō*, by this; fourteen occurrences in 1 John, only five in the Fourth Gospel) clause looks ahead to the ἐάν (*ean*) clause (marked by the colon in my translation).[22] John offers a means of acquiring secure knowledge of Christ or, more likely, God (so R. Brown 1982: 249). The means is ethical in nature: "we keep his commandments" (on "commandments" in 1 John, see von Wahlde 1990). John is not saying that keeping commandments alone is a sufficient condition to vouchsafe true knowledge of God. As the discussion associated with the figures in the exegesis of 2:1a indicated, "knowing God" in the full sense is a multiplex matter and involves pistic and agapic dimensions as well; it "describes not only a theoretical belief that something is true but a being involved with something" (Strecker 1996: 40; Strecker might have more aptly written "with someone"). John is, however, affirming that keeping commandments is necessary as appropriate response to the God who is light (R. Brown 1982: 248 notes that the verse points back to 1:5)—yet not as a condition but as "a sign of knowing God" (Strecker 1996: 40).

What does John mean by "commandments"? The word ἐντολή (*entolē*) is common in the LXX (240 times), most often translating Hebrew מִצְוָה (*miṣwâ*, commandment). A commandment is closely related to νόμος (*nomos*, teaching, guidance, law; cf. Hebrew תּוֹרָה, *tôrâ*). In the OT the two terms may be roughly synonymous, or *miṣwâ* may denote an individual stipulation within a larger didactic or legal corpus—within *tôrâ* (Moses's teaching) are the Ten Commandments, the ten *miṣwôt* (מִצְוֹת). In the fifteen occurrences of νόμος in the Fourth Gospel, John always has the broader classification in mind, often referring explicitly to the law of Moses. The word νόμος itself is absent from John's Letters.

Ἐντολη, on the other hand, is present in both John's Gospel (ten times) and John's Epistles (eighteen times). In the Gospels it refers to a commandment, charge, order, decree, or other imperative (e.g., John 10:18; 11:57; 12:49). In John's writings NIV never translates it "commandment," which in English might connote a more sweeping and comprehensive standing rule than "command." (Think of the difference between saying "The Ten Commandments" and "The Ten Commands.") The RSV prefers "commandment" in nearly every case.[23]

It may be that in 1 John 2:3 and elsewhere in 1 John where ἐντολή appears, John has in mind not merely a command in the situationally limited sense but

22. Turner 1963: 45 calls the construction "a characteristic usage in Paul and John." R. Brown 1982: 248–49 catalogs each occurrence to determine whether the reference is backward, forward, or a combination of both.

23. In fact the word "commandment" has disappeared from the NIV NT, except in those passages (a total of fourteen occurrences) thought to refer specifically to the Ten Commandments or other stipulations of the law of Moses. ("Commandments" [pl.] is used an additional twenty times with the same meaning.) The RSV NT refers to "commandments" over fifty times and "commandment" thirty-four times.

a commandment in the more encompassing and transcendent sense. John's Gospel and other early Christian proclamation make clear that Jesus comes in a prophetic role like that of Moses (cf. Deut. 18:15 and John 1:21; Acts 3:22; 7:37). Moses quotes God as saying, "I will put my words in his [i.e., the coming prophet's] mouth, and he will tell them [i.e., God's people] everything I command him" (Deut. 18:18 NIV). God's commands to the prophet like Moses (cf. John 6:14; 7:40), to be passed on to the people of God, are no less than commands, but by virtue of the high authority of the one who delivers them, they are somewhat more: they are commandments. Jesus's self-awareness in John's Gospel as speaking from and for God comports with this Mosaic depiction of his prophetic office.

If by ἐντολή John usually means a commandment, a standing directive with entailments and potential applications for every situation (as opposed to a command, which can be understood as more situation-specific),[24] what commandments does he have in mind in 1 John 2:3? Two answers may be given, the first quite definite: the commandment to love one another.[25] This is prominent in John's Gospel (13:34; 15:12) and is directly reflected in John's Epistles, where the noun or verb for "love" occurs a remarkable fifty-two times in the Greek text (most discussed by R. Brown 1982: 254–55). In a Christian community rent by schism, the love commandment is clearly apropos.

Ἐντολή also has a second, broader connotation. This is implied by John's parallel use of "word" (λόγος, *logos*). The commandments in 1 John 2:3 are equivalent to Jesus's "word" in 2:5. Jesus's "commandment" and "word" to love are identical in 2:7. John's Gospel speaks of "keeping" Christ's word in the same sense as keeping his commandment (8:51, 52; 14:23, 24) or of Christ "keeping" the Father's word in the same sense as he heeds the Father's commandment (8:55; 17:6). "Commandment" in 1 John 2:3 can therefore mean the "word" delivered by Jesus, a concept as specific as his didactic discourse recorded in the Gospels and as broad as the apostolic gospel and its application as seen in other NT writings. Nor can "commandment" in John's usage be sharply separated from OT directives, since both Jesus and his followers (as exemplified by NT authors) so clearly regard them as oracular, ethically suggestive if not binding, and through proclamation and associated sacrament constitutive of God's living presence in their communities.

John writes that keeping Christ's commandments is "how we know that we truly know him," that is, know Christ.[26] The word "truly" is not in the

24. This distinction would seem to hold true in John's Gospel at 12:49, 50; 13:34; 14:15, 21; 15:10 (2x), 12.

25. Augustine (*Hom. 1 John* 1.9) agrees that the commandment has love in view but understands "perfected in love" as "to love even enemies, and love them for this end, that they may be brethren."

26. Rensberger 1997: 57 flirts with reductionism by denying any associations between light and right knowledge or right belief, reducing John's whole concern to behavior, which he then conflates with love. In fact belief, action, and affection seem to be equally vital in John's portrayal of life in Christ.

Greek text but may be inferred from the context, where the first occurrence of "know" (γινώσκομεν, *ginōskomen*) is simply present tense and refers to the ongoing awareness of John and his readers, which may or may not constitute a state of assurance, while the second use of "know" is perfect (ἐγνώκαμεν, *egnōkamen*) and may connote a full and settled state (so Schnackenburg 1992: 95; see also first additional note on 2:3). The sense is, "This is how we maintain the awareness that we have come to know him fully." As the figures in the exegesis of 2:1a projected, Christian assurance in the sense of knowing God and reflecting that knowledge ethically (and in other ways) is a high priority for John, because the absence of these factors spells a bogus belief. John's pastoral instincts are too strong to let people limp along with a religion that merely apes aspects of the complete gospel that Christ brought, with its full complement of pistic, ethical, and agapic dimensions. First John 2:3 contains the first of a series of twenty-six occurrences of γινώσκω (*ginōskō*, know) in John's Letters, the fuller meaning of which will unfold in the exegesis of individual passages.

b. Disqualification from Assurance (2:4)

Just as 1 John 1:6–10 depicted religious postures with the help of an "if we say" device, in 2:4 (cf. 2:6, 9; 2 John 11) John uses "the one who says" (ὁ λέγων, *ho legōn*) to dramatize a possible response to Christ among those claiming to follow him. John envisions an individual ("I truly know") who claims the full and settled knowledge of Christ of which John speaks in corporate terms in 1 John 2:3 ("we truly know"), but who does not keep the commandments. Such an individual, John states, is "a liar." We have already encountered the general notion of Christian-looking people belying their confession by their deeds in 1:6 ("we lie"; cf. 1:8, 10). But these passages are perhaps a bit more diplomatic; John has not yet called the transgressor a liar. Here he does. A person of similar description crops up later in the epistle, too, as the person who denies true christological doctrine (2:22). But John's reference in 2:4 is more closely parallel to the one who is a liar in the sense of failing to love his or her brother while claiming to love God (4:20), because at the center of "his commandments," as demonstrated above, is the love command. It can also be said of this person, as John states in 2:4, that "the truth is not in him" (see exegesis of 1:8).

Is John's hateful-sounding denunciation—in American English, at least, to call someone a liar sounds bitterly denunciatory—not a contradiction of his ubiquitous exhortations to love elsewhere in the epistle? Culpepper (1998: 255) feels that "the pluralism of the church today makes it difficult for us to grasp the exclusiveness of the spirit of 1 John." Sloyan (1995: 2–3) uses words like "harshness of tone," "vituperative," and "obloquy" to characterize John's rhetoric. While it is possible simply to convict the writer of hypocritical blindness or a cynical double standard (he can hate, but hatred is a sin when his enemies do it), it is worth asking whether a more sympathetic reading is possible. Several observations may be made (beyond the obvious but important one that vulgar or denunciatory rhetoric in one language, directly translated, may not have the same tawdry connotations in another). First, John is portrayed elsewhere as one of two "sons of thunder" (Mark 3:17), who were ready to call down fire from heaven, if possible, to destroy people for what they perceived to be the kingdom's sake (Luke 9:54). This indicates a personality type given to strong feelings and probably a social ethic, not absent from the Middle East today, in which violent revenge on enemies is among accepted mores. Second, the word "liar" was part of Jesus's verbal repertoire, too, to refer not only to the devil (John 8:44) but also to people who claim to know God but actually do not (8:55). The parallel with 1 John 2:4 is direct, and the question is raised whether John's characterization is something learned from Jesus. Third, that Jesus uses similar language (cf. other denunciatory flourishes and epithets like "hypocrites," "blind guides," "blind fools," "snakes," "brood of vipers," and the like in Matt. 23:13–33) tells us that strong denunciation of blatant evil is not necessarily a sin (though it certainly can be)—unless we think that Jesus sinned in some of his verbal displays or that such harsh words attributed to Jesus must be the work of later writers and not faithful representations of what he actually said. Fourth, it is possible that John's language, coming from a personal disciple of Jesus exercising the special leading of the Holy Spirit promised the apostles in John 14–16, simply reflects God's pastoral verdict on the kind of disingenuousness that 1 John 2:4 describes. It *is* a serious thing that that person *is*, objectively speaking, a liar who flaunts Christ's commandments while claiming to be his loyal follower. We may not like John's verbal style, but he may simply be stating a fact in God's sight as a pastoral messenger to God's people who need a wakeup call.

It is possible, therefore, to reject John's strong words as a template for our own speech conduct under normal circumstances, while retaining their force for our instruction and, with great hesitation, regarding them as examples in very rare cases for circumstances that are abnormal.[27] John may be a reminder that somewhere between Yeats's "best" people, "who lack all conviction" (and therefore lack moral sense and courage to denounce), and his worst, who "are full of passionate intensity" (and for whom spleen might be the normal rhetorical mode), there is room in the Christian community both for seemingly infinite forbearance and for piquant prophetic forthrightness.[28]

c. Expansion of the Basis for Assurance: The Perfection of Christian Love (2:5)

First John 2:5 augments the picture sketched in 2:3. There the connection was made between a full and settled state of knowing God and compliance with divine commandments. Now John makes a similar statement, but with important

27. Klauck 1991: 174 speaks disapprovingly of the extreme polemic in 1 John, yet concedes: "The right, indeed the necessity of contending for the truth remains . . . untouched."

28. The reference is to W. B. Yeats's poem "The Second Coming."

expansions. Instead of "commandments" in 2:3, he now speaks of Christ's "word." Moreover, the word "love" (ἀγάπη, *agapē*) makes its first appearance in the epistle. Love, the agapic aspect without which knowing God is incomplete, has truly been perfected[29] in the person who keeps that word. Finally, from a literary or rhetorical point of view, the phrase ἐν τούτῳ γινώσκομεν (*en toutō ginōskomen*, by this we know) of 2:5 demarcates the *inclusio* that commenced with the identical words of 2:3. First John 2:6, though outside the *inclusio*, will complete it by way of summary and slight expansion.

Some comments are in order about my translation of 2:5. "On the other hand" translates δέ (*de*) understood as if μέν (*men*) were present at the beginning of 2:4; several NT writings reflect the Hellenistic Greek tendency to omit μέν in de facto μέν . . . δέ constructions (BDF §447.2). "Christ's" translates αὐτοῦ (*autou*, his) to make explicit that the antecedent seems to be Ἰησοῦν Χριστόν (*Iēsoun Christon*, Jesus Christ) in 2:1–2. Admittedly John at times segues from Father to Son without making the transition explicit, and this could be the case here. "God has perfected his love" translates ἡ ἀγάπη τοῦ θεοῦ τετελείωται (*hē agapē tou theou teteleiōtai*, lit., the love of God has been perfected); at work here are two convictions: (1) that ἡ ἀγάπη τοῦ θεοῦ should be understood as subjective (Loader 1992: 17) or perhaps qualitative (Schnackenburg 1992: 97 with note 118) and (2) that the verb τετελείωται is a so-called divine passive (BDF §130.1; Zerwick 1994: §236 ["theological passive"]; Moule 1994: 26; cf. also the explanation and cautions against overuse and misuse of this category in Wallace 1996: 437–38). It is not that John is reluctant to use God's name here for theological reasons; it is rather that the phrase "God has perfected the love of God" would be intolerably awkward, while "God has perfected his love" (ὁ θεὸς τετελείωκεν τὴν ἀγάπην αὐτοῦ, *ho theos teteleiōken tēn agapēn autou*) might be taken to refer to the person's love and rather than God's.[30]

The person who keeps Christ's commandments and in whom God is perfecting his love[31] knows himself or herself to be "in him" (ἐν αὐτῷ, *in autō*). The phrase calls to mind Paul's frequent use of the words "in Christ (Jesus)" (M. A. Seifrid, *DPL* 433 likens the Pauline expression to "pronominal references to Christ in the Johannine materials"). First John's ἐν αὐτῷ refers to "in Christ" or "in God" rather indiscriminately (Christ in 2:5, 6, 8; 3:6, 9[?]; God in 4:13; either Christ or God in 2:27, 28; 3:24). To these occurrences may be

29. The Greek perfect (τετελείωται) used futuristically is "entirely in conformity with classical usage" (BDF §344). But John is not referring here only to the future.

30. Τελειόω (*teleioō*, perfect, complete) occurs only in the passive in 1 John, and only in connection with the noun "love." In every case divine activity can be understood as lying behind the passive voice (besides 2:5 see 4:12, 17, 18). In John's Gospel the perfect tense divine passive of τελειόω is likely at 17:23 and 19:28 (in the latter verse, the subsequent aorist passive construction ἵνα τελειωθῇ ἡ γραφή [*hina teleiōthē hē graphē*, in order that the Scriptures might be fulfilled] further underscores God's contextual proximity).

31. Strecker 1996: 41 stresses the eschatological overtones of this perfecting action. But John seems to be trafficking primarily in the present effects. Marshall 1978: 125 helpfully comments on John Wesley's doctrine of "perfect love" derived from this verse and rightly rejects "the closely related phrase 'Christian perfection'" as lacking scriptural warrant.

added more corporately oriented references to Christ (3:24[?]) or God (3:24[?]; 4:12, 13, 16) dwelling ἐν ἡμῖν (*en hēmin*, in/among us).[32] To be in Christ or God, as 1 John depicts the state, is to be in the positive domain marked out by the pistic, ethical, and agapic trajectories sketched in the exegesis of 2:1a. It is to know God the Father fully through relationship to him via the Son. It is to have the Father living in oneself, doing his work, if Jesus's own description of being "in the Father" and having "the Father . . . in me" is any indication: "Don't you believe that I am in the Father, and that the Father is in me? . . . It is the Father, living in me, who is doing his work" (John 14:10 NIV).

The ethical-agapic link should be noted as John underscores in 1 John 2:5 that keeping Christ's word is a demonstration of the perfection of God's love.[33] This would not come as a surprise for anyone versed in Jesus's repeated teaching in John's Gospel that to love him is to obey his commandments and vice versa (John 14:15, 21, 23; cf. 14:24; 15:10). It might sound strained or foreign to someone who understands love and moral constraint as mutually exclusive. But "John knows nothing of a tension between love and righteousness" (Schlatter 1999: 123; on the correlation between the two, see Law 1909: 80–87). In the immediate context of 1 John 2:5, John is leaving unvoiced the dimension of faith (pistic dimension) that, like loving God and keeping his commandments, is integral to knowing God in the full sense, as John's Gospel and passages later in 1 John make clear. He cannot always mention everything at once, and he would have assumed a general measure of pistic integrity in communities having at least a degree of allegiance to Christ. Rensberger (1997: 61) seems to overlook this in claiming that knowing God "does not mean knowing correct facts or doctrines about God, but having an intimate relationship with God." This either/or is foreign to this epistle. It is rather the case that ethical uprightness, agapic devotion, and pistic integrity function in a correlative balance in the life of the authentic recipient of John's message. First John 2:5 just happens to stress only two of these three dimensions.

d. Ethical Obligation of the Professing Christian (2:6)

The section that began with 2:1 can be seen as concluding at 2:6. The "saying" denoted here ("the one who *says*") carries the sense contextually of making an affirmation or claim, and the claim is to "abide" (μένειν, *menein*) in Christ.[34] To make that claim stakes the speaker to a certain ethical responsibility: *imita-*

32. Other references could be added that use ἐν ὑμῖν (in/among you; e.g., 4:4) or that in combination with a form of μένω (*menō*, abide) speak of abiding in the Son or Father (e.g., 2:24).

33. A generation or less after John's death, Ignatius sends similar instruction and exhortation to the Asia Minor region that may have first received John's First Epistle. He warns the Ephesian Christians against people who traffic in God's name but disobey his commands: "For there are some who maliciously and deceitfully are accustomed to carry about the name while doing other things unworthy of God" (*Eph.* 7.1). But he commends the Ephesians: "So you are all fellow pilgrims . . . adorned in every respect with the commandments of Jesus Christ" (*Eph.* 9.2).

34. Neander 1852: 66 thinks that "to abide in Christ, designates something more than to be in Christ. It means, not merely to have entered through faith into fellowship with Christ,

tio Christi (imitation of Christ).[35] The concept is more profound than merely mimicking externals or even obeying Christ's expressed will in a formal way. It has to do with "living the whole of life" *coram deo*, as in God's presence (a plausible rendering of περιπατέω, *peripateō*, to walk), as Jesus did (on καθώς [*kathōs*, just as], see exegesis of 3:3). Jesus did the will of the Father (fulfilling the ethical component of right human response to God: John 4:34; 5:30; 6:38, 40). Further, Jesus seems always to have lived in loving fellowship with God, as both lengthy seasons of private prayer and explicit references[36] indicate, modeling the agapic dimension of appropriate human response to God. The imitation that John commends is probably centered in these twin pillars of Jesus's piety: his ethical faithfulness to God (stressed by Kruse 2000: 82 and most other commentators) and manifest love of God.

"Walk" in the sense of living the whole of life *coram deo* has rich OT associations (Smalley 1984: 22; Rensberger 1997: 51–52), whether in terms of Hebrew הָלַךְ (*hālak*, to go, walk; cf. Prov. 2:7, 20; 3:23; 4:12; 6:22; 8:20; 10:9; 14:2) or דֶּרֶךְ (*derek*, way, road), used metaphorically to refer to the "way" or "walk" of both righteous and unrighteous people (Ps. 1:1 NIV speaks of "not *walk*[*ing*]" in the counsel of the wicked or stand[ing] in the *way* of sinners"). H. Wolf (*TWOT* 1:197) notes that in OT usage "the way [*derek*] of the righteous is closely linked with 'the way of the Lord.'" Throughout the history of Israel, God's people were to emulate God's ways. (For the LXX use of περιπατέω, see the exegesis and second additional note at 2:11.)

The imperative to imitate God (cf. Eph. 5:1) implied in 1 John 2:6 understandably takes on particular urgency once God is understood to have assumed human form as a leader who called disciples. At the footwashing, Jesus made a telling application: "I have set you an example that you should do as I have done for you" (John 13:15 NIV). While any number of Jesus's acts (notably his atoning sacrifice for sin) and attributes (notably his essential oneness with the Father) are not presented by NT writers as goals for humans to imitate directly, in broad terms Jesus's life does indeed present a pattern to be duplicated, *mutatis mutandis*, in his followers (Sloyan 1995: 18; Culpepper 1998: 260). And even the cross and Jesus's filial consciousness have important analogies in the Christian life. "The bond between Jesus and believers is determinative for the community's ethical norms" (Hays 1996: 143), and a sizable component in that bond is how Jesus lived his life. John had seen that life lived out (recall

but also to persevere therein steadfastly." For a classification of John's uses, see R. Brown 1982: 259–61.

35. Strecker 1996: 43 prefers the term *imitatio Jesu*. This is most appropriate if one has concluded that Jesus was not the Christ of biblical promise and theology and therefore that the two names must be distinguished. But it would limit the possible extent of imitation to the level of mimicking.

36. E.g., John 14:31 points to both the ethical and agapic aspects of Jesus's relationship with the Father: "I love the Father and . . . I do exactly what my Father has commanded me" (NIV). Cf. Jesus's love for the Father in 15:10 (includes ethical aspect) and 17:26.

1 John 1:1–4), and believers since then have had either oral or written apostolic testimony (i.e., the four Gospels) to inform and instruct them.

This "noble exemplar" motif is not surprising. The leader-follower dynamic is an important OT motif extending into the NT. Alexander (1901: 121) speaks of "the law of restoration by living example through personal influence." Whether in covenantal-family terms (with Jacob following Isaac who followed Abraham in the matter of which Ancient Near Eastern god to serve) or in terms of godly leader or parent inspiring dedicated worshipers (Moses-Joshua, Hannah-Samuel, David-Solomon, Elijah-Elisha, Isaiah-disciples, and perhaps Jeremiah-Baruch [cf. Jer. 45]), knowing God often involves patterning life along lines bequeathed by a spiritual forebear or mentor. It finds rich expression in the phenomenon of Pharisaism with its stress on teachers of encyclopedic range and pupils of comprehensive responsibility—even Jesus said, "Do everything they tell you" (Matt. 23:3 NIV). The pattern is only intensified in the NT, with the God and the faith of the patriarchs coming in for renewed praise, the Scriptures of Judaism and Israel receiving renewed application, and the leaders of renewed covenant existence in Christ calling for imitation of their convictions and ways (S. E. Fowl, *DPL* 428–31). It is within this nexus that 1 John 2:6 appeals for imitation of Christ. Moreover, John taps into a trajectory extending directly back to Jesus's "ought" (ὀφείλετε, *opheilete*) in John 13:14 ("now that I, your Lord and Teacher, have washed your feet, you also ought to wash one another's feet") and moving forward to include 1 John 2:6 and two other affirmations in 1 John calling for imitation of Jesus (3:16) or God (4:11).

But what exactly does it mean "to live the whole of life in the manner he did" (2:6)? There are several senses in which John would likely find possible notions of the *imitatio Christi* insufficient in themselves:

1. Imitation could be construed in a simplistic or crude way—like a mimic affecting the voice and mannerisms of another. This could even amount to "aping" how someone else acts. In the early 1980s, a preacher traversed Scotland on foot, carrying a large wooden cross as he went. This might have been effective in drawing crowds to hear his message, but it falls short of what John refers to. (Even Jesus did not lug around a cross to attract listeners.) When imitation runs the risk of looking like parody, John's sense has been lost. Augustine (*Hom. 1 John* 1.9) uses humor to good effect in asking whether walking like Christ walked might mean that his followers should try to stride across the surface of a stormy sea like Jesus is reported to have done (John 6:19).
2. Imitation could connote forming oneself after the pattern of another, inasmuch as some things or people are worthy of imitation. John is at least calling for living as Jesus did in the sense of making him an exemplar for our own ways (Smalley 1984: 53). It is here that the "What would Jesus do?" approach to life and decisions might at its best be placed.[37] Augustine

37. For the limitations of this mode of direction seeking, see Schlatter 1950: 25.

(*Hom. 1 John* 1.9) adopts a somewhat limiting interpretation of this sort in concluding that the epitome of proper emulation of Christ would be to pray for enemies even as they unjustly persecute the righteous.

3. Imitation could be understood in the sense of Jesus's command to "follow" (ἀκολουθέω, *akoloutheō*) him (Preuschen 1963: 15).[38] This is an imitation that does not merely ask at points how someone else might act but rather involves a root-and-branch subsuming of one's own life under what someone else stands for and is (cf. Origen, *First Principles* 4.1.31). Rensberger (1997: 69) says it well: "Those who claim to be enlightened, to know God, can verify that claim only by their concrete correspondence to the one who brought this knowledge into the world, and to the nature of the God that he revealed as love." Rensberger thinks this excludes imitation either as "mimicry of Jesus's lifestyle" or "attempting to become like him through moral behavior."

Johannine imitation means to follow as a disciple, a completely dedicated adherent and advocate.[39] This was, in obedience to Jesus's call, the way of life that John had embraced for himself (Matt. 4:21–22; John 1:37–39[?]). It is accordingly the way he now commends to his readers. In Johannine terms it far exceeds what imitation of any other human might involve, because following Christ is a two-way street: not only do believers reach out toward him, but he also takes up residence within his followers by his Spirit, according to his promise (John 14:17–19; 15:7–14) and John's claims in this epistle (1 John 2:20, 24, 27; 3:24; 4:4, 13; cf. Malatesta 1978). "As there is a literal, so there is a mystical walking as Christ walked" (Alexander 1901: 129). Christ's life (taken in conjunction with his saving death) truly becomes "both a model to be imitated, and . . . the means for that imitation to become a possibility" (Smalley 1984: 53).

First John 2:6 states in laconic indicative form what the self-proclaimed Christian "ought" to be doing. The next section sharpens this descriptive statement and others that John has made (like "God is light") into imperatives that touch the whole range of human age groups across the totality of their lives.

Additional Notes

2:1. The correct reading is surely the aorist subjunctive ἁμάρτητε. Even if the poorly attested present subjunctive ἁμαρτάνητε were preferred, current understanding of the semantic difference between

38. Cf. Rothenberg 1965: 50, who defines *imitatio Christi* as "mimicking Christ" but adds, "more correct, properly speaking: following Christ as a disciple."

39. Disputed by Schnackenburg 1992: 99n126: "imitation, not discipleship." But the argument is largely from silence and pits Synoptic use of ἀκολουθέω against a different use in John's Gospel. This confuses a word with a concept: the reality of discipleship is as palpable in John as in the Synoptics. R. Brown 1982: 286 concludes: "The 'just as Christ' comparison involves more than the imitation of a model. Christians have the same eternal life that Jesus had and has; this life, as an internal principle, must express itself in the same way it did and does in him." It may be questioned, however, whether Christians have precisely "the same eternal life that Jesus had and has."

the two would furnish little sure ground for interpretative conclusions (contra Holtzmann 1908: 331, who quoting B. Weiss argues that "habitual sinning" would have required the present tense as in 3:6, 8; 5:18). Linguistically speaking, the aorist is less heavily marked and perfective (Porter 1989: 360–61), "perfective" here meaning that the action is viewed from the point of view of being complete. Cf. Wallace 1996: 559, who uses the term "consummative."

2:1. Many translations take παράκλητος in John 14–16 as something besides "Advocate" (JB, NRSV, TNIV): "Comforter" (KJV, LB), "Counselor" (RSV, NIV, HCSB, NLT), "Helper" (TEV, NASB, ESV).[40] Such renderings have hoary precedent stretching back at least to Luther, who in his September-Bibel (1522) rendered παράκλητος as *troster* (Comforter). Augustine (*Homilies on the Gospel of John* 94.2) had already taken the same tack. But in 74.4 he notes that Greek παράκλητος "is in Latin called *advocatus*." The connotation of "comforter" seems to derive from a possible meaning of the Greek verb παρακαλέω (to exhort, encourage, console), which cannot be assumed without contextual justification to attach to the cognate noun παράκλητος. Irenaeus combines understanding παράκλητος as both Spirit and Son in the same passage:

> This Spirit . . . did confer upon the church, sending throughout all the world the Comforter [Latin *Paracletum*] from heaven, from whence also the Lord tells us that the devil, like lightning, was cast down. Wherefore we have need of the dew of God, that we be not consumed by fire, nor be rendered unfruitful, and that where we have an accuser there we may also have an Advocate [Latin *Paracletum*]. (*Ag. Her.* 3.17.3; Latin text in Harvey 1857: 93)

Origen defines Paraclete as "Intercessor" when referring to Christ and "Comforter" when referring to the Holy Spirit (*First Principles* 2.7.4).

2:2. A few manuscripts, among them B, read μόνων rather than μόνον. The latter reading is to be taken adverbially (along with οὐ, another adverb) as specifying "how" Christ is the propitiation: "not only" for believers' sins. Translation of the variant would make little difference to the verse's meaning. The adjectival and adverbial uses of μόνος had grown similar in Classical Greek and by the Hellenistic period were occasionally confused (BDF §243).

2:3. While facile generalizations about the perfect tense are to be avoided (cf. Porter 1989: 257), inductive reflection on the NT's twenty-one perfect-tense occurrences of the verb ἐγνώκαμεν indicates that a connotation of "know fully" makes better sense than simply "know" without further qualification. This is borne out most forcefully when ἐγνώκαμεν occurs in close parallel with the unusual perfect form of πιστεύω (John 6:69, 1 John 4:16).

2:3. Instead of the present subjunctive τηρῶμεν (we keep), Ψ and 1852 have the aorist subjunctive τηρήσωμεν. Any possible difference in meaning is hard to ascertain, and external evidence for the latter form is weak. But consideration of the forms does point to the curious fact that in John's Gospel τηρέω occurs as a subjunctive only in the aorist (8:51, 52; 12:7; 15:10a; 17:15), while in 1 John it occurs only in the present (2:3, 5; 5:3). Instead of τηρέω, א* here reads φυλάξωμεν, aorist subjunctive of the virtually synonymous φυλάσσω. But in the Johannine corpus, τηρέω is much the more common word. Perhaps the copyist sought to avoid the distracting repetition of τηρέω (which occurs also in 2:4 and 2:5).

2:4. Most manuscripts omit ὅτι *recitativum* (BDF §470.1), which serves as de facto quotation marks around the phrase "I truly know him." Neither omission nor inclusion affects the sense.

2:4. א, shortening καὶ ἐν τούτῳ to καί, reads "is a liar and there is no truth." The omission of a single ἐν τούτῳ in this immediate context may have been encouraged by its occurring four times in 2:3–5. Further confusion in the same phrase comes to light in nearly a dozen manuscripts that

40. CEV replaces the noun with a verbal clause: "The Holy Spirit who will help you."

omit καί and thus read "is a liar; in him there is no truth." Καί here was a function of John's paratactic style to start with, and scribes were probably copying *ad sensum* (my translation does not render καί for the same reason).

2:4. No importance can be attached to the omission of the article before ἀλήθεια by a handful of witnesses (including Ψ); the meaning is very nearly if not completely the same. א, joined by a scant few other manuscripts, underscores that this is the truth τοῦ θεοῦ. Other manuscripts took this tack in 1:8 (see first additional note on 1:8).

2:5. A handful of Byzantine witnesses (322, 323, 1241, 1739, 1881) omit ἀληθῶς, which makes the apodosis in the second clause slightly less forceful.

2:5. In Ψ, indirectly supported by a few Latin witnesses, 2:5 ends with the insertion of ἐὰν εἰς αὐτὸν τελειωθῶμεν (if we are perfected in him). This may improve the flow of the diction by allowing a full stop after τετελείωται. This gives the verse's second ἐν τούτῳ something definite to point ahead to and relieves the uncertainty of what ἐν τούτῳ refers to when it points back, as it must without the addition. But while it is not a malicious addition in any sense, it is not likely to have been part of John's original document.

2:6. NA[27] reads οὕτως but encloses it in brackets to indicate editorial uncertainty as to whether it belongs. Καθὼς . . . οὕτως is attested several times in John's Gospel (3:14; 12:50; 14:31; 15:4). Manuscript evidence is too evenly balanced to decide the original reading on external grounds, and its presence or absence does not affect the sense.

II. Primary Commandment: Embody the Age-Old Message (2:7–17)

The opening section of 1 John affirms and applies the conviction that God is light; the second section stresses the need for that conviction not only to be affirmed personally and cognitively but also acted on practically.

True, John has already called for active response to the message of God's light in his Son. His readers are to walk in the light as God is in the light (1:7), confessing their sins (1:9). They are to forsake sin (2:1). They are to keep his commandments (2:3). Their lives should be a living reflection of Jesus's own earthly life (2:6). An ethical stress has already been prominent, crowning a less prominent agapic subtext (e.g., 1:8; 2:5) and a thus-far tacit dimension of personal faith.

But beginning with 2:7 John narrows the focus to a particular commandment: love others (2:7–8). He grounds the commandment's validity in its combination of antiquity and contemporaneity. Whether one hallows ethical lore of temporally distant or of recent extraction, the love command stands. It stands precisely because of darkness's flagging power and the strong countervailing force of the light (2:8). Mention of light renews the force of the light metaphor for God that was first advanced in 1:5 and justifies (in conjunction with additional references to light and darkness in this section) seeing the metaphor's theological power as undergirding the whole of the epistle's second section.

Another link with the earlier section is John's return to "the one who" rhetoric (2:9–11; cf. 2:4, 6). Here John teases out the implications of the love command for two kinds of people: those who dislike others, and those who find it in their hearts to love rather than despise ("hate" in John's parlance). Light and dark are again very much a part of John's imagery. It is important for people's actual, practical lives to be engaged in the activity of caring for others. Apostolic (and ultimately dominical) doctrine is to find bodily expression. The age-old message must not only enlighten minds but also direct feet and hands. Nothing less befits an ethic rooted in Jesus's bodily self-sacrifice (2:2) and issuing in emulation of the way he lived out his earthly days for the sake of others (2:6).

The section climaxes with the epistle's first overt imperative (2:15): "Do not love the world!" As if to prepare for this rhetorically aggressive counsel, John first poignantly commends his readers for both how God has touched them and how they have responded (2:12–14). John's imperative does not come from a pitiless ivory tower but from the soul of a pastoral leader with heartfelt ties to his readers (Lloyd-Jones 1993: 147; this is a commonplace in the secondary literature). This praise gives the subsequent imperative a positive ring of promise and not a negative sting of censure. John's diplomatic softening prior to voicing a somewhat incriminating and sweeping order increases the likelihood that readers would not stop their ears when the command comes. Despite John's potentially offensive directness, they could listen calmly to the rationale for heeding such a difficult and possibly confusing imperative (2:16–17).

There is a logic to this section's placement, not only with respect to the preceding section, but also vis-à-vis the one that follows (2:18–3:8). There John will move into a combined hortatory and didactic mode. The single imperative of 2:15 is followed by five more in the next section. Since there are only ten imperatives in the entire epistle, this means that the next section is weighted heavily with counsel. The ground for this is prepared by the directions taken in 2:7–17 in three ways. First, John's pastoral diplomacy establishes a deposit of goodwill on which he can draw when he later issues still sterner warnings. Second, his continued veiled references to ostensibly hypothetical individuals who say one thing but do another (2:9, 11; cf. analogous allusions in section I at 1:6, 8, 10; 2:4) prepare the way for outright identification of anti-Christian elements in section III. Third, the author's sustained emphasis in section II on ethical and agapic concerns places pressure on him to acknowledge the third element of saving knowledge of God, the pistic. This comes in for repeated emphasis in section III from several angles, both subtle and overt.

A. The Nature and Implications of the Message (2:7–11)

It is significant that the portion of John's epistle that builds toward issuing the first imperative (2:15) initially lays a foundation of clarifying the apostolic message. This continues the indicative-imperative structure of John's thinking already noted above (see exegesis of 1:5; 2:1b–2, 6).

John clarifies the content of the message by relating it to the past (2:7) while at the same time defining it with respect to the present (2:8). He thus avoids either a hidebound appeal to tradition alone or a neophyte's breathless fascination with late-breaking news exclusively. He rather manages to hallow the past in which God worked without idolizing it (because something epochal has occurred) and at the same time to elevate recent developments without cutting them off from the history that substantially defines them.

Yet John's focus on the message's simultaneous antiquity and novelty does not result in a fixation on information alone or theory primarily. The proclamation that reveals itself in commandments is rendered comprehensible by the way people react to it—whether for or against. The nature of the message and its implications are organically and inextricably linked. Thus in 2:9–11 it is once again natural for John to concretize the meaning of the message he stands for by presenting examples of human response to it.

The substance of 2:7–11 may be characterized as follows:

1. The message old yet current (2:7)
2. The message new yet true (2:8)
3. Implications for the misanthrope (2:9, 11)
    a. The futility of mere confession (2:9)
    b. The darkness of lovelessness (2:11)
4. Implications for the philanthrope (2:10)

Exegesis and Exposition

7⌜Beloved⌝, I am not addressing a new commandment to you but an old
commandment, one you have had all along. The old commandment is the message
that you heard. ⌜ ⌝ 8On the other hand, I am addressing a new commandment to
you—speaking now about that which is ⌜true in him⌝ and in ⌜you⌝; for the darkness
is dissipating and the true light already shines. 9The one who claims to be in the light
but hates his fellow believer ⌜ ⌝ is as yet still in the darkness. 10The one who loves his
fellow believer abides in the light; there ⌜is no offense in him⌝. 11But the one who

hates his fellow believer ⌜is⌝ in darkness. He lives his whole life in darkness and does not understand where he is going, because the darkness has blinded his eyes.

1. The Message Old yet Current (2:7)

John calls his readers ἀγαπητοί (*agapētoi*, beloved; also 3:2, 21; 4:1, 7, 11). "St John while enforcing the commandment of love gives expression to love" (Westcott 1883: 52). "Beloved" (RSV, NRSV, ESV; cf. W. Klassen, *ABD* 4:389, 391) as a noun of direct address carries an archaic ring for some today. Perhaps for that reason, modern translations have opted for "(my) dear friends" (TEV, NIV/TNIV, NEB, NLT, HCSB; cf. BDAG 7) or even the folksy "my dear people" (JB).

A range of older commentators translates "beloved" (Westcott 1883: 52; Holtzmann 1908: 332; Schlatter 1950: 25 ["Geliebte"]), with no thought of a connotation of "friends" (cf. LSJ 6, where no gloss suggestive of "friends" is offered). For that the word φίλος (*philos*, friend) was available. But φίλος is never used in the NT to denote the relatedness that exists among Christian believers because of their shared union with Christ.[1] Rather, lexical treatments often center on the connotation of the word "beloved," not in familiar terms of human friendship, but with reference to "the community of the new spiritual life in Christ" (D. M. Pratt, *ISBE* 1:432; cf. Westcott 1883: 52), which in turn is associated with divine election (W. Günther and H.-G. Link, *NIDNTT* 2:544–45). Christians are "beloved" (not just "dear friends") because God has set his affection on them, in the same sense that his own Son was at once both "the beloved" (Matt. 3:17; 12:18 [cf. Isa. 42:1]; Matt. 17:5) and "the chosen" one (Luke 9:35; 23:35). Old Testament precedent for the close association between divine love and divine election is clear and extensive.[2] In expressing affection for one another, God's people are acknowledging God's prior benevolent regard for them, which makes their loving community possible and fills mere human love with transcendent promise. "Christians are 'beloved' because God has loved them" (R. Brown 1982: 264).

John's term of address likely identifies his readers, with a conviction frequently found in Paul, as "God's chosen people, holy and dearly loved [ἠγαπημένοι, *ēgapēmenoi*]" (Col. 3:12 NIV; cf. 1 Thess. 1:4; Rom. 11:28). They are not just "dear friends" (which according to Burge 1996: 100 "misses the power of John's endearing language") in the normal interpersonal sense and nothing more. It is noteworthy that recent lexical semantic treatment of ἀγαπητός makes no mention of "friends" (LN 1:294, 591). E. Stauffer's assertion that "beloved" in John's Epistles "has nothing to do with the thought

1. John 15:14–15 only proves the point; by "friends" (φίλοι, *philoi*) Jesus means human companions held in high regard, not something akin to what "brothers" (Rom. 12:1; 1 Cor. 1:10), "saints" (Rev. 18:20), or "beloved" (Heb. 6:9; James 2:5; 1 Pet. 2:11) came to signify in early Christian circles.

2. See Deut. 7:6–7; 10:15. See also the confluence of loving or having compassion with election in Deut. 4:37; Pss. 47:4 (47:5 MT); 78:68; Isa. 14:1; cf. Rom. 11:28. On broader issues that this raises, see Ellis 2002.

of election but refers quite simply to the relation of brother to brother (3 Jn. 5; 1 Jn. 4:7)" (*TDNT* 1:53) lacks basis. John's usage is of a piece with other General Epistles whose authors frequently use "beloved" to connote both heartfelt human closeness and grateful acknowledgment of the corporate experience of undeserved divine favor. This same usage was continued into the postapostolic age, and Lightfoot (1891) rightly translates "dearly beloved" and never "dear friends" in the fifteen or more passages where ἀγαπητοί appears in 1 Clement and Ignatius (Goodspeed 1960: 3). It is unfortunate that a recent revision of Lightfoot does not follow suit (Holmes 1999).

John insists that he is bringing his beloved readers a familiar edict (on "commandment," see exegesis of 2:3), not a novel one (καινήν, *kainēn*, new, in the sense of previously unknown; cf. Schnackenburg 1992: 104n143). By "commandment" in this section, John most likely refers to Jesus's imperative to love. It is "old" in the sense that, even as formal moral instruction, it goes back at least to Moses's time, as John would have learned in the synagogue as well as from Jesus (the dour disparagement of the OT law in Darby 1907: 33–34 is to be rejected as out of sympathy with John's Gospel and First Epistle alike).[3] In fact it is even more ancient than Moses in that it is grounded in God's eternal character and existence and was integral to the creation order reflected in the rapport between Adam and Eve (in Matt. 19:4, 8 Jesus uses the language of ἀπ' ἀρχῆς [*ap' archēs*, from the beginning] to refer to God's creation of humans in the garden). Therefore, apostolic teaching on love, underscored in Jesus's teaching particularly in John's Gospel, is not something that either the apostles or Christ inaugurated[4] but something profoundly embedded in God's world and subsequently codified redemptively in the Hebrew Scriptures.[5] It was also not absent from pre-NT Judaism (see third additional note on 2:7). When Jesus taught (Matt. 22:37–40 NIV), "All the Law and the Prophets hang on these two commandments," he had just quoted "Love the Lord your God with all your heart and with all your soul and with all your mind [Deut. 6:5]" and "Love your neighbor as yourself [Lev. 19:18]" (cf. Rom. 13:8). This twofold ancient commandment is the heart of the message that Christians receive. Its primeval quality (cf. Calvin 1988: 248) helps explain why John grounds the love that people express in the love that God has revealed (1 John 4:10)—the latter is prior to and constitutive of the former.

3. It is argued that John "is implicitly equating the commandment of Jesus with the Decalogue, the covenant demand of the OT" (R. Brown 1982: 265), though this may be an overly specific inference.

4. Far less does "from the beginning" refer simply to the time of arrival of Christian faith in the hearts of John's readers, as Holtzmann 1908: 332–33 proposes (cf. Loader 1992: 19: "the beginning of their faith journey").

5. Strecker's contention (1996: 49n11) that John here "shows no interest in tracing his proclamation to the OT" is *e silencio* and therefore weak. It does not face the question of how a disciple of Jesus of Nazareth, who taught so studiously from the OT, could speak of the love of God, of Christ, and of God's people in isolation from OT precepts and the history of redemption. Schlatter's exposition (1950: 26–28) is likewise bereft of proper OT reference.

The commandment is old not merely in terms of its content. It is also old with respect to how people are to respond to it: with full compliance. That is, acknowledgment of the commandment to love, while necessary to please God, is not sufficient for justification in the sight of God. This is an OT commonplace. *Actions* reflective of love are as important as understanding and endorsing the love commandment. John states this explicitly elsewhere: "And this is love: that we walk in obedience to his commands. As you have heard from the beginning, his command is that you walk in love" (2 John 6 NIV). W. Klassen (*ABD* 4:384) rightly defines the Greek verb ἀγαπάω (*agapaō*, to love) as "a life-enhancing action," not an intellectual postulate or emotional disposition alone. Speaking of an old command that requires action in 1 John 2:7 makes good sense after John has just insisted that his readers walk as Jesus did in 2:6.

The readers have been in possession (εἴχετε, *eichete*, you had)[6] of this commandment "all along" (lit., "from the beginning"; see exegesis of 1:1). Of the nineteen uses of this expression in the NT, twelve are in John's writings. John can use the phrase to refer to Satan's point of origin (John 8:44; 1 John 3:8), the beginning of Jesus's public ministry (John 15:27; cf. Luke 1:2), the invisible (to humans) horizon of eternity past (1 John 1:1; 2:13, 14), and the time when a particular individual or group first heard and received the gospel (1 John 2:24 [2x]; 3:11; 2 John 5, 6). First John 2:7 likely belongs in this last category (though none of the categories is hermetically sealed from the others). John confirms this when he explains at the end of the verse, "The old commandment is the message that you heard." The commandment is the message of Christ, whose saving death (2:2) makes possible the perfection of divine love (2:5) in those who hear the gospel message. John numbers his readers among this group.

John's stress on the oldness of his teaching is distinctly impolitic in a consumerist age, increasingly common in both the West and the East, which places high value on the "new" because of its marketability in a materialistic and pragmatic world economy. Today, if something is new, profitable, and useful, it defines personal and social reality for many and is in that sense "true."[7] But in John's world, among at least some reflective individuals, for something to be true it needed to have an ancient heritage and not just offer novel utility (M. McVann in Pilch and Malina 1998: 19–21). This conviction lies behind the Gospel genealogies (Matt. 1; Luke 3). Jesus assumes it in his disputes with opponents: he is more ancient than their ancestor Abraham (John 8:58). Eusebius (ca. 300) commends his *Ecclesiastical History* because by it "the real antiquity and divine character of Christianity will be . . . demonstrated to those who suppose that it is recent and foreign, appearing no earlier than

6. Imperfect tense, despite the stem change from the first principle part ἔχω, which might in itself suggest a second aorist. This verb is one of the relatively few whose stem changes in the imperfect. Imperfect forms of ἔχω occur just over fifty times in the Greek NT. The third principle part (second aorist) is ἔσχον, forms of which are found twenty times in the Greek NT.

7. Calvin 1988: 248 decries a similar dilettantism in his own time.

yesterday" (1.2.1). Celsus (Hoffmann 1987: 55) derides the Christian faith precisely because he considers it derivative rather than original. Apparently even Moses, as he compiled Genesis, intuited the importance of showing that his account connects with the world's primal beginnings (Gen. 1:1). It is therefore understandable that for John the issue of origins begs attention. "To hold fast to the old, to what was preached from the beginning, is for the author the seal of truth" (Schnackenburg 1992: 104). D. Smith (1991: 62) draws this corollary: "The Christian faith has an essential historical dimension or component; its past is authoritative."

2. The Message New yet True (2:8)

The problem with old messages is that they are easy to forget. Old Testament writers remind readers many times not to forget past divine disclosures: "Remember the wonders he has done, his miracles, and the judgments he pronounced" (Ps. 105:5 NIV; cf. Deut. 8:2; Neh. 4:14 [4:8 MT]; Isa. 46:9; Mal. 4:4 [3:22 MT]). Further, even when memory is active, response may be lacking. Xenophon (*Respublica Lacedaemoniorum* 10.8) mentions that the very oldest laws of the Greeks were widely praised, but they were not heeded.

Old messages may also be overlooked because they are out of step with the times. In the modern West a basic belief is "individualist realism" (Pilch and Malina 1998: xxxii). In such an outlook I am the center of my life, not other people. Love for others becomes a secondary concern; self-love is primary. John was not addressing the twenty-first century, but it is likely that in all times and places a certain degree of individualist realism is present—note, for example, the brutal self-preoccupation of tribal leaders and the engrossing private misery of the powerless in the so-called primitive Yanomamö tribe of southern Venezuela (Ritchie 1996). As for classical antiquity, Cynic philosopher Diogenes lays down the grim observation that "every living thing is to nothing so devoted as to its own interest" (cited in W. Klassen, *ABD* 4:383). Self-interest, he concludes in the same passage, ultimately overshadows loyalty to "father and brother and kinsmen and country and God." This will sound to some like Cynic overstatement, but the basic fact of culpable human selfishness (cf. Luther's *curvatus in se*) seems an anthropological constant. In contrast, the age-old reality to which John's "God is light" calls is love—for God and for others, especially brothers and sisters in the faith.

In 1 John 2:8 the author now asserts that the central commandment implied by his core message is not only old, in the best sense, but also new. (For rabbinic parallels to John's old-new rhetoric, see Strecker 1996: 48n8. But John offers "a hidden reminder of Christ, not just an ingenious play on words!" [Schnackenburg 1992: 104].)

It has already been observed that John often writes in terms of black-white contrasts (see exegesis of 1:5). But here he speaks not of "either-or" but of "both-and." Πάλιν (*palin*, again) at the beginning of 2:8 is correlative and can be translated "on the other hand" (BDAG 753; cf. Luke 6:43). The love command is very old. Yet it is also very new. The command is new because Jesus reaffirmed and exemplified it in five notable ways.

First, Jesus exemplified love by the way he experienced it in fellowship with God: "The Father loves the Son and has placed everything in his hands" (John 3:35 NIV). "For the Father loves the Son and shows him all he does" (5:20 NIV). "I have obeyed my Father's commands and remain in his love" (15:10 NIV). "You loved me before the creation of the world" (in Jesus's prayer to the Father in 17:24 NIV). Jesus's filial consciousness was not an experience that those around him could enter into fully, but it was powerfully (and for some repugnantly; 5:18) visible, and it undoubtedly informed his command to love. It must be seen as contributing to what made that command new.

Second, Jesus reaffirmed love in the way he loved others, whether friends like Martha, Mary, and Lazarus (John 11:5); lost souls like the rich young ruler (Mark 10:21); his close disciples (John 13:1); his mother at the hour of his own execution (19:26–27); a largely hostile city over which he wept (Luke 19:41); or those who carried out the crucifixion (23:34). Even his detractors seemed to have noted this (John 11:36). Jesus's charitable character gives point to his command (cf. Thompson 1992: 58). There is a sense in which, just as "no one ever spoke the way" Jesus did (7:46), few if any have been seen to love as he did.

Third, Jesus taught his disciples to love others as he had loved them—with humility. He illustrated this in a preliminary way by washing the disciples' feet (John 13:1–17). Jesus expressly termed the teaching that he gave on that occasion a new command: "A new command I give you: Love one another. As I have loved you, so you must love one another" (13:34 NIV). While Jesus was probably not thinking of how his teachings stacked up against those of classical philosophers, the quality and degree of love he advocated have no real parallels among the Greco-Roman ethicists of the age (W. Klassen, *ABD* 4:382–84). "This self-effacing, dedicated love is the new element in the Christian commandment of love" (Schnackenburg 1992: 105). A love suffused with humility was a new concept in an era where humility was no virtue.[8]

Yet it was not the admittedly impressive but still imitable servant-love of footwashing that for Jesus plumbs love's depths. A fourth sense in which Jesus's command is new is its connection with the willing sacrifice of his life for others (John 10:11, 15, 17–18; 15:13; 1 John 3:16). Peter claimed he would rally to die for Jesus if necessary (John 13:37). So did the rest of the Eleven (Matt. 26:35). But their avowed love faltered. Paul concedes that self-sacrifice for another, while rare, is not unheard of (Rom. 5:7).[9] But such a gesture would assume a noble person or cause for which to die. Jesus the righteous (1 John 2:1) died for a people manifestly unrighteous (1 Pet. 3:18). The command to

8. "In the Gr[eek] world, with its anthropocentric view of man, lowliness is looked on as shameful, to be avoided and overcome by act and thought" (H.-H. Esser, *NIDNTT* 2:260).

9. Examples abound in modern military history; cf. the moving chronicles of the "World War II Commemorative Series" commissioned by the United States Marine Corps Historical Center. See also examples throughout Ambrose 1997.

love as he loved is new because of the way that he, sinless and sent from God, embodied love on the cross (Thompson 1992: 58).

Fifth, the command is new not only because it is grounded in a unique act but also because it possesses a unique efficacy: the power to regenerate those who would otherwise be eternally lost (cf. John 3:16). But to appreciate this, more attention to John's wording is necessary.

In 1 John 2:8 John reiterates a commandment that (ὅ, *ho*) is "true in him and in you" (on ἀληθής [*alēthēs*, true], see the third additional note on 2:8; on "in him," see exegesis of 1:5; on "in you," see exegesis of 2:27). The neuter ὅ is unexpected since the proper relative pronoun for the feminine ἐντολή (*entolē*, commandment) is ἥν, as in 2:7. Moule (1994: 130) cites Eph. 5:5 as a possible parallel for John's usage here and suggests that John has in mind "the 'whole idea' of the preceding clause rather than . . . the single word which is the immediate antecedent" (so also Thompson 1992: 59n; cf. Persson 1990).[10] The problem with this suggestion is that the preceding clause contains no "whole idea" that is larger than "a new commandment." It is, however, possible that rather than pointing primarily back, the relative points mainly forward (cf. Zerwick 1993: 727; Strecker 1996: 47). In this case John does not have in mind the simple moral directive to love but the broader reality of what animates the present living Christ ("is true in him") and his readers ("and in you"). This is no less than discrete acts of love. But it is considerably more, since that love has its existence and dynamic not first of all in human ethical expression but in the living Christ. Thus the translation "I am addressing a new commandment to you—speaking now about that which is true in him and in you; for the darkness is dissipating and the true light already shines." By avoiding the expected relative pronoun, John has ensured that he does not reduce Jesus to a cipher for nothing more than moral action.[11]

John is saying, then, that he is not merely recapitulating a familiar imperative but explicating and evoking a living truth. And precisely here lies the fifth way in which the commandment is new in the fullest sense. It is no longer merely typological of the divine love shown in Christ like Moses's love commandments were. Nor is it simply a restatement of Jesus's precept to love, a command that chronologically preceded his own definitive self-sacrifice and for that reason could not be appropriated fully by those who first received it. John is urging on his readers a pattern of response to others around them—a pattern of love—that is new because Christ is on location as promised (John 16:10, 28) in his mediatorial role (1 John 2:1) to enable such love. Jesus had said that through faith the Eleven would "do even greater things than" what Jesus accomplished, "because I am going to the Father" (John 14:12 NIV).

10. Holtzmann 1908: 333 (followed by Strecker 1996: 50) thinks John means to stress the commandment's newness. This does not sufficiently explain the shift in pronoun gender. Strecker (citing Acts 2:32; Gal. 2:20; Col. 1:29; 1 Pet. 2:8; Rev. 21:8; cf. BDAG 689) points out that the neuter relative can at times summarize a whole sentence.

11. In a sense John exercised the same syntactical shrewdness with the first word of the Greek text of this epistle (ὅ).

John is testifying to a time of fulfillment of this projection. His testimony is true, in Christ and in believers, because (note ὅτι [*hoti*] in 2:8) it can now hold sway among those who follow Christ with an assurance and missionary effect not possible prior to the salvation-historical juncture that John and his readers now occupy. "The newness of the commandment is eschatological; it is part of the realization of God's promises in the last times" (R. Brown 1982: 267; cf. Rensberger 1997: 64).

The verse concludes with reference to this temporal juncture. Something remarkable is happening: "The darkness is dissipating [παράγεται, *paragetai*] and the true light already shines." (On "darkness," see the exegesis of 1:5 and 1:6; on παράγεται, see the fourth additional note on 2:8.) Calvin (1960: §4.8.7) grasps John's doxological excitement: "Since Christ, the Sun of Righteousness, has shone, while before there was only dim light, we have the perfect radiance of divine truth, like the wonted brilliance of midday." John is sounding both an ethical and a christological note of triumph here.[12] He is not alone among apostolic leaders in airing this sentiment; Paul uses the active voice of the same verb to convey a similar truth: "For this world in its present form is passing away [παράγει, *paragei*]" (1 Cor. 7:31 NIV). Elsewhere he states, "The night is nearly over; the day is almost here" (Rom. 13:12 NIV). John's claim is not his isolated opinion but echoes an early Christian consensus (a verbal parallel is found in Jewish apocalyptic; see 1 Enoch 58.5).

"Darkness" in 1 John 2:8 is the moral and spiritual gloom that enshrouds current human existence. It is "the realm of evil, deprived of God's presence and ruled by Satan" (R. Brown 1982: 268). With the coming of Christ, this darkness, never sovereign in the world even in OT times, receives a decisive setback and weakening; John's Gospel uses very similar language in announcing the incarnation:

John 1:5	τὸ φῶς ἐν τῇ σκοτίᾳ φαίνει, καὶ ἡ σκοτία αὐτὸ οὐ κατέλαβεν.	The light shines in the darkness, and the darkness did not extinguish [*or* comprehend] it.
1 John 2:8	ἡ σκοτία παράγεται καὶ τὸ φῶς τὸ ἀληθινὸν ἤδη φαίνει.	The darkness is dissipating and the true light already shines.

Jesus promised his followers that they need not walk in darkness (John 8:12). He came "into the world as a light, so that no one who believes in [him] should stay in darkness" (12:46 NIV). Now John testifies to a time in which the light Jesus promised is an increasing[13] reality in the community he founded.

12. Sloyan 1995: 20 misses the christological note in asserting that the Johannine community's obedience "causes the darkness to pass away."

13. Wallace 1996: 522 sees a stative lexical connotation inhering in the darkness passing away and the light shining. But the simultaneous waning of darkness and appearing of light may imply not only stative continuation but also progressive strengthening of the light (cf. Westcott 1883: 54: "The change is pictured as a process"). So, e.g., Schnackenburg 1992: 106: "The divine realm of light is expanding and the power of the good is advancing victoriously."

True, "the process will be fully consummated only when Christ the redeemer personally returns to earth to banish the darkness" decisively (Hiebert 1991: 87). But despite the problems that his epistle addresses, John is sure that "the true light" (on ἀληθινόν [*alēthinon*, true] see third additional note on 2:8) already has the upper hand. This light "is the real thing" (Marshall 1978: 130). The challenge is for this reality to be embodied in the life and lives of his readers.

3. Implications for the Misanthrope (2:9, 11)

The nature of John's message that God is light (1:5) carries with it the corollary command to love, which is both old and new (2:7–8). But it also carries implications, both for those who are misanthropic and those who love as they have been loved. In 2:9 John characterizes the class of misanthrope who makes a verbal claim (ὁ λέγων, *ho legōn*, the one who says; the same construction appears in 2:4, 6; 2 John 11) that belies the truth. In 2:11 he adds additional description to the assertion of 2:9.

a. The Futility of Mere Confession (2:9)

John characterizes a person who "claims to be in the light but hates[14] his fellow believer [ἀδελφός, *adelphos*]" (cf. Strecker 1996: 51: "The ἀδελφός is the fellow Christian").[15] Being "in the light" means being in fellowship with both God and other believers as the result of the cleansing effected by Christ's death (1:7). It is a condition made possible by the nature of God, who is light (like Christ himself; John 12:46), as the gospel message goes forth and is received (1 John 1:5). It is fitting and natural that believers should openly claim their allegiance to the light that is God and Christ; 1 John is itself an extended example of such testimony.

But the claim can be bogus. Καί (*kai*) in 2:9 is adversative and can be translated "but" or "yet" (see exegesis of 1:6). The claim is one thing; the reality is something else. In fact the person does not love his or her ἀδελφός, referring here not exclusively to flesh-and-blood kin (although obviously a natural sibling

14. It is unnecessary to repeat the definite article found at the beginning of the verse (ὁ λέγων) before the second, parallel participle μισῶν due to the Granville Sharp rule (Wallace 1996: 273–75).

15. Edwards 1996: 91–92 questions the wisdom of translating John's ἀδελφός as "brother and sister" or other generic label (cf. NRSV, NLT; cf. also English translations of Strecker 1996: 47 and Schnackenburg 1992: 89). CEV reads, "If we claim to be in the light and hate someone." TNIV opts for "those who claim to be in the light but hate a fellow believer," thus avoiding "brother" but also losing the individual focus of the assertion by changing the particular "one who says" into an unspecified collection of persons. The original spotlights an arrogant individual (ὁ λέγων), not an impersonal group. (Paul's periphrastic rendering of Ps. 32:1–2 in Rom. 4:7 is reasonable and legitimate, but it hardly justifies a translation philosophy that would render Ps. 32:1–2 plural or Rom. 4:7 singular.) The words of Porter 1989: 33–34 on the CEV and gender language come to mind: "At points the biblical text may well be considered hopelessly insensitive in matters of gender, but I am not convinced that it is in the best interests of making the meaning of the original text clear if the clear meaning that exists is in fact obscured."

might also be a Christian "brother") but in an extended sense to fellow professors of faith in Christ (cf. Rensberger 1997: 66). This person rather "hates" the ἀδελφός. This is the first of five uses of the verb μισέω (*miseō*, to hate) in this epistle (also 2:11; 3:13, 15; 4:20). What does John mean by it? "In the modern climate of ecumenism and inter-faith dialogue," John's word choice can make his epistles "seem intolerant and uncharitable" (Edwards 1996: 90–91).

"Hates" conjures up the specter of pathological and even violent animosity along with clear intentionality to harm. Hitler hated the Jews (as did Stalin; Bullock 1993: 1037–38, 1049) with more calamitous but hardly less intense passion than some in Greco-Roman times (Feldman and Reinhold 1996: 305–95; but see Rutgers 1998). Ahab hated Micaiah son of Imlah (2 Chron. 18:7). Haman hated Mordecai and his people (Esth. 3:5–6).

If John had this intensity of hostility in mind, many recipients of the epistle could probably have assured themselves of being exempt from his criticism. But it is unlikely that John means "hate" in this very strong sense. While the NT word for "hate" can have extreme, even homicidal associations (e.g., Matt. 24:9), John refers to a disposition that he warns ought not characterize fellow believers. We lack proof that members of local congregations were plotting each other's murder. Jesus himself may help define what "hate" in John's sense might have looked like, as he glossed it in a statement preserved in Luke 6:22: "Blessed are you when men hate you, when they exclude you and insult you and reject your name as evil, because of the Son of Man" (NIV). Exclusion, insult, and rejection because of doctrinal belief or religious practice generally fall short of murder (though of course there have been many exceptions to this in times of persecution both ancient and recent). In fact people can exclude, insult, and reject simply by failing to accord due respect, quite without intentional and active malice. This is the basic sense in which "the world" hates Jesus's disciples: it dismisses as silly, wrong, or dangerous their attachment to Jesus's ideals rather than to worldly ones (John 15:24). This is generally not so much open bitter persecution (though it has too often heightened to that point) as refusal duly to acknowledge Christ's kingdom and its subjects.

It is likely that John is thinking of "hate" in this softer yet insidious sense in 1 John. The light of God in Christ transforms those who embrace it, and the seal of this is heartfelt response to the old-yet-new command (see exegesis of 2:7–8). Failure to love as Christ commands and enables is tantamount, in the kingdom economy as John presents it, to hating.[16] "Love for God requires concrete expression in love of the sisters and brothers" (Strecker 1996: 52). "For either love, to the exclusion of the selfish element, is the animating principle; or self is made the centre of all, and selfishness governs" (Neander 1852: 80).

Nineteenth-century theologian Charles Hodge observed, "It often happens . . . that men are very pious without being very good. Their religion expends itself in devotional feelings and services, while the evil passions of their nature

16. "Hate" understood as "not loving" is a familiar OT usage (Deut. 21:15–17; 2 Sam. 19:6 [19:7 MT]; Prov. 13:24; Mal. 1:2–3). This could contribute to John's dualistic language here.

remain unsubdued" (Calhoun 1994: 348).[17] Selfishness issuing in lovelessness, and masked in the "spiritual" claim to be dwelling in the light, answers to what Hodge laments and is an illustration of what John warns against.[18] Saying one thing while doing another is currently defended as a Mediterranean norm (termed "equivocation") that even Jesus and Paul practiced (J. H. Neyrey in Pilch and Malina 1998: 63–67), but John (no less Mediterranean in Neyrey's sense) concludes here that it is evidence that one "is as yet still in the darkness." Such a person's spiritual and practical condition is out of conformity with salvation-historical possibility (see exegesis of 2:8) and indeed divine expectation. In 2:11 John elaborates on this sorry state.

b. The Darkness of Lovelessness (2:11)

The first clause of 2:11 ("but the one who hates his fellow believer is in darkness") merely restates the last words of 2:9, adding the initial δέ (*de*, but) to set 2:11 in contrast with 2:10 (on the grammar of 2:9, see Turner 1963: 146). John's "hate" often amounts to failure to love rather than to some lethal antipathy (see exegesis of 2:9). In subsequent clauses of 2:11, John expands on the dilemma posed and faced by the confessing believer who does not love others.

First, such a person "lives his whole life [περιπατεῖ] in darkness." The LXX uses περιπατέω (*peripateō*, to walk) as a metaphor for the tone and direction of the whole of life (see exegesis of 1:6; 2:6). About half of the ninety-five NT uses of περιπατέω are metaphorical, a usage that H. Seesemann calls "alien" to Classical Greek (*TDNT* 5:941).[19] Metaphorical περιπατέω seems to be first amply attested in the LXX, where six of its forty uses of the word are of this type (2 Kings 20:3; Prov. 8:20; Eccles. 4:15; 11:9; Sir. 38:32; Isa. 59:9; see the second additional note on 1 John 2:11 for more on LXX occurrences). Paul uses περιπατέω thirty-two times, always metaphorically. In John's Gospel and Revelation, metaphorical περιπατέω is limited to John 8:12; 12:35 (2x); Rev. 21:24. But John's Epistles employ the metaphorical sense exclusively: 1 John 1:6, 7; 2:6 (2x), 11; 2 John 4, 6 (2x); 3 John 3, 4.

By saying that someone walks in darkness, John means that his or her ethical and spiritual life is benighted. This person is not walking with God and may not admit or even recognize it, as John will make clear later in 2:11. This is

17. A North American parish experience illustrates this point: a young couple visited a church, and during a subsequent appointment the man interrogated the pastor closely and at length on his views of the Great Tribulation, a staple fixation of the Left Behind series. He informed the pastor that unless he could endorse the pastor's point of view, he feared to sit under his preaching on a regular basis. The man did not mention what the pastor knew from other sources—that the woman at his side, with whom he was living, was not his wife.

18. Cf. Calvin 1988: 250: "Fictitious sanctity dazzles the eyes of almost all, whereas love is neglected or at least put in a corner."

19. Less specifically Semitic in heritage are the noun ἀναστροφή (*anastrophē*, way of life), which occurs thirteen times in the NT, and the verb ἀναστρέφω (*anastrephō*, to conduct oneself), which occurs nine times. But neither word is found in Johannine writings.

hardly a surprise, since in John's Gospel, Jesus teaches that people, far from abhorring darkness, typically have a strong preference for it (John 3:19). The alternative of having light shed on their evil deeds is unthinkable. It is easier to justify darkness and call it light, a tactic not foreign to OT annals: "Woe to those who call evil good and good evil, who put darkness for light and light for darkness" (Isa. 5:20 NIV).

In the early church, darkness connoted the realm of Satan, in which all who do not know Christ languish and from which the message of the cross delivers (Acts 26:18; Eph. 5:8; Col. 1:13; 1 Pet. 2:9). It is sobering to contemplate John's allegation that in the congregations he addressed could be ostensible believers who actually were strangers to saving grace. But the absence of communal love mentioned in 1 John 2:9 and now 2:11 was prima facie evidence of this very thing. Out of compassion, if nothing else, a pastoral leader like John would be bound to say something.

And John does, continuing with a second allegation regarding unloving "believers": they do not understand (see exegesis of 2:20–21) where they are going. John is practically quoting words of Jesus recorded in John's Gospel:

John 12:35	ὁ περιπατῶν ἐν τῇ σκοτίᾳ οὐκ οἶδεν ποῦ ὑπάγει	and the one who walks in the darkness does not understand where he is going
1 John 2:11	καὶ ἐν τῇ σκοτίᾳ περιπατεῖ καὶ οὐκ οἶδεν ποῦ ὑπάγει	and walks in the darkness and does not understand where he is going

Literary dependence, while theoretically possible, is unlikely here since there is little evidence for it elsewhere in the epistle. Rather, this must have been a theme of Jesus's teaching that lodged itself firmly in the young John's mind, perhaps aided by reminders from dominical traditions circulating in early Christian decades (Ellis 1999: 183–200). Followers of Christ in the early church were on "the Way" (ὁδός, *hodos*; cf. Acts 9:2; 19:9, 23; 22:4; 24:22), whose destination was assured. Jesus consoled his baffled disciples that despite their momentary confusion (John 14:5), they "know the way to the place where [Jesus is] going," because Jesus himself is the way (14:4, 6). John voices no such assurance regarding those who do not love fellow believers. In their aversion to love they are charting a course toward the abyss.

There is a reason for this pitiful groping, and it is the third piece of information John offers about the person whose love is deficient: "The darkness has blinded his eyes" (1 John 2:11). This is the third mention of darkness in the verse, and a logical progression is possible (cf. Neander 1852: 83–84), from being and living in darkness (which may imply an ongoing conscious choice) to a state of blindness that the darkness produces (and that may not be evident to the blinded person). John's Gospel told of high-ranking religious leaders who were blind in this sense, although they thought their vision was acute (John 9:41). Their commitment to a theological point regarding the relationship between sin and human suffering, as well as their growing antipathy toward Christ,[20] crushed any possible compassion for a man born blind who suddenly could see. They had opted for darkness so long that it now seemed perfect daylight to them (9:40). But the illumination Jesus brought worked in two directions: to give sight to the blind and to render blind all self-proclaimed seers (9:41). Elsewhere John evokes a prophecy of Isaiah to account for blindness among the people of God: the Lord blinds their eyes in just response to their self-directed ways (12:40; cf. Isa. 6:10). The person "is gripped by the force of the delusion that drives him" (Schlatter 1950: 30). "When we have been in the darkness for a long time . . . , we can no longer see" (Schnackenburg 1992: 109). It is just such blindness that John writes of now.[21] Absence of love between professing believers bespeaks a condition of the heart to be avoided at all costs.

The troubling fact, true in John's day as well as ours, is that religion not seldom fosters and sanctions the kind of darkness that John rejects here. In 1994 perhaps a million people were massacred in Rwanda; by one reckoning, more than 70 percent of the Hutus and Tutsis who slaughtered each other were Christian (Roman Catholic 58 percent, Protestant 15.2 percent, Adventist 6.3 percent; see Bayinsana 1996: 23). Jesus alludes to a popular opinion that regarded honoring God and hating certain people as compatible: "You have heard that it was said, 'Love your neighbor and hate your enemy'" (Matt. 5:43 NIV). Jesus rejected this, and so does John in this epistle. But not all religious teachers of the time thought that hatred was necessarily a bad thing. The Community Rule, found among the Dead Sea Scrolls, teaches that community members are to "love all the sons of light, each according to his lot in God's design, and hate all the sons of darkness, each according to his guilt in God's vengeance" (1QS 1.9–11). This hatred could be seen as a reflection of God's own loathing of evil: since God abhors the wickedness of the world, his people would be justified in abhorring wicked people (1QS 4). An OT apocryphal book voices this sentiment: "I have hated many things, but none to be compared to [the evil man]; even the Lord will hate him" (Sir. 27:24 RSV). John's insistence on love among community members stands in stark contrast to such outlooks.

Commentary literature resounds with the insistence that in speaking of brotherly love, John is in no way excluding the imperative for believers to be loving toward all people and not just each other (e.g., Neander 1852: 85; Hiebert 1991: 89; Edwards 1996: 90). The love that Christians have for each other is to be a springboard for reaching out, not a wall of exclusion. "Nowhere does the author preach hatred" (Schnackenburg 1992: 113); like Jesus (Matt. 5:44–48) and Paul (Gal. 6:10; Titus 3:1–2), John calls for an all-embracing charity (cf. John 3:16). By stressing reciprocal love among Christians in 1 John, he is not repudiating love for humanity at large (rightly Marshall 1978: 131).[22]

20. Holtzmann 1908: 334 aptly comments, "Hatred blinds."

21. Lieu's conclusion (1988: 91; followed by Strecker 1996: 53n34) that John's Gospel and 1 John portray very different conceptions of blindness seems overstated.

22. Westcott 1883: 55 appears to be correct in saying that "there is, as far as it appears, no case where a fellow-man, as man, is called 'a brother' in the N.T." R. Brown 1982: 270–73

He is rather underscoring the necessity of Christ's followers first practicing among themselves what they preach that God offers to the world through the gospel.

4. Implications for the Philanthrope (2:10)

In 2:10 John traces out three characteristics of the person who honors the love commandment. The first characteristic is implied, not stated: the person who loves stands in contrast to the person (falsely) claiming to be in the light (2:9) as well as to the person who fails to love (or "hates") a fellow believer (2:11). By depicting a positive response to the love commandment between the negative examples of 2:9 and 2:11, John makes it difficult for readers to mistake proper response to the old-yet-new directive.

Second, the person who "loves his brother abides in the light." The light, we saw at 1:5 and 1:7, refers to God. This person is living on a consistent basis (μένει [*menei*, abides] implies constancy and steadfastness) in a manner acceptable to God. Light also refers to the brilliance of what Christ's earthly ministry revealed and set in motion (2:8). It is not far-fetched to conclude that by "abides in the light" John means "to live in conformity with the gospel as an authentic disciple of Christ" (Malatesta 1978: 155). Schlatter (1950: 29; cf. Westcott 1883: 56) rightly notes, "The light does not arise from our love; for the light comes from above, shines on us from God above, has come to us in Christ, and reaches us by his word." Loving others as a result of knowing God's love in Christ is central to living in the fellowship that John writes to promote (1:4). "Love for Christ and for fellow Christians is necessary for salvation" (Peterson and Williams 2004: 79).

Third, the person who loves a fellow believer is in no danger of being a σκάνδαλον (*skandalon*, offense): "There is no offense in him." This is naturally important for a writer whose aim is that his readers not sin (2:1). By σκάνδαλον John could have any of several things in mind. He could mean offense in the sense of committing personal transgression. The person hurts himself or herself by stumbling morally. Such a meaning is definitely attested only once among its twenty-three LXX occurrences (Sir. 7:6; possibly also Pss. 69:22 [68:23 LXX]; 106:36 [105:36 LXX]; 119:165 [118:165 LXX]; cf. Jubilees 1.21 and 1QS 2.11–12) and is not attested at all in the NT (although Neander 1852: 82 and R. Brown 1982: 274–75 find it here). Or, John could mean offense in the sense of what directly offends God. The person incurs God's displeasure. This stress is clearly present only rarely in the LXX (Jud. 5:20; 12:2) and not at all in the NT. John's likely meaning is an action (or culpable inaction) that is detrimental to another person (so Kruse 2000: 86). This connotation predominates among the NT's fifteen occurrences of the word. The person

pushes very hard in the direction of suggesting that 1 John supports a loveless attitude toward non-Christians.

who loves a fellow believer places no obstacle in the believer's path.[23] This person promotes rather than deters the kingdom progress of others. This is the delightful fruit of abiding in the light.

Jesus had taught that σκάνδαλα (offenses) are inevitable. But he pronounced a woe on those who cause them (Matt. 18:7; Luke 17:1; cf. Rev. 2:14). Paul likewise warned against placing stumbling blocks in the way of other believers (Rom. 14:13). He took "pains to do what is right, not only in the eyes of the Lord but also in the eyes of men" (2 Cor. 8:21 NIV). The clear lesson, underscored in 1 John 2:10, is that followers of Christ must place a high premium on love for others, "for the gospel is about 'faith expressing itself through love' (Gal. 5:6), and anything else is counterfeit" (Marshall 1978: 133).

Yet what John calls for, while clear, is not without ambiguity. The Father appointed the Son to be a σκάνδαλον (Rom. 9:33; cf. 1 Pet. 2:8). The message of Christ crucified is a σκάνδαλον that believers are to embrace rather than circumvent (1 Cor. 1:23; cf. Gal. 5:11). If zeal for love requires avoidance of σκάνδαλον in one sense, zeal for truth—the truth of the saving meaning of Christ's death—requires identification with and promulgation of σκάνδαλον in another (so rightly Darby 1907: 40). John's message is not a simplistic call to indiscriminate tolerance and affirmation of all human expression and action. Not being a σκάνδαλον does not mean "unconditional love" in the sense of sentimental endorsement of whatever anyone might decide to be and do. Nor does it mean cutting the cloth of the gospel message to suit those with no desire to don robes washed clean in sacrificial blood (1 John 1:7; cf. Rev. 7:14; 19:13). It means, rather, selfless regard for others in the community of faith that Christ founded and that he upholds by the apostolic message. Such regard entails faithful word no less than loving deed. An illustration here might be the combination of verbal action and Christian affection affirmed in Paul's "speaking the truth in love" (Eph. 4:15).

Additional Notes

2:7. K, L, 049, 69, and 𝔐 read ἀδελφοί instead of ἀγαπητοί. The manuscript support for ἀδελφοί is chronologically late. Usage in 1 John may tend against it (though this is hardly decisive), with 3:13 being the only other place where the vocative plural of ἀδελφός appears (but see ℵ at 3:21), while ἀγαπητοί is quite common in 1 John. An error of hearing or of the eye is a possibility. Metzger 1994: 640 also points to influence from the customary use of ἀδελφοί in Byzantine lectionaries to introduce NT pericopes "attributed to apostles" (R. Brown 1982: 263).

2:7. Regarding the "old commandment," there was in OT religion and Judaism a long-standing tradition calling for love for others. This extended even to enemies: the Letter of Aristeas 227–28 (ca. 170 BC?) describes a banquet in which an Egyptian king poses difficult questions to Jewish scholars. One of the questions is, "To whom must a man be generous?" The answer is, first, that one should be magnanimous to friends, which is called "the general opinion." But like John, though for different reasons, the scholar being questioned takes the matter a step farther: "My belief is that we must also

23. Smalley 1984: 62 suggests than John refers both to personal offense and to causing others to sin.

show liberal charity to our opponents so that in this manner we may convert them to what is proper and fitting to them." And to the question, "To whom must one show favor?" the same scholar replies, "To his parents, always, for God's very great commandment concerns the honor due to parents. Next (and closely connected) [God] reckons the honor due to friends, calling the friend an equal of one's own self. You do well if you bring all men into friendship with yourself." This is not identical to 1 John's appeal to love one's brother and not hate, since it lacks the distinctive christological component (see exegesis of 2:8) and reflects a family loyalty and patronizing tone foreign to both Jesus's and John's pedagogy. But it is at least consistent with John's thrust and shows that he is not calling for some completely unheard-of measure.

2:7. 𝔐 (and thus the KJV) repeats the prepositional phrase ἀπ' ἀρχῆς at the very end of the verse. Several minuscules omit it, as do most uncials. Without the words the verse does seem to end on a bit of an abrupt note, and the addition may have been an attempt to smooth a rough literary edge (cf. Metzger 1994: 640).

2:8. Ἀληθὲς ἐν αὐτῷ appears in a slightly different order in A, with no real change in meaning. A weightier group of witnesses (among them ℵ and Jerome) inserts καί after ἀληθές, so that instead of "true in him and in you" we read "true both in him and in you." This friendly amendment is too spottily attested to be considered original.

2:8. Uncials A and 049, several minuscules, and a wide range of versional evidence speak for ἐν ἡμῖν (in us) rather than ἐν ὑμῖν (in you). "In us" is likely to be secondary, its widespread presence possibly stemming from similarity in sound between the two pronouns. If the secondary reading were original, it would simply mean that John was including himself and other apostles among those in whom the commandment "is true."

2:8. The adjectives ἀληθής and ἀληθινός, both translated "true," appear in this verse. Ἀληθής occurs twenty-six times in the NT, seventeen of these in John's writings. Ἀληθινός appears twenty-eight times, twenty-three times in John's writings (including ten times in Revelation). When John wants to use "true" as a predicate adjective, his predilection is to use ἀληθής, as here. His use of ἀληθής attributively is rare (only John 6:55 [2x]). Equally rare in John is ἀληθής as a substantive (only 19:35). On the other hand, while John can use ἀληθινός as a predicate adjective (e.g., 4:37; 7:28; 8:16; 19:35) or a substantive (e.g., 1 John 5:20 [3x]), he prefers to use it when he wishes to attribute the quality of "true" to a person or thing (as in 2:8: "the true light"). It can be concluded that the basic definition of the two words is the same, with their respective usages (which are not identical) being a function of stylistic preference or syntactical feel. As to the meaning of the words, Neander 1852: 76 helpfully suggests that for John "'the true,' when used with a word applicable both to what is divine and to objects of sense, means only and always the divine" or what partakes of the divine, as in "true food" (John 6:55) or "true light" (1:9). See also the exegesis of 5:20.

2:8. Παράγεται (*paragetai*) is used intransitively (cf. BDF §308) in the active voice seven times in the NT to refer to someone "passing by" or "walking along" (Matt. 9:9, 27; 20:30; Mark 1:16; 2:14; 15:21; John 9:1). Here, however, it is used figuratively and in the passive voice (so also 2:17).

2:9. A major Alexandrian (ℵ) and (sometimes) Western (614)[24] witness add ψεύστης ἐστίν καί. The addition may have been suggested by analogous language in 2:4 or, for scribes who had read or copied 1 John before, in 4:20.

2:10. A few witnesses, some impressive (e.g., ℵ, A, C), change the word order so that instead of ἐν αὐτῷ οὐκ ἔστιν one finds οὐκ ἔστιν ἐν αὐτῷ. The latter, surely secondary reading might by

24. On the Western proclivities of 614, see K. Aland and B. Aland 1987: 108, 131. At the same time the Alands (244) rank 614 as Byzantine in the Catholic Epistles.

explicit parallelism ensure that the antecedent of αὐτῷ would be understood to be ὁ ἀγαπῶν τὸν ἀδελφὸν αὐτοῦ and not φωτί.

2:11. Instead of ἐστίν, P and 1243 are among a very few witnesses that read μένει. The meaning is virtually the same; the secondary reading has the rhetorical advantage of creating formal symmetry with the two following verbs (περιπατεῖ and ὑπάγει).

2:11. Expressing the same idea but using the verb εὐαρεστέω (*euaresteō*, to be well pleasing) to translate Hebrew הָלַךְ (*hālak*, to walk) are the following: Gen. 5:22, 24; 6:9; 17:1; 24:40; 48:15; Pss. 26:3 [25:3 LXX]; 35:14 [34:14 LXX]; 56:13 [56:14 MT/55:14 LXX]; 116:9 [114:9 LXX]. Did LXX translators feel that to "walk" with or in the presence of the Lord presented theological difficulties, so that they chose a word free from the literal associations of περιπατέω? On the danger of assuming too facilely that the LXX goes to great lengths to avoid anthropomorphisms, see Jellicoe 1968: 271, 300, 311.

B. Pastoral Appeal in View of the Message (2:12–17)

The foundational message of this epistle, I have argued, is that God is light. The previous verses (2:7–11) explored the nature and implications of that message especially with respect to love for others. Now John moves from exposition of the love commandment (a primary corollary of God's nature; cf. 4:8) to poignant appeal to his readers (2:12–14). This is a more positive interpretation than suggested, for example, by D. Smith (1991: 62), who states: "The theme of this section is the polarity or hostility between God and the world." Candlish (1866: 149–50) calls 2:12–14 "a trumpet-call, summoning all the faithful to a recognition of their real and true position before God." The flow from exposition to exhortation (and then to imperative in 2:15) is natural, so that the connection between 2:12–14 is hardly "tenuous" (contra Burge 1996: 110; Smalley 1984: 66–67 makes convincing sense of the literary flow).

While the precise literary structure of 2:12–14 is disputed (for a rhetorical analysis, see Watson 1989 and Klauck 1990), it seems at first glance that two groups are in mind, each broken into three subgroups. But on closer examination τεκνία (*teknia*) in 2:12 is parallel with παιδία (*paidia*) in 2:14. Taken in connection with a possible meaning of the writer's shift from present tense γράφω (*graphō*, I write) in 2:12–13 to aorist tense ἔγραψα (*egrapsa*, I wrote) in 2:14, this fact suggests that the two groups are essentially just one, addressed twice from slightly different angles.

The appeal will culminate in a direct imperative (2:15), the first of only ten found in 1 John. (By comparison with two other NT epistles that also contain five chapters, 1 Peter has thirty-five imperatives and James has fifty-five; see table in the exegesis of 2:15a.) The imperative warns of devotion to the world and of what such devotion implies for the person unwise enough to succumb to it. Following the warning is a terse and dark assessment of the essence of temporal existence seen in isolation from the heavenly Father. The world as an ephemeral sphere of folly (contra Rusam 1993: 231, "world" is hardly the specific embodiment of Jews, apostates, and rulers) is contrasted with the bright prospects awaiting the person whose top priority is doing the will of God.

The content of 2:12–17 may be outlined as follows:

1. De facto greeting: Reflexive appeal (2:12–13)
2. De facto greeting continued: Reflective appeal (2:14)
3. Imperatival appeal in view of the message (2:15–17)

a. Heart of the imperative: Warning against world-love (2:15a)
b. Warning regarding absence of love for God (2:15b)
c. Explication of warning (2:16–17)
   i. The origin of world-love (2:16)
   ii. The bane of world-love and the promise of doing the will of God (2:17)

Exegesis and Exposition

[12]The reason I am writing to you, ⌜little children⌝, is because ⌜your⌝ sins have been forgiven on account of his name; [13]I am writing to you, fathers, because you know him who was from the beginning; and I am writing to you, young men, because you have conquered ⌜the⌝ evil one.

[14]The reason ⌜I have written⌝ to you, little ones, is because you know the Father; to you, fathers, I have written because you know ⌜him⌝ who was from the beginning; and to, you young men, I have written because you are strong, and the word ⌜of God⌝ abides in you, and you have conquered the evil one.

[15]Do not set your affection on the world, nor on the things belonging to ⌜the⌝ world! Whoever sets his affection on the world forfeits the love of the ⌜Father⌝. [16]For everything that belongs to the world—what the body hankers for and the eyes itch to see and what people toil to acquire—is not from the Father. It is rather from the world. [17]Now the world, like the lusts found in ⌜it⌝, is passing away. But whoever does the will ⌜of God⌝ abides forever. ⌜ ⌝

1. De Facto Greeting: Reflexive Appeal (2:12–13)

To whom is John speaking here? The τεκνία (*teknia*, little children) of 2:12 are probably the entire readership, conceived of by John as children of God through their reception of the gospel (cf. the parenting language of John 1:12–13). By extension, because of John's apostolic ministry to them, they are referred to affectionately as his "little children." (Note Paul's self-perception as spiritual father and those he ministered to as children in 1 Cor. 4:15; 1 Tim. 1:2, 18; Titus 1:4; Philem. 10.)

Against this, it can be argued that the τεκνία are to be understood as a very young (whether chronologically or spiritually) set of individuals who are complemented by the much older πατέρες (*pateres*, fathers) and the somewhat younger νεανίσκοι (*neaniskoi*, young men). Three different groups are in view. This understanding is viable (and allows an analogous reading of 2:14). But it assumes a choppy flow, from the very young to the old and then back to the not so young (or not so old).

Others argue that John addresses one group. The different terms of address bespeak various aspects of their experience. They are children in that they are begotten of God, fathers in that they acknowledge the ultimate Father, and young men in that they possess great spiritual strength (Augustine, *Hom. 1 John* 2.5–6; cf. Marshall 1978: 138). It can be asked whether this does sufficient justice to the differences that John predicates of each class of people, both by the words of address he uses and the truths he asserts regarding them.

It may be preferable to view τεκνία as a blanket term (like παιδία [*paidia*, little ones] in 2:14) with the subsequent terms subordinate (so also Holtzmann 1908: 334). The flow in 2:12–13, paralleled in 2:14, would then be as follows:

1 John 2:12–13 [2:12–13b NIV]	1 John 2:14 [2:13–14 NIV]
τεκνία (little children), that is . . .	παιδία (little ones), that is . . .
πατέρες (fathers)	πατέρες (fathers)
νεανίσκοι (young men)	νεανίσκοι (young men)

In this organizational scheme, John addresses the whole of his audience under two general terms of endearment (τεκνία and παιδία) and then, more specifically, subdivided into the older and the younger. Because it seems to make the best literary and logical sense, this understanding is assumed in the exegesis below.

It is often noted that 1 John lacks a personal greeting. This is not quite true, since in 2:12–14 the writer personally addresses his readers. The greeting is simply delayed, not absent altogether. He addresses them not by name but by age group. What might be lost here in terms of interpersonal specificity (cf. Paul's greetings in Rom. 16, also not at the epistle's beginning) is offset by a certain gain in universality of application: no one can feel unaffected by virtue of having not been cited by name.[1] Additionally, and strategic from a pastoral point of view, no one need feel accused or singled out maliciously. Paul is vague about the names of his addressees when discussing obvious controversy in both Corinthian letters, and a similar vagueness is apparent in most of the NT's so-called Catholic Letters, a common element of which is stiff prophetic correction.

The de facto greeting may be seen as reflexive. It is a spontaneous and natural rhetorical turn in which John fixes his readers (or hearers) firmly in mind to heighten rapport with them. He has not been strictly impersonal to this point in the epistle, making several direct appeals and personal disclosures (cf. the first-person verbs used in 1:3, 4; 2:1, 7). But his pastoral concern, so far expressed mainly in doctrinal and ethical exposition, now erupts in direct address that should probably be understood as laden with considerable emotion[2]—expressed in my translation by the addition of the words "the reason," which

1. Calvin 1988: 251 remarks with pastoral shrewdness that John here "accommodates the Gospel" to various subgroups because "such is our malignity that few think that what is directed at all belongs to themselves. The old for the most part steal away as if they had exceeded the age of learning. Children refuse to hear, as if they were not yet old enough. Middle-aged men do not attend, because they are occupied with other cares." By addressing demographic subgroups, Calvin thinks, John anticipates his readers' ingenious evasiveness.

2. Cf. Candlish 1866: 151: "It is a very emphatic reiteration, having in it a pathos that should be very affecting."

are meant to convey urgency (cf. R. Brown 1982: 318), slight consternation, or possibly exasperation.[3] Four points argue for this in 2:12–13: the threefold repetition of γράφω, the diminutive form τεκνία heading up the verses, the comprehensive sweep of the horizon of address (embracing the gamut of age groups), and the weightiness of the theological truths adduced.

Repetition of Γράφω

John's three uses of γράφω in 2:12–13 (followed by three more in 2:14) constitute an infamous crux that has long defied an agreed-on solution (for delineation of possibilities, see R. Brown 1982: 294–97). Moule (1994: 12) confesses, "No really convincing explanation is known to me." The first three uses are present tense (γράφω). The second three are aorist (ἔγραψα). Some argue that John speaks of two bodies of writings. In this view, the present tense refers to 1 John itself, which the author is currently in the process of composing. The aorist refers to some previous writing (so, e.g., Turner 1963: 73), whether John's Gospel (Holtzmann 1908: 335), 2 John or 3 John, a nonextant Johannine letter, or even a source that underlay 1 John (for details of these positions and representative advocates, see Klauck 1991: 49–50). The theory that with the aorist John may be referring to an earlier writing has been widely abandoned of late (e.g., Schnackenburg 1992: 118; Porter 1989: 229; R. Brown 1982: 294–97; Thompson 1992: 62; Burge 1996: 111),[4] being incapable of verification thus far. It is entirely possible that all six occurrences of γράφω/ἔγραψα have 1 John in view.

For our purposes, the repetition highlights John's intensity of focus. Whether one speaks of anaphora (repetition of a word at the beginning of two or more sentences) or of repetition more generically, the effect of his chosen literary strategy is "to secure emphasis" (Holman 1977: 446). The page layout of NA[27] reflects the dramatic effect of John's rhetoric, which takes on the weight of an apostrophe of sorts, a dramatic aside permitting John to underscore that at stake in his epistle are matters of eternal moment.[5] It is as if John's prior concentration on the theological considerations that promote fellowship and joy (1:3–4) via the force of a transcendent message (1:5) as it is ethically

3. Few find here "compliments" that "then become a rhetorical device (a kind of *captivo benevolentiae*) to attract their favorable attention" (D. Smith 1991: 63).

4. Strecker 1996: 4 thinks that ἔγραψα in 2:14 "could refer to 2 (and 3) John." But he fails to answer the objections of R. Brown 1982: 294–97 to this theory. In fact Strecker (55n5) appears to misread Brown, adducing him in support of the view that 2:14 refers "to earlier Johannine Letters," a view that Brown firmly rejects. Strecker's alleged parallels between 1 John and 2 John (55n6) are unconvincing. It should also be noted that Strecker (4n11) cites Schnackenburg as supporting the view that ἔγραψα in 2:14 does not refer to 1 John. The truth is exactly the opposite (Schnackenburg 1992: 118).

5. The passage is apostrophic (so also Schnackenburg 1992: 116n183: "brief apostrophes") in its directional shift of discourse and emotional level. It is going too far to call it a digression (as does Klauck 1991: 49, following Watson 1989), if digression means "the insertion of material unrelated or distantly related to the specific subject under discussion" (Holman 1977: 161). Pastoral appeal is of the essence of the entire apostolic corpus.

appropriated (1:6–2:11) is broken by the seasoned communicator's intuition that by this point in the discourse readers (or hearers) stand in need of fresh exhortation to take heed. Therefore he employs an altered angle of address that clamors for the full engagement of their interpretive faculties. It is the literary equivalent of hitting a mule between the eyes with a two-by-four.

Diminutive Τεκνία

Caution is advised in reading too much into John's use of a form of τεκνίον (*teknion*, little child) rather than the more prosaic τέκνον (*teknon*, child). What the words share semantically is greater than what separates them, and in some cases they are no doubt synonymous. Τέκνον can be used to connote not just family relationship (whether literal or figurative) but also endearment (MM 628), though in the NT this meaning seems limited to the twelve vocative occurrences of the word (Matt. 9:2; 21:28; Mark 2:5; 10:24; Luke 2:48; 15:31; 16:25; Gal. 4:19; Eph. 6:1; Col. 3:20; 1 Tim. 1:18; 2 Tim. 2:1), and endearment may not always be connoted even there. Yet it can be argued that each of 1 John's uses of τέκνον connotes the objective status of being a descendant—whether a child of God (1 John 3:1, 2, 10a; 5:2), a child of the devil (3:10b), or a spiritual descendant of a church or believer (2 John 1, 4, 13; 3 John 4). The same pattern obtains in John's Gospel (1:12; 8:39; 11:52). In contrast to this, τεκνίον (a word absent from the LXX and not common in the Hellenistic period) always appears to imply endearment in John's writings, to which corpus it is limited in the NT (John 13:33; 1 John 2:1, 12, 28; 3:7, 18; 4:4; 5:21). A τεκνίον is a τέκνον (in John always figurative) regarded personally and with deep filial love. It is therefore fitting that the NIV translates "dear children" in all 1 John occurrences. The word is used "as an affectionate address of Jesus or the apostles to their spiritual children" (A. Oepke, *TDNT* 5:639) and is a second pointer in the direction of the emotion and intended force of these verses.

Age Groups

A third indicator of the feeling reflected in John's words is the breadth of the net he casts. It covers everyone, and it does so in a way calculated to attract rather than repel or accuse. Τεκνία, as already suggested, is probably a term of affection. Πατέρες is a term of respect, for two reasons.

First, in society generally, "the cornerstone of the patriarchal and patrilineal social edifice [was] the father" (Pilch in Pilch and Malina 1998: 145). In the covenant life of God's people, mothers likewise came in for high respect; the fifth commandment mandated "honor your father and your mother," not just father alone (Exod. 20:12 NIV; cf. Lev. 19:3 [where the mother is mentioned before the father]; Matt. 15:3–6; Eph. 6:2). "Father" in broader OT usage could apply to a prophet (2 Kings 2:12), priest (Judg. 17:10), and teacher (Prov. 1:8). John's appeal dignifies those of parental standing, spiritually speaking.

Second, in biblical parlance earthly fathers (and by extension all God-fearing adults) have the privilege of in some ways mirroring the character and prerogatives of the heavenly Father.[6] Believers are accordingly called to be "sons of your Father in heaven" and to "be perfect . . . as your heavenly Father is perfect" (Matt. 5:48 NIV; cf. 5:45). They are told, "Be merciful, just as your Father is merciful" (Luke 6:36 NIV). "Be imitators of God," Paul tells the Ephesians (Eph. 5:1). Fathers' largesse to children is a mirror of the heavenly Father's bounty (Luke 11:11–13), and their loving discipline of sons is a picture of their own tutelage under the Father above (Heb. 12:9). Fatherhood may be a beleaguered institution in the postmodern West, but in antiquity "father" could serve as "a title of respect or honour" (MM 498) even outside the quasi-sacred bounds of family. To appeal to Christians as fathers was to evoke their sense of responsibility and their humble yet lofty privilege under the Father par excellence.

Those who might feel too youthful, in age or in spiritual wisdom, to see themselves as πατέρες would be included in νεανίσκοι (*neaniskoi*, young men). In Philo (*Creation* 105), following Hippocrates, the term refers to the fourth of a man's seven stages, identified as the period between twenty-two and twenty-eight years of age. This is typically a period of high energy, idealistic vision, willingness for conflict when necessary,[7] and great potential for service (cf. Burge 1996: 120); for this reason, Timothy is urged to capitalize on advantages associated with his νεότητος (*neotētos*, lit., youth; 1 Tim. 4:12). The nineteenth and twentieth centuries were a period when many of youthful age responded to great spiritual awakenings (Orr 1971). In American colonial days it was observed: "When the elders are still, sometimes a young Phineas rises up and shows his zeal for Christ" (Cotton 1962: 148; cf. Num. 25:1–13; Ps. 106:30–31). Loader (1992: 23) raises the possibility, however, that John commends these "young men" because it was from their demographic ranks that troublemakers arose in the first place.

In early Christian times νεανίσκοι are among the recipients of Pentecostal promises (Acts 2:17). In the Gospels, people of this age are pictured as being influenced by Jesus's ministry (Matt. 19:20; Mark 14:51; Luke 7:14). In the LXX, νεανίσκοι are the heroic spies who rescued Rahab and her family (Josh. 6:23), the recruit pool for the devoted Nazirites (Amos 2:11), and the courageous men who along with Daniel maintained faithfulness to God despite the pressure of foreign enslavement (Dan. 1:4, 17). In calling readers νεανίσκοι, John most likely appeals to the promise and spiritual vitality of believers who are relatively new on the scene of Christian faith yet capable of great things by virtue of their developmental level.[8]

Recent translations are uneasy with John's words πατέρες and νεανίσκοι, which are variously rendered as "fathers/young people" (NRSV, TNIV), "you

6. John even exemplifies this by adopting the OT Wisdom literature convention of assuming the role of a parent addressing children; cf. R. Brown 1982: 318.

7. Westcott 1883: 60 notes John's assumption in this passage that "conflict is inevitable unless men passively yield to the power of evil."

8. Contra Bruns 1967: 453, it is unlikely that John presents Jesus as victor over death à la Herakles and hopes to attract young men by this appeal to classical heroism.

who are mature/you who are young" (NLT), and "parents/young people" (CEV). Edwards (1996: 92) concludes that "by modern standards, the formulation of 1–3 John's teaching is androcentric in that males are perceived as the norm, though it is probably too much to call it 'sexist.'" She expresses confidence that "the author(s), if pressed, would agree that all that is said about love, faith, and obedience applies also to Christian women" (cf. Burge 1996: 113). Thompson (1992: 62–63) concurs, noting that the Bible often refers to the whole people of God under the rubrics "young and old" (so also R. Brown 1982: 299). As long as men refrain from handling these verses as if they referred only to males, women have no reason to feel that the masculine form of the words πατέρες and νεανίσκοι excludes them (on the inclusive nature of the Greek masculine plural, see Turner 1963: 22). The author "includes all Christians who will permit themselves to be addressed by this homily" (Strecker 1996: 56).

Weighty Theological Truths

A fourth reason for seeing 2:12–14 as conveying considerable emotion and therefore serving a prominent place in John's tacit rhetorical strategy is provided by the weightiness of the theological truths adduced. Based on the author's use of verb forms, Porter (1989: 230) concludes that the ὅτι (*hoti*) clauses in 2:12–14 "summarize the entire theology of the epistle" (on whether the ὅτι clause are causal or declarative, see exegesis of 2:14). Even if overstated, this rightly captures the considerable force of the three perfect-tense affirmations that fill out the literary unit. Having grabbed his readers' attention in the ways outlined above, John characterizes the divine benefits they have received.

First, speaking generally to all his readers, John writes that their "sins have been forgiven on account of his name" (2:12; cf. 3:23; 5:13; on ἀφίημι [*aphiēmi*, to forgive], see third additional note on 2:12). Their redemption is secure insofar as their confession of sin is genuine and Christ's atoning work is accordingly in effect (1:9). Jesus's "name" probably points to the high status he possessed as the unique, God-sent savior, who in his humanity shared the very divine nature in unique fashion.[9]

The image of "this Jesus" (cf. Acts 2:32, 36; 17:3; Bockmuehl 1994) forgiving needy sinners of their transgressions (already alluded to repeatedly in 1 John) would have been etched in the minds of many of John's readers from the Gospel narrative, whether in written or preached form (cf. Jesus's explicit pronouncement of forgiveness of sins using the same language as 1 John in Matt. 9:2; Luke 5:20; 7:48; 23:34). The same motif is implicit in virtually every chapter of John's Gospel; from his baptism to his resurrection Jesus is "the Lamb of God, who takes away the sin of the world!" (John 1:29 NIV). "Forgiveness

9. As illustrative of John's high Christology, cf. John 3:35; 4:34; 5:18, 19, 22, 30; 6:38; 7:28; 8:42; 10:17, 36; 13:3; 14:9; 16:32; 17:24; 20:17. The Johannine Epistles move in this same christological sphere. On the Semitic associations of this use of "name," see Ps. 25:11; R. Brown 1982: 302. More broadly, see Painter 2002: 187–88.

of sins" in Christ and him alone[10] was apparently at the center of apostolic proclamation across the three decades spanned by Acts (e.g., 2:38; 5:31; 10:43; 13:38; 26:18); "the proclamation of the forgiveness of sins was the message of the Gospel" (Westcott 1883: 59). Current Western thought easily trivializes the Christian doctrine of sin (see McLeish 1995: 680–81) and therefore the magnitude of the redemption that Christ brought. In this spirit, Funk (1996: 306, 312) can demand that we "give Jesus a demotion" and "abandon the doctrine of the blood atonement." But the author of 1 John retains early Christian (and proleptic OT) joy and wonder at the assurance that the curse of sin (Gen. 3) has been overcome by the cross of Christ (cf. John 17:4; 19:30). In reminding his readers of their forgiveness of sins, John renews the note of joy with which the epistle began (1 John 1:4; contra R. Brown 1982: 303, it is unlikely that this passage reflects a baptismal background).

Second, John reminds the more seasoned community members (πατέρες) that they "have come to the true knowledge of him who existed from the very beginning" (Cassirer 1989: 448), a plausible rendering of τὸν ἀπ᾽ ἀρχῆς (*ton ap' archēs*) given the presence of "the most heavily marked perfect" ἐγνώκατε (*egnōkate*, you have known; Porter 1989: 230). John has already called attention to bogus knowledge (2:4); here he commends knowledge that is sound.[11] He has already warned against deception and departure from the truth (1:6, 8, 10; 2:4); now he commends those who give evidence of an authentic[12] grasp of the eternal one (on "who was from the beginning," see exegesis of 1:1 and 2:7).[13] Despite widespread agreement among commentators that this refers to Christ rather than God (Loader 1992: 22; Kruse 2000: 90; Akin 2001: 105; but see Dodd 1946: 38; Stott 1964: 97; Bruce 1970: 58), it is not easy to see how the two can be separated here from the standpoint both of contextual factors (cf. R. Brown 1982: 303)[14] and of Johannine theology (in which Father and Son are closely intertwined [e.g., John 14:7; 17:7]). It is possible that to some degree John is conflating the two (Smalley 1984: 74). "In any case it is clear

10. Weight is placed on Christ's work and not human cooperation by John's διά (*dia*, because of) with the accusative rather than the genitive. The latter would make Christ's name instrumental in salvation, while the construction John has chosen presents Christ as the primary cause.

11. D. Smith 1991: 64 correctly notes: "Whether this description of fathers is to be pressed historically—the fathers knew Jesus personally, is an unanswerable question. More than likely they did not but are representative of the generation contemporary with Jesus."

12. On the full-orbed entailments of forgiveness of sin in 1 John, which involve pistic, ethical, and agapic dimensions, see exegesis of 2:1a.

13. Wallace 1996: 236 points out that in τὸν ἀπ᾽ ἀρχῆς the article is used to make a prepositional phrase function like a noun.

14. To the factors mentioned by R. Brown that, he concedes, make a reference here to God "not an inconceivable position" should be added that even the epistle's opening ὃ ἦν ἀπ᾽ ἀρχῆς, while clearly a pointer to the Son, is an entrée to a fellowship in which the Father is mentioned first (1:3) and a message at whose epicenter is God (ὁ θεός; 1:5). For John, Christology remains subordinate to "theos-ology"; theology is not replaced by a facile "Jesus-ology." Having said that, in John's writings elsewhere the perfect of γινώσκω always expresses the disciple's knowledge of the Son (John 6:69; 14:7, 9; 17:7; 1 John 2:3, 4; 3:6) except in 1 John 2:13. The other apparent exception (John 8:55) expresses Jesus's knowledge of the Father.

that the author does not wish to separate Jesus from the Father" (Strecker 1996: 57n16). The mark of maturity in the Christian community is sound knowledge of God through his Son or, in Marshall's words, "knowledge of the Godhead" (1978: 140).

Third, John affirms that those of less seniority among his readers "have conquered [νενικήκατε, *nenikēkate*] the evil one." In John's Gospel (17:15), Jesus prays for his followers to be protected from the selfsame figure. References to Satan under this title are otherwise limited in John to a few other passages in 1 John (2:14; 3:12; 5:18, 19). From additional mention of this adversary in the NT (Matt. 5:37; 6:13; 13:19, 38; Eph. 6:16; 2 Thess. 3:3) it is clear that he is a formidable opponent. "His activity continues and is dangerous for the Christian" (R. Brown 1982: 305). But compared to the one in whom John's readers have placed their trust, his powers are negligible (1 John 4:4) because Christ came to destroy his works (3:8)—and in John's understanding obviously succeeded.[15] Therefore with the same perfect-tense settledness of the previous two ὅτι clauses, John praises his readers for "their" victory. It is a victory clearly won on their behalf by Christ, whom John presents as using the same verb of himself in stating, "I have overcome [νενίκηκα, *nenikēka*] the world" (John 16:33 NIV; cf. Painter 2002: 189). The picture of Christ as conqueror is augmented by several comparable uses of νικάω (*nikaō*, conquer) in Revelation (3:21; 5:5; 6:2; 17:14). John reminds readers that Christ's victory is also their own. "For our Head, Christ, has overcome the whole world once for all for us" (Calvin 1988: 252). In this particular context, John does not make clear which aspect of Jesus's life and ministry constituted the devil's definitive defeat. The effect of this is for the victory to seem related to the whole sweep of Christ's activity rather than to be reduced to a particular act or event.

2. De Facto Greeting Continued: Reflective Appeal (2:14)

Throughout 2:12–14, the question arises whether the six appearances of ὅτι (*hoti*) are causal ("I write because"; cf. Noack 1960) or declarative ("I write that"; cf. Zerwick 1994: §416; Kruse 2000: 88n62; Painter 2002: 186). If the latter, John's statements are somewhat tautological (cf. Smalley 1984: 71), and it is not clear what purpose is served by such laconic summaries of what he has said or will say later in greater detail.[16] Causal ὅτι, on the other hand, would be inclusive of the declarative sense—John must assume *that* these things are true in order to treat them as somehow causative of his act of writing. And a causal understanding fits well with an understanding that John's

15. Cf. Culpepper 1998: 261: "As deep as the dualism of the Johannine literature is, it is not an absolute dualism; God in Christ has triumphed over the powers of darkness. The assurance of victory, therefore, is a recurring theme of these writings."

16. R. Brown 1982: 318–19 makes sense of a declarative understanding of ὅτι by relating it to the readers' "danger of being confused and divided over the interpretation of 'the gospel' because of seductive secessionist propaganda." The readers need to be told what a Christian is, not assured of what they already are. Interpreters who see 1 John as less permeated with antisecessionist polemic may find the causal understanding more plausible.

sixfold repetition of γράφω/ἔγραψα (*graphō*/*egrapsa*) is a rhetorical device to refresh reader attention, which he undertakes precisely *because* there are weighty reasons (forgiveness of sin, knowledge of God, victory over the evil one) to think that his words will have the salubrious effect he intends. Further, causal ὅτι would comport with what appears to be the parallel passage of 2:21. "Because" is accordingly the translation and understanding adopted here (cf. D. Smith 1991: 63; Loader 1992: 24; Rensberger 1997: 71).[17]

I observed above that in some respects 2:12–13 serves the purpose of a greeting. First John 2:14 continues in this vein and follows an identical syntactical pattern. Yet there is an obvious change in the initial verb. It may be granted that the shift from γράφω in 2:12–13 to ἔγραψα in 2:14 marks stylistic preference rather than temporal reference; by ἔγραψα John is not referring to something that he did in former times, as opposed to what he is doing currently as reflected in the use of γράφω. Ἔγραψα is simply an epistolary aorist (Zerwick 1993: 728; Burge 1996: 111).[18] Temporally there is no reason why the acts denoted by the respective verbs cannot be simultaneous. Yet even Porter (1989: 230), who rejects any temporal differentiation in the morphological shift, sees a change in emphasis. In my view the change (reflected in my translation) may be explained as follows. The first-person present form of γράφω (more heavily marked than the aorist, according to Porter) is used to convey a relatively higher degree of feeling and urgency, as indicated in the exegesis of 2:12–13. My translation "the reason I am writing" attempts to express in English the gist of John's direct, personal, and emphatic tone. (Thompson 1992: 65 does not document her claim that the aorist here is "more emphatic.")

In contrast, the slightly deemphasized aorist ἔγραψα befits 2:14's restatement and slight elaboration of 2:12–13 (contra Calvin 1988: 253, 2:14 is not "superfluous" or the result of misplaced scribal creativity). Whereas γράφω comported with John's *act* of writing, ἔγραψα views the *fact* of having written, regarded in its entirety (not because of "the individual semantic value" of the aorist component, but because of the meaning of ἔγραψα as "an entire proposition in context," to adapt words from Porter 1989: 184).

My translation "I have written" in 2:14 seeks to reflect this understanding. It also characterizes the second phase of John's extended de facto greeting as reflective whereas 2:12–13 is reflexive. First John 2:14 is reflective in the sense of being corroborative and explicatory of the two verses preceding it—the author reflects on and slightly extends what he has already substantially expressed.

John writes to the same twofold group addressed in 2:12–13, but now he calls them παιδία (*paidia*, children). This is a much more common word for child (52 NT occurrences, 169 in the LXX) or even baby (cf. frequent uses in the birth narratives of Matthew and Luke) than the rare τεκνίον of 2:12.

17. Akin 2001: 103 seems to say that to select either option is to commit an exegetical fallacy.

18. An epistolary aorist is "an aorist tense verb that is past from the reader's point of view but actually present from the writer's point of view" (Demoss 2001: 52).

The word can connote tender age (John 16:21) or the innocence associated with childhood (Luke 18:16). Jesus addressed his disciples as τεκνία once in John's Gospel (13:33) and also calls them παιδία one time (21:5). In 1 John 2:14, παιδία is likely simply another way for John to express his warm regard for his readers, although Caragounis (2006: 573) suggests that the word connotes superior social standing in addition to familiarity.

He commends them because they "know the Father." Whereas 2:12–13 may key on the Son's benefits (esp. if τὸν ἀπ' ἀρχῆς [*ton ap' archēs*] in 2:13 refers to Christ), with "on account of [Jesus's] name" serving as a sort of heading, 2:14 begins with a clear reference to God. Readers as a whole are reminded of their relationship with the Father, γινώσκω in John often being a relational (cf. Schnackenburg 1992: 117) as well as cognitive verb (well illustrated in John 17:3, 7, 8, 23, 25; cf. already in 1 John the use of γινώσκω in 2:3, where relational and cognitive aspects are in view).

In close parallelism to 2:13, John says of the "fathers" in 2:14 that they know τὸν ἀπ' ἀρχῆς (him who was from the beginning). The proximity of this phrase to "the Father" in the previous clause makes it slightly more possible that John speaks of God here than of Jesus.

It is to the "young men" that John enlarges on the statement he made in 2:13. Not only have they "conquered the evil one," but John also credits them in 2:14 with being ἰσχυροί (*ischyroi*, strong). The term ἰσχυρός is used some 160 times in LXX. It can refer to strength and power as possessed, for example, by nature, people, or armies. But it is also used adjectively to describe the Lord's might (Deut. 10:17; Josh. 4:24; 2 Sam. 22:48; Neh. 1:5; 9:31, 32; 2 Macc. 1:24; Ps. 7:11 [7:12 LXX]; Sir. 15:18; Jer. 50:34 [27:34 LXX]; 32:18 [39:18 LXX]; Dan. 9:4) and substantively as a title for the Lord: ὁ ἰσχυρός (*ho ischyros*, the Mighty One; 2 Sam. 22:31, 32, 33; 23:5; Job 22:13; 33:29; 34:31; 36:22, 26; 37:5, 10). In the NT the term, largely absent from John's writings, is used by John the Baptist to describe Jesus (Matt. 3:11) and by Jesus in depicting himself obliquely as the ἰσχυρότερος (*ischyroteros*, stronger man) who overpowers ὁ ἰσχυρός (*ho ischyros*, the strong man) Satan (Luke 11:21–22). None of this constitutes lexical proof that with ἰσχυροί in 1 John 2:14 John has in mind strength peculiarly associated with or directly derived from God. But the concept of God and Christ being strong is well established in both Greek Testaments. With a cognate noun, Paul voices a familiar biblical motif: "Be strong in the Lord and in the strength of his might [ἰσχύος, *ischyos*]" (Eph. 6:10). It might be difficult to prove contextually, whether in terms of Johannine theology or earliest Christianity generally, that in 1 John 2:14 John does not have in mind strength provided by God rather than purely human power alone. "The biblical concept of strength is not purely physical" (R. Brown 1982: 305).

Closely associated with their power (at least in part) from God is the abiding presence of the word of God: "The word of God abides in you" (for negative examples, see 1:10; John 5:38; for "in you," see exegesis of 2:27). The phrase "word of God" (ὁ λόγος τοῦ θεοῦ, *ho logos tou theou*) appears over three dozen times in the NT (in John at John 10:35; cf. Rev. 1:2, 9; 6:9; 19:13; 20:4). To these occurrences may be added "the word of the Lord" (ten times in the NT, well over two hundred times in the OT). John points to appropriation of God's verbal self-expression as integral to the strength and character of the young (whether in age, spiritual maturity, or both) believers he addresses. The link between youth, moral strength, and God's word was well established from OT times: "How can a young man keep his way pure? By living according to your words [τοὺς λόγους σου, *tous logous sou*]" (Ps. 119:9 [118:9 LXX]). This "word of God" is for John likely a complex combination of God's creational activity and redemptive witness to himself in the many forms attested in salvation history (contra Smalley 1984: 79, it is surely not the generic "reality of God"). In the present context, it would especially encompass (1) the apostolic preaching and instruction (cf. Ellis 2000: 270: "general Christian truth") and (2) its twofold foundation, the OT and Jesus's life and teaching (crowned by his death, resurrection, and triumphant return; the conquering Christ of Rev. 19:13 is called "the Word of God"). The truths of these words and events "abide," are enduringly and effectively present, in John's addressees. Marshall (1978: 141) rightly speaks here of "the importance of Christian assurance" as "one of the notes in this Epistle which has aroused surprisingly little echo among expositors."

As a result, John repeats that they "have conquered the evil one" (see exegesis of 2:12–13). The victory is explicitly if loosely connected with "the word of God." The nature of the connection calls for comment. It can be surmised that John was not ignorant that "the word of God" inaugurated the new dimension of salvation history that the incarnation marked, whether in terms of the word that came to John in the Judean desert (Luke 3:2), the word of Jesus (called "the word of God" in 5:1) that he taught the people, "the word of God" in the sense of the OT writings (Matt. 15:6) that Jesus and later his apostles (including John in his Gospel) famously explicated, or "the word of God" that was the apostolic focus and message (the phrase occurs about a dozen times in Acts). "The word of God" even as a set phrase (to say nothing of implied or explicit references to it in its scriptural crystallization)[19] looms large enough in the NT epistles (1 Cor. 14:36; 2 Cor. 2:17; 4:2; Eph. 6:17; Phil. 1:14; Col. 1:25; 1 Thess. 2:13; 1 Tim. 4:5; Titus 2:5; Heb. 4:12; 6:5; 13:7) that the impression given by Acts is confirmed: the word in both its broad sweep and conceptual particularity gave primary impetus to the early Christian movement. Stark (1997: 211) even argues that early Christian doctrine (in my understanding not to be widely separated from the word) is the ultimate explanation for the survival and gradual widespread acceptance of Christianity in the Roman Empire leading up to the time of Constantine: "It was the religion's particular doctrines that permitted Christianity to be among the most sweeping and successful revitalization movements in history." John's

19. The phrase "the word of God" does not appear in Romans—an epistle heavily laden with OT quotations and allusions.

early enthusiasm for the word and its potential for overcoming evil with good was, it seems, not misplaced.

Since at least the time of Harnack, it has been popular to characterize early Christianity at its purest as solely spiritual and spontaneous (1904: 167–70; cf. the seminal sketch of this position in Harnack 1886: 36–44), the opposite of a religion of teachings or a book. Yet there quickly arose the temptation to make doctrine, and particularly Christology, a touchstone for Christian faith (1904: 185). Largely from Greek thought, "assent to a series of propositions about Christ's person" allegedly began to intrude into Christianity (1904: 188), which for Harnack is emphatically not about theological verities (at least not Trinitarian ones) but rather about ethics and untrammeled individual religious feeling. In this view, a religion in which "the word of God" would take on such definite doctrinal form was a lamentable disaster; for this reason especially the OT "was a menace to Christian freedom" (1904: 190) from earliest times.

What emerges from Harnack's picture of the early church is a scenario in which "the Word of God" would be at best perhaps a cipher for spiritual experience or later (as early church experience quickly became tainted by Greek ideas) an allegiance to doctrinal truths that did not characterize the very earliest Christians themselves. "The Word of God" is in any case not to be understood as doctrine or written Scripture. This animus against equating "Word of God" and the Bible had roots extending back over a century earlier.[20] It became a primary and dominant assumption of much Western theology and biblical scholarship of the twentieth century and for that reason is very much a factor in biblical scholarship currently.

In considerable contrast to such an understanding, John extols "the word of God," an entity certainly vaster than Scripture and doctrines alone can exhaust, but hardly to be understood in contradistinction to these. John's usage is closer to that of the psalmist, for whom God's "words" (Ps. 119:9 [118:9 LXX]: λόγους, *logous*) can also be called his "oracles" (119:11 [118:11 LXX]: λόγια, *logia*), a term referring to written Scripture (Rom. 3:2; Heb. 5:12). Or one could think here of Jesus himself, who under deadly moral bombardment took refuge behind the revetment of God's word and then, in brilliant confirmation of the temporal locus of that word, returned fire with Moses's writings (Matt. 4:1–10). Thus in John's Gospel, Jesus can say to his detractors, "If you believed Moses, you would believe me, for he wrote about me" (John 5:46 NIV). Here is a point where Jesus and Harnack seem to be at odds. For Harnack and many since, "the gospel is not a doctrine" (1886: 47n2), while in John's epistle "the word of God" can be taken as an apostolic reminder that apart from doctrine—and the divine word by which apostles formulated, applied, and disseminated it—the "gospel" would hardly have made the impact that history indicates it did. Historically speaking, the view of Hiebert (1991: 99) that "the Word of God" in John's understanding would

20. Johann Salomo Semler (1725–91) generally gets credit for effectively establishing "a wall of separation between the Bible and the word of God" (Baird 1992: 123).

signify "the message of God as brought by Christ and now embodied in the inspired Scriptures" has at least as much to say for it as Harnack's theory.

3. Imperatival Appeal in View of the Message (2:15–17)

a. Heart of the Imperative: Warning against World-Love (2:15a)

John's message is that God is light (1:5). He has traced out many implications of this in previous verses. Most of all for present purposes, in 2:12–14 he has at some length detailed the spiritual status and profile of his readers in whose lives the divine light shines (2:8) and who are therefore not groping blindly in Stygian gloom (2:11). Thanks to their standing vis-à-vis the light of Father and Son, great benefits are theirs, among the greatest of which is that they are not helpless before the predations of the liar and murderer (John 8:44) who is the evil one (1 John 2:13–14). Rather, they have conquered him.

On this basis John is in a position to move from an expository or indicative mode to the imperative.[21] He does so in 2:15a with the sudden turn of phrase: μὴ ἀγαπᾶτε τὸν κόσμον μηδὲ τὰ ἐν τῷ κόσμῳ (*mē agapate ton kosmon mēde ta en tō kosmō*), which may be rendered, "Do not set your affection on the world, nor on the things belonging to the world!"

First a word about imperatives in John's writings (for changes underway in the history of the language at that time, see Caragounis 2006: 167–68). Among the Gospels, the Fourth Gospel contains the fewest imperatives, both in raw number and in relative frequency (the following list includes prohibitive subjunctives).

Imperatives

NT Book	Present	Aorist	Perfect	Total	Frequency per 1,000 Words
Matthew	121	165		286	13.50
Mark	82	65	1	148	11.34
Luke	129	155		284	12.68
John	58	74		132	7.26
Acts	41	83	1	125	6.01
Romans	34	28		62	7.51
1 Corinthians	85	14		99	12.24
2 Corinthians	13	9		22	4.24
Galatians	16	5		21	7.93
Ephesians	34	6	1	41	14.74

Continued

21. Technically speaking, ἀγαπᾶτε is subjunctive, not imperative, but in Hellenistic Greek a prohibitive imperative combines a negative particle (typically μή) with a subjunctive verb for an imperatival sense. The computer software Accordance rightly tags such "subjunctive" forms as imperatives when they occur with this meaning. See Wallace 1996: 487, who points out (note 99) that there are only eight true aorist imperatives in prohibitions in the NT; the rest are morphologically subjunctives.

Imperatives

NT Book	Present	Aorist	Perfect	Total	Frequency per 1,000 Words
Philippians	22	3		25	13.11
Colossians	23	7		30	16.37
1 Thessalonians	19	1		20	11.66
2 Thessalonians	7			7	7.42
1 Timothy	41	2		43	23.14
2 Timothy	16	17		33	22.90
Titus	11	3		14	18.11
Philemon	2	2		4	10.36
Hebrews	23	6		29	5.11
James	31	23	1	55	26.53
1 Peter	10	25		35	17.96
2 Peter	4	3		7	5.63
1 John	8	2		10	4.01
2 John	2	1		3	10.79
3 John	2			2	7.87
Jude	3	2		5	9.42
Revelation	27	62		89	7.93

First John follows in the steps of John's Gospel by containing a relatively low frequency of imperatives. Unlike John's Gospel and Revelation, 1 John favors present imperatives. Given their relative paucity, it makes sense to pay careful attention to those few that occur.

John strongly discourages undue attachment to the world and the things "belonging to the world" (cf. James 4:4; Schlatter 1999: 98). His disparagement of the world may be accounted for by the simple observation that "there must be conflict with the world if the soul is to grow up into Christ" (Darby 1907: 44). Reasons for this will become clear as the meaning of "the world" for John is examined below. The words τὰ ἐν τῷ κόσμῳ (*ta en tō kosmō*, the things in the world) require nuanced handling, for two reasons. First, the article τά (the things) should be regarded as cataphoric (cf. Wallace 1996: 220), pointing forward to the fuller definition of what John has in mind, which he will detail in 1 John 2:16 (see exegesis). Without this fuller understanding, it would be premature to demonize all worldly "things" on the basis of 2:15. Second, John's warning about "things in the world" notwithstanding, people are things insofar as they are created objects, and they are in the world, and they are certainly to be loved—in the NT there are dozens of exhortations to love one another. Even enemies are to be loved (Luke 6:27, 35)! In fact, so powerful is the portrayal of divine love for the world in Scripture—epitomized by John 3:16, in which God is said to "love the world," that is, people in the world (cf. Pss. 33:5; 57:10 [57:11 MT])—that we can withdraw human beings from the set of objects John has directly in mind when he warns against undue world-love in 1 John 2:15 (cf. Schlatter 1950: 35). "There is no suggestion that the Christian is to hate the material world or its inhabitants" (Marshall 1978: 142–43).

Then what does John mean? In using "world" negatively in 2:15a, he reverses the more positive connotation the word has elsewhere (2:2; 4:9, 14) and anticipates the more negative associations that emerge as the letter progresses. For John, the κόσμος (*kosmos*, world) is passing away (2:17). As a whole it is a realm that does not (or will not) recognize Christ (3:1) and that despises people who follow Christ (3:13). It is shot through with the influence of dangerous deceivers like false prophets (4:1) and antichrist himself (4:3), the evil one "who is in the world" (4:4). "The world" is conceived of as the stronghold of those who ignore the apostolic testimony (4:5; cf. 4:6). While "the Father has sent his Son to be the Savior of the world" (4:14 NIV), this saving work consists in equipping believers to "overcome the world" (5:4–5), not benignly acquiesce to its ways. In the end, in a sense "the whole world is under the control of the evil one" (5:19 NIV). In the light of such numerous and pervasive negative associations, the κόσμος is a sinister sphere indeed; it is an image "of life where God does not rule" (Loader 1992: 24). It is therefore not surprising that, viewed this way, things that "belong to" the κόσμος (i.e., that are characteristic of the fallen world order rather than of God's redemptive order unfolding in the world) can hardly be the legitimate objects of the highest devotion of Christ's followers. Cyprian asks his readers, "Since the world hates the Christian, why do you love that which hates you? and why do you not rather follow Christ, who both redeemed you and loves you?" (*Treatise* 7.24).

This raises the issue of what John has in mind by the verb ἀγαπᾶτε in this context. Because John's writings so strongly teach "love" for others *in the world*, it seems warranted to seek an equivalent expression in English that will discourage any simplistic ascetic temptation to demonize the world (and possibly people with it). The life of Jesus, who enjoyed (loved?) the world sufficiently to be charged with hedonistic excess (Matt. 11:19), cautions against too swashbuckling of an abnegation of "world" viewed as God's creation (and not merely as the evil one's domain), for it is also true that "the earth [LXX γῆ, *gē*] is the Lord's, and everything in it, the world [LXX οἰκουμένη, *oikoumenē*], and all who live in it" (Ps. 24:1 NIV). Hence I suggest "set affection on" as the sense of what John forbids. God (along with God's name [Ps. 119:132; Isa. 56:6] and salvation [Ps. 70:4 (70:5 MT)]) is to be the primary object of human love (Deut. 6:5; Mark 12:30). In addition to loving God, his people are to love what God loves—for example, the people of God (Lev. 19:18, 34; Deut. 10:19; John 13:34–35; Rom. 13:8; 1 Pet. 1:22), the dwelling place of God (Pss. 26:8; 84:1 [84:2 MT]), and the commandments of God (Ps. 119). The devotion of the heart is to be oriented in these redemptive directions, all of which lead back to God himself. Conversely, believers are not to love, set their affection on, other objects or allurements of the world (viewed as under the evil's one sway) that would detract from full engagement with what constitutes and mediates God's grace.

John, unlike Cyprian, for example, who centuries later quotes these verses to urge women to modesty and austerity (*Treatise* 2.7), is not calling for blanket condemnation of the world.[22] He is not commanding "love not the world" in the sense of "to blazes with it!" This is why I chose to avoid the obvious, most straightforward translation. He is not raising an alarum, Chicken Little-like, that the sky is falling. In fact, a certain love of the world is called for (cf. Augustine, *Hom. 1 John* 2.11),[23] as I intimate above. But he counsels strategic disavowal of loyalties to features of the world that would surely compromise the total devotion that is appropriate to God alone. In the remainder of 1 John 2:15, John tells why such disavowal, such measured and directed setting of affection, is crucial.

b. Warning Regarding Absence of Love for God (2:15b)

What if someone loves the world in the inappropriate fashion John forbids in 2:15a? In 2:15b John takes up this question. Regarding anyone who sets affection on the world as defined in 2:15a, John asserts that οὐκ ἔστιν ἡ ἀγάπη τοῦ πατρὸς ἐν αὐτῷ (*ouk estin hē agapē tou patros en autō*, the love of the Father is not in him).

This is perhaps the juncture to pause and ask a question pressing to some: What's so bad about the world? "For many readers the seemingly negative attitude to the world . . . raises difficulties" (Edwards 1996: 14; cf. R. Brown 1997: 392–93; Klauck 1989). It is possible to dismiss John's darkly pessimistic words in this section as parochial extremism or partisan overreaction to doctrinal or political reversals, in hindsight rather trivial, in one or more churches known to him. Especially those in Western lands may feel that economic prosperity, political stability, material plenty, and intellectual refinement combine to make John's warnings sound a little gauche, at least as regards their application today. Perhaps *he* could not lighten up; but let *us* steer clear of such negativism and melodrama. Of course today no one can reconstruct precisely what factors moved John, so we really lack evidence to convict him of situational exaggeration. But in all events the structure of current world

22. D. Smith 1991: 65 calls attention to an overwrought "Christian pietism" in which "anything that affords sensate pleasure is suspect, if not downright evil."

23. R. Brown 1982: 324–25n22 agrees that Augustine is right but thinks that John is "one-sided" (like James 1:27; 4:4) and that Augustine has read into John "other NT authors who were more open to a mission to the world." It is hard not to see a little of the scholar's condescension in Brown's assertion that Augustine (and others) "felt a pastoral need" and because of this misrepresented the text. This points to a methodological question: is John to be read as necessarily denying all that he does not explicitly affirm (e.g., a positive understanding of the world as God's domain and fertile field for positive mission) in these few verses? Or can he be assumed to be in basic agreement with other biblical writers, and with Christ as presented even in John's Gospel, in their obvious urgency to take the good news to the world and be a positive influence, salt and light, in the world? If one chooses the latter option, Augustine is not being unfaithful to John.

existence is sufficiently of a piece with John's times that the following observations may be relevant.

As I write this section, word has arrived of the in utero death of a colleague's baby. Doctors turned the perfectly healthy firstborn son-to-be to correct a breech positioning scant days before the due date. The umbilical cord was apparently pinched in the process. The funeral will be private. Meanwhile, a retired colleague's wife and primary caregiver just sustained a sudden, massive, and fatal heart attack. Another colleague's wife is battling terminal cancer, without notable success thus far. The chemotherapy is proving to be more debilitating than the radical surgery that preceded it. An e-mail just in tells of another kidnapped Christian in Sudan. He has a wife and small children, and no one can find him. Another report documents the torture and slaying of more Christian political prisoners in that same country. On the local front, a high school hockey player was left totally and irreversibly paralyzed last night by a late cross-check. Meanwhile I read in Harnack, that great theological scholar of yesteryear whose views are still common coin today, that apostolic Christianity never was true, in the sense that church fathers claimed for it, and that it is certainly not to be embraced from the pages of Scripture and lived out today. Christ is denied in precisely the sense warned about in John's letter, and this denial is normative for the teaching of the Christian religion in academic centers around the world. Many of them are training ministers for the church.

These are matters coming to my attention in the span of just a few hours, not because I have looked for evidence of death and oppression and theological drift but because it encroaches from all directions and, if one cares to see, at virtually all times. By the time these words are published, what is outlined above will be old news. But there will be no shortage of more of the same to replace it—the seemingly endless aftermath of 9/11, the disintegration of the space shuttle *Columbia*, the tsunami of Christmas 2004, the carnage of the US occupation in Iraq, and the multiplied provocations of terrorists that precipitated and perpetuate it.[24]

This is the κόσμος. Granted, it is not without an amazing plenitude of joy and delight. Laughing and dancing have their place, just like weeping and mourning (Eccles. 3:4). But John reminds us of important truths about the world's underlying structure and eschatological destiny. The evil one is present, even dominant, wherever divine light is suppressed. "Quite simply, the world is a dangerous place for its human inhabitants" (Sloyan 1995: 24). People either conquer by the Son or they are conquered. There is light and darkness. There is love and hate. There is salvation and perdition. Elsewhere capable of expressing the profound hope of deep affection, John seems here to be gripped by the starkness of the alternatives and the great gulf that separates life in the Son from everything else that exists.[25] It is possible to smile wanly at his

24. For effective identification and discussion of these and related issues, see Carson 2002.

25. Cf. Rensberger 1997: 75: "In 1 John's dualism, god and the world are opposed in such a way that things originate in, and are determined by, either the one or the other."

apocalyptic-sounding pronouncements. Or is it perhaps the case that we are to be pitied to the extent that we have lost John's wistful acuity regarding life's daily deathliness and the barely restrained darkness that seeks to extinguish all true light? His clarity of vision of Christ as cure may be inseparable from his (easily parodied) readiness to diagnose malaise—and to do so with the same emotional élan that his teacher Jesus not seldom displayed.

When a person sets affection on the world, John claims in 2:15b, it means that the Father's love (ἡ ἀγάπη τοῦ πατρός) is not in that person. The expression "love of the Father" occurs nowhere else in Scripture, though "love of God" is found nearly a dozen times (Luke 11:42; John 5:42; Rom. 5:5; 8:39; 2 Cor. 13:13 [13:14 NIV]; 2 Thess. 3:5; 1 John 2:5; 3:17; 4:9; 5:3; Jude 21). Here it makes sense to take it as an objective genitive: the Father is the object of believers' love (so Schnackenburg 1992: 120; Wallace 1996: 121n136; Rensberger 1997: 73–74; contra Painter 2002: 193). The person who sets affection on the world cannot exercise true love for the Father. There are two reasons for this.

First, authentic love for the Father requires reception of God's love as revealed in his Son through the cross: "This is love: not that we loved God, but that he loved us and sent his Son as an atoning sacrifice for our sins" (1 John 4:10 NIV). The love for the Father that John is thinking of is not a natural affection innate to all people but a gracious enablement brought about by the gospel (cf. Zerwick 1993: 728). For there to be "love for the Father" (objective genitive), there must be a prior "love by the Father" (subjective genitive) received by a sinner willing to seek it; "in the final analysis . . . love toward the Father is only the flowering of the love granted by God to the believers" (Schnackenburg 1992: 120). This means that the objective genitive of 2:15b presupposes a subjective genitive. This is reflected in my translation.

Second, authentic love for God exists only when it has no essential rivals. "There can be but one supreme object of moral devotion" (Westcott 1883: 63). "You shall have no other gods before me. . . . I, the Lord your God, am a jealous God" (Exod. 20:3, 5 NIV; cf. Josh. 24:15). "No one can serve two masters" (Matt. 6:24 NIV). The extended lesson in John 13–17 on the near equivalency of loving Christ, on the one hand, and obeying him, on the other, points in the same direction. "There is an expulsive power in all true affection" (Alexander 1901: 147), and to set one's heart on the world is effectively to expel God from the heart. To attempt to love God in multitasking fashion, dedicating a portion of one's love worldward and then the remaining amount godward, is fruitless because it fails to acknowledge God as he truly is: sole, unique, sovereign, alone deserving one's core allegiance. He accepts nothing less than the love that Christ's death exemplified and, when appropriated, generates. Even on largely Hellenistic, pre-Christian premises, Philo anticipated John's insight: "It is impossible for love of the world to coexist with love for God, just as it is impossible for light and darkness to be present at the same time."[26]

26. A Philo fragment cited in Strecker and Schnelle 1996: 1431 (my translation), from John of Damascus, *Sacra parallela* §370/382.

The one who does not tender God this magnitude of love "forfeits the love of the Father," as my translation has it. This rendering captures John's bare "the love of the Father is not in him," understood as the person's love for God. I noted above that God's love for the person is in fact a prerequisite for a person's love for God acceptably to arise. "Forfeits the love of the Father" covers both senses: the person who sets affection on the world has neither set it properly on the Father (probably John's explicit intended sense) nor received that love in its fullness from the Father so that the Father's love truly can be "in him" (implicit in the epistle's pronouncements elsewhere on "the love of God").

c. Explication of Warning (2:16–17)
i. The Origin of World-Love (2:16)

In 2:15a John warned against love for τὰ ἐν τῷ κόσμῳ (*ta en tō kosmō*, the things in the world). As noted above, the article τά (the things) should be regarded as cataphoric, pointing forward to 2:16. In other words, the imperative of 2:15 looks ahead to a further explanation of why the imperative is needed. It is not an arbitrary edict. The opening word of 2:16, ὅτι (*hoti*, because), confirms this. "Love not," John admonishes in 2:15, "because" or "inasmuch as" there is good reason for the warning. First John 2:16 gives the reason, or more precisely two reasons.

The reason lies primarily in the place of origin of "the things" John has in mind: πᾶν τὸ ἐν τῷ κόσμῳ . . . οὐκ ἔστιν ἐκ τοῦ πατρὸς ἀλλ' ἐκ τοῦ κόσμου ἐστίν (*pan to en tō kosmō . . . ouk estin ek tou patros all' ek tou kosmou estin*, everything that belongs to the world is not from the Father but is from the world). John is thinking of things that can be regarded as detrimental because they lack sanctifying ties with the Father. They are not rooted and grounded in him and can therefore be regarded as not coming from him. What are those things?

The core of 2:16 answers that question and thereby gives the second reason for the warning of 2:15. Characteristic of the world are things that emanate from human ἐπιθυμία (*epithymia*, craving). The κόσμος in one sense is the Father's domain, because it was created by the agency of his Son (John 1:10) and therefore is the sphere in which the Father's will comes to pass. A prominent stress of Jesus in John's Gospel is the will of the one who sent him (4:34; 5:30; 6:38; 7:17), which he terms τὸ θέλημα τοῦ πατρός μου (*to thelēma tou patros mou*, the will of my Father). When 1 John 2:15 speaks of things that are not from the Father, it is tacit acknowledgment of Jesus's teaching that there are things in the world that *are* central expressions and effects of the Father's will. Examples would include what Christians petition as often as they pray "your will be done on earth" (Matt. 6:10). First John 2:17 explicitly refers to that will.

But there is another will in the world, too, the will of the κόσμος that αὐτὸν οὐκ ἔγνω (*auton ouk egnō*, did not recognize him), that is, did not recognize

God's Son (John 1:10). The will of this wayward κόσμος is what John means by ἐπιθυμία. Although the word need not have pejorative connotations (Luke 22:15; Phil. 1:23; 1 Thess. 2:17), in about thirty-five of its thirty-eight NT occurrences it is not a positive term (see exegesis of 2:17). This is the case here. John's sense is nicely captured by Peter's explicit distinction between human ἐπιθυμία and God's θέλημα, between human craving and God's will (1 Pet. 4:2). In 1 John 2:16 John describes a quality of human desire that is inimical to God's desire. The dark reference to "what was in a man" that kept Jesus from entrusting himself to people could be relevant here (John 2:25). This degraded desire is apparently what John sees as prominent in the world at this stage of the discourse. He therefore warns against it. John seeks "to turn them from frivolity of misapplied craving" (Charry 1994: 50).

John not only warns but also explains. He glosses his expression πᾶν τὸ ἐν τῷ κόσμῳ with three phrases (see R. Brown 1982: 307–8 for a compilation of analogous diabolical triads in ancient, patristic, and medieval literature).

First is ἡ ἐπιθυμία τῆς σαρκός (*hē epithymia tēs sarkos*), translated "the lust of the flesh" by KJV, RSV, NASB, and HCSB. This phrase is variously rendered because the language is generic yet suggestive enough to justify a wide range of translations:

TEV	what the sinful self desires
NIV	the cravings of sinful man
TNIV	the cravings of sinful people
JB	the sensual body
NEB	all that panders to the appetites
CEV	our foolish pride
NLT	the lust for physical pleasure
LB	the craze for sex
Cassirer 1989	the appetites deriving from our carnal nature

Most of these capture a facet of what the original suggests (though LB seems to press a bit far). My translation "what the body hankers for" (taking τῆς σαρκός as objective, though Turner 1963: 213 suggests a genitive of quality and Moule 1994: 40 a subjective genitive) is simply one more idiomatic rendering of the danger to which John seeks to call attention: things originating in innate human nature regarded as unredeemed by God. This interpretation relates "body" more to the OT and Jewish frame of reference in which "'flesh' is the human as distinct from the divine" (R. Brown 1982: 310; cf. Lazure 1969; arguing for a more Hellenistic cast to "flesh" is Schweizer 1957) rather than to Greek background where physical desire was often regarded a priori as inimical to piety.

Second is ἡ ἐπιθυμία τῶν ὀφθαλμῶν (*hē epithymia tōn ophthalmōn*, the lust of the eyes). In Jesus's teaching the eyes have the capacity to mislead: "If your eyes are bad, your whole body will be full of darkness" (Matt. 6:23 NIV). Blindness is a biblical metaphor for spiritual deadness (23:16, 17, 19, 24, 26); it denotes insensitivity to God and rebellion against him (13:15; cf. Isa. 6:9–10 and the exegesis of 1 John 2:11). Reception of sight, on the other hand, becomes a symbol for spiritual regeneration (Matt. 9:27; 15:31). The godly person directs his or her eyes heavenward (Ps. 123:1–2), fixing them in the direction God calls for: "Let your eyes look straight ahead, fix your gaze directly before you" (Prov. 4:25 NIV). Wording in Prov. 6:25 LXX directly connects ἐπιθυμία and the eyes: μή σε νικήσῃ κάλλους ἐπιθυμία μηδὲ ἀγρευθῇς σοῖς ὀφθαλμοῖς (*mē se nikēsē kallous epithymia mēde agreuthēs sois ophthalmois*): "Do not let lust for beauty [of a harlot] conquer you; do not be caught with your eyes." The eyes, with obvious design and capacity for good, can sadly serve evil ends.

In 1 John 2:16 John is thinking of their capacity for evil. Eyes are parallel with flesh, which in this context we have seen is pejorative (in Prov. 27:20, eyes parallel Sheol and Abaddon). Characteristic of the κόσμος are foolish "eyes [that] wander to the ends of the earth" (17:24), eyes of "a proud heart" that are "the lamp of the wicked" (21:4). "The lust of the eyes" is the moral short-sightedness that obscures higher and better realities; we could render it "visual decadence," the moral bankruptcy of the spiritually blinded heart. We can also think of eyes in terms of what they see. Then "the lust of the eyes" becomes an illicit thing that godless eyes dart about hoping to glimpse—"what . . . the eyes itch to see" in the translation above. Internet pornography is a readily available example. John's words can be understood as referring to either of these two senses of the eyes' propensity for godless activity (though translators necessarily choose one or the other). Neither sense can be understood as from God; it is rather part of the world; believers must not set their affection on the world to the extent that this kind of thing defines the world.

The third component in John's explanation of what characterizes the κόσμος is ἡ ἀλαζονεία τοῦ βίου (*hē alazoneia tou biou*, the arrogance of life). The expression is difficult because the nouns in tandem are not particularly easy to pin down. Ἀλαζονεία occurs in the LXX only in the apocryphal writings (2 Macc. 9:8; 15:6; 4 Macc. 1:26; 2:15; 8:19; Wis. 5:8; 17:7), where it connotes arrogance and not seldom boastfulness. Schnackenburg (1992: 122n207) points out that the word refers to external expressions of braggart overconfidence and not the hidden root of interior self-satisfaction (for a contrary assertion see Alexander 1901: 140). In the NT it occurs elsewhere only in James 4:16, again with the sense of boastfulness. But what would, for example, "the boastfulness of life" mean? The word for "life" (βίος) can mean simply "everyday life" (Luke 8:14; 2 Tim. 2:4), but it often means "livelihood," "material goods," or "property." Thus the storied poor widow gave "all her livelihood," that is, all she had to live on (Luke 21:4). The father appportioned a share of his "property" to the son who would become prodigal (15:12, 30).

The NLT proposes "pride in our possessions" (cf. ESV's "pride in possessions"),[27] but that is too indiscriminate. Is all pride in all possessions to

27. TNIV is an improvement; it speaks of people's "boasting about what they have and do."

be renounced? Even more infelicitously sweeping is the TEV's "everything in this world that people are so proud of," which verges on gnostic-sounding world-negation.[28] The NRSV goes with "the pride in riches" (following "the desire of the flesh, the desire of the eyes"), which is an improvement. But the problem with "riches" could be that no one thinks he or she is rich (enough), so that "the pride in riches" (apart from being too sweeping in condemning pride—what kind of pride are we talking about?) almost ensures that many readers will not see themselves addressed. Perhaps better would be "what people toil to acquire," as in my translation above. This conveys the idea of vain (and ostentatious?) pursuit of earthly goods (on βίος in this sense, see the helpful note in Strecker 1996: 59n24). It also comports with the rendering of ὁ βίος upcoming in 3:17. It must be conceded, however, that no single translation is apt to capture John's full sense perfectly—even if we could be certain of exactly what it is.

John's indisputable point to his readers is that much of what surrounds them, insofar as it "belongs to the world," is "not from the Father. It is rather from the world." More specifically, the world is characterized by an unholy trinity[29] of "what the body hankers for and the eyes itch to see and what people toil to acquire." This toxic mix poisons and destroys. "The world is not simply a passive entity, but a rival for the allegiance of every person" (Thompson 1992: 67). Because of this, one must not set one's affection on the world (1 John 2:15). Believers' prayer should be that of Sir. 23:4–5, a passage that combines the same elements of desire, the eyes, and pride that John mentions: "O Lord, Father and God of my life, do not give me arrogant eyes [μετεωρισμὸν ὀφθαλμῶν, *meteōrismon ophthalmōn*], and remove evil desire [ἐπιθυμίαν, *epithymian*] from me."

But John has an additional, more global reason for the admonition of 1 John 2:15.

ii. The Bane of World-Love and the Promise of Doing the Will of God (2:17)

The logic of 2:7–17, as it comes to a close, runs like this: do not set your affection on the κόσμος (*kosmos*; 2:15), insofar as what characterizes the κόσμος is foreign if not hostile to the Father and what he represents (2:16). Further, the

28. TEV pales in comparison, however, with NLT's overwrought "for the world offers only the lust for physical pleasure, the lust for everything we see, and pride in our possessions," a rendering that is linguistically indefensible (cf. R. Brown 1982: 306: John "does not state that these three factors are all that is in the world; they are examples of what is in the world") and seriously out of sympathy with biblical writers' affirmation of the world as the sphere of God's reign and blessing. See exegesis of 2:15a; cf. Schnackenburg 1992: 125–28 and his careful delineation of "world" in this context.

29. Augustine (*Hom. 1 John* 2.14) attempts to show that each kind of desire is a category of temptation faced by Jesus when tested by the devil. He battled "lust of the flesh" when tempted to turn stones to bread, "lust of the eyes" when urged to perform a miraculous descent from the temple pinnacle, and "pride of life" when a kingdom was dangled before him. Alexander (1901: 141–43) follows Augustine (though without attribution) and likens the desires John mentions to Eden's allurements.

κόσμος and the human desire dominant in it are ephemeral—in contrast to the permanence of those who conform to the Father's will (2:17). First John 2:17, then, highlights two ideas: the fleeting nature of the world and the lasting quality of what compliance with God's will brings about.

The idea of the world "passing away" (παράγεται, *paragetai*) was already encountered in 2:8 (see exegesis). There the darkness was dissipating because it was being routed by the light. In 2:17 John assumes rather than states the reason for the world's passing. Contextually, he has spoken of the evil one's defeat just a few verses previous (2:13–14). It is the devil's ongoing demise and the corresponding victory of God's people that John likely has in mind as he speaks of the present world order passing into oblivion.

Alongside this world's passing, John sets the termination of the godless human craving (ἐπιθυμία, *epithymia*) spoken of in 2:16. It too is bound for destruction. As in the previous verse, John here seems to be articulating a theological anthropology that quickly became dominant in apostolic Christendom. Jude 18 (cf. similar language in 2 Pet. 3:3) records that the apostles warned against end-time "scoffers who will follow their own ungodly desires [ἐπιθυμίας]" (NIV; cf. Jude 16). In 2 Pet. 1:4 redemption itself is characterized as "escape [from] the corruption in the world caused by evil desires [ἐπιθυμίᾳ]" (NIV). Life apart from Christ is conformity with ignorant and evil desires (ἐπιθυμίαις; 1 Pet. 1:14); abstinence from these desires (2:11) and living "for the will of God" (4:2) is of the essence of Christian existence. James likewise locates the fallen human dilemma in ἐπιθυμία (1:14–15). In doing so, he has precedent in Paul, who repeatedly uses the word pejoratively at central junctures of his teaching (Rom. 1:24; 6:12; 7:7, 8; 13:14; Gal. 5:16, 24; Eph. 2:3; 4:22; Col. 3:5; 1 Thess. 4:5; 1 Tim. 6:9; 2 Tim. 3:6; 4:3; Titus 2:12; 3:3). John's statement in 1 John 2:17, then, is consistent with other apostolic pronouncements of the era. There is allure but no future in ἐπιθυμία (cf. Kruse 2000: 96). John's use of the word is also not without foreshadowings in Jesus's teaching (Mark 4:19; John 8:44) and the OT (Pss. 10:3 [9:22 LXX]; 106:14 [105:14 LXX]; 140:8 [139:9 LXX]; Prov. 12:12; 21:26; Sir. 5:2; 18:30, 31; 20:4; 23:5). This will need to be recalled later when his doctrine of Christian sinlessness (1 John 3:6, 9) is presented.

In itself John's teaching that the things of the world are not ultimate is hardly unique. Third-century philosopher Porphyry commends a life of self-contentment rather than pursuit of luxury, for riches and fame bring nothing but problems (*De abstinentia* 1.54.3–4). Other pagan thinkers (Dio Chrysostom, *Orations* 4.83–84; Lucian, *Hermotimus* 7, 22) voice the same conviction. Hellenistic Jewish writer Philo, reflecting Stoic values, writes, "One should practice being contented with a little, for this is being near God; but the contrary habit is being very far from him" (in Yonge 1993: 890). Philo (*Decalogue* 142, 153) sees "the desire of money, or fame, or pleasure" as the source of wars, not well-being; the tragedy is that "the human race has its heart set on these things."[30]

30. Kruse 2000: 94n77 calls attention to the wisdom text of the Cairo Genizah (ca. AD 100) and its numerous parallels to John's teaching about the world.

What these writers are vague about is the benefit of such self-denial. Based on classical paganism's ideas alone, one would be forced to conclude that "the true symbol for humanity is . . . a skull and an hour glass" (Alexander 1901: 155). But John has the clear notion of a goal with promise both for this age and the age to come. In contrast to (δέ [*de*, but] in 2:17 is adversative) the world and the banal desire that characterizes it stands ὁ . . . ποιῶν τὸ θέλημα τοῦ θεοῦ (*ho . . . poiōn to thelēma tou theou*, the one who does the will of God). For John, this is obviously a person of enviable standing. The reason is not hard to see.

Jesus commends the person of this description in the Sermon on the Mount (Matt. 7:21). Such a person is figuratively his "brother and sister and mother" (12:50; cf. Luke 11:27–28). The son who did the will of his father is the focus of a famous parable (Matt. 21:28–32) with direct implications for those who do on earth the will of Jesus's Father.

As presented in John's Gospel, Jesus's own life modeled doing God's will, even in contradistinction to his own: "I have come down from heaven not to do my will but to do the will of him who sent me" (6:38 NIV). He is credited with the same selfless attitude in Hebrews (10:7, 9; cf. Ps. 40:8 [40:9 MT/39:9 LXX]), an attitude enjoined on slaves by Paul, who urged them to do "the will of God [τὸ θέλημα τοῦ θεοῦ, *to thelēma tou theou*] from the heart" (Eph. 6:6).

From this emerges a profile of a person who, faced with a choice between the world's lust (ἐπιθυμία) and its Lord, wisely chooses the latter. Simply by virtue of the correspondence of such behavior with Jesus's life (cf. 1 John 2:6) and early church teaching, the advantage of this choice seems self-evident. But augmenting immediate earthly benefit, John factors in an additional consideration: the person who does God's will "abides forever." The background for this expression is likely OT and perhaps even specifically LXX usage in which, for example, God's righteousness (Pss. 111:3 [110:3 LXX]), praise (111:10 [110:10 LXX]), truth (117:2 [116:2 LXX]; cf. 1 Esd. 4:38), and word (Isa. 40:8) "abide forever." Jesus's extensive discourses on eternal life epitomized in the Fourth Gospel will also have informed John here. By doing God's will with reference to his Son, John's readers (like David's seed: Ps. 89:37 [89:38 MT/88:37 LXX]) will be able to share endlessly in the transcendent glory of the God they have seen fit to serve. "The righteous live forever" (Wis. 5:15). Augustine (*Hom. 1 John* 2.10) rightly exhorts, "Hold fast Christ. For you he became temporal, that you might become eternal."

Whether John has in mind a here-and-now ("realized") understanding of this promised blessing, on the one hand, or a futurist-eschatological understanding, on the other, is not exactly clear.[31] The answer probably lies in John's overarching view of time (see Anderson 1990: 41). He does not reflect

31. Schnackenburg 1992: 123 is eloquent but unconvincing in asserting the absence of what he terms "eschatological accent" here. The claim would have merit only if it could be shown that John's doctrine of world and last things were at odds with that of other NT writings, including John's Gospel, which contra Schnackenburg (1992: 124) is "interested in future judgment" and "the world to come" (see, e.g., John 12:48 and references to "eternal life" in John's Gospel, which

on that extensively in this context. He does make clear that the world is passing away; things are not an endless cycle. History is moving, then, toward a grand goal, for John is certainly not a nihilist, Christ having gone to prepare a place (John 14:2). Till then, John has a conviction that with Christ's first coming completed, it is now "the last hour" (1 John 2:18). The redemption of the world, the dawn of the long-awaited age to come, is as close as the light that is already shining (2:8). Christ's followers have already conquered the prince of darkness. If John's views are in harmony with those of Jesus and other disciples, he probably has in mind both present and future eschatological benefits. This is one of several fresh elements of John's message that crystallize in the next section.

Additional Notes

2:12. To the word τεκνία, a single minuscule (630) adds the possessive pronoun μου. In place of τεκνία some half dozen minuscules, in addition to Jerome, read παιδία. In both cases, such sparse and late attestation points to readings not apt to be original.

2:12. Two majuscules and a half dozen later witnesses (including Didymus of Alexandria from the late fourth century) have ἀφέωνται ὑμῶν αἱ ἁμαρτίαι (your sins have been forgiven) instead of NA[27]'s ἀφέωνται ὑμῖν αἱ ἁμαρτίαι (the sins have been forgiven you). See first additional note on 1:9 for discussion of the same phenomenon with respect to "our sins" and "the sins" there. The Synoptics have Jesus saying both ἀφίενταί σου αἱ ἁμαρτίαι (Mark 2:5; cf. Matt. 9:2) and ἀφέωνταί σοι αἱ ἁμαρτίαι σου (Luke 5:20), suggesting that the essential meaning of either reading is not vastly different.

2:12. Five other times the perfect indicative of ἀφίημι is used in the NT to refer to forgiveness of sins (Luke 5:20, 23; 7:47, 48; John 20:23b). When ἀφίημι bears this meaning, it is used in the aorist indicative only at Matt. 6:12 and Rom. 4:7, the latter of which is a citation from the LXX (there are six additional aorist subjunctives of ἀφίημι in the NT: Matt. 6:14, 15; 18:35; Mark 4:12; John 20:23a; 1 John 1:9). The perfect tense in 2:12 may imply stative importance, giving grammatical expression to "the speaker's conception of the verbal process as a state or condition" (Porter 1989: 257).

2:13. ℵ reads the neuter pronoun τό, in which case reference is to "evil" rather than to "the evil one." A single witness is unlikely to preserve the original wording. A scribal slip of hearing or seeing is the likely explanation of the variant.

2:14. Instead of NA[27]'s ἔγραψα, the 𝔐 group (joined by Old Latin and two Vulgate editions) reads γράφω as the first word of the verse. Metzger 1994: 640 speaks of scribal absentmindedness affected by the previous three present tenses. By external criteria, NA[27] is likely correct.

2:14. B and Ψ* along with Augustine (in some passages) read τό instead of τόν, so that reference is to "that which was from the beginning" instead of "him who was from the beginning." The thinly attested variant has the advantage of conforming more closely to the epistle's opening neuter reference to ὃ ἦν ἀπ' ἀρχῆς but is unlikely to have been original.

2:14. In an obvious scribal oversight, B leaves out the words τοῦ θεοῦ. Perhaps to the scribe the abiding word was self-evidently the word of God.

---

are hardly irrelevant for John's doctrine of the coming age). R. Brown 1982: 314 and Burge 1996: 116 argue for the eschatological overtones of 1 John 2:17.

2:15. Several minuscules read ἐν κόσμῳ rather than John's normal ἐν τῷ κόσμῳ (eight times in John's Gospel; cf. 1 John 2:16; 4:3, 4, 17). The shorter reading may be a scribal assimilation to Paul's typical ἐν κόσμῳ for "in the world" (Rom. 5:13; 1 Cor. 8:4; 14:10; Phil. 2:15; Col. 2:20; 1 Tim. 3:16; ἐν τῷ κόσμῳ occurs in Paul only at 2 Cor. 1:12; Eph. 2:12). Certain nouns like κόσμος might or might not take an article, with no difference in meaning (BDF §253.4). This is particularly the case when the noun is the object of a preposition (Wallace 1996: 247, with references to other grammars).

2:15. A, C, and some other witnesses read ἡ ἀγάπη τοῦ θεοῦ instead of ἡ ἀγάπη τοῦ πατρός. The secondary reading assures that divine and not familial love is in view. Minuscule 614 and a few other witnesses conflate the two readings, a good example of how some longer readings come into existence.

2:17. A, P, and several minuscules and versions omit αὐτοῦ, so that instead of "the world and the lust of the world" reference would be to "the world and lust" passing away. Since αὐτοῦ seems otiose, its omission is understandable.

2:17. A few manuscripts replace τοῦ θεοῦ with αὐτοῦ, and even fewer read τὸ θέλημα with no genitive at all. But there is no example of τὸ θέλημα without a modifying genitive in either John's Gospel or John's Epistles, and it is unlikely that he violated his custom here.

2:17. At the end of 2:17, some versions and patristic witnesses add "just as God abides forever." The reading voices a noble theological sentiment but remains unattested in Greek manuscripts.

I. Central Burden: God Is Light (1:1–2:6)
II. Primary Commandment: Embody the Age-Old Message (2:7–17)
➤ III. Key Counsel: Abide in His Anointing (Truth) and Receive Eternal Life (2:18–3:8)
IV. Core Teaching: Love, Works, Trust (3:9–4:6)
V. Foundational Imperative: God's Love (4:7–14)
VI. Illustrative Appeal: Renewed and Expanded Invitation to Love (4:15–5:15)
VII. Concluding Admonition: Pastoral Counsel, Assurance, and Warning (5:16–21)

III. Key Counsel: Abide in His Anointing (Truth) and Receive Eternal Life (2:18–3:8)

In the previous two sections, John set forth his foundational message—God is light (1:5)—and advanced a central corollary of that fact in the form of the love command (2:7–8). Although to some degree all of 1 John's sections contain each of the emphases—pistic, ethical, and agapic—outlined in the exegesis of 2:1a, the epistle's first section (1:1–2:6) focused on the pistic (what is true about God and Christ and therefore to be believed), and section II (2:7–17) stressed the ethical (what God in Christ commands and is therefore to be done).

But belief and embodied response, as vital as these are, in themselves yield an incomplete picture of the spirituality to which John calls his readers. An interpersonal axis extends (or not) from each human heart to the person of God, an axis marked by the reality and dynamic of love. Termed "agapic," from Greek ἀγάπη (*agapē*, love), this axis stretches forth like a bridge from God, its earthly terminus cemented in the human soul when the gospel of Christ is savingly believed. It is that bridgehead, that locus of God's presence in the heart and life of his people, that John is most concerned with in the present section (2:18–3:8).

An occasion for the key counsel that John now offers is the existence of perceived gospel enemies who at some earlier point left the community or communities that John addresses (2:19). The apparent earthquake of their departure has left aftershocks, and this explains John's allusion to the incident. Its vagueness suggests that we should not exaggerate the extent to which the epistle is primarily a reaction to this event or group. Other NT epistles that directly address the problem of gospel enemies are much more forthright that they are written for this reason—one thinks here of Galatians, the Corinthian correspondence, Jude, or perhaps even Hebrews. These treatises emit the heat of impassioned debate more or less from the outset and with more or less express reference to the problems raised by the respective troublemakers. First John is more to be compared with Colossians or the Thessalonians letters. Problems to address abound, but they are not the sole or primary raison d'être of the documents. In the case of 1 John, schism may precipitate but does not generate or even dominate the discourse.

In this section, taking up the walkout of former members as a point of shared interest and therefore a communicative bridge, John rather undertakes the positive task of explicating his readers' privilege to live in the strength of the "anointing" they have received (2:20, 27), which vouchsafes to them the eternal life they were promised (2:25). John's idiom for steadfast existence in this state of grace is "abiding." This state (and ultimately act) translates various verbs and participles related to the Greek word μένω (*menō*, to remain), a word that occurs twenty-four times in 1 John, with peak usage in the third chapter, as seen in this graph.

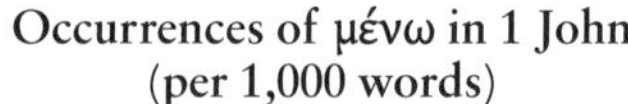

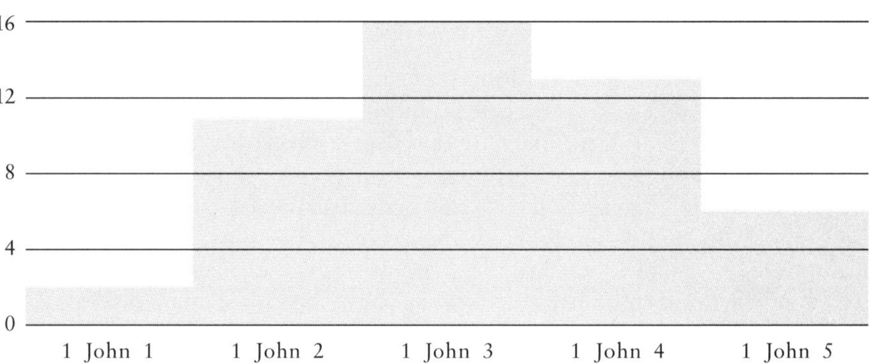

John's didactic counsel in the epistle is in some ways concentrated and summed up in this section's eight μένω passages (2:19, 24 [3x], 27 [2x], 28; 3:6). Their presence is not a bolt out of the blue, since the previous section assumed readers' awareness of the motif (2:6), commended them for the relational steadfastness associated with abiding in the light (2:10), mentioned the abiding work of the divine word in the believer (2:14), and contrasted the lustful world with the one who does God's will and therefore "abides forever" (2:17). But now the μένω passages, previously incidental to other themes, take on conceptual dominance in the flow of the discourse.

A. Three Considerations Informing the Counsel to Abide (2:18–21)

The message that "God is light" resulted in an ethical focus in the previous section. Now John's application of that message shifts to relational ground. At the outset the discourse is still in an indicative rather than hortatory mode (2:18–21), continuing in the same vein that marked the close of the preceding verses (2:16–17). Another point of contact with earlier verses is endearment language (first word of 2:18). But this subsection breaks new ground in explicating conditions both positive and negative that are relevant to the readers' exercise of steadfastness. Specifically, John begins to move from the ideal of the one who "abides forever" (2:17) to the command to let the message "abide" in his readers (2:24) by laying a foundation for the counsel that 2:18–3:8 as a whole contains. The subsection can be understood as follows:

1. Eschatological consideration in view of antichrist (2:18)
2. Ecclesiastical consideration in view of schism (2:19)
3. Charismatic consideration in view of anointing (2:20–21)

Exegesis and Exposition

18My dear little ones, it is the last hour, and just as you heard ⌜that⌝ antichrist is coming, even now many antichrists have arisen. By this we know that it is the last hour. 19They separated from us, but they were not part of us, for if ⌜they had been part of us⌝, they would have remained among us. But so that ⌜they might be seen for what they are⌝—that ⌜they were not all⌝ of us—they separated. 20But you have anointing from the Holy One, ⌜and you all understand⌝. 21I have written to you not because you do not understand the truth but because you do understand it, and because ⌜no⌝ lie comes from the truth.

1. Eschatological Consideration in View of Antichrist (2:18)

John's opening παιδία (*paidia*, little ones; see exegesis of 2:14) is another reminder of the emotional stake he has in his readers' spiritual welfare. The reality of a unique religion centered on redemptive love deserves underscoring in an age when the equivalency of all religions is frequently asserted. In John's time, at least, the religion he championed was quite different from surrounding outlooks[1] (which is not to deny that there were similarities, too).

1. Underscored, but also overstated, by H. Smith 2005: 10–11.

The message that John advances establishes a personal relationship with God through Jesus Christ (1:3). This God is known personally and intimately, cares for each of his worshipers, and unites them to other community members in a bond of love. Such a doctrine was virtually unknown in the Greco-Roman religions that were indigenous to Asia Minor. Bell (1994: 149) comments that the Egyptian goddess Isis, whose worship was widespread across the Roman Empire, "is virtually the only ancient divinity who displays any love or concern for her devotees." But even this did not translate into a community whose members' high calling was to love one another. The blessings of the mythological Isis pale in comparison to the promises of the real-world, incarnate Christ.

Similarly, Stoic philosophy of the day reflected an impersonal ideal. Life's goal was not to be united with others but to be free from the demands they might make. For the Roman moralist Seneca, "not to be disturbed" was a very high priority—to know "tranquility of mind" (Hadas 1961: 58). In Epictetus's teaching this called for maintaining distance from people and not being too attached to them, not even to wife and children (1961: 88–89). Very different is the Christian mandate of loving others (as John evidently cared for his "little ones") and finding joy even in sacrifice for them.

John is aware that the blessed status of steadfastness (abiding) in the will (2:17) and light (2:11) of this loving God because of the abiding divine word (2:24) cannot be taken for granted. Militating against his readers' well-being is, first, the very structure of temporal reality, for it is, he asserts, ἐσχάτη ὥρα (*eschatē hōra*, the last hour).[2]

In Johannine parlance, there seem to be three decisive "hours." The first was when Jesus laid down his life for the salvation of God's people (John 2:4; 7:30; 8:20; 12:23, 27; 13:1; 16:32; 17:1). J. Schneider (*TDNT* 2:673; cf. Strecker 1996: 62; Wallace 1996: 525) sees this as "fundamentally . . . not the hour of earthly human history, but the hour of divine salvation history," yet this distinction is foreign to John's thinking. The hour is both phenomenal and noumenal. The second was when Jesus through the Spirit would confirm to the apostles the meaning of Jesus's life and ministry for their gospel mandate (John 16:2, 4, 25). The third is yet to come, the time when Christ appears (cf. 1 John 2:28) and final judgment takes place (John 4:21, 23; 5:25, 28). In 1 John 2:18 John speaks as though this time of judgment might be imminent. He expresses his conviction that "his own time has an eschatological importance" (Schnackenburg 1992: 133). The tone is like Paul's characterizing his generation as the time "upon which the ends of the ages have come" (1 Cor. 10:11), a note echoed also by Peter (1 Pet. 4:7) and in Hebrews (9:26). John's sense of history at a crossroads is mainstream apostolic (cf. Kruse 2000: 98). "The apostle, after the common manner which Scripture adopts, warns believers that no more remained but for Christ to appear for the redemption of the world" (Calvin 1988: 255).

2. For the (unlikely) theory that the expression is a historicization of an existentialist historical perspective in John's Gospel, see Klein 1971.

How does John know this? In broad terms such prophetic admonition reflects OT convictions that could have informed John (cf. Schlatter 1950: 42). More directly, John's apocalyptic awareness might have come with the experience of having heard Jesus's preaching (which proclaimed the arrival of God's kingdom) and witnessed such eschatological harbingers as the Baptist's preaching (John 1:19–34), the sick being healed (4:46–54), the dead being raised (11:43), and the crucified Christ being resurrected (20:20).[3] If John was ministering around Ephesus late in the first century as he wrote 1 John, he was perhaps displaced from Judea by the Roman legions and would have seen Jesus's prediction of Jerusalem's razing (Matt. 24:2) fulfilled in unnerving fashion (cf. Schlatter 1950: 41). How could he not think that the end was near?[4]

In this context, however, John says it is because there have presently (νῦν, *nyn*, now) come to be many antichrists (ἀντίχριστοι πολλοὶ γεγόνασιν, *antichristoi polloi gegonasin*, many antichrists have come into being; cf. Schnackenburg 1992: 129). Jesus had taught his disciples to expect false prophets and false Christs (Matt. 24:11, 24; cf. Ellis 2000: 33). From the topics that John has broached thus far in this epistle, we can infer that he addresses readers in one or more churches that have been touched by the nemeses of ethical laxity and doctrinal aberration. Jesus's prophetic counsel seems to have been given for application to the world at hand, and that is exactly what John does if he is reasoning from Jesus's predictions to the apparent state of things as ripe for judgment. The antichrists, presumably, would be the ringleaders or leading devotees of church subgroups (so Rensberger 1997: 78) whose aims and practices are turning out to be unacceptable to norms and outcomes established under Christ's direct lordship by handpicked apostolic leaders like John (cf. Akin 2001: 115). Subsequent discourse will establish that the issue was in large measure christological (Culpepper 1998: 262, citing 1 John 4:1–2).

John says that his readers have already heard[5] that antichrist is coming. The Johannine Letters "are the earliest extant works to employ the technical term 'Antichrist'" (Jenks 1991: 328). Taken in conjunction with other occurrences of the title (2:22; 4:3; 2 John 7; the word does not occur elsewhere in the NT), it seems that an individual is in mind. "The Antichrist envisioned by the author of 1 John must have been conceived of as a supernatural being" (Lietaert Peerbolte 1996: 103). Who is this figure?[6] It is probably not directly related to "the Babylonian Tiamat opposed to Marduk" (Reinach 1930: 265). Lorein (2003: 232, 241) rather finds the basis for Second Temple antichrist beliefs, which inform NT beliefs, in the OT. This basis consists of five components: (1) "the concepts of the good and wicked prophet," (2) "the history of David and his opponents," (3) "the concepts of the good and wicked shepherd,"

3. Cf. Rensberger 1997: 77, citing 1 John 2:22: "Eschatological events had already occurred in the coming of Jesus the Messiah."

4. For discussion on John's sense of the end, see Burge 1996: 125–27.

5. Schnackenburg 1992: 133–34 notes that John's appeal here is "to the tradition, to the official Christian teaching."

6. Sloyan 1995: 28–29 surveys answers given across a wide slice of church history.

(4) "the horn," and (5) "the actions of Antiochus IV Epiphanes." Or in the words of Lietaert Peerbolte (1996: 113), the antichrist "tradition is probably a Christianisation of the Jewish tradition on an eschatological coming of Beliar."[7]

While Lorein (2003: 231) also argues that in the Johannine passages "it is not immediately clear whether we are actually dealing with an eschatological individual," the cumulative NT evidence seems to indicate at least eschatological overtones to his origin and activity (as he later seems to conclude; 2003: 236). He is likely a human representative or incarnation of the evil one whom Christ explicitly acknowledged in his teaching (Matt. 6:13), prayers (John 17:15), temptation, and elsewhere (e.g., 8:44). Paul spoke of this same sinister being (2 Thess. 3:3; cf. Sloyan 1995: 26–27). In the devil's service, he will exalt himself against God and Christ's kingdom (2 Thess. 2:1–12), perhaps following a pattern foreshadowed by Antiochus IV Epiphanes (1 Macc. 1:10–64), the Seleucid ruler who desecrated the temple and slaughtered God's people. His coming and wiles were seen as foretold in OT Scripture (Dan. 7:7–8, 21–22). The book of Revelation too "knows of one empowered by Satan who will oppose Christ in the last days" (Morris 1979: 40).[8] John's distinctive "many antichrists" apparently refers to forerunners of this end-time figure. They would be people of influence straying from the path of faith to which John and others bore testimony (cf. 1 John 1:1–4), leading others behind them on their ruinous course (cf. Thompson 1992: 75).

Early Christian writers identified the antichrist in various ways (for a fuller study, see Schnackenburg 1992: 135–39). Polycarp (early second century) has a threefold description of such a figure (*Phil.* 7; cf. Kruse 2000: 98n86; Lietaert Peerbolte 1996: 112). He first quotes 1 John 4:2–3: "For every one who shall not confess that Jesus Christ is come in the flesh is antichrist." He then issues two parallel warnings: "And whosoever shall not confess the testimony of the cross is of the devil; and whosoever shall pervert the oracles of the Lord to his own lusts and say that there is neither resurrection nor judgment, that man is the firstborn of Satan." John may have been near the beginning of a line of early Christians who kept their eyes peeled for opponents of Christ and the Christian message (see also Did. 16.3–5; Apocalypse of Peter 2), viewing them as opponents of Christ himself (hence the term "antichrist" in the sense of opponent of, rather than replacement for, Christ).

In the course of urging the steadfastness of abiding on his readers, then, John touches on an eschatological consideration that would not have been foreign to them because they had heard it before. Some things bear reiteration, however, and apparently John thinks that this is one of them. They must *remain* cognizant of the dark implications of antichrist's nearness, whether

7. On the other hand, "the Johannine epistles provide direct evidence for very few of the elements which comprised the Antichrist myth in later literature" (Jenks 1991: 341).

8. For references to antichrist in post-NT apocalyptic literature, see, e.g., the apocalypses of Daniel, Sedrach, Elijah, and Ezra (*OTP* 1:761–70, 609–13, 735–53, 571–79).

temporally or morally or both, if they wish to *remain* true to the faith as John will soon explicitly exhort them to do. "Each person ought to question his own conscience, whether he be an antichrist" (Augustine, *Hom. 1 John* 3.4).

But there is a further (and related) consideration: problems with views and movements in the Christian community that have disturbed the fellowship that John writes to promote (1 John 1:3). As John continues, "he confirms the faithful against offences which might have disturbed them" (Calvin 1988: 255; cf. Schlatter 1950: 40) and that are somehow abetted by antichrist's threat. With all due allowance for the love commandment, "at times erroneous teaching which is plainly at variance with the truth of the gospel has to be named, and its origins exposed" (Kruse 2000: 102).[9]

2. Ecclesiastical Consideration in View of Schism (2:19)

My argument here continues to be that 2:18–21 should be seen as an undergirding rationale for John's larger overarching counsel to remain or abide in what Christ's saving work and message mediate. In 2:19 John touches on a rift that has occurred—people have left the community. A breach, or schism, has taken place.

John speaks first of the fact of the schism: "They separated from us." The Greek word order, in which ἐξ ἡμῶν (*ex hēmōn*, from us) begins the sentence, may reflect John's conviction that the group he addresses, who maintain loyalty to the apostolic "we" (see 1:1–5) among whom John locates himself, was prior and primary—to paraphrase: "We were here first and doing fine; *they* were the ones who diverged and departed." The verb ἐξῆλθαν (*exēlthan*, they went out; on the -αν ending, see the second additional note on 2:19) is a euphemism or at least an understatement. The normal connotation of the verb ἐξέρχομαι can be joyous (Matt. 25:1; John 12:13) or suggestive of nothing more than spatial movement (Matt. 26:30; Luke 8:35; John 21:3; Acts 16:40). It can be a positive activity, as in 3 John 7's description of traveling missionaries: "It was for the sake of the name that they went out [ἐξῆλθον]" (NIV: cf. similar usage in 1 Clem. 42.3). But here it describes action more suggestive of such verbs as ἀφίημι (*aphiēmi*, to move away from, resulting in separation) or χωρίζω (*chōpizō*, to depart, leave, separate; see LN 1:187–90 for a graded range of possible expressions). BDAG 348 concedes here a use of ἐξέρχομαι amounting to "leave a congregation," proposing a discrete semantic category into which it also places 2 Cor. 6:17. John makes do with a simple and generic word rather than a more technically descriptive one, which might have had the effect of accusing or even condemning those who departed (note the pejorative effect of words that overtly describe morally dubious or even malicious departure in John 6:67 [ὑπάγω, *hypagō*] and Jude 6 [ἀπολείπω, *apoleipō*]). John is being diplomatic, alluding without histrionics to what has taken place.

9. Rensberger 1997: 78, 83 is seemingly critical of John's "rather bold move" of identifying proponents of false Christology with "the single expected false" Christ.

This restraint is too seldom noted in the literature and weakens the theory that sees polemics and bitter division as the essential dynamic of the letter. John, at least, is maintaining the calm spirit without which the message of love he upholds would become hypocrisy (see, e.g., Cyprian, *Epistle* 75.1, for an overly exclusivistic application of John's words).

If the first few words of the verse assert the fact of schism, the next few (ἀλλ' οὐκ ἦσαν ἐξ ἡμῶν, *all' ouk ēsan ex hēmōn*, but they were not of us) assert the meaning of that separation. People have left the community, in John's estimation, because in one or more fundamental respects they were not truly part of it (Kruse 2000: 102). John's language continues to be free of specific charges and colorful description, and therein lies its major challenge: who exactly went out? why? what were the issues? what did they do once they departed? With the evidence currently available, none of these questions can be answered with certainty. It can only be observed that repeatedly in this epistle, and with an inexorable cumulative effect, John has been sketching the parameters of authentic knowledge of God in Christ. There is one central saving fact of Christ's coming, but appropriate human response to it is variegated, involving not merely affirming words but also transformed wills and, with that, altered lives. Implicit in these parameters is a certain chain of transmission of the message on which all depends, from the Father to the Son to those chosen to witness (and witness to) the Son's saving work and proclamation.

John writes as one of the privileged apostolic testifiers, and the schism he describes makes tolerable sense if we think of it as refusal of some in the community to abide by the meaning and implications of the Christian gospel as John (along with other apostles) upheld it. Elsewhere in the NT, Acts 15 is an obvious example of how within the early church profound differences of opinion arose about how to understand and apply without essential attenuation the apostolic message. Second Corinthians reflects a similarly dire ecclesiastical setting in which, at least as Paul sent the letter, issues about the basic definition of gospel belief were very much in question. John's "but they were not of us" accounts for the breach of fellowship by asserting that those who made the break were simply showing their true colors (stressed by Tertullian, *Against Heretics* 3). At issue is not the possibility that faith in Christ admits of no unitary essential definition (for John it clearly does), or that the apostolic definition of it might be mistaken, or that the gospel's effect is to fragment rather than unite God's people. Those who have departed condemn themselves; they do not imperil the integrity of the Christ whom John represents. John's words are, then, words of assurance (so also Cyprian, *Epistle* 54.7). Flightiness and social dislocation need not deter his readers' resolve from the central ideal and virtue of abiding in what—and whom—they have received. In 1 John 3:4, 6, John may be sketching on an individual basis the contours of persons who have gone out; I will argue there that such persons are outside the pale of Christ's followers as the result of their willful apostasy.

If John's "they were not of us" is a word of assurance, interpreting the meaning of separation by some, his next words, "for if[10] they had been part of us, they would have remained among us," give at least the beginning of a reason for the schism. Quite simply, these people did not see fit to *remain* within the apostolic parameters that for John were inclusive of true Christians. The occurrence here of the verb μεμενήκεισαν (*memenēkeisan*, they would have remained; Moulton 1908: 148 thinks this pluperfect could as easily have been an aorist), whose root is μένω (*menō*), should not be overlooked in a context where the steadfastness implied by the verbal actions of remaining or abiding is the paraenetic center of the discourse.

But the reason for the schism is more complex than simply the unwillingness of some to remain steadfast. The last clause in the verse attempts a substantial though highly compressed characterization of a more fundamental reason why some have departed the community that, according to John, is intent on upholding the truth of Christ's incarnation and redemption: "But so that they might be seen for what they are—that they were not all of us—they separated."

On all accounts, it is agreed that the Greek text contains a considerable ellipsis here (on elliptical ἵνα, *hina*, see BDAG 476). One could translate literally, "But in order that they might be[11] manifest, that they are not all of us." This falls short of being a coherent sentence in that it is all predicate, or protasis, with no subject, or apodosis. Translations therefore rightly supply words to express what John must have assumed but did not bother to write (or dictate):

NIV	but their going showed that none of them belonged to us
Cassirer 1989	indeed . . . this was to make it evident that it is not everybody that belongs to our company
KJV	but they went out that they might be manifest that they were not all of us
JB	but they left us, to prove that not one of them ever belonged to us

While completing John's thought for him has proved not too daunting for translators, catching the force of John's logic is a less straightforward affair. It is not easy, at first glance, to appreciate why John bothers to make such a remark, unless it were just a vindictive expression of an I'm-right-and-they're-all-wrong sentiment. In principle this is a possibility, but there may be a better explanation.

John may be reflecting a conviction articulated by other NT writers and even by Jesus himself, a conviction that in turn has OT roots as well: God

10. The εἰ/ἄν (*ei*/*an*, if/then) combination signals a contrary-to-fact assertion; cf. Wallace 1996: 694–96. They are not, and in fact never had been, part of the community to which they ostensibly belonged (cf. Peterson and Williams 2004: 81).

11. The conviction that ἵνα is imperatival (Turner 1963: 95; Moule 1994: 145), so that the translation would be "must be," is followed by few if any translations. Wallace 1996: 477 mentions it as a possibility.

is continually at work showing forth his glory, and for his people this means their ongoing sifting and purifying (cf. Akin 2001: 117, who speaks of both purifying and educating). When ostensible members of the people of God turn away from the beliefs and practices authorized by God and subsequently depart the community, God is glorified in that the truth of who are his and who are not is revealed. Paul tells the Corinthians, "No doubt there have to be differences among you to show which of you have God's approval" (1 Cor. 11:19 NIV).

God is glorified in an immediate and then a potential sense. Immediately, as separation unfolds, gospel truth is highlighted via opposition to it. God's people who remain are kept from being overwhelmed by elements ultimately unfriendly to God as they hold the line on what they have received (cf. 1 Cor. 11:2). Potentially, out of such separation may come reconciliation, as those who part company later awaken to the error of their ways. John Mark left Paul (Acts 13:13) but later was restored to fellowship with him (Col. 4:10). Peter denied Christ (Matt. 26:75) but later reversed course. Paul holds out hope even for those who oppose apostolic doctrine because there is the chance "that God will grant them repentance leading them to a knowledge of the truth, and that they will come to their senses" (2 Tim. 2:25–26 NIV; cf. the incident alluded to in 2 Cor. 2:6–11). None of this could have taken place if the reality of separation, whether ideological or spatial or both, had not been underscored. The pain of an open parting of the ways (unavoidable even under Jesus's own direct leadership; see, e.g., John 6:66) can be the necessary prelude to a higher level of community cohesion and doctrinal integrity.[12]

3. Charismatic Consideration in View of Anointing (2:20–21)

John now takes up matters relating to the "charism" implicit in eternal life in Christ. That is, he speaks of the "anointing" (χρῖσμα, *chrisma*; found in the NT only here and twice in 2:27) that believers have received (2:20) and the implications of it for his readers' steadfastness in "the truth" (2:21). In the wake of eschatological (2:18) and ecclesiastical (2:19) considerations, John now points to a charismatic reason why his readers ought indeed to abide. The force of this reason, in turn, lies in several components: the anointing itself, the anointing's source, and the anointing's effect.

The Anointing

The first word of 2:20, καί (*kai*), is adversative and appropriately translated "but" (see exegesis of 1:6). The contrast is between those who went out (2:19)

12. Bede (in Bray 2000: 188) likens the separation to the benefit of the removal of a tumor. The language of Calvin 1988: 258 will scandalize some but repays reflection: "He tells them that the trial of the Church is useful and necessary. From this it follows . . . that there is no good reason for worrying. The Church is like a threshing-floor and the chaff has to be blown away so that the pure wheat may remain. This is what God does when He casts hypocrites out of the Church, for He cleanses it from rubbish and filth."

and those who remain and therefore constitute John's readership. The contrast is probably underscored by the second word of the verse: ὑμεῖς (*hymeis*, you [plural]). This often superfluous but in this case emphatic[13] pronoun has the effect of heightening the distinction between those who departed and those who remain.

These readers "have an anointing." This probably refers to the effect of the apostolic message they have received (La Potterie 1959, who defends a metaphorical interpretation; others opt for a ritual interpretation—the "anointing" is baptism or some other rite [Lietaert Peerbolte 1996: 100]).[14] Clearly John treats this anointing as beneficial. The reason may be near to hand in the sacred writings of the Jewish people with which John was familiar both as a Jew and as a follower of Jesus.

John would have been aware that from the days of Moses fine olive oil was rubbed or poured on objects to mark them off for God's special use. That is, these objects were anointed. Aaron and his sons were anointed in like fashion for their service in the tent of meeting: "They shall minister to me as priests, and it will be that they will have an anointing of priesthood forever" (Exod. 40:15; related LXX uses of χρῖσμα are found in 29:7; 30:25 [2x]; 35:15 [2x] [35:14, 19 LXX]; 40:9). The connection between the priests' anointing and the expectation that they would "continue" in God's service and blessing is worth noting in light of John's focus on abiding in the same section of 1 John in which he speaks of Christians' anointing.

Later in the history of Israel, prophets like Samuel anointed men chosen by God to be king. David was honored in this way. On that occasion the Holy Spirit "came upon David in power" (1 Sam. 16:13). Still later, and in John's very lifetime, Jesus Christ, the Son of David, was viewed by the early Christians as God's Anointed One par excellence (Acts 4:26; cf. Ps. 2:2 NIV: "The kings of the earth take their stand and the rulers gather together against the LORD and against his Anointed One").

13. The second-person plural nominative of the Greek personal pronoun appears six times in John's Letters, all in 1 John and all arguably with emphatic force: 1:3; 2:20, 24 (2x), 27; 4:4. Analogous emphatic uses of ὑμεῖς are not absent from John's Gospel, where the form occurs sixty-eight times and appears to have emphatic force at, e.g., 1:26; 3:28; 4:20, 22; 6:67; 7:8, 47; 8:15; 9:27; 18:31; 19:6, 35.

14. An ancient and still-prominent view equates the anointing of 2:20 with the Holy Spirit (e.g., Augustine, *Hom. 1 John* 3.5, who goes on to equate the Spirit with the sacrament; Holtzmann 1908: 336; Persson 1990; Burge 1996: 128; Culpepper 1998: 262; Kruse 2000: 103, 109–10; Akin 2001: 118). Since saving knowledge of God is not possible without the Holy Spirit, the theology implied in this view is not wrong. But *in this context* John's reference seems primarily to the teaching that believers have received. The Holy Spirit has not even been mentioned in the epistle so far, whereas the apostolic word and message has been a recurrent theme. Nor is it necessary to equate anointing with the Holy Spirit to make sense of 2:27. If any background theological concept informs the word "anointing," it is perhaps as likely to be election (because of the close correlation between anointing as reflecting God's choosing) or the grace implicit in the illumination of the heart with the gospel message.

As John writes[15] to believers who "have anointing from the Holy One" who was himself anointed, it is hard to imagine him not recalling this heritage of blessing and setting apart for service dating back both to Christ's own life and then many centuries earlier to God's people in OT times.[16] The climactic coming of the "Anointed One" (Greek χριστός, *christos*, from which derives the title "Christ") results in a whole community that revels in a derivative anointing. While some have recently departed from their community, John addresses those who remain. As they listen to the apostolic message in which John's epistle confirms them, their anointing is a source of comfort and hope.

The Anointing's Source

The anointing is ἀπὸ τοῦ ἁγίου (*apo tou hagiou*, from the Holy One). The adjective "holy" (ἅγιος, *hagios*) occurs nowhere else in John's Epistles. Here it is used substantivally (Wallace 1996: 294–95). In the LXX the same prepositional phrase refers to God's dwelling place, whether the holy of holies (Ezra 2:63; Neh. 7:65) or his heavenly abode (Isa. 26:21; Jer. 25:30 [32:30 LXX]). Yet 1 John 2:27 makes clear that the anointing John has in mind derives from a person, not a place. The conviction that his readers can and will weather the storm of the recent separation, and abide in what they have received (2:24), is grounded not least in this exalted figure bestowing on them their privileged status.

"The Holy One" in the OT is God himself (Ps. 71:22; Hab. 1:12; 3:3), often linked with his people in the phrase "the Holy One of Israel" (about thirty OT occurrences, mostly in Isaiah). This Holy One taught his people (Isa. 48:17) and bestowed splendor or glory on them (55:5; 60:9). This parallels the didactic and gifting functions of the Holy One in 1 John 2:20, 27. New Testament occurrences of "the Holy One" are sparse but telling. In Mark 1:24 (cf. Luke 4:34) "the Holy One of God" is Jesus, confessed as such by a demoniac in the synagogue. In John 6:69 NIV, Peter states to Jesus that he and other disciples "believe and know that you are the Holy One of God" (cf. 1 Pet. 1:15, drawing on Lev. 11:44; Balla 2006: 216). "The Holy One" is also the Christ who speaks through his angel to the church in Philadelphia (Rev. 3:7).

John's Gospel is perhaps most helpful in delimiting the meaning of "from the Holy One" in 1 John 2:20. The adjective "holy" occurs there only five times. Three times it refers to the Holy Spirit (John 1:33; 14:26; 20:22), once to Jesus (6:69), and once to God the Father (17:11). These references, in light of the context of 1 John 2:20, suggest that John could have in mind Christ, God, the Spirit, or some combination of the three viewed in their joint function.[17] The outcome is the same, whichever referent be chosen: God himself

15. Ἔγραψα in 1 John 2:21 is an epistolary aorist; see also 2:14, 26; 5:13. It appears to mean much the same thing as John's first-person present tense γράφω (1:4; 2:1, 7, 8, 12, 13 [2x]), allowing for slight differences in particular contexts.

16. Extra-OT Jewish literature refers to anointing in 2 Enoch 22.8–9 (cf. Strecker 1996: 66), but this appears to have little direct relevance to 1 John.

17. Calvin 1988: 259 relates the anointing to all three persons of the Godhead. Sloyan 1995: 27 and Rensberger 1997: 80 think it is either God or Christ. Akin 2001: 119 opts for Jesus but

has graced them in such a way that the departure of some need not demoralize those who are still standing fast.

The Anointing's Effect

The anointing has a prominent cognitive dimension—"and you all understand" (2:20; see additional note for discussion of textual variants). The separation would have sown confusion and was doubtless precipitated by *mis*understanding, whether inadvertent or willful. John reminds those who have remained of the knowledge latent in their God-given anointing. The understanding implied in the verb used here (οἴδατε, *oidate*, you understand) plays a noteworthy role in 1 John, occurring fifteen times in thirteen verses:

1 John	Form	Translation	Comment
2:11	οἶδεν	he does not understand where he is going	Hatred and darkness obscure an understanding that spawns love and light.
2:20	οἴδατε	you all understand	Divine anointing results in an understanding that enables steadfastness.
2:21 (2x)	οἴδατε	[John writes] not because you do not understand the truth but because you do understand it	The understanding that God gives admits of augmentation, as, for example, from the apostolic writer here.
2:29	εἰδῆτε	if you understand that he is righteous	An initial level of understanding of God's character may be requisite for right discernment of human behavior.
3:2	οἴδαμεν	we know that when he appears	The understanding that God gives extends to things promised but not yet seen.
3:5	οἴδατε	you know that he appeared so that he might take away our sins	The understanding that God gives extends to the effects of the atonement.
3:14	οἴδαμεν	we know that we have passed from death to life	The understanding that God gives extends to things promised but not yet seen.
3:15	οἴδατε	you know that no murderer has eternal life	The understanding that God gives enables practical discernment.
5:13	εἰδῆτε	[John writes] so that you may know that you have eternal life	The understanding that God gives enables assurance of eternal life.
5:15 (2x)	οἴδαμεν	if we know that he hears us, . . . we know that we have what we asked of him	The understanding that God gives has a role in the mechanics of prayer.
5:18	οἴδαμεν	we know that anyone born of God does not continue to sin	The understanding that God gives enables practical discernment.
5:19	οἴδαμεν	we know that we are children of God	The understanding that God gives enables assurance of eternal life.
5:20	οἴδαμεν	we know that the Son of God has come and has given us understanding	The understanding that God gives confirms facts about the incarnation and its fruits.

underscores that the difference is insignificant "due to the intimate fellowship that exits between the Father and the Son" in John's understanding.

The table shows that a strong point of contact between John and his readers is the understanding that their shared experience of the gospel message (see 1:5) imparts. The understanding is both factual and doctrinal in nature. As I suggested in the exegesis of 2:1a, knowledge alone is not a sufficient condition for full-orbed Christian life; perhaps the devil himself would grant a measure of validity to the facts tabulated above (cf. James 2:19). But for John it appears to be a necessary condition. The Holy One's anointing brings powerful and specific cognitive entailments. John takes heart in, and encourages his readers with, what he knows they grasp and will resonate with as his pastoral counsel continues.

The subsection consisting of 2:20–21 concludes with a statement too weighty to be called an afterthought yet sufficiently secondary to be called parenthetical. The first half ("I have written to you not because you do not understand the truth but because you do understand it") reflects diplomatic savvy (not helplessness in the face of an "egalitarian" church order [so Rensberger 1997: 82], which makes it impossible for John to "teach the readers").[18] Dominical and apostolic authority are effective when administered with a shepherd's care rather than a tyrant's force (cf. John 10:1–17; 13:1; 1 Thess. 2:7–9). Addressing a community that has until recently harbored those of deviant belief or practice or both, John knows that reasserting apostolic truth is a delicate undertaking. He must not alienate readers by seeming to talk down to them. So in good faith—love hopes all things (1 Cor. 13:7)—he affirms his solidarity with them, no doubt seeking to rally reciprocal response (to say that his aim is to "arm" them against those who have left [so Kruse 2000: 97, 102] may be questioned; John's aim seems more to stir up zeal for truth and love than to furnish weaponry). His counsel assumes not their ignorance but their sophistication in the matters at hand. They understand the truth (for truth as the testimony of divinely chosen eyewitnesses, see exegesis of 1:1–3), and because of this he writes with confidence. Admittedly, like other apostles John is zealous to broaden the base of believers' practical and doctrinal comprehension (cf. Phil. 1:9; 1 Thess. 3:12; 4:1, 10; 2 Pet. 1:8; 3:18).

John writes with confidence also for a second reason: "no lie comes from the truth."[19] I suggest "comes from" (cf. TEV, NIV/TNIV, JB, HCSB, NRSV) rather than the literal "is from" or "is of" (KJV, RSV, ESV) because John seems to be stressing not just the existence but also the point of origin of this lie; "comes" conveys the sense of originating somewhere and going forth without in any way denying that the lie "is." John has already implied that lying and

18. Culpepper 1998: 262 likewise stresses the egalitarian impulse that causes John to "show that his authority is limited." This is to impute weakness to words behind which in reality stands great strength (cf. 1 Cor. 4:21). Loader 1992: 30 notes that with this remark John "in no way has . . . abdicated his own teaching role!"

19. The Greek words πᾶν ψεῦδος ἐκ τῆς ἀληθείας οὐκ ἔστιν could be rendered "every lie is not of the truth." But English translations rightly shape the wording differently to avoid an awkward locution that would add nothing in accuracy or rhetorical force.

liars are, or until recently have been, part of the social context he addresses (1:6, 10; 2:4). He is about to elaborate on this very problem (2:22; cf. 4:20; 5:10). He writes to those who have not departed, who have remained steadfast because of the understanding they have embraced (2:20). That understanding encompasses truth (see exegesis of 1:8) that excludes what is not true; what his readers have endorsed in the Christian message cannot be the source of the untruths that have bedeviled their community and split their ranks. "No lie comes from the truth" that they have affirmed. This is the bedrock that John builds on as he shifts the discussion in the next section from lies that cannot be true to the truth that remains steadfast and gives his readers a basis for doing likewise.

Additional Notes

2:18. Some few manuscripts (among them A, L, 1881) replace ὅτι with ὁ in the phrase ὅτι ἀντίχριστος ἔρχεται. This confers on the antichrist a more definite identity but does not account for the presence of ὅτι in all other manuscripts. Some (ℵ*, B, C, Ψ, 1739) have ὅτι with no definite article. This is the shorter reading and is preferred in NA[27]. ℵ[2], 33, and 𝔐 read ὅτι ὁ. It is possible that this is original, and that ℵ*, B, C, Ψ, and 1739 represent an economizing that does not change the meaning but streamlines the diction. Elsewhere ἀντίχριστος in the singular always has a definite article (1 John 2:22; 4:3; 2 John 7). Ὅτι is recitative, and because it introduces indirect discourse, the present tense ἐστίν is appropriate (Wallace 1996: 458, 539).

2:19. Ἐξῆλθαν is one of sixteen occurrences of the third-person plural form of ἐξέρχομαι in the NT. Only in Acts 16:40 does the identical ἐξῆλθαν appear; in the other fourteen cases (including John 4:30; 12:13; 21:3; 2 John 7; 3 John 7; Rev. 9:3; 15:6) the form is ἐξῆλθον. Like Luke (cf. ἐξῆλθον in Luke 8:35), John can use either form. The -αν suffix (common in the LXX and a striking departure from Classical Greek; see Conybeare and Stock 1905: 35–36) is the result of the first aorist ending -σαν being added to the second aorist stem (*sigma* drops out after *theta*). This form was used to distinguish the third-person plural from the identical first-person singular form (ἐξῆλθον). The -ον suffix was the more prevalent second aorist ending.

2:19. Manuscripts are divided on the word order ἐξ ἡμῶν ἦσαν (NA[27], following some half dozen witnesses, among them B and C). 𝔐, ℵ, A, P, and numerous patristic witnesses read ἦσαν ἐξ ἡμῶν. The latter may be slightly smoother and could have become prevalent for that reason. NA[27]'s reading appears to throw emphasis on the prepositional phrase (see exegesis).

2:19. A very few manuscripts read φανερωθῇ (third-person singular) instead of φανερωθῶσιν (third-person plural). The former reading makes sense ("but in order that it might be manifest that . . ."), and the singular form is found soon thereafter in 1 John 2:28 and 3:2, but it is too weakly attested to be considered original.

2:19. Some of the same manuscripts that select φανερωθῇ (see previous additional note) omit πάντες in the phrase εἰσὶν πάντες. Attestation for the shorter reading is too weak to take seriously and may be explained as an expedient to make better sense of the φανερωθῇ already chosen by copyists. A few Latin and Syriac witnesses assume that ἦσαν stood where NA[27] reads εἰσὶν πάντες, but no Greek copies preserve this reading, which makes it unlikely to have been original.

2:20. Apparently the difficulty of the idea of believers knowing all things, or the obscurity of all believers knowing (knowing what?), occasioned some textual turbulence in the clause καὶ οἴδατε πάντες. Here are the options:

Reading	Translation	Witnesses
οἴδατε πάντες	you all know	B, Sahidic
καὶ οἴδατε πάντα	and you know all things	A, C, (049), 33, 1739, 𝔐 (partial list)
καὶ οἴδατε πάντες	and you all know	ℵ, P, Ψ (very few others)

The first reading may be omitted as too sparsely attested. The second may have suggested itself because it expresses an idea found elsewhere in Scripture (see exegesis of 2:20–21). But it cannot be completely ruled out as expressing an apostolic teaching that seemed less subversive prior to later gnosticism than it did afterward; D. Black 1992 defends the reading. The third reading has B (in essence) and ℵ on its side, but otherwise support is not strong. Here copyists in the wake of gnostic controversy could conceivably have changed πάντα to πάντες. It is difficult to decide between the second and third readings, since both make contextual sense, and witnesses are strong on both sides (barring unreasonable prejudice in favor of the ℵ-B combination).

2:21. Codex C omits πᾶν from the phrase πᾶν ψεῦδος. This singular reading is clearly a scribal miscue.

B. The Truth That Abides (2:22–26)

I am arguing that the present section (2:18–3:8) urges readers to abide in the truth and receive eternal life. This is in the wake of affirmation that God is light (1:1–2:6) and that he commands his followers to love (2:7–17). How is this to be achieved? John's counsel in 2:18–3:8 seems straightforward: by abiding in the truth.

The counsel seems feasible because the readers have been anointed (2:20), resulting in understanding sufficient for the challenges they face. Yet 2:21 with its mention of falsehood serves notice that the readers' grasp of the truth is by no means unchallenged. There are counterfeit construals of the Christian message to contend with. First John 2:22–26 serves as a parenthesis to clarify details that are pertinent to the counsel John is offering. The parenthetic nature of these verses is indicated by the rhetorical flow that frames them beginning and end in an A-B-B′-A′ pattern:

A you have an anointing
  B I am not writing to you because . . .
  B′ I am writing to you . . .
A′ the anointing you received . . .

Within this rhetorical bracketing, John explicates the truth that his readers, in his view, understand (2:21). To make it possible for this truth to remain intact, John identifies "the liar" (presumably the source of the lies implied in 2:21) in 2:22, contrasts the liar with the person who makes a true confession (2:23), urges his readers to abide in what they have received (2:24–25), and brings the parenthesis to a close with a declaration of why he felt constrained to touch on such matters (2:26). The subsection therefore breaks down like this:

1. Who the liar is (2:22)
2. Who is on the side of the truth (2:23)
3. Who will abide in the truth and their reward (2:24–25)
4. Who imperils those seeking to abide (2:26)

Exegesis and Exposition

[22]Who is the liar? It is none other than the one who expresses the denial, "Jesus is not the Christ!" This person is the antichrist, the one who denies the Father and the

Son. [23]Anyone who denies the Son does not have the Father, either; ⌜the one who confesses the Son has the Father too⌝. [24][But as for] you⌜ ⌝, that which you heard from the beginning—let it abide in you! If that which you heard from the beginning abides in you, you too will abide ⌜in the Son and in the Father⌝. [25]And this is the promise that he himself promised ⌜to us⌝: eternal life. [26]I⌜ ⌝ write these things to you concerning those who are trying to deceive you.

1. Who the Liar Is (2:22)

Mention of "lie" in 2:21 now prompts a brief excursus on the profile of those who promulgate the untruth that John apparently has in mind. He enlarges on the matter by means of a rhetorical question: "Who is the liar?" (on John's apparently bitter language, see exegesis of 2:4). The word ψεύστης (*pseustēs*, liar) is found elsewhere in the NT only at John 8:44, 55; Rom. 3:4; 1 Tim. 1:10; Titus 1:12; 1 John 1:10; 2:4; 4:20; 5:20 and in the LXX only at Ps. 116:11 [115:2 LXX]; Prov. 19:22; Sir. 15:8; 25:2. In early post-NT times, being a liar is discouraged for pragmatic reasons (Did. 3.5; Herm. *Sim.* 6.5.5). But in 1 John 2:22, the folly of the liar is connected with theological, not ethical, shortcoming (cf. Tertullian, *Against Praxeas* 28).

In other Johannine passages εἰ μή (*ei mē*) can be translated "except" (e.g., John 3:13; 6:46; 14:6; 17:12) or "if not" (e.g., 9:33; 15:22; 18:30). But here it should be understood as mirroring LXX usage in which εἰ μή in the sense of "verily" precedes a virtual oath (LEH 172; see Judg. 11:10; 1 Kings 20:23 [21:23 LXX]; 2 Kings 5:20; 9:26; Job 12:10; 22:20; Jer. 15:11; 48:27 [31:27 LXX]; Ezek. 5:11; 20:39; for NT parallels, see Gal. 1:7; 1 Cor. 7:17; possibly Rom. 14:14; Eph. 4:9; Heb. 3:18). This yields the translation "it is none other than . . ." (or less idiomatically "verily, it is . . ."). First John 5:5 offers a similar construction that calls for a similar translation. The liar's identity and status are obvious and definite, given a particular indicator.

That indicator is a denial. The liar denies that Jesus is the Christ. The verbal action implied in the substantival participle ὁ ἀρνούμενος (*ho arnoumenos*, the one who denies) is best rendered intransitively (contra BDAG 132), making the following ὅτι (*hoti*) recitative. This in turn allows the statement Ἰησοῦς οὐκ ἔστιν ὁ χριστός (*iēsous ouk estin ho christos*, Jesus is not the Christ) to be understood as a direct quotation.[1] Analogous intransitive use of a form of ἀρνέομαι (*arneomai*, to deny) followed by ὅτι is found at Matt. 26:72 ("he denied with an oath, 'I do not know the man!'"; cf. 26:70; Mark 14:68; Luke 22:57). Another close parallel is John 1:20 ("he did not deny but confessed, 'I am not the Christ'"; cf. 18:25, 27).[2]

1. This differs, then, from the widespread view (e.g., Strecker 1996: 68 with note 39) that we are dealing here with a double negative. Painter 2002: 200 gets the right sense in his translation: "Who is the liar if not the person who denies [saying] the Christ is not Jesus?"

2. BDAG 132 rightly notes that the opposite of ἀρνέομαι in such contexts is ὁμολογέω (*homologeō*, to admit, say yes). For intransitive ὁμολογέω followed by ὅτι recitative and a quotation, see Matt. 7:23 and possibly Acts 24:14; 1 John 4:15.

The person who proclaims this anticonfession is the antichrist (see exegesis of 2:18). This means not that he is the one and only antichrist but rather that he is one of the many antichrists that John has already said have made their appearance. Such persons deny "the Father and the Son." Here the verbal action implied in the participial construction ὁ ἀρνούμενος is transitive. The emphasis shifts from the act of denial to what the denial repudiates. It repudiates Jesus's messiahship, which for John apparently entails also the near equivalency of Father and Son. The logic of 2:22 seems to be this: the one who rejects that Jesus is the Messiah = the antichrist = the one who denies the Father and the Son. (On Jesus as God's Son, see exegesis of 3:7–8.)

Jesus's de facto oneness with the Father—his sonship implying essential oneness with God (cf. John 5:18)—is an issue in John's Gospel from the prologue (1:1–18) onward and was understandably denied, indeed attacked, from the earliest days of postresurrection Christian preaching (cf. Irenaeus, *Ag. Her.* 3.15.5, who cites this portion of 1 John against "these blasphemous systems which divide the Lord"). Hardly less prominent in John is the issue of Jesus's kingship, his identity as Messiah (μεσσίας, *messias*, occurs in the whole NT only twice, both times in John [1:41; 4:25]). The word "king" with reference to Jesus occurs in Matthew (seven times), Mark (six times), and Luke (five times) considerably less frequently than in John's Gospel (sixteen times). Whereas God glorified Jesus by vindicating his status as both Son of David (or Messiah) and Son of God (cf. Rom. 1:1–7), detractors handed him over to death by disowning him (Acts 3:13–14) and rejecting (7:35) the proposition that he was Israel's chosen one (or anointed king: the meaning of "Christ"). These passages in Acts use ἀρνέομαι to describe denial-type disavowal.

A considerable amount of theological conviction is packed into the few lines of 1 John 2:22. This is not surprising. John is intimately familiar with and committed to Christ and to the theological verities that undergird the message his letter bears (1:5). He writes to urge that message on apparently wavering readers. He can speak of the central importance of Jesus being "the Christ" (cf. 5:1) without any qualification or explanation;[3] apparently it is common coin in the Christian circle(s) he addresses. Naysayers are jeopardizing the integrity of Christian faith with flat negations of the *conditio sine qua non* of authentic Christian existence (so also Kruse 2000: 105). The sudden segue from 2:21 to 2:22 may be literarily abrupt, but the reader sympathetic to John's christological convictions can probably intuit the psychological justification for the direction in which he veers and the bluntness of his rhetoric.

2. Who Is on the Side of the Truth (2:23)

First John 2:22 identifies the liar, the antichrist, the archdenier, as the person who "denies the Father and the Son" by rejecting Jesus's messiahship. First

3. "Christ" occurs eight times in 1 John, but six times it is preceded by the word "Jesus" (1:3; 2:1; 3:23; 4:2; 5:6, 20).

John 2:23 drives this point home by making a negative and then a positive statement.

The negative statement asserts that to deny the Son means not to "have the Father, either." "Have the Father" means to be heir of the privileges passed down through a family heritage. John the Baptist's detractors appear to have refused his baptism on the basis of the statement "we have Abraham as our father" (Matt. 3:9; Luke 3:8). They were, they felt, already Abraham's descendants, with the rights and privileges appertaining thereunto, to put it in legal terms. Later, Jesus's Jerusalem opponents made a similar claim, not about Abraham but about God: "We have one Father [ἕνα πατέρα ἔχομεν, *hena patera echomen*]—God!" (John 8:41). Their language bears comparison with τὸν πατέρα ἔχει (*ton patera echei*, has the Father) in 1 John 2:23. But Jesus discounted this claim because they rejected him (John 8:42). First John 2:23 employs similar logic: not to embrace ("have") the Son is a de facto disavowal of the Father.

For John, what it means to "have the Father" likely is closely tied to what the Father "has" and then bestows on his people. It seems to work like this: the Father has (eternal) life. Then, "as the Father has life in himself, so he has granted the Son to have life in himself" (John 5:26 NIV). This life shared by Father and Son is in a subsequent step available to humans—John's epistle began by testifying to the appearance and proclamation of it (1 John 1:3). Issuing from this life and then extended to penitent sinners through the gospel message, believers "have" (ἔχω, *echō*) the following benefits according to 1 John: fellowship (1:3, 6, 7), an advocate (2:1), the command to love (2:7; 4:21), anointing (2:20), confidence (2:28; 3:21; 4:17; 5:14), hope (3:3), God's love (4:16), acceptance of God's testimony about himself (5:10), eternal life (5:12, 13), and answers to requests made in prayer (5:15). This does not exhaust, though it does characterize, things *not* possessed by the one who denies the Son (2:23) by disputing Jesus's messiahship (2:22). That person has forfeited the blessing of the Father that the Son mediates. Denial of Jesus's messiahship, if he really was the Messiah, carries grave implications.

The second half of 2:23 makes a positive assertion. Like the first half, it is to be understood against the background of 2:22. There the issue was whether Jesus is the Christ. The liar says no. The Gospels record that this was a disputed question during and immediately after Jesus's life in his native environs. As the gospel went forth into the Roman world, the theological question was doubtless complicated by the sociological scandal of universal salvation (2:2) coming through one particular people, and a people widely despised in the ancient world at that. How could it be that "salvation is of the Jews" (John 4:22)? Just as Judaism was divided into largely disparate sects, pagan intellectual authorities found little agreement on the most fundamental questions about the gods (e.g., Cicero, *Nature of the Gods* 1.1–5). Overall, if to "have the Father" means to know God personally and assuredly and savingly, then it can be said that there was a great deal of confusion as to what "have the Father" means. For that reason there would have been widespread agreement on what "have the Father" could *not* mean: it could hardly mean something as straightforward, definite, and restrictive as John's message claimed—that the key to having the Father was acknowledging and confessing that in Jesus of Nazareth the promised Christ of God had come. For a variety of reasons, this proved not to be very palatable for either Jews or pagans. But confession of Jesus and truths about him is at the core of 1 John's claims (see exegesis of 4:2–3, 15–16). This is plausibly traceable to Jesus's own claim that to "confess" him has eschatological consequences (Matt. 10:32), a notion that only gained strength as the early church expanded (Rom. 10:9–10; cf. 2 Clem. 3.4; 4.3; Pol. *Phil.* 7.1; Martyrdom of Polycarp 12.1; Herm. *Sim.* 9.28.7; Ign. *Smyrn.* 5.2).

3. Who Will Abide in the Truth and Their Reward (2:24–25)

In 2:24–25 John's key counsel, to be most plainly stated in 2:28, is mooted more explicitly than anywhere else in the epistle thus far: "But as for you, that which you heard from the beginning—let it abide in you!" (2:24) "But as for" is not in the Greek text but may be inferred from the flow of the discourse. First John 2:22–23 is third person and descriptive; 2:24 is second person and hortatory. Many Greek manuscripts add οὖν (*oun*, therefore) to mark tangibly the patent discourse shift (see first additional note on 2:24). I have chosen "but as for" to reflect this shift as well as to call attention to the emphatic reference to "you" that begins the Greek sentence (on emphatic ὑμεῖς [*hymeis*], see exegesis of 2:20–21, including footnote 13).

What they "heard from the beginning" is not the same as "what was from the beginning" in 1 John 1:1 (see exegesis of 1:1). The exegesis of 2:7 explored the various uses of the phrase "from the beginning," including the time when a particular individual or group first heard and received the gospel (1 John 2:7; 2 John 5–6), the category in which 1 John 2:24's occurrences likely belong. All along there has been a certain quality, intent, efficacy, and consistency characterizing the saving message they embraced. They should continue to let it do its work and not seek to make drastic revisions in the message or their response to it now. Paul uses a similar rhetorical strategy with the Corinthians (1 Cor. 15:1–8; cf. Kruse 2000: 107). The departure of some members (1 John 2:19) and the threat of false teaching and teachers (2:18, 21–23) give John's advice its point.

The readers, or at least the "young men" among them, have already been commended for letting "the Word of God abide [NIV: live]" in or among them (2:14; on "in you," see exegesis of 2:27). They have been assured that "the one who does the will of God abides [NIV: lives] forever" (2:17). In both cases the NIV captures an important dimension of what μένω (*menō*, to remain, abide) connotes. But "live" and "abide" are slightly different. The former term is more generic; the latter term connotes a particular mode of living in which Christ himself is the root and branches upon which human lives are dependent like leaves on a grapevine. This is the imagery of John 15, a passage that crystallizes and defines the "abide" concept in John's cognitive world as known to us from his writings. There Jesus utters the word "abide" (or a form of it) eleven times in seven verses. To abide is to be assured fruitfulness (15:4 [3x], 5; cf. 15:16), preservation from destruction (15:6), and hearing of petitions (15:7a). With his words abiding in them (15:7b; cf. 5:38; 8:31), believers are to abide in Christ and in Christ's love (15:9). They are promised that if they obey his commands (15:10a), they will remain in his love, just as he obeyed the Father's commands and remained in his love (15:10b).

John's strategy for steadfastness in 1 John 2:24 is, then, well founded in past dominical instruction and precedent. And in the same vein he continues, "If that which you heard from the beginning abides in you, you too will abide in the Son and in the Father." To abide in the Son and Father is akin to "having" the Father by confessing the Son à la 2:23. John describes a state of blessedness. It should be underscored that the blessing is the direct result of the word of God (or of Christ; Sloyan 1995: 30), which takes the initiative and carries saving force, not the labor of human abiding, however successful, itself; John's understanding of the salvation process is consistently monergistic (worked by God alone) and not synergistic (the result of God and humans working together on substantially equal terms; Yarbrough 1995). This is not to say that human response is unnecessary for John, but at no point does John view human response to the saving message as on par with the message itself. Nor does he regard people as competent to render decisions by which they save themselves through autonomous appropriation of the message. Rather, human response, when it arises, is always conditioned and brought forth by the Word. In a famous Reformation-era debate, it is likely that Erasmus would have found John siding with Luther (Winter 1966).

Rhetorically his stress is on the addressees, with emphatic ὑμεῖς (*hymeis*, you [plural]—a hanging nominative or *nominativus pendens* according to Moulton 1908: 69) heading up both halves of 2:24. Moreover, the prepositional phrases "in [*or* among] you" (ἐν ὑμῖν, *en hymin*) may also be emphatic by virtue of their placement (suggested but not demonstrated in Akin 2001: 123).[4] If so, then we can use italic type and unnatural English word order to depict the force of John's wording: "But as for *you*, that which you heard from the beginning—*in you* let it abide! If *in you* abides that which you heard from the beginning, *you too* will abide in the Son and in the Father." The point of John's stress may be to continue the contrast between those who are troubling or have left the community (2:19–23) and those who remain to receive John's pointed appeal.

The future tense μενεῖτε (*meneite*, you will abide) in 2:24 throws attention forward to coming days. This is language of future promise, and promise is the note on which John begins to wrap up 2:22–26. Father, or Son, or perhaps the

4. In the Johannine corpus, emphatic uses of ἐν ὑμῖν (that is, when it precedes the main verb or participle it modifies) are John 5:38; 12:35; 14:17; 15:7, 11; 1 John 2:14. Nonemphatic occurrences of ἐν ὑμῖν, with the prepositional phrase following the main verb and not seeming to call attention to itself, include John 8:37; 14:20; 15:4; 1 John 2:8, 27. Ἐν ὑμῖν does not occur in Revelation.

combined ministry of both assures readers of "eternal life" (2:25); "this is the promise that he himself promised us" (a cognate accusative; see BDF §153.2; Moule 1994: 32). The noun "promise" (ἐπαγγελία, *epangelia*) occurs fifty-two times in the NT but only here in the whole Johannine corpus. Similarly, the verb ἐπαγγέλλομαι (*epangellomai*, to promise) occurs fifteen times in the NT but only here in John's writings. This does not mean that John has little regard for the future.[5] It rather invites the observation that where other NT writers talk of the *ground* of future blessing—God's promise—John stresses the *effect*. By God's promise, his people receive eternal life (see exegesis of 1:1–2). In 2:24–25, this is a baseline assurance and incentive for John's readers to let that word abide in them that will make it possible, in a few more verses, for John to summon them to "abide in him" (2:28).

"Eternal life" can bear a hackneyed ring to ears overfamiliar with biblical language. It may help to salvage a degree of John's obvious delight in 2:25 to recall that a classical writer like Plutarch (*Parallel Lives*, Marius 46.2–4) could inveigh against the notion of future hope and assume the high moral ground in doing so. For Plutarch, it is essential to dwell on and be grateful for the boon (if any) of past and present, for "what happens in the future is subject to fortune." It is "quite uncertain." Plutarch would presumably trade John's messianic assurance for "a firm foundation based on reason and education" by which things here and now can be rightly apprehended (translations from Warner 1972).

Plutarch speaks from within a classical antiquity in which life was constantly overshadowed by the threat of death. (It still is, of course, but technology can sometimes insulate people able to afford its benefits from ravages like plague and pain that in former times were ubiquitous.) Life expectancies were short by modern standards and medical care primitive. Coping mechanisms had to be devised. One notable philosophical response was denial, or more precisely apathy, a posture of resolute indifference to the surrounding world. This is seen in Epictetus's strategy of pretending that death is not what troubles people; it is rather the idea of death (*Manual* 16). Informing this counsel of despair is the Stoic belief that life is a never-ending cycle of purely material recurrence in which there is no transcendent good or evil or indeed eternal meaning of any kind: "Born from nothingness, [people] go back to nothingness" (Seneca, *On Tranquility of Mind* 15.4). "The future, either in this life or after it, is nothing to look forward to" (Bell 1998: 172).

John proclaims, however, "the eternal life, which was with the Father and has appeared to us" (1 John 1:2). While Plutarch may be right to excoriate obsessive future gazing, there *is* hope for times and ages ahead. But it does not lie in Plutarch's "reason and education" per se: in 2:25 John points rather to God's promise through which appeared "the resurrection and the life"; whoever believes in him "will live, even though he dies" (John 11:25). In light

5. Still less likely is the proposal that "the notably non-Johannine motif" of promise "may show the infiltration into 1 John of ideas from other Christian groups" (Rensberger 1997: 82).

of this promise, it makes sense that John seeks to lift his readers' gaze above the confusion and deception of their current community setting.

4. Who Imperils Those Seeking to Abide (2:26)

It is hard to know whether to take 2:26 as concluding the prior section or introducing the next one. Perhaps it evenly straddles a literary seam and could be treated either way. NA[27] handles what we might call "transitional ταῦτα" in the Johannine corpus as they think best fits the context, apparently, and while some of the time this means that ταῦτα (*tauta*, these things) sums up the previous section (John 1:28; 7:9; 8:20; 16:33; 20:31; 1 John 1:4), more often ταῦτα introduces a new paragraph or chapter (John 8:30; 11:11; 13:21; 14:25; 16:1, 25; 17:1; 18:1; 1 John 2:1, 26; 5:13). I will handle it as summative despite NA[27]'s contrary paragraphing because "these things I write" seems to restate and wrap up the parenthesis that began with "I am not writing to you" in 2:21. And 2:27 ("but you—the anointing you received . . .") seems to start a new section using impetus gained from restating an earlier allusion to anointing in 2:20 that was prematurely dropped but will now be taken up again.

Using another epistolary aorist (see already 2:14, 21; cf. 5:13), John affirms that a major motive for writing is because of τῶν πλανώντων (*tōn planōntōn*, the ones who are deceiving) them. Since the readers are apparently not yet deceived to the point of breaking fellowship with John, we may take the verbal action implied in the participle as conative[6]—these shadowy figures are trying to deceive but have not yet actually succeeded, at least not completely. John has already spoken of the danger of self-deception (on the meaning of the word πλανάω [*planaō*, to deceive], see exegesis of 1:8). In the LXX the term πλανάω is used particularly of the subversive lure of idols, idolatry, and those who tempt others to worship them. In John's Gospel, Jesus is accused of being a deceiver by some (7:12, 47). Jesus warns against false prophets and "Christs" who deceive (Matt. 24:24). Paul warns that in the last times "evil men and impostors will go from bad to worse, deceiving and being deceived" (2 Tim. 3:13 NIV). He reminds Titus that prior to conversion Christians "too were foolish, disobedient, deceived and enslaved by all kinds of passions and pleasures" (Titus 3:3 NIV). The motif of deceived or straying believers, or pseudobelievers, is not limited to 1 John.

The exact identity of the would-be deceivers must be inferred from the letter and perhaps from patristic evidence (see the introduction to 1 John). But in a literary context where antichrist and the liar have already been mentioned, it is not surprising that elsewhere in the Johannine corpus, one of many strung-together epithets for the devil is "the deceiver" (ὁ πλανῶν, *ho planōn*; Rev. 12:9; 20:10). Moreover, in the church at Thyatira, an Asia Minor church where 1 John may well have circulated, Revelation warns against "Jezebel, who calls herself a prophetess" and who "by her teaching . . . misleads [πλανᾷ, *plana*]

6. Cf. Wallace 1996: 534–35, where, however, the discussion relates to finite verbs rather than participles; Strecker 1996: 76.

[God's] servants into sexual immorality and the eating of food sacrificed to idols" (2:20 NIV). Spiritual subversion as implied in the verb πλανάω is likewise the theme elsewhere in Revelation (13:14; 18:23; 19:20; 20:3, 8, 10). We cannot assign names, dates, and specific locales to the subverters whom John has in mind. But we can note that the danger he points to is not anomalous in the historical setting traditionally associated with 1 John. And the action implied in John's warning is as frequently elsewhere pastoral in intent: "It is the duty of a good and diligent pastor not only to gather the flock but also to drive away wolves. . . . And so no one can faithfully teach the Church unless he is set on banishing errors wherever he finds them spread by seducers" (Calvin 1988: 262–63).

Additional Notes

2:23. Most minuscules omit the words in half brackets, possibly because of homoioteleuton involving the words τὸν πατέρα ἔχει, which occur twice in the strongly attested longer reading adopted by NA[27] and supported by, for example, ℵ, A, B, C, P, Ψ, and many minuscules.

2:24. 𝔐, with the sole patristic support of Augustine, inserts οὖν. By providing a formal transition between 2:23 and 2:24, this smoothes what is otherwise an abrupt locution. But weighty external evidence, combined with the principle of the harder reading, is decisive for omission.

2:24. Instead of NA[27]'s ἐν τῷ υἱῷ καὶ ἐν τῷ πατρί (A, C, P, Ψ, 33, 1739, 𝔐), B and a few other manuscripts omit the second ἐν. The meaning is not affected since in all manuscripts ἐν already appears before υἱῷ. ℵ and others reverse the word order to read ἐν τῷ πατρὶ καὶ ἐν τῷ υἱῷ. Again, the sense is not affected, but the external evidence is suspect and the reading is rightly rejected. Two minuscules (69, 945) read ἐν τῷ υἱῷ καὶ ἐν τῷ πνεύματι, theologically feasible but textually indefensible. NA[27] rightly opts for the reading with widespread support that also plausibly explains the existence of the other readings.

2:25. B and two minuscules read ὑμῖν instead of NA[27]'s ἡμῖν. The discrepancy may lie in a hearing error involving the initial sounds of the respective pronouns. The latter reading has superior external attestation.

2:26. Just as 𝔐 and Augustine read the transitional particle οὖν at the beginning of 2:24 (see first additional note on 2:24), ℵ, 1852, and a Syriac version insert postpositive δέ. But NA[27] rightly accepts the widely attested noninclusion of δέ. Of the seven NT books in which δέ occurs at a frequency of fewer than ten times per thousand words, four of them are traditionally ascribed to John:

2 John	0.00
Revelation	0.63
Colossians	2.73
1 John	4.41
Ephesians	7.19
3 John	7.87
1 Thessalonians	8.75

The frequency of δέ per thousand words in John's Gospel is 11.71, with the Synoptics all higher than this: Matthew (23.31), Mark (12.49), and Luke (24.20).

III. Key Counsel: Abide in His Anointing (Truth) and Receive Eternal Life (2:18–3:8)
  A. Three Considerations Informing the Counsel to Abide (2:18–21)
  B. The Truth That Abides (2:22–26)
➤ C. The Imperative to Abide (2:27–29)
  D. The Glory of Abiding (3:1–8)

C. The Imperative to Abide (2:27–29)

The entire subsection reaches its climax in 2:27–29. These three verses form the core of a block (2:24–3:1) in which nearly half of 1 John's ten imperatives occur (see exegesis of 2:15a). The key counsel of 1 John—that believers should and must abide—comes to the fore explicitly. John urges this in 2:28 after first reaffirming the readers' anointing and the instruction they have embraced (2:27). What they were taught and have believed all along retains its validity and superiority to rival construals of Jesus that have arisen.

First John 2:28 not only articulates the heart of John's pastoral counsel to abide, it also introduces a new (in the flow of the epistle thus far) incentive: Christ's return. The allusion is not oblique but direct and even threatening. From the parousia imagery, John moves quickly, in 2:29, to an appeal to Christ's ethical example. This makes sense if latent in John's appeal to abide is the call for ethical uprightness that has wavered, either among those who have departed (2:19) or those who remain part of the community. Christ's righteous character, which issued correspondingly in a holy life, is the reasonable template for his followers to contemplate as they ponder their own ethical expression. If they have been "born of him," John's expectation is that their lives will show it.

The subsection can be subdivided as follows:

1. The basis for the imperative: Anointing and instruction (2:27)
2. The imperative and its incentive: The parousia (2:28)
3. The basis for heeding the imperative: Christ the Righteous One (2:29)

Exegesis and Exposition

[27]Now as for you—the ⌜anointing⌝ you received from him ⌜abides in you⌝, and you have no need for anyone to teach you; ⌜but as⌝ ⌜his anointing⌝ teaches you regarding all things—and it is true and not a lie—⌜indeed⌝ just as it did teach you: ⌜Abide⌝ in him! [28]⌜So now, dear children, abide in him⌝, so that ⌜we might have⌝ confidence ⌜if⌝ he is revealed and not be put to shame ⌜by him at his appearing⌝. [29]If you know that he is righteous, you know that ⌜likewise⌝ everyone who does righteousness has been born of him.

1. The Basis for the Imperative: Anointing and Instruction (2:27)

The initial καί (*kai*) introduces a result from the previous discussion (cf. BDAG 495). Contrary to the subterfuge of deceivers (2:26), readers can steer a higher course. "Now," whatever the subverters are up to, "as for you [ὑμεῖς, *hymeis*], . . . abide in him!" John addresses them emphatically (on emphatic ὑμεῖς, see exegesis of 2:20–21). The verb μένετε (*menete*, abide) that accompanies the second word in the sentence (ὑμεῖς) occurs nearly forty words after it, almost at the end of the verse. This gapping (or hyperbaton) makes the verse's logic difficult to follow on first reading. While my translation conforms largely to the word order of the original, the explication below will reconfigure John's wording for ease of explanation.

Imperative: Abide in Him!

John's counsel is likely informed by Jesus's teaching as epitomized in John 15:1–10. His readers are to "abide" in the one whose anointing they have "received" (ἐλάβετε, *elabete*).[1] They are to remain steadfast in the message about him that mediated salvation to them. This assumes the pistic dimension of Johannine salvation (see exegesis of 2:1a). They are not simply to articulate or confess but actually to live out the reality of abiding in him (cf. 2:6). This implies the ethical dimension of Johannine salvation that John returns to frequently in the epistle. Finally, abiding is relational and not merely doctrinal (pistic) and behavioral (ethical). Essential to it is the personal relationship that permeates the John 15 discourse and recurs in 1 John with notable frequency (forms of a Greek noun or verb for "love" occur 46 times in 1 John's 105 verses).

The personal relationship is assured because the reality of abiding is already inherent in Christ's being. It is therefore something that John as his apostle can offer. From the standpoint of Johannine theology, the basis for their abiding is that "the Christ will remain forever" (John 12:34; cf. Heb. 7:24). In the Fourth Gospel this serves as an apologetic assertion of "the eternal character of the dignity of Jesus in the face of Jewish protests which deny His Messiahship on the basis of His transitory earthly existence" (F. Hauck, *TDNT* 4:575). First John takes up analogous challenges (2:22). But just as the supremacy of truth abides in Second Temple Jewish thought (1 Esd. 4:38), so also LXX usage of μένω (*menō*, to abide) takes on quasi-technical status by virtue of association with the immutability of the Lord (Pss. 9:7 [9:8 LXX]; 102:12 [101:13 LXX]), the Lord's counsel (33:11 [32:11 LXX]), the messianic line (89:36 [88:37 LXX]), God's righteousness (111:3 [110:3 LXX]; 112:3, 9 [111:3, 9 LXX]), God's praise (111:10 [110:10 LXX], and God's truth (117:2 [116:2 LXX]). Neither Jesus nor John was ignorant of the Psalter, and the theological truths expressed by the use of μένω there are likely relevant to the theology of steadfastness that informs John's μένω imperatives.

John continues the indicative-imperative pattern already observed repeatedly (1:5; 2:1b–2, 6, 15a). The command he voices is not an arbitrary decree.

1. It is possible to take ἐν αὐτῷ in 2:28 as referring to their anointing ("in it") rather than to Christ. Since Christ's anointing is virtually tantamount to Christ, no great difference would seem to inhere in the distinction.

It grows by logical necessity from four facts, grammaticalized by indicative mood clauses, that make up the bulk of the verse.

Relevant Indicative #1: The Anointing You Received from Him Abides in You

John reminds readers that they have received an immense blessing from God, one analogous to that received by Christ ("the Anointed One") himself: anointing (see exegesis of 2:20–21). It has come to them "from him," meaning either the Father or the Son or perhaps both viewed as one (for John's gliding back and forth between God and Jesus, sometimes not making clear who the subject of a verb is, see exegesis of 2:5).

"In you" (ἐν ὑμῖν, *en hymin*) should not be interpreted in an overly individualistic sense. The preposition ἐν combined with this pronoun can result in the meaning "among/with you" (BDAG 326–27), connoting "association (often close personal relationship)" (Wallace 1996: 372; cf. Moule 1994: 75). This observation is relevant to other occurrences of the phrase in 1 John (2:8, 14, 24 [2x]; 4:4). In Western exegesis this dimension of the meaning of ἐν ὑμῖν is generally overlooked.[2] The result of the anointing tends to be seen as primarily interior and self-focused. It is likely that John views it as a divine act that heightens horizontal ties among fellow believers no less than vertical relationship with God. The anointing and its effects abide among them, with them, in their midst corporately, and not merely *in* them as discrete individuals.

Relevant Indicative #2: You Have No Need for Anyone to Teach You

John's next indicative possibly reflects proselytizing activity on the part of the deceivers (2:26). Have they been teaching things that are not only erroneous but also simply superfluous, since what John's readers already possess is in no need of this particular augmentation? In any case, John affirms here a second basis for the imperative he issues. The anointing has a residual effect: it is instructive. The Johannine Jesus is one whose public identity was largely defined by his teaching activity (John 6:59; 7:14, 28, 35; 8:2, 20; 18:20). He is commonly addressed as "teacher" (1:38; 3:2; 11:28; 13:13; 20:16). It is his anointing they have received. It is understandable that John attributes a didactic force to it.

John obviously uses slight irony here.[3] If they had no need for instruction beyond some inner light imparted by their anointing, his epistle would be unnecessary (cf. Thompson 1992: 82). So in a sense John's high praise of what they have received is hyperbolic. His epistle is proof that the anointing does not result in unerring guidance by intuition (and may be evidence that

2. It is lacking, e.g., in the otherwise magisterial treatment of prepositions by M. J. Harris, *NIDNTT* 3:1190–93.

3. Herod Agrippa II uses almost the same idiom in a letter to Josephus (*Life* 366).

the anointing is not the Holy Spirit). John's statement cannot be taken as grounds for minimizing the office of pastor-teacher (cf. Eph. 4:11) in the early church (contra Rusam 1993: 231–32, who sees a radical leveling here between John and his readers). John means that what he is urging on them is fairly self-evident: the false teachers and their claims are wrong. The point needs no belaboring, so John simply reminds them. Yet of course they, like God's people in all times and places, *do* need to be taught in the sense of continually abiding in Christ and Christian doctrine—teaching—and living out their lives as disciples, which means learners, which implies continual exposure to teachers and teaching. John's statement must not be isolated from its context within the apostolic oversight, ecclesial order, and ongoing internalization of the didactic witness (preaching and teaching) through which the Lord guides and nurtures his followers in the church until the eschaton—at which point John's statement will no longer be hyperbolic (Jer. 31:34).

Relevant Indicative #3: His Anointing Is Sufficient and Trustworthy

Ἀλλ' ὡς (*all' hōs*, but as) contrasts this clause with the previous one. "You have no need for anyone to teach you—as some have attempted to do" is a possible sense of the preceding clause. But a veiled allusion to the deceivers is by no means certain. What is certain in this clause is that John's readers' anointing teaches them περὶ πάντων (*peri pantōn*, regarding all things; cf. Prov. 28:5). It is sufficient in its scope. Again there is a hint of irony. If the anointing granted them knowledge of all things, John's words would be superfluous. But John is not ascribing omniscience to them. He asserts simply that they have enough understanding to honor God in the touchy situation in which they find themselves.

Their anointing is also trustworthy. In John's words, it "is true and is not a lie" (ἀληθές ἐστιν καὶ οὐκ ἔστιν ψεῦδος, *alēthes estin kai ouk estin pseudos*). It performs the function that God intends for it. John's allusion corresponds well to what Paul tells the Corinthians when he says that God (or Christ) anointed them and makes both Paul and the Corinthians "stand firm in Christ" (2 Cor. 1:21). Paul's "stand firm in Christ" is virtually identical to John's "abide in him." For both, anointing is foundational to abiding.

Again the question can be raised whether some had charged that Christian doctrine as John understood it was false. Why else would he protest that it is not a lie? On repeated occasions Paul found it necessary to deny explicitly that he was "lying" (Rom. 9:1; 2 Cor. 11:31; 1 Tim. 2:7). His message and teaching did not constitute a "lie" (Gal. 1:20). Jesus, faced by detractors who questioned his veracity, accused them of being liars (John 8:55). He traced such lying back to Satan, who does not hold "to the truth, for there is no truth in him. When he lies, he speaks his native language, for he is a liar and the father of lies" (8:44 NIV). In alluding to lying, 1 John 2:27 takes up an issue that seems to have been close to the surface in many discussions relating to first-century belief and practice in the community that Christ founded. From an early Christian perspective, untruth was the essence of Greco-Roman religious conviction as a polytheistic civilization "exchanged the truth of God for a lie, and worshiped and served created things rather than the Creator" (Rom. 1:25 NIV; cf. 2 Thess. 2:11). In contrast to this, God does not and cannot lie (Titus 1:2; Heb. 6:18). Through Christ comes truth, for he told the truth that he "heard from God" (John 8:40). The correspondence of John's doctrine, for which he confirms direct connection with Jesus (1 John 1:1–3), to reality is yet another aspect of the basis for his readers to abide.

Relevant Indicative #4: His Anointing Served You Well in the Past

John's readers are to abide "just as" (καθώς, *kathōs*; see table in the exegesis of 3:3) their anointing taught them. The same idea appeared in 2:6, when John urged readers that those who say they abide ought to live "as" (καθώς) Jesus did. The spirituality of abiding apparently often involves analogy. This is certainly true in John's Gospel, where καθώς appears thirty-one times, frequently to draw a comparison between the Father or Son and how people should reflect the divine character. For example, Jesus speaks "just as" the Father "taught" (ἐδίδαξεν, *edidaxen*) him (8:28). Now John's readers are to abide "just as" their anointing "taught" them.[4]

The verb ἐδίδαξεν (*edidaxen*, taught) probably refers to an earlier period when John's readers were taught and confirmed in the faith. Each of the eleven times that this verb occurs in the aorist indicative in the NT, it refers back to a particular event (Matt. 28:15; Mark 6:30; Luke 11:1; 13:26; John 8:28; 18:20; Gal. 1:12; Eph. 4:21; Col. 2:7; 2 Thess. 2:15; 1 John 2:27). Three of these passages refer specifically to the didactic grounding of new believers (Eph. 4:21; Col. 2:7; 2 Thess. 2:15). Anointing is intertwined with instruction. Out of this activity grows the potential for those who receive John's message (1 John 1:5) to remain firm in it—to abide in Christ.[5]

2. The Imperative and Its Incentive: The Parousia (2:28)

The initial καὶ νῦν (*kai nyn*, and now) can be understood as a logical inference from what precedes: "So now."[6] The editors of NA[27] indicate this by making 2:28 start a major new discourse unit (so also Kruse 2000: 112). John addresses his readers for the third time as τεκνία (*teknia*, little children; see exegesis of

4. The subject of ἐδίδαξεν could be God or Christ rather than "anointing." The meaning would not be greatly affected; see p. 165n1 above.

5. It is not clear how Rensberger 1997: 83 finds "a powerfully antiauthoritarian, nearly anarchic concept of the church and of Christian doctrine" in this section, with John "declaring that the only teaching needed is that which comes directly from the Holy Spirit." If John really believed that, his letter would have been superfluous, along with its appeals to God, Jesus, and commandments. It would also seem to reduce the meaning of their vaunted anointing to a charismatic individualism hard to square with John's summons to shared particular beliefs and behaviors throughout the epistle.

6. Thrall 1962: 32 calls καὶ νῦν here a "development of the classical use of νῦν following an imperative" and gives the expression "an inferential sense 'and so.'" Cf. Acts 22:16 and Epictetus, *Discourses* 4.11.17.

2:1a and 2:12–13), which may be understood as a reaffirmation of his affection for them. He repeats the counsel that they should "abide in him" (see the final words of 2:27). The repetition of this directive lends credence to the theory that it is the rhetorical center of this section.

But John now adds a new incentive: Christ's return. "Not only the Antichrist but also the Christ is coming" (Schlatter 1950: 52). The final words of 2:28 speak of his παρουσία (*parousia*, coming, appearing). Since Christ has already come and departed at the time John writes, he must be speaking of the second coming.[7] This is the only time that παρουσία occurs in the Johannine corpus. But the expression plays a prominent part in the Olivet Discourse (Matt. 24:3, 27, 37, 39) and in Paul's writings (1 Cor. 15:23; 1 Thess. 2:19; 3:13; 4:15; 5:23; 2 Thess. 2:1, 8). Christ's return denoted by the word παρουσία is also found in James (5:7–8). It seems to have been a fairly widespread early Christian expression, and its meaning is hardly obscure despite John's sparing use of it. If he was present at the Olivet Discourse, he would have heard it (or a Semitic equivalent) from Jesus's own lips.

"At his appearing" at the end of 1 John 2:28 answers to "if he is revealed" (φανερόω [*phaneroō*, to reveal]; see exegesis of 3:2) in the middle of the verse. This "if" (ἐάν, *ean*) does not denote uncertainty as to *whether* Christ will show up but *when*. Since Jesus himself was not sure when the Son of Man would return (Matt. 24:36), John cannot be either. But there is need to be ready when it takes place (24:44; 25:13). On that occasion two things are desirable.

First, John, using the first-person plural (σχῶμεν, *schōmen*, we may have) to include himself among his readers, wants believers to have παρρησία (*parrēsia*)[8] when Christ appears. The word can mean confidence, fearlessness, joyousness (cf. CCC §2778) in the face of possible threat. In 1 John 4:17 John clearly has in mind eschatological judgment,[9] and that seems to be the idea in 2:28 (where wordplay with *parousia* at the end of the verse is likely) as well. By abiding in Christ when he is physically absent, believers can be assured of confidence on the day when he takes his stand again on earth (if John is a chiliast) or ushers in the final age (if John is not).

Second, John wants believers to abide so that they will avoid condemnation. Again John uses the first-person plural, thus assuming a position alongside and not over his readers: "So that . . . we might not be put to shame by him" (ἵνα . . . μὴ αἰσχυνθῶμεν ἀπ' αὐτοῦ, *hina . . . mē aischynthōmen ap' autou*). "Shame" is a euphemism for the utter disgrace of a sinner (e.g., Pss. 97:7 [96:7 LXX]; 119:80 [118:80 LXX]) or God's enemies (e.g., Ps. 6:10 [6:11 LXX]; Zech. 9:5) exposed before him and subject to his wrath (for a litany of warnings against things that bring shame, see Sir. 41:17–23 [41:17–42:1 LXX]). Since

7. Παρουσία refers to the first coming in 2 Pet. 1:16. It refers to a dramatic appearance of "the lawless one," which precipitates Christ's own second παρουσία, in 2 Thess. 2:9.

8. The word occurs nine times in John's Gospel, but always in the dative case (παρρησίᾳ) and always adverbially to mean "plainly, clearly, publicly."

9. For παρρησία as aplomb in the face of more mundane threat, see Acts 4:13, 29.

John writes to promote his readers' joy (1 John 1:4), his concern that they circumvent divine displeasure is well placed.

3. The Basis for Heeding the Imperative: Christ the Righteous One (2:29)

The translation of 2:29 may be straightforward ("if you know that he is righteous, you know that likewise everyone who does righteousness has been born of him"), but the logical flow from 2:28 is not. Perhaps the thought runs as follows: 2:28, in calling for readers to abide and not be put to shame, sheds indirect light on former community members who did not abide but departed (2:19). Their behavior was disloyal to the Righteous One who saves them and inconsistent with the divine parentage, so to speak, that is the birthright of the spiritually reborn (cf. John 1:12–13; 3:1–16).[10]

In this case it makes sense for John to wrap up the subsection with a fresh allusion to Christ (for the view that John refers to God here rather than Jesus, see von Wahlde 2002: esp. 322). Readers who have remained to receive John's counsel do indeed "know that he is righteous" (2:29a). He is righteous (δίκαιος, *dikaios*) to forgive sin (1:9) and to intercede before the Father (2:1). His righteous life is a model for those who confess to be his followers (3:7). With the assurance of Christ's righteous status and example firmly before them, they can reaffirm the basic truth that is their consolation in the wake of community dislocation.

That truth is that in standing firm ("abiding"), they are upholding the heritage into which their confession of Christ has placed them. "Everyone who does righteousness has been born of him." Those who departed were never really part of the family; those who remain steadfast know that their righteous stand verifies their divine parentage. It is at once both a credit to the one they know to be righteous (2:29a) and a confirmation that they have been born of God (2:29b).

All of this suggests that the function of 2:29 is, as the subheading above indicates, to reaffirm the basis for the key counsel that 2:27–29 offers. It is Christ. He is righteous and his followers know it, and they can therefore reasonably be expected to conduct themselves in keeping with his identity. This means staying put and staying fruitful ("abiding") in the anointed community (2:20, 27) to which John writes.

The words πᾶς ὁ ποιῶν τὴν δικαιοσύνην (*pas ho poiōn tēn dikaiosynēn*, everyone who does righteousness) are difficult. What does it mean to "do righteousness"? Is it simply to "do/does right" (LB, RSV/NRSV, NEB, CEV) or "do/does what is right" (TEV, NIV/TNIV, HCSB, NLT)? It is remarkable that since the KJV's "doeth righteousness," so many translations have translated δίκαιος in 2:29a as "righteous" but the cognate δικαιοσύνην at the end of the

10. The idea of being somehow "born of" God is mentioned in 2:29 for the first time in this epistle, but it is an expression that John will return to repeatedly (3:9; 4:7; 5:1, 4, 18). He assumes reader familiarity with it and does not go into particulars; 1 John "is far more concerned with the results of divine birth than with its mechanics" (Rensberger 1997: 86).

verse in a more moralistic fashion (most pointedly JB: "everyone whose life is righteous"). Exceptions are Cassirer (1989: 449: "does what is righteous") and ESV ("practices righteousness"). If these sound Pauline and not Johannine, it may be because John here "appears to be associating himself with Pauline tradition" (Strecker 1996: 82).

The expression takes on at least some clarity once its prominence in the LXX is noted (e.g., Gen. 18:19; 24:49; 2 Sam. 8:15; 1 Kings 3:6; 2 Chron. 9:8; Tob. 4:6 [4:7 LXX]; 12:9; 13:6 [13:8 LXX]; Pss. 106:3 [105:3 LXX]; 119:121 [118:121 LXX]; Isa. 56:1; Jer. 22:3; Ezek. 18:17). Often the sense is to act in keeping with God's righteous character. Since he *is* righteous, what he *does* reflects that quality. The lives of his people should follow suit. The assumption of 1 John 2:29 seems similar: Christ is righteous, and those born of God will respond in the current situation[11] by appropriating and upholding the steadfast stance that is called for. This means they will abide. As they do so, they will enjoy the fullness in which John rejoices in the next section.

Additional Notes

2:27. B and 1505 are among witnesses that read χάρισμα (*charisma*, gift) instead of χρῖσμα. Sparse attestation and the likelihood of confusion between χάρισμα and χρῖσμα make the NA[27] reading irresistible.

2:27. The NA[27] reading, μένει ἐν ὑμῖν, supported by א, A[c], B, C, and 𝔐 (𝔐 with different word order) has external evidence and the principle of the harder reading on its side. The complicated grammar of the verse may account for two variants. (1) Some minuscules, joined by two late uncials (P, Ψ) and a scattering of versions, read μενέτω ἐν ὑμῖν. As external evidence, this is not impressive, and it looks like an effort to replicate the rhetoric of 2:24 in order to ease the verse's tortured syntax. (2) The original hand of A stands alone in apparently reading μένει ἐν ἡμῖν. Because it nearly replicates NA[27], this supports NA[27]; it varies only in reflecting scribal confusion between ἡμῖν and the original ὑμῖν.

2:27. Instead of ἀλλ' ὡς as NA[27] has it, a few witnesses, including B, read simply ἀλλά. This would simplify the verse and for that reason, in the absence of stronger external evidence, is not likely to have been original.

2:27. Witnesses offer three alternatives to NA[27]'s τὸ αὐτοῦ χρῖσμα, which while defensible is only marginally better attested than the first alternative. (1) A, K, L, 𝔐, and some versions read τὸ αὐτὸ χρῖσμα (the same anointing). External evidence is impressive but has א, B, and other witnesses against it. Moreover, the adjectival use of αὐτός to mean "same" "occurs nowhere else in either the Fourth Gospel or the three Johannine Epistles" (Metzger 1994: 642). The intrinsic probability of the reading is therefore low. (2) A few witnesses, including 33 and 1505, read αὐτοῦ [or αὐτό] χάρισμα. External evidence is too weak to be convincing. (3) Instead of τὸ αὐτοῦ χρῖσμα, one finds τὸ αὐτοῦ πνεῦμα in א* and the Bohairic Coptic. This singular reading is not likely to be original.

11. It is important to keep the context clearly in mind. Otherwise, moralistic translations of 2:29 can sound like John is affirming salvation by works—a notion foreign to the theology of his writings. An example is NEB: "Every man who does right is his child." It is possible to do a great deal that is right without being born of God.

2:27. A few manuscripts omit καί. It is not needed because the previous ὡς already works coordinately with the καθώς clause. Weak external attestation and the omission of καί constituting a slight simplification argue against the variant.

2:27. Codex 049 and 𝔐 read future indicative μενεῖτε instead of NA[27]'s present imperative μένετε. If 𝔐 were original, it is hard to see how so many, and such a range of, earlier witnesses could have emended the text to the imperative. The future tense could be an assimilation of the end of 2:27 to the end of 2:24, the only other Johannine use of μένω in the future except for John 15:10.

2:28. ℵ, 69, 630, and some Vulgate witnesses omit the six words (καὶ νῦν, τεκνία, μένετε ἐν αὐτῷ). Homoioteleuton may be suspected. The omission of ἐν αὐτῷ by a single minuscule (81) could be to avoid pedantic repetition of the identical final words of 2:27.

2:28. Instead of ἐάν (if), 𝔐 reads ὅταν (when). This is understandable as an attempt to make the second coming a definite rather than a possible event. On the other hand, is it possible that ℵ, A, B, C, P, and others reflect the antichiliastic convictions that increasingly held sway after the time of Origen? Even if one reads ἐάν, the sense of the statement is not far from the English term "when."

2:28. It is not easy to decide between NA[27], which reads the aorist subjunctive σχῶμεν (following ℵ[2], A, B, C, P, Ψ), and ℵ*, 33, and 𝔐, which opt for the present subjunctive ἔχωμεν. With certain verbs like ἔχω, the difference between present and aorist can be significant (Moulton 1908: 110, 145).

2:28. ℵ moves ἀπ' αὐτοῦ to the end of the verse. As the sole witness to this reading it is unlikely to preserve what John first wrote.

2:29. It is not easy to decide whether καί should be retained as the harder reading (NA[27], following ℵ, A, C, P, and many minuscules and versions; so Cernuda 1977) or rejected with B, Ψ, 𝔐, and many versions. The difference in English translation between the two readings will be more formal than material.

III. Key Counsel: Abide in His Anointing (Truth) and Receive Eternal Life (2:18–3:8)
A. Three Considerations Informing the Counsel to Abide (2:18–21)
B. The Truth That Abides (2:22–26)
C. The Imperative to Abide (2:27–29)
➤ D. The Glory of Abiding (3:1–8)

D. The Glory of Abiding (3:1–8)

This subsection is best understood as operating at two levels. First, as a self-contained unit it makes several notable, even urgent[1] observations relating to such matters as divine love, being God's children, the prospects of seeing Christ and experiencing transformation as a result, the nature of sin, Christ's mission vis-à-vis sin, and the contrast between Christ and the devil. Just in terms of pithy propositions and admonitions, the passage is dense.

Second, the subsection plays an even more important role in bringing to a close the larger unit that began at 2:18. Abiding in Christ continues to concern the writer (3:6), so that we are justified in seeing these verses as linked with the preceding ones. But the passage makes the best sense if we take the verses as extolling the excellence of the course that John has counseled in 2:18–29: abide in him! He has already given justification and incentive for doing so. Now he will cover various and seemingly somewhat random aspects of the mandate he has laid down. It may be assumed that 3:1–8 deals with lore that John deems essential to his readers' understanding and behavior if they are to remain steadfast in keeping with John's overall message—and if they are not to depart or become otherwise aberrant in ways that others have already chosen.

It is as if the specter of further community fragmentation still lingers in the air, and John writes to dispel it.

The verses may be organized as follows:

1. The marvel of the Father's love (3:1)
2. The promise of divine transformation (3:2–3)
   a. Future transformation (3:2)
   b. Present ethical urgency (3:3)
3. The ethics of Christ's presence (3:4–8)
   a. Defiance of Christ's presence (3:4, 6)
   b. Purpose of Christ's presence (3:5)
   c. Victory of Christ's presence (3:7–8)

Exegesis and Exposition

[1]See what great love the Father ⸢has given us⸣, in order that we might be called children of God—⸢and we are!⸣ Because of this the world does not recognize ⸢us⸣, for it did not recognize him. [2]Beloved, now we are children of God, and what we shall be has not yet been revealed. We know ⸢ ⸣ that if he is revealed, we will be like him, because we will see him just as he is. [3]And everyone who has such hope in Christ purifies himself

1. Note the exclamatory first word of 3:1: ἴδετε (*idete*, look!); cf. Schnackenburg 1992: 155.

just as he is pure. 4Everyone who does sin also does lawlessness, and sin is lawlessness.
5And ⌜you know⌝ that that one was revealed in order that he might take away ⌜sins⌝,
and there is no sin in him. 6Everyone who abides in him does not sin; everyone who
sins has neither seen him nor known him. 7⌜Dear children⌝, let ⌜no one⌝ deceive you:
the one who does righteousness is righteous, just as that one is righteous; 8⌜the one
who⌝ does sin is of the devil, because the devil sinned from the beginning. The Son
of God was revealed so that he might destroy the works of the devil.

1. The Marvel of the Father's Love (3:1)

In the context of other biblical writers, John is preoccupied with the divine love, if usage of ἀγάπη (*agapē*, love) and ἀγαπάω (*agapaō*, to love) is any indication. New Testament uses of these two words show that frequency is by far highest, in comparison with other Gospels and epistles, in John's Gospel and John's Epistles.[2] Whereas a (jaded?) modern scholar can speak of the "magnificent monotony" of John's references to love (E. Stauffer, *TDNT* 1:53), on another reading his penchant for the words is evidence of ongoing wonder and joy.[3] The high frequency of love language in John's writings can be depicted graphically and numerically:

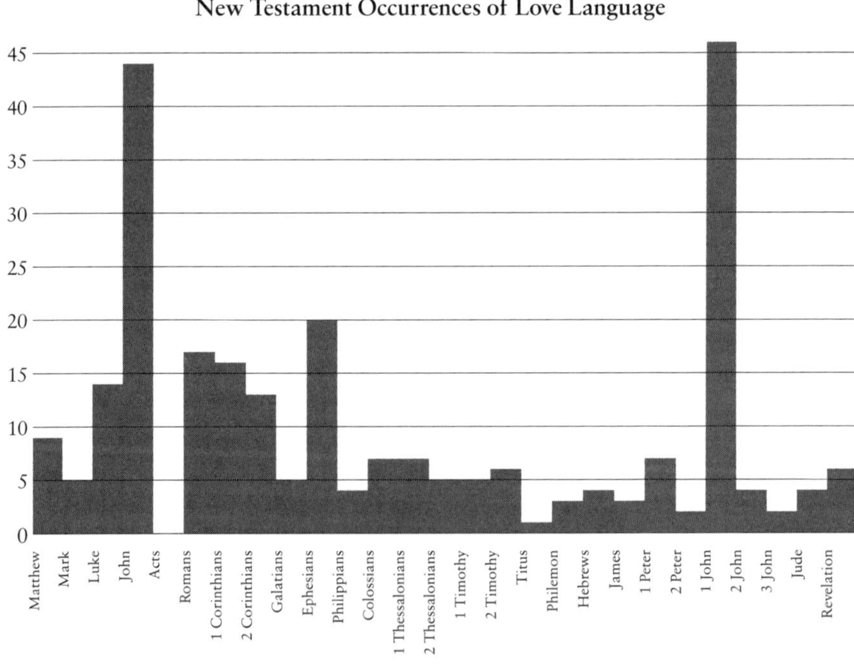

2. If φιλέω is added to the search (thirteen occurrences in John's Gospel, five times in Matthew, once in Mark, twice in Luke), his relatively frequent use of love language becomes even more evident.

3. Sloyan 1995: 31 speaks of "the marvelous intimacy of abiding in the Son and in the Father" and of "the magnificence of the gift of God's love." Cf. CCC §1692.

	Total Occurrences	Per 1,000 Words
Matthew	9	0.42
Mark	5	0.38
Luke	14	0.63
John	44	2.42
Acts	0	0.00
Romans	17	2.06
1 Corinthians	16	1.98
2 Corinthians	13	2.51
Galatians	5	1.89
Ephesians	20	7.19
Philippians	4	2.10
Colossians	7	3.82
1 Thessalonians	7	4.08
2 Thessalonians	5	5.30
1 Timothy	5	2.69
2 Timothy	6	4.716
Titus	1	1.29
Philemon	3	7.77
Hebrews	4	0.70
James	3	1.45
1 Peter	7	3.59
2 Peter	2	1.61
1 John	46	18.44
2 John	4	14.39
3 John	2	7.87
Jude	4	7.53
Revelation	6	0.54

First John's use of the noun or verb for love begins to peak in 1 John 3 (nine occurrences) and climaxes in 1 John 4 (twenty-seven occurrences). In 3:1 it is the wonder of this love that John underscores. He marvels at "what great" (ποταπός, *potapos*) love the Father has bestowed. The adjective appears on only six other occasions in the NT and only twice with this same connotation of greatness (Mark 13:1 [2x], describing the magnificence of the massive stones of the Jerusalem temple).[4] John uses an unusual word to magnify an incomparable love.

The love's greatness lies in its effect: it makes people τέκνα θεοῦ (*tekna theou*, children of God). The phrase is found elsewhere in 1 John at 3:2, 10; 5:2. Paul uses the expression in connection with the ideas of adoption (Rom. 8:16) and election (9:8); he exhorts people to live as God's children (Phil. 2:15). In John's Gospel this status is the result of God's procreative act—those who believe in Jesus's name are "born of God" (1:13). In broad terms all humans are children of God in that God is their maker (Isa. 45:11–12). More particularly, Israel has God as its father (Deut. 32:6–12; Isa. 43:6–7; Mal. 2:10). But Christians are children of God in a still fuller sense. "By God's creative act of love, we belong to God as surely and permanently as children belong to their parents. . . . We do not simply *look at* a love that is external to us and marvel at its greatness; we *know* a love that resides *within* us" (Thompson 1992: 88, emphasis original).[5]

The love's greatness also lies in its purpose. The Father bestows such love "in order that" (ἵνα, *hina*) John and his readers might enjoy his familial favor (on the encroachment of consecutive ἵνα into usage formerly reserved for ὥστε [*hōste*, so that], see Caragounis 2006: 224–26). John's Gospel portrays the

4. In Matt. 8:27; Luke 1:29; 7:39; and 2 Pet. 3:11 ποταπός carries the meaning "what kind" or "what sort."

5. Schlatter 1950: 55 points out that this joyful awareness of God's gift of love is, in essence, faith.

benefits of Jesus's death as extending not only to Jews, "sons of Abraham" (cf. 8:39), but also to "the scattered children of God [τὰ τέκνα τοῦ θεοῦ], to bring them together and make them one" (11:52 NIV). John has not lost his sense of wonder at this truth, which likewise causes praise to well up in Paul (e.g., Eph. 3:6–7).

The love's greatness lies also in its quality. The Father's love stands in grim contrast to some expressions of parental love of the era. While the natural love of father for children was of course present, it is also true that human fathers in the Greco-Roman world were not always affectionate or even equitable. Children might be abused and were often unwanted. When they were born, a father was free to order them to be "exposed," taken to an out-of-the-way place and left to die. Church father Tertullian notes that under the proconsulship of Tiberius in North Africa, children were sacrificed to Saturn; across the empire children were killed "by drowning or by exposure to cold and hunger and dogs" (*Apology* 9). Childhood was by no means always a time of safety and nurture in such an age.[6]

The status of being God's children enables John to address a question that may have been nagging at his readers. Given God's great love and the resultant joy and fellowship within his community (1:3–4), why has there been schism (2:19)? Why does "the world" seem sinister and hostile in some respects (2:15–17)? The answer, John says, lies in the alienation that results from owning God as Father. It is "because of this" (διὰ τοῦτο, *dia touto*)—which in 3:1 most likely points backward—that "the world does not recognize" John and his readers. It does not see them in the same light in which they see themselves. This flawed perception is in turn a function of ignorance of the Father (or perhaps the Son; so Culy 2004: 68).[7] That they "did not recognize him [οὐκ ἔγνω αὐτόν, *ouk egnō auton*]" likely refers to the world's rejection of the Father via its rejection of Christ: "He was in the world, and though the world was made through him, the world did not recognize him [αὐτὸν οὐκ ἔγνω]" (John 1:10 NIV). Even when Jesus was present, the Father's representative presence in him was unrecognized: "They did not understand [οὐκ ἔγνωσαν] that he was telling them about his Father" (8:27 NIV; cf. 16:3). It is not surprising that Jesus's servant John diagnoses the same malady still at work.[8]

Later John will affirm that "the whole world is under the control of the evil one" (1 John 5:19); for now he sets before his readers a fresh glimpse of the

6. Nor is childhood today a time of safety, with child neglect a perennial problem and abortion on demand an international, and especially North American, horror.

7. As Culy notes elsewhere (2004: xx), there is "Trinitarian ambiguity" at many junctures in 1 John. Culy thinks John wrote both the Gospel and this letter and conjectures that "the writer's emphasis on the absolute unity, mutuality, and equality of the Father and the Son evidenced in the Fourth Gospel . . . has led him to feel under no compulsion always to distinguish between members of the Godhead within his letter."

8. Rensberger 1997: 89 seems to locate the problem in John and his readers: their "self-understanding is typical of sectarian and countercultural groups." He warns against carrying such views to extremes. John's point is to warn against obliviousness to the fundamental incompatibilities between God's people in Christ and all other human societies.

wonder of the Father's love as antidote to estrangement and incentive to abide. Rensberger (1997: 89) feels that John's declaration "is not gracefully put." An earlier commentator anticipated this issue: "There is, indeed, an imprecision in the language. But the apostle preferred imprecision to not declaring what needed to be known" (Calvin 1988: 265).

2. The Promise of Divine Transformation (3:2–3)

The Father's love may be breathtaking in grandeur, but John and his readers are yet very much part of a troubled and troubling world. Encouragement is needed if the commendation of divine affection is to be regarded as something more than cant. In order to abide, the readers need an anchor for their souls. In 3:2–3, John furnishes it.

a. Future Transformation (3:2)

John again appeals to his readers by terming them ἀγαπητοί (*agapētoi*, beloved; see exegesis of 2:7). He repeats that "now," not in some future state but already, they are "children of God." First John 3:1 alluded to the wonder of this. The present possession of believers requires constant reaffirmation because of what daily life presents them with, as seen in Calvin's (1988: 266) memorable words: "Physically, we are dust and a shadow, and death is always before our eyes. We are exposed to a thousand miseries and our souls to innumerable evils, so that we always find a hell within us. The more necessary is it that our senses should be withdrawn from the view of present things, lest the miseries . . . should shake our trust in that happiness which as yet is hidden." And so John underscores that a greater glory awaits: "What we shall be has not yet been revealed." John echoes the eschatological note already sounded in 2:28 and continued in 3:3 with mention of hope.

In 2:28 talk was of the parousia, Christ's appearing. In 3:2 the perspective shifts from what Christ will be in that day to what his followers will one day be (cf. CCC §163). Presently this can only be adumbrated, not parsed in detail,[9] because what they will be "has not yet been revealed [οὔπω ἐφανερώθη, *oupō ephanerōthē*]." The word φανερόω occurs nine times in 1 John (1:2 [2x]; 2:19, 28; 3:2 [2x], 5, 8; 4:9). While it can mean simply "to be evident or manifest," as in 2:19 (cf. John 3:21; 7:4), it more often suggests divine revelatory activity apart from which a truth would not be redemptively appropriated and perhaps not even seen. Things revealed in 1 John include eternal life (1:2), the incarnation (3:5, 8), and God's love in his Son (4:9).[10] All of these occurrences are in the passive voice, and it is possible that God is to be seen as the active agent lying behind the verbal activity in each case (on the so-called divine passive, see BDF §130.1; Zerwick 1994: §236 ["theological passive"]; Moule 1994:

9. Cf. Schnackenburg 1992: 157: "All he says is 'what we shall be.' Otherwise he is quite vague about it. He thus avoids all the problems about the intermediate state which figured so largely in Jewish apocalyptic."

10. For similar usage in John's Gospel, see 1:31; 2:11; 9:3; 17:6; 21:1 (2x), 14.

26; cf. also the explanation and cautions against overuse and misuse of this category in Wallace 1996: 437–38).

John's allusion may be clarified by Paul's fuller statement on the same subject in Col. 3:4: "When Christ . . . appears [φανερωθῇ, *phanerōthē*], then you also will appear with him in glory" (NIV). The link between the parousia and future glorification of believers is patent. John is making the same connection in 1 John 3:2 by asserting that when Christ appears,[11] believers will be fundamentally transformed. This should be an encouragement to them despite the cold shoulder the world may give them.

The full truth of their future state has not yet been revealed, but this does not mean that nothing whatsoever can be said for sure about it. Using the distinctively Johannine locution οἴδαμεν (*oidamen*),[12] John affirms what "we know," likely referring to himself and those who receive the apostolic faith he upholds. Among these would naturally be his readers. John knows that when Christ appears again, his followers will be like Christ (ὅμοιοι αὐτῷ ἐσόμεθα, *homoioi autō esometha*, we will be like him). How does he know this, and what does he mean?

Such knowledge, from John's viewpoint, is implicit in the incarnation. Later in 1 John he will affirm, "We know [οἴδαμεν] also that the Son of God has come and has given us understanding, so that we may know him who is true" (5:20). Those like John who lived with Jesus and were taught by him, and by extension those who received Christ's first followers as faithful interpreters of Christ, have access to privileged and transforming information. This calls to mind the anointing already mentioned, through which John said his readers "all know" gospel verities (2:20). They know by virtue of Christ's coming to earth and then his ongoing presence with them through their faith in him.

The meaning of what "we know" is in John's estimation transformational. This understanding does not leave people unchanged; if it does, they have not really opened themselves to the fullness of what they profess to believe. Paul wrote that by Christ's Spirit, believers "are being transformed into [the Lord's] likeness with ever-increasing glory" (2 Cor. 3:18 NIV). In the same context he wrote that through the gospel, God "made his light shine in our hearts to give us the light of the knowledge of the glory of God in the face of Christ" (4:6 NIV). Light and knowledge of God are themes prominent in 1 John, too. But whereas Paul's allusions are primarily to what is "already" true for Christians, John eyes the "not yet" of things to come. Yet here too Paul may shed light on the truth that John affirms. Speaking of the awaited parousia, Paul predicts that Christ "will transform our lowly bodies so that they will be like his glorious body" (Phil. 3:21 NIV). John is not so

11. Greenlee 2000 correctly opts for the translation "if" for ἐάν. He defends both "Christ" and "it" as possible understood subjects of the verb φανερωθῇ. I opt for "Christ" because it seems to be the foremost implication of the discourse flow.

12. The verb οἴδαμεν occurs more frequently in 1 John (also 3:14; 5:15 [2x], 18, 19, 20) and John's Gospel (eighteen times) than in any other NT books. On the verb οἶδα more generally, see exegesis of 2:21–20.

explicit about the bodily dimension. But he is no less explicit that a coming glimpse of Jesus will complete the redemptive work that the incarnation inaugurated. Is this a modified application of Jesus's statement, "Blessed are the pure in heart, for they will see God" (Matt. 5:8 NIV)? In any case the promise of the future is part of John's admonition to remain steadfast in the present.[13]

Believers "will see him just as he is," with eternal consequences. But it is the present implications of those consequences that John wishes to highlight, as the next verse shows.

b. Present Ethical Urgency (3:3)

First John 3:3 does not contain an imperative but is tantamount to one. It is a descriptive statement with prescriptive force. To have the hope[14] of which 3:2 speaks is to have a zeal for ethical uprightness. This is true for "everyone," that is, every child of God, according to 3:3, and not just some among John's addressees. Closely related conceptually is Paul's exhortation to the (ethically suspect) Corinthians in the light of God's promises: "Since we have these promises, . . . let us purify ourselves . . . , perfecting holiness out of reverence for God" (2 Cor. 7:1 NIV). For both John and Paul, eschatological eventualities are a catalyst for close attention to personal holiness in the here and now (cf. Schnackenburg 1992: 161: "The dynamic of the Pauline ethic . . . permeates the Johannine theology too"). The same conviction is present for James (5:8) and Peter (1 Pet. 1:13). John leaves no place for a dreamy heavenly mindedness that renders believers no earthly good.

The standard for being holy (ἁγνός, *hagnos*) is Christ: John's readers are to purify themselves "just as [καθώς, *kathōs*] that one is pure" (1 John 3:3). (On the importance of imitation of Christ, see exegesis of 2:6.) Analogies denoted by καθώς are frequent in 1 John. They often either ground an imperative or constitute an indicative with imperative implications. In every case Painter's observation (2002: 228) holds true: "The use of this word [καθώς] suggests that Jesus is the source and mode of the believer's righteousness."

"Just as" passage in 1 John	Implication
2:6: Whoever claims to live in him must walk as [καθώς] Jesus did.	Jesus's ethical example has a normative force for his followers.
2:27: Just as [καθώς] his anointing teaches you, abide in him.	Believers' anointing is instructive for living.
3:7: He who does what is right is righteous, just as [καθώς] he is righteous.	Christ's righteousness furnishes an ethical and character norm for his followers.

Continued

13. Sloyan's statement (1995: 33) that "the preparation for the self-disclosure of God at the end that is enjoined is a life of fidelity in sinlessness" appears to underestimate John's earlier assertions (e.g., 1:8, 10; 2:1) that sinlessness is not possible.

14. The combination of the noun ἐλπίς (*elpis*, hope) with a form of the verb ἔχω (*echō*, to have) is attested in the NT at Acts 24:15; Rom. 15:4; 2 Cor. 3:12; 10:15; Eph. 2:12; 1 Thess. 4:13.

"Just as" passage in 1 John	Implication
3:12: [Love one another,] not like [καθώς] Cain.	Cain's example of hostile lovelessness illustrates a *via negativa* for Christ's followers, who are to love and not hate.
3:23: Let us love each other just as [καθώς] he gave us command.	Christ's command to love is an ongoing mandate for his followers.
4:17: Because just as [καθώς] Christ is, so are we in this world.	The love Christ manifested, which is appropriated and lived out among believers, is their confidence in the day of judgment.

The general structure of John's counsel here is accordingly straightforward: there is a concern for ethical rigor among Christ's followers, rooted in Jesus's own example of purity and given urgency by eschatological expectation.[15]

But what is the nature of the hope of which John speaks? Translations like "everyone who has this hope in him" (NIV; cf. KJV, TNIV) may give the impression of a hope that is resident within the believer (cf. 1 Pet. 3:15 NASB: "the hope that is in you") or that the believer truly makes his or her own (LB, JB). Other translations render τὴν ἐλπίδα ταύτην ἐπ᾿ αὐτῷ (*tēn elpida tautēn ep' autō*) as "hope in Christ" (TEV) or "hope in him" (NRSV; cf. RSV, NASB). Underscored here is the proper object of valid hope: Christ who will come again. This understanding of ἐλπίς plus the preposition ἐπί (*epi*, on, upon) finds support in Jer. 17:5: Cursed is "the one who places hope in man" (ὃς τὴν ἐλπίδα ἔχει ἐπ᾿ ἄνθρωπον, *hos tēn elpida echei ep' anthrōpon*). A third view is that this is a hope that lies "before" the believer (NEB; Cassirer 1989)—it is central to his or her perceptual horizon. This view reflects the possible connotation of ἐπί with the dative as "immediate proximity" (BDAG 363); it would be roughly equivalent to ἐνώπιον (*enōpion*) or ἐναντίον (*enantion*).

None of these senses can be excluded as possibilities. My translation, "everyone who has such hope in Christ," favors the second view.[16] "Such hope" is for John an expectation of Christ's future return, which is so certain (1 John 3:2: "we know"), complete, and compelling that it has a spillover effect in the present. One might liken this to a person who knows that a large tax refund is in the mail and who with expectant assurance lays plans to spend the money. Its arrival, after all, is just a matter of time.

3. The Ethics of Christ's Presence (3:4–8)

In the subsection 3:1–8, so far John has written of the marvel of the Father's love (3:1) and the promise of divine transformation (3:2–3). In the remaining five verses (3:4–8) he applies these promises to the ethical sphere. He envisions and comments on scenarios in which people fall short of the implications of

15. The verb ἁγνίζω (*hagnizō*, to cleanse, purify) can have either a ceremonial (John 11:55; Acts 21:24, 26; 24:18) or ethical (James 4:8; 1 Pet. 1:22) connotation. Here the latter is in view.

16. Cf. ESV: "And everyone who thus hopes in him." Akin 2001: 138 states: "There is nothing within the believer that creates hope and security for the future. The foundation for hope, now and forever, is Christ alone."

God's love and promise (3:4, 6). He reiterates the purpose of Christ's coming in terms of the destruction of sin (3:5). The final two verses of the subsection (3:7–8) make a summary appeal to the reader and affirm truths that serve to ground John's paraenesis. Many of these truths have already been stated in slightly different form in the epistle.

a. Defiance of Christ's Presence (3:4, 6)

Three times in 3:4 and 3:6, John uses the expression πᾶς ὁ (*pas ho*, everyone who). The phrase is used fifty-six times in the NT, but of these thirteen are either πᾶς ὁ ὄχλος (*pas ho ochlos*) or πᾶς ὁ λαός (*pas ho laos*), either of which generally mean "all the people." Most of the remaining occurrences are either on Jesus's lips (Matt. 5:22, 28, 32; 7:21, 26 [Matthew's Sermon on the Mount]; Luke 6:47; 14:11; 16:18; 18:14; 20:18) or in 1 John (thirteen times total). John's Gospel is particularly replete with this usage (eleven occurrences: 3:8, 15, 16; 4:13; 6:40, 45; 8:34; 11:26; 12:46; 16:2; 18:37). This raises the question of whether John's πᾶς ὁ (like that of other Gospel writers) is not in some measure an echo of Jesus's distinctive rhetoric. First John 3:4's πᾶς ὁ ποιῶν τὴν ἁμαρτίαν (*pas ho poiōn tēn hamartian*, everyone who commits sin) is directly paralleled in the NT elsewhere only on Jesus's lips in John 8:34.

In any case John in 1 John 3:4 appears to envision the case of those who do not emulate Christ's purity in their own lives as 3:3 asserts. Not to purify oneself in the fashion upheld in 3:3 is to sin, apparently (3:4). John uses the phrase ποιῶν τὴν ἁμαρτίαν. A similar parallel phrase, "do righteousness," is based in LXX usage (see exegesis of 2:29).

The contrast between the hope-filled and purified person of 3:3 and the transgressor of 3:4 is obvious. Less transparent is the nuance of John's assertion in 3:4 that "everyone who does sin [ἁμαρτίαν] also[17] does lawlessness [ἀνομίαν, *anomian*]." The rhetorical flow seems to demand that the first word for sin denote a less heinous or more generic moral miscue, while the second points to a more diabolical and grave infraction (cf. Schnackenburg 1992: 171; Strecker 1996: 94).[18] This is confirmed by NT uses of ἀνομία on Jesus's lips, in which those guilty of it deserve or receive eschatological punishment (Matt. 7:23; 13:41; 24:12; cf. Thompson 1992: 93).[19] It also comports with many of the LXX's more than 220 occurrences of ἀνομία in which an utterly despicable transgression is denoted (e.g., Gen. 19:15; Lev. 19:29; 20:14; Deut. 31:29; 2 Sam. 22:5; Isa. 53:8; Zech. 5:8; Mal. 1:4; Manns 1988 even suggests the translation "sin is Belial"). For example, because of ἀνομία God's people were captives in Babylon (1 Chron. 9:1). A variation of ποιῶν τὴν ἀνομίαν in

17. Καί (*kai*) is adverbial and not conjunctive.

18. In three NT uses that draw on the LXX, the two words seem basically synonymous: Rom. 4:7; Heb. 1:9; 10:17.

19. Paul associates the word with the mysterious "man of sin [ἀνομία]" of the end times (2 Thess. 2:3; cf. 2:7) and like John uses the word in antithesis to moral purification (Titus 2:14) or "righteousness" more generally (Rom. 6:19; 2 Cor. 6:14).

the LXX is ἐργαζόμενος τὴν ἀνομίαν (*ergazomenos tēn anomian*, performing sin), a phrase that occurs sixteen times in the Psalms and always refers to those who have resolutely turned away from God, to the point that they can no longer be regarded as his people but are in fact now his enemies (Pss. 5:5 [5:6 LXX]; 6:8 [6:9 LXX]; 14:4 [13:4 LXX]; 36:12 [35:13 LXX]; 53:4 [52:5 LXX]; 59:2, 5 [58:3, 6 LXX]; 64:2 [63:3 LXX]; 92:7, 9 [91:8, 10 LXX]; 94:3, 15 [93:4, 16 LXX]; 119:3 [118:3 LXX]; 125:5 [124:5 LXX]; 141:4, 9 [140:4, 9 LXX]; cf. the comparable conclusion in Kruse 2000: 118–19 [citing La Potterie]; see also Lyonnet 1957 and Cooper 1972).

There seems to be sufficient lexical warrant to posit that by ἀνομία John has in mind transgression so weighty that the perpetrator is outside the pale of Christ's followers.[20] He or she is walking in darkness, having turned aside from, or having never truly received, the dominical message in its full ramifications (Baylis 1992). In that sense, Kruse (2003b: esp. 69–70) may be correct that "*anomia* is the key" to understanding this passage and the larger problem of John's baffling assertion that Christians do not sin. The objections of Witherington (2006: 503–4) to Kruse are insubstantial. If Kruse is correct, the second half of 1 John 3:4, "and sin is lawlessness," may be regarded as explicative. That is, it explains what goes before it (for this use of the clause's initial καί [*kai*, and], see BDAG 495). To commit sinful acts (many of which John has alluded to in the epistle thus far) is to flirt with apostate behavior and consequences (3:4a); this is so because, quite simply, chronic sin (which bedevils all humans [1:8, 10] but can be forgiven if repented of [1:9; 2:1]) can progress to the level of ἀνομία, at which point it saddles one with a guilt from which there is no remission because it is not inadvertent but rather heinous rebellion that reflects one's confirmed inner character, not just incidental (though serious) misdeeds. First John 3:4 implies that for some this has taken place and indirectly admonishes the readers to take heed. There is probably a close relation to "sin" in this sense and the "fatal sin" spoken of in 5:16 (see exegesis of 5:16–17).

First John 3:6 is a second πᾶς ὁ (*pas ho*, everyone who) verse, like 3:4, and can be bracketed with it. "Everyone who abides in him" does not sin. First John 3:5 will underscore the christological reason for this. What John does in 3:6 is affirm the freedom from sinning enjoyed by the one who abides in Christ. He also, in the verse's latter half, sheds additional light on characteristics of those who do sin.

First John 3:6a is difficult because it apparently affirms that the person abiding in Christ does not sin (Segalla 1981 attempts a solution through structural analysis; Swadling 1982 suggests that the sinlessness sayings of 3:6, 9 were slogans used by gnostics, which John refutes).[21] Yet John has already stated

20. Cf. 2 Tim. 2:19 NIV: "Everyone who confesses the name of the Lord must turn away from wickedness [ἀδικία, *adikia*]"; or Heb. 3:12: "Beware . . . lest there be among some of you an evil heart of unbelief [καρδία πονηρὰ ἀπιστίας, *kardia ponēra apistias*] in falling away from the living God." Like the language of redemption, the early Christian vocabulary of apostasy is rich and varied.

21. For a summary of nine major views, see Akin 2001: 143n373.

that no one is free from sin (1:8, 10) and presented Jesus as the advocate if believers do sin (2:1). It is unlikely that John has forgotten what he wrote earlier or changed his mind in the interim. Nor is it advisable to resort to the understandable but unsatisfactory expedient of stressing the alleged continual nature of the sinning John has in mind (e.g., NIV/TNIV: "No one who lives in him keeps on sinning"). This may be true, but "keeps on sinning" (adopted also by ESV) probably overreads the verb tense (cf. Wallace 1996: 524–25; contra Kruse 2000: 120 and many other commentators). Smalley (1984: 159–60) effectively unmasks this misuse of the present tense, along with the dubious proposal that 2:1 in contrast uses aorist forms to connote isolated sinful acts. This is oversubtle. In addition, as Smalley points out, 5:16 uses the present tense to describe specific sinful acts, not chronic transgression. The present tense cannot bear the weight that the translation "keeps on sinning" places on it in 3:6, 9 (cf. Culy 2004: 73; yet note Caragounis 2006: 90: the issue is complicated!).

A better solution may lie along one of two lines, which arrive at much the same destination in the end.[22] First, by οὐχ ἁμαρτάνει (*ouch hamartanei*, does not sin), John may have in mind sin in the sense of the ἀνομία that he has been discussing. In this case he is commending the necessity of abiding in Christ—the overall theme of this section—on the ground that it delivers one from the abyss that awaits those guilty of ἀνομία (as defined above). The best defense against spiritual disaster is aggressive pursuit of Christ.

Or John may have a slightly broader frame of reference in mind. By ἀνομία he may refer to those kinds or degrees of transgression that he has already warned against frequently, both implicitly and explicitly. Here the exegesis of 2:1a comes into full play. I suggested there that for John full-orbed reflection of the God who is light in the Christian's life is a three-dimensional reality. The domain of the true believer's existence lies in a positive response to God in Christ doctrinally (faith), ethically (works), and relationally (love). Figure 4 in the exegesis of 2:1a schematizes major components of what it means to abide in Christ.

To apply this to 3:6a: John may be assuming a definition of "sins" that extends primarily to the transgressions that threaten his readers and have already led some to desert the faith (cf. 2:19), as John sees it. This is, in other words, a contextual solution to the problem. Some run aground at points of doctrine (2:22), others at points of ethics (2:4), and still others at points of love for God (stressed later in the epistle) or for other people (2:9–11). They have sinned not in the inadvertent sense of the word (see again Caragounis

22. For a third possibility, see Calvin 1988: 269–70: "But inasmuch as Christ's kingdom flourishes in them, sin is abolished. Meanwhile [believers] are reckoned according to the chief part; that is, they are said to be righteous and to live righteously because they sincerely aspire to righteousness. They are said not to sin because, although they labour under the infirmity of the flesh, they do not consent to sin, but in fact struggle and groan, so that they can truly testify with Paul that they do the evil they would not." At the same time Calvin writes: "Many would like to persuade themselves that they have this righteousness buried in their hearts while iniquity openly occupies their feet, hands, tongues and eyes."

2006: 90) but in the sense distinct to the discourse of this section, in which John has argued (3:4) that the ἁμαρτία of some constitutes ἀνομία. In this view, John can use the same word, ἁμαρτάνω (*hamartanō*, to sin), with significantly different connotations. In 3:6a, as compared with, for example, 2:1, he apparently does so (Caragounis 2006: 326 directly contradicts Porter here in relating this to the aspect of aorist versus present).

First John 3:6b makes a contrasting declaration: "Everyone who sins has neither seen him nor known him." The meaning of "sins" in 3:6b will be closely linked to the meaning of "sins" in 3:6a. If the explanation above is correct, then John is speaking of someone who sins to the extent of committing ἀνομία. What would possess someone to do this? The question is of obvious relevance in a social setting in which the integrity of doctrine, ethics, and love for others is apparently under siege. In 3:6b John furnishes a twofold answer.

First, the one guilty of such sin has not "seen him," which likely refers to Christ, explicitly mentioned in the previous verse. The form of the word for "has seen" (ἑώρακεν, *heōraken*) occurs in the NT almost exclusively in John's writings.[23] Jesus uses the word to speak of seeing the Father (John 6:46 [2x]; 14:9; cf. 1:18; 3:32). Both 1 John 4:20 and 3 John 11 mirror this usage. The sense in 1 John 3:6b seems to be explained best by Jesus's remark in John 14:9: "The one who has seen [ὁ ἑωρακώς, *ho heōrakōs*] me has seen [ἑώρακεν] the Father." John has already made clear that the overall message of this epistle concerns God—namely, he is light with no admixture of darkness (1 John 1:5). In the immediate context of 3:6b, God is very much present, in that he is the offended party of the sins and sinning that dominate 3:4–6. What would account for such flagrant offense against God? John's answer is, first, the sheer blindness of not seeing Christ with the perception that would drive the transgressor to believing and abiding in him.[24]

Second, the one guilty of such sin lacks a certain knowledge; he or she does not "know [ἔγνωκεν] him." The perfect tense of γινώσκω (*ginōskō*, to know) occurs twenty-one times in the NT, five times in Paul's writings (1 Cor. 2:8, 11; 8:2, 3; 2 Cor. 5:16) and the rest of the time in John (seven times in the Gospel). First John uses the perfect tense eight times, five of which have appeared earlier (2:3b, 4, 13, 14 [2x]). John seems to refer to a knowledge that is distinguished at least by depth of conviction (cf. Akin 2001: 144). In the broad sweep of the epistle, though, depth of conviction is not all that John has in mind; true knowledge of Christ also involves doctrinal, ethical, and relational considerations. The person guilty of sin à la 3:6b falls short in part because he or she lacks this quality and scope of knowledge.[25] Paul stresses that there is

23. The exception: in Luke 1:22 ἑώρακεν refers to the vision that Zachariah "saw" in the temple.

24. Calvin 1988: 270 suggests that "by seeing and knowing" in this section "we are simply to understand faith."

25. A linguistic parallel for 3:6b is found in John 14:7. Jesus tells Thomas, and by implication the rest of the Eleven, that from that time forth they both γινώσκετε αὐτὸν καὶ ἑωράκατε αὐτόν (*ginōskete auton kai heōrakate auton*, know him [the Father] and see him).

a kind of knowledge that transforms the knower because in its highest sense such knowledge is love for God, which in turn is a function of being "known by God" (1 Cor. 8:2–3; Gal. 4:9). The form of John's statement is different, but the underlying theology seems closely related.

The effect of 1 John 3:6, in summary, is to join with 3:4 to depict an antithesis to the person who has eschatological hope and therefore lives an ethically rigorous life (cf. 3:3). First John 3:4 and 3:6 identify those who do not abide in Christ but rather languish in ἀνομία, an advanced or confirmed posture of noncompliance with John's message. Their blindness and ignorance stand in sharp contrast to the vision and understanding that John claims to have (1:1–5). Their defiance of Christ (as opposed to hope-generated ethical transformation because of him [3:3]) violates the very purpose of his coming, as 3:5 is at pains to emphasize.

b. Purpose of Christ's Presence (3:5)

If 3:4 and 3:6 are veiled imperatives that warn by negative examples how John's readers are not to conduct themselves, then 3:5 is the indicative that grounds the imperatives. John speaks of a shared understanding ("you know") that extends to why Christ[26] appeared and then to the absence of sin in him. This is one of fifteen uses of οἶδα (*oida*, to know) in 1 John (see table in the exegesis of 2:20–21) and as in other cases denotes some aspect of the facts of the gospel message as well as their implications, whether doctrinal, ethical, relational, or some combination of these three.

What John wants his readers to "know," first, is that Christ "was revealed." This is the seventh of nine occurrences of φανερόω (*phaneroō*, to appear) in this epistle (see exegesis of 3:2). While it can mean simply to be evident or manifest, as in 2:19 (cf. John 3:21; 7:4), it more often suggests divine revelatory activity apart from which a truth would not be redemptively appropriated and perhaps not even seen. Things "revealed" in 1 John include eternal life (1:2) and God's love in his Son (4:9). In 3:5 (and 3:8) John uses the same verb to speak of the incarnation.

Their knowing "that" (ὅτι, *hoti*) Christ appeared is more assumed than asserted in 3:5; what John wants to stress is his purpose in coming: to "take away [αἴρω, *airō*] sins." In John's Gospel, Jesus is identified as "the Lamb of God, who takes away [αἴρω] the sin of the world!" (1:29 NIV; cf. Isa. 53:4, 11–12). John has already spoken of Jesus's propitiatory work (see exegesis of 2:2) through his death[27] and intercession. Now he points to an application of it. The presumed sins of some (3:4, 6) stand in contrast to a central purpose of Christ's coming: to remove sin, both in terms of forgiveness of sins past and elimination of sin (esp.

26. Ἐκεῖνος (*ekeinos*, that one, he) assumes but does not refer to "the historical reality of Christ's incarnation" (contra Akin 2001: 141). It rather denotes Christ himself (Painter 2002: 227), particularly as the one who through his atoning work dealt with the human sin problem.

27. In Col. 2:14 Paul uses αἴρω when describing how Christ "took away" the certificate of indebtedness by "nailing it to the cross."

in the sense of ἀνομία, *anomia*) in daily life. In the immediate context, the upshot would be that the behavior presumed in 3:4, 6 would render profession of faith in Jesus null and void. Positively, John's readers can hold out for more upright conduct. This possibility is assured by the very goal Christ had in coming. "If sin is opposition to God, Jesus's work stands in opposition to sin" (Thompson 1992: 93; cf. the eloquent observation in *CCC* §457).

Readers know not only *that* and *why* Christ came: they also know that sinlessness marked his character. Jesus asked his detractors, "Can any of you prove me guilty of sin?" (John 8:46 NIV). The tacit answer is no, at least from John's point of view. In contrast to humans, who will "die in [their] sins . . . if [they] do not believe that" Christ is the one he claimed to be (8:24), Jesus lived without sin so that he could destroy it (see exegesis of 3:7–8). This same conviction of Jesus's purposeful sinlessness underlies 1 John 3:5: "there is no sin in him" (on Jesus's sinlessness, see also Matt. 3:14; Acts 2:27; 3:14; 4:30; 7:52; 2 Cor. 5:21; Heb. 4:15; 7:26; 1 Pet. 1:19; 2:22). "As the sacrificial animal must be unblemished, so also for Christ as the sacrificial lamb the necessary precondition of his atoning efficacy is sinlessness" (Strecker 1996: 96). A prophecy of Isaiah hints at this in speaking of the Suffering Servant as one who "had done no violence, nor was any deceit in his mouth" (53:9 NIV).

But the assertion of Jesus's purity is not a random theological utterance. As everywhere in 1 John, doctrine informs and generates vibrant practical life. Because the model and precedent for believers' lives is Christ (2:6; 3:3, 7), and in view of the direct connection between his presence in the world and the lives of his followers (4:17), they are to reflect the freedom from sin that he announced to those willing to abide in his teaching (John 8:31) and live as his disciples. "Then you will know the truth, and the truth will set you free" (8:32 NIV). Part of this freedom is liberation from the tyranny of a life lived in darkness rather than in God's good light (cf. Heb. 9:26 NIV: Christ has been manifest "to do away with sin by the sacrifice of himself").

The message that God is light without darkness (1 John 1:5), coupled with the reality of abiding in God's Son (2:18–3:8), means that the malaise of 3:4, 6, while virulent, is not sovereign. Christ is. John sets this sinless one before his readers as both hope and mandate.

c. Victory of Christ's Presence (3:7–8)

First John 3:7–8 in many ways sums up much of what the epistle has stated thus far. Several terms or themes are repeated: τεκνία (*teknia*, dear children; 2:1, 12, 28), ὁ ποιῶν (*ho poiōn*, the one who does) certain things (2:29; 3:4), righteousness and righteous (1:9; 2:1, 29), sin (ten references in earlier passages), "from the beginning" (1:1; 2:7, 13, 14, 24), the manifestation of God's Son (2:28; 3:2, 5), deceivers seeking to lead John's readers astray (2:26). But while most elements are not new, this particular configuration in 3:7–8 is fresh.

First John 3:7 begins with by-now familiar endearment language ("dear children"). The sharp appeal that John aims at his readers is sheathed in affection for them. He issues the fourth imperative of this section: "let no one deceive you" (cf. imperatives at 2:24, 27, 28; 3:1; for discussion of πλανάω [*planaō*, to deceive], see exegesis of 1:8 and 2:26). Each of 1 John's imperatives bears scrutiny since the epistle contains a total of only ten of them. This one is important because, taken in tandem with similar language in 2:26 about deceivers,[28] it confirms that throughout the section thus far, stretching back to the mention of antichrists and schism (2:18–19), John has had in mind the threat to his readers posed by those of aberrant faith (2:22) or ethics (3:4, 6). He battles a spirit of deceit (4:6) that works within "many deceivers" who "have gone out into the world" (cf. 2 John 7). The subversion of God's people by idolatry (Deut. 13:6 [13:7 MT]; 2 Kings 21:9) or evil angelic beings is a recurrent theme of both OT Scripture and later Jewish literature (1 Enoch 6–10; Jubilees 5.1–10). The Testament of Levi, in warning of end-time transgression, uses a word related to John's "lead astray" (10.2; 16.1). John is warning of missteps that could have consequences of eschatological proportions.

In the remainder of 1 John 3:7–8, John counters this threat with three affirmations. First, on the positive side, "the one who does righteousness is righteous, just as that one is righteous" (3:7b). This is a reaffirmation of much of the substance of 2:29: "If you know that he is righteous, you know that likewise everyone who does righteousness has been born of him." Christ's status as "righteous" (δίκαιος, *dikaios*) has already been firmly established (see exegesis of 1:9 and 2:1b). To be like him in this aspect of his character calls for practical living that comports with his example and teaching. This is the likely message of 3:7b. It is clear that John feels that elements who have left the community have not "done righteousness"—embraced the doctrine, ethics, or love fitting for those who abide in Christ (on "doing righteousness," see exegesis of 2:29). This could mean that they have made verbal claims without living them out (so Schnackenburg 1992: 173–74; cf. Luke 6:46), or it could mean that they have baldly transgressed elements of Christian faith and practice, from the standpoint of an apostolic guardian like John (cf. Jude 4). Since Christ is righteous, such unrighteous response to him is clearly illicit. It would be fatal for John's readers to succumb to it. This is why John pleads that they let no one lead them astray.

Second, if 1 John 3:7b sets forth the positive model of conformity to Christ, 3:8a sets forth the negative. Instead of "the one who does righteousness," there is "the one who does sin." Instead of the exemplary Christ, there is the execrable devil and his miserable consistency through all epochs: he "sinned from the beginning" (taking the present tense ἁμαρτάνει [*hamartanei*] as gnomic).[29] The contrast between light and darkness, between abiding in Christ and languishing in the devil's grip (cf. 2 Tim. 2:26, speaking of persons in

28. The attempt of Strecker 1996: 97 to sever any connection between 2:26 and 3:7 seems strained in light of the verses' rhetorical proximity and linguistic similarity.

29. Schnackenburg 1992: 174 draws on John 8:44 to suggest that John refers to the Gen. 3 narrative. See also Strecker 1996: 100.

the church hostile to apostolic leadership), is total. By eliminating gray areas, John may hope to clarify to readers what their real choices are; in times of community crisis, the fog of ambiguity can result in crippling indecision or creeping compromise.

"The devil" (ὁ διάβολος, *ho diabolos*) is mentioned in 1 John only here (three times) and in 3:10. In John's Gospel, Jesus calls one of his followers (Judas) a "devil" (6:70). He accuses his detractors of having the devil as their ideological father; he adds that "he was a murderer from the beginning" (8:44 NIV). John portrays the devil as inciting Judas to betray Jesus (13:2; cf. Acts 13:10). Revelation refers to "that ancient serpent called the devil or Satan, who leads the whole world astray" (12:9 NIV; cf. 20:2). His end is to be "thrown into the lake of burning sulfur, where the beast and the false prophet had been thrown. They will be tormented day and night for ever and ever" (20:10 NIV). John desires neither the leadership nor the fate of this sinister figure for the congregations he addresses. Because he is the archtempter (Matt. 4:1–11) as well as the liar and murderer par excellence (John 8:44),[30] God's people should be as keen to avoid him as they are zealous to follow Christ. John's implied teaching here is that central to achieving this is doing righteousness rather than sin.

A third affirmation serving to ward off possible deception is that "the Son of God was revealed so that he might destroy the works of the devil" (3:8b). "To destroy . . . the works of the devil means their radical annihilation" (Schnackenburg 1992: 174). The parallel with Heb. 2:14 NIV is striking: Christ assumed humanity so that "by his death he might destroy him who holds the power of death—that is, the devil" (cf. also 2 Tim. 1:10; Acts 10:38). If the first clause of 1 John 3:8b refers to the incarnation (ἐφανερώθη [*ephanerōthē*, was revealed] appeared earlier, in 1:2; 2:28; 3:2, 5), the latter refers to his triumphant death and resurrection. By these Christ destroyed "the works of the devil" in two senses that become visible in 1 John. First, death itself has been destroyed. This is implicit in every Johannine reference to eternal life (1:2; 2:25; 3:15; 5:11, 13, 20), and it is explicit in 3:14: "We know that we have passed from death to life." This insight lies at the core of an early and influential view of the atonement, the so-called classical view (Aulén 1960: 199–200). Second, "works" hostile to God, or characteristic of the devil, have been destroyed. While ἔργα (*erga*, works) can have a good connotation (e.g., Titus 2:7, 14; 3:1, 5, 8, 14), in John's Epistles they are usually negative (1 John 3:12; 2 John 11; 3 John 10; the exception is singular ἔργον [*ergon*] in 1 John 3:18). In essence they correspond to Paul's "works of darkness" (Rom. 13:12) or "works of the flesh" (Gal. 5:19) or "evil work" (2 Tim. 4:18). Such works are the stuff of the sin that John so steadily decries throughout his epistle and mentions twice in this verse alone. Because Christ is victorious over the devil in death, he can

30. When Jesus says in John 8:44 or John writes in 1 John 3:8 that the devil committed misdeeds ἀπ' ἀρχῆς (*ap' archēs*, from the beginning), he is probably making a statement dealing more with character than chronology. However long he has been at work, nothing but malice and woe attends his activity.

mentor daily ethical victory in the lives of followers who would otherwise be "held in slavery by their fear of death" (Heb. 2:15 NIV).

This means that God's people in Christ, far from regarding sin with weary resignation or fearful foreboding, are assured that their struggle against it has both purpose and promise. Christ himself stands behind them as they wrestle with the forces and ideas and behavior against which John warns. The dramatic portrait of *Christus victor* dominates the literary horizon as the section comes to a close. The epistle's key counsel—to abide in Christ and receive eternal life—is not a counsel of despair but a straightforward and compelling application of what Christ has already accomplished.

He is, after all, the Son of God. "Son of God" is the title for Jesus Christ that occurs most frequently in the Johannine Epistles (also 4:15; 5:5, 10a, 12b, 13, 20a). Its shortened version "Son" is even more common (1:3, 7; 2:22, 23 [2x], 24; 3:23; 4:9, 10, 14; 5:9, 10b, 11, 12a, 20b; 2 John 3, 9). It refers to Jesus's divinity, his unique oneness with God the Father. In Hellenistic religion there was talk of divine sonship via human cohabitation with a god; the offspring would be a "son of a god." Caesar Augustus was alleged to have divine parentage as the result of his mother's impregnation by a snake in the temple of Apollo (Suetonius, *Augustus* 94). In a religious setting where the gods were both numerous and essentially human in their characteristics, the notion of a human attaining some semblance of divinity is hardly startling.

Very different is the idea of Jesus's divine sonship. He is the one and only (μονογενὴς θεός, *monogenēs theos*; see John 1:18) Son of the God who is holy—utterly unique. His conception by the Holy Spirit was without male human agency. His relationship to God is unparalleled because he had been "with God" and "came from God" in a sense true of no other human ever (1:1; 8:42). He was sinless (see exegesis of 3:5). He fully shared humanity's lot but at the same time transcended it. His complete mastery over all that ails sin-plagued people who must someday face judgment is John's springboard for instruction regarding love, works, and trust in the verses ahead. (For more on "Son of God," see exegesis of 5:4–5.)

Additional Notes

3:1. Some half dozen variants exist of NA[27]'s δέδωκεν ἡμῖν (based on ℵ, C, P, 𝔐). Instead of the perfect tense δέδωκεν, a few uncials and minuscules read the aorist ἔδωκεν, retaining ἡμῖν. Two minuscules (81, 623) read the aorist but replace the first-person ἡμῖν with the second-person ὑμῖν. B, K*, 049, and a few other witnesses combine the perfect δέδωκεν with ὑμῖν. Minuscule 1241 appears to be unique in reading the perfect tense and ὁ πατὴρ ὑμῶν (your Father) instead of NA[27]'s "the Father." Errors of hearing would account for the divergences, along with the sense of the verse remaining essentially the same no matter which variant is read. The NA[27] reading has in its favor a superior range and depth of support as well as intrinsic plausibility (cf. 4:13; 5:20). The aorist of δίδωμι is, however, found at 3:23, 24; 5:11. In 1 John, when a form of δίδωμι is used with a plural personal pronoun, it is always ἡμῖν.

3:1. Several manuscripts omit καὶ ἐσμέν (e.g., K, L, 049, 69, 𝔐), whether to omit a phrase deemed superfluous or because of the similarity of -μεν endings in two of the last three words of the clause (κληθῶμεν, καὶ ἐσμέν). But many others, including important uncials, contain it, and it is not easy to imagine how the words would have been added so uniformly to so many copies, while its omission is readily explicable.

3:1. An impressive range of manuscripts, including ℵ* and 𝔐, prefers ὑμᾶς to ἡμᾶς. But the predominance of first-person plural references in the context (but see 3:5), combined with the respectable external evidence for ἡμᾶς ($\mathfrak{P}^{74}$, $ℵ^{2}$, A, B, Ψ, numerous minuscules and versions), suggests that ἡμᾶς is the better reading.

3:2. 𝔐 and a few versions insert δέ, which may be a stylistic improvement. Uncial testimony, however, is unanimous for omission, and this is corroborated by minuscules 33, 81, 323, 945, 1241, and 1739. Of the four other times in 1 John that the author uses οἴδαμεν in a context where δέ could also be used (3:14; 5:18, 19, 20), only in 5:20 can a case be made for John's use of δέ.

3:5. ℵ is joined by only a few versions in reading οἴδαμεν. External attestation for the second-person plural οἴδατε is decisive.

3:5. There is strong evidence (ℵ, C, Ψ, 𝔐, some versions) for including ἡμῶν, making it "our" sins that Christ came to take away. Scribes might have added the pronoun to bring 3:5 into line with 1:9; 2:2; and 4:10.

3:7. Some witnesses have παιδία (in 1 John only at 2:14, 18) instead of the more common (in 1 John) τεκνία (six other occurrences in the epistle). But both intrinsic and extrinsic evidence tend against παιδία.

3:7. Uncial A is unique in reading μή τις instead of μηδείς. Such a solo voice is not likely to reflect the original.

3:8. Ψ adds καί before ὁ. Uncial A and a few versions insert postpositive δέ after ὁ. In neither case can this be termed weighty evidence, and NA^{27} should be followed.

IV. Core Teaching: Love, Works, Trust (3:9–4:6)

The previous section ended on the strong note of Christ's victory over the devil's works. This was coupled with the dark reminder that the person who "commits sin" (3:8) is of the devil. In the larger context of that section, these remarks served as incentive for John's readers to avoid the ruinous course of those who might otherwise deceive them (2:26; 3:7). They are to reaffirm the anointing they received (2:20, 27) and stand firm ("abide") in the Son (2:27, 28; 3:6) and in the Father (2:24). In quite literal terms, they are to abide in the sense of not walking out as those had who did not remain with the community (2:19). The notion of abiding was central to the section.

The present section is linked with the previous one by the "abiding" concept (3:9, 14, 15, 17, 24). But different emphases emerge. Love comes in for more attention (eight explicit occurrences of ἀγαπ- [*agap*-, love] words) than in the three previous sections combined (six occurrences total). The importance of good works as the practical manifestation of religious confession and love for God comes to the fore in a variety of ways. And faith or trust receives its first explicit mention (3:23) in close connection with love (fully explored in Barrosse 1957). It has already been seen that the essence of saving response to the apostolic message lies in the triad of faith, obedience, and love (see exegesis of 2:1a). In this section John will move toward a fuller explanation or application of each of these components of authentic knowledge of God in Christ.

In the sevenfold division of 1 John adopted in this commentary, the present section stands exactly in the middle. There is a certain aptness to this. True, the beginning section sets the stage for all that follows and voices John's central burden that God is light. The final one likewise carries great weight by virtue of the summative and provocative last words it delivers. Sections II–III, as well as V–VI, fully justify concentrated scrutiny by virtue of their strategic place in John's overall presentation; in such a concise and pithy letter, no section seems superfluous or amounts to fluff. But to the extent that John's apparent intention in the epistle is to push readers toward a more authentic expression of faith, obedience, and love, 3:9–4:6 is rightly central in placement because of the distinctive and effective way this section advances that intention.

There is first a summons to love (3:9–18). It is important not to let the many negative allusions of these verses overshadow the predominately positive agapic stress. References to hating, Cain, and coldness toward others are a foil for John's real focus, not discrete and independent themes. His gospel is not law (though it is also not without very definite directives) or moral negativism but love. To urge love on his readers, John speaks in dualistic terms regarding two paternities (3:9–10), two options (3:11–12), and two ways of life (3:13–18). The third of these pairs receives a fairly extensive explication, one that begins (3:13) and ends (3:18) with piercing commands.

The intense progression running through 3:9–18 levels off by confirming the readers in their projected response to John's teaching (3:19–24). There can be peace of heart despite the high expectations that faith affirms. There can be confidence before God and in prayer. Final confirmation, John concludes, is administered by the Holy Spirit, mentioned in 3:24 for the first time in the epistle (although some find the Holy Spirit in 2:20 and 2:27; see exegesis of these verses).

Next John summons his readers to be canny in their religious loyalty and expression (4:1–3). Deception apparently continues to be a real danger and therefore is a notable theme of the epistle. Prophets with false christological conceptions threaten to make inroads, if indeed they have not already done so. The word "antichrist" flashes across the screen once more, building upon the previous mention (2:18). There is need to be wary and discriminating in the voices they choose to heed. To "test the spirits" is to make a choice from among competing claims.

The section concludes with a second confirmation, this time not of love but of their choice, which assumes that they will have decided rightly despite the challenges they are facing (4:4–6). John is frank that readers find themselves in an "us-them" situation; worldly forces both human and diabolical lurk on the fringes of the community that John addresses. While there is indeed a "spirit of truth," there is also a "spirit of deceit" (4:6). But there is a clear path through the jumble of conflicting claims, practices, and behaviors that apparently vie for the readers' attention and loyalties. They have the resources to live lives true unto God because the one in their midst, Christ, is greater than the one who confounds and misleads "the world" (4:4). Christ's presence among them ensures that their choice will have been sound.

IV. Core Teaching: Love, Works, Trust (3:9–4:6)
➤ A. Summons to Love (3:9–18)
B. Confirmation of Love (3:19–24)
C. Summons to Choose (4:1–3)
D. Confirmation of Choice (4:4–6)

A. Summons to Love (3:9–18)

In previous sections John's stress has been on the character of God, the commandment to love, and the need to abide. These things are of the essence of eternal life as believers appropriate it in the present order of things. Now he directs extended attention to the love commandment, like Moses in the desert (Deut. 30:19) or Joshua at the Jordan (Josh. 24:15) setting the options of life or death before God's people. In the process, he revisits themes already introduced (e.g., children of God) but also speaks in new or more emphatic terms (e.g., God's seed, Cain, abiding in death, the vicarious death of Christ as incentive for believers to lay down their lives for others, the necessity that profession of faith translate into ethics and thereby transcend mere words). He paints with broad strokes, some light and some dark, portraying both God's offspring and his enemies. But as Paul could write that the goal of his instruction was "love . . . from a pure heart and a good conscience and a sincere faith" (1 Tim. 1:5 NIV), John's eventual point is not to demonize outsiders but to galvanize the faithful toward consistent expression of love for each other. This is, after all, the flip side of true belief (1 John 3:23). Both are hallmarks of authentic response to the God and Christ of whom John is an apostle.

The subsection can be broken down as follows:

1. Two paternities: Divine versus devilish origins (3:9–10)
2. Two options: Love or hate (3:11–12)
3. Two paths: Life or death (3:13–18)
   a. The world's hostility and believers' charity (3:13–14)
   b. Cain's progeny and Christ's precedent (3:15–16)
   c. Love's practicality (3:17–18)

Exegesis and Exposition

[9]No one begotten of God sins, because his offspring abide in him. They are not
able to sin, because they are begotten of God. [10]By this the children of God and the
children of the devil are obvious. Everyone not ⌜doing righteousness⌝ is not of God,
nor is the one who does not love his brother. [11]For this is the ⌜announcement⌝ that
you heard from the beginning: that we love each other—[12]not like Cain was of the
evil one and slew his brother. And why did he slay him? Because his works were
wicked but those of his brother righteous. [13]⌜So⌝ do not marvel, ⌜ ⌝ brothers, if the
world hates you. [14]We know that we have passed out of death into life because we
love the ⌜ ⌝ brethren. The one who does not love ⌜ ⌝ abides in death. [15]Everyone who

hates ⌜his⌝ brother is a killer, and you know that no killer has eternal life abiding ⌜in
him⌝. [16]By this we know love: that one laid down his life for us. So, ⌜for⌝ the brethren
we ought ⌜to lay down⌝ our lives. [17]But whoever ⌜has⌝ material plenty and ⌜notices⌝
his brother having need, but then ⌜is callous⌝ toward him—how is the love of God
⌜abiding⌝ in him? [18]⌜ ⌝ Dear little children, let us love not with words ⌜and⌝ mouth
alone but with actions and in fact.

1. Two Paternities: Divine versus Devilish Origins (3:9–10)

First John 3:9 reaffirms that God's offspring do not sin: "No one begotten of God[1] sins."[2] This comes as a direct result of their divine parentage. John's assertion has points of contact with previous verses but makes its claim in slightly different ways. Thus 3:9, taken together with 3:10, lays the foundation for the summons to love that is the major theme of 3:9–18.

First John 3:9–10 accomplishes that, first, by affirming the divine parentage of believers. Passive forms of γεννάω (*gennaō*, beget), with God the tacit active agent, stand like bookends at the beginning and end of 3:9. The word appeared earlier (2:29) and persists in later discussions (4:7; 5:1 [3x], 4, 18 [2x]). It is this parentage that enables believers to be called "children of God" (see exegesis of 3:2). They "have been begotten" (Greek perfect passive participle conveying a stative sense) along the lines of all "children of God" (John 1:12), who are "begotten of God" and are not products of human procreative or volitional resolve (1:13). No wonder John will go on to make ambitious demands of them: they are a unique reality, divinely fathered and therefore graced with a higher ethic than those only naturally born.

The meaning of "children of God" can be clarified by a comparison. First-century rhetorician Dio Chrysostom (*Orations* 4.21–23) relates a conversation between Alexander the Great and a philosopher named Diogenes. Alexander asked Diogenes what he thought of the claim made by some that Alexander was begotten by a god. Diogenes replied that if Alexander lived austerely and embodied "the divine art of being king," then he might rightly be termed "a son of Zeus."

Like Diogenes, John sees a connection between human behavior and divine blessing. But "God" for John is not Zeus, one of the pantheon of pagan gods and goddesses. Consequently, John calls for "doing righteousness," that is, living in keeping with the nature and commandments of the very different God whom Jesus revealed. Likewise John calls for love—something essential to the Hebrew-Christian God (cf. 1 John 4:16) but alien to the nature and concerns of the deities of Greco-Roman polytheism. "Children of God" in John's sense and "son of Zeus" à la Diogenes are two very different things.

1. On the phrase ἐκ τοῦ θεοῦ (*ek tou theou*, of God), see exegesis of 4:1.

2. One could also translate, "Everyone begotten of God does not sin." This seems needlessly awkward. My translation is semantically equivalent.

As God's children, they do not sin.[3] Moreover, they "are not able to sin" (for the likely meaning of this affirmation, see exegesis of 3:4, 6). John is not talking of some abstract ideal with no relation to lived experience (contra Holtzmann 1908: 343). Nor does he have in mind sinless perfection (cf. the lengthy excursus in Kruse 2000: 126–32). He speaks rather of types or degrees (or both) of sins that are tantamount to defection from God's people. He probably refers in particular to aberrant doctrine, ethics, or devotion that have recently marred the community's integrity. There may be a close relation between "sin" in this sense and the "fatal sin" spoken of later (see exegesis of 5:16).

Why they do not succumb to sin in this sense is specified in the observations that they are God's σπέρμα (*sperma*, seed, offspring) and that "his offspring abide in him" (3:9). This is not (contra Schlatter 1950: 67; Schnackenburg 1992: 175; Kruse 2000: 125) a reference to some growth-inducing agent from God (e.g., his word or divine nature; cf. James 1:18, 21; 2 Pet. 1:4) that enters and transforms believers. Nor is it the message they have received, their anointing, or the Holy Spirit. It is rather a term denoting believers' status as God's offspring. Dryden (1998: 96) offers plausible demonstration that John uses σπέρμα here as tantamount to τέκνα (*tekna*, children) in the same sense that Paul toggles between σπέρμα and τέκνα in Rom. 9:6–8. "Descendants" is an established lexical meaning of σπέρμα in the LXX (LEH 563).

John assumes that God's "seed," his true descendants, reflect his character in their actions. They "abide[4] in him" (3:9b). "The fruit and effect of divine adoption always appear in the life" (Calvin 1988: 274). The logic that reasons from family or genus to visible fruit was employed to good effect by Jesus (Matt. 7:6, 18; cf. James 3:12). What this means may be clarified by comparing John's teaching with that of Roman moralist Seneca, who attributes virtuous behavior to the power of human goodness. Virtuous action comes from within and by one's own volition. He speaks of "the man of perfect wisdom" who is impervious to lapses of good judgment and behavior (*Epistle* 72.6). "Moral perfection" was recognizable in Horatius Cocles, a mythical one-eyed military leader of Rome's early history who modeled consistency and was good, not by dint of conscious planning but simply because that was his character (*Epistle* 120.10).

In contrast to this, John refers not to human virtue in the Greco-Roman sense but to response to the message that God is light (1 John 1:5), compliance with God's commandments (mentioned fourteen times in 1 John) through faith in Christ, and conformity to Jesus's daily walk (2:6). This is not a function of autonomous virtue but the inexorable result of divine parentage. If John senses a tension between divine sovereignty in regeneration and human responsibility to respond and obey, he does not show it in this epistle.[5]

3. Schlatter 1950: 68 draws a parallel with Paul's doctrine of dying to sin (Rom. 6:2).

4. Μένει (*menei*, abides) is singular, appropriate since σπέρμα, a collective noun, is formally singular as well.

5. In this sense John is surprisingly current. Concluding a historical survey of the doctrine of perseverance through the whole history of Christianity, Henžel 2003: 148 states: "The positive

The second way that 1 John 3:9–10 lays the foundation for a summons to love is by affirming the visible nature of the social distinction between those of divine and those of devilish origins. "By this [ἐν τούτῳ, *en toutō*] the children of God and the children of the devil are obvious" (3:10a; on the devil, see exegesis of 3:7–8). Ἐν τούτῳ may point forward to the latter half of 3:10, but it may also look back to 3:9 (cf. Schnackenburg 1992: 176n181: it points "both backwards and forwards"). Based on his readers' divine parentage, John is confident that God's true children, like those of the devil, ultimately cannot conceal their identity. The nature of their inner identity will be "evident" (φανερά, *phanera*) from their actions. This word occurs repeatedly in the NT (though only here in John's writings) to describe the laying bare of the inner truth about deeds (Mark 4:22; Luke 8:17 [2x]; Acts 4:16; 1 Cor. 3:13; 11:19; Gal. 5:19), God's attributes (Rom. 1:19), or Jesus (Matt. 12:16; Mark 3:12).

The danger of John's assertion is that it could foment the very judgmentalism that Jesus forbade (Matt. 7:1). Painting groups in black-white terms is hazardous because not even John's readers, as we have seen, can claim to be without sin (1 John 1:8, 10), nor are enemies of the gospel to be written off by Christ's followers (cf. Titus 3:2–3). After all, long before this epistle appeared, Jesus had addressed the issue of what it means to be children of God: "Love your enemies and pray for those who persecute you, that you may be sons of your Father in heaven" (Matt. 5:44–45 NIV).

And yet to make black-white distinctions is not always to commit a black-white fallacy. For one thing, John's tendency toward hyperbolic dualisms needs to be borne in mind; passages elsewhere in 1 John that forbid hate qualify his identification of the devil's children here. Moreover, Jesus himself seemed to combine a strong sense of group identity (e.g., as master of the disciples) with an equally strong commitment to extend himself even to detractors (e.g., dining with critical Pharisees). John's distinction between children of God and children of the devil is foundational to the love command (the major theme of 3:11–18) in that it seeks to guard the sanctity of the very basis of Christian love: the integrity of community members before God. While overfine or haughty distinctions could imperil that integrity, abolishing all distinctions would constitute a moral leveling and community dilution sure to destroy it. Zeal for in-house purity (cf. 3:3) need not be tantamount to xenophobia and hate.

A third way that 3:9–10 lays the foundation for a summons to love is by affirming the ethico-relational nature of the social distinction between the two groups that John describes—in particular, that some fail, first, to obey God, and then, second, to love others: "Everyone not doing righteousness is not of God, nor is the one who does not love his brother" (3:10b). By touching on the matter of not doing righteousness (see exegesis of 2:29), John reiterates the

way forward is not in defusing the tension between divine grace and human responsibility but in maintaining this tension." If this is correct, numerous groups today have yet to arrive at the level of insight attained by John.

ethical dimension of knowing God (see exegesis of 2:1a). This foreshadows paraenesis in later verses of the section.

By bringing love for others into focus, John introduces the dominant theme of this section.[6] He diagnoses the perennial shortcoming of any group, whether vis-à-vis others or vis-à-vis God: love (hence Jesus's teaching on the two great commandments; Matt. 22:38–40). He makes it clear that any crisis in group identity that he may seek to pinpoint, whatever else may be true of it, is irreducibly relational in nature. It spotlights people's deficiency in terms of the interpersonal rapport (fellowship) with God and other people that John writes to promote (1 John 1:3). This means that the author is not making or assuming the kind of ethnic, racial, socioeconomic, or gender distinctions that one might expect in ancient moral exhortation. Readers with postmodern sensitivities need to ponder carefully before concluding that John's pungent remarks are as intolerant as a cursory reading might indicate. Perhaps he knows of a quality and strength of love made possible by God's light that are foreign to the shadowlands of vogue Western relativism. Augustine summarizes John's counsel this way: "Love, and sin is undone" (Bray 2000: 200).

2. Two Options: Love or Hate (3:11–12)

First John 3:11–12 continues to build the case that John's readers ought to love one another. The ὅτι (*hoti*, for) that begins 3:11 loosely relates it to what precedes (cf. BDF §456). Such love is what was announced[7] to them "from the beginning." This refers to the general time at which they heard and received the gospel message (on ἀπ' ἀρχῆς [*ap' archēs*], see exegesis of 1:1 and 2:7).

The announcement of which John reminds them is "that" (ἵνα, *hina*) they ought to love each other. Ἵνα expresses the "content" (cf. Moule 1994: 145; Painter 2002: 233 calls it epexegetical) of what they heard. Love is a topic already broached in this epistle repeatedly (2:5, 15; 3:1, 10). It is easy to imagine why John would be issuing this reminder. When differences arise within a community, hard feelings can be the result. Enmity has been a feature of human social existence since early on (see exegesis of 1:6), and Christian groups are not immune to its ugliness. Many NT epistles address the problem of strife (e.g., 1 Cor. 6:1; 2 Cor. 12:20; Eph. 4:31; Col. 3:8; 1 Tim. 2:8; 2 Tim. 2:23–24). Nor was it absent from Jesus's own followers even when he was with them (Luke 22:24; cf. Acts 15:2), despite the high premium he placed on peacemaking (Matt. 5:9; cf. James 3:18). In the wake of schism, it is no wonder that John emphasizes it here (other references to loving "one another" [ἀλλήλους, *allēlous*] in John's Epistles are found at 1 John 3:23; 4:7, 11, 12; 2 John 5).

6. "From here until verse 18 the theme is brotherly love as the content of the righteousness demanded" (Holtzmann 1908: 343).

7. On whether John wrote "message" (ἀγγελία, *angelia*) or "promise" (ἐπαγγελία, *epangelia*), see additional note on 3:11.

The tack John takes to address the danger of lovelessness is first of all narratival or even typological.[8] That is, he adduces the story or precedent of Cain (Gen. 4:1–16), who slaughtered Abel (4:8).[9] Barmash (2005: 12–19) helpfully calls attention to particulars of this drama as a historical account in its primordial setting. John's critique of Cain, a faithful application of the Genesis account, is simple: he murdered Abel because of (on χάριν τίνος [*charin tinos*, why?], see additional note on 3:12) the righteous nature of Abel's works in contrast with the evil nature of his own. This points to jealousy on Cain's part because Abel's sacrifice was acceptable to God, while his own sacrifice was rejected (cf. Heb. 11:4). Cain's behavior and underlying attitude were the utter antithesis of love. John uses Cain, the epitome of treachery (cf. Jude 11), as an example of how God's people must *not* regard each other (on οὐ καθώς [*ou kathōs*, not like], see exegesis of 3:3). The message that God is light (1:5; cf. D. Smith 1991: 90) and the announcement that John's readers have had "from the beginning" ought to be issuing in active goodwill for others, not murderous impulses toward them. A major Johannine assurance of salvation is not just the confession but also the exercise of love (3:14).

In the twentieth century names like Hitler, Stalin, Pol Pot, Idi Amin, Saddam Hussein, and Slobodan Milošević became synonymous with murderous intrigue and social oppression if not chaos. In ancient Jewish literature, Cain played a similar role. Opinions vary as to the exact nature of his heinousness. Philo thinks Cain's sin lay in his focus on "earthly and inanimate things," his love for himself, and his offhand attitude toward God's standards of acceptable sacrifices (*QG* 1.59–60). For Philo, virtue lies in attention to the things of the soul, not of the earth.

Josephus (*Ant.* 1.54) accuses Cain of greed and of impropriety in plowing the earth; this meant that the sacrifice he offered to God was "forced from nature by the ingenuity of grasping man." He introduced great evil into the world by "rapine and violence"; further, he corrupted "that simplicity in which men lived before by the invention of weights and measures: the guileless and generous existence which they had enjoyed in ignorance of these things he converted into a life of craftiness" (1.61). Josephus continues (1.66): "Even while Adam was alive, it came to pass that the posterity of Cain became exceeding wicked, every one successively dying one after another more wicked than the former. They were intolerable in war, and vehement in robberies; and if anyone were slow to murder people, yet was he bold in his profligate behavior, in acting unjustly and doing injuries for gain."[10]

8. Cf. D. Smith 1991: 90: "Here is a brief but fundamental exercise in narrative theology and ethics."

9. Akin 2001: 155 calls this the "only direct Old Testament reference in the entire epistle." But it is hard to imagine that John would agree that all his talk of God, light, sin, righteousness, judgment, faith, and other themes so redolent of both Hebrew Bible and LXX passages had no direct grounding in the OT.

10. Additional biblical and extrabiblical references to Cain are collected in Kruse 2000: 235–42.

Other sources suggest that Cain was "led by the adversary" (Apocalypse of Abraham 24.5), largely agreeing with John's assertion in 1 John 3:12 that he was ἐκ τοῦ πονηροῦ (*ek tou ponērou*, from the evil one). He is "a son of wrath" (Apocalypse of Moses 3.2). "Cain's seed" (1 Enoch 22.7) comprises a social force analogous to "the children of the devil" in 1 John 3:10. "Until eternity those who are like Cain in their moral corruption and hatred of brother shall be punished" (Testament of Benjamin 7.5).

John's restrained allusion to the Cain incident is less speculative or midrashic than extrabiblical sources but in harmony with what they insinuate. His readers are not to be like Cain in their behavior. Otherwise the love commandment of the previous verse becomes impossible to honor. John will return to Cainlike behavior in 1 John 3:15, but he first deals with the hostility from outside the community that might tend to generate harsh feelings within it.

3. Two Paths: Life or Death (3:13–18)

In the remainder of this section John contrasts the status, loyalties, and actions of his readers with those of "the world" (3:13). Characteristic of one group is life and of the other group death (3:14–15). Without explicit utilization of the "two ways" language found in postapostolic sources (e.g., Did. 1.1; Barnabas 18.1; cf. 1 Clem. 31.1; but see also Prov. 4:18–19; 15:9), John reflects a comparable viewpoint. His summons to love continues to grow out of a combined critique of evildoing and commendation of agapic attitudes and actions.

a. The World's Hostility and Believers' Charity (3:13–14)

The initial καί (*kai*) is transitional, introducing a result from what precedes (BDAG 495), and may be translated "so." The command μὴ θαυμάζετε (*mē thaumazete*, do not marvel) most closely resembles two sayings of Jesus in the Fourth Gospel (3:7; 5:28; cf. Eccles. 5:8 [5:7 LXX]; Sir. 11:21). John seems to have assumed that readers (whom he calls ἀδελφοί ⌊*adelphoi*, brothers or "fellow-Christians" (so Loader 1992: 41)], the only time in 1 John he uses this form of address)[11] were grappling with the reality of some kind of social rejection or ostracism. They should not be upset by such challenges (cf. 2 Thess. 2:2; 1 Pet. 4:12).

John does not cite a reason why they ought not be upset. He merely underscores the inevitability of the hostility they apparently face (on the world's "hate" toward believers, see exegesis of 2:9) from the world (see exegesis of 2:15a). "World" in 3:13 denotes the realm of the devil's influence and human opposition to God; it is not a denigration of the created order in toto. Jesus taught his disciples that they would be hated: "All men will hate you because of me" (Luke 21:17 NIV). He told them that the world's rejection of his followers was the result of his selection of them and their association with him

11. More commonly John uses τεκνία or ἀγαπητοί; see exegesis of 2:1a. Some manuscripts read ἀδελφοί at 2:7 and 3:21 (see first additional note on both 2:7 and 3:21).

(John 15:19). Jesus himself was hated, he said, because he pointed out people's evil deeds to them (7:7). Even before he passed from the earthly scene, Jesus warned his followers that they would be hated by "the world" (17:14). He seemed to believe that knowing opprobrium would come on them just as it came on him would help fortify his followers to face it bravely as he did: "If the world hates you, keep in mind that it hated me first" (15:18 NIV). The language and rhetorical strategy of the Johannine Jesus and the author of 1 John in 3:13 have close resemblances. This extends right down to the use of the first-class conditional sentence structure of both John 15:18 and 1 John 3:13 (Wallace 1996: 690–94; see exegesis of 4:11).

Because of John's paratactic style and the graphic images that Cain imagery and words like "hates" conjure up, it is easy to forget that the dominant theme of this section is love. But in 3:14 the love command of 3:11 again comes to the fore. In 3:11 John reminded readers that love for each other is intrinsic to the gospel message. In 3:14 he portrays love as a primary sign, or perhaps means of assurance, of salvation. Human expression of love is not the *cause* of salvation. Calvin (1988: 275) rightly notes that John does not make "man . . . his own deliverer, as if by loving the brethren he could rescue himself from death and procure life for himself." Schnackenburg (1992: 180) notes, "Otherwise it would suggest that one can attain to life through love, an idea not found in John."

The expression οἴδαμεν (*oidamen*, we know) occurs more frequently in 1 John (also 3:2; 5:15 [2x], 18, 19, 20) and John's Gospel (eighteen times) than in any other NT books (on the fifteen uses of οἶδα in 1 John, see exegesis of 2:20–21). In 3:14 John takes his stand alongside the readers and affirms what as believers they all confess: passage from death to life.

"We have passed" in 3:14 translates a form of μεταβαίνω (*metabainō*, to go, pass over). Normally in the NT this word has a straightforward and literal sense: Jesus "*went on* from there to teach" (Matt. 11:1; cf. 8:34; 12:9; 15:29; 17:20 [2x]; Luke 10:7; John 7:3; Acts 18:7). But in its three other occurrences, all in John, it is used figuratively of transferring from the present age or world to the next. Jesus's words in John 5:24 are most reminiscent of 1 John 3:14 NIV: "I tell you the truth, whoever hears my word and believes him who sent me has eternal life and will not be condemned; he has *crossed over* from death to life" (cf. John 13:1 NIV: "Jesus knew that the time had come for him to leave this world and *go* to the Father"). John's affirmation in 1 John 3:14 would comport with the view that John had been taught by Jesus.

What John affirms as a present reality ("we have passed") is viewed as God's past act by some NT writers (e.g., Col. 1:13). Clearly John speaks proleptically; he knows that ultimate deliverance awaits Christ's appearing (1 John 3:2). But believers already experience life in the sense of the eternal life the gospel grants (see exegesis of 1:1–2 and 2:24–25). Their possession of this life is evidenced by their exercise of love toward each other.

The opposite is likewise true. "The antithetical statement in v. 14c gives a negative exposition to underscore what has already been said" (Strecker 1996:

112). Not to love is to abide in death. Believers are to abide in Christ (see esp. 2:18–3:8), having been transferred out of the reign of death. But there is always the possibility, and in John's community the apparent recent reality, of believers giving ostensible assent to Christian faith but not matching it with agapic expression toward those around them. John reminds them what a grating inconcinnity this is. "Whatever else they may claim . . . , they basically deceive themselves about their state of salvation" (Schnackenburg 1992: 181).

The way of (eternal) life is the way of love. Love's absence testifies to death's dominance (cf. Akin 2001: 157). This is not a very subtle point in theory, but experience suggests that it is a truth easily overlooked in any given community at any given time. Apparently due to the elusiveness of this implication of John's message, he continues to urge it on his readers in coming verses.

b. Cain's Progeny and Christ's Precedent (3:15–16)

John's language reflects the same "two ways" orientation seen in previous verses. In 3:12 he alluded to Cain's killing his brother. In 3:15 he reverts to the harrowing image of fratricide. Just as 3:4 apparently wished to show the utter heinousness of all sin, in that it ultimately amounts to rebellion against God, so in 3:15 John apparently wishes to show the utter wretchedness of lovelessness, in that it amounts to murder.

The first half of 3:15 makes this very point. "Everyone who hates his brother is a killer." In the rhetorical scope of 1 John, to not love is to hate (see 2:10–11), and to hate is to be a murderer. This is not very satisfactory as a strictly logical argument, because in fact there seems to be a whole spectrum of orientations lying between the relational termini of love and hate. Similarly, it is not literally true that if we do not love someone, we have murdered them in exactly the same sense that Cain murdered Abel. John is, however, not marshaling a strictly logical and literal argument. He is rather using the sort of either/or imagery found in the Sermon on the Mount (Strecker 1996: 113n36 calls attention to rabbinic parallels). There, too, to be angry is to murder (Matt. 5:21–22), just as to lust is to fornicate (5:28). It is widely conceded that Christ was speaking hyperbolically (but see Calvin 1988: 276). John is likewise using overstatement to clinch his point in 1 John 3:15.

He makes his point by using the word ἀνθρωποκτόνος (*anthrōpoktonos*, murderer), a word occurring elsewhere in the NT only on Jesus's lips (John 8:44) to describe the devil.[12] Since he has mentioned "children of the devil" a short while earlier (1 John 3:10), and since Cain's ties with the devil are clear (3:12: he is "from the evil one"), it is understandable that John applies the term to people bereft of love here.

In the second half of 3:15 John avers what his readers, he feels, will readily intuit to be true: "you know [see exegesis of 2:20–21] that no killer has eternal life

12. The word is also not attested in the LXX, Philo, Josephus, or the apostolic fathers. Even in classical sources it is "rare" (BDAG 81) and thought to have made its way into Hellenistic prose via the poetry of Euripides (MM 44).

abiding in him."[13] "It does not require searching inquiry or research to confirm this fact. It is self-evident" (Akin 2001: 158). The punch of John's statement lies in what he has previously confirmed about both eternal life and abiding. The former is a major theme of the epistle (1:1–2), the core of God's saving promise (2:25), and the assured possession of those who love others (3:14). The latter theme, abiding, has come to be almost ubiquitous shorthand in 1 John for believers' habitual personal attachment to Christ (e.g., 2:6, 28) or for the presence in believers of God's saving truth (e.g., 2:24, 27; 3:9). In 3:15b John breaks no new ground; he just brings previously voiced convictions to bear on the present equation that lovelessness = hatred = murder. His point in the context will be that to fail to love is to emulate the behavior of Cain. But his readers' model is supposed to be Christ (2:6). First John 3:16 will make this explicit.

Love for others may be considered easy in affluent Western settings where insulation from them is possible. But Seneca, writing approximately AD 50, is more realistic and honest. He frankly points out how "hatred of the human race seizes us" because of the corruption and foolishness we see on every hand (*On Tranquility* 15.1). Dishonesty and stupidity could easily foment despair. But Seneca suggests a better strategy: not John's strategy of love but the Stoic's strategy of contempt. Laugh! Scoff and be cynical! "Therefore all things must be derided and borne with a calm mind. It is more manlike to scoff at life than to bewail it" (15.2, adapted from Hadas 1961: 77). Seneca's forthrightness is admirable, but John points to a better solution. It is easy to write people off, but believers are called to a road higher than either flippant ridicule or bitter resignation.

Seneca prescribed cynicism as an antidote for hatred of others; John calls for attention to Christ's saving death: "By this we know love: that one laid down his life[14] for us" (1 John 3:16). "By this" (ἐν τούτῳ, *en toutō*)[15] points ahead; hence the colon in my translation. "We know" (ἐγνώκαμεν, *egnōkamen*) is one of eight perfect-tense occurrences of γινώσκω (*ginōskō*, to know) in 1 John; each connotes a full and settled experiential knowledge (2:3b, 4, 13, 14 [2x]; 3:6; 4:16). John refers to Jesus as "that one" (ἐκεῖνος, *ekeinos*; see also 2:6; 3:3, 5, 7; 4:17), a usage common in John's Gospel—where it functions as a circumlocution for God (1:33; 5:19, 37, 38; 6:29; 7:29; 8:42), Messiah (4:25), Son of Man (9:37), the Holy Spirit (14:26; 15:26; 16:8, 13, 14), or Jesus (1:18; 2:21; 3:28, 30; 5:11; 7:11; 9:12, 28; 19:21, 35[?])—but completely absent from other Gospels.[16]

13. In the interest of clarity I rendered the literal Greek wording ("every killer does not have eternal life abiding in him") in a way more appropriate to English expression. See exegesis of 3:9–10 and footnote 2 there.

14. Description of Jesus's death in words similar to 1 John 3:16's distinctive τὴν ψυχὴν αὐτοῦ ἔθηκεν (*tēn psychēn autou ethēken*, he laid down his life) is found elsewhere in the NT only in John's Gospel (10:11, 15, 17; cf. 13:37–38).

15. The phrase occurs fourteen times in 1 John; see exegesis of 2:3.

16. Ἐκεῖνος refers to Jesus in Matt. 27:19, 63, but the construction is attributive and not substantival as in the Fourth Gospel.

While in any culture various definitions of love vie for acceptance, for John's readers there is a central defining image: Christ's death for others.[17] In the ancient world "it was the Cross on the Hill rather than the Sermon on the Mount which produced the impact of Christianity upon the world" (Atkinson cited in McGrath 1988: 7). There is of course no utter disjunction between the two. Yet Jesus himself taught that self-sacrifice was the ultimate expression of love: "Greater love has no one than this, that he lay down his life for his friends" (John 15:13 NIV; cf. Rom. 5:7). John passes on to readers the same lesson that Jesus taught him. It was a lesson that confirmed him in love—"by this we know love."

The last third of 1 John 3:16 draws the inference that Jesus's followers ought to lay down their lives for fellow believers. "Ought" language (ὀφείλω, *opheilō*) occurs only three times in 1 John, in each instance pointing to Christ's (2:6) or God's (4:11) example that should in turn be a template for God's people. In the Fourth Gospel, Jesus told his disciples that in keeping with his example they "ought to wash one another's feet" (13:14). John makes the same point here but uses a metaphor from Golgotha rather than from the Upper Room. Early Christians frequently had to lay their necks on the line in the course of their duties (e.g., Acts 15:26; Rom. 16:4; Phil. 2:30). Christ's precedent furnishes believers with a mandate even when response will be costly.

c. Love's Practicality (3:17–18)

First John 3:17–18 rounds off a section that summons readers to love. First John 3:17 employs a lesser-to-greater argument: if a person cannot even share earthly goods with a needy believer, how can this person have God's love abiding in him or her? Similar reasoning appears later, in 4:20. First John 3:18 concludes with a terse exhortation to match confession with tangible action.

The opening words of 3:17, ὃς δ' ἂν (*hos d' an*, but whoever), are found also in 2:5; otherwise they occur in the NT only on Jesus's lips (Matt. 5:19, 21, 22; 12:32; 16:25; 18:6; 23:16, 18; Mark 3:29; 8:35; Luke 9:24; 17:33; John 4:14). Is this a rhetorical mark that John's teacher left on various Gospel writers or their sources? Or is the echo purely accidental, so that John merely sets forth a general and purely hypothetical case (Holtzmann 1908: 345)?

John describes a selfish believer of whom three things are true. First, this believer "has material plenty" (τὸν βίον τοῦ κόσμου, *ton bion tou kosmou*, the property of the world). Βίος (*bios*) refers here to "livelihood, material goods, property" (Luke 15:12, 30; 21:4; see exegesis of 2:16). When βίος is taken in conjunction with τοῦ κόσμου, the phrase "material goods of the world" in this context translates into "material plenty," at least when compared with the one in need. John describes a person with an adequate though perhaps not lavish physical livelihood.

17. Cf. Strecker 1996: 114: "Knowledge of love is founded on Christ's self-sacrifice." Akin 2001: 158 makes the important point that Jesus's "act was not one of mere martyrdom but of atonement." Following Christ's example in the fullest sense is therefore neither necessary (because he paid the price for sin) nor possible (no other human could furnish a sinless offering).

Second, this believer sees a fellow believer (ἀδελφόν, *adelphon*, brother) in need (χρείαν ἔχοντα, *chreian echonta*, having need). Similar language in other NT texts reveals that this was a frequent issue in the early church: some "had need" in the Jerusalem congregation (Acts 2:45; 4:35); Paul labored to supply the "needs" of himself and his coworkers (20:34); Paul commanded that "the needs of the saints" be met via sharing (Rom. 12:13; cf. Eph. 4:28; Titus 3:14). Such activity requires not only industry and economy but also willingness to give. In the scenario that 1 John 3:17 envisions, the former may have been present, but the latter was not.

Third, this believer with means "is callous toward" the one in need. A literal rendering of κλείσῃ τὰ σπλάγχνα (*kleisē ta splanchna*, closes his intestines) would be grotesque and would fail to note that while σπλάγχνα can refer to the viscera (Acts 1:18), in the OT it frequently is a metaphor for what modern English speakers call the heart—the location of deep feelings of affection (cf. Marshall 1978: 194n22; Schnackenburg 1992: 183n205). It can accordingly refer to the mercy or compassion that arises from within (Luke 1:78; 2 Cor. 7:15; Col. 3:12). To "close" this faculty is to be hardened, whether through indifference or brazen heartlessness.

In a sense what John condemns here was widely decried in at least Jewish religion of his day, which went to great lengths to care for the poor. There was an overt OT command about this (noted also by Kruse 2000: 138):

> If there is a poor man among your brothers in any of the towns of the land that the Lord your God is giving you, do not be hardhearted or tightfisted toward your poor brother. Rather be openhanded and freely lend him whatever he needs. . . . Give generously to him and do so without a grudging heart; then because of this the Lord your God will bless you in all your work and in everything you put your hand to. (Deut. 15:7–8, 10 NIV)

Josephus boasted that "no Jew depended on outsiders for charitable support, since the Jews cared for all of their destitute and disabled brethren" (Wylen 1996: 92). Writers like Ben Sira extolled the virtues of giving to the needy (ἐλεημοσύνη, *eleēmosynē*, almsgiving; Sir. 7:10). But the motivation is different than one finds in 1 John. Giving to the needy atones for sin (Sir. 3:14, 30; 35:1–3; Tob. 12:8–10). The motivation is not love but the expectation of getting something in return, whether from the person helped or from God (Sir. 12:1–3; cf. 17:22; 29:8–13; 40:24; Tob. 4:4–11). There is a fine line between appropriating God's promise (Heb. 11:6) and serving him with too mercenary an interest.

In any case sinners and the ungodly are not to receive aid (Sir. 12:4–7; Tob. 4:16–17). But in the community that John addresses, no one is free from sin (1 John 1:8, 10; 2:2), yet all are to abide in God's love. Caring for the needy as the result of having Christ's cross in view appears to be very different from giving primarily to honor the commandment to give alms, a recurring motif in Ben Sira, or to be delivered from misfortune, a stress in Tobit (e.g., 14:11).

The answer to John's rhetorical question "How is the love of God[18] abiding in him?" is obvious: it is not. There is a stark contradiction between the Scroogelike portrait that John paints, on the one hand, and much that he has already written about God's love (e.g., 3:1) and Christ's selfless example that taught love (e.g., 3:16), on the other hand. Love has profound theological underpinnings (see exegesis of 4:7–14) and a sublime exemplar in Christ. But God has sent love forth to be taken up, not admired at a distance. The first test of gospel profession is the practical expression of love toward fellow believers in proximity. Absent this, the claim to know and have God's love is a sham. In an e-mail, internet, and global age, the number of believers in proximity lends even more sting to John's barb than it carried in the first century. This is particularly true of most Westerners vis-à-vis believers in needy lands around the world—to say nothing of the destitute that are never far away from the doorways of homes and churches everywhere.

John concludes his summons to love with a direct exhortation (3:18): "Dear little children [see exegesis of 2:1a], let us love not with words and mouth alone but with actions and in fact." John has the affection of a shepherd as he delivers the message of a prophet. He takes his place alongside the readers as he makes his plea; in fact, the hortatory subjunctive form ἀγαπῶμεν (*agapōmen*, let us love) is found in the NT only in John's Letters (1 John 3:11, 14, 18, 23; 4:7, 12, 19; 5:2; 2 John 5). This is not to say that other NT writers love less. It is only to note that no other writers appear to have made love the major component in their paraenetic thrust in the same way found in the Johannine corpus (see exegesis of 3:1). Since so many of the references to love in John's Gospel are on Jesus's lips, this may be another fairly direct reflection of the influence of Jesus's rhetoric and spirit on John.

The final summons is to deeds and not just words. It is easy to feel a sentiment and call it love, yet fail to perform the acts that actually constitute love's reality as a redemptive manifestation. "God so loved that he gave" (John 3:16). The comparable stress of James comes immediately to mind (James 1:22; cf. Matt. 7:26; Testament of Gad 6.1: "Love one another in deed and word and inward thoughts"). The expression μὴ . . . λόγῳ μηδὲ τῇ γλώσσῃ (*mē . . . logō mēde tē glōssē*, not . . . in word nor in tongue) may connote both things said and the bodily organ that says them; I have followed this understanding in my translation "not with words and mouth alone." Or the expression could be hendiadys (CEV: "not merely by talking"). The corresponding ἐν ἔργῳ καὶ ἀληθείᾳ (*en ergō kai alētheia*, in deed and truth) clearly points to tangible deeds done in reality and not just in theory, "participating in the divine reality that is revealed by Christ, and realizing it in one's own life" (Hass, de Jonge, and Swellengrebel 1994: 2). Jesus's own words come to mind: "Why do you call me, 'Lord, Lord,' and do not do what I say?" (Luke 6:46 NIV). From Jesus, John learned well the lesson that mere outward show—hypocrisy—is deadly.

18. The phrase "love of God" is probably to be understood as a subjective genitive, i.e., the love that God expresses toward people; cf. Strecker 1996: 117.

He not only urges but also shows love by employing sufficient directness that his readers can respond to the question gladly now, rather than quail before Christ on a day when it is too late (cf. 1 John 2:28; 3:3).

Additional Notes

3:10. A, C, K, P, and some minuscules insert the definite article τήν, making NA[27]'s ποιῶν δικαιοσύνην (B, 33, and 𝔐) into ποιῶν τὴν δικαιοσύνην. The sense is hardly affected either way, but NA[27] may be slightly harder since in the only two analogous phrases in the whole NT, 1 John 2:29 and 3:7, the article is present; it is not easy to explain why John would suddenly have omitted the article in his third use of the expression. The anarthrous construction is attested in the LXX only twice (Psalms of Solomon 9.5; 17.19), the articular not at all. A sparse assortment of witnesses replaces ποιῶν δικαιοσύνην with ὢν δίκαιος, so that John speaks of the one who is not "being righteous" rather than the one not "doing righteousness." Poor external attestation combined with the principle that the easier reading is suspect rules it out.

3:11. "Message" (ἀγγελία, *angelia*; A, B, 049, 33, 𝔐; NA[27]) competes in the manuscript tradition with ἐπαγγελία (*epangelia*, promise or declaration) in ℵ, C, P, Ψ, and many minuscules and versions. The latter may well be original, with ἀγγελία having been introduced (1) to conform usage to 1:5 and (2) to avoid making 3:11 appear to speak of a "promise" when the context speaks rather of an announcement or declaration. MM 226 speaks of the "original sense" of ἐπαγγελία as "announcement," a sense that it clearly has in, for example, 4 Macc. 12:9. LEH 219 gives "announcement" as its first gloss. Schnackenburg 1992: 178n187 points out its occasional use to mean "commandment." On ἐπαγγέλλομαι as a virtual technical term for civic "announcement of public sacrifices," see MM 227. Of course the lexical meaning of a verb is not necessarily the same as that of its cognate noun.

3:12. The improper preposition χάριν is found eight times elsewhere in the NT but always with its accompanying genitive preceding it, which is standard Hellenistic Greek usage (BDAG 1078). John's use of it with the genitive object following it adheres to LXX custom. The exact phrase χάριν τίνος is, however, attested in the LXX only at 2 Chron. 7:21.

3:13. Manuscript evidence is well balanced between including καί (which here introduces a result; NA[27]) and excluding it (NA[25]). The context implies what καί makes explicit even if καί is omitted.

3:13. 𝔐 and some Vulgate and Syriac manuscripts add μου. Ἀδελφοί μου is prominent in James (eleven times) and Paul (eight times) but would be an anomaly in the Johannine corpus. This combines with strong external evidence (ℵ, A, B, C, P, Ψ, 33, etc.) to justify omission.

3:14. ℵ is among a very few witnesses to insert ἡμῶν. This is weak external evidence. Ἀδελφοὺς ἡμῶν would be a NT, and not just a Johannine, hapax legomenon.

3:14. C, Ψ, 𝔐, and others include τὸν ἀδελφόν, with another group (P, four minuscules, some versions) reading τὸν ἀδελφὸν αὐτοῦ. The manuscript divergence combines with the rule of the shorter reading to make NA[27] (supported by ℵ, B, 33, and others) plausible though not decisive: there is a motive for the shorter reading in the superfluity of a τὸν ἀδελφόν so quickly after τοὺς ἀδελφούς.

3:15. B has ἑαυτοῦ. A single witness is normally and rightly suspect.

3:15. B, K, 049, and a handful of minuscules furnish evidence for αὐτῷ in NA[27]. External evidence for the reflexive ἑαυτῷ is superior (ℵ, A, C, P, Ψ, 1739, 𝔐), and the reading comports with, for example, 5:10 (NA[27]; but the same textual question exists there). Also, nowhere else in the NT is a μένω +

ἑαυτούς combination found (Acts 28:16 is really not parallel). This makes the better attested reading the harder reading, too, and it should be preferred.

3:16. Very few manuscripts prefer περί to NA[27]'s ὑπέρ, which carries the same meaning here and has superior attestation.

3:16. The aorist infinitive θεῖναι (NA[27]) is much better attested than the present infinitive τιθέναι (𝔐). The present infinitive (found in the NT elsewhere at Acts 5:15; Rom. 14:13) might convey the idea of ongoing sacrifice whereas the aorist (elsewhere in the NT at Luke 5:18; John 10:18; 1 Cor. 3:11) seems to contemplate action that is summary or complete. But the NT database is slender.

3:17. An unimpressive collection of later manuscripts (including L, which also prefers the indicative in the next two variants) has indicative ἔχει, when the subjunctive ἔχῃ is expected after ὃς δ' ἄν (the only exception in the NT is Mark 8:35, but the indicative there is future tense, close to the sense of the subjunctive).

3:17. Three late uncials (K, L, 049) and a few minuscules read indicative θεωρεῖ instead of NA[27]'s subjunctive θεωρῇ. The subjunctive is preferable because of external evidence and the grammar of the clause.

3:17. External evidence as well as grammar support NA[27]'s aorist subjunctive κλείσῃ rather than future indicative κλείσει found in L and a few minuscules.

3:17. A few manuscripts read future tense μενεῖ. NA[27] opts for the present tense μένει, attested by Ψ, 1739, 𝔐—and presumably attested by uncials like ℵ, A, B* C, P, which, however, lack the accent mark to make the determination certain.

3:18. K, L, 049, and minuscules (including 𝔐) add μου, which is then identical to 2:1 but different from John's normal τεκνία without the personal possessive (2:12, 28; 3:7, 18; 4:4; 5:21). Μου would appear to be a later addition.

3:18. Instead of μηδὲ τῇ two uncials (P, Ψ) and some minuscules omit τῇ. ℵ substitutes καί for μηδὲ τῇ. In this case the longer reading is better, due to external backing, and the shorter reading is suspect because it brings a symmetry into the clause (λόγῳ is anarthrous). The text of NA[27], in other words, is the harder reading syntactically.

IV. Core Teaching: Love, Works, Trust (3:9–4:6)
   A. Summons to Love (3:9–18)
➤ B. Confirmation of Love (3:19–24)
   C. Summons to Choose (4:1–3)
   D. Confirmation of Choice (4:4–6)

B. Confirmation of Love (3:19–24)

Having summoned readers to love in 3:9–18, and having employed some strong language in doing so, John now pauses to dispense encouragement. But the comfort he offers is bracing, not saccharine. To be confirmed in love is to assess the state of one's heart before God, never a light matter. On the contrary, it is weighty, because the heart can be a means of both assurance (3:19) and accusation (3:20). Reaching a point of justified boldness before God (3:21), while attainable, must always be regarded as elusive.

The section is bracing also because the logical flow is not transparent, or may seem arbitrary, and many verses (esp. 3:21–24) are weighed down in the armor of Johannine nomenclature. The juxtaposition of so many Johannine themes (truth, heart, boldness, prayer requests, commandments, pleasing God, believing, loving, abiding, receiving the Spirit) in such short compass threaten the interpreter with conceptual overload. Yet there is a luminous thread visible throughout the thick tapestry: despite the human propensity to fall short of the summons to godly love, there can be comfort and confidence in the knowledge of God through faith in Christ and love for one another (3:23). Such assurance, facilitated by divine commandments that make "abiding" in Christ possible, is enabled by God's Spirit (3:24).

The verses may be analyzed as follows:

1. Assurance of the heart (3:19)
2. God's sway over the heart (3:20)
3. Assurance of confidence (3:21–22)
4. Assurance of valid faith (3:23)
5. Assurance of abiding (3:24)

Exegesis and Exposition

19⌜And by this⌝ ⌜we will know⌝ that we are of the truth, and ⌜we⌝ ⌜ ⌝ will set our hearts
at ease⌝ before him, 20⌜whenever⌝ our hearts ⌜ ⌝ condemn us, ⌜for⌝ God is greater than
our hearts and knows all things. 21⌜Beloved⌝, ⌜if our hearts do not condemn⌝, ⌜we have⌝
confidence before God 22so that we receive whatever we request ⌜from⌝ him, for ⌜we
keep⌝ his commandments and do the things that are pleasing in his presence. 23And
this is his commandment: that ⌜we believe⌝ ⌜in the name⌝ ⌜of his Son⌝ Jesus Christ
and love one another, just as he gave ⌜us⌝ commandment. 24And the one who keeps
his commandments abides in him, and Christ abides in that person. And we know by
this that he abides in our midst, by the Spirit whom ⌜he gave to us⌝.

1. Assurance of the Heart (3:19)

In the wake of a stern command against the hypocrisy of a do-nothing love (3:18), John extends an olive branch of assurance. "And by this" probably looks back to the previous verse (Schnackenburg 1992: 184; Burge 1996: 163) and assumes positive response to it. By loving others with integrity, "we will know." Ethically, confirmation in relationship to Christ often comes by compliance with his commands: "If you know these things, you are blessed if you do them" (John 13:17 NASB). By the same token in the cognitive realm, if one does the things appropriate to full-orbed faith, a deepened understanding results.

What will John's readers know as a result of loving each other? They will know that they are ἐκ τῆς ἀληθείας (*ek tēs alētheias*, of the truth).[1] This could have a social connotation. The previous section placed people in one of two groupings (3:10): "children of God" (τέκνα τοῦ θεοῦ, *tekna tou thou*) or "children of the devil" (τέκνα τοῦ διαβόλου, *tekna tou diabolou*). Cain was "of the evil one" (ἐκ τοῦ πονηροῦ, *ek tou ponērou*; 3:12). To be "of the truth" would mean to be among those whose spiritual vitality grows out of the truth.[2] This comports with Johannine usage elsewhere: Jesus said he testified "to the truth" and that "everyone who is of the truth [ἐκ τῆς ἀληθείας] listens" to him (John 18:37). John writes this epistle to readers who "know the truth" and who recognize that "no lie comes from the truth [ἐκ τῆς ἀληθείας]" (1 John 2:21). To love, then, in both word and deed is to know more clearly that the source of one's identity and life as a believer is the truth—which is to say, in John's frame of reference, Christ (John 14:6; cf. 1:14, 17; 8:32). John's first word of assurance points readers to Jesus.

The second "and" of 1 John 3:19 introduces a result: "And we will set our hearts at ease before him." The main question here relates to the verb πείσομεν (*peisomen*). It can mean either to persuade, convince, and thus reassure; or it can mean to conciliate, pacify, set at ease (Schnackenburg 1992: 185). The second option has good lexical backing (BDAG 791–92; an analogous future tense occurrence is Matt. 28:14) and makes sense in the context. On the heels of the nearly incriminating 3:18, there might be need for words of encouragement. Who loves sufficiently to be free of pangs of conviction in this matter? On the other hand, the meaning "to persuade, convince" could make sense as a restatement of the clause "we are of the truth." That is, readers are convinced of their origin and identity in Christ despite the conviction produced by being called into question in the preceding section. I have translated "set our hearts at ease" in order to make better sense of the apparent doubled ὅτι (*hoti*) in the next verse.

"Before him" (ἔμπροσθεν αὐτοῦ, *emprosthen autou*) may speak of John's readers in the presence of the ἀδελφός (*adelphos*, brother) of 3:17 (and implied in 3:18), whom they are supposed to love. But that would be a remote

1. No other NT writers use this phraseology, nor does it occur in the LXX.

2. This assumes the Johannine doctrine of spiritual (re)birth. Alongside natural origin is the occurrence of divine regeneration (John 3); cf. γεννάω (*gennaō*, to beget) language in 1 John 2:29; 3:9 (2x); 4:7; 5:1 (2x), 4, 18 (2x).

antecedent of αὐτοῦ. More likely it envisions God as ongoing observer of believers' actions.[3] Or it may have eschatological reference (πείσομεν is future tense): when Christ appears, our hearts, which might well have been full of consternation, will rather be set at ease (the meaning "to persuade, convince" seems to make less sense here). Or "before him" may refer to truth in the previous clause, which for John is synonymous with Christ—not that the two terms are completely congruent, but they do overlap significantly. John would then be saying, "And by this we will know that we are of the truth [i.e., belong to, originate in, God in Christ], and in Christ's presence we will set our hearts at ease [despite deficiency in compliance with the command to love others]."

2. God's Sway over the Heart (3:20)

John now gives a reason why hearts may be assured. But first he affirms that they may very well be accusatory: "whenever[4] our hearts[5] condemn us." The word translated "condemn" (καταγινώσκω, *kataginōskō*) occurs in the NT outside 3:20–21 only at Gal. 3:11. In the LXX it is likewise scarce (Deut. 25:1; Prov. 28:11; Sir. 14:2; 19:5). Yet uses are adequate to establish lexical meaning (see also MM 325). Sirach 14:2 speaks of a person who is blessed because his "heart [ψυχή, *psychē*] does not condemn him" (RSV). If one thinks of the phenomenon of self-abasement and estrangement from God brought about by internal misgiving, for example, in the Psalms, and not simply of the word καταγινώσκω, what John speaks of has rich OT precedent.

In the event that one senses condemnation, presumably in connection with lack of love for the brethren (3:17–18) and in the wake of putting such wrong right, then John assures readers that "God is greater than our hearts." This points to two truths. First, God is great. This confession is axiomatic in the OT, serving practically as a refrain (e.g., 1 Chron. 16:25; Pss. 48:1 [48:2 MT]; 96:4; 99:2; 145:3; Mal. 1:5; cf. Sir. 43:5; 46:5) (all quotations from NIV):

Ps. 77:13 (77:14 MT)	Your ways, O God, are holy. What god is so great as our God?
Ps. 86:10	For you are great and do marvelous deeds; you alone are God.

3. Yet the LXX's ἔμπροσθεν (162 occurrences) seems never to be used in connection with God's presence; ἐνώπιον (*enōpion*) is much preferred (558 occurrences). Even in the NT there is only slight blurring of this dividing line (Acts 10:4; 2 Cor. 5:10; 1 Thess. 1:3; 3:9, 13). Jesus speaks of himself, but never humans, as ἔμπροσθεν God and uses ἐνώπιον when depicting humans in the divine presence (Luke 16:15; cf. 12:9). Overall NT writers overwhelmingly use ἐνώπιον to refer to people in God's presence. This may argue against the view that with ἔμπροσθεν αὐτοῦ John means "in God's [or Christ's] presence."

4. NA[27]'s ὅτι ἐάν should be read as ὅ τι ἐάν, with ἐάν equivalent to ἄν (cf. BDF §107), yielding "a generalizing relative clause with a conditional character" (Schnackenburg 1992: 185; cf. Strecker 1996: 120).

5. As elsewhere in Johannine literature (e.g., John 12:40; 14:1, 27; 16:6, 22), the singular καρδία (*kardia*, heart) is used where English demands the plural "hearts." Cf. Turner 1963: 23, who speaks of the "distributive singular," i.e., "something belonging to each person in a group of people is placed in the sing[ular]." But some Greek texts have the plural in 3:19; see third additional note on 3:19.

Ps. 89:7 (89:8 MT)	In the council of the holy ones God is greatly feared; he is more awesome than all who surround him.
Ps. 95:3	For the LORD is the great God, the great King above all gods.

In the NT this lofty regard for God is reflected in, for example, doxological passages that ascribe eternal glory to him (by Paul in Rom. 16:27; Gal. 1:5; Eph. 3:21; Phil. 4:20; 1 Tim. 1:17; 2 Tim. 4:18). In John's Gospel the glory of God (11:4, 40; 17:5, 22, 24) and Christ (1:14; 2:11; 8:54; 12:41; 17:5, 22, 24) is likewise prominent. A solitary created human, when confronted with overwhelming conviction, does well to call God's greatness to mind.

Second, God's greatness is relevant to the state of the human heart. "God is greater than our hearts" for John, not in the sense that he so transcends them that there is no personal point of contact (as, e.g., with Allah in Islam), but in the sense that precisely as the exalted Lord, he ministers comfort to the individual. Another set of OT passages dramatizes the point of God's identification with the lowly (all quotations from NIV):

Ps. 18:27 (18:28 MT)	You save the humble but bring low those whose eyes are haughty.
Ps. 25:9	He guides the humble in what is right and teaches them his way.
Ps. 147:6	The LORD sustains the humble but casts the wicked to the ground.
Ps. 149:4	For the LORD takes delight in his people; he crowns the humble with salvation.

The NT, too, contains passages that affirm God's compassion for the humble (Luke 1:48; James 4:10; 1 Pet. 5:5) and lowly (1 Cor. 1:28). All this suggests that if the heart is weighed down with the conviction of wrongdoing, the place to turn is not farther inward but outward and upward toward God. Burge (1996: 164) states, "We do not look into our hearts to see if we feel secure and then use this as evidence of our security. . . . If our conscience condemns, God overrides the verdict." John has already intimated how this takes place in 1 John 1:9.

Doubtless numerous reasons could be given for John's optimism that God is the place to turn when the heart is pricked with guilt, but John underscores just one in 3:20: God "knows all things." God's omniscience is as axiomatic in Scripture as his greatness (e.g., Job 28:12–24; Ps. 33:13–15; Isa. 46:9–11; Matt. 6:8; Rom. 11:33; Heb. 4:13). Again John's point is not to advance an academic assertion. It is to remind readers that in coming before God, they approach one who knows everything about all hearts (Acts 1:24; Luke 16:15) yet is still able to forgive (1 Kings 8:39). He knows human folly and guilt (Ps. 69:5 [69:6 MT]), disgrace and shame (69:19 [69:20 MT]), even thoughts and words before they are spoken (139:2, 4; cf. Jer. 12:3). Yet at the right hand of this God is Christ the advocate (1 John 2:1). Through his intercession, God's knowledge of human misery can result in exoneration that the heart longs for rather than the condemnation that the soul conjures up and fears. "Blessed is he whose heart does not condemn him" (Sir. 14:2 RSV).

3. Assurance of Confidence (3:21–22)

With "an emphatic turning toward the readers" (Strecker 1996: 123), John reaffirms rapport with his third use of vocative ἀγαπητοί (*agapētoi*, beloved) in this epistle (cf. 2:7; 3:2; see exegesis of 2:7). Though the Gospels do not record Jesus using the expression, it seems to have been common coin among the early generation of apostolic or subapostolic Christian leaders, as seen in its use by Paul (eight times), Hebrews (once), James (thrice), Peter (twice in 1 Peter, four times in 2 Peter), and Jude (thrice).

John addresses his "beloved" readers as those whose hearts now do *not* condemn them (3:21a). At first glance this is jarring, since in the previous verse he writes, "If our hearts *do* condemn us" (emphasis added). Are their hearts adversarial or not? The answer may lie in a shift of perspective. First John 3:20 assumes a reader who is convicted of sin regarding love for the fellow believers. This reader has a tortured or at least troubled soul. First John 3:21 seems to assume that the afflicted person has now availed himself or herself of the assistance latent in acknowledging God's greatness and benevolent omniscience (3:20). With those uplifting truths in view, believers can move from a defensive or defeatist mode to a positive one.

They can, namely, "have confidence [παρρησία, *parrēsia*] before God" (3:21b). The word appeared earlier, in 2:28.[6] Confidence in the presence of God is no small thing. Hebrews urges believers to hold on to it (3:6; 10:35) since it enables them to "enter the Most Holy Place by the blood of Jesus" (10:19 NIV). One of the most memorable exhortations in Hebrews is this: "Let us then approach the throne of grace with confidence, so that we may receive mercy and find grace to help us in our time of need" (4:16 NIV). Later, 1 John relates confidence to the perfection of love prior to the last day: "Love is made complete among us so that we will have confidence on the day of judgment" (4:17). In a religion that sets forth a God both merciful in forgiveness and stern in judgment (Rom. 11:22), the sense of unfettered access to his presence is of primary importance.

For John's readers such confidence would appear to have been threatened by both internal impediments (deficiency in faith, ethics, or relationship, as discussed frequently above) and external challenges (e.g., the deceivers of 2:26; cf. 3:7). In the immediate context it would be threatened by an accusing heart—but John has already affirmed that God transcends the heart's self-condemnation (3:20). And so it is that John can affirm a sure confidence despite the numerous exhortations, teachings, and even warnings he has directed to his readers thus far.

6. Παρρησία occurs nine times in John's Gospel but always in the dative case (παρρησίᾳ) and always adverbially to mean "plainly, clearly, publicly."

This confidence is a means, however, not primarily an end. The initial καί (*kai*) in 3:22 probably connotes result. They have confidence "so that" their prayers are effective: "We receive whatever we request from him." (On whether this should be regarded as a carte blanche to "name and claim" whatever one wishes from God, see exegesis of 5:13–15.) This is the first mention of prayer in the epistle (though it is presupposed in 1:9). It may be regarded as important from John's viewpoint for two major reasons.

First, Jesus was a man of prayer. In the wake of Lazarus's death, Martha said to Jesus, "I know that even now God will give you whatever you ask" (John 11:22 NIV). This assurance and precedent of Jesus's effectiveness in prayer is the tip of an iceberg limned more fully in other Gospels, especially Luke, in which Jesus's praying is noted at his baptism (3:21), during his ministry (5:16; 9:18; 11:1), prior to choosing the Twelve (6:12), at his transfiguration (9:28–29), prior to his crucifixion (22:32, 41–42), and on the cross (23:46). How to pray was a memorable point in his pedagogy, a fact still reflected around the world as often as Christians recite the Lord's Prayer in worship public or private. But prayer is halfhearted, if not absent, when confidence about entering the divine presence is weak. So John affirms the assurance with which believers whose hearts have been set at ease may approach God.

Second, Jesus instilled in his inner circle the conviction that to be his follower is to be reliant on requests made to and granted by the Father. He promised the Eleven, "I will do whatever you ask [ὅ τι ἂν αἰτήσητε, *ho ti an aitēsēte*] in my name, so that the Son may bring glory to the Father. If you ask me for anything [ἐάν τι αἰτήσητέ με, *ean ti aitēsēte me*] in my name, I will do it" (John 14:13–14). In the closing hours of his earthly ministry, he placed high priority on urging his close followers to focus their upcoming apostolic ministries on making requests of the Father (15:16; 16:23, 24, 26). All of this echoes in 1 John 3:22 as John writes, ὃ ἐὰν αἰτῶμεν λαμβάνομεν ἀπ' αὐτοῦ (*ho ean aitōmen lambanomen ap' autou*, whatever we request we receive from him). Confidence in God's presence turns the possibility of petitioning God as Jesus taught into a reality. To John's way of thinking, there is no need to stress "in Jesus's name" in 3:22 like Jesus did in the Fourth Gospel; his very person (implied by "his name") is the foundation of 1 John (1:1–4). The passing reference to Jesus's name in 2:12 shows that John does not need to harp on the point that he writes with this authorization because it is presupposed. Its explicit mention in 3:23 is additional evidence that it is not far from John's mind in 3:22.

Access to God can be confident but not flippant. Believers have their requests "for we keep his commandments and do the things that are pleasing in his presence" (3:22; on commandments, see exegesis of 2:3). The relational (confident access) presupposes the ethical (doing what God commands). The prayer that John envisions would not be self-indulgent or whimsical; it would grow out of close attention to what pleases God and furthers his intention. Honoring God as he is revealed in his commandments has already been presented as key to knowing God (2:3–4). It is also key to loving others, since it is the commandment that Christ's followers heard from the beginning (2:7–8). Such commandment-keeping need have nothing to do with rote or sterile subservience; "the things that please him" (τὰ ἀρεστὰ ἐνώπιον αὐτοῦ, *ta aresta enōpion autou*) is precisely the expression used by Jesus to characterize his lively faithfulness to the Father (John 8:29).[7] Moreover, this honoring response is "pleasing in his presence." Ἐνώπιον αὐτοῦ often connotes God's nearness (see exegesis of 3:19, esp. footnote 3). Acts of obedience are not acceptable as minimal responses to an abstract moral code. Yet as means of knowing God, they are integral to a complex of factors (Christ's intercession, true belief, love for one another) that fit believers to stand confidently before the God they confess in Christ.

4. Assurance of Valid Faith (3:23)

Mention of ἐντολή (*entolē*, commandment) in 3:22 brings up a subject not broached explicitly since 2:8. It is a theme that John now expands on in 3:23–24. Previously "commandment" has been associated with knowing God, loving others, and answered prayer. Now John enlarges the boundaries of commandment-keeping still further with a two-part statement. The effect will be to assure readers of the confidence of which he has been speaking.

First, "his commandment"—whether Christ's or God's is not clear—is "that[8] we believe in the name of his Son Jesus Christ" (3:23). While the pistic dimension of Johannine salvation has been implicit throughout the epistle (see exegesis of 2:1a), this is the first time that believing has been referred to explicitly. The call to believe is an ethical imperative.[9] John's Gospel also presents believing as an ethical expectation: "The work of God is this: to believe in the one he has sent" (6:29 NIV). The act of believing is at the heart of ethical compliance before God.

Believing is to have a particular substance. Not only "that" there be belief but also "what" is believed is critical. Schnackenburg (1992: 189) points out this epistle's stress "on confessional statements" laden with "christological content." Belief is to be placed "in the name" of someone (cf. John 1:12; 2:23; 3:18). This means trust in the person, "name" being redolent of an individual's identity. In this case the person is "[God's] Son Jesus Christ," already designated in 1 John as God's Son (1:3) and the righteous advocate in God's presence (2:1). Jesus is referred to elsewhere by this specific designation in 4:2; 5:6, 20 (cf. 2 John 3, 7; John 1:17; 17:3; Rev. 1:1, 2, 5). These additional references are reminders that for John, Jesus's identity (his "person"

7. The adjective ἀρεστός is found elsewhere in the NT only at John 8:29; Acts 6:2; 12:3 and denotes things that are fitting or pleasing.

8. Ἵνα is appositional, linking ἐντολή with believing (Wallace 1996: 475).

9. The verb πιστεύω (*pisteuō*, to believe) is notoriously prominent in John's Gospel, occurring nearly one hundred times: John the Baptist came to facilitate belief in "that light" who was Christ (1:7; cf. 12:46). Believing is the key to divine sonship (1:12; 12:36), eternal life (3:15, 16; cf. 5:24; 6:40, 47; 11:25; 20:31b), knowing God (6:69; 10:38b; 17:8), receiving the Spirit (7:38–39), worshiping Christ (9:38), and seeing God's glory (11:40). Not to believe brings wrath (3:36) and death (8:24).

in classic theological terms) is not only a matter of his being but of his doing (his "work").[10] His incarnation (1 John 4:2; 2 John 7), his baptism and atoning death on the cross for sin (1 John 5:6; cf. Rev. 1:5), his self-disclosure and divinity (1 John 5:20), his role as heavenly witness and "ruler of the kings of the earth" (Rev. 1:5)—all of these are encompassed by "the name of . . . Jesus Christ." This formal-sounding reference out of the blue is made with an apparent presumption that readers will know exactly what John is talking about. If so, it is probably because both the act and the object of believing are so basic to the message they have received that John can mention them here without needing to explain what he is talking about. If readers had been ignorant of the fundamental structure and substance of Christian faith, they would not have been in the community who received this communiqué.

First John 3:23 also underscores that concomitant with believing in Jesus Christ is loving one another (cf. 3:11; 4:7, 11–12; 2 John 5). The understanding that trust and love are mutually conditioning[11] and defining is not only a legacy of OT theology (Deut. 6:5; 7:9; 10:12; 11:13; 19:9; Pss. 13:5 [13:6 MT]; 52:8 [52:10 MT]; 143:8); it was also underscored by Jesus on the night he was betrayed (all quotations from NIV):

John 13:34	A new command I give you: Love one another. As I have loved you, so you must love one another.
John 15:12	My command is this: Love each other as I have loved you.
John 15:17	This is my command: Love each other.

This may be what John has in mind as he adds that readers must love each other "just as he gave us commandment" (1 John 3:23), but it is unlikely that Jesus's teaching on this subject was confined to that particular occasion. Christ continually called for trust but did so in such a way that trust was not mere assent to his statement but also personal commitment to his person [illegible] love. In the same vein, love as Christ showed it to his followers throughout his ministry was to be the norm for his followers' regard for each other. First John 3:23 is an adapted restatement of (1) Jesus's personal counsel to John and others on the eve of his passion and (2) the object lesson that Jesus's life embodied (cf. 2:6).

5. Assurance of Abiding (3:24)

In 3:24 John concludes the section that began at 3:19 and that grants readers assurance in the light of the command to love each other. John relates themes

10. In biblical literature this is true for God the Father as well (e.g., Exod. 3:15; 6:3; 15:3; 1 Kings 18:24; Pss. 20:1 [20:2 MT]; 54:1 [54:3 MT]; 83:18 [83:19 MT]; Isa. 18:7; 30:27; 42:8). For a comprehensive listing and classification of Scriptures speaking of the divine name, see Elwell 1991: 5–34 (God), 117–34 (Christ).

11. It is unnecessary, and for Johannine thinking perhaps an impermissibly foreign conception, to rank love as "secondary to faith in Christ" as Schnackenburg 1992: 190 does. The faith that John recognizes is a personal commitment to Christ, whose very character is one of love.

touched on earlier in a slightly new way in 3:24a–b. In referring to the Spirit in 3:24c, he segues into the next section.

He first relates keeping Christ's commandments with abiding in him and with Christ abiding in the obedient person. "Abiding" has earlier been correlated with loving the brother (2:10), doing the will of God (2:17), honoring what was heard from the beginning (2:24), and receiving God's anointing (2:27). Now it is correlated with commandment-keeping. This points to the multidimensional nature of what abiding entails. In light of 3:23, "the commandments" that John has in mind are likely believing in Christ and loving one another. This is a fitting summary observation in a section (3:19–24) that seeks to confirm readers in a truly Christian love. Faith and love work together, for John as for Paul (1 Cor. 13:2, 13; Gal. 5:6; Eph. 1:15; Col. 1:4; 1 Thess. 1:3; 3:6; 5:8; 1 Tim. 1:14; 2:15; 6:11; 2 Tim. 1:13), to effect the abiding that for John (like Jesus) is a fruit of true knowledge of God in Christ.

John concludes by stating, "And we know by this that he abides in our midst, by the Spirit whom he gave to us" (3:24c). An important question arises. Does "by this" (the expression occurs fourteen times in 1 John; see exegesis of 2:3) point forward to the Spirit? In this case the Spirit could be understood as the proof that the believer abides. Presumably the Spirit confirms to the believer that the commandment-keeping just mentioned is adequate to assure that the believer abides in Christ and Christ in the believer. Keeping the commandments sufficient to achieve a state of abiding is a means to the end of having the Spirit.

Or does "by this" point back to the abiding that comes with the commandment-keeping John has just mentioned? In this case the Spirit is not a proof that one has achieved the preliminary step of abiding; the Spirit is rather the means that God uses to effect the knowing of which John speaks. Believers know, by the Spirit that God (or Christ) gives them, that they abide in Christ and Christ in them as they keep the commandments to trust and love.

The latter interpretation seems more likely for two reasons: (1) it avoids elevating possession of the Spirit to a level even higher than abiding in Christ. In John's theology, abiding is the epitome of trust in Christ, like being "in Christ" for Paul. Neither John nor Paul seems impressed by claims to have the Spirit if the claimant lacks this fundamental grace. (2) It keeps concrete response to God's revealed will central in arbitrating claims to know God. John writes, it seems, to help a community upset by some who say, "I have come to know him," but do not keep Christ's commandments (2:4). Why could they not simply say, "Look, I have the Spirit, and this gives me the knowledge that I abide in Christ and he in me"? In the first interpretation above, it would be difficult if not impossible to adjudicate this claim. But in the second interpretation, the claim could not arise. No one could appeal to possession of the Spirit as a step or stage beyond concrete, often public responses to God like keeping commandments, loving others, and doing the will of God.

The likelihood that 3:24 is meant to head off mystical appeals to possession of the Spirit, not to encourage them, is confirmed in the next section. False prophets and bogus spirits make the matter of deciding who truly hears and echoes God's voice acute.

Additional Notes

3:19. NA[25] and some manuscripts (e.g., A, B, and a few others) omit the initial καί. A half dozen or so minuscules include καί but follow it with ἐκ τούτου instead of ἐν τούτῳ (Harklean Syriac lacks καί but reads ἐκ τούτου). NA[27] is supported by ℵ, C, P, Ψ, 1739, 𝔐, and many versions. Of the fourteen occurrences of ἐν τούτῳ in John's Letters, only three are preceded by καί (2:3, 4; 3:24). Both intrinsic and extrinsic considerations make certainty as to the original text impossible. Yet the difference for interpretation is minimal.

3:19. Three late uncials, 𝔐, and Latin versions support present tense γινώσκομεν (cf. 2:3, 5, 18; 3:24; 4:6, 13; 5:2). NA[27] prints future tense γνωσόμεθα, a NT hapax legomenon (but found in the LXX eight times) with superior external support. In addition, intrinsic criteria make the future the harder reading.

3:19. Remarkable diversity exists in the phrase rendered in NA[27]'s πείσομεν τὴν καρδίαν (so A* B and a few other witnesses):

πείσωμεν τὴν καρδίαν	a few minuscules
πείσωμεν τὰς καρδίας	a few minuscules
πείσομεν τὰς καρδίας	ℵ, A^{c}, C, P, 𝔐, a Latin manuscript, Vulgate (Clementine edition)

External support for the subjunctive πείσωμεν is weak, and the reading may be set aside. The singular τὴν καρδίαν is perhaps a harder reading than the plural τὰς καρδίας (the plural verb could be expected to have a plural object: "we" have multiple "hearts"), which apart from ℵ has external support that is not particularly impressive. Internal evidence is slightly in favor of the singular τὴν καρδίαν, in that there are only two occurrences of a plural form of καρδία elsewhere in the traditional Johannine corpus (Rev. 2:23; 17:17) but six occurrences of a singular in John's Gospel where a plural might be expected (12:40 [2x]; 14:1, 27; 16:6, 22) and three others in 1 John (3:20 [2x], 21). In the end it is hard to eliminate both the first and last possibilities listed above.

3:19. R. Bultmann (*TDNT* 6:3) conjectures that οὐ should precede πείσομεν, so that John writes that "we cannot assure our hearts before him." But he concedes that the conjecture "is not necessary," and there is no manuscript support for it.

3:20. To overcome the difficulty of the apparent repetition of ὅτι, some commentators propose that 3:20 open with ὅ τι instead. This would take "the first *ho ti* as the neuter of *hostis* and *ean* as equivalent to *an*, as frequently happens in Koine" (Schnackenburg 1992: 185). But the more difficult reading with the doubled ὅτι, supported by almost all extant manuscripts, is more likely original.

3:20. A scant few witnesses (Ψ, Latin manuscripts t and w, some Vulgate manuscripts) insert μή before καταγινώσκῃ. The external support is too weak to be more than a failed attempt to make better sense of a difficult passage.

3:20. To overcome the difficulty of the doubled ὅτι in the manuscript tradition, it appears that A, 33, and a few other witnesses simply dropped the second one.

3:21. As in 2:7, ἀδελφοί is preferred to NA[27]'s ἀγαπητοί by a few witnesses, among them ℵ. Both external and internal evidence (ἀδελφοί is unambiguously attested in 1 John only at 3:13; John much prefers ἀγαπητοί or τεκνία) are decisive against ἀδελφοί.

3:21. For full tabulation of the eleven different permutations of the phrase rendered in NA[27] as ἐὰν ἡ καρδία [ἡμῶν] μὴ καταγινώσκῃ, see Metzger 1994: 643–44. No great difference in meaning attends the various options, and NA[27] has come as close to a defensible result as the evidence permits.

3:21. B, Ψ, and several minuscules read ἔχει, so that ἡ καρδία is the subject of the clause rather than the implied subject of ἔχομεν. This makes sense, but the evidence is too slender. Even less well attested is the hortatory subjunctive ἔχωμεν (e.g., 33, 1243), though the sense is plausible.

3:22. Late uncials K, L, and 049 join 69, 2298, and 𝔐 in reading παρ' αὐτοῦ instead of NA[27]'s ἀπ' αὐτοῦ. The latter reading is supported by better manuscripts. Παρ' αὐτοῦ is found in John's Gospel (7:29, 51; 8:26) but not in John's Letters, whereas ἀπ' αὐτοῦ appears in 1 John six other times (1:5; 2:27, 28; 3:17; 4:21; 5:15). Ἀπ' αὐτοῦ occurs in John's Gospel at 10:5.

3:22. Instead of indicative τηροῦμεν several manuscripts have subjunctive τηρῶμεν (e.g., א, A, K, Ψ). Τηρῶμεν would be nicely parallel with αἰτῶμεν earlier in the verse and would also comport with 1 John's usage in 2:3 and 5:3. For that reason the indicative (found nowhere else in the Johannine corpus) may be considered the slightly harder and preferred reading.

3:23. Impressive manuscript support exists for both the aorist subjunctive πιστεύσωμεν (NA[27], following B and 𝔐) and the present subjunctive πιστεύωμεν (א, A, C, Ψ, about a dozen minuscules). The difference in meaning would not be great, and the balanced evidence between the two readings makes a clear decision difficult.

3:23. A few minuscules and versions have made slight changes to τῷ ὀνόματι, whether by adding an initial ἐν or by changing it to the familiar Johannine εἰς τὸ ὄνομα (cf. John 1:12; 2:23; 3:18; 1 John 5:13) or by changing ὀνόματι to υἱοῦ. Lack of uncial support renders all these possibilities unlikely.

3:23. A few witnesses (e.g., A, 1846, some Vulgate manuscripts) omit τοῦ υἱοῦ, but the external evidence is overwhelming for inclusion.

3:23. Codex 049 and 𝔐 omit ἡμῖν. Strong and varied support from uncials, minuscules, and versions suggests that the original did indeed contain the personal pronoun.

3:24. א, K, a half dozen minuscules, and a few versions opt for the word order ἔδωκεν ἡμῖν. This order might feel a little smoother and is found in the NT at John 4:12; 2 Tim. 1:7; 1 John 5:11. But the external evidence for it is not strong, and the reading of NA[27] is perhaps the harder reading in that Johannine usage tends to place the dative personal pronoun after the verb δίδωμι (as in 1 John 3:23; 5:11; and eighteen passages in John's Gospel), not before (only here in 1 John; possible parallels in John's Gospel only at 6:52 and 17:6).

C. Summons to Choose (4:1–3)

John's earlier summons to love (3:9–18) was followed by a series of assurances (3:19–24), culminating in mention of the Spirit that believers possess (3:24). But there is Spirit, and then there are spirits. A disciple of Jesus would have had ample occasion to witness both in connection with Jesus's ministry (Hawthorne 1991: esp. 145–78). Nor, for John, would the decades since Jesus's earthly life have been bereft of encounters with spiritual forces and beings, if Acts (seventy explicit references to πνεῦμα [*pneuma*, spirit]) is any indication. John therefore toggles back to the summons mode, this time urging readers not to love but to choose. Lest confidence in the Spirit's presence induce sloppiness in readers' religious life, John calls for keen diligence. Love as John understands it is apparently not indiscriminate affirmation but discerning devotion.

This summons to choose lasts only three verses, comprising eight full lines in NA^{27}. In contrast, this section's earlier summons (3:13–18) ran to more than thirteen lines. But 4:1–3 relates the issue of spiritual discernment to Christology and antichrist. These are matters already touched on in this epistle. It is unnecessary for John to dwell on them at greater length here. He can rather simply mention them, extend his earlier comments as necessary, and then draw the inferences that are appropriate for the subject now at hand.

The verses may be analyzed as followed:

1. Admonition and basis (4:1)
2. Identification of the Spirit of Christ and the spirit of antichrist (4:2–3)

Exegesis and Exposition

[1]Beloved, do not give credence to every spirit. Rather, subject ⌜the spirits⌝ to testing
whether they are of God, because many false prophets have gone out into the world.
[2]This is how ⌜you recognize⌝ the Spirit of God: every spirit that confesses ⌜Jesus Christ⌝
as ⌜having come⌝ in the flesh is of God. [3]But every spirit that ⌜does not confess⌝ ⌜this
Jesus⌝⌜ ⌝ is not ⌜of⌝ God. In fact this is the spirit of the antichrist—⌜the spirit that⌝ you
heard is on the way and is already, now, in the world.

1. Admonition and Basis (4:1)

John again calls his readers ἀγαπητοί (*agapētoi*, beloved; see exegesis of 2:7). This noun of direct address[1] occurs at key junctures in 1 John:

2:7	Beloved, I write to you not an old but a new commandment.
3:2	Beloved, we are children of God; it is not yet evident what we will be.
3:21	Beloved, we have confidence before God, if our hearts do not condemn.
4:1	Beloved, do not give credence to every spirit.
4:7	Beloved, let us love one another.
4:11	Beloved, if God loved us this way, we ought to love each other.

John employs ἀγαπητοί primarily to introduce weighty statements of fact. In 4:1, however, as also in 4:7, "beloved" precedes a command. In all occurrences this word implies a close rapport between John and his readers. In 4:1 and 4:7, it lends a particular weight to the commands that follow. John writes not as a distant authority figure but as a mentor with a personal regard for his addressees.

They are not to "give credence to every spirit." The imperative is a form of πιστεύω (*pisteuō*, to believe). But John is not warning readers against placing their faith in spirits. It would be axiomatic that religious trust belongs to God and the Son of God alone (John 14:1; cf. 12:36; Acts 16:31). The construction of 1 John 4:1 (πιστεύω + dative; cf. John 4:21; 10:37, 38; 14:11; Moulton 1908: 67–68) connotes rather a prohibition against accepting what these spirits claim or the dark ethical impulses they may encourage. While the Spirit of God is to be heeded and welcomed, these spirits are to be assessed and, if need be, resisted (Moulton 1908: 125 detects an iterative force to the prohibition). They are not to be given a gullible reception.

Specifically, they are to be tested. The verb δοκιμάζω (*dokimazō*, to examine, put to the test) occurs imperativally twice in the LXX (Pss. 26:1 [25:2 LXX]; 139:23 [138:23 LXX]). In both cases the psalmist implores the Lord to test or search his heart, mind, thoughts, or some combination of these. In NT usage the same verb is used as an imperative in connection with doctrinal or ethical self-assessment (1 Cor. 11:28; 2 Cor. 13:5; Gal. 6:4). Prospective deacons, Paul tells Timothy, are to be "tested" (1 Tim. 3:10). Likewise, in 1 John 4:1, when spirits manifest themselves, they are to be scrutinized closely.

A multiplicity of spirits need not point to a sinister presence. Angels can be regarded as "spirits" rendering benevolent service to believers (Heb. 1:14; cf. 1:7), and Christ is represented as sending forth "seven spirits" into the churches (Rev. 3:1; cf. 4:5) and indeed into all the earth (5:6). Ellis (2000: 204) assumes that the spirits here are angels. More commonly, however, NT writings associate πνεύματα (*pneumata*, spirits) with evil (Matt. 12:45; Luke 11:26; Acts 19:12–13), uncleanness (Mark 3:11; 5:13; Acts 8:7), false prophecy

1. For the nominative form filling a vocative function, see BDF §147.

(Rev. 16:13), and demons (16:14). It is therefore well advised to check to see "whether[2] they are of God."

Spirits not "of God" are to be rejected. Implementing John's command hinges on grasping positively what "of God" entails. Things "of God" or "from God" (ἐκ θεοῦ, *ek theou*) in NT annals include regeneration (John 1:13), charismatic giftedness (1 Cor. 7:7), apostles like Paul (2 Cor. 2:17), the resurrection body (5:1), and the righteousness that is by faith (Phil. 3:9). First John 4:1 adds an article before "God" (ἐκ τοῦ θεοῦ, *ek tou theou*). The phrase still means "of God" but in this particular form is more redolent of Jesus's words in John's Gospel (John 7:17; 8:42, 47 [2x]).[3] The phrase occurs with notable regularity (sixteen times in a total of twelve verses) in 1 John:

3:9a	No one born *of God* commits sin.
3:9b	He cannot sin because he is born *of God.*
3:10	Anyone who does not do righteousness is not *of God.*
4:1	Subject the spirits to testing whether they are *of God.*
4:2	Every spirit that confesses that Jesus Christ has come in the flesh is *of God.*
4:3	Every spirit that does not confess this Jesus is not *of God.*
4:4	You are *of God.*
4:6a	We are *of God.*
4:6b	The one who is not *of God* does not listen to us.
4:7a	Love is *of God.*
4:7b	Everyone who loves has been born *of God.*
5:1	Everyone who believes that Jesus is the Messiah is born *of God.*
5:4	Everyone born *of God* overcomes the world.
5:18a	We know that everyone born *of God* does not sin.
5:18b	The one who was born *of God* keeps him.
5:19	We know that we are *of God.*

From this listing we see that the phrase "of God" describes the identity of those who confess Jesus aright: they are "of God."[4] True christological confession and love are likewise "of God." This same quality is, however, lacking where sin is dominant and particularly where aberrant christological confession prevails.

2. For εἰ in the sense of "whether," see Luke 14:31; John 9:25; Acts 4:19; 2 Cor. 13:5.

3. For the same construction in Paul, see Rom. 2:29; 1 Cor. 2:12; 11:12; 2 Cor. 3:5; 5:18. "From God" (ἐκ θεοῦ or ἐκ τοῦ θεοῦ) occurs in the NT only in writings traditionally ascribed to John and Paul and is absent from the LXX. The near synonym ἀπὸ θεοῦ (*apo theou*) occurs in James 1:13 and 2 Pet. 1:21.

4. I avoided the translation "from God" because it could connote a more direct descent from God the Father, and in Johannine parlance this answers to ἀπὸ θεοῦ (*apo theou*, from God). In John 3:2; 13:3; and 16:30 Jesus is said to have come "from God." It is unlikely that John, either in the Gospel or in the epistles, sees himself and believers as coming "from God" in the same sense. For John, Jesus is ἀπὸ θεοῦ; John and other believers are ἐκ θεοῦ. D. Smith 1991: 100 rightly calls attention to NRSV's unfortunate decision to render ἐκ as "from" throughout this passage.

Spirits "of God," then, would be impulses, presumably reflected in the lives of people that John addresses, conducive to the christological integrity and ethical probity that John associates with knowledge of the God who is light (1:5). John's readers are to be alert as to whether doctrines and behavior cropping up in their midst truly reflect the character of the God they worship as revealed in Jesus Christ.

The reason for the warning is simple: "Many false prophets have gone out into the world." This statement begs comparison with John's earlier claim that "now many antichrists have appeared" (2:18; so also Beale 2004: 292). It also echoes Jesus's predictions of false prophets (Matt. 24:11, 24). And it resonates with still broader first-century concerns. Greco-Roman religion of the time trafficked heavily in secret or privileged knowledge of sacred mysteries. There was "proliferation of personal dream revelations, oracles and their interpretation, magic and astrology"; in addition, there were "numerous exclusive groups offering initiates higher knowledge for their personal weal and salvation" (Bockmuehl 1990: 20).

A Roman commander kept a Syrian prophetess named Martha with his army to give advice on important decisions; the Roman senate could settle an issue according to the prophetic pronouncement of a priest or priestess (Plutarch, *Parallel Lives*, Marius 17.1).

In Jewish settings both Philo (*Spec. Laws* 1.315) and Josephus (*J.W.* 6.285–88) warn against false prophets. Qumran literature speaks of "two spirits" that steer persons (1QS 3.13–4.14). One of these is the destructive spirit, which seeks the overthrow of God's people. Discernment is called for to keep from falling prey to this spirit's ways, which are carefully cataloged in 1QS 4.10–11 (Vermes 1997: 102):

1. greed
2. slackness in the search for righteousness
3. wickedness and lies
4. haughtiness and pride
5. falseness and deceit
6. cruelty and abundant evil
7. ill temper and much folly and brazen insolence
8. abominable deeds [committed] in a spirit of lust
9. ways of lewdness in the service of uncleanness
10. a blaspheming tongue
11. blindness of eye and dullness of ear
12. stiffness of neck and heaviness of heart

The outcome, says this Qumran document, is "that man walks in all the ways of darkness and guile."

No wonder John instructs readers to regard spiritual manifestations warily. They were widespread (although John's "antichrist tradition" took on "a unique form"; Jenks 1991: 346), and their effects were not always benign, as

NT exorcism accounts in both Gospels and Acts document. But how were readers to know when a spirit or spirits were leading them astray? In the next two verses, John provides at least a partial answer to this question.

2. Identification of the Spirit of Christ and the Spirit of Antichrist (4:2–3)

"This is how you recognize the Spirit of God," John states. The exact expression "the Spirit of God" (τὸ πνεῦμα τοῦ θεοῦ, *to pneuma tou theou*) is found elsewhere in the NT only at Matt. 3:16; 1 Cor. 2:11; 3:16 (and with anarthrous θεοῦ in Rom. 8:9 and 1 Cor. 7:40). But the reality and active role of God's Spirit—extending far back into OT times, even to creation (Gen. 1:2)—has long been recognized (see Warfield's classic 1932 study; for updated discussion, see Hamilton 2003). As inheritors of the biblical tradition, John's readers would have been no strangers to God under this rubric. God is heavenly Lord and incarnate Son, yet also ubiquitous Spirit. It is important that they not mistake his identity.

The initial words of 1 John 4:2 (ἐν τούτῳ, *en toutō*, lit., "by this") look ahead to the next clause (cf. Schnackenburg 1992: 200); John is going to give a yardstick for measuring the Spirit's presence.

The measure is christological. Spirits from God confess "Jesus Christ as having come in the flesh" (for an exhaustive study of "the Coming One," see Cuadrado 1993; cf. Silva 1995). The perfect participle ἐληλυθότα (*elēlythota*, having come; cf. Mark 9:1; Luke 5:17; Acts 18:2) points to a settled status: Christ did not merely make an appearance in a fleshly guise but fully assumed the bodily existence common to humanity. It is important that this truth be affirmed in the course of the confessional activity that defined Christian identity from the church's earliest days (see the confessional connotation of ὁμολογέω [*homologeō*, to acknowledge or confess] at Matt. 10:32; Acts 24:14; Rom. 10:9–10; 1 Tim. 6:12). "The criterion that aids discernment of spirits is confession" (Strecker 1996: 134).

This is often and plausibly taken as a rebuttal of the docetism that arose in the early church and competed with the view that Jesus was both fully God and fully human. John would have been in a good position to speak to this issue. As the epistle's prologue (1 John 1:1–4) makes clear, John was among those who had physical contact with Jesus. His full humanity could not be questioned. Yet John's Gospel (in Christian history often styled the "eagle" Gospel [cf. Rev. 4:7] because of its high Christology) makes astounding claims regarding Jesus's full divinity. True, he was not God the Father (John 1:18). But he somehow possessed a commonality with God that no other human ever has or could (if God is one, i.e., a singular unity). A spirit from God will not distort this two-sided truth: Jesus's full humanity as well as his full divinity. A primary gauge of a spirit's authenticity is, then, doctrinal.

It should be remembered that the doctrinal test, however, is not the only test. From what John has already written, his readers would understand that, along with doctrine, ethics and love are equally important calling cards of gospel truth. A spirit or its human lackey spouting doctrinal correctness but encouraging ethical laxness or hatred would hardly receive John's approval. But in 1 John 4:2 he apparently envisions a social setting, perhaps communal worship, where utterances reflecting religious spirit, if not spirits proper, are in evidence (cf. 1 Cor. 12:3; 14:32). D. Smith (1991: 99) proposes that "Christian prophets claiming the authority of the Spirit (or of Christ) have been addressing the community." Burge (1996: 173) speaks of "pneumatics, teachers claiming that their words are inspired by the Spirit of God." In such a setting full fidelity to the apostolic teaching about Jesus Christ, both human and divine, is a sine qua non of authentic Christian worship.

John acknowledges two very different kinds of spirit manifestations, and this is why some yardstick is necessary. First, a spirit may be "of God" (see exegesis of 4:1). It may represent and express ideas or sentiments that are in line with God's assessment of things. Paul wrote his epistles with a consciousness of having God's Spirit (1 Cor. 7:40). As an apostle, John writes with a similar sense of presence. His letter typifies an expression that is "of God" in the sense of conveying God's wisdom and truth about the matters at hand.

Or a spirit may give a very different impression: it may seem to indicate that "Jesus is not of God." This is probably an elliptical expression that in context means that Jesus as God's Son did not really and fully assume human nature and with it full corporeality. The writer of 2 John 7 issues a warning with at least formal parallels: "Many deceivers, who do not acknowledge Jesus Christ as coming in the flesh, have gone out into the world." The Jesus of the Qur'an comes to mind (cf. Jomier 2002: 65–73); he is a creature and in no sense an incarnation of God (sura 3.59; 18.4–5). Nor did he die on the cross (E. M. Caner and E. F. Caner 2002: 220; sura 4.157). The readers of 1 John are to be alert to misrepresentation of Christ in the midst of the spiritual manifestations that arise within their community. "The Spirit does not work in a vacuum or independently of any other authority in the church" (D. Smith 1991: 101). At issue is not a fine point of doctrine but rather the specter of antichrist himself (1 John 4:3), who, as John has already said (2:18), has come and is active in the world. Satan will stoop to any level to deceive people, including God's people, who are apparently susceptible to such hoodwinking. John appeals to his readers to exercise discernment. Just as Christ has come and remains present in the world with glorious redemptive potential, so also the adversary is on the scene to disrupt and mislead where he can (cf. 1 Pet. 5:8). But as the next subsection will insist, Christ maintains a firm upper hand.

Additional Notes

4:1. Two uncials seek to intensify John's counsel, K by making it clear that they should test "all the spirits" (πάντα τὰ πνεύματα, *panta ta pneumata*) and Ψ by stating that "every" (πᾶν, *pan*) spirit should be put to the test.

4:2. Ψ*, 𝔐, and two versions have the present passive γινώσκεται. This would make τὸ πνεῦμα the subject: "By this the Spirit of God is recognized." Against this reading is the quality of external attestation and the principle of the harder reading (γινώσκεται fits in perfectly with the context and is therefore suspect). But it still deserves consideration, because if scribes were going to choose a truly "easier" reading, they could have opted for the first-person plural γινώσκομεν (like ℵ* and 630), as the phrase ἐν τούτῳ γινώσκομεν is common in 1 John (2:3, 5; 3:24; 4:13; 5:2). The reading chosen by NA[27] is, however, also a harder reading, since nowhere else in John's Letters does ἐν τούτῳ γινώσκετε appear. And the external witnesses are weighty: ℵ², A, B, C, L, Ψᶜ, 33, and others.

4:2. Uncial C is alone in reading χριστὸν ἰησοῦν, a locution that occurs only ten times in the NT, five times each in Acts and Paul. Ἰησοῦν χριστόν has vastly superior external support and a better claim to be Johannine (cf. John 17:3; 1 John 2:1; 2 John 7).

4:2. B and a few other witnesses have ἐληλυθέναι (perfect active infinitive) instead of ἐληλυθότα (perfect active participle). The difference in meaning is nil, but the variant is too sparsely attested to be considered original.

4:3. The Vulgate and (according to a marginal reading in 1739) Irenaeus, Clement of Alexandria, Origen, and Lucifer read λύει (destroys) instead of μὴ ὁμολογεῖ (does not confess). The variant is intriguing but lacks serious external support. Even if the variant were accepted, the net effect of the clause would be much the same from the point of view of John's Christology: not to confess a Jesus of apostolic proportion is tantamount to confessing no Jesus at all.

4:3. NA[27]'s τὸν ἰησοῦν is supported by A, B, Ψ, and other witnesses (including Origen and, according to a marginal reading in 1739, Irenaeus and Clement of Alexandria). ℵ stands alone in offering "Jesus [as] Lord"; 1881 and 2464 stand alone in reading the anarthrous ἰησοῦν; 1846 alone reads τὸν χριστόν; 𝔐 and others preserve the reading τὸν ἰησοῦν χριστόν (K has the same but omits the article; 614 contains the article but has ἰησοῦν after χριστόν). NA[27]'s reading is likely to be original, but the passel of variants testifies to the pressure that scribes faced to make their version fully reflect the christological import of the phrase.

4:3. Probably borrowing from 4:2, many witnesses add ἐν σαρκὶ ἐληλυθότα: ℵ, Ψ, (33), 𝔐, and some versions and church fathers. Omitting the phrase are A, B, several minuscules, and other versions and fathers. The external evidence is rather evenly divided. The sense of the additional phrase is implied in the discourse whether or not John penned the actual words.

4:3. K, L, 049, and others omit ἐκ, which would yield a translation "of God": John would be saying that a spirit making such a confession is not doing God's bidding. This is close to the same sense that reading the preposition ἐκ yields. In any case ἐκ is surely original, since external evidence for it is overwhelming.

4:3. External support for ὅ, whose antecedent would be "the spirit," is strong. ℵ and a few others read ὅτι ("for you have heard"); Ψ and a few Latin witnesses read οὗ ("whom you have heard"). Support for neither variant is weighty enough to be taken seriously.

D. Confirmation of Choice (4:4–6)

The preceding apocalyptic-sounding declaration of threats posed by false prophets, false spirits, and antichrist (4:1–3) amounts to a summons for John's readers to choose. This appeal is now both grounded and offset by assurance that readers are in fact on the right track and therefore beyond the reach of evil's ravages. Danger is real, but its destructive power pales alongside the bright force of Christ that gives God's people their identity. It is hazardous to infer from John's language that opponents of the faith were enjoying widespread success outside of Johannine circles (rightly Strecker 1996: 139). All that is certain is that some were willing to hear distortions of the gospel, just as those with at least equal zeal found a place in their hearts for the truth.

To underscore the confidence that John's message warrants despite the deceptive power of spirits that work against them, John focuses on the victory that believers have won (4:4), the self-referential deludedness of the faith's detractors (4:5), and the truth of the apostolic message (4:6). Full and continual reception of that message, John implies, is the confirmation that believers are rightly discerning the spirits that seek to direct their devotion either heavenward, toward Christ and his ways, or elsewhere. The verses may be analyzed as follows:

1. God's victory in his people (4:4)
2. The world's self-fixation (4:5)
3. The apostolic testimony (4:6)

Exegesis and Exposition

4You are of God, dear children, and you have prevailed over them, because the one who is among you is greater than the one who is in the world. 5They are of the world; for this reason they speak from the world's vantage point and the world listens to them. 6We are of God; the one who knows God listens to us. ⌜The person who is not of God does not listen to us⌝. ⌜This is how⌝ we know the spirit of truth and the spirit of deception.

1. God's Victory in His People (4:4)

In contrast to the antichrist and spirits that work in league with him (4:3), John reminds readers of their identity as God's possession. They are "of God" (see exegesis of 4:1). The direct and perhaps plaintive tone of John's appeal is underscored not only by the emphatic ὑμεῖς (*hymeis*, you; see additional note) but also by his use of τεκνία (*teknia*, dear children; see exegesis of 2:12–13). It is possible that "children" refers here particularly to their status as God's children and not merely to their relationship to the author (Balla 2006: 224). In either case, the warning implied in 4:1–3 is heartfelt.

But John is optimistic. His readers, he asserts, "have prevailed over" the forces arrayed against them. It is not clear whether John has in mind antichrist and allied spirits, evil people in the world generally, those who have left the church (2:19), or some combination of these. Whether he has any or all of these in view, John declares victory. His readers, in the midst of wrestling with the forces of evil, have already defeated them. There are direct parallels here with Paul's theology of the cross as it emerges in the latter half of Rom. 8 (esp. 8:37).

The perfect tense use of νικάω (*nikaō*, to conquer) occurs in the NT only in John's writings (John 16:33; 1 John 2:13, 14). Jesus's use of the term is instructive. On the eve of the cross he declares his own triumph: "But take heart! I have overcome the world!" (John 16:33 NIV). On the lips of a man who was accurately predicting his imminent death and admitting his profound travail of soul (12:27), the words are baffling. They seem to contradict the reality of surrounding circumstances. But that is probably the point. Surrounding circumstances are not the ultimate consideration. For Christ on that evening, the overarching will of God was rather the controlling image. That image promised the light of glory beyond the abyss of the cross.

John may be offering an analogous consolation to his readers. He is not denying the struggle they face or even the threat of slippage if not failure by some. He well understands that defection from the community of the faithful is a real possibility. But he appeals to those who, he trusts, will hold fast to his words (1 John 4:6). The perseverance of those who hear is a fait accompli.

Yet John's confidence, while it extends to his readers, is not grounded in them. They will prevail only "because the one who is among you[1] is greater than the one who is in the world." The one "in the world" is antichrist and the beings or forces he commands. The one whom believers share is Christ. He is, in traditional Johannine parlance, the one "who holds the seven stars in his right hand and walks among the seven golden lampstands" of the churches (Rev. 2:1 NIV). His powerful presence guarantees his followers' arrival at the destination to which he beckons them.

It can be asked how Christ does this. In the flow of the letter thus far, we can relate Christ's omnipotence as John presents it here to the being and nature of God as transformative light, which he asserts earlier (see exegesis of 1:5). Flowing from the redemptive action of God in his Son, John sees true faith (3:23), obedience to commandments (2:3; 3:24), and pure love (2:10) arising in

1. Most translations prefer "in you." Here as in 1:10 (see exegesis) the distributive sense, which includes the individual sense but enlarges the reference to the corporate society, is preferable. Christ is not present in the individual to any greater extent than the individual participates in the presence of Christ amid the apostolic fellowship as a whole.

the lives of Christ's followers, who are those who receive John's message. As surely as Christ came in the flesh (4:2), died (2:2), rose (implied in every reference to Christ's present existence), and intercedes (2:1), believers can be assured that they will not fall prey to God's opponents. It needs to be underscored, however, that the victory is ever Christ's and then only in a derivative sense their own. It becomes theirs in the course of their experience of "abiding" in him (2:27–28) and is completed only in the age to come (3:2). The "already/not yet" structure of Christian existence frequently noted in Paul is present likewise in John's thinking.

2. The World's Self-Fixation (4:5)

Apostolic writers frequently admonish disciples with clear reference to what those regarded as outside the community of faith may be saying, thinking, or doing (to take examples just from Paul: Rom. 1:18–32; 1 Cor. 1:20; 2 Cor. 4:4; Gal. 5:12; Eph. 4:17; Phil. 3:2; Col. 2:8; 1 Thess. 2:15; 2 Thess. 2:9; 1 Tim. 1:6; 2 Tim. 3:6; Titus 1:16). These extrusions into the Christian fellowship of elements are, to use John's language, ἐκ τοῦ κόσμου (*ek tou kosmou*, of the world). John adopts this same culture-critical strategy here in stating, "They are of the world." Even if he refers directly to those who have left the church or who remain but secretly sympathize with those who have departed, his words have an obvious broader reference. Elements foreign to the good and holy will of God constantly challenge the thoughts and lives of God's people. "The church must be equipped to combat all forms of evil" (Burge 1996: 183).

Jesus stressed two things that relate to John's talk of people who are "of the world." First, Jesus claimed he was *not* of the world. To detractors he said, "You are from below; I am from above. You are of this world; I am not of this world" (John 8:23 NIV). Second, his followers, while obviously ἐν τῷ κόσμῳ (*en tō kosmō*, in the world), are not of the world: "If you belonged to the world, it would love you as its own. As it is, you do not belong to the world, but I have chosen you out of the world" (15:19 NIV; cf. 17:6, 14–16). In this sense Jesus envisions a clear polarity between the community of his followers and everyone else.

John reflects this same social vision. First John 4:5 speaks of a "they" for whom the world, not Christ, is the decisive point of reference. "Because of this" (διὰ τοῦτο, *dia touto*)[2] orientation, "they speak from the world's vantage point"—just as they are of the world (ἐκ τοῦ κόσμου), so they speak.

And naturally, John continues, "the world listens to them." "The world welcomes their message gladly because they are saying just what the world wants to hear" (Schnackenburg 1992: 204). John's reasoning here is a direct reflection of an axiom laid down by Jesus: "He who belongs to God hears what God says. The reason you do not hear is that you do not belong to God"

2. The prepositional phrase διὰ τοῦτο occurs three times in John's Letters (cf. 3:1; 3 John 10) and each time points back.

(John 8:47 NIV). By inference John would know that those who are of the world listen to voices from the world, and vice versa.

John's strategy in 1 John 4:5 is clear. In 4:1–3 he urged readers to exercise spiritual discernment. They must regard the religious claims they encounter with wide-open eyes, and they must be prepared to make hard decisions to distinguish wheat from chaff. In 4:5 John gives concrete definition to those who would be vehicles for the aberrant spiritual impulses that 4:1–3 warns against. Their origin is "of the world," their point of view is likewise "from the world," and as a result the message they are predisposed to hear is not the message that Christ has brought "from above" (John 8:23). This is the message that 1 John seeks to interpret and apply.

John does not stop here, however, but in the next verse moves to set forth a positive alternative and thereby bring the present discussion to a close.

3. The Apostolic Testimony (4:6)

Like another "we" passage of 1 John (1:1–5), where the "apostle addresses church" nature of John's epistle is unmistakable, 4:6 refers first of all to John and others of the apostolic circle. By extension, then, it applies to readers who receive John's message and thereby join the circle. Together this "we" is "of God," in contrast to those in 4:5 who are "of the world."

The function of 4:6 in the context is to reaffirm the apostolic origin of John's message, in contrast to the deceptive currents implied in 4:1–3. There are two corollaries to this as 4:6 continues. First, those who know God hear and accept what John says or writes, and those who are "not of God" do not heed John's voice. Second, the division of the house that John's message generates has a salubrious result: "This is how we know." Such polarity validates the "spirit of truth" that John thinks he upholds, just as it sheds light on the mistaken aspects of "the spirit of error" that John has been warning against.

It is hard to ponder 4:6 without being reminded of the schism implied earlier in 2:19. Division is painful, but sometimes it is necessary, and when necessary it may even have a consoling aspect. In 4:6 John seems to be stating that the clarity that results from people showing their true colors is valuable. Out of the crucible of disagreement or error may come an occasion for discerning God's Spirit (τὸ πνεῦμα τῆς ἀληθείας, *to pneuma tēs alētheias*, the spirit of truth) from the spirit of imposters or pretenders (τὸ πνεῦμα τῆς πλάνης, *to pneuma tēs planēs*, the spirit of deception).[3] On such occasions the apostolic testimony provides resources for informed deliberation and confirmation of wise choice.

Additional Notes

4:4. Ὑμεῖς, the second-person nominative plural form of the personal pronoun, occurs elsewhere in John's Letters only at 1:3; 2:20, 24, 27. In each case it can be seen to have emphatic force. The same

3. 1 John 1:8 juxtaposes truth and deception in comparable fashion; see exegesis.

pattern can be observed in John's Gospel, where the form appears far more than in other Gospels: Matthew has 1.46 occurrences per one thousand words, Mark has 0.77, Luke has 0.89, and John has 3.74; its frequency in 1 John is 2.41. For comparison, the frequency of ὑμεῖς in the thirteen-letter Pauline corpus is 1.74 per one thousand words.

4:6. A, L, two minuscules, and a few other witnesses omit an entire clause. It is possible that the eye of a copyist skipped as the result of homoioteleuton from the first occurrence of ἀκούει ἡμῶν to the final clause beginning with ἐκ τούτου (see Metzger 1992: 189). The Latin witness that follows this pattern might have been led astray by its Greek *Vorlage*, or a Latin scribe could have independently made the same mistake with the repeated phrase *audit nos*.

4:6. A few manuscripts or versions (A, 81, Vulgate, Peshitta, Coptic) prefer the almost synonymous ἐν τούτῳ. Since this phrase occurs fourteen times in 1 John, it is understandable that a scribe might conform ἐκ τούτου (which otherwise occurs nowhere else in the epistle and only six times in the whole NT: once in Jesus's words at the Last Supper [Matt. 26:29] and four times in John's Gospel [6:51, 66; 8:23; 19:12]) to the more common locution.

V. Foundational Imperative: God's Love (4:7–14)

If 1 Cor. 13 is the premier Pauline articulation of God's love, then this section of 1 John (4:7–14) is the premier Johannine statement of that theme (for the same comparison, see D. Smith 1991: 106, 109).[1] In just eight verses, some fifteen words built on the Greek ἀγαπ- (*agap-*) stem appear, all conveying the idea of love, whether as a noun or an action. But John's strategy here is different from Paul's in 1 Cor. 13 (as are aspects of his orientation; see Hoffmann 2002: 78). There Paul gives a lofty exposition, the better to inform an overarching discussion of the use of spiritual gifts in the church.[2] Here John's rhetoric is not lofty but thickly terse. It is not expositional but hortatory. He now prevails on the readers to reflect in their lives the fundamental application of the commandments (1 John 2:7–17), counsel (2:18–3:8), and teaching (3:9–4:6) that he has given earlier. "The true knowledge of God of necessity begets love for God in us" (Calvin 1988: 290).

Nor does John, like Paul in 1 Cor. 13, speak of love as a means to a larger goal. Love is important here not in the first instance for reasons of utility (though that will enter the picture) but for the sake of identity: since love is so inextricably bound up in the nature and work of God as revealed in his Son, those claiming to follow the Son must be inextricably involved in love (beautifully expressed in Schlatter 1950: 85–86). John's burden in the epistle, I argue, is that God is light (1:1–2:6), but that light in its ineffable glory is invisible (4:12), and the essential form it assumes in the created world is love. God's light takes visible shape when God's people reflect his love.

Two occurrences of ἀγαπητοί (*agapētoi*, beloved) in the span of only five verses demarcate the discourse. Since John uses this noun of direct address somewhat sparingly in his epistle (it occurs elsewhere only at 2:7; 3:2, 21; 4:1), we are justified in seeing a certain emphasis in what he says here. He is "expressing his pastoral, heartfelt concern for the welfare of his followers" (Burge 1996: 186). The first ἀγαπητοί (4:7) directly introduces the hortatory subjunctive ἀγαπῶμεν (*agapōmen*, let us love), which is in effect a first-person

1. Culpepper 1998: 269 calls 4:7–21 "the third and most profound treatment of love in 1 John."

2. For a different view of 1 Cor. 13, see Patrick 2004, who stresses formal rhetorical strategies and their impact on Paul's language and themes. I do not think his findings prove, however, that Paul's concern over spiritual gifts does not remain a key issue in interpreting the chapter.

imperative (cf. Strecker 1996: 143).[3] John commands readers to love, but he does so in a humble way by including himself in the order. The second ἀγαπητοί (4:11) introduces a similar exhortation in a somewhat different form and is followed by a slightly contrasting discussion. Yet the two subsections are roughly symmetrical, as the analysis below will show.

3. Painter 2002: 265 calls attention to the alliteration of the first three words of 4:7: ἀγαπητοί, ἀγαπῶμεν ἀλλήλους (*agapētoi, agapōmen allēlous*), commenting that "it shows a certain skill in the use of words."

A. First Exhortation to Love (4:7–10)

The section begins with the first of two appeals for the readers to love. A plain second-person plural imperative might be expected; John is not shy about asserting apostolic privilege (e.g., 1:1–5). Elsewhere in the NT the imperative of ἀγαπάω (*agapaō*, to love, i.e., other people) occurs in the second person:

Reference	Greek Text	Translation
Matt. 5:44; Luke 6:27, 35	ἀγαπᾶτε τοὺς ἐχθροὺς ὑμῶν	love your enemies
Eph. 5:25; Col. 3:19	ἀγαπᾶτε τὰς γυναῖκας	love your wives
1 Pet. 1:22	ἀλλήλους ἀγαπήσατε ἐκτενῶς	love one another fervently
1 Pet. 2:17	τὴν ἀδελφότητα ἀγαπᾶτε	love the brotherhood of believers

It will be seen that only Jesus, Paul, and Peter issue commands to love other people in second-person imperatival form (and even they do so sparingly). John's preferred mode of address is different and in fact unique. His epistles stand alone among all NT books in using a first-person plural form of ἀγαπάω to call readers to love others (1 John 3:11, 18; 4:7, 12, 19; 2 John 5).[1] John's peculiar but appropriate choice of words reinforces his popular reputation in Christian history as "the apostle of love."

As often elsewhere in the epistle, John's style is paratactic. No conjunctions or connective particles join 4:7–10 together. Logical development, if any, must be inferred. In general it can be said that John uses a loose collection of meditative observations about God's love to furnish a basis for exhorting readers to let that same agapic light shine in their lives.[2] D. Smith (1991: 111) rightly affirms, "The integral theological and ethical relationship between indicative (God's love for us) and imperative (our love for others) is the crux of this text."

The verses may be analyzed as follows:

1. Origin and effect of God's love (4:7)
2. Status of the one who does not love (4:8)

1. It can be further observed that all eleven NT occurrences of first-person plural of ἀγαπάω are found in either 1 John or 2 John. In addition to references above, see 3:14, 23; 4:10; 5:2 (2x). The LXX contains only two occurrences: Song 1:4 and Amos 5:15.

2. It is not clear on what basis Hoffmann 2002: 78 sees here "an ancient Christian hymn dating from about 60 CE." The hymnic arrangement of 4:7–10 in NA[27] is without adequate justification according to Strecker 1996: 143.

3. God's goal in revealing his love (4:9)
4. God's means of revealing his love (4:10)

Exegesis and Exposition

7Beloved, let us love each other, because love is from God, and the one who loves
⌜ ⌝ has been born of God and recognizes God. 8The one who does not love ⌜does not
know God⌝, for God is love. 9The love of God was revealed among us in this: God sent
his one and only Son into the world, so that through him we might live. 10This is what
love ⌜ ⌝ is: not that ⌜we loved⌝ God but that ⌜he⌝ loved us—that is, he ⌜sent⌝ his Son
to be a propitiation for our sins.

1. Origin and Effect of God's Love (4:7)

The opening appeal, "Beloved, let us love each other," echoes not only 1 John 3:11, 23 and Jesus himself (John 13:34) but also 1 John 4:1. There are at least three reasons why the command is fitting at this juncture of the discourse.

First, in 4:1–6 John called for discernment and the distinguishing of false spirits from true. This is sometimes a necessary operation in a Christian community, but it is risky. Even those on the right side of an issue theologically may seek to rectify wrongs in harsh, loveless, thoughtless, or prideful ways. Luke's Gospel records that John once wanted to call down heavenly fire on Samaritans who did not receive Jesus and the disciples (Luke 9:54). When Paul urges believers to restore to full fellowship those who have fallen into sin, he simultaneously warns that the rescuers are liable to disaster themselves (Gal. 6:1; cf. Jude 22–23). Church discipline can be carried to unproductive extremes (2 Cor. 2:6–11). Dialogue between dissidents can lead to mutual destruction (Gal. 5:15). For their part, those in error are understandably likely to resent any challenge and may respond vindictively to questioning. Paul knew the joy of seeing errant believers repent (2 Cor. 7:8–13), but he also knew the frustration of believers unwilling to give up their sins (12:21). John himself was apparently the target of malicious opposition to his leadership in the church (2 John 9–10). In all such matters, there is need to preserve the unity that love produces—where this is possible (Rom. 12:18). There is considerable pastoral wisdom in John's summons to mutual love immediately after a warning to be on the alert against deceiving spirits. He knows he must anticipate possibly deleterious effects of his own counsel as readers take it to heart.

Second, if godless spirits are actually at work, the deeds of the flesh that they are apt to spawn cannot be far behind. Many of these deeds, judging from NT *Lasterkataloge* (lists of illicit behavior; see R. N. Soulen 1981: 105–6; R. N. Soulen and R. K. Soulen 2001: 98–99), involve attitudes or practices that are far from expressive of love: "envy, murder, strife, deceit and malice" (Rom. 1:29 NIV); "hatred, discord, jealousy, fits of rage, selfish ambition, dissensions, factions" (Gal. 5:20 NIV); "quarreling, jealousy, outbursts of anger, factions, slander, gossip, arrogance and disorder" (2 Cor. 12:20 NIV).

Schism of some considerable proportion has recently rent the community to whom John writes (1 John 2:19). As John envisions the possible influence of deceiving spirits, it is natural that he urge readers to exhibit what Paul lists as not only the firstfruit of the true and good Spirit (Gal. 5:22) but also the cardinal Christian virtue (1 Cor. 13:13).

Third, by this point in the epistle, John has spoken frequently of love, but he has given it very little theological grounding. First John contains a total of forty-six occurrences of noun or verb forms of the ἀγαπ- (*agap-*) word group, and prior to 4:6 there have been over a dozen mentions. But most occurrences thus far speak of the exercise of love in the ethical sphere (e.g., 2:10; 3:10, 11, 14) or merely assume the existence of love in connection with God (e.g., 2:5; 3:16). John has made no substantive and explicit assertion as to where such love comes from or what its character might be. Of course, these things ought to have been well known already to a Christian community. But if John found it necessary earlier to spell out with almost pedantic clarity the command that Christians have had "from the beginning" (2:7–8), it is no wonder that he now moves to fortify the theological foundation of the imperative to love. He does this by clarifying love's origin (cf. Painter 2002: 265) and love's effect.

John's readers should love each other because love is "from God" (ἐκ τοῦ θεοῦ, *ek tou theou*). Love, John seems to be saying, is to be sought, hallowed, nurtured, and guarded simply by virtue of its inherent God-rootedness. Of course, many things are depicted in Scripture as being or coming ἐκ τοῦ θεοῦ:[3] Jesus's teaching (John 7:17), Jesus himself (8:42), people who respond to God's Word (8:47), praise of the person who is a true Jew (Rom. 2:29), God's Spirit (1 Cor. 2:12), the sufficiency of apostles like Paul (2 Cor. 3:5), and spiritual regeneration (5:18). In a sense, "all things" are from God (1 Cor. 11:12). But love for John is not merely one among many things finding distinctive rootage in God. It is rather a primary attribute of God (1 John 4:8, 16). Its supernal origin in the Father makes it most to be cherished among those who claim to be God's children. John will go on to state that to fail to love aright is to belie one's Christian confession (4:20). Love among Christian believers (and, judging from Jesus's example, love for nonbelievers too) is a nonnegotiable necessity in the household of faith. "If anyone separates faith from love it is as if he were trying to take away heat from the sun" (Calvin 1988: 290).

John also points to the effect of God's love. It gives rise to love in those to whom God grants spiritual rebirth: "The one who loves has been born of God." To love as John counsels is to be confirmed in the faith he is explicating. (Note the close connection between love and faith affirmed earlier in 3:23; more broadly, cf. Barrosse 1957.) This means that "love alone . . . is not a sign of being born of God" (Marshall 1978: 212; Rensberger 1997: 117) if we take the broader context of John's letter into account. Further, love is a means of knowing God: "The one who loves . . . recognizes God." John has just given advice regarding how his readers can "recognize the Spirit of God" (4:2) in

3. For comments on the synonymous phrase ἐκ θεοῦ, see the exegesis of 4:1.

terms of christological doctrine. But 4:7 implies that doctrine is not the entire issue. An agapic reality likewise comes into play in order for spiritual discernment to take place. A key component in effective discernment is love.

And so John has exhorted readers to love. He has linked that love directly to God. But John realizes that to persuade often requires more than mere assertion. Ever the pastoral realist, John can imagine that there will be those who do not heed his counsel. To address this contingency, in the next verse he anticipates the problem of the person who fails to love.

2. Status of the One Who Does Not Love (4:8)

Of the eighteen NT occurrences of 4:8's opening words, ὁ μή (*ho mē*, the one who does not), nearly half are on Jesus's lips (Matt. 12:30 [2x]; Luke 11:23 [2x]; 22:36; John 5:23; 10:1; 14:24). Paul uses the phrase three times (Rom. 14:6, 22; 1 Cor. 7:38). The other seven occurrences are in 1 John (3:10 [2x], 14; 4:3, 8; 5:10, 12). John has already spoken of "the one who" does not do righteousness (3:10a) and does not confess Jesus as having come from God (4:3). He has also spoken twice of "the one who" lacks love, in this case brotherly love: such a person is not from God (3:10b), and, worse, he or she "abides in death" (3:14).

In 4:8 John makes a third affirmation about the person without love: he or she does not know God. The negated aorist form of γινώσκω found in 4:8 (οὐκ ἔγνω, *ouk egnō*, does not know) sees a curiously consistent use in the NT: in all six of its occurrences it denotes failure to know God. The subject of this failure is most often "the world" (John 1:10; 17:25; 1 Cor. 1:21; 1 John 3:1), though once it is Israel (Rom. 10:19). But in nearly every case (Rom. 10:19 may be the only exception), God is the object of the verbal nonaction implied in οὐκ ἔγνω (for similar LXX usage see Isa. 1:3 and Jer. 8:7).

It would not be necessary here for John to spell out the implications of this dismal condition. He has called for believers to love one another (1 John 4:7). To fail here, 4:8 asserts, is not merely to fail ethically; it is to fail in the whole matter of salvation. Loving other people and knowing God are components of one inseparable whole: "Love alone opens access to all God's words and works, and whoever lacks love is blind to God" (Schlatter 1950: 88). "Lovelessness is godlessness and proves inability to grasp and understand God" (Holtzmann 1908: 350).

John explains why this is true: "God is love."[4] No other biblical writing makes this explicit assertion, but the claim is strongly implied in both John's Gospel and throughout the OT wherever God's steadfast covenant love is mentioned (cf. Rensberger 1997: 117). To John it is self-evident that this aspect of God's nature makes a sham of any claim to know God on the part of a

4. Marshall 1978: 212 rightly points out that "we do wrong to exalt the love of God as his supreme feature just because it is more congenial to our thinking." God is also light (1:5) and spirit (John 4:24). The temptation to reduce God to a single quality to the exclusion of others is to be resisted.

so-called believer who is deficient in love. What is the relation between God being love and John's certainty that to know God is to be impelled to love? The relationship may be explained like this: God's communicable attributes, like light and love and truth (or faithfulness), are transformative. The person who receives Christ's cleansing from sin (1:9) and seeks Christ's mediation with the Father (2:1) has a relationship with the Father established by which the Father's traits increasingly mark the believer. For example, this relationship actualizes a will to obey divine commands (2:5) and follow Christ's example (2:6). No trait is more inherent to God as depicted in 1 John than the active will to love. Therefore, to know God results, quite simply, in loving like God loves. Paul breaks down this same religious psychology into more explicit and christologically specific terms in Eph. 5:1–2: "Be imitators of God, therefore, as dearly loved children and live a life of love, just as Christ loved us and gave himself up for us as a fragrant offering and sacrifice to God" (NIV). For both Paul (who speaks more of love for God than love for people; but see Rom. 13:8–9; 1 Thess. 4:9) and John, loving people goes hand in hand with saving knowledge of God.

In an age of increasing tolerance of the notion that all religions amount to the same thing, it is worth noting that John's picture of God is part of a unique affirmation. "Outside the pages of Scripture there is no comparable picture of God" (Marshall 1978: 213; cf. Holtzmann 1908: 350). Further, John does not say that love is God, a statement found nowhere in Scripture. "There have always been some who wished to apotheosize human love, but it cannot be done" (Sloyan 1995: 45; cf. Loader 1992: 52). To do so would be to replace a living, personal, and active God with an intellectual, ethical, volitional, or emotional abstraction. This is the last thing that the language of 1 John, or the graphic portrayal of God incarnate in the Gospels, would permit.

3. God's Goal in Revealing His Love (4:9)

First John 4:9 might be taken as a statement of means rather than goal: God reveals himself by sending his Son. But it is possible to see the real point of 4:9 in the final clause: "So that through him we might live." In the love-laden context of 4:7–14, to "live" in the full, God-enabled sense is to love as God demands and deserves. First John 4:9 may be taken, accordingly, as an affirmation in support of 4:7's imperative to love each other. Such love is a possibility, according to 4:9, because God's very purpose in sending[5] his Son into the world was to bring about the God-given life of regeneration. John makes abundantly clear, in both his Gospel and in this epistle, that to "live" in this sense is also to love.

First John 4:9 begins with the tenth of fourteen of this epistle's ἐν τούτῳ statements (see exegesis of 2:3). This one seems to point ahead rather than back. "The love of God" is apt to be a subjective genitive here (so Rensberger 1997: 119;

5. For the theory of a Hellenistic-Jewish wisdom background, along with Alexandrian Logos speculation, informing both Johannine and Pauline "sending" formulas, see Schweizer 1966.

Painter 2002: 266)—it is the love that God exercises, not human love for God. John says this love "was revealed" (ἐφανερώθη, *ephanerōthē*), the passive voice verb probably connoting the divine activity in the incarnation. "Particularly important is the fact that God has taken the initiative" (D. Smith 1991: 107). Calvin (1988: 290) rightly sees here "a more than wonderful goodness which ought to ravish our minds with amazement" (Spicq 1958 also extols God's expression of love). John goes on to state where, how, and why it was revealed.

As for *where* God's love was revealed, John describes the locus as ἐν ἡμῖν (*en hēmin*, in us). In the exegesis of 1:10, we saw that ἐν ἡμῖν can have a distributive/corporate as well as locative/personal sense (cf. Moule 1994: 75). When this is the case, the translation can be "among us" or "in our midst" (e.g., Luke 1:1; 7:16; John 1:14; Acts 1:17; 2:29; Eph. 3:20; Heb. 13:21). The corporate sense may be preferable here (so Painter 2002: 266) in that the incarnation was not a private individual event but something that "was not done in a corner" (Acts 26:26). God revealed his love "among" and not merely "inside" people, although the former did pave the way for the latter.

As for *how* God revealed his love, the central event was the sending of his "one and only Son into the world." "One and only" is the NIV rendering of μονογενῆ (*monogenē*)[6] and as a translation is hard to improve on, since it conveys both the exclusivity and the uniqueness of the Father's revelation in the Son. The Son's status as one "sent" from God (Luke 4:18; John 5:36; 20:21) and more broadly God's "sending" forth people (John 1:6; Acts 7:35; 9:17; 10:17), angels (Luke 1:19), and spirits (Rev. 5:6) to do his bidding are motifs encountered frequently across the sweep of the NT. John speaks here from well within a broad tradition.

As for *why* God brought about this revelation, John attempts no comprehensive account. He contents himself with just one facet of a very large truth: the Son was sent "so that through him we might live." John has already correlated the life received through faith in Christ with love for others: "We know that we have passed from death to life, because we love our brothers" (3:14). It is that correlation that he seems to be pointing toward as 4:9 concludes. A major purpose behind God's sending his Son into the world is so that, through faith in him, people might receive life that produces love. This is an aspect of the mechanism, so to speak, that John thinks will galvanize readers to respond to the imperative of 4:7.

4. God's Means of Revealing His Love (4:10)

That 4:9 deals ultimately with the goal of God's love, not its means, does not indicate that John thinks that means are unimportant. Rather, he turns immediately in 4:10 to extending the theological foundation for the love imperative

6. The same word is used of the Son elsewhere in the NT only at John 1:14, 18; 3:16, 18. Although older translations rendered it "only begotten," it is recognized today that this was due to the influence of patristic interpretation on early English translators through the Vulgate (cf. Pendrick 1995). More commonly it refers to what American English calls an "only child" (Luke 7:12; 8:42; 9:38; Heb. 11:17 [there may be double entendre in this occurrence]).

precisely by explicating the means through which God has established his love. "Here love is defined in the act" (Painter 2002: 270).[7] He does this in two movements, the first debunking an anthropocentric notion of love, the second affirming and defining the redemptive love to which 4:7–14 is a summons.

The opening ἐν τούτῳ of 4:10, like the identical words that begin 4:9, points forward. "This is what love is," John announces, and then he proceeds to his twofold explanation.

Love is not, in the first instance, what people do from themselves (cf. Loader 1992: 53). How could it be, when prior to being touched by God's love in the gospel, people are at their root his enemies (cf. Rom. 5:8, 10), when they are "of the world" (ἐκ τοῦ κόσμου, *ek tou kosmou*), in John's parlance (1 John 2:16; 4:5)? Perhaps John envisions a scenario in which readers will note John's love command and then peremptorily or facilely resolve to obey it. First John 4:10 sounds a cautionary note. Whether the verb "we loved" is aorist or perfect (the witnesses are divided; see second additional note), human response is not the measure of the love that John calls for but the divine act that established and sustains ἀγάπη (*agapē*). The self must look beyond itself in order to access divine love.

John's theological anthropology is not rosy. The Jesus of John's Gospel told listeners, "I know that you do not have the love of God in your hearts" (John 5:42 NIV). Later in this epistle, John will lament, "The whole world is under the control of the evil one" (1 John 5:19). The perversity of the human heart made it impossible for Jesus to "entrust himself" even to his disciples (John 2:24). John portrays Christ has having addressed himself to people—"the world" (1:10–11)—whose hearts were blinded and deadened (12:40). It is only through spiritual rebirth that people are infused with capacities that make reception of divine love, and thereby expression of divine love, a possibility.

Considerations like these probably inform John's insistence that human love is not the norm for the care of others that he calls for. First John 4:7's "love one another" is not a request to exercise natural affections as such. This is not about being nice, winning friends, and influencing people. John is calling for a love grounded in God's perfection in contradistinction to human fallenness, a hallmark of which is selfishness rather than love. This is not to disparage generic human affection (as D. Smith 1991: 111–12 rightly points out) but to call it to a higher plane and theocentric definition.

Yet this raises an unavoidable question. If, when told to love each other, people cannot simply look to their innate inner resources, then where are the resources to be sought? John's answer is clear and immediate. "This is what love is: . . . that God loved us and [καί, *kai*] sent his Son to be a propitiation for our sins." Καί here is not simply connective, in which case John would be speaking of two different things: (1) God loving and (2) God sending. Rather, καί should be understood as explicative (BDAG 495): God's sending provides

7. Painter 2002: 269 argues, however, that 4:10 defines "the nature of love itself" and "is not a statement about the way love is revealed." In my view it is both.

the fuller demonstration of his loving (cf. Rom. 5:8). Hence my translation "he loved us—that is, he sent his Son to be a propitiation for our sins." (On propitiation, see exegesis of 2:2; the suggestion of Thornton 1968 that the meaning in both 2:2 and 4:10 is expiation, not propitiation, is unconvincing.) The resources for believers to love are rooted in the efficacy of Jesus's saving death (so also D. Smith 1991: 107, referring to Rom. 5:8 and Gal. 2:20).

John assumes but does not unpack the relation between Christ's propitiatory mission and the love command. Several possible connections may be suggested, all interrelated. One is that since his readers' sins have been dealt with by Christ, they are freed from their self-limitations and empowered to love as they have been loved (cf. Eph. 5:1–2). Another is that receiving the benefit of Christ's propitiation makes possible love for him and with it obedience to his commands (John 14:15, 23). First among these is the command to love. A third connection may be that knowing God's love in Christ's cross infuses believers with a capacity for love (cf. 1 John 3:1) that enables them to extend themselves openly to others. Knowing God's love produces an ebullient generosity that touches those around (cf. John's hope in 1:4 that his readers' joy would be enhanced by this epistle). A fourth connection has already been laid down explicitly a few verses earlier: "This is how we know what love is: Jesus Christ laid down his life for us. And we ought to lay down our lives for our brothers" (3:16). Christ's costly propitiatory atonement uncaps an artesian well of selflessness in which believers find resources for sacrificial care for each other.

Such fine distinctions might seem too subtle or even beside the point. It could be argued that since "love one another" lies way back at the beginning of 4:7, we are extending the idea too far when we see 4:9–10 as giving 4:7 a foundation. But there is decisive evidence in the text that John, in talking of incarnation and atonement, does indeed have the love command directly before his eyes: he restates and continues to ground it, beginning with 4:11 in the next section. He has been theologizing with an eye to praxis all along.

Additional Notes

4:7. Codex A adds τὸν θεόν. This would ensure that readers not suppose that merely human love is somehow tantamount to spiritual rebirth. But this truth is obvious from other passages and does not need this enrichment to support it.

4:8. While NA[27] reads οὐκ ἔγνω τὸν θεόν, there is divergence in several manuscripts:

οὐ γινώσκει τὸν θεόν	A, 33, 81, a few others
οὐκ ἔγνωκεν τὸν θεόν	Ψ*, (69)
οὐκ ἔγνωκεν	א[2]

The last reading is recognized as an error (homoioteleuton) by a corrector, and the other two are obvious attempts to improve the grammar by changing the aorist ἔγνω to either present or perfect tense. Little is achieved by the changes, which are rightly set aside on the basis of external evidence.

4:10. As in 4:7, so here some manuscripts (א, some Vulgate witnesses, the Sahidic Coptic version) want to insert τοῦ θεοῦ. For the same reason cited in 4:7 above, the insertion is superfluous.

4:10. Weighty witnesses line up on both sides of the question whether the original is the aorist ἠγαπήσαμεν (the corrector of א, A, 33, 𝔐) or the perfect ἠγαπήκαμεν (NA[27], following, e.g., B, Ψ). If the perfect is original, it would be the only finite perfect verb form of ἀγαπάω to appear in the entire NT. Finite aorist forms, in contrast, occur about seventeen times. The perfect would seem to be the harder reading, especially in conjunction with the aorist form later in the verse. On the other hand, external evidence could be taken to favor the perfect. The difference between the two forms for interpretation will be slight.

4:10. Codex A stands alone in reading ἐκεῖνος (exceedingly common in John: seventy-five times in John's Gospel, seven in 1 John) rather than αὐτός here. A single dissenting witness is unlikely to preserve the original.

4:10. א prefers the perfect ἀπέσταλκεν to the aorist ἀπέστειλεν in NA[27]. א may have been conforming 4:10 to the perfect of ἀποστέλλω found in 4:9 and 4:14. But the aorist is more likely to be original on external grounds.

B. Second Exhortation to Love (4:11–14)

This subsection in many ways mirrors the previous one. The major difference is that while 4:7–10 focuses on the nature of God (Rensberger 1997: 116), 4:11–14 focuses on the knowledge of God. That is, while the earlier verses explicate implications of God seen as love (4:8), these verses affirm that knowledge of God's saving nature and ways is credibly present within the community. John's summons to love is, accordingly, not to be received fideistically or as an ex cathedra apostolic pronouncement. Rather, there are good and necessary warrants for the love that John commands. He will now set forth a few of these warrants. He appeals to the effect that God's love ought to have (4:11), the importance for the community that it express God's love (4:12), and the assurance of God's love that the community can enjoy (4:13). And in a final first-person declaration (4:14), he brings closure to the immediate discussion surrounding the imperative to love each other by reaffirming his credentials for issuing the mandates of this section. The verses may be analyzed as follows:

1. Effect of God's love (4:11)
2. Importance of expressing God's love (4:12)
3. Assurance of God's love (4:13)
4. Apostolic confirmation that the Father sent the Son (4:14)

Exegesis and Exposition

[11]Beloved, if God loved us like this, we too ought to love each other. [12]No one has ever seen God. If we love each other, God abides among us and his love ⸢is perfected among us⸣. [13]This is how we know that we abide in him and that he abides with us: by his Spirit that ⸢he gave⸣ to us. [14]And we ⸢have beheld⸣ and testify that the Father sent the Son to be savior of the world.

1. Effect of God's Love (4:11)

John's direct appeal in the form of the vocative "beloved" mirrors the opening of 4:7 (see exegesis). "If [εἰ, *ei*] God loved us" marks the second of only three first-class conditional sentences in this epistle (also 3:13 and 5:9; the other times that εἰ appears [2:19, 22; 4:1; 5:5] are not really parallel). This construction assumes the facticity of the if-clause for the sake of the current discussion (Wallace 1996: 692). Οὕτως (*houtōs*, like this) points back to 4:9–10. If God's love really does consist in his sending and sacrificing the Son, this has unavoidable consequences for John's readers. They are freed from the constraints of human selfishness and can love others as they have been loved: "Freely you have received, freely give" (Matt. 10:8 NIV). This love, while perhaps finding its primary expression in the fellowship of believers, no doubt has an aspect that extends to those outside as well (cf. Gal. 6:10; Titus 3:2; Loader 1992: 53–54).

Within the horizon of 1 John 4:11, the major consequence is the onus that God's love places on both John and his readers: "We too[1] [i.e., like God] ought to love each other." This conviction and its underlying rationale are not unique to John. Jesus's parable of the unmerciful slave (Matt. 18:21–35) illustrated the same point in a graphic way, and the logic at the parable's core parallels the logic of 1 John 4:11: "Shouldn't you have had mercy on your fellow servant just as I had on you?" (Matt. 18:33 NIV; cf. Col. 3:13). Paul uses a similar grammatical construction (a form of ὀφείλω [*opheilō*] plus the infinitive of ἀγαπάω [*agapaō*]) on two occasions. (1) He tells the Romans, "Let no debt remain outstanding, except the continuing debt to love one another" (Rom. 13:8 NIV). (2) He tells husbands, "Husbands ought to love [ὀφείλουσιν . . . οἱ ἄνδρες ἀγαπᾶν, *opheilousin . . . hoi andres agapan*] their wives" (Eph. 5:28 NIV).

Paul also tells readers that they are "taught by God to love each other [θεοδίδακτοί ἐστε εἰς τὸ ἀγαπᾶν ἀλλήλους, *theodidaktoi este eis to agapan allēlous*]" (1 Thess. 4:9). John has already noted that believers are divinely instructed (1 John 2:20, 27). For John as for Paul, the command to love assumes the fact of divine instruction and motivation, the inner working of the divine word (cf. 2:14), not natural human ability alone.

In sum, 4:11 restates the imperative of 4:7, albeit in a slightly softened manner by using "we ought to love" rather than a direct imperative. The command to love in 4:11 is presented as the effect of God's prior action in sending and sacrificing his Son (4:10). But now John advances a new set of arguments for taking this directive to heart.

2. Importance of Expressing God's Love (4:12)

Among central emphases earlier in the discourse is the need for readers to "abide" or "remain" in what they have been taught and in Christ (e.g., 2:6, 10, 14, 17, 24, 27, 28). John has also stressed the perfecting or making complete of God's love in believers through obedience to God's Word (2:5). First John 4:12 sees the confluence of these two strands, "abiding" and "perfecting," as closely tied with the expression of love among believers: "If we love each other, God abides among us and his love is perfected among us."

1. Καί (in the phrase καὶ ἡμεῖς) is adjunctive (Wallace 1996: 671) and may be translated "also" or "too."

The additional consideration of 4:12 is John's categorical observation that "no one has ever[2] seen[3] God." The invisibility of God[4] is a corollary to the conviction that God is Spirit, not a being possessing material properties (cf. John 4:24). In OT thought that spills directly over into the NT, God is a personal being, but he is not a human (all quotations from NIV):

Num. 23:19	God is not a man, that he should lie, nor a son of man, that he should change his mind. Does he speak and then not act? Does he promise and not fulfill?
1 Chron. 21:13	David said to Gad, "I am in deep distress. Let me fall into the hands of the LORD, for his mercy is very great; but do not let me fall into the hands of men."
Job 9:32	He is not a man like me that I might answer him, that we might confront each other in court.
Job 33:12	But I tell you, in this you are not right, for God is greater than man.
Ps. 50:21	These things you have done and I kept silent; you thought I was altogether like you. But I will rebuke you and accuse you to your face.
Hos. 11:9	I will not carry out my fierce anger, nor will I turn and devastate Ephraim. For I am God, and not man—the Holy One among you.

This ontological truth has very definite liturgical and ethical ramifications: God's otherness as signified by his invisibility lies at the heart of the Decalogue, which forbids the construction and veneration of idols (Exod. 20:4; cf. Deut. 4:12–19). God tells Moses, "No one may see me and live" (Exod. 33:20 NIV). Such a high view of divine transcendence and utter prohibition against physical representation of his being could easily create a religion highlighting the vast distance between people and God. Islam, whose ninety-nine names for God do not include "Father" and for whom "God's many names do not describe his essence, only his will and law" (Braswell 1996: 46, 48), is a case in point.

The OT's insistence that God is invisible is fully endorsed in the NT (John 5:37; 6:46; 1 Tim. 1:17). But in 1 John 4:12, John makes a very different point. He points to the importance of believers actualizing God's love among themselves in view of God's not being seen. God's invisibility, then, is not only a reason to exalt and venerate him in his heavenly loftiness; it is at the same time an implicit mandate for God's people to render his presence concrete by their response to him. Foremost in that response is the expression of love to others.

2. The word πώποτε (*pōpote*, ever) is rare in the NT. Of its six occurrences, five are in John's writings (John 1:18; 5:37; 6:35; 8:33; also Luke 19:30).

3. For the possibility of a play on words involving τεθέαται (*tetheatai*, has seen) and θεόν (*theon*, God), see van der Horst 1972.

4. On both OT/Jewish and Hellenistic foundations of the belief that God cannot be seen, see Strecker 1996: 156–57.

By loving others, believers can be assured that "God abides among us" (ὁ θεὸς ἐν ἡμῖν μένει, *ho theos en hēmin menei*). Here as earlier (see exegesis of 4:9), ἐν ἡμῖν can be taken to have a distributive and corporate meaning. God dwells, or "abides," in the midst of his people as they respond to each other with the love that he has extended to them. Moreover, John states, "and his love is perfected among us." The repetition of "among us" (ἐν ἡμῖν) suggests that John insists on seeing concrete local manifestations of love for believers. God's essential nature implies an ethic for his redeemed human creatures. "The love of God for human beings intends, by its very nature, to actualize itself in the Christian community in the form of mutual love of human beings for one another" (Strecker 1996: 157).

"Perfected" in 4:12 is unlikely to refer to a state of sinless perfection in believers, which John has already rejected. Nor is John suggesting that there is something imperfect in God's love (subjective genitive; cf. Painter 2002: 272) that believers by loving bring to perfection or fill out. The root of the perfect participle τετελειωμένη (*teteleiōmenē*) means "to finish, complete, or bring to the desired outcome" (cf. John 4:34; 5:36; 17:4; Rensberger 1997: 119). John speaks here not of perfect people (cf. D. Smith 1991: 110) but of God's already pristine love finding its fullest possible earthly expression as people respond to the message of Christ and reach out to one another as a result.

John takes a backseat to no one in Scripture in advancing a lofty view of God the Father's essential being. But in direct proportion to God's transcendence, for John, is the mandate that believers incarnate God's character, central to which is his love (1 John 4:8, 16). "God is accessible to us only as we love" (D. Smith 1991: 108). This is important if John's readers are to avoid the lovelessness that other portions of 1 John warn against. It is also important for the sake of believers' own in-house and personal assurance, as the next verse goes on to assert.

3. Assurance of God's Love (4:13)

The expression of God's love among believers is important because it renders visible the God who in himself cannot be seen (4:12). But human response to the love imperative does not by itself fully exhaust the assurance that God extends. There are in fact multiple dimensions of confirmation (cf. Marshall 1978: 219), and among these is the Spirit that God bestows on believers. "This is how we know that we abide in him and that he abides with us: by his Spirit that he gave to us," John writes (4:13). This is no doubt the Spirit called "holy" in John 14:26.

The initial ἐν τούτῳ (*en toutō*, by this, this is how) of 1 John 4:13 echoes the identical openings of 4:9 and 4:10.[5] There the phrase clearly looked ahead to the substance of subsequent ὅτι (*hoti*) clauses. First John 4:13 can be understood

5. First John is alone among NT books in containing the exact formulation ἐν τούτῳ γινώσκομεν (*en toutō ginōskomen*, by this we know; 2:3, 5; 3:24; 4:2 [variant reading], 13; 5:2).

as following the same pattern.[6] John and his readers know or recognize their abiding in God and his abiding in them, by virtue of the Spirit, whom God has given them (see 2:18–3:8). This is similar to the statement John already made in 3:24. There, however, the stress was more generic and focused on commandment-keeping. First John 4:13's concern is more strictly limited to the love command alone.

John sounds a Pauline note in correlating the presence of love in 4:11–12 and the giving of God's Spirit in 4:13: "God has poured out his love into our hearts by the Holy Spirit, whom he has given us" (Rom. 5:5). But the distinctive feature of 1 John 4:13 is not God's largesse in giving the Spirit (stressed also, e.g., in John 3:34) but the connection between the Spirit and Christians' cognizance of what John calls them to embrace. The way that believers recognize God's presence and his love (1 John 4:12) is by the Spirit (cf. Calvin 1988: 293). The Holy Spirit plays a vital role in believers' grasp of both God and love. "The Spirit teaches the truth about God's sending Jesus as the Saviour of the world and knowing this provides believers with the basis of assurance" (Kruse 2000: 163).

There is no indication here of magical impartation of purely cognitive data. This might be the case if John were speaking of some mysterious infusion of knowledge that readers had no natural means of acquiring. But John's doctrine of the Spirit, if his Gospel is any indication, makes no such assertion about the Spirit's operation. The Spirit is closely correlated with Jesus's words or teaching, which are called "Spirit" and "life" (John 6:63). John speaks of "the Spirit of truth," concealed from the world's view but recognized by the Eleven because of his abiding presence with them (14:17; cf. 15:26). This Spirit teaches the first disciples and calls to mind the words of the earthly Christ (14:26). God sent the Spirit to instruct Jesus's first followers in things they did not understand at first but would need to know later (16:13). Strecker (1996: 158) rightly speaks here of "the spirit of right knowledge."

In 1 John 4:13 John speaks of the Spirit's role in believers' assurance that God is indeed in their midst as they reach out to others with the divine love that has touched them. Soteriologically, John is not a synergist (cf. Yarbrough 1995), but this does not mean there is no synergy between God and his people as he gives and they, receiving, respond. The Spirit is the link, even agent, who permits believers to see this reciprocity for what it is: a token of God's very presence among them, assuring them of the veracity of the message they have received and the importance of the ethic they are being called to embrace. First John 4:13 encourages them, then, with the apostolic insight that it is divine presence and not merely human impulse that moves them to selfless regard for each other. Within the discourse this is not merely an interesting theological

6. Admittedly, in 4:13 the ὅτι clause could look back on the previous statement that God abides and his love is perfected. In that case John would be saying that the Holy Spirit corroborates what the exercise of love has already established. This would require taking ὅτι as causal (for, because) rather than continuative (that), as above.

observation; it rather raises the stakes of the imperatives of 4:7 and 4:11 by implying that failure to love would be to grieve if not completely spurn the Spirit of God. In John's cognitive universe of interconnected divine being and beings, that would be to spurn Father and Son as well.

4. Apostolic Confirmation That the Father Sent the Son (4:14)

In a statement heavy with hortatory implication, the writer apparently feels the need to underscore the authority with which he writes. This is not a human authority but the authority of God's own action in sending his Son—the note on which this subsection began (4:11). And yet God has seen fit to delegate the revelation of the transforming message to people—whether to John the Baptist or Jesus (see opening verses of John's Gospel) or to the apostles (Acts 1:8; 1 Pet. 5:1) and other early disciples (Acts 13:31). It is as one of these delegates that John now concludes by reaffirming that he is one of those who personally "beheld and testify that the Father sent the Son to be savior of the world" (1 John 4:14).

The primary reference of "we" in 4:14 ("we have beheld") is apostolic (so also Schlatter 1950: 90); few if any of the readers would have viewed Jesus in his earthly days.[7] The unnecessary stated pronoun ἡμεῖς (*hēmeis*, we) may be slightly emphatic, marking a contrast between John and his readers. This is not to deny that to an extent John "includes the readers with himself" (Loader 1992: 55, Rensberger 1997: 120). Yet writer and readers do not meld into a single indistinguishable voice. John's language may be understood to exclude the shadowy opponents whose errors his epistle periodically has in view.

Forms of the verb τεθεάμεθα (*tetheametha*, we have beheld) occur also at 1:1 (see exegesis) and 4:12. In Johannine usage (see also John 1:14, 32, 38; 4:35; 6:5; 11:45) it seems to have the sense "to see and draw a certain inference from." John and others "saw" Jesus in this intensive and reflective manner. This "does not mean [just] any sort of seeing, but what is joined to faith and by which they recognized the glory of God" (Calvin 1988: 293). This qualifies him to point to the implications that logically follow. Foremost among these is the command to love. To be confirmed in the knowledge of Christ's coming is to be confirmed in the expression of love for others.

John not only "beheld," referring back either to Jesus's life as a whole or perhaps even to his crucifixion in particular when the divine love was manifest in a climactic way (cf. 1 John 4:10); he also now "testifies" (on the identical form μαρτυροῦμεν [*martyroumen*, we testify], see exegesis of 1:2). This action is so closely linked with the action of "seeing" or "beholding" that this may be a hendiadys. "Seeing is believing," goes the old saying; for an appointed

7. Possibly John has in mind the "seeing" that believing reception of the gospel message implies. In that case his readers are more directly included in his circle of reference. Strecker's suggestion (1996: 158) that this is "a contemplative, spiritual vision in contrast to the realistic seeing that the author claims for himself as an apostolic witness" unnecessarily separates the "we" of 1 John's opening from "we" of 4:14.

spokesperson like John (cf. John 15:27), to see is to testify (cf. Acts 4:20 [Peter and John]; John 1:34 [John the Baptist]; 3:11, 32 [Jesus]).

Such testimony in biblical usage often connotes a sort of deposition with binding force (e.g., John 1:7, 15, 32), and that is probably the case here. The readers are accountable for what has been revealed to them on the basis of God's act in Christ. It has been revealed "that[8] the Father sent[9] the Son to be savior of the world." This divine act grounds the imperative to love in several ways, none of which John spells out:

1. God's loving act in sending Christ is, or should be, an impetus for his children to follow suit (cf. 1 John 4:11). In this case 4:14 simply restates 4:11 in slightly different fashion. As John will write in a few more verses, "We love because he first loved us" (4:19).
2. God's act of sending Christ had a saving intent and effect—he was sent to be σωτῆρα (*sōtēra*, savior). A God who is love (4:8, 16) would surely send a savior who would call for and facilitate love. However, "savior" (which occurs in John's writings only here and at John 4:42) is not directly associated with love in any other of its twenty-two NT occurrences.
3. God's saving act in sending Christ had a horizon as wide as all creation; he was sent to be savior "of the world" (see exegesis of 2:2), an expression occurring elsewhere in the NT only at John 4:42. "Savior" is a title for God with rich OT associations (e.g., Pss. 24:5; 25:5; 27:9; 65:5 [65:6 MT]; 79:9; Isa. 45:15; 62:11; Mic. 7:7; Hab. 3:18). For an apparently Jewish writer like John to apply it to Christ points to his belief in Jesus's divinity. Since God's love is so expansive and so clearly attested by witnesses, his followers can afford to be generous with their affection for one other. Recent schism may have aroused hard feelings among those who remained. It is important that the wideness of God's love overcome any residual relational stinginess in the community that John addresses.

Additional Notes

4:12. Witnesses vary regarding word order. The choices (with sample support) are the following:

8. Ὅτι (*hoti*) in 4:14 should be seen as continuative ("that"; cf. the translation of Painter 2002: 272, who uses a colon) rather than causal ("because") based on the logical demands of the discourse: John testifies "that" the Father sent the Son because it is this sending act by which he showed his love, and it is that love that stands at the head of this subsection (4:11). It is admittedly possible to see causal force instead, but this is semantically less likely.

9. Of the approximately 130 occurrences of the verb ἀποστέλλω (*apostellō*, to send) in the NT, 22 are perfect, 17 are present, 88 are aorist, and 5 are future. Hard distinctions between perfect and aorist (both of which would often refer to past events) cannot always be detected, but in John's Gospel, where the perfect occurs 7 times, it can at least be said that John views the action not just as a past event but as one that is connected to the present (also John 1:6, 24; 3:28; 5:33, 36; 20:21). This would also comport with the two perfect occurrences of ἀποστέλλω in 1 John 4:9, 14. In 4:14, John would be testifying to the event of God's sending in connection with the Son's being or becoming savior of the world.

τετελειωμένη ἐν ἡμῖν ἐστίν	NA[25], ℵ, B
τετελειωμένη ἐστίν ἐν ἡμῖν	Ψ, 𝔐
τετελειωμένη ἐστίν	1241
ἐν ἡμῖν τετελειωμένη ἐστίν	NA[27], 𝔓[74vid], A, 048[vid], nine other minuscules, and a few Old Latin manuscripts

The differences between these options in translation relate at most to word order or emphasis. All but 1241 (which may be set aside as reflecting a scribal slip) agree that God's love is perfected among believers.

4:13. NA[27] has the perfect δέδωκεν, which is better attested on external grounds: only A and a few minuscules have the aorist ἔδωκεν. The internal evidence is uncannily evenly divided: the perfect form of δίδωμι occurs twenty-three times in John's Gospel and three times in 1 John, while the aorist occurs twenty-eight times in the Gospel and three times in 1 John. Either perfect or aorist seems equally Johannine.

4:14. A, Ψ, and several minuscules read the aorist middle ἐθεασάμεθα rather than the perfect τεθεάμεθα (NA[27]). External evidence for the aorist is not overwhelming, and the aorist is an easier reading, first, because the aorist of θεάομαι predominates in the NT (nineteen times), with the perfect appearing only thrice (John 1:32; 1 John 4:12, 14 [if original]). It is easier also because the aorist would conform exactly to the first-person aorist ἐθεασάμεθα seen in 1:1. The harder and better attested perfect should stand.

VI. Illustrative Appeal: Renewed and Expanded Invitation to Love (4:15–5:15)

As explained in the introduction (see "Literary Structure"), this commentary outlines 1 John using the seven divisions made by scribal copyists. At first, it is not easy to see why they felt 4:15 ought to begin the sixth major division of 1 John. The lack of a conjunction might be one clue. But a more important hint may lie in 4:15's opening words: ὃς ἐάν (*hos ean*, whoever). This precise expression occurs only eleven times in the NT (twenty-four times in the LXX). It always appears on Jesus's lips (Matt. 5:19, 32; 11:6; 12:32; 18:5; 20:26; Luke 7:23; 9:48; 17:33) except for one occurrence in James (4:4)—an epistle noted for reflecting the teaching if not the exact words of Jesus—and here.

If one broadens the search by adding in three semantic equivalents (ὃς δ' ἄν [*hos d' an*], ὃς ἄν [*hos an*], and ὃς γὰρ ἄν [*hos gar an*]), there are a total of fifty-six such expressions in the NT. Forty-nine of these are sayings of Jesus (twenty-three are from Matthew, thirteen from Mark, twelve from Luke, and only one from John). The other seven are found in 1 John (2:5; 3:17; 4:15), James (4:4), a pair of LXX quotations (Acts 2:21 and Rom. 10:13, quoting Joel 2:32 [3:5 LXX]),[1] and Paul's traditional language regarding the Lord's Table (1 Cor. 11:27).

It is possible, though of course less than certain, that Greek-speaking scribes heard a dominical note in both the context and the diction of 1 John 4:15's opening ὃς ἐάν. John in 4:14 and 4:16 underscores that he (and others) has seen, testifies to, knows, and believes the savior and the love he revealed. First John 4:15 can be understood as marking a literary transition because it amounts to a dominical-sounding appeal[2] to respond in the light of the epistle's discourse to this point.

Understanding the opening words of 4:15 this way—as reflecting Jesus's and the LXX's authoritative appeals to acknowledge (the sense of ὁμολογήσῃ [*homologēsē*, confess] in this context) the salvation revealed as love in the savior that God sent—I conclude that John is illustrating the love that he taught

1. Both quotations are oracular in tone, since they are universal invitations to call on God's name and be saved: "Everyone who [πᾶς ὃς ἄν, *pas hos an*] calls on the name of the Lord will be saved."

2. Or one might speak of a declarative invitation. The semantic weight of such an expression is to declare a state of affairs that amounts to an open invitation for the reader or hearer to respond with benefit or profit (Matt. 5:19b; 10:42; 11:6; 12:32a; 16:25; 18:5; 20:26, 27). Jesus also made pronouncements of this type that function, not as veiled invitations, but as veiled threats (Matt. 5:19a, 21, 22 [2x], 32; 10:14; 12:32b; 18:6; 19:9). Here an invitation to repent may be implied.

about in 4:7–14. That love, as John presented it, is the love of a God who takes the initiative, acts on behalf of those in need, and sends word of his action to be proclaimed to them. It is appropriate, then, that John moves from an indicative-imperative pattern designed to promote assurance of God's love in 4:7–14 to a de facto appeal for readers to respond to that love in 4:15–5:15.

Their response needs to be as comprehensive and as variegated as the epistle has already presented authentic faith, obedience, and love to be. To this end, in 4:15–5:15 he invites readers to respond by recapitulating and expanding various themes already touched on.

The section begins by expressing John's, and ultimately God's, commendation of full acknowledgment of Christ (4:15). This is backed up by a declaration, reminiscent of 4:14, that John's authorial "we" (referring at least to John and to some extent his readers too) is authorized to set forth such an appeal. He does not speak from hearsay but from personal knowledge sealed with personal commitment (4:16).

The next cluster of verses amounts to a commendation of Christ that, if affirmed, results in love (4:17–21). Along the way John anticipates several challenges or hindrances to such love: pusillanimity (4:18), lack of assurance (4:19), and lovelessness toward other people (4:20–21). Succumbing to any of these would be breaches of the authentic acknowledgment of Christ that 4:15 announces at the head of the section.

From love, John moves to trust and faith (5:1–5). As the epistle has affirmed already repeatedly, this is not something ancillary to or removed from love; faith as John defines it is rather the conduit through which God's love reaches people, changes them, and makes them centers of selfless outreach to others. John reiterates both the ethical proactiveness of this love and its high promise of victory in a sometimes hostile world.

From faith as human response and experience, John shifts slightly to that in which faith is placed: God's self-testimony (5:6–12). The core of this testimony relates to Jesus, and John has already intimated that the name "Jesus" is capable of misrepresentation among his readers. So he spells out what God's testimony is regarding the one he has sent. He also states consequences of accepting or rejecting, respectively, the divine witness.

From God's witness, John moves finally both to clinch and to expand slightly or apply the affirmations already made in this section. He assures readers that his purpose in writing is their appropriation of eternal life (5:13). He also spells out a couple of major benefits from the relationship that results when God's self-testimony is embraced with due seriousness (5:14–15). Chief among these is the boldness of access that enables unfettered, believing, and uncalculating prayer.

A. Declarative Invitation with Supporting Warrant (4:15–16)

This brief two-verse block serves to state the aim of the verses following in this section: to urge reception of the message that John's epistle conveys. It does so, first, by stating that God himself sanctions the confession that John wants readers to embrace (4:15). It also restates the essence of the desired confession. It does so, second, by reiterating apostolic and early church certainty regarding the nature of the love that John commends (4:16).

Exegesis and Exposition

15Whoever ⸢confesses⸣ that Jesus ⸢ ⸣ is the Son of God—God abides in that person, and that person ⸢abides⸣ in ⸢God⸣. 16And we have come to know and ⸢fully believe⸣ the love that God has for us. God is love, and whoever abides in love abides in God, and God ⸢abides⸣ in him.

This pair of verses amounts to an appeal to the readers to open themselves fully to the love that God offers. First John 4:15 grounds the appeal by underscoring the happy state of the person who responds to it. "God abides in" this person and vice versa. John has already used the word "abide" (μένω, *menō*) twenty times in this epistle (2:6, 10, 14, 17, 19, 24 [3x], 27 [2x], 28; 3:6, 9, 14, 15, 17, 24 [2x]; 4:12, 13).

The notion of God "abiding" in someone has rich associations with John's Gospel, where μένω occurs more than three dozen times. The word can mean simply to dwell somewhere; one's domicile is where one "abides" (John 1:38, 39a; 2:12; 4:40 [2x]; 7:9; 8:35 [2x]; 10:40; 11:6, 54). But there is a fuller sense. God's Spirit descended and "remained" on Jesus, according to John the Baptist (1:32, 33). The Spirit was Jesus's constant companion. To "remain" or "abide" in Jesus's teaching is to be his true disciple (8:31). A disciple will be informed and steered by all that Jesus commanded and taught. God the Father "remained" or "abode" with Jesus during his earthly days (14:10). The Father was the source of the very words he spoke, and Jesus "remained" continually in the Father's love (15:10b). "Abiding" describes a reality involving Father, Son, and Spirit.

It is therefore a momentous thing, from the Johannine standpoint, to think of God "abiding" with someone. It carries overtones of the very identity of God in his Trinitarian being. It is a privilege as rich and fruitful as enjoying the constant companionship of Christ himself, God's Son—the very thing that Jesus promised to his disciples (John 15:4–10). It is this rich prospect that John holds before his readers in 1 John 4:15. The literary structure itself carries a certain attraction with the help of chiasm:

ὁ θεὸς ἐν αὐτῷ μένει	God in him abides
αὐτὸς ἐν τῷ θεῷ	he in God [abides]

John's categorical affirmation of God's presence with the believer, and the believer with God (Strecker 1996: 159 rightly speaks of "reciprocity," Akin 2001: 184 of "mutuality"), is an indicative full of hope and promise.

But it is a promise that assumes a condition. The condition is confession that "Jesus is the Son of God." The phrase "Son of God" appears several other times in 1 John (3:8; 5:5, 10, 12, 13, 20; see exegesis of 3:7–8). In addition Jesus is called "Son" (with God as his Father) in many other passages (1:3, 7; 2:22, 23, 24; 3:23; 4:9, 10, 14; 5:9). To confess (see exegesis of 1:9; cf. 2:23 and 4:2–3) that Jesus is God's Son here means to regard, obey, and commit to Jesus as the writer of this epistle and other true believers do. I have frequently noted that there is a threefold texture to the faith that John commends in this epistle: pistic, ethical, and agapic. While none of these three qualities exists in pure form without the other two, the first is primarily doctrinal, the second behavioral, and the third relational (see exegesis of 2:1a). In 4:15 stress is on the doctrinal. John's declarative invitation is extended to the person whose confession is true to who Jesus really was and is. "The abiding of God within is confined to those who can make this Johannine profession of faith" (Sloyan 1995: 47).

The effect of this statement is to affirm that "fellowship with God depends on the historical fact of the incarnation; we must confess that the Father sent the Son, and that the Son is Jesus" (Marshall 1978: 220; cf. Holtzmann 1908: 351). True discipleship "*has theological content*" (Burge 1996: 189, emphasis original). "Faith must approve itself by an open confession of the Son of God . . . in opposition to the world which ignores him and hates his followers" (Neander 1852: 267). Commentators spanning many decades and settings recognize John's loving appeal to his readers that they not stop short of the fullest possible acknowledgment of Christ. Augustine (*Hom. 1 John* 8.14) misses the mark here by relating 4:15 to deeds of charity; John is rather concerned to affirm yet again the terms of apostolic belief without which, in his opinion, confession of God or Jesus is aberrant. John's statement is a rebuttal of those whose representation of Jesus differed in fundamental ways. John's "opponents might agree that God sent the Son to save us and give us life; but for the author this confession is not complete if it is not the human Jesus who is this Son sent from God" (Rensberger 1997: 121).

In the same way that a solemn affirmation of the truth of John's message concluded the previous section (4:14), in 4:16 John lays down the basis for the appeal of 4:15 by another somber confession. The opening καί (*kai*) signals the linkage between the two verses. The "we" echoes other occurrences of the nominative pronoun ἡμεῖς (*hymeis*) that are clustered more in this section of the epistle (4:6, 10, 11, 14, 16, 17, 19) than elsewhere, where the word's appearance is sparse (nominative ἡμεῖς otherwise occurs in 1 John only at 1:4; 3:14, 16). In light of the previous verse, this "we" refers not only to the writer but also to readers who share in his robust confession of Jesus (come in the flesh; cf. 4:2) as God's saving Son (cf. 4:14). John's statement is not starkly individual but richly if guardedly social. "Through the love of God and Christ we come to the love of God the Father and of our neighbor" (Luther 1967: 300).

The basis relates to John's experience of God's love. John counts himself among those who "have come to know" and "fully believe" God's love. Both verb tenses are perfect: ἐγνώκαμεν (*egnōkamen*, we have come to know) and πεπιστεύκαμεν (*pepisteukamen*, we fully believe). A nearly equivalent expression, with only the order of the verbs reversed, occurs in John 6:69, when Peter confesses, "We believe [πεπιστεύκαμεν] and know [ἐγνώκαμεν] that you are the Holy One of God" (NIV). Too much weight should not be placed on the perfect tense in light of ongoing discussions of verbal aspect; some translations read the perfects in 1 John 4:16 as presents (e.g., RSV, TEV, NIV). Yet others find a fuller sense:

KJV	We have known and believed.
Phillips	So have we come to know and trust.
JB	We ourselves have known and put our faith in.
NEB	We have come to know and believe.
ESV	We have come to know and to believe.

Since the perfect tense of γινώσκω (*ginōskō*, to know) is fairly rare in the NT (only twenty-one occurrences total, sixteen of them in Johannine literature), with perfects of πιστεύω (*pisteuō*, to believe) occurring even less frequently (eighteen times total, eight of them in the Johannine writings),[1] it is fair to find at least slight emphasis in John's word choice here. This explains my translation, "We have come to know and fully believe." If this stress is justified, John is affirming a reflected and settled state of knowledge and trust rather than describing a mood of the moment as he composes the epistle or a conviction recalled from some event or era of the past. He would be particularly well placed to register this confession as a follower of Jesus in his earthly days: he had been part of a band who came to place full trust in Jesus's leadership (John 6:69), were helpless to save him in his hour of direst need (19:25–30), and yet enjoyed complete restoration to fellowship with Jesus in the end (John 21). As the opening verses of the epistle have already made clear, John's confidence in Christ and the fellowship he established on the Father's behalf is boundless.

The object of John's knowledge and confidence is love (ἀγάπη, *agapē*)—yet not just any love, but that "love that God has for us [ἐν ἡμῖν, *en hēmin*]." The

1. By comparison, in the NT there are 80 occurrences of γινώσκω in the present tense (20 in John's writings) and 97 in the aorist (25 in John's writings). There are 113 occurrences of πιστεύω in the present tense (52 in John's writings) and 99 in the aorist (22 in John's writings).

expression is curious. While "love" is often the object of the verb ἔχω (*echō*, to have; John 5:42; 13:35; 15:13; 1 Cor. 13:1, 2, 3; 2 Cor. 2:4; Phil. 2:2; Col. 1:4), seldom is this construction followed by the preposition ἐν (*en*, in). There are two exceptions in the whole NT: in John 5:42 Jesus tells listeners, "You do not have the love of God in yourselves [ἐν ἑαυτοῖς, *en heautois*]," and in 13:35 he informs disciples that the world is watching to see "if you have love for one another [ἐν ἀλλήλοις, *en allēlois*]." The expected expression is love "for" (εἰς, *eis*; cf. 2 Cor. 2:4; Col. 1:4; Philem. 5). Apparently in 1 John 4:16, the writer follows the usage found in John 13:35. Since God's love is not merely a projection of divine favor from some transcendent realm but the personal, abiding presence of a God whose painstaking care has been demonstrated in the cross of Christ (4:10), his love can be described as "in" his people. God's acceptance, favor, and affection is vested in and lavished on those who have received his Son.

The remainder of 4:16 restates the proposition of 4:8 that "God is love." But it extends this assertion: "God is love, and whoever abides in love abides in God, and God abides in him." NA[27] and many modern translations (TEV, NIV, TNIV, NEB, NRSV [but not RSV or ESV], CEV, NLT) begin a new paragraph here. This is an unnecessary disruption of the discourse. It is just as likely that John is putting the finishing touch on the reprise that began at 4:15. First John 4:16b does not elaborate a new thought but seals the relational assurance voiced in 4:16a ("and we have come to know and fully believe the love that God has for us"). This assurance is a function of God's very nature as revealed in his Son, which is to reach out in love and to claim those he touches. The logical progression of 4:16 can therefore be understood as follows: John asserts full acceptance of the divine love that God sends forth; this is fully consistent with the essence of God's character in terms of love as manifested in the Son; whoever dwells in this love continually dwells in God, and God likewise dwells in that person. While "dwelling" here is deeper than a mere feeling, Luther (1967: 300) is right to affirm that it is no less: "It is impossible for a heart, provided that it really knows Christ and the love of God, not to have a friendly feeling toward Him."

The effect of 4:16 is to ground the christological affirmation of 4:15 in the eternal divine character of the Father and to pave the way for the commendation of love that is set forth in 4:17–21.

Additional Notes

4:15. Codex A and two minuscules have the present subjunctive construction ἐὰν ὁμολογῇ rather than NA[27]'s aorist subjunctive ἐὰν ὁμολογήσῃ. External evidence sides overwhelmingly with NA[27]. Across the NT, the present subjunctive occurs only in 1 John 1:9, while the aorist subjunctive is slightly more frequent (Luke 12:8a; John 9:22; Rom. 10:9). Codex Ψ reads the future indicative ὁμολογήσει (without ἐάν), a form found elsewhere in the NT (Matt. 7:23; 10:32; Luke 12:8b; Rev. 3:5). The meaning of the future differs little from the aorist subjunctive but is not apt to be original due to its singularity.

4:15. Codex B and some Vulgate manuscripts attest to the insertion of Χριστός after Ἰησοῦς. First John uses both forms: Ἰησοῦς alone (1:7; 4:3; 5:5) and Ἰησοῦς Χριστός (1:3; 2:1; 3:23; 4:2; 5:6, 20). The insertion is apt to be secondary on external grounds.

4:15. $\mathfrak{P}^{9}$ supplies ἐστίν. Such meager attestation marks the insertion as secondary. It is semantically superfluous, since it (or μένει) is latent in the context.

4:15. A few witnesses replace τῷ θεῷ with αὐτῷ. Ἐν τῷ θεῷ is not a common phrase in the NT, occurring elsewhere only in 1 John 4:16 and in Paul's writings (Rom. 5:11; Eph. 3:9; Col. 3:3; 1 Thess. 2:2). Ἐν αὐτῷ carrying the sense of "in God" is common in 1 John (e.g., 1:5; 2:5, 28; 3:5; 4:13) and would therefore be the easier reading in 4:15. That and its weak external support speak decisively in favor of τῷ θεῷ.

4:16. Codex A, 33, and a couple of Latin versions attest to the present form of πιστεύω rather than the perfect. Such external evidence is too slender to be taken seriously. Semantically, the present captures enough of the sense of the perfect to be regarded as a benign alteration.

4:16. The end of 4:16 parallels the end of 4:15:

4:15 ἐν αὐτῷ μένει καὶ αὐτὸς ἐν τῷ θεῷ
4:16 ἐν τῷ θεῷ μένει καὶ ὁ θεὸς ἐν αὐτῷ μένει

Codex A and at least six minuscules omit μένει at the end of 4:16. External evidence speaks for its inclusion. So does the principle of the harder reading (which here trumps the principle of the shorter reading), since it is not easy to explain why the preponderance of manuscripts would so uniformly add such an unnecessary word at precisely this location of the clause. The superfluous μένει must be original.

VI. Illustrative Appeal: Renewed and Expanded Invitation to Love (4:15–5:15)
  A. Declarative Invitation with Supporting Warrant (4:15–16)
➤ B. Commendation of Love (4:17–21)
  C. Commendation of Faith as *Fides Qua Creditur* (5:1–5)
  D. Commendation of Faith as *Fides Quae Creditur* (5:6–12)
  E. Commendation of the Full Assurance of Eternal Life: Confident Prayer (5:13–15)

B. Commendation of Love (4:17–21)

First John 4:17–21 commends love in powerful ways. Each verse has an independent assertion to make. Yet as a literary unit these five verses have a cumulative weight that may relate to the setting John addresses, which is a community tempted not to embody the same proactive love that God in Christ has extended to community members. When groups split (cf. 2:19), hard feelings normally result. Defensiveness and perhaps even a hateful attitude toward those who have walked out can dominate. Those left behind may be prone to infighting (cf. Gal. 5:15), because love is the unifying bond of believers (cf. Col. 3:14), and when this tie is loosened, suspicion of one another and self-centered behavior can easily surface.

The first step in calling readers to reaffirm divine love is to bear witness to it, and that is what John undertakes in 1 John 4:17–21. The verses may be analyzed as follows:

1. Triumph of divine love (4:17–19)
2. Necessity of human love (4:20–21)

Exegesis and Exposition

[17]In this way God's love is fully perfected with us, in order that we might have boldness in the ⸢day of judgment⸣⸢ ⸣. For just as that one⸢ ⸣is present, so ⸢are⸣ we in this world. [18]There is no fear in love. Rather, perfect love casts out fear, because fear grows out of the dread of punishment, and the one who fears has not been made perfect in love. [19]We⸢ ⸣love⸢ ⸣because ⸢he first⸣ loved us. [20]If anyone says, "I love God," but hates his fellow believer, he is a liar. For the one who does not love his brother whom he sees⸢ ⸣cannot love God whom he does not see. [21]And this commandment we have ⸢from him⸣: he who loves God should love his brother, too.

1. Triumph of Divine Love (4:17–19)

The opening words of 4:17, "in this way" (ἐν τούτῳ, *en toutō*), refer back to the previous verse (so also Marshall 1978: 223n17; Strecker 1996: 162n1; cf. Burge 1996: 189): the God known through Jesus Christ is love, and as a result love should characterize the community of those who confess trust in this God. The definite article that appears with "love" in 4:17 (ἡ ἀγάπη, *hē agapē*) identifies it as the same love that John has been talking about throughout this context (cf. Painter 2002: 277–78), a christologically and theologically defined and revealed love. But the retrospective "in this way" has an immediate prospective application: boldness on the final day of judgment (cf. Holtzmann 1908: 352: John offers "a clear glimpse into the future").

John has spoken of "boldness" (παρρησία, *parrēsia*) twice already in connection with eschatological judgment. In 2:28 John urges readers to "abide in him" to avoid being put to shame at the parousia. In 3:21 John sounds a similar note, speaking of "boldness toward God" rather than the self-condemnation of a disobedient heart. While this epistle contains no systematic exposition of a doctrine of divine judgment, it is clear that the author assumes his readers will be familiar with the concept. This should not be surprising. Eschatological expectation is well known from the OT (e.g., Zeph. 1:14–18) and is the note on which the OT concludes (Mal. 4). It is present in abundance in Jewish apocalyptic writings (cf. Schnackenburg 1992: 222n79; Painter 2002: 278). It is a theme that sounds prominently in the preaching of John the Baptist, who announced about Christ, "His winnowing fork is in his hand, and he will clear his threshing floor, gathering his wheat into the barn and burning up the chaff with unquenchable fire" (Matt. 3:12 NIV). If any conviction was common to the early Christian community, it was the doctrine of coming divine judgment.[1]

The Jesus of the Fourth Gospel is likewise no stranger to this doctrine.[2] Far from it: the very context that harbors the beloved assurance of John 3:16 bristles with the conviction that the Father's love for the world through his Son is matched by a judgment of the world by his Son. The light of Jesus's first coming already amounts to a κρίσις (*krisis*, judging, judgment) of the world (3:19). The Father has delegated this judgment to the Son (5:22, 27). It can be averted through hearing the Son's message and trusting the God who sent him (5:24). But those who spurn the Son will be resurrected unto judgment just as surely as believers are resurrected unto life (5:29). The notion of eternal punishment is perennially unpalatable to those threatened by it, but Christ asserts that his judgment is just and true (5:30; 8:16). It is also necessary, because judgment is the means by which "the ruler of this world" is ultimately overthrown (12:31). Conviction of judgment is administered by Christ's Spirit, whom Christ sent to his disciples and to the world (16:8, 11). Clearly, the author of the Fourth Gospel was no stranger to the idea of a coming day of judgment. Even if the accent is placed on the "realized" eschatology of a present judgment, implicit in Jesus's earthly presence, there can be no doubt that Jesus looked ahead to an ultimate and eternal day of reckoning: "There is a judge for the one who rejects me and does not accept my words; that very word which I spoke will condemn him at the last day" (12:48 NIV). This would be the same day of judgment of which 1 John 4:17 speaks.

1. Cf. Guthrie 1981: 874: "The theme of judgment occurs throughout the NT." See also Strecker 1996: 164: "For the author of 1 John there can be no doubt that the traditional idea of a future judgment applies also to him and his community."

2. Holtzmann 1908: 352 marks the Synoptic feel of 4:17's "day of judgment."

The gloom of judgment is dispersed[3] by the light of love, which "is fully perfected with us" (4:17). John writes "with us" (μεθ' ἡμῶν, *meth' hēmōn*)[4] in keeping with his awareness from the previous verse that God is abidingly present. Love is perfected not at some remote distance but by dint of the God who in his Son lives "up close and personal" with his people. Love "is Jesus' image in us" (Schlatter 1950: 92). The words "is fully perfected" render the perfect passive τετελείωται (*teteleiōtai*). If God, who is the consummate manifestation of love, is with a people in such an intimate and ongoing way (4:16), then that perfecting activity may be termed "full." Hence the adverb "fully" in my translation, an amplification perhaps supported also by the verbal form used. Calvin's gloss is apropos: God's love "is abundantly poured forth and really bestowed and is complete in every respect" (1988: 294). God's direct and transformative presence is probably the active agent in the voice of the verb, which should be understood as a divine passive (see exegesis of 2:5).

In support of the assertion that love is perfected in such a way that fear of judgment is put to flight, John adds: "For just as[5] that one is present, so[6] are we in this world" (4:17c). "That one" (ἐκεῖνος, *ekeinos*) is probably Christ (so Kruse 2000: 167; Holtzmann 1908: 352), present in the world via gospel proclamation and the Spirit and God's people. But it could also refer to God (so Calvin 1988: 295),[7] abiding with his people as they manifest his powerful love. If the reference is to Christ, then John is saying that just as the Son was and is present in the world in a loving fashion that in no way attracts divine displeasure, so are the Son's followers. If the reference is to the Father, John is drawing the obvious inference that if the God who is love abides with his people, they need not fear heavenly wrath; divine love that they appropriate and manifest puts any hint of morbid fear to flight (cf. Thompson 1992: 127). Whatever the reference, the assurance that John proffers is utterly complete because Christ's work is a fait accompli; it is for that reason baffling that Schnackenburg (1992: 224) asserts, "The author knows that his readers have not yet attained to perfect love." Has anyone in this life? No, except for Christ.

3. Schnackenburg 1992: 222 seems out of touch with John's confidence when he explains this verse as affirming that "we are still in an incomplete state of salvation, still under the threat of future judgment." To the extent that this is true, it is hard to see how John can talk about a perfected love that confers confidence in the day of judgment.

4. Moule 1994: 61 thinks the meaning may be "among us (in our community)." This is a true statement about God with his people, but μεθ' ἡμῶν is better understood here as asserting that God is present proximally and *in addition to* those with whom he takes up residence, not simply diffused among them. The thought is of the personal and discrete *presence* of transcendence, not some distributive immanence. This is the promise of Immanuel in Matt. 1:23: μεθ' ἡμῶν ὁ θεός, *meth' hēmōn ho theos*, God with us).

5. For the six uses of καθώς in 1 John, all with imperatival implications, see exegesis of 3:3.

6. Adverbial καί (*kai*) means "also."

7. Strecker 1996: 165 points out that the grammar favors Calvin's interpretation, though most commentators take Christ to be the antecedent.

But the discourse of this section turns on John's insistence that the divine act in the cross (4:10) is complete in its scope and effect. "On that day the believer need not fear because Christ has atoned for his sins" (Akin 2001: 185). Human assurance does not depend on human attainment but on completed divine action and promise.

It bears repeating that this love, however, is not a vague emanation or the impersonal attribute of a universal divinity, as Plato's god was the good, the true, and the beautiful. The religious philosopher's query, "Should fear or love play the leading role in religion?" (Schnackenburg 1992: 224; cf. Philo, *Unchangeable* 69), may be something of a universal question admitting of general solution, but for John, God's love is not known apart from the Son who came and bled to effect redemption. Luther (1967: 301–2) is therefore not far from John's sentiment in commenting, "If consciousness of a great sin weighs you down, comfort yourself with this blood of love. . . . No human religion can hold its own in the face of the judgment, but it is solely in the blood of Christ that we have confidence on the Day of Judgment." Both Luther and Calvin dwell on the fear of guilt, death, and hell that was more prominent in late medieval thought than today; their ruminations are salutary in an age possibly more richly deserving of divine judgment, though paradoxically chillingly dismissive of it.

Foreign to John's thought is medieval counsel that Christians can hope to survive judgment to the extent that they merit divine favor by making progress in virtuous imitation of God (see Augustine, Hilary of Arles, and Andreas in Bray 2000: 216). It is not that "faithfulness to Jesus removes any need to fear the day of judgment" (D. Smith 1991: 114), because no amount of human faithfulness can counteract the judgment that human faithlessness calls forth. Rather, the love of which John writes, God's love, Christ's love, abides in believers through the gospel to such an extent that their confidence in that love is more assured than the prospect of death itself.

But fear of death, hinted at with reference to "the day of judgment" in 4:17, is so deeply ingrained in the human psyche that John now takes it up in greater detail in 4:18.

The first clause of 4:18 ("there is no fear in love; rather,[8] perfect love casts out fear") speaks of that fear as φόβος (*phobos*). While it is tempting to think of this as the Bible's familiar "fear of God," in the Johannine corpus φόβος refers either to "fear of the Jews" who held political power (John 7:13; 19:38; 20:19) or to the abject terror caused by witnessing ghoulish or calamitous events (Rev. 11:11; 18:10, 15). This cautions against leaping to the conclusion that "fear [of God]" is something that John rejects categorically when other biblical writers regard it positively.[9] John is more likely to have in mind the fear of

8. For ἀλλά (*alla*) as "rather," see Mark 7:15; Luke 17:8; Rom. 3:31; 6:13; 11:11; 12:3; 13:14; 15:21.

9. See, e.g., 2 Chron. 19:7, 9; Job 28:28; Pss. 19:9 (19:10 MT); 34:11 (34:12 MT); 111:10; Prov. 1:7; 2:5; 10:27; 15:33; 19:23; 22:4; 23:17; Isa. 11:2–3; 33:6; Acts 9:31; 2 Cor. 5:11; 7:1; Eph. 5:21; 1 Pet. 1:17; 2:17; Rev. 15:4; 19:5. Schlatter 1950: 93 summarizes, "Scripture plants the fear

eschatological judgment (so most commentators).[10] The previous verse (1 John 4:17) has just ruled that out on the basis of the love that God perfects among his people. The biblical commendation of a healthy fear of God is therefore not mitigated by 4:18 (contra Loader 1992: 57).[11] Also, John's statement should not be taken to suggest that fearlessness is a sure sign of confidence before God. He would hardly be making a virtue of brazen swagger.[12] Perfect love may well cast out fear, but as Schlatter (1927: 138–39) shrewdly notes:

> Fear is also cast out by perfect lovelessness, the utter minimizing of God. It is not simply a matter of fear being cast out; the question must also be asked how it is cast out. . . . Love drives out fear in a different way than minimizing God does. Love does not subtract from God that which fear grants to him; it grants him still more. Love does not fight with God over who is on the throne and does not try to make him its slave. Love gives God his due honor, grants wisdom and goodness to him alone. Perfect love is total surrender; it says totally and from the heart: not what I will. This was the love shown by Jesus, the one whom perfect love moved to such deep prostration before God, as only perfect fear can do.

God's love is "perfect" (τελεία, *teleia*), and such love "casts out fear."[13] God's abiding love as demonstrated in Christ's death (4:10) and manifested among believers (4:12) leaves no room for morbid fear to fester and spread. John might term it "perfect" for several reasons: it originates in God, who as pure heavenly light (1:5) is flawless in every attribute; it was proved in the sending of his Son, through whom eternal life has come (4:9); it works powerfully among believers[14] to produce the same quality of love that both Father and Son have shown in the world (4:17). A love so comprehensive and effectual forcibly expels or throws out (βάλλει, *ballei*) the dread of judgment on the last day. Other NT writers express a comparable sense of relief here:

---

of God in us as the beginning of wisdom, and the apostolic word likewise nurtures it in us and makes it a powerful force working hand in hand with faith."

10. This is a present fear in the light of a possible future, however, not "a fearless confidence on the day of judgment" alone (as Culpepper 1998: 27 has it).

11. Cf. Marshall 1978: 224: "There is, of course, a place for fear in the life of the Christian." Calvin 1988: 296 elaborates: "Fear is not cast out in such a way that it does not assault our minds; but it is so cast out that it does not disturb us or hamper the peace that we obtain by faith." See also Painter 2002: 283. Bede (in Bray 2000: 217) is among those who misguidedly suppose that God's love explicitly banishes even the fear of the Lord that is the beginning of wisdom. Burge 1996: 196–97 tends in this direction: "Whenever our perception of God is shaped by fear and anxiety, . . . we have not plumbed the depth of his love."

12. Cf. Neander 1852: 272: John "would, indeed, by no means banish that holy awe, which impels him who lives in the consciousness of still inhering sin, to watch continually over himself, to shun everything which might mar his fellowship with God." Cf. Burge 1996: 197.

13. Schnackenburg 1992: 224 draws from John's flat indicative an anthropocentric inference: "We should therefore do all we can to banish fear." This may be true, but John's point is that God by his love has already done this.

14. Yet Neander 1852: 270 wisely counsels: "It is not the believer's own worthiness, or perfectness, which John regards as the ground of this confidence." John is commending first of all God's love, not human appropriation of it (cf. Thompson 1992: 128).

"For you did not receive a spirit that makes you a slave again to fear" (Rom. 8:15 NIV). Christ freed "those who all their lives were held in slavery by their fear of death" (Heb. 2:15 NIV). In a setting where judgment was generally expected,[15] the assurance of exoneration would be welcome news.

John states that for his readers, fear is banished, "because fear has punishment [κόλασιν, *kolasin*],[16] and the one who fears has not been made perfect in love." The logic seems to be that fear as John defines it here is rooted in the expectation of punishment at God's hands: "The one who fears has not been made perfect in love." But John addresses his readers as if they have been thus perfected (4:17). Therefore such fear of retribution is a thing of the past for them. John speaks of a fear still clinging to those who have left the community, not a fear that should be plaguing readers who remain.

It is not perfectly clear what triggers John's mention of fear.[17] Perhaps it is simply John's pastoral instinct to comfort due to the disquieting reminder of the existence of divine wrath. More contextually, it may be recalled that John addresses readers among whom there have been recent quarrels over the apostolic message. Possibly John's opponents used fear as a part of their anti-apostolic panoply. Follow us or else! Do not follow leaders like John![18] Throughout the ages leaders have used misinformation and intimidation to discourage allegiance to the gospel and to encourage its opposite (warning against abuse of power either against or for the gospel is Rensberger 1997: 123). It is accordingly possible that "the one who fears" (4:18c) is an oblique reference to those who already have been, or still might be, stampeded, enticed, or otherwise cajoled into adopting a formulation of Christ's message deemed aberrant by John. John calls *his* followers, Christ's followers, to a love free from eschatological terror because this love has united them perfectly with Christ.

Seen from this angle, John's remarks in 4:18, while anomalous in form, are hardly foreign in spirit to much else that the First Epistle offers. There is no fear of estrangement from God in the love that by definition establishes intimacy with God. "We arrive at a calm rest outside fear by being aware of God's love towards us" (Calvin 1988: 296). The one who fears has not been perfected in that love, but John is convinced of better things concerning his readers. In case anyone needs explicit assurance, John's testimony here furnishes it. Burge

15. Cf. Jesus's words in Matt. 8:12; 25:30; also 1 Enoch 62.10: "But the Lord of the Spirits himself will cause them to be frantic, so that they shall rush and depart from his presence. Their faces shall be filled with shame, and their countenances shall be crowned with darkness" (*OTP* 1.43).

16. The word κόλασις appears over a dozen times in the LXX but elsewhere in the NT only at Matt. 25:46: "Then they will go away to eternal punishment" (NIV). In Hellenistic writings it was a well-established term for divine retribution (J. Schneider, *TDNT* 3:816–17, esp. 817n5; Painter 2002: 278; Strecker 1996: 167n38).

17. D. Smith 1991: 117 suggests: "Having introduced the theme of judgment, John must address the possibility of fear." But plenty of biblical writers do the former and not the latter.

18. Paul seems to have encountered this strategy among detractors of his leadership at Corinth (see esp. 1 Cor. 1; 2 Cor. 11).

(1996: 195–96) gives impressive anecdotal evidence that this is a message still much needed in the church today.

First John 4:19 concludes John's affirmation of the triumph of divine love: "We love because he first loved us."[19] Any lack of assurance caused by fear of judgment is thereby overcome. The summary function of the verse is reflected by οὖν (*oun*, therefore) inserted by copyists of some manuscripts (see first additional note on 4:19). John restates a point he expressed slightly differently in 4:10 (and that Paul states in Rom. 5:8). The "we" of 1 John 4:19 contrasts with the "the one who fears" in 4:18. That person lacks the full assurance of God's love, while "we" of 4:19 possess that assurance based on God's initiative; they have discovered that "God always makes the first move in the game of love" (Sloyan 1995: 49). This discovery has made a difference in the way they regard one another: they love.

But response to God's proactive and transformative love has not extended to all parties with sufficient force. If it had, John might not have needed to pen this epistle or to make love such a prominent topic in it. The final two verses of the chapter take up a challenge that God's superfluity of love poses for the community John addresses.

2. Necessity of Human Love (4:20–21)

First John 4:20 begins with a word pair that echoes Jesus's language in the Fourth Gospel: ἐάν τις (*ean tis*, if anyone).[20] In the Synoptic Gospels the words occur on Jesus's lips at only two junctures: when Jesus tells two disciples to go and untie a colt for Jesus's entry into Jerusalem (Matt. 21:3/Mark 11:3/Luke 19:31), and when Jesus foretells the announcement of false Christs (Matt. 24:23/Mark 13:21). In marked contrast to this, John's Gospel quotes Jesus to this effect in some ten passages:

John	Greek Text	Translation
6:51	<u>ἐάν τις</u> φάγῃ ἐκ τούτου τοῦ ἄρτου ζήσει εἰς τὸν αἰῶνα	*If anyone* eats of this bread, he will live forever. (NIV)
7:17	<u>ἐάν τις</u> θέλῃ τὸ θέλημα αὐτοῦ ποιεῖν, γνώσεται περὶ τῆς διδαχῆς πότερον ἐκ τοῦ θεοῦ ἐστιν ἢ ἐγὼ ἀπ' ἐμαυτοῦ λαλῶ	*If anyone* chooses to do God's will, he will find out whether my teaching comes from God or whether I speak on my own. (NIV)

Continued

19. JB ("we are to love") is one of the few translations following the view of Schnackenburg 1992: 225 that "we love" here is imperatival: "let us love," a rendering favored also by Rensberger 1997: 125–26 and Strecker 1996: 170.

20. Painter 2002: 284 thinks this is "the seventh and final claim of the opponents" against whom John writes, the other six being found in 1:6, 8, 10; 2:4, 6, 9 (see also Schnackenburg 1992: 226). The form of these claims varies enough to make the theory uncertain. For other objections, see Strecker 1996: 170–71.

John	Greek Text	Translation
7:37	ἐάν τις διψᾷ ἐρχέσθω πρός με καὶ πινέτω	*If anyone* is thirsty, let him come to me and drink. (NIV)
8:51 (cf. 8:52)	ἐάν τις τὸν ἐμὸν λόγον τηρήσῃ, θάνατον οὐ μὴ θεωρήσῃ εἰς τὸν αἰῶνα	*If anyone* keeps my word, he will never see death. (NIV)
10:9	ἐγώ εἰμι ἡ θύρα· δι᾽ ἐμοῦ ἐάν τις εἰσέλθῃ σωθήσεται	I am the gate; *if anyone* enters through me, he will be saved.
11:9	ἐάν τις περιπατῇ ἐν τῇ ἡμέρᾳ, οὐ προσκόπτει	*If anyone* walks in the daylight, he will not stumble.
12:26	ἐὰν ἐμοί τις διακονῇ, ἐμοὶ ἀκολουθείτω . . . ἐάν τις ἐμοὶ διακονῇ τιμήσει αὐτὸν ὁ πατήρ	*If anyone* serves me, let him follow me; . . . *if anyone* serves me, the Father will honor that person.
12:47	ἐάν τίς μου ἀκούσῃ τῶν ῥημάτων καὶ μὴ φυλάξῃ, ἐγὼ οὐ κρίνω αὐτόν	*If anyone* hears my words and does not keep them, I do not judge him.
14:23	ἐάν τις ἀγαπᾷ με τὸν λόγον μου τηρήσει	*If anyone* loves me, he will keep my word.

As in 1 John 4:15 (see exegesis), it is possible that in 4:20 Jesus's own diction is affecting the way that John frames the discourse here (see also 2:1, 15; 5:16).

John envisions a situation in which someone professes love for God but fails to love—in John's parlance, "hates"—a fellow believer.[21] This problem was marked early in church history[22] and has already come up elsewhere in this epistle. In 2:9, 11 John describes the incompatibility of failing to love others while claiming to be "in the light," and in 3:15 John characterizes failure to love others as tantamount to murder (see exegesis of these passages). Now John warns against lovelessness, or even active hostility, in light of the freedom from fear of judgment that 4:17–19 sets forth. A Synoptic parable tells the sordid tale of a slave forgiven a great huge debt by his lord (Matt. 18:21–35).[23] Upon release this man seizes and beats a fellow slave who owes him a tiny debt. Jesus warns of dire consequences from God for such behavior (18:35). First John 4:20 takes a similar tack: given God's great love that frees from judgment (4:17–19), love for others becomes an inexorable corollary. That John brings

21. This, too, is an echo of Jesus's language as recorded in the Fourth Gospel: see John 3:20; 7:7; 12:25; 15:18, 19, 23, 24, 25; 17:14. Schnackenburg 1992: 226 notes a further parallel in the a fortiori nature of the argument, "a tactic favored by Jesus himself (Mark 2:9ff.) and in the rabbinic schools."

22. Ign. *Smyrn.* 6.1: "Beware of those who hold strange doctrine regarding the grace of Jesus Christ which came to us. . . . They have no care for love, none for the widow, none for the orphan, none for the afflicted, none for the prisoner, none for the hungry or thirsty."

23. Other commentators (e.g., Rensberger 1997: 127) find a parallel in Mark 12:28–34.

up the subject suggests that it was a corollary not being embraced completely among his envisioned readership.

To profess love for God while not loving others makes one "a liar." The author has a penchant for framing issues in either/or terms; "there are no half measures" (Painter 2002: 285). In the exegesis of 1:10; 2:4, 22–23, we saw that this is not an example of Johannine "hate speech" but straightforward description. It is, we might say, blunt application of the law of noncontradiction. John offers a commonsense warrant for this assertion: "For the one who does not love his brother whom he sees cannot love God whom he does not see." John has already alluded to God's invisibility (4:12; cf. John 1:18), which, however, is partially offset when his people show love for one another. The invisible God who is love (1 John 4:8, 16) takes on form indirectly as his people love.[24] This is axiomatic for John (as it was for Paul; see Rom. 13:9–10; Gal. 5:14) and helps account for the strong conviction of his statement. God is infinitely remote; Christians are all around, and our help can touch them immediately, directly, and effectively. It is therefore pure self-delusion to view love for God (who is far away) as fulfilled when love for others (who are nearby) is lacking (cf. Schlatter 1950: 94–95). Such a person "cannot love God": it is impossible. Even if someone "goes through the outward motions of devotion to God, prayer, attendance at worship, and so on, it may still be all empty show" (Marshall 1978: 225). Jesus warned against a piety that showcased prayer but shunned widows (Mark 12:40/Luke 20:47; cf. James 1:27).

First John 4:21 summarizes and extends[25] John's point: "And this commandment [ἐντολή, *entolē*] we have from him:[26] the one who loves God should love his brother, too." "From him" could mean either from God (so Painter 2002: 287) or from Jesus (Holtzmann 1908: 353 is too dogmatic that John could be referring only to Jesus). The personal reference is significant; John's counsel here is grounded in a relationship with the Father or the Son, not the command of an impersonal moralism. John could be recalling the incident where Jesus was asked about the "great commandment" (ἐντολὴ μεγάλη, *entolē megalē*; Matt. 22:36). Or he could be recalling the OT passage on which Jesus based his answer (Deut. 6:5 NIV): "Love the Lord your God with all your heart and with all your soul and with all your strength." The point is the same. The imperative to love others is implicit in the claim to love God. As Bede (in Bray 2000: 218) states, "Who is there who would say that he loves the emperor but cannot abide his laws? The true lover of God is one who loves his commandments also, as Ps. 119 makes perfectly clear."

24. Calvin 1988: 297 makes the point that true love of God will result in love for people because they are made in God's image; he also cites the psalmist's love for God that issues in delight "for the saints who are in the land" (Ps. 16:3).

25. Cf. Strecker 1996: 173: "The copulative καί has not only a connective but also an epexegetical function."

26. The conjunction ἵνα (*hina*, in order that) marks the clause as imperatival; see Caragounis 2006: 220 and numerous examples given there.

John has spoken elsewhere of divine commands (1 John 2:3, 4, 7–8; 3:22–24; see exegesis of 2:3) and has already given the counsel contained in 4:21: "And this is his command: . . . to love one another as he commanded us" (3:23). Here he simply applies this now-familiar directive to readers whose realization of freedom from eschatological punishment should transform the way they regard their peers. Citation of a command "makes us careful how we cultivate love, giving love a holy necessity and inviolable importance" (Schlatter 1950: 95).

Additional Notes

4:17. Codex ℵ and a few other witnesses daringly replace ἐν τῇ ἡμέρᾳ τῆς κρίσεως with ἐν τῇ ἀγάπῃ. Expunging "in the day of judgment" removes a jarring note from an otherwise love-soaked context, but John has shown repeatedly that he is fully capable of unexpected turns of phrases. And it is unlikely here that an almost solitary reading can make a claim to be original.

4:17. A few minuscules (1505, 1611, 2138) add πρὸς τὸν ἐνανθρωπήσαντα (with respect to taking on human form). This nicely explains a sense in which we will have confidence on judgment day, but it has scant claim to stem from John's own pen.

4:17. Minuscule 2138 continues in an expansive vein (see previous additional note) by replacing "just as that one *is present in this world*, so are we" with "just as that one *was in the world blameless and pure*, so are we in this world" (italic type emphasizes the particular points of contrast). Weaker external evidence can hardly be imagined. The longer reading, in this case secondary, serves to explain the sense in which Christ was in the world and bears a resemblance to us.

4:17. ℵ and 2138 read the future ἐσόμεθα instead of ἐσμέν. This changes John's meaning from how Christians currently resemble Christ in this world to how they may do so in the future. The evidence favors John's making a statement about Christians' current state of being, not just their future one.

4:19. A respectable though decisively small collection of witnesses inserts οὖν, a word occurring elsewhere in John's Letters only at 3 John 8. While οὖν is a favorite conjunction in John's Gospel (two hundred times) and is found in Revelation (six times), it is unlikely to be original here.

4:19. Some dozen manuscripts or versions, ℵ among them, furnish an object of this love: τὸν θεόν. Bearing much the same sense is αὐτόν, found in Ψ and 𝔐. This is a benign insertion, comparable to English translations adding "they went out" to 2:19 to fill what feels like a slight ellipsis, for ἀγαπῶμεν is normally transitive in 1 John (see 3:11, 14, 23; 4:7, 12; 5:2; intransitive only at 3:18), and it is understandable that scribes might tweak their copies to render a transitive form here. (If they understood ἀγαπῶμεν as a hortatory subjunctive [Metzger 1994: 645], supplying an accusative is even more intelligible.) But the absence of τὸν θεόν (and αὐτόν) from uncials A and B makes its originality less than certain. The shorter reading gets a cautious nod. Moreover, given John's stress elsewhere on love for others, he might object to restricting the object of love in this clause to God.

4:19. While NA[27] follows ℵ, B, and most other manuscripts in reading αὐτὸς πρῶτος, there are two other attested possibilities. One, ὁ θεὸς πρῶτον (or ὁ θεὸς αὐτὸς πρῶτον), is clearly late and secondary. (Πρῶτον, an adverbial neuter to denote time, means the same as πρῶτος, of which it is a derivative form [BDAG 892].) The other possibility, ὁ θεὸς πρῶτος, has the backing of A, 33, and a few others. But this is scanty external evidence. All three possible readings convey much the same meaning.

4:20. NA[27] reads the relatively awkward τὸν θεὸν ὃν οὐχ ἑώρακεν οὐ δύναται ἀγαπᾶν, awkward in that the predicate of the sentence (the last three words) is widely separated from the subject (ὁ

. . . μὴ ἀγαπῶν). Scribes of two uncials (A, 048) and 𝔐 transformed the predicate to a question: πῶς δύναται ἀγαπᾶν (How can he love?). NA[27]'s declaration becomes a very Johannine-sounding question (for πῶς combined with a form of δύναμαι in John's Gospel, see John 3:4, 9; 5:44; 6:52; 9:16; 14:5). But external evidence (א, B, Ψ, several minuscules and versions) and the principle of the harder reading rule out the improvement.

4:21. A, probably 048, and a couple of Latin witnesses attest to the more explicit ἀπὸ τοῦ θεοῦ. But context makes specifying the referent of αὐτοῦ unnecessary. With such sparse manuscript support, the variant is clearly secondary.

VI. Illustrative Appeal: Renewed and Expanded Invitation to Love (4:15–5:15)
  A. Declarative Invitation with Supporting Warrant (4:15–16)
  B. Commendation of Love (4:17–21)
➤ C. Commendation of Faith as *Fides Qua Creditur* (5:1–5)
  D. Commendation of Faith as *Fides Quae Creditur* (5:6–12)
  E. Commendation of the Full Assurance of Eternal Life: Confident Prayer (5:13–15)

C. Commendation of Faith as *Fides Qua Creditur* (5:1–5)

The next block of verses only appears to change the subject. Since believing and faith frame the passage (5:1, 5), it is natural to see "faith" as the main subject, and it is undoubtedly important. Painter (2002: 289) sees here a new section, though he concedes that "there is a close connection between the theme of love in the previous section and the focus on the christological confession in the present section" (2002: 292). The beginning of a new chapter should not obscure the real continuity with the end of 1 John 4. "John does not change his subject, but here gives it a different nuance" (Burge 1996: 191). The "commandment" of 4:21 is linked with "commandments" in 5:2–3, just as "love" that dominates much of 1 John 4 is also prominent in 5:1–3. Love and faith "are combined without a strict break in thought" (Akin 2001: 188).

There is, however, a shift in emphasis. The latter half of 1 John 4 stresses the agapic and ethical dimensions of relationship with God in Christ: love and obedience are rhetorically paramount. The only mention of faith relates it to God's love (4:16). Now in 5:1–5 John will begin to shift emphasis in a pistic (faith) direction—of the ten occurrences in 1 John of the Greek noun or verb for "faith" or "believe," seven of them are in 1 John 5. Specifically, 5:1–5 begins and ends with affirmations of personal Christian faith, the subjective act of Christian belief (*fides qua creditur*). Not surprisingly, Jesus is the central focus, but the stress is on the *that* of believing, not the *what* of what faith affirms (*fides quae creditur*), which will come to the fore in 5:6–12 (cf. Schnackenburg 1992: 227). The verses may be analyzed as follows:

1. Believing as entrée into free love of God (5:1–3)
2. Personal faith victorious over (the lovelessness of) the world (5:4–5)

Exegesis and Exposition

[1]Everyone who believes that Jesus is the Christ is born of God, and everyone who loves the one who grants spiritual rebirth loves ⌜also the person⌝ to whom he grants it. [2]This is how we know that we love the children of God, when we love God and ⌜keep⌝ his commandments. [3]For this is the love of God: that we keep his commandments, and his commandments are not onerous. [4]For everyone given spiritual rebirth from God overcomes the world. And this is the victory that triumphs over the world: ⌜our⌝

faith. [5]⌜But who is⌝ the one who conquers the world? It is none other than the person who believes that Jesus is the Son of God.

1. Believing as Entrée into Free Love of God (5:1–3)

The key to Christian identity, John has been insisting, is love. The road to love, he will now affirm, is paved with faith.

The faith John has in mind has a particular content,[1] as we have already seen, particularly in 4:2–3: "Every spirit that acknowledges *that* Jesus Christ has come in the flesh is from God, but every spirit that does not acknowledge Jesus is not from God" (emphasis added). To "acknowledge" (or not) is to affirm (or deny) faith, and this faith has a particular christological substance (see exegesis of 4:2–3). John will say more about that substance in 5:6–12.

Here, however, he wants to draw out a central implication of the experience of Christian faith, perhaps in contrast to the powerful but false religiosity that has rent the community he addresses.[2] The central implication is that true faith leads to a particular quality and depth of love. This is not a hit-and-miss phenomenon but a universal feature of faith: "everyone who believes" (an expression found on Jesus's lips in John 3:15, 16; 12:46; cf. Acts 13:39; Rom. 10:11 [quoting Isa. 28:16]) is affected by faith in this way. Believes what? Believes that Jesus is the Christ. This means, at the very least, "to hope from Him everything that has been promised about the Messiah" (Calvin 1988: 298; Loader 1992: 60 stresses that John "goes far beyond saying that [Christ] is the fulfilment of Jewish hopes for the Messiah"). John has already spoken explicitly of "Christ" five times in this epistle: he is the one with whom believers enjoy fellowship (1:3), the Righteous One who makes intercession with the Father (2:1), the one whom the antichrist denies (2:22), the one in whose name (alone) people are commanded to trust (3:23), and the one who has come from God in the flesh (4:2). John does not need, at this juncture, to spend more time sketching Christ's identity and character for his readers; they both know of whom he is writing.

What John wishes to stress is that to believe is to have been acted upon in a dynamic, transformative way by God. It is to have been "born of God." Holtzmann (1908: 353) rightly notes that whereas for Paul, faith is the condition for being a child of God, John refers to it here as the result.[3] Marshall (1978: 226n31) reasonably observes that the perfect tense γεγέννηται (*gegennētai*,

1. Painter 2002: 292 points to ὅτι (*hoti*, that) in "everyone who believes *that*" as indicating "the content of belief." Cf. Kruse 2000: 171.

2. Strecker 1996: 174 correctly notes that any opponents "are only indirectly in view."

3. The comment of Marshall 1978: 226 (echoed in Strecker 1996: 174n6, who necessarily decouples 1 John 5:1 from John 1:12–13) that "John is not trying to show how a person experiences the new birth" is unconvincing. Like Marshall, Sloyan 1995: 49 thinks that "belief . . . brings about birth from God in 5:1," but John can be understood as expressing the opposite. Kruse 2000: 171 is closer to the mark in observing that spiritual rebirth here "is something initiated by God and effected through his Spirit, and it takes place in conjunction with faith in Christ."

has been born) points to "the present state of the believer."[4] The language of spiritual rebirth (γεννάω, *gennaō*, to cause to be born) is a memorable feature of John's Gospel (1:12–13; 3:3–8). It has also already figured prominently in this epistle. Spiritual rebirth is closely related to "doing righteousness" (1 John 2:29), forsaking sin (3:9), and experiencing the love and knowledge of God (4:7). To be "born of God" is not cant, however popular it may be to parody born-again Christians in some quarters; it is essential to saving faith. In Johannine theology, spiritual rebirth seems to precede and ultimately create faith: those who believe do so not so much as the result of human volition as of prior divine intention (cf. John 1:12–13; Akin 2001: 189 misses this by citing 1:12 but not 1:13; more aptly, see Peterson and Williams 2004: 188–89). Whoever confesses faith in Christ, then, has been visited by God. This can be expected to result in profound change of the person so visited.

It results, first, in love for God. John does not state this in 1 John 5:1 but assumes it: every believer "who loves the one who grants spiritual rebirth" is a clear reference to the believer's love for God. John has already accounted for this: "We love because he first loved us" (4:19). In 5:1 John assumes rather than describes or enjoins the believer's love for God (cf. 4:21; also Painter 2002: 293).

It results, second, in love for other believers: "Everyone who loves the one who grants spiritual rebirth loves also the person to whom he grants it." To love God as the result of having been touched by his regenerating force is to love others who have likewise been divinely transformed (to call them "divinized" [Sloyan 1995: 50] probably goes beyond what John meant to convey, which was that believers are united in their savior by faith, not that they have achieved his status vis-à-vis God in every sense).[5] Love for fellow believers has already been a consistent emphasis in this epistle (2:10; 3:10, 14, 18, 23; 4:7–8, 11–12, 19, 21), more prominent in fact than love for God, which John has mostly assumed. Now John merely draws out its catalyzing source (God who grants spiritual renewal) and its necessary object (fellow believers). Just as siblings in a family normally hold each other in high regard, members of God's household care for one another and regard each other with the affection of personal kin in key respects. (Nothing indicates, however, that John intends this to be a criticism of natural family affection.)

4. The view (see, e.g., Akin 2001: 189) that the perfect "suggests a past action with results that continue in the present," whatever its status vis-à-vis current aspect theory, points to the Johannine conviction that the one who believes does so due to circumstances that are prior to the personal act of faith.

5. Patristic writers like Augustine (*Hom. 1 John* 10.3) and Cyril of Jerusalem (in Bray 2000: 221) held that John is speaking here not of the Christian brother or sister but of Christ himself (also Luther 1967: 308 and Akin 2001: 190). Everyone who loves God will also love the one born from God (i.e., Christ). This may be a valid assertion, but it is contextually unlikely, because John's overarching topic seems to be love for God leading to love for fellow believers, not love for Christ per se (a self-evident Johannine desideratum).

The preponderance of birth language in 5:1 has the effect of highlighting God's being explicitly at work in the community John addresses (cf. Phil. 2:12–13), not just human factors like natural affection and religious assent. A contemporary writer looks at Christian experience as merely phenomenal and virtually delusional: "According to popular orthodoxy, we are promised eternal life . . . for believing the right things, for being theologically correct" (Funk 1996: 312). This may or may not be an apt account of what some believe today, but it definitely does not describe Christian experience as John understands it. Faith's tie to God is not grounded in its own tenacity, much less in a self-serving spiritual autism; it is rather a response to a saving message brought home by the grace of divine regeneration. The sublime authorship of saving Christian faith—for which John gives God primary credit—makes possible a sublime outcome: love for others. The singular nature of early Christianity's cardinal characteristic, love, which had no close parallels in pagan religions of the era, may help to explain John's determination to show that the impulse that gives rise to faith and then results in love comes from God and not from humans themselves.

The next verse (1 John 5:2) begins with the epistle's fifth and final occurrence of ἐν τούτῳ γινώσκομεν (*en toutō ginōskomen*, by this we know; cf. 2:3, 5; 3:24; 4:13). First John 5:1 spoke of divine parentage producing a faith that results in love; 5:2 ("almost the Johannine equivalent of the Jewish *Shema*," according to Culpepper 1998: 271) speaks of a love for fellow believers that consists of love for God *and* compliance with his commandments (Calvin 1988: 299 aptly notes: "The love of God is no idle thing"). The phrase ἐν τούτῳ γινώσκομεν is therefore most likely cataphoric (forward looking),[6] although John's diction is so intertwined here that most clauses are related somehow with most other clauses in both directions.[7] Accordingly, I translated it "this is how we know," anticipating the coming ὅταν (*hotan*, when)[8] that introduces the two clauses that conclude the verse. This knowledge, as elsewhere in the epistle, is both theoretical and practical, not merely one or the other (cf. Strecker 1996: 176).

Mention of "commandments" (see exegesis of 2:3) in 5:2 begins an inclusio pointing back to 4:21 and extending to the end of 5:3. In 4:21, John noted that believers have received the commandment (from either God or Jesus) to love not only the Father but also the Son. Now John broadens the singular in 4:21 to a plural; while 4:21 spoke specifically of the love

6. So also D. Smith 1991: 117; Thompson 1992: 130; Strecker 1996: 176; Rensberger 1997: 128; Akin 2001: 191. For the argument in favor of taking it as anaphoric (backward looking), see Marshall 1978: 227–28; for fuller discussion taking careful note of Dodd and R. Brown, see Painter 2002: 290–91, 293–94.

7. Holtzmann 1908: 354 notes that this has caused some as far back as Grotius to posit a textual dislocation here calling for an emendation. But there is no textual evidence for this, and the author's diction often meanders.

8. Loader 1992: 60 seems to construe ὅταν (wrongly) as "if." Strecker 1996: 176 points out that it could be translated "because." Cf. BDF §394.

imperative, 5:2 speaks of obeying God more generally. The logical flow of 5:2 runs like this: there is a way to confirm that we love our fellow believers ("children of God" in 3:1–2, 10): it is when we love God in such a way (or to such an extent)[9] that we are obedient to what he commands. In 5:2, John takes his stress on love for others, which beginning in 4:20 he grounded in the divine love commandment as well as in love for God, and extends it as an assurance of these very things. The circularity is obvious (cf. Kruse 2000: 172), but it is not vicious. It merely indicates the simultaneity of three components of reborn Christian experience: the pistic (faith), the ethical (obedience to commandments), and the relational or agapic (love for God and others). This triad has already been discussed repeatedly and at length (see exegesis of 2:1a). First John 5:2 therefore continues John's commendation of the personal experience of Christian faith (*fides qua creditur*) by underscoring the assurance that attends it in terms of love for God expressed as compliance with what he commands his people to do. John's overall goal continues to be an appeal for readers to reflect the full measure of love that has come to them via their spiritual rebirth and faith. The juxtaposition of love and commandment-keeping has a significant OT counterpart that no doubt informs John's Christian understanding and is worth underscoring (all quotations from NIV, emphasis added):

Deut. 6:2, 5	Fear the LORD your God as long as you live by *keeping all his decrees and commands. . . . Love the LORD your God* with all your heart and with all your soul and with all your strength.
Deut. 10:12	And now, O Israel, what does the LORD your God ask of you but to fear the LORD your God, to *walk in all his ways, to love him*, to serve the LORD your God with all your heart and with all your soul.
Deut. 11:1	*Love the LORD your God and keep his requirements, his decrees, his laws and his commands* always.
Deut. 11:13	So if you *faithfully obey the commands* I am giving you today—to *love the LORD your God* and to serve him with all your heart and with all your soul. . . .
Deut. 11:22	If you carefully *observe all these commands* I am giving you to follow—to *love the LORD your God*, to walk in all his ways and to hold fast to him. . . .
Josh. 22:5	But be very careful to keep the commandment and the law that Moses the servant of the LORD gave you: to *love the LORD your God*, to walk in all his ways, to *obey his commands*, to hold fast to him and to serve him with all your heart and all your soul.
Josh. 23:6, 11	Be very strong; be careful to *obey all that is written in the Book of the Law* of Moses, without turning aside to the right or to the left. . . . So be very careful to *love the LORD your God*.

9. I translate καί (*kai*) as "and," but it probably introduces a result that follows from what precedes (cf. BDAG 495).

First John 5:2 rules out that common oversimplification of Christian faith, which contends that how we treat other people is, in the end, all that matters; ultimately church is, in this view, mostly about interpersonal or social ethics. While decent treatment of others, particularly fellow believers (cf. John 13:34–35; Gal. 6:10), is always in order, it cannot be separated from the christologically grounded love for God and the resultant pursuit of God's commandments that 1 John 5:2 commends. "Men are loved rightly and duly when God stands first" (Calvin 1988: 299). Bede (in Bray 2000: 221) states more colorfully, "Only someone who is on fire with the love of his Maker can be said to love his fellow humans in the right way." D. Smith (1991: 120) puts it, "The gospel cannot be reduced to a kind of benign humanism with a horizontal, but no vertical, direction. Our love for each other is beautiful, ennobling, but tinged with sadness and ultimately tragic apart from love of God."

Therefore the surest way to fail in the responsibility to love others is to come up short in our love for God and his injunctions. This is perhaps the largest miscalculation of the world's millions of nominal Christians (and of those who mislead them), who suppose that being nice to other people (and perhaps religious on occasions like Christmas and Easter) in the general name of "God" and "Jesus Christ" is an adequate expression of faith. Such a minimalist understanding will find little validation in 1 John. "If God means little to you, people will become worthless to you too, and love even for them will die out" (Schlatter 1950: 98). Prospects are no brighter, eschatologically speaking, for people who manage to attain a high standard of humanitarian expression but do so without reference to Christ.

First John 5:3 concludes this subsection's commendation of personal faith as the means of a full love of God. It does so by setting forth love in activist terms. While love can be viewed as primarily emotion or sentiment, and while there is no doubt a relational component of affection in love as John conceives it, he here portrays it as keeping God's commandments with an élan that bespeaks glad acceptance, if not joy, rather than some grim moral resignation.

The verse begins with an expansive αὕτη γάρ ἐστιν ἡ ἀγάπη τοῦ θεοῦ (*hautē gar estin hē agapē tou theou*, for this is the love of God). Only 2 John 6 offers any close parallel of the near demonstrative pronoun with ἀγάπη (*agapē*, love). Γάρ (*gar*, for) is inferential (cf. Strecker 1996: 177n28); John's statement takes its point of departure from the previous verse, in which love and God's commandments were positively juxtaposed, but only implicitly. First John 5:3 makes this connection explicit. This "love of God" is clearly an objective genitive (Painter 2002: 291, 295): God is the object of the verbal action implied in the head noun. John is talking about human love for God, not God's love for people.

This love is expressed by[10] doing what God says—his ἐντολαί (*entolai*, commandments). The word has already occurred some dozen times in this epistle

10. Ἵνα in 5:3 is explanatory or epexegetical (BDF §394). It introduces a clause ("we keep his commandments") that explains what John understands by "the love of God." Cf. BDAG 476.

(2:3, 4, 7 [3x], 8; 3:22, 23 [2x], 24; 4:21; 5:2; see exegesis of 2:3). Commandment-keeping is clearly an important component in Christian faith as John understands it (cf. 2:5; 2 John 6; John 14:15, 21). Though in this subsection John is stressing faith as the means to loving God, here he reminds the reader that love has definite character and structure. It draws its definition, namely, from divine commandments (one of which, in John, is faith in God through faith in Christ [John 6:29; cf. Luther 1967: 308], making his teaching here perfectly circular). John is commending neither a vague and uncertain faith nor a weak and self-determined love. Rather, love for God means complying with his known directives. Love is not *only* obedience to commandments,[11] of course, but John's point is that it is not less.

To conclude this verse, John adds that for those who love God, what he commands is not βαρύς (*barys*, onerous; for rich theological reflection, see Calvin 1988: 299–301).[12] The fuller reason for this becomes evident in the next verse (Schnackenburg 1992: 229). The word is used negatively by Jesus to refer to the crushing ethical impositions of certain Pharisees (Matt. 23:4; cf. Acts 15:10) and positively to refer to the "weightier" matters of God's law like justice, mercy, and faith (Matt. 23:23).[13] In the OT itself Moses insists, "Now what I am commanding you today is not too difficult for you or beyond your reach" (Deut. 30:11 NIV). Jesus taught that heavy-laden people should come to him, "For my yoke is easy and my burden is light" (Matt. 11:30 NIV). Moses and Jesus agree that from one viewpoint, the closer one grows to God, the more delightful his moral and ethical guidelines become (cf. Ps. 119). John has already implied that "God's commands do not oppress or cause us fear and pain" because "love drives out such fear" (Schlatter 1950: 99; cf. 1 John 4:18). It can also be said that "God's power enables people to keep the commands God gives" (Thompson 1992: 131n; cf. Burge 1996: 192). Yet, pastoral leader that he was, John would have known that God's commandments are typically felt as a burden to humans in their native estrangement from God. Here the Pauline insight that the flesh (which infects human will) wars against the Spirit (which affirms God's law) comes into play (cf. Rom. 7; Gal. 5). Particularly those from societies dominated by autonomous individualism may feel claustrophobic when contemplating a philosophy of religion in which love and law are mutually defined. John, however, was a disciple of Jesus, who said, "I always do what pleases him [i.e., the Father]" (John 8:29 NIV). Jesus knew an intimacy with God in which submission to his will, while often not easy, was by far the highest good (cf. Loader 1992: 61).[14]

11. D. Smith's unguarded assertion (1991: 118) that loving God and keeping his commandments "are now equated" calls for nuancing (so also Thompson 1992: 130–31).

12. On the rabbinic distinction between easy and difficult commandments, which is probably not highly relevant to this passage, see Strecker 1996: 178n33. For lengthy discussion on the role of commandments vis-à-vis valid faith in Christ, see Luther 1967: 309–10.

13. The three other NT occurrences (Acts 20:29; 25:7; 2 Cor. 10:10) are less relevant to 1 John 5:3.

14. Contrast Jesus with the figure described by Neander 1852: 280: "To him whose spirit is ruled by the world, who feels himself drawn to the world and finds in it his highest good, to him

Hence the words of the Lord's Prayer: "Your will be done." Jesus was conscious of no guilt whatsoever before God (John 8:46), making commandment-keeping a touchstone of Christlike relationship with the Father. Perhaps in part for this reason, John has already stated to his readers, "We obey his commands and do what pleases him" (1 John 3:22).

John concludes this subsection, then, with an assertion that commends love in terms of faithfulness to God's expressed will. "John is not speaking of the bare Law, which contains only commands, but joins with it the fatherly kindness of God, by which the rigour of the Law is softened" (Calvin 1988: 300). Law-compliant love is a marker of personal faith in "the one who believes that Jesus is the Christ" (5:1). Believing in Christ is infinitely rich in ethical and agapic implications and serves John well as a basis for appealing to readers to love one another, the overarching theme of 4:15–5:15.

2. Personal Faith Victorious over (the Lovelessness of) the World (5:4–5)

The first word of 5:4, ὅτι (*hoti*, for), signals a close tie with 5:3. But it also signals a shift in focus, from a generous love for God (5:1–3) to a victorious faith in Christ (5:4–5).

The reason why God's commands are not a bitter burden (5:3) is that personal faith enables believers to break free of the world's downward pull (Loader 1992: 61; Akin 2001: 192). That is the gist of 5:4. John states that "everyone given spiritual rebirth from God overcomes the world." The neuter πᾶν τὸ γεγεννημένον ἐκ τοῦ θεοῦ (*pan to gegennēmenon tou theou*, everything that has been begotten of God) is to be understood in personal terms here; "the neuter is sometimes used with reference to persons if it is not the individuals but a general quality that is to be emphasized" (BDF §138.1; cf. John 3:6, where τὸ γεγεννημένον is used to refer to people born of flesh or spirit; also 6:37, 39; 17:2; Painter 2002: 296). Caragounis (2006: 237) says that this neuter denotes "an all-encompassing significance . . . especially when strengthened by πᾶν" as it is here. I accordingly translate "everyone given spiritual rebirth," the participle of γεννάω (*gennaō*, to cause to be born) in the passive voice to denote God's giving of spiritual life. The (neuter) "everyone" of 5:4 is parallel with "the one who believes" in 5:5. John chooses a construction in 5:4 that emphasizes the quality and elite status that believers possess by virtue of having received spiritual renewal by a regenerating act of God appropriated by faith (cf. 5:1).

Persons thus renewed "overcome the world." The verb νικάω (*nikaō*, to conquer, overcome) has seen use earlier in the epistle: "young men" have "overcome" the evil one (2:13–14), and believers in general "overcome" the antichrist and those who follow his sinister lead (4:4). "The one who overcomes"

the commands appear difficult." Positively, note the explanation of Strecker 1996: 179: "The commandments given by God should not be seen as 'difficult,' because in the life that is lived in community with God they are *eo ipso* fulfilled."

is repeatedly extolled in John's letters to the seven Asia Minor churches (Rev. 2:7, 11, 17, 26; 3:5, 12, 21; cf. 12:11; 15:2; 21:7). But most glorious of all is the overcomer par excellence, Jesus Christ (5:5; 17:14), for he has "overcome the world" (John 16:33).

In this context John appears to have in mind victory defined as a love for God through faith that joyfully embraces God's commands (1 John 5:1–3). "The world" substantially lacks these things. Therefore believers "overcome the world" by their appropriation of them. This is not cheap triumphalism. For one thing, it is all of Christ. He is the victor, and his followers prevail only because their master has made a way for them (cf. John 16:33); the Word of God lives in them (1 John 2:14), and the one who is in them "is greater than the one who is in the world" (4:4). For another thing, it is a victory that the world would regard as Pyrrhic. While Jesus asked, "What good will it be for a man if he gains the whole world, yet forfeits his soul?" (Matt. 16:26 NIV), those outside the church essentially turn the question around: What good is eternal redemption if it costs you temporal benefit? Many value the world's enticements more highly than the benefits of spiritual rebirth through the message of Christ. Like the rich young ruler, if they even take the trouble to understand the gospel, they go away sad (19:22), because its benefits pale alongside the putatively superior advantages of allegiance to the current world order. But their loyalty to the ephemeral is ultimately a mistake and utter loss. Therefore to receive the gospel promise—to be spiritually born "from God"—is an incalculable victory.

That world-overcoming victory so closely related to love is comprehended in the experience of personal faith, "our faith" (1 John 5:4). The author includes himself with his readers. He writes with authority but not gratuitous self-elevation. Even an apostle is saved only through faith. This is "a living apprehension of Christ which applies to us His strength and office" (Calvin 1988: 302). There is no other "victory that triumphs over the world." John speaks of ἡ νίκη ἡ νικήσασα (*hē nikē hē nikēsasa*, the victory that triumphs). The aorist form of νικάω is used in Revelation to denote Christ's victory (3:21; 5:5; 6:2) and should probably be understood as connoting victory regarded in its entirety.[15] Schnackenburg (1992: 230), drawing on Revelation, thinks that "the thought is intimately connected with the victory that Christ won once for all in salvation history" (for other possibilities, see Akin 2001: 193).

Commentators commonly note that πίστις (*pistis*, faith) in 1 John 5:4 is the only occurrence of this noun in either John's Epistles or John's Gospel (but see Rev. 2:13, 19; 13:10; 14:12; in some of these passages, however, it may mean "faithfulness"). Keeping commandments is salutary, even necessary (1 John 5:2–3), but faith is paramount. John does not equate faith with acts

15. Schlatter 1950: 100–101: "John speaks believingly of the power of faith and writes therefore of the victory as a possession already achieved." And the victory is great because of the one in whom is placed the faith that results in victory: "In all the world there is only one single person that is superior to it and juts up like a rock above its raging flood" (1950: 101). Cf. Kruse 2000: 174.

of obedience but subordinates the latter to the former. With that clarity of insight that helped launch the Reformation, Luther's excursus on 5:4 brings out elements that should not be forgotten (1967: 311–13). He notes that "in Augustine one finds too little faith, in Jerome none at all. . . . They frequently commend the virtues and good works: too seldom do they commend faith." In a brief personal testimony, Luther laments the works-rich asceticism that he says almost destroyed him when he was a monk. He continues:

> I, too, once believed that the first four chapters of . . . Romans are not useful for teaching, that only the chapters that follow, which urge the virtues, are efficacious. But by the grace of God I was enlightened, so that from Paul's first chapters I learned about the righteousness of Christ, which makes us Christians, and from the later chapters I learned to know what the marks and ornaments of a Christian are.

Luther helps us see that John's singling out of faith amounts to an important bridge from John to Paul. Although John stresses commandments, these are for him, as they are for Paul in Romans, "the marks and ornaments of a Christian." Redemption lies in Christ's work, not human works. John upholds the supremacy of faith and in that sense commends *sola fide* (faith alone) with the same conviction as Paul (Rom. 3:28; Gal. 2:16). Interpretation of 1 John must not minimize any of the elements like love, Christology, and commandments that the epistle highlights. But it should also not obscure the element without which no entrée into the gospel's soteriological riches is possible: faith.

NA[27] begins a new paragraph with 1 John 5:5, and this is understandable because it asks a question that 5:6 answers. Therefore 5:5 can be seen as the start of a thought unit that extends to 5:6 and beyond. On the other hand, 5:1 speaks of "the one who believes" (ὁ πιστεύων, *ho pisteuōn*), and 5:5 uses the identical wording. It is at least equally plausible to regard the two verses as an inclusio, particularly since 5:1–5 places emphasis more on the experience of faith, while 5:6–12 directs attention more explicitly to faith's object. I therefore regard 5:5 as the final verse of the thought unit beginning in 5:1.[16]

First John 5:5 takes the victory attributed to faith in 5:4 and extends it to the person who exercises it. To accomplish this, John uses a rhetorical question, for which he supplies the answer: "But who is the one who conquers[17] the world? It is none other than[18] the person who believes that Jesus is the Son of

16. Painter 2002: 296 likewise groups 5:5 with 5:4, not with 5:6. So also Rensberger 1997: 124–30 and Akin 2001: 193.

17. The present tense implies that the struggle is in progress. Believers may be free of sterile legal burdens (5:3), but they are not free from conflict. Cf. Calvin 1988: 301: "It is, of course, true that our warfare lasts all through our life, that our conflicts are daily, that new and manifold battles are every moment begun against us by the enemy from every side"; and Luther 1967: 311: "He who believes in Christ is now a warrior." Yet Calvin and Luther, like John, emphasize the fait accompli nature of the victory.

18. Εἰ μή (*ei mē*) can be translated "except" or "if not" in other Johannine passages. But here it should be understood as mirroring LXX usage in which εἰ μή in the sense of "verily"

God." The conqueror is that very person who makes this particular[19] profession of faith. "To believe anything less about Jesus is to believe in somebody who does not have the ability to save us from the power of the godless world" (Marshall 1978: 231). Such confession of Jesus as the Son of God should be regarded here as including his status as the Christ (5:1) and his coming in the flesh (4:2). The meaning of the phrase is obviously informed by all that the epistle has said of "the Son" thus far (1:3, 7; 2:22–24; 3:23; 4:9–10, 14; cf. Holtzmann 1908: 354; Loader 1992: 62). "Son of God" proper has already occurred in this epistle twice (3:7–8 and 4:15; see exegesis of 3:7–8) and is plausibly related to its use in John's Gospel. "Son of God" is what John the Baptist, Nathanael, and Martha the sister of Lazarus all called Jesus (John 1:34, 49; 11:27). Martha combines all of the elements stressed so far in 1 John: "I believe that you are the Christ, the Son of God, who was to come into the world" (NIV).

The problem with "Son of God" applied to Jesus, in John's presentation, is that it seems to equate the man Jesus with the eternal God.[20] This would seem to violate the first word of the Decalogue, to have no other gods next to the Father (Exod. 20:3; Deut. 5:7). God forbade Israel from "imaging" the true and living God as a human: "Do not become corrupt and make for yourselves an idol, an image of any shape, whether formed like a man or a woman" (Deut. 4:16 NIV). John agreed that Jesus was different from the invisible eternal Father (John 1:18). And yet John affirmed the Son's essential divinity—Jesus showed forth "the glory of the One and Only" (1:14). His disciples came to confess him as "the Holy One of God" (6:69). Jesus said, "I and the Father are one" (10:30). It is understandable that religious leaders in Jerusalem were bent on taking Jesus's life, if necessary, for appearing to be a false prophet who elevated himself to God's level (5:18; cf. Deut. 13). At Jesus's trial they insisted, "We have a law, and according to that law he must die, because he claimed to be the Son of God" (John 19:7 NIV). "Son of God" could connote a status warranting the charge of blasphemy.

Or it could denote a sober truth about Jesus's identity, in which lies eternal salvation for those willing to affirm it. John writes as one convinced that this is the proper understanding. And in 1 John 5:5, he reiterates that to embrace that understanding with due seriousness—to believe—is to frustrate the ravages of a world that is for the most part hostile to God and what God values (see 2:15–17; 3:1, 13). It is to avoid the deception of the false prophets (4:1)

---

precedes a virtual oath (LEH 172). This yields the translation "it is none other than." See exegesis of 2:22.

19. Cf. Oecumenius (in Bray 2000: 222–23): "It is not faith in the abstract that overcomes the world. It must be faith in Jesus Christ, as John makes plain." Similarly Painter 2002: 299: "Thus the one *correct* faith is seen as the victory" (emphasis original).

20. It is not easy to see why Schnackenburg 1992: 232 wants to exclude "the metaphysical nature of the Son" from John's concern here (the soteriological reason given seems thin). Throughout John's Gospel and first epistle, (metaphysical) person and (soteriological) work are inextricably intertwined.

and the antichrist, who are already "in the world" (4:4). It is in that sense to "conquer the world."[21] No higher tribute could be paid to the value and excellence of a personal faith[22] in the Son of God that manifests itself also in the love and obedience that dominate the landscape of 5:1–5.

Additional Notes

5:1. Confusion characterizes the manuscripts. B, Ψ, and others, including a range of versions, omit the adverbial καί that is here translated "also." This reading was accepted in NA[25], apparently on the strength of B's support. א and 69 contain καί but read τό instead of τόν. This is fatally weak external attestation. Internally, it is an easier reading because the neuter τό corresponds to the same peculiar usage, undoubtedly original, coming up in 5:4 (πᾶν τὸ γεγεννημένον). The harder reading, which here happens to be also the longer reading, is NA[27]'s καὶ τόν. This reading is supported by A, P, 1739, 𝔐, and two versions. NA[27] aptly recognizes the difficulty of arriving at textual certainty with its bracketing of καί.

5:2. Did John write "do [ποιῶμεν] his commandments" or "keep [τηρῶμεν]" them? The former reading is harder, but perhaps so hard as to be improbable from the standpoint of Johannine usage: "doing" commandments (combining a form of ποιέω with ἐντολή) is found elsewhere only as a variant reading in Rev. 22:14. Yet it is the choice of NA[27], in part because of the support of B. In favor of τηρῶμεν is the support of א, other uncials, and 𝔐. The usage corresponds with John's usual combining of τηρέω with ἐντολή (1 John 2:3, 4, 5; 3:22, 24; cf. John 14:15, 21; 15:10). Even if NA[27]'s ποιῶμεν is accepted, the translation is still something like "we keep," because in English it is idiomatically preferable to speak of "keeping" commandments; "doing" them conveys the idea satisfactorily but sounds a little lame—hence NIV's "carrying out" his commandments. Other English versions use a form of "obey."

5:4. "Your" (ὑμῶν) faith has weak external backing (barely a half dozen witnesses, none of them weighty) and is an example of the ubiquitous confusion of "your" and "our" in the textual tradition. NA[27]'s choice of "our" (ἡμῶν) follows compelling external evidence.

5:5. Manuscripts vary on the order of the verse's opening words. B and NA[25] begin τίς ἐστιν δέ, but since B stands alone, it is unlikely to preserve the original reading. A and Ψ join 𝔐 in omitting the connective particle δέ. Including δέ are א, three other uncials, and some minuscules. Τίς [δέ] ἐστιν of NA[27] gives the likeliest word order, with the brackets showing the uncertainty attaching to δέ.

21. Neander's missiological note (1852: 283) deserves attention: "From this we learn the important lesson, that all true reformation of the world can only proceed from this faith, from the energy of the divine life residing therein. We cannot, therefore, but be distrustful of all attempts to cure the evils of the world, which build not upon this one foundation. Even though they may accomplish many single reforms, yet a radical cure of the disease is not to be effected by such means."

22. Rensberger 1997: 130 rightly notes that while the content of Christian faith comes into view here, overall "faith still means believing, the act of belief rather than its object."

D. Commendation of Faith as *Fides Quae Creditur* (5:6–12)

In a portion of 1 John (4:15–5:15) that overall, I argue above, declares the high status of God's love and invites readers to appropriate it in their lives, faith continues to receive particular attention, since it is the divinely ordained avenue of receiving that love. But whereas 5:1–5 laid stress on the experience of faith (*fides qua creditur*), 5:6–12 emphasizes the object and content of faith (*fides quae creditur*). John is concerned to affirm empirical truth regarding Jesus Christ, in whom faith is placed (cf. Culpepper 1998: 272). By extension this would establish the truth of the whole message of this epistle, which from its opening verses has made clear that everything depends on God's Son.

"Witness" language is concentrated more heavily in these verses than in any other portion of the Johannine corpus: in 5:6–12 there are ten occurrences of either μαρτυρέω (*martyreō*, to testify) or μαρτυρία (*martyria*, testimony). This points to a dual conviction on the part of the writer: (1) his message meets the highest standards of verification, and (2) it is critical that his readers heed and internalize this message if they wish to know for themselves the eternal life that Christ came to make available—and to avoid the repercussions of making God out to be a liar.

This section also calls attention once again to the pastoral concern of the writer. It is not a sterile truth for which he vies but one that is of eternal import for readers, for to "have" the Son of whom he writes is to inherit eternal life, while not to have him, or to affirm a distorted image of his true identity, is to miss out on the life that John's message mediates.

The verses may be analyzed as follows:

1. God's testimony to Jesus Christ, the object of saving faith (5:6–9)
2. Human reception of God's testimony (5:10–12)

Exegesis and Exposition

6He is the one who came through water and ⌜blood⌝, Jesus Christ—not by water
⌜alone⌝ but by the ⌜water and by the blood⌝. And the Spirit is the one who testifies,
because ⌜the Spirit⌝ is the truth. 7For there are three who testify, 8⌜the Spirit and the
water and the blood, and the three are one⌝. 9If we accept the testimony of humans,
the testimony of God is greater. For this is the testimony of God⌜:⌝ he bore witness
concerning his Son⌜ ⌝. 10The person who believes in the Son of God has the testimony
⌜ ⌝ within ⌜himself⌝; the one who does not believe ⌜God⌝ has made him out to be liar,

because he has not believed in the testimony to ⌜which God testified⌝ concerning his Son. [11]And this is the testimony: ⌜God gave to us⌝ eternal life, and this life is in his Son. [12]The person who has the Son has that life. The person who does not have the Son does not have that life.

1. God's Testimony to Jesus Christ, the Object of Saving Faith (5:6–9)

The previous subsection ended on a note of affirmation of personal faith in Jesus, the Son of God (5:5). Now John proceeds to underscore elements of Jesus's identity. This has the effect of shifting attention from the experience of faith to the truth and character of what faith affirms (*fides quae creditur*).

First, faith's proper object is "Jesus Christ." This word combination reversed ("Christ Jesus") occurs ninety-five times in the NT but not once in the traditional Johannine corpus. In the NT, apart from five occurrences in Acts and one in 1 Peter, "Christ Jesus" is found only in Paul's Letters, where it occurs in all of his thirteen epistles except 2 Thessalonians. It is in any case absent from John. "Jesus Christ," on the other hand, appears twice in John's Gospel (1:17; 17:3), five times elsewhere in 1 John (1:3; 2:1; 3:23; 4:2; 5:20), twice in 2 John (3, 7), and three times in Revelation (1:1, 2, 5).[1] When occasion calls for reference both to the man in full, the historical person of Nazareth ("Jesus"), as well as to the anointed Son of God ("Christ"), this is 1 John's preferred usage.

Second, faith affirms that this[2] Jesus Christ is ὁ ἐλθών (*ho elthōn*)—"the one who came." The Synoptics speak prospectively of an awaited figure who would come: ὁ ἐρχόμενος (*ho erchomenos*, the coming one; Matt. 11:3/Luke 7:19). John records that due to the signs he did, Jesus was thought to be "the prophet who is coming [ὁ προφήτης ὁ ἐρχόμενος, *ho prophētēs ho erchomenos*] into the world" (John 6:14; cf. Deut. 18:15–19; Acts 3:22). Martha confesses faith in Jesus as "the Christ, the Son of God, the one who comes [ὁ . . . ἐρχόμενος] into the world" (John 11:27). On Palm Sunday, Jesus was hailed as some such exalted figure; all four Gospels picture the crowds greeting his entrance into Jerusalem by using words found in Ps. 118:26 [117:26 LXX]: "Blessed is ὁ ἐρχόμενος [the one who comes] in the name of the Lord" (Matt. 21:9/Mark 11:9/Luke 13:35/John 12:13).

Now 1 John 5:6 uses the same expression, but in aorist participle form (ὁ ἐλθών) rather than the present participle ὁ ἐρχόμενος. The aorist is appropriate for a narrator retrospectively describing someone's coming—as when John's Gospel using the same participle refers to Nicodemus as "the one who came" to Jesus by night (7:50; 19:39). Reference to Jesus's coming likely implies his

1. For sake of comparison, "Christ" occurs (without "Jesus") 20 times in John (16 times in the Gospel, 1 time in 2 John, 3 times in Revelation). "Jesus" occurs without "Christ" 255 times in John (241 times in the Gospel, 4 times in 1 John [1:7; 4:3, 15; 5:5], and 10 times in Revelation).

2. John refers to Jesus by using the demonstrative pronoun οὗτος (*houtos*, this one). Sloyan 1995: 51 sees "special solemnity" in this.

heavenly origin.[3] He was the light "coming [ἐρχόμενον, *erchomenon*] into the world" (1:9), having been "with God" in unique fashion "in the beginning" (1:1; cf. 1:18). He was the one whom John the Baptist promised was "coming" (ἐρχόμενος, *erchomenos*) after him (1:15, 27), of whom he was not worthy. Jesus was the one "coming" from above, from heaven (3:31). In other words, in John's understanding, Jesus is God incarnate (Culpepper 1998: 272 finds the incarnation rather in John's reference to water). Full-orbed, redemptive faith in Jesus Christ recognizes that he, and no other, is the one who came from heaven to be God's saving agent in the earthly domain.

Third, Jesus Christ came "by water and blood."[4] Water is likely to be a reference to his baptism by John the Baptist (so Marshall 1978: 231 and many others).[5] By extension it may also include Jesus's own ministry of baptizing those who believe in him by the Holy Spirit (so Kruse 2000: 177 and Thatcher 2001: 247; but this is rejected by Painter 2002: 304). What can hardly be disputed is that Jesus Christ is that very figure who came and who received the baptism of repentance offered to all of Israel—but which was received by only some. Jesus identified himself with the lost he came to save precisely "by water."

He came also "by blood." "Blood" is likely to be a reference to Jesus's atoning death (cf. 1 John 1:7; Rev. 1:5; 5:9; 7:14; 12:11). The association of Jesus's blood, his sacrificial death, with the salvation he came to effect is a unifying feature of a wide range of NT writings, as this sample of citations illustrates (all quotations from NIV):

Matt. 26:28	This is my blood of the covenant, which is poured out for many for the forgiveness of sins (cf. Mark 14:24; Luke 22:20; 1 Cor. 11:25).
Acts 20:28	Be shepherds of the church of God, which he bought with his own blood.
Rom. 3:25	God presented him as a sacrifice of atonement, through faith in his blood.
Rom. 5:9	Since we have now been justified by his blood.
Eph. 1:7	In him we have redemption through his blood.
Col. 1:20	Making peace through his blood, shed on the cross.

3. Holtzmann 1908: 355 prefers "his messianic appearance." But the Messiah is sent from God and, contrary to many expectations of the day, turns out to be of heavenly origin. The view of Sloyan 1995: 51 that the coming refers to Jesus's mission is an understatement.

4. John's use of διά (*dia*, through, by) plus the genitive seems to be equivalent to ἐν (*en*, in, by) plus the dative in this verse; cf. Heb. 9:12 (δι' αἵματος) and 9:25 (ἐν αἵματι). Painter 2002: 301, 303 points here to John's penchant for stylistic variation.

5. Little in the context justifies seeing here a reference back to the "blood and water" issuing from Jesus's side when he was pierced by a spear (John 19:34; contra Schnackenburg 1992: 236 and others). Thus the CEV rendering ("water and blood came out of the side of Jesus Christ") should be rejected as fanciful (cf. Marshall 1978: 233n8). Calvin 1988: 302 is followed by few in seeing "the ancient rites of the Law" in "water and blood." Nor are the Christian sacraments of baptism and the Eucharist likely to be in view (Burge 1996: 201; Schlatter 2005: 522–23).

Heb. 9:12	He entered the Most Holy Place once for all by his own blood, having obtained eternal redemption.
Heb. 13:12	And so Jesus also suffered outside the city gate to make the people holy through his own blood.

Even NT books that do not explicitly use such language exalt Jesus as a savior figure. But historically speaking, this is a status he attained via his death for sin (and subsequent resurrection; cf. 1 Pet. 3:18). Jesus's saving "coming by blood" is the very core of the redeeming work to which 1 John bears testimony. For that reason, it is part of the nonnegotiable *fides quae creditur* that his epistle upholds.[6]

Parenthetically John adds "not by water alone but by the water and by the blood." The doubled "the" serves to point back to his earlier mention of water and blood in this verse. This could be evidence that opponents accepted Jesus's baptism but did not regard his blood sacrifice in the same way that John did (cf. Schlatter 1950: 103). It could be a way of affirming the superiority of Jesus's ministry to that of John the Baptist. Or it could simply be John's way of stressing the importance of Jesus's death. That water and blood correspond to elements of baptism and communion in Christian practice is a useful meditative insight but not likely to have been a conscious factor in John's message here (Marshall 1978: 233n8, 238; Thatcher 2001: 237).

In any case, John now calls in the artillery to back up his pronouncement about Jesus's coming through water and blood. This is not John's belief alone; it is the very testimony of God: "And the Spirit is the one who testifies, because the Spirit is the truth." John has already mentioned the Spirit repeatedly (3:24; 4:1 [2x], 2, 3, 6, 13). In John's writings, truth is associated with the Father (John 15:26), the Son (1:14, 17; 14:6; 18:37), and the divine Word (associated with Father, Son, and Spirit alike) that sanctifies believers (17:17). But truth is linked most frequently with the Holy Spirit (14:17; 15:26; 16:13; 1 John 4:6; 5:6). It is therefore fitting to adduce the Spirit to corroborate John's sober affirmation of Jesus's incarnation, his baptism, and his sacrificial death. The faith of which he speaks is rooted in the truth, not human tradition or speculation or imagination. Attestation by God's Spirit is either implicitly or explicitly a factor in divine confirmations of Jesus's ministry at his baptism (Mark 1:10–11), transfiguration (9:7), and crucifixion (John 12:28). Without the Spirit, there is little benefit to the water and blood: "No matter how much the Gospel is preached, no one accepts it unless the Spirit is present" (Luther 1967: 315). John is more likely to be referring generally to the veracity and efficacy of the Spirit's testimony than he is to be making a veiled allusion to "what the Beloved Disciple [i.e., the author of 1 John] has said comes from the Spirit" (Burge 1996: 204).

6. Thatcher 2001: 247–48 argues that blood refers to Jesus's "human physicality," which he then equates with "the established traditions about Jesus' life and death." It seems more plausible to link blood with its common connotation elsewhere in the NT as referring to Jesus's atoning death.

First John 5:7–8 states John's basis for commending to his readers this Jesus Christ, who came by water and blood and was testified to by God's very Spirit. First John 5:7's opening ὅτι (*hoti*, for) signals the explanatory nature of the two-verse unit. John is backing up what he just wrote, not breaking new ground. Although "water and blood" refer to past events, it is fitting that John uses the present participle construction (οἱ μαρτυροῦντες, *hoi martyrountes*) to describe them, since in conjunction with the Spirit their testimony is ongoing and current. Readers cannot evade Christ's relevance for them, because authoritative attestation to his rule is not a relic of the past but a component of the present due to the persistence of testimony to it.[7]

John stresses not only *that* there is binding testimony to his words: he also cites *who* and *what* constitute his testimony. Regarding *what*, see exegesis of "water and blood" above. Regarding *who*, for John τὸ πνεῦμα (*to pneuma*, the Spirit) is not an impersonal "it" or force. He is rather the virtual presence of *Christus in absentia*. Jesus's disciples know this "Spirit of truth" because after Jesus's resurrection he "lives with" them and "will be in" them (John 14:17). Moreover, "he will testify about" Jesus (15:26). John seizes on that promise here (and no doubt experiences it existentially as Jesus's former follower who heard him deliver it). He stresses the personal nature of God's testimony to Christ's ministry through his baptism and his crucifixion. John knows this will be highly persuasive to readers who share his sense of personal relatedness to the Father through the Son.

In citing three witnesses, John may have been influenced by the "two or three witnesses"[8] called for by Moses (Deut. 17:6; 19:15), Jesus (Matt. 18:16), and Paul (2 Cor. 13:1; see exegesis of 1:1–3). He may have been moved by the insight that just as the threefold Father, Son, and Spirit constitute God's heavenly self-disclosure, so there are three foundational underpinnings to Christ's earthly self-disclosure. (Some such chain of association may explain the expansion of this passage found in Latin versions going back to the third or fourth centuries as well as in the KJV; see additional note on 5:7–8.) Or the mention of three witnesses may be explained simply by observing that Jesus's baptism and death more or less bracket his entire public ministry (so

7. Schlatter 1950: 104–5 extends this considerably: "The Spirit gives us an internal, hidden witness, while water and blood give an external and visible one. We must not despise one in favor of the other. Only in their unification do they present to us the whole of the Christ and give us a solid basis for faith. Water and blood testify that he came to us; the Spirit testifies that he is with the Father. The former attest his work in time, the latter attests his life in eternity. The former testify that he is our reconciliation, the latter testifies that he is our salvation and transfiguration. Through both together is he our savior and revealed to us fully."

8. Even if John does not have this criterion in mind, Strecker's view (1996: 192) that "neither here nor elsewhere in 1 John is there any suggestion of OT influence" seems strained. Strecker's positive suggestions that John's usage reflects "the principle of round numbers" or that "the testimony of the 'three' expresses the divine plenitude that always characterizes God's revelation in and to the community (John 1:16; Eph 1:23; 4:10)" are more credible.

also Holtzmann 1908: 355 and Burge 1993: 202),[9] while the Spirit's witness summarizes Jesus's ongoing self-disclosure until he returns. In this case no particular importance need be attached to there being three witnesses.

John says these three εἰς τὸ ἕν εἰσιν (*eis to hen eisin*). In theory this could be read literally as "are into the one [thing]," but such a slavish rendering would be nonsensical. Most translations understand this to signify that the three witnesses "agree" (RSV/NRSV, NLT, CEV, ESV) or are "in agreement" (HCSB, NIV/TNIV). Contextually this is a reasonable rendering. "The three are one" (not in essence but in witness) is an equally valid translation, since NT writers occasionally use a state-of-being verb with εἰς (*eis*, in, into) and an object in place of a predicate nominative, probably due to Semitic influence (BDF §145.1; cf. Caragounis 2006: 147, who terms this construction "totally unknown in purely Greek Demotic speech"). There is no great difference between being "one" and being "in agreement." John's point is that given this wealth of irrefragable testimony, readers are logically, historically, and theologically bound to receive his message as binding.

First John 5:9 underscores this point. John argues from a commonsense conviction (so Loader 1992: 69–70 and many others): "we accept the testimony of humans."[10] "Witness" is an everyday phenomenon. The word "we" probably refers to people in general, although it is not impossible that John has John the Baptist and OT prophets in mind, for they were all humans testifying to divine truths, and their testimony was widely felt to carry God's own authority (cf. Hilary of Arles and Bede in Bray 2000: 224). Christians accept the human testimony of prophets; why would they hesitate to heed a witness from God himself? The importance of μαρτυρία (*martyria*, witness) comes to the fore in John's Gospel, where the noun appears over a dozen times and the cognate verb nearly three dozen times. As John views life and particularly Jesus's ministry, he now argues from the lesser to the greater (*qal wahomer*). If (lesser) human testimony is generally accepted as significant—and the Greek clause beginning with εἰ (*ei*, if) implies that John is assuming here it is—then God's (greater)[11] testimony is all the more inescapable. "To reject it is therefore a serious evil, and to oppose it a futile project" (Schnackenburg 1992: 239).

The phrase ἡ μαρτυρία τοῦ θεοῦ (*hē martyria tou theou*, the testimony of God) occurs nowhere else in the NT (though Revelation speaks of "the testimony of Jesus" at 1:2, 9; 12:17; 19:10; 20:4) and is absent from the LXX. It is likely a subjective genitive construction: God is the subject, the active agent, in

9. Cf. the Apostles' Creed, in which almost the whole of Jesus's life is comprehended by the two phrases "born of the Virgin Mary, suffered under Pontius Pilate."

10. Luther 1967: 317 points to the tragic dimension of this fact. People are fairly ready to accept what other people say, but they are skeptical or apathetic about what God says regarding Christ, the gospel, and human sin.

11. The comparative adjective μείζων (*meizōn*) has already been used to speak of the Father who is "greater" than shaky hearts (3:20) and of the Spirit who is "greater" than "the one who is in the world" (4:4).

the verbal action implied in the head noun "witness." God, through his Spirit[12] and ultimately also through the water and blood mentioned in 1 John 5:6–8, has registered eloquent testimony. This refers to external, publicly manifested witness, not the internal witness of the Holy Spirit, which will come up in the next verse. Since he is infinitely superior to humans, his testimony should be regarded as infinitely weightier and tenaciously embraced.

The second half of 5:9, like 5:7, begins with ὅτι (*hoti*, for). The clause answers the question of what makes God's testimony so important. While the reply could be that God being God, whatever he says is true and eternally significant (cf. Rom. 9:20), John takes a different tack. God's testimony is greater than that of humans for a christological reason: "For [ὅτι] this is the testimony of God: he bore witness concerning his Son." The colon renders a second ὅτι in this half verse, which serves to set off the substance of what follows (cf. an analogous construction in 1 John 1:5). This hardly results in nothing but a "tautology," as Rensberger (1997: 134) concludes. John's diction may be a little repetitious, but his concern for verbal elegance takes a backseat to his elevated regard for God's Son, in whom all divine testimony through the ages finds its apex (cf. Holtzmann 1908: 357). From the focus of God's testimony, Luther (1967: 318) draws a pastoral inference: "It is the whole function of our preaching to establish this testimony concerning the Son of God in the hearts of men."

The perfect form of μαρτυρέω (here μεμαρτύρηκεν, *memartyrēken*, bore witness) occurs nine times in the NT and frequently connotes a solemn and lasting verdict (John 1:34; 3:26; 5:33; 19:35; Heb. 11:5). Particularly suggestive is John 5:37, in which Jesus uses the same verbal form to state, "The Father who sent me has himself testified [μεμαρτύρηκεν] concerning me" (NIV). John merely repeats and applies a teaching of Jesus. God's testimony is permanent and final, not to be set aside or altered by neglect or human tampering. "One time in the course of world history God appears as witness, speaks clearly, and gives proof and secure direction. That took place at the sending of the Christ" (Schlatter 1950: 104). "And thus we also, from the stand-point of our own age, may appeal to it as something at once past and present" (Neander 1852: 293; cf. Schnackenburg 1992: 239).

This subsection's commendation of the substance of victorious faith in terms of God's witness to it is complete. Next John takes up the matter of human response.

2. Human Reception of God's Testimony (5:10–12)

A doctrinaire ideologue or polemicist might be content with harshly affirming the truth and letting the chips fall where they may. But as a servant of Christ, John's pastoral bent will not permit this. He turns from the divine witness to human appropriation of it. It will be recalled that John's purpose in writing is

12. It should not be overlooked that the de facto equating of "God" in 5:9 with "Spirit" in 5:6–8 amounts to an affirmation of the full personhood and divinity of the latter.

to promote fellowship and joy, not to win an argument or put down a shadowy opposition (1:3–4). Moreover, as I outline the epistle, this section (4:15–5:15) is an appeal to readers to love. The agapic theme of the larger context should not be forgotten.

For God's love to flourish, there must be faith in Christ (recall the close association of believing and love in 5:1; see also the stirring words of Calvin 1988: 305–6). "This passage presents the content of the confession about Jesus Christ that believers are to have and to hold" (Thompson 1992: 138). From God's witness to his Son in 5:9, John turns to the issue of acceptance or rejection of that testimony in 5:10.[13]

He first envisions the believing recipient of God's witness. "The person who believes in the Son of God has the testimony within himself." John speaks of the *testimonium spiritus sancti internum* (the inner witness of the Holy Spirit)[14] (cf. Rom. 8:16; 9:1; also 1 John 4:15: "If anyone acknowledges that Jesus is the Son of God, God lives in him and he in God"). The testimony possessed by the believer grows out of God's self-attestation via Spirit, water, and blood mentioned in previous verses. These three are one (5:8); they amount to the gospel message of salvation in Jesus Christ. To engage that testimony in a seeking and trusting fashion is to be cleansed from sin (cf. 1:7, 9), making it possible to welcome God's personal, living presence into one's inner life where the hidden religious impulse dwells. The witness moves from what God affirms in the public sphere (5:9) to what the individual appropriates in his or her private domain (5:10). This person possesses God's self-disclosure "within himself" (ἐν ἑαυτῷ, *en heautō*)[15] in such a way that the divine redemptive aim is set in motion and sustained. The result would be the fellowship and joy for the sake of which John writes the epistle.

If the objective pole of this transaction is God's true and faithful self-disclosure, his testimony, then the subjective pole is the act of believing. It is ὁ πιστεύων (*ho pisteuōn*, the one who trusts), and that one alone, who has the ability to receive God's testimony. John has already linked spiritual rebirth

13. It is unwarranted to see in John's either/or scenario here the arrogance imputed to him by Sloyan 1995: 54: "He is of the truth party and that is all there is to it." For apostolicity to be partisanship, either God would have to be untrue or his envoys would have to misrepresent him.

14. So Neander 1852: 293; Holtzmann 1908: 357; D. Smith 1991: 125; Loader 1992: 70; Thompson 1992: 137; Sloyan 1995: 53; Strecker 1996: 194; Culpepper 1998: 272; Akin 2001: 200; and Painter 2002: 310. But see next footnote.

15. Marshall 1978: 241 rejects NIV's translation "in his heart" and denies that John refers to the internal witness of the Spirit (similarly Schnackenburg 1992: 239–40; Rensberger 1997: 135; Kruse 2000: 181). Marshall's understanding is reflected in, e.g., TNIV, NLT, and CEV. Marshall (like Schnackenburg) appeals to Rev. 6:9; 12:17; 19:10—where "have a testimony" means to hold it firmly. So 1 John 5:10 is just saying that to believe in the Son "is to accept and keep God's testimony." But NIV is not alone in its rendering (see TEV, JB, NEB, NRSV; cf. RSV, ESV, HCSB). The Revelation passages lack the phrase ἐν ἑαυτῷ. They are not really parallel to 1 John 5:10 at the point in question. It is hard to see how better to render ἐν ἑαυτῷ than as denoting possession of the Spirit's witness internally. If John wished to say no more than that believers received the witness, then ἐν ἑαυτῷ seems largely otiose, and it is hard to explain why John wrote it at all.

with this ability (5:1). Elsewhere John speaks of an authorization, a sort of passkey, to the status of being a child of God. That key is the ongoing act of placing trust and personal commitment in the Christ: "To all who received him, to those who believed in his name, he gave the right to become children of God" (John 1:12 NIV). In John's Gospel as well as in this epistle, God's saving act is depicted as the result of divine conception somehow precipitating human will or decision (1:13). The dynamic nature of the believing that John promotes is implied by his very word choice: the noun "faith" occurs only one time in John's Gospel and John's Epistles (1 John 5:4). But verbal forms connoting the action of believing occur some 107 times in the same corpus, and about 82 of these are in the present form, which tends to suggest an ongoing (as opposed to a static or once-and-done-with) response.

The first half of 5:10, then, is a commendation of the faith (*fides quae creditur*) made possible and constituted by God's self-testimony. Believing "God"[16]—shorthand here for that fullness of God's self-disclosure in Jesus Christ that is a major theme of the whole epistle—is the desired outcome of his letter. The one who believes receives that testimony and enjoys its beneficial, transformative working within.

The second portion of the verse is marked by extreme parataxis: no conjunction joins the two sentence halves, heightening the antithetical effect of the contrasting assertions. John's continuing pastoral orientation should be noted in that his rhetoric is not flat condemnation but essentially an appeal: "The entire verse with its sharp antithesis calls for a decision" (Schnackenburg 1992: 240). Starkly parallel to the one who believes is "the one not believing [ὁ μὴ πιστεύων, *ho mē pisteuōn*] God." While saving belief in 5:10a was εἰς (*eis*, in, into) the Son, implying personal commitment, the negative counterpart is the simple dative τῷ θεῷ (*tō theō*, in God; on this distinction, see Moulton 1908: 67–68). This probably means (not) to give him credence (cf. John 4:21; 8:31; Painter 2002: 310). This person not only fails to trust God personally; he or she does not even accord God the respect of a careful hearing. This is consistent with Jesus's statement in John that those who belong to God hear his voice (8:47). Those who listen to God and learn from him come to Christ (6:45). The person in 1 John 5:10b has not listened or learned and therefore does not come.

Opposite to dynamic trust (5:10a) lie any number of contrasting postures (summarized in 5:10b), as some Johannine examples may illustrate: willful ignorance (John 4:22), apathy (12:37), cowardly or disenchanted withdrawal (6:66), hypocritical lip service (8:31, 48), malicious misappropriation (12:6), secret contempt (7:28; 8:19), open hostility (11:57; 15:21), misplaced skepticism (20:25). The consequence is all the same, and it is lethal: not to believe is to predicate untruth of God—it is to "make him out to be a liar" (ψεύστην πεποίηκεν αὐτόν, *pseustēn pepoiēken auton*; see exegesis of 1 John 1:6, 10; on

16. John is not saying that bare theism is salvific, any more than he implies in 4:16 that the person who loves is thereby transformed into a Christian.

the ethics of the use of rhetoric like "liar," see exegesis of 2:4). Two features of the wording make it somewhat emphatic: the frontal placement of the accusative direct object "liar" and the perfect form of the verb ποιέω (*poieō*). John's diction underscores the monstrous folly of unbelief. "Implicit in opposition to Jesus is renunciation of God" (Schlatter 1950: 106; cf. Schnackenburg 1992: 240, who speaks of a "contradiction of God" that is "catastrophic").[17]

First John 5:10c concludes with a ὅτι (*hoti*, because) clause that explains how the unbeliever in effect charges God with being a liar. This happens, John says, when someone "has not believed in the testimony to which God testified concerning his Son." The concentration of witness-language (awkward sounding in English) continues. Perhaps John is addressing a situation in which some are claiming faith in Christ but questioning features of the testimony that leaders like John claim to mediate from God. John's words here have the effect of leaving no room between believing in (εἰς) the Son of God (5:10a) and believing in (εἰς) the witness that God gives (5:10c). The three consecutive perfect verbal forms (πεποίηκεν [*pepoiēken*, made]; πεπίστευκεν [*pepisteuken*, believed]; μεμαρτύρηκεν [*memartyrēken*, testified]) give an air of gravity and irrevocability to John's statement. To withhold belief in the face of God's self-testimony is a fateful course of action. Even mere humans do not appreciate having their sworn testimony cast aside; how much more of an affront is skepticism toward the God who has given such palpable and magnanimous notice of his person, work, and will (cf. 1:1–2, in addition to all the other witness rhetoric in the previous verses)? Luther (1967: 320) aptly summarizes: "God should not be sought or known except through the testimony; for to be unwilling to be content with the manner in which God wants to be found by us but to seek and prescribe one's own manner is to find the devil, not God."

But John has no desire to dwell on the tragic spectacle of people who need divine grace spurning it. "We should not miss . . . the overwhelmingly positive nature of the author's attitude towards the gospel. It is not primarily about escape from evil or even forgiveness of sins. It is about *life*" (Loader 1992: 71, emphasis original). First John 5:11, in frank yet very positive fashion, states what the unbeliever throws away, and the believer receives, through affirming God's testimony.

The first word of 5:11, καί (*kai*, and), is explicative (BDAG 495), drawing out an implication of 5:10. Objectively, God's testimony is *that* he has made a saving disclosure regarding his Son (5:9–10). But in 5:11, John specifies *what* this witness means (cf. Marshall 1978: 241n42) or amounts to: "God gave to us eternal life."[18] "Eternal life" is placed in emphatic position in its clause.

17. Cf. Calvin 1988: 305: "He makes the ungodly guilty of extreme blasphemy, because they charge God with falsehood. There is undoubtedly nothing more precious to God than His truth. Therefore, no more atrocious injury can be done to Him than to despoil Him of this honour."

18. On eternal life, see exegesis of 1:1–2 and 2:24–25. "Eternal life" in 5:11 is equated with God's witness; in 2:25 it is equated with God's promise in a similar grammatical construction. It is not a function of holy baptism per se, contra Oecumenius (in Bray 2000: 225); Strecker

That "God gave" it is a reminder "that we are destitute of it" without Christ and "it cannot be acquired by merits" (Calvin 1988: 306; cf. Akin 2001: 202). Strecker (1996: 195) suggests that the word "gave" "describes the uniqueness of the past Christ-event" (though verbal aspect theory rightly takes a dim view of his reasoning). Ὅτι (*hoti*) functions as a colon (cf. the second ὅτι in 5:9) to conjoin the forward-looking[19] αὕτη ἐστὶν ἡ μαρτυρία (*hautē estin hē martyria*, this is the witness) with the next clause, which sets forth a central benevolent outcome of God's testimony. This makes the unbelief of 5:10 all the more poignant, because not only has God in his Son proclaimed the truth and attested richly to it, but his gracious act also has as its goal the gift of eternal life to its recipients. Some, however, would rather make God a liar than stoop (as they would see it) to receiving the gift.

John has a further word to say on this matter: "This life is in his Son" (5:11). The tie here is still back to 5:10, where God's witness to his Son met with rejection by the one who withholds faith. God's testimony, his Spirit, water and blood, promise, faith, love—numerous elements of the broader context converge on the central component of John's saving message. That component is the person and work of Jesus Christ. Schnackenburg (1992: 241) notes that 5:9, 5:10, and 5:11 "all end with 'his Son.'"

But the tie is also ahead to 5:12. With the same abrupt parataxis found in 5:10, John lays out an absolute either/or in 5:12. "The person who has the Son has that life. The person who does not have the Son does not have that life."[20] To "have" the Son is to trust in him continuously (cf. Strecker 1996: 196). This life has an eschatological fulfillment but is also a decisive element of believers' lives here and now. The language and syntax are reminiscent of 2:23: "Anyone who denies the Son does not have the Father, either; the one who confesses the Son has the Father too." In 5:6–12 as a whole, according to my outline, John has been commending faith in terms of its material content (*fides quae creditur*). Rensberger (1997: 136) speaks of "a *regula fidei*, a rule of faith," that comes to the fore in this passage. "Eternal life is not possible apart from true belief in Jesus as the Son of God" (Marshall 1978: 242). The faith that John articulates has definite parameters and substance (cf. D. Smith 1991: 127) because of the Son who came to ground faith, the Spirit who testifies to the Son's work, and the Father toward whom personal trust is directed through the Son. Without *this* faith there is no eternal life. Even the word order at the end of 5:12, in which "that life" is placed before the verb, stresses what is lost when the Son is denied (cf. Akin 2001: 202–3).

1996: 195 likewise ties eternal life to acceptance of a particular sacramental understanding of baptism and the Eucharist.

19. Cf. Strecker 1996: 195. For other forward-pointing αὕτη ἐστίν clauses, see 2:25; 3:11, 23; 5:3, 4, 9.

20. I translate τὴν ζωήν (*tēn zōēn*, lit., the life) as "that life," recognizing that "occasionally, the article is practically equivalent to a demonstrative pronoun" (Moule 1994: 111). Contextually, it is clear that John is referring to "that" life of which he spoke in 5:11.

Tacit is the theological assumption that humans untouched by the saving work of Christ are lost and headed for destruction. They need not do anything extra to draw divine displeasure; they attract and deserve it by nature as well as deed (cf. 1 John 1:8, 10). Calvin (1988: 306–7) takes up the problem of seemingly honorable people being consigned by John's message to judgment. His reply is twofold. First, as Jesus taught, what people exalt, God despises (Luke 16:15). External appearances hide the impure heart that all are born and struggle with—but it is not hidden from God, who sees all (cf. 1 Sam. 16:7). No matter how upright people appear, therefore, "there is . . . nothing praiseworthy save in Christ." Second, Calvin points out that in biblical understanding, human righteousness grows directly out of forgiveness of sins. "If you take this away, the certain curse of God and eternal death awaits us all." John's laconically grim assessment of the human condition vis-à-vis Christ may raise eyebrows in Western cultures that have constructed a god figure toward whom all religions are alleged to be striving by their various means—and who regard all religious beliefs as equally valid.[21] Stark (1997: 209) notes that among historians of the NT era, "it is deemed bad taste nowadays to suggest that any religious doctrines are 'better' than any others." But John's perspective is fully in line with the logic and teaching of redemption found throughout Scripture and championed by John's teacher Jesus himself.

First John 5:12 aptly concludes the subsection by explaining why John has been focused so intently on Christ since 5:6. In a word, to "have the Son"—or in the words of 5:10 to believe in him—is to have the benefit of the eternal life mentioned in 5:11. Not to have him, or not to give him a hearing and thereby come to faith in him (cf. 5:10), is to forfeit that same life. "Break the tie between the life of God and the human self-giving of Jesus and eternal life has vanished" (Painter 2002: 311). John has been setting before his readers eternal blessedness, on the one hand, and eternal perdition and wrath (cf. John 3:36), on the other. Life or death: the reader can choose. "Claiming a divine enlightenment that neglects the Son is eternally perilous" (Burge 1996: 205). Here is powerful incentive to respond with verve to John's appeal to live a life of love, the overarching theme of 4:15–5:15. "The long theological discussion of the nature of faith thus has a significant practical conclusion" (Marshall 1978: 242).

It also has a scandalous historical and theological edge, to which Rensberger (1997: 137) perceptively calls attention. While in a sense John's language is graphic in the alternatives it sets forth, it is actually euphemistic in its understated mention that preparatory for Christ's glory was his gore: "First John

21. Almost obligatory for many in the West is the outlook reflected in a Chicago-area newspaper (J. Masterson, "Lake County United Committed to Common Good," *The News Sun*, May 1, 2003, A-3), which speaks of "Muslims, Catholics, Protestants, Jews, Hindus" who "worship the one God" and together "help build the kingdom." Reflecting an ignorance of religion too common among journalists, this overlooks that the Qur'an deplores the Christian doctrine of God, that Hindus do not believe in one god but in many gods, and that Jews are unlikely to exalt the kingdom of a Christ whom they deny ever came.

is right to insist that it is in his death—his bloody death—that the Johannine Jesus" makes possible eternal life. "The victorious God of eternal life is revealed, and proffers this life, in the violent death of a human victim of oppression." Talk of "victim" and "oppression" risks politicizing a death that was not a senseless martyrdom but a divinely ordained, willful sacrifice for sin. Jesus put it this way, "No one takes it [i.e., my life] from me, but I lay it down of my own accord. I have authority to lay it down and authority to take it up again" (John 10:18 NIV). Yet Rensberger is right to underscore the concrete, historical, and gruesome headwaters of the eternal life flowing forth from this passage. John offers no "spiritualized resolution" to human deathliness, and "however obscure his wording may sometimes be, our author has grasped this truth" of the costly nature of eternal life "with a grip of iron." Burge (1996: 206, emphasis original) draws the proper lesson from the section as a whole: "*John urges that 'the blood'—the cross—must remain central to all we are and preach.*"

Additional Notes

5:6. An interesting array of readings exists here:

1. A very few minuscules replace "blood" (αἵματος) with "spirit" (πνεύματος), scribes possibly taking a cue from John 3:5. The paucity and quality of witnesses eliminates this reading from being considered original.
2. A slightly larger number of witnesses read "through blood and (Holy) Spirit" (δι᾽ αἵματος καὶ [ἁγίου] πνεύματος). Codices ℵ and A are among these, offering serious external support.
3. A less impressive array of minuscules joins a pair of uncials (P, 0296) in reversing the previous reading: δι᾽ πνεύματος καὶ αἵματος. If these are the correct objects of the preposition, then ℵ and A are more likely to be original.
4. The reading in NA[27] is supported by B, Ψ, 1739*, 𝔐, and a few other witnesses. As a shorter, multiply attested reading, it is preferable, because if πνεύματος were original, it is hard to see why this collection of manuscripts would have omitted it, while its inclusion in other manuscripts is readily explicable as an assimilation drawing on 5:8.

5:6. B and possibly 81 make the adverb μόνον (the singular neuter accusative of μόνος; see BDF §243) into an adjective (μόνῳ). This almost singular reading can be safely set aside on the basis of external evidence, to say nothing of Johannine style, for which μόνον is common, but μόνῳ is unattested and is rare in the NT generally (seven occurrences).

5:6. The six words τῷ ὕδατι καὶ ἐν τῷ αἵματι appear in various orders and forms in the tradition:

τῷ αἵματι καὶ ἐν τῷ ὕδατι
τῷ ὕδατι καὶ ἐν τῷ πνεύματι
τῷ αἵματι καὶ ἐν τῷ πνεύματι
τῷ αἵματι καὶ ἐν τῷ ὕδατι καὶ πνεύματι

External evidence makes the NA[27] reading the most attractive.

5:6. Virtually all manuscripts agree that John wrote τὸ πνεῦμά ἐστιν ἡ ἀλήθεια. But a single minuscule (61, dating from ca. 1500) reads χριστός ἐστιν ἡ ἀλήθεια, a reading echoed in the

Vulgate's "Christus est ueritas." This is a true statement (cf. John 14:6), but the manuscript evidence rules out its originality.

5:7–8. The Greek text underlying the KJV translation of 5:7–8, and NA[27] as rendered in the NIV, are clearly very different. The KJV's additional material is in italic type:

KJV	NIV
For there are three that bear record *in heaven, the Father, the Word, and the Holy Ghost: and these three are one. And there are three that bear witness in earth*, the spirit, and the water, and the blood: and these three agree in one.	For there are three that testify: the Spirit, the water and the blood; and the three are in agreement.

There are few critical issues on which there is greater agreement among scholars of all persuasions: the Greek text underlying these italicized words (often termed "the Johannine comma," *comma* here being Latin for "clause" [cf. Greek κόμμα, also meaning "clause"]) did not come from John's hand (Carson and Moo 2005: 682). They contain great truth, but they are not original. Only a single Greek text (fourteenth-century cursive 629) dating from before ca. 1500 contains them in the original scribal hand. Where pre-Erasmus Greek texts do contain them, we are dealing with secondary back-translations from the Vulgate (Klauck 1991: 12). For the story of how they came to be included in the KJV, see Metzger 1992: 62, 101–2 and de Jonge 1980. The summary of R. Brown 1997: 388n14 is apt: the suspect words first appear among Latin writers in the third and fourth centuries and represent "dogmatic trinitarian reflection on the shorter original" (cf. R. Brown's full and important discussion elsewhere [1982: 775–87]). See also, for example, Strecker 1996: 188–91; Akin 2001: 198–200; Painter 2002: 301. For older sources arguing for the KJV reading, see Maynard 1995.

5:9. Did John write ἡ μαρτυρία τοῦ θεοῦ ἥν or ἡ μαρτυρία τοῦ θεοῦ ὅτι? Codex P and the tradition represented by 𝔐 attest to the former ("the witness of God *which*"). But this is weak attestation compared to the latter's support by ℵ, A, and B, among other witnesses. John almost certainly wrote ὅτι.

5:9. Some manuscripts of the Vulgate and Beatus of Liébana (died 798) attest to the inclusion of a phrase that, translated from Latin, reads: "Whom [the Son] he [God] sent to earth as savior, and the Son gave testimony on earth, by fulfilling Scripture. And we give testimony that we have seen him, and we proclaim to you, so that you may believe" (Strecker 1996: 193n48). It has no claim to be part of the Greek text of 1 John.

5:10. A few manuscripts insert τοῦ θεοῦ after "testimony," most notably Codex A. But the support is weak, and it adds little to John's assertion to say that the believer's testimony is "of God" when one's entire status as a believer is attributed to God's regenerating work anyway (5:1, 4).

5:10. Witnesses are somewhat evenly divided between the reflexive pronoun ἑαυτῷ (NA[27], ℵ, Ψ, and others) and the simple personal pronoun αὑτῷ (NA[25], A, B, P, 𝔐). These nearly synonymous forms were in transition at this stage of Hellenistic Greek (BDF §283), and the translation is not greatly affected regardless of the reading chosen.

5:10. In whom did John say belief should be placed? Codex A and other witnesses (including the Vulgate) say "in the Son." A few insignificant witnesses attest to "the Son of God." An obscure fifth-century Latin writer attests to "Iesu Christo." Some Vulgate manuscripts totally lack a stated object of belief. Greek manuscript evidence is overwhelming that τῷ θεῷ is original.

5:10. A few witnesses, primarily Latin, leave out ὁ θεός. These words are implicit in the verb anyway. A fifth-century codex (048) leaves out the whole clause ἣν μεμαρτύρηκεν ὁ θεός—scribal carelessness that does not materially alter the thrust of the verse.

5:11. Word order is disputed: did John write ἡμῖν ὁ θεός (NA[27], ℵ, A, P, 𝔐, and others) or ὁ θεὸς ἡμῖν (NA[25], B, and others)? NA[27] appears to have better support, but the two versions translate identically into English. The reading of 1241 (ὑμῖν ὁ θεός) is singular and most unlikely to preserve John's original wording.

E. Commendation of the Full Assurance of Eternal Life: Confident Prayer (5:13–15)

The literary structure of the epistle from 5:13 forward is disputed. The JB and NRSV have 5:13 standing alone. In that position it appears to summarize all that has been written thus far and also introduce the few verses remaining. That would also appear to be the understanding of Rensberger (1997: 138). Most commentators, however, prefer to view 5:13, not as a freestanding or swing statement, but as beginning a new major section of which it is the head verse. "To conclude John summarizes the major principles that point the way for the church in contrast to the world and to every false direction in its own midst" (Schlatter 1950: 106, referring to 5:13–21). The section is regarded as the concluding portion of the epistle, a sort of epilogue.[1] NA[27] typifies this understanding by separating 5:13–21 from 5:12 with a line space. English versions that follow suit are RSV, ESV, TEV, NIV/TNIV, NEB, and NLT.

Following the divisions entered by Byzantine copyists, I relate 5:13 more directly to what precedes it (among modern translations see HCSB; CEV could also be taken this way; see also Stott 1988: 186; D. Smith 1991: 127; Strecker 1996: 197–98). The verse can be plausibly related to the verses immediately preceding (Schnackenburg 1992: 247) as well as to the whole of 4:15–5:12. Further, I make 5:13 part of a literary unit that includes 5:14–15. Most translations follow this course. John's goal in these three verses taken together is clear: to commend to his readers the full assurance of eternal life that his message overall makes possible. Apparently because prayer is for John such an integral aspect of fellowship with the Father and Son (cf. 1:3), the bulk of this subsection deals with God's promise to give the prayers of his children a hearing (5:14) and with the nature of their assurance that God does indeed listen to their petitions (5:15).

It is fitting that a section of the epistle (4:15–5:15) that appeals to readers to love God avidly should return to fundamentals without which relationship to God is impossible. Among them are faith, eternal life, and trusting prayer.

Exegesis and Exposition

[13]These things I have written to you ⌜ ⌝ so that you might know that you have life eternal—⌜you who are believing⌝ in the name of the Son of God. [14]And this is the

1. Bultmann 1973: 2 argues that 5:13 originally concluded the epistle, with 5:14–21 added later by a redactor. Against this, see Strecker 1996: 198–200 and Rensberger 1997: 138.

confidence ⸢we have⸣ in his presence⸢:⸣ if we request anything according to his ⸢will⸣, he hears us. [15]And if we know that he hears us, whatever we request, we know that we have the requests that ⸢we requested⸣ ⸢from⸣ him.

First John 5:13 begins with ταῦτα ἔγραψα ὑμῖν (*tauta egrapsa hymin*, these things I have written you). The verb is sure to be an epistolary aorist (Painter 2002: 312; see exegesis of 2:14): John reflects on how the readers will receive his words in the days following his authoring of them. Identical words appear in 2:26. The word ταῦτα is in emphatic position, but this does not necessitate viewing it as beginning a major new section in either 2:26 (where it clearly does not) or here. John 20:31 offers a parallel: ταῦτα . . . γέγραπται (*tauta . . . gegraptai*, these things . . . I have written; the perfect γέγραπται is not appreciably different in meaning from the aorist ἔγραψα of 1 John 5:13). Like 1 John 5:13, John 20:31 summarizes what precedes more than it sets apart or even introduces what follows.[2]

What precedes 1 John 5:13 is a series of commendations to love God and others. Already we have seen many times that love in John's sense is intertwined with the ethical integrity of keeping God's commandments and the confessional integrity of a faith that conforms to the truth of Jesus's coming, his work, and his nature. To "have" Jesus Christ in this full sense (5:12), to trust implicitly in the witness God has furnished regarding him (5:10), results in eternal life. It is the assurance of this life of which 5:13 speaks. "Eternal life" therefore becomes shorthand for the full breadth and depth of benefit available via the message of Christ received broadly and deeply.

John writes that readers may "know." First Maccabees 11:31 uses the same verb (εἰδῆτε, *eidēte*, that you may know) to denote the same idea: arriving at a state of understanding via a written communication.[3] Understanding serves experience; assurance has a solid basis in what God has shown through Christ that believers learn from teachings like this epistle (cf. D. Smith 1991: 129). Jesus (Matt. 9:6 and parallels) and Paul (Eph. 6:21) use the identical verbal form in other connections. What is distinct is not the act of knowing[4] but what John commends that they may know: eternal life. This is a central theme of the epistle, mentioned numerous times already (1:1–2; 2:25; 3:14–15; 5:11–12). And John will speak of this life still more (5:16, 20). It is obviously a major

2. This point is steadfastly overlooked by commentators intent on making 5:13 the beginning of an alleged epistolary epilogue and looking to John 20:31 as a parallel (e.g., Holtzmann 1908: 358; Marshall 1978: 243; Culpepper 1998: 273).

3. "This copy of the letter that we wrote . . . to . . . Lasthenes we have written to you also, so that you may know" (τὸ ἀντίγραφον τῆς ἐπιστολῆς, ἧς ἐγράψαμεν λασθένει . . . γεγράφαμεν καὶ πρὸς ὑμᾶς ὅπως εἰδῆτε) (NRSV).

4. "Knowing" is, however, important, as Calvin 1988: 307 comments: "We must pay heed to our duty of learning, that our faith may increase throughout the whole of our life. For there are still many remnants of unbelief in us, and our faith is so weak that what we believe is not yet really believed without more confirmation."

concern for him—doubtless because it was a major theme in Jesus's ministry, the word appearing in John's Gospel some three dozen times, frequently on Jesus's lips. The way that John separates "life" from "eternal" in 5:13 by the verb "have" (ζωὴν ἔχετε αἰώνιον, *zōēn echete aiōnion*, lit., life you might have eternal) is unique in Johannine usage. It is a literary touch shedding particular light on the eternal quality of the life the readers may enjoy (noted also by Burge 1996: 213 with note 3).

It might seem strange to stress near the end of the epistle an apparently basic reality—eternal life—to which John has already alluded repeatedly. But Luther's words (1967: 321) may well capture an awareness that moved John to yet another mention of a now-familiar topic: "Because [eternal life] is a difficult mystery, we must treat of it constantly in order that we may retain it and grow in faith. It is not like geometry, which suffices once it has been grasped; but these things must be learned assiduously, and it is through tribulations that we must be exercised in learning them." One of those tribulations is no doubt the constant challenge to relate aright to God and the world through prayer.

"To you" in 5:13's opening words is in apposition to the clause that concludes the verse: "You who are believing in the name of the Son of God." The awkward syntax makes "you who are believing" emphatic (Marshall 1978: 243n2), and this emphasis serves a couple of pastoral aims. First, the present aspect of the participle gives a dynamic sense to John's counsel. His readers may well be under continual pressure. The proper response is continual vigilance. This was, of course, a memorable aspect of Jesus's pedagogy: always be prepared (e.g., Matt. 24:44; Mark 13:32–37; Luke 12:35–48; 21:36; John 9:4; cf. also Paul in 1 Cor. 15:58; this counsel is almost ubiquitous in the Catholic Letters). Second, John does not want to give false assurance. The first half of the verse might convey a wrong impression if readers failed to grasp that assurance is conditional on authentic relationship with Jesus Christ himself, not any mere human being (cf. Luther 1967: 322). The person and work of Christ, the Son of God in the fullness of his identity and accomplishment—that is the import of "in the name of the Son of God."[5] The name is tantamount to the fullness of his being, work, and word. To believe in that name means "total surrender in faith" (Strecker 1996: 200n10).

The eternal life of the Son is mediated by faith. John's assurance is for those "who are believing" (emphasized by Culpepper 1998: 273). John's stress is in keeping with the *sola fide* (faith alone) affirmation of the Reformation and since. This does not mean that a sterile affirmation of correct doctrines is

5. The precise expression "in the name of the Son" appears only here in the whole NT (but cf. Matt. 28:19; John 1:12; 2:23; 3:18; Acts 8:16; 19:5). "In his name" referring to God is found in Heb. 6:10. "In the name" (εἰς τὸ ὄνομα) appears in the LXX only at 2 Macc. 8:4, referring to blasphemies "unto [= against] the name" of God. The more common LXX phrase is ἐν ὀνόματι κυρίου (in the name of the Lord), which occurs some eighteen times. As usual in Jewish literature, God's name is his person or being (as reflected, e.g., in the parallelism of Pss. 5:11 [5:12 MT/LXX]; 9:2 [9:3 MT/LXX]; 18:49 [18:50 MT/17:50 LXX]; 20:1 [20:2 MT/19:2 LXX]). See also Westcott 1883: 243–45.

salvific. It does, however, repudiate any number of conflicting notions of how to achieve access to the benefit of the Christian message. Already in the second century, for example, eternal life was linked with human morals rather than with Christ's death received trustingly: "If we shall have done the will of the Father and kept the flesh pure and guarded the commandments of the Lord, we shall receive life eternal" (2 Clem. 8.4; cf. 8.6; the entirety of 2 Clement is suffused with an air of works-righteousness). John agrees that God's commandments are obligatory for believers. But he commends obedience as the result and not the means of arriving at saving faith (cf. 1 John 5:2–3).

John can commend a full assurance of eternal life to his readers because the full requirements of salvation were met by Christ. To affirm this message humbly and heartily—and the whole of this epistle is a commentary on what such faith looks like and how counterfeit faith may be opposed and corrected—is to enter into a transforming and joyful relationship with God and God's people (cf. 1:3–4). Some religions (e.g., Islam) reject the notion of assurance of salvation, and a predominant segment of the church (e.g., Roman Catholicism) teaches that assurance of personal salvation is not only unattainable but presumptuous. Yet it is clearly what John aims at here. Stott (1988: 187) aptly observes, "If God's revealed purpose is not only that we should hear, believe, and live, but also that we should know, presumptuousness lies in doubting his word, not trusting it."

To affirm John's message also means to affirm a confident and mature understanding of prayer. This is the focus of 5:14–15. The centrality of prayer to fellowship with God should surprise no one familiar with the Bible generally (perhaps most notably the Psalms) and with Jesus's life as portrayed in the Gospels particularly (most notably Luke). Schlatter (1950: 107) notes that prayer largely defines the meaning of being Christian and "comprises the calling of the congregation." He captures biblical precedent and precept well:

> Since prayer is that act by which we turn our will to God, prayer is of the very essence of religion. . . . Prayer is the most direct expression of faith, because prayerfully turning our thoughts and will to God is the initial step from thought about God to full assurance of God. By the same token prayer is the most direct expression of love. It is an offering of highest priority, since the first thing we owe God is our thinking and willing. (English translation in Neuer 1995: 159)

In a lengthy section appealing for readers to love (4:15–5:15), John's final words fittingly turn to prayer, because without that active, interactive, and personal component, the joyful fellowship to which he calls readers would be at best a religious sham. "Prayer he makes the soul of the whole [C]hristian life" (Neander 1852: 299).

John speaks first of παρρησία (*parrēsia*, boldness): "And this is the confidence we have in his presence [πρὸς αὐτόν, *pros auton*]." The initial "and" could mean "therefore," so that 5:14 introduces the result of the knowledge of eternal life affirmed in 5:13. This knowledge leads to a confidence, assurance, and even boldness in God's presence (*coram deo*). The prepositional phrase πρὸς αὐτόν is most frequently used with a form of λέγω (*legō*, to speak) or ἔρχομαι (*erchomai*, to come, go) to denote the direction of someone's speech or movement, but it can also connote interpersonal proximity and rapport (John 14:23; Rev. 3:20). Paul writes that Abraham had no boasting πρὸς θεόν (*pros theon*), meaning "before God" (Rom. 4:2 NIV) or in his presence (cf. 2 Cor. 3:4; Kruse 2000: 189). Christ was πρὸς τὸν θεόν (*pros ton theon*, with God, in God's presence) in eternity past, according to John 1:1 (Painter 2002: 312). It is no small claim to affirm confident access into the very presence of the invisible, eternal, and almighty God, but this is not the first time in the epistle that John has voiced this conviction (3:21; cf. 2:28; 4:17). It is, however, plausible under the assumption that God in his Son has made the bloody sacrifice claimed in preceding verses, registered such unimpeachable testimony to his action (5:7–11), and offered eternal life as freely as John and other apostolic writers represent.

But when John writes "this is the confidence," the phrase points ahead. Ὅτι (*hoti*) in 5:14 serves as a colon to introduce the clause that follows (cf. the second ὅτι in 5:9). Believers have assurance that prayerful requests to God will certainly be heard: "If we request anything according to his will, he hears us." Does "his will" refer to the Father's will or to Christ's? Since Jesus is the advocate in the Father's presence (2:1), it would not seem to matter a great deal (Sloyan 1995: 57). That may be part of the basis for confidence. God in his fullness, Father and Son and by implication Spirit, unites in hearing the prayers of God's people.

The "anything" (τι, *ti*) of which John speaks is in emphatic position, perhaps calling attention to the limitless span of what believers might bring before God for his consideration.[6] They may "request"[7] whatever they wish. The question that arises is this: what is a believer free to wish?

The prayer that Jesus taught his disciples makes clear that prayer is always to be for the furtherance of God's kingdom and will: "Thy kingdom come, thy will be done," in KJV parlance. So to request "anything" in 5:14 is unlikely to be a carte blanche for attaining selfish human desire (so also Marshall 1978: 244). Rather, the thought is more apt to be along the lines of OT teaching that was already ancient in John's time: "Delight yourself in the Lord, and he will give you the desires of your heart" (Ps. 37:4 ESV). Prayer is the means that God uses to give his people what he wants (the thesis of Hunter 1986; see also Stott 1988: 188). This is an implication of Jesus's stress, particularly in

6. In some cases where τι in the accusative case immediately follows a conditional particle (John 5:19; 14:14; 2 Cor. 10:8; Eph. 6:8; cf. 2 Macc. 9:24; 3 Macc. 7:9), its default positioning appears to be immediately following the particle. In these cases, no particular emphasis can be attributed to the word order.

7. First John and the Fourth Gospel seem to use the active αἰτέω and middle αἰτέομαι interchangeably (active in 1 John 3:22 and John 14:13, 14; middle in 1 John 5:14 and John 15:7; 16:26). There is no immediately discernible difference in meaning between the two voices in John's usage (Painter 2002: 313; but cf. Moulton 1908: 160).

John, that prayers are to be offered "in the name" of the Son—meaning under his authority and consistent with his teaching and purposes (John 14:13, 14; 15:7, 16; 16:23, 24, 26). In a word, as 1 John 5:14 explicitly states, "anything" that believers may request is immediately qualified by "according to his will." Believers are free to pray whatever they wish as servants of Christ, but the requests that they can be confident God will comply with are those that lay hold of his intentions and plans.[8] It is God's will (τὸ θέλημα αὐτοῦ, *to thelēma autou*), not the believer's whim, that is the cardinal criterion of prayer that God honors. No Christian "can pray against God's will" (Schlatter 1950: 107). This is hardly a restriction on prayer, for there is an infinity of needs and opportunities to pray and work for under God's direction. It is admittedly a challenge to views of human freedom that vest in human will an ultimate autonomy from God and vest in God an ultimate dependence on humans.

To the "confidence" of 5:14 corresponds what John speaks of as *knowing* in 5:15: "And if[9] we *know* that he hears us" (cf. Schnackenburg 1992: 248). Twice previously in the epistle, John has affirmed matters "we know" (οἴδαμεν, *oidamen*), including the conformity of believers to God's Son when he appears (3:2) and the transfer of believers from death to life (3:14). The knowing connoted by forms of οἶδα (*oida*, to know) in 1 John (2:11, 20, 21 [2x], 29; 3:2, 5, 14, 15; 5:13, 15 [2x], 18, 19, 20) may tend to refer to a settled state of awareness or a grounded conviction, as contrasted with an inference drawn from immediate perception when a form of γινώσκω (*ginōskō*, to know) is used (γινώσκομεν [*ginōskomen*, we know] occurs at 2:3, 5, 18; 3:24; 4:6, 13). John affirms a knowledge that God hears with respect to "whatever we request" (ὃ ἐὰν αἰτώμεθα, *ho ean aitōmetha*). There are no explicit limits set to such requests, although it is likely that John assumes that believers will pray in keeping with God's purposes. Yet Paul notes (Rom. 8:26) that, just what believers should pray for, they do not always precisely know (οὐκ οἴδαμεν, *ouk oidamen*, we do not know). Gethsemane illustrates this even in Jesus's case. John's point is to affirm *that* we know God hears when we request, not that we have unerring discernment as to what we should be requesting or how we should set about campaigning for it.

The "if" part of 1 John 5:15, the protasis, is followed by the "then" part, the apodosis. If we know that God hears, regardless of what we ask, "we know that we have the requests that we requested from him." D. Smith (1991: 133) notes, "Such a blanket assurance by Jesus of the fulfillment of petitions in

8. How are these discerned? Calvin 1988: 309 replies: "God supplies a twofold remedy, lest we should pray outside the command of His will. He teaches us in His Word what He wants us to ask, and He has also set over us His Spirit as our leader and ruler to restrain our affections, that we may not let them stray beyond due bounds."

9. Ἐάν, which is normally followed by a subjunctive but here is not, is equivalent to εἰ (BDF §372.1a; cf. Schnackenburg 1992: 248n144). The construction is unusual but not unparalleled (Zerwick 1994: §336). The explanation for it may lie in the intermingling of subjunctive and indicative modes underway at that time in the history of the language: see Caragounis 2006: 117, 188, 191, 557.

prayer has, through the succeeding centuries, doubtless puzzled a great many Christians whose prayers have not been answered in the way they would have hoped." On the face of it, there are two ways to understand John's assertion. First, he could be saying that whatever believers ask, if they feel they know that God hears, then they can be assured that God will grant their requests if they have sufficient faith.[10] Marshall (1978: 245, in disagreement with Stott) seems to hold this view, at least insofar as requests for spiritual gifts are concerned (a qualification that seems foreign to the context; it is, however, stressed by Schnackenburg 1992: 248).

This is unlikely given several examples from salvation history in which prayer, even from the most godly, is hardly represented as a surefire means of securing God's favorable intervention. Moses prayed for rebellious people's sins to be forgiven, but God refused (Exod. 32:31–35). He turned down Moses's request to cross the Jordan (Deut. 3:23–27). Prayers offered under certain auspices are detestable (Prov. 28:9; cf. 15:8, 29) and obviously not granted. God ignores presumptuous prayers when they are lifted up with unclean hands (Isa. 1:15). There are times when God's people cry out and he refuses to answer (Mic. 3:4; Jer. 11:11). Divine wisdom even laughs at their calamity when they cry out to him (Prov. 1:26, 28). However adamantly they may affirm the knowledge that God answers prayers, prophets also remind God's people of the possibility that "your iniquities have separated you from your God; your sins have hidden his face from you, so that he will not hear" them (Isa. 59:2 NIV).

And it is not only transgressions that hinder answers to prayer: sometimes God has higher aims in mind than the petitioner may wish to accept. Jeremiah was told not even to bother praying; there was no use in wasting his breath (Jer. 7:16; 11:14; 14:11). Other passages in Amos and Ezekiel attest to what Tiemeyer (2006: 191) calls "divine restriction on intercession." Paul's thorn in the flesh could not be removed (2 Cor. 12:7–9), nor could Jesus's cross (Matt. 26:39 and parallels; cf. Heb. 5:7–8), despite repeated prayers by each.[11] In incarnate form the Son of God made it clear that neither he nor the Father was at the beck and call of whimsical or selfish supplicants and their requests (Mark 10:35–40; Luke 9:54–55; John 21:21–22). Paul prayed ardently for the salvation of his fellow Jews (Rom. 10:1), but the return seems to have been meager (cf. 1 Thess. 2:14–16; Col. 4:7).

Despite the attraction of verses that, taken out of context, may be thought to set very few bounds to "believing prayer" (e.g., Matt. 21:22 and parallels), the weight of biblical testimony is that prayer is not a means of wresting

10. Bede (in Bray 2000: 226) thinks the key lies in asking "in the right way."

11. Charles Finney (*Revivals of Religion*, 85) contended that Paul's not praying in faith was the reason his thorn was not removed. Finney also believed that Jesus was praying, not that the cup of suffering (the cross) would be taken from him, but that he would not "die in the garden [of Gethsemane] before He came to the cross" (83). But it is not easy to understand Mark 14:36 (cf. Luke 22:42) as a request not to drop dead in the garden, particularly against the backdrop of Jesus's earlier repeated predictions that he would be put to death by crucifixion (Mark 8:31; 9:12, 31; 10:32–34).

concessions from God that he previously had no thought of granting (supporters of open theism would of course see the matter differently). Jesus's promise that "if you ask me anything in my name, I will do it" (John 14:13) needs to be unpacked frankly in the light of important contextual qualifications: (1) he speaks to the Eleven in the upper room, a group to whom he made other assurances that night that we would hardly apply undiluted to ourselves and whose specific mission as apostles none of us shares (14:26, 29; 15:16, 27; 16:2, 4); (2) he makes a parallel statement in 15:7 that qualifies 14:13, with the result that those who do not abide in Christ and in whom Christ's words do not abide cannot expect their petitions to be granted; (3) he says in 14:13, "if you ask *me* anything *in my name*" (emphasis added), a reminder of both the *identity* and the *authority*, or *commission*, that the Son bears, both of which serve to define what apostolic petitioners would be free to expect him to grant.

These considerations suggest a second interpretation of John's statement in 1 John 5:15. John may understand prayer not primarily as *communicating* in order to acquire petitions or to somehow force God's hand but as *communing* with God. "God's simple hearing of our requests . . . is tantamount to receiving a favorable answer" (Sloyan 1995: 56–57). The loftiest attainment of errant mortals petitioning before the heavenly throne is not to gain God's compliance but to be fully assured of his listening ear—whatever external results our prayers do or do not precipitate from God's side. "If we know that he hears us, whatever we request," it is enough. The highest divine response to the petitioner is not to put human prayer in the driver's seat of destiny but to assure the one who prays that all requests are duly considered and acted on so as to maximize the coming of God's kingdom and the fulfillment of his will—the attitudinal common denominator that Jesus taught should characterize all his disciples' prayer.

Therefore, when John writes that "we know that we have the requests[12] that we requested from him," he is affirming that to know that God hears, to trust that he always acts in a wise and timely fashion, and to commune prayerfully with him in that settled assurance is in itself the deepest gratification of those who have eternal life in his Son (cf. 5:11; for extensive reflection on applying John's teaching, see Burge 1996: 222–25). Proof of Moses's high esteem in God's sight lay in his "face-to-face" interchange with God, not his ability to direct God's ways with his prayers (Exod. 33:11; cf. Num. 12:8; Deut. 34:10). Jesus's Gethsemane request for the cup to be removed was not granted, but far from diminishing his sense of the Father's closeness, it intensified it (as implied, e.g., by John 17). Paul's eschatological vision of believers *coram deo* is not God's unlimited "yes" to human petitions but seeing God "face to face" (1 Cor. 13:12). John has already placed a high value on precisely this level of intimacy at the parousia (1 John 3:2), in which believers (including, presumably, their wills)

12. On αἰτήματα (*aitēmata*, requests), see Strecker 1996: 201n17.

are transformed in a godly direction, not God in the direction of humans. John does not present prayer as essentially convincing God what, in our estimation, he had best do.

Affirmation of a posture of full personal trust and mutual love is a fitting capstone to this section of 1 John (4:15–5:15), which has so eloquently, subtly, and searchingly affirmed the priority of reflecting God's love in all human dealings as well as in face-to-face fellowship with the Lord in prayer. "The assurance of faith certainly does not beget sloth" (Calvin 1989: 309) but promotes informed and energetic internalization and actualization of the wide-ranging counsels found in this section.

Additional Notes

5:13. Codex P and 𝔐 are chief among witnesses that apparently move τοῖς πιστεύουσιν εἰς τὸ ὄνομα τοῦ υἱοῦ τοῦ θεοῦ from the end of the verse and insert it near the beginning, after ὑμῖν. This makes for much smoother reading. But this also means that it is less likely to be original: why would earlier manuscripts have uniformly made the verse jarring by shifting the clause to the end of the sentence?

5:13. Instead of τοῖς πιστεύουσιν (supported by the original hand of ℵ, B, and some versions), the tradition offers two alternatives. One is καὶ ἵνα πιστεύητε (P, Ψ, 323, 𝔐, and others). This makes for nice parallelism with ἵνα εἰδῆτε earlier in verse, but as an easier reading, it is suspect. Another option, favored by the second corrector of ℵ, A, probably 33, 623, and a few others, is οἱ πιστεύοντες (a pair of words that occurs in the NT only at Acts 2:44; cf. John 6:64). This attempted grammatical improvement, which changes the syntax of the sentence but not its meaning, has weak external attestation.

5:14. Instead of ἔχομεν (we have), a few manuscripts (among them A, 1243, and some copies of the Vulgate) have the subjunctive ἔχωμεν (we may have; cf. variant reading at Rom. 5:1). The external witnesses are too few and insignificant for this reading to be accepted, and the subjunctive adds a note of conditionality that runs counter to the assurance that John is more apt to be asserting.

5:14. Instead of ὅτι ἐάν τι, two minuscules and all Latin witnesses testify to the reading ὅτι ὃ (ἐ)άν. A few other manuscripts (e.g., A, 049, 69*) read ὅ τι (ἐ)άν or something very similar. Both ranges of variants look like slight scribal confusion, or perhaps attempts to increase clarity, or perhaps an effort to conform this verse to John 14:13, where Jesus uses the words ὅ τι ἂν αἰτήσητε. No matter which of the three possible readings is chosen, the difference in meaning is negligible. The NA^{27} reading has the best external support by far.

5:14. Instead of requesting "according to his will [θέλημα]," Codex A reads "according to his name [ὄνομα]." This is an obvious scribal slip or perhaps intentional change. A single manuscript is unlikely to be correct against the preponderant weight of so many others, many of respectable quality.

5:15. Instead of the perfect ᾐτήκαμεν, a cluster of minuscules reads the aorist ᾐτήσαμεν. Minuscule testimony alone is unconvincing.

5:15. The last two words of the verse, ἀπ' αὐτοῦ, are supported by ℵ, B, 33, 81, and a few other witnesses. Far more numerous are manuscripts that have παρ' αὐτοῦ. The meaning and nuance of the two prepositions followed by this pronoun are indistinguishable: compare the use of αἰτέω + παρά (Acts 3:2; 9:2; James 1:5; cf. Matt. 18:19) with the use of αἰτέω + ἀπό (Matt. 20:20; Luke 6:30; cf. 1 John 3:22). Interestingly, based on the limited sample that the Gospels provide, John's apparent ἀπ' αὐτοῦ comes more frequently from Jesus's lips. The original hand of 2464 dispenses with the preposition altogether. This is notably weak support externally. The NT offers no true examples of αἰτέω having this meaning and followed by a genitive that is not in apposition either to παρά or ἀπό. This, combined with the singular external attestation, makes the reading all but impossible to accept as original.

VII. Concluding Admonition: Pastoral Counsel, Assurance, and Warning (5:16–21)

The shortest of seven scribal divisions of the epistle reads like a pastoral postscript (although Marshall 1978: 245 thinks that 5:16–17 is John's "main topic"). In six verses John takes up five pressing miscellanies: sin in the life of believers and intercession for that sin by others (5:16–17), believers' relationship to sin and to God (5:18), believers' identity vis-à-vis God and the world (5:19), believers' assurance of Christ's nature and ministry to them (5:20), and a concluding warning (5:21).

The section begins with the writer seemingly anticipating a question that will arise as the epistle's message is assimilated by the readers. What should they do about those in the church who are out of compliance with John's teaching (5:16–17)? There are two possibilities. It is conceivable for some to be found sinning μὴ πρὸς θάνατον (*mē pros thanaton*, not to death). There is hope for them, as there has been since the beginning of the epistle (cf. 1:9; 2:1), and John outlines a retrieval strategy. Others may be entangled in sin from which there is no easy exit,[1] succumbing to ἁμαρτία πρὸς θάνατον (*hamartia pros thanaton*, sin to death). John has other advice to cover that contingency, including additional clarification of what constitutes "sin." Little of the precise meaning of all this is transparent to modern readers (Sloyan 1995: 57; Burge 1996: 226), as the exegesis will show.

Next John moves to a threefold affirmation of assured understanding shared by him and his readers. First John 5:18, 5:19, and 5:20 all begin with οἴδαμεν (*oidamen*, we know). This block of verses nicely restates several points that John has made previously but puts a sharper edge on some of them and adapts them to John's immediate hortatory purposes in moving toward the conclusion of the epistle. The repetition of οἴδαμεν followed by the apparent overt ascription of divinity to Jesus Christ at the end of 5:20 lends considerable rhetorical force to this subsection.

John concludes with perhaps the most unusual epistolary ending found in the NT: an enigmatic exhortation to avoid idolatry.

1. Strecker 1996: 202 goes too far in saying "no petition is allowed" for it.

A. Counsel regarding Sinners and Sin (5:16–17)

First John 5:16–17 is among the most discussed passages in the whole NT since these verses treat the notorious "sin unto death." On this topic lengthy periodical treatments and commentary excurses abound (see recently Kruse 2000: 193–94; Painter 2002: 317–20; Witherington 2006: 551–56). D. Smith (1991: 133–34) writes of "an avalanche of exegetical and theological discussion." Interpretation is complicated by the long history and strong convictions associated with the application of these verses in various church traditions (see Westcott 1883: 209–14; R. Brown 1982: 614–19; Strecker 1996: 203–8 with literature cited). Discussion continues (Tan 2002). I propose an interpretation that seeks to make sense within the nexus of pistic, agapic, and ethical concerns that have dominated the epistle throughout. I also note the affinity of this section with concluding portions of other NT epistles.

Exegesis and Exposition

16If anyone sees a fellow believer committing sin that is not unto death, he should petition and God will grant that person life—⌜to those sinning not unto death⌝. There is sin that is unto death. Making request in prayer for those committing that sin is not something I am saying to do. 17All wrongdoing is sin, but there is sin that is ⌜not⌝ unto death.

The language of this passage is fairly straightforward. The initial ἐάν τις (*ean tis*, if anyone) echoes Jesus's language in the Fourth Gospel (see exegesis of 4:20–21; the same words occur at 2:1, 15). John envisions a situation in which one believer "sees" (ἴδῃ, *idē*)[1] a brother or sister in the faith "sinning a sin" (ἁμαρτάνοντα ἁμαρτίαν, *hamartanonta hamartian*). This cognate accusative (Moule 1994: 32) or accusative of content (cf. BDF §151.1, reflecting Hebrew influence [cf. Lev. 5:6; Ezek. 18:24]) yields awkward English if literally translated. Hence my translation "committing sin." The scenario is not one of religious moral police keeping each other under surveillance but of any individual becoming aware of some transgression on the part of τὸν ἀδελφὸν αὐτοῦ (*ton adelphon autou*, his brother), which I render as "a fellow believer" (cf. Burge 1996: 215). The closeness connoted by the possessive pronoun "his" should not be overlooked. These are followers of Christ living in the close ties of fellowship with God and each other that John writes to promote (cf. 1:4).

1. That is, the sin is evident and unmistakable, not simply suspected or alleged.

What happens when attitudes or acts fall short of the norms that Jesus taught and John's epistle reinforces?

First of all, believers are to pray. "Surely it is an iron hardness not to feel pity when we see souls, redeemed by Christ's blood, going to ruin" (Calvin 1988: 310). Prayer for erring community members is as old as Abraham and Moses (Gen. 18:23–33; 20:7; Exod. 32:9–14). The one who sees sin is to make request or petition (αἰτήσει, *aitēsei*, he will request), not point fingers, turn a blind eye, initiate gossip, or bask in a feeling of superiority. The future tense verb αἰτήσει has the weight of an imperative (cf. Exod. 3:22 LXX; Conybeare and Stock 1905: §74; Painter 2002: 315); John is not making a prediction (contra Stott 1988: 188, followed by Akin 2001: 207) but prescribing a strategy.

Prayer for transgressions, whether one's own or those of others, is as basic to Christian faith as the Lord's Prayer: "Forgive us our trespasses, as we forgive those who trespass against us." To their consternation, Jesus taught his followers that they must reckon with forgiving each other repeatedly and ongoingly (Matt. 18:21–22; Luke 17:4). Violation of the high standards of Christian devotion are inevitable. When a sibling in the family of God stumbles, the first response is to be intercession for the person in prayer in the presence of the divine head of the household. First John 1:9 is normally understood in terms of individuals confessing their own sin, but it may well be equally concerned with praying when others stumble. God, not the person who prays (so Marshall 1978: 246n17, but this point is disputed by many commentators),[2] will respond by giving that person "life" (cf. James 5:15, 20). This is surely reference to the benefits of "eternal life" already alluded to frequently in the epistle (1:1–2; 2:25; 3:14–15; 5:11–13). God will keep that person in his fellowship despite his or her (perhaps even grave) transgression. The picture of Jesus saying that he would pray for Peter so that he would return after his denials comes to mind (Luke 22:32).

Petition is to be offered on behalf of those[3] committing sin μὴ πρὸς θάνατον (*mē pros thanaton*, not unto death). The expression occurs twice in 1 John 5:16 and again at the end of 5:17 (where οὐ [*ou*] rather than μή [*mē*] is used, with no discernible difference in meaning; see Turner 1963: 281). Moreover, John also speaks of sin that is πρὸς θάνατον (*pros thanaton*, unto death). What do these expressions signify?

That John does not use the definite article and seems to stress the act of sinning rather than precisely to delineate some particular misdeed weakens the case for seeing here one specific heinous sin (cf. Westcott 1883: 192; Witherington 2006: 553). Blasphemy of the Holy Spirit (Matt. 12:31; Mark 3:29; Luke 12:10; cf. Henry ca. 1710: 1096; Calvin 1988: 311, though Calvin

2. Cf. Akin 2001: 207n237. Yet Calvin 1988: 310 points out that, either way, "the sense will stay the same, that the prayers of believers will avail even to rescuing a brother from death." From a slightly different angle, Loader 1992: 75 says: "It would have to be God's action ultimately, so that the meaning amounts to the same whichever way we identify *he* in the text."

3. The hypothetical individual of 5:16a (τις, *tis*, someone) is expanded to a larger general class of persons in the appositional clause "to those sinning not unto death."

speaks primarily of apostasy as the violation that John has in mind) is a traditional popular proposal (perhaps with references to Heb. 6:4 and 10:26 thrown in; see *SHNT* 936; Holtzmann 1908: 359).[4] But Jesus gives that sin a clear definition—attributing his earthly work done by the Holy Spirit to the powers of darkness—which is not easy to integrate with John's language here (cf. Witherington 2006: 554–55). To see blasphemy of the Holy Spirit as something different from the sin unto death is not necessarily to create *two* sins that are unforgivable. If my argument below is correct, the sin unto death will amount to specific manifestations of unregenerate conduct for which "blasphemy against the Spirit" serves as an umbrella rubric. Such blasphemy includes, but is not strictly limited to or identical with, transgressions that John breaks down into finer, but not *essentially* dissimilar, terms appropriate to the setting he addresses. That is not the same setting that Jesus faced in his earthly days.

Nor is it likely that John means sin that does not cause physical death (as contrasted with sin because of which people die; cf. Acts 5:1–11; 1 Cor. 5:3–5; 11:30). This would suggest that he was also addressing the issue of prayers for the dead, something foreign to this epistle as well as in the rest of the NT. More plausible is the idea that John has been influenced by the OT "distinction between inadvertent sins and intentional sins" (Burge 1996: 216; cf. D. Smith 1991: 134; Lev. 4:2, 13, 22, 27; 5:15–18; Num. 15:27–31; Deut. 17:12), a differentiation that persists in Qumran documents. But even if that is the case, the OT background has not left a very definite or explicit mark on John's stipulations in these two verses.

I propose that it makes the most sense to understand sin "not unto death" as violation of God's will for which forgiveness is possible because (1) people seek it and (2) God therefore grants it. From other 1 John passages we know that John expects that believers will sin (2:1a) and seek forgiveness and divine cleansing, which God faithfully bestows (1:9). First John 5:16, then, is saying that as Christians fall short of fully reflecting the character of a God who is infinite pure light (1:5), there is continual restoration available on the basis of Christ's blood and intercession (2:1b), appropriated by his followers as they prayerfully commit their own and others' transgressions to God. He can expunge it from the record and, in due course, eradicate it from his people's lives. There is sin that does not irrevocably separate the believer from God—it does not lead to spiritual death[5]—and John expects the community to be diligent in spotting it and offering prayer on behalf of those succumbing to it. As in all things, Jesus's precedent (see 2:6) is normative.[6]

4. For an extended interpretation combining apostasy and blasphemy of the Holy Spirit, see Loader 1992: 75 78.

5. Cf. Culpepper 1998: 273 with most other commentators: "Death refers to a spiritual condition—separation from the life that is available only in Christ."

6. Conversely, in John 17:9 Jesus states, "I am not praying for the world" (NIV). That Christ at times limited his own prayers may have conditioned John's counsel later in this verse that there are ways that believers may need to limit theirs.

Any explanation of sin "not unto death" must dovetail with sin that is "unto death." John gives several clues to what he means by this.

First, he says there is such a thing (5:16b). All sin is serious, but some does not lead to forfeiture of eternal life; it is not "unto death." Other sin does lead to loss of eternal life; it is sin "unto death." There is no avoiding the necessity of the Christian community's reckoning with sin's existence, even in the church, and dealing with it as prescribed if compliance with John's teaching is thought to be a priority.

Second, John writes that petitioning God for forgiveness of such sinning is *not* something he is saying to do.[7] The rendering of 5:16c's οὐ περὶ ἐκείνης λέγω ἵνα ἐρωτήσῃ (*ou peri ekeinēs legō hina erōtēsē*, not concerning that [sin] do I say he should request) is not greatly disputed among major translations:

TNIV	I am not saying that you should pray about that.
NIV	I am not saying that he should pray about that. (cf. HCSB)
RSV	I do not say that one is to pray for that.
ESV	I do not say that one should pray for that.
NRSV	I do not say that you should pray about that.
KJV	I do not say that he shall pray for it.

It will be seen that all agree that John's ἐρωτήσῃ means "pray." What is at issue is whether John means pray "for that" to be forgiven (cf. RSV, ESV, KJV). Since the Greek word for "that" is feminine singular, it can refer only to the "sin [feminine singular] unto death" of the previous clause. John is not, of course, talking about prayer for the sin itself, that is, prayer on behalf of some undetermined offense in the abstract; he means prayer for the person guilty of such sin, analogous to the forgiveness through prayer granted to those who sin not unto death. The NLT nails the sense exactly: "I am not saying you should pray for those who commit it."

On another reading, John is being enigmatic: there is most definitely a sin unto death—but "I do not say that you should pray about that" (NRSV; cf. TNIV, NIV; also JB, NEB, TEV). Contextually this seems to yield a less than satisfactory sense. First, John would be leaving believers to make up their own counsel, for he would be evasive about his own opinion: "I do not say that you should"—leaving the reader clueless as to what John *does* say they should. Second, he would be acknowledging that they are apt to pray "about that," but not encouraging about the help they may receive by doing so. Third, in English "pray about that" begs to be understood as meaning either (1) "pray about what the sin unto death is," or (2) "pray about that, period." If the first view, then John is discouraging seeking guidance from God in prayer regarding the sin unto death to determine what it is. This is unlikely, since the Bible virtually nowhere encourages believers to determine Christian doctrine by direct

7. Contra Sloyan 1995: 57, John does not propose "not praying for such sinners." He rather leaves the question open.

personal revelation. Why would John be acting like this were a possible option here? If the second view, he might be understood to imply that any prayer about this sin or its perpetrators whatsoever is not recommended. In John's world of so much black-white admonition, if such prayer were somehow ill advised, it seems likely he would come out and say so.

I conclude that John's counsel is, as my translation indicates: "Making request in prayer for those committing that sin is not something I am saying to do." The distinctive word order is an attempt to emphasize what John's diction may seek to stress in Greek. But the statement raises two further questions. Just what is "that sin"? And why is John so uncharacteristically nuanced in the counsel he gives?

"That sin" has already been alluded to in the exegesis of 3:4, 6, 9–10 (cf. also the exegesis of 2:1a). It is best understood in a way that comports with a close reading of the entire epistle[8] rather than in the broader dogmatic context in which questions about the "sin unto death" are understandably most frequently posed. In the exegesis of 2:1a, I proposed that John's notion of saving knowledge of God is three dimensional, involving faith or doctrine, ethics or obedience, and love or personal relationship. I subsequently noted that John speaks of ἀνομία (*anomia*), which I concluded was sin of a diabolical and grave nature (3:4), as well as Christians' inability to sin (3:6, 8, 9). It was determined that John rules out sin in the Christian life when defined as doctrinal convictions, ethical patterns, and relational tendencies—or any combination of these three—which belie one's claim to know the God of light (1:5). To know God is to have been born of God. Divine parentage does not generate the breaches of faith, ethics, or love that John warns against. Christians, accordingly, are not chronically characterized by these fundamental deficiencies or lapses. If they are, they are not Christians, in John's outlook.[9]

If this captures John's drift, then the "sin unto death" is simply violation of the fundamental terms of relationship with God that Jesus Christ mediates.[10] This is sin that marks a person's confession, behavior, or affections as defective in God's sight. A couple of examples, ventured with fear and trembling, may clarify. A churchgoing woman well known and liked in her church beats two sons to death (ages eight and six) with rocks and bashes in the head of her infant in its crib. She states that God told her to do it (*World*, May 24, 2003, p. 7). In our age we think first of derangement, a medical pathology that excuses the perpetrator of criminal responsibility. This possibility should not be minimized. But suppose it could be determined that organic pathology is

8. Cf. Painter 2002: 316: "All the reader has are clues implied by the context."

9. Cf. D. Smith 1991: "Those who have committed the sin unto death are the Johannine Christians who have separated themselves and now lie beyond the pale." Cf. Thompson 1992: 143n: "For John, these people were never truly children of God."

10. Cf. Marshall 1978: 247: "John means the sins that are incompatible with being a child of God." Sloyan's view (1995: 58) that "no certainty about the author's meaning is forthcoming" is probably unduly pessimistic.

not the cause, that the murders were a true reflection of the person and are never repented of.

Many who read these lines will have received e-mail messages promising millions of dollars in commissions for helping someone abroad transfer money into a US bank. One such e-mail begins: "Dear Beloved in Christ, It is by the grace of God that I have received Christ, knowing the truth and the truth have [*sic*] set me free. Having known the truth, I had no choice than to do what is lawful and right in the sight of God for eternal life and in the sight of man for witness to God's mercy and glory upon my life." Later in this unremittingly unctuous letter, the reader learns that God by direct revelation has told the letter-writer to e-mail the reader, for the sake of showering millions of dollars upon him or her: just send personal information including bank account number, please.

Murder and mail fraud in the name of God, even Christ. Setting aside for the moment the individual personages of this pedicidal parent and scam artist—their souls are in God's merciful hands—looked at objectively John teaches that, unrepented, this kind of behavior or its informing credo or its animating devotion or any combination of these is utterly incommensurate with the regenerating work of the God who redeems the lost by the message of Jesus Christ. No legally sane and morally responsible person who functions like this can be a Christian, to the extent that these acts are true depictions of their soul as God knows it (and again: this is something that in the end only God *can* know; these persons are not being placed on trial but used as examples to concretize the issues involved).

To "sin unto death" is to have a heart unchanged by God's love in Christ and so to persist in convictions and acts and commitments like those John and his readers know to exist among ostensibly Christian people of their acquaintance, some of whom have now left those whom John addresses.

As to why John's counsel is nuanced, telling readers neither to pray nor not to pray, this probably reflects first of all a wise humility that knows better than to seek to micromanage other people's lives when it comes to a habit of the heart like prayer.[11] Without denigrating public prayer, which Jesus frequently practiced and witnessed in the synagogue, he taught that prayer must also be profoundly private: "But when you pray, go into your room, close the door and pray to your Father, who is unseen" (Matt. 6:6 NIV). To suppose that a church leader should or could mandate all its particulars in blanket fashion would be to violate its basic character. John leaves primary responsibility for personal prayers in this matter with individuals.

A second reason involves the inscrutability of human acts to all but God. What human observer would have seen in Judas's kiss (Luke 22:48) a precursor to perdition but in Peter's oath (Matt. 26:72) the Lord's subsequent pardon?

11. Stott 1988: 189 suggests that John does not advise prayer because "he clearly doubts its efficacy in this case." Its propriety or advisability more than its efficacy seems to be the issue. Marshall 1978: 251n31 rightly notes that private prayer rather than public is likely to be in view.

"John cannot give a clear marker to indicate in every case whether someone's lapse is unto death and unforgivable, or whether God's pardon may still extend to him. No person can furnish that" (Schlatter 1950: 109). The command to pray or not pray must remain to some extent beyond human ken in any given particular case. John's reserve here leaves room for the Pauline (and Mosaic) dictum: "Do not take revenge, my friends, but leave room for God's wrath, for it is written: 'It is mine to avenge; I will repay,' says the Lord" (Rom. 12:19 NIV; cf. Deut. 32:35; Lev. 19:18). Even if we were to ascertain the guilt of the pedicidal parent or blasphemous scam artist (above), John is not saying we *must* not pray for them.

A third reason might involve the soul of the one who prays. To pray for another is, to an extent, to take up that person's case. It is to identify with the person and sustain a travail for him or her. There is no danger of making God do something against his own will. But there could be a danger of disenchantment with God if prayers are not answered in the desired way. I have already noted that God told Jeremiah to quit praying for his compatriots (Jer. 7:16; 11:14; 14:11). At some point he had to be willing to affirm the righteousness of God's judgment against them and cease allying himself with their cause. So it might have been with John's readers. John does not tell them they must pray for every person in every case, because there comes a time when intercession has to cease for the sake of the person who intercedes. "We should not pray where God's will stands against us" (Schlatter 1950: 108; cf. Calvin 1988: 311). An intercessor's final loyalties must remain with God and not with the transgressor, in spite of Jesus's command to pray even for persecutors (Matt. 5:44). Just as John's nuanced counsel gave readers leave to pray, it also left them free to cease their prayers when the time arrived.[12]

A fourth reason may lie in the integrity of the entire message that 1 John upholds (cf. Thompson 1992: 144; this is essentially also the concern of Luther 1967: 324–25). To pray that eternal life be granted to individuals who commit sin that God deems worthy of death—and John underscores that there is such a thing—is at least a risky gambit. At worst it signals an unwillingness to abide by God's emphatic testimony that fellowship with him is contingent on acknowledgment of sin and embracing of Christ as savior. Believers should be wary of condemning themselves by what they too brazenly agitate for God to grant (cf. Rom. 14:22 NASB: "Happy is he who does not condemn himself in what he approves"). Offsetting this caveat is Jesus's praying for the people who crucified him (Luke 23:34). Yet it is unlikely that Jesus was asking God

12. This seems a better solution than Rensberger's charge (1997: 140) that, because "the forgiveness of the opponents' deadly sin and their restoration to fellowship with the community" is precisely what John ought most to encourage his readers to pray for, and because he leaves open the option of not praying, then we have here "a particularly unhappy example of the restriction of love to 'one another.'" Rather, we have here a weighty qualification to love: it must ultimately cling to God and not other humans, especially when those humans reject God and tempt others to do likewise.

to grant eternal life to individuals who ultimately rejected the truth he died to establish.[13]

First John 5:17 rounds off John's teaching on this subject. In the statement "all wrongdoing is sin," ἀδικία (*adikia*, wrongdoing) is the same word used in 1:9 (God "is faithful and just to forgive us our sins and cleanse us from all *wrongdoing*"). As the exegesis of 1:9 showed, the word is best understood as denoting specific evil deeds. It is likely a blanket term for the transgressions that John is addressing, whether they are unto death or not unto death. Sin brings death, and the wrongdoing that John addresses is certainly sin. But,[14] John hastens to add, "there is sin that is not unto death." As grave as all sin is, and granting that particular evil deeds can bespeak terminal opposition to God, there is also sin that can be overcome through prayer, repentance, and renewed faith resulting in reform and restoration. John's instruction ends on a cautionary and hopeful note (Holtzmann 1908: 359). Augustine in his *Retractions* wrote, "We must not despair of anyone, no matter how wicked he is, while he lives, and we should pray with confidence for him of whom we should not despair" (Bray 2000: 226; cf. Witherington 2006: 555–56). Readers should not be oblivious to each other's sin, but neither should they assume the worst about every violation of God's will they may observe, even when the violation is clearly heinous. In God's sight, what violation is not (James 2:10)?

A final word on the context in which the "sin unto death" should be seen. While it is often singled out as a virtually anomalous reference, it begs comparison with closing verses in every other NT epistle that addresses Christian communities and calls them to unity, prayer, repudiation of evil and evildoers, concern for one another, or some combination of these (Rom. 16:17; 1 Cor. 16:14, 16, 22; 2 Cor. 13:11; Gal. 6:1, 9–10; Eph. 6:18, 23; Phil. 4:2, 9; Col. 4:2, 12; 1 Thess. 5:12–18; 2 Thess. 3:6–15; Titus 3:10; Heb. 13:1, 9, 18; James 5:19–20; 1 Pet. 5:5, 12; 2 Pet. 3:14, 17; Jude 20–23). While it is legitimate and helpful to focus on 1 John 5:16–17 for careful analysis, in broad terms it reflects concerns and counsel common to other NT writers (so also Luther 1967: 324–25). The passage has its distinctive features, but it is hardly anomalous in either tone or substance.[15]

13. Note Peter's similar gracious assessment: "Now, brothers, I know that you acted in ignorance, as did your leaders" (Acts 3:17 NIV). But this did not keep him from proclaiming a judgment from which there could be no recovery without repentance and faith.

14. Καί is adversative; cf. Strecker 1996: 203n25 (also Zerwick 1994: §455).

15. Loader 1992: 75–77 proposes that John represents a "strict position" that dominates the NT, while "the story of Peter who disowned and cursed Christ but was rehabilitated to become Peter the apostle suggests another way." Loader calls this way "the compassion of restoration." Interpreters must decide which is the more faithful representation of God's will for his people in everyday church life: John's admittedly stiff counsel or Loader's attenuation of it. Those who fail to see an honest way around what John (like other NT writers) says may see in Loader's view an unfortunate accommodation to contemporary sensitivities having little grounding in Christian views of grace and judgment. It is doubtful that we can credibly lay claim to John's high view of God's love—so powerfully transformative that it frees believers from sin's crippling and

Additional Notes

5:16. Instead of the plural τοῖς ἁμαρτάνουσιν, a handful of minuscules and a smattering of versions read the singular τῷ ἁμαρτάνοντι. The singular fits well with the singular τις earlier in the verse, but as an easier and poorly attested reading, this one has little claim to be original. Codex A and a few other minor witnesses have the expanded τοῖς μὴ ἁμαρτάνουσιν ἁμαρτίαν (to those not committing sin) not unto death. Unless this is an intentional double negative, this would seem to affirm that God gives life to those who do *not* commit the sin that is not unto death—in other words, who do not sin at all. More likely the vast preponderance of manuscripts is correct in recording John's teaching as just the opposite: eternal life is available to those *not* sinning "unto death."

5:17. Some minuscules and versions omit οὐ. Since there has always been debate about what John meant both by sins unto death and sins not unto death, the omission does not seriously affect the meaning of the passage. Nor does the change of οὐ to μή, as found in a scant few minuscules and Clement of Alexandria change the sense. But neither reading is likely to be original to John.

---

dehumanizing mastery—if we decline to endorse his robust sense of God's implacable rejection of people who, impenitent to the end, indulge in certain types or degrees of transgression.

VII. Concluding Admonition: Pastoral Counsel, Assurance, and Warning (5:16–21)
- A. Counsel regarding Sinners and Sin (5:16–17)
- ➤ B. The Tie That Binds: Shared Certainties (5:18–20)
- C. Final Pastoral Appeal (5:21)

B. The Tie That Binds: Shared Certainties (5:18–20)

Hard on the heels of the "sin unto death" passage comes assurance in 5:18–20. The vagaries and complexities of human sin can leave even an apostle taking an agnostic stance on how to pray in certain situations (5:16), just as in Gethsemane Jesus voiced a short-term personal preference but left ultimate resolution of his acute prayer concern in the Father's hands (Mark 14:36).

Three "we know that" statements, "an effective rhetorical device" (Strecker 1996: 208), are the backbone of the passage. John articulates points of doctrine that refocus reader attention in the wake of the astringent counsel immediately preceding. He recites bedrock truths that bind believers to God, inasmuch as their standing is radically and irrevocably ἐκ τοῦ θεοῦ (*ek tou theou*, from God). These certainties also bind them to each other, implicit in the first-person plural "we" at the head of each verse. They are a buffer and bulwark between readers and the opposition they face from the evil one and the world (5:18–19). Around them threats loom, but in their corner is one who "is the true God and eternal life" (5:20). Confident rather than quailing declaration of faith's triumph is likely John's intent in these ringing phrases that draw the epistle to a close.

Exegesis and Exposition

18We know that every one born of God does not sin. Rather, ⌜the one born of⌝ God keeps ⌜him⌝, and the evil one does not touch him. 19We know that we are of God, and the whole world languishes under the evil one. 20⌜But we know⌝ that the Son of God has come ⌜ ⌝, and ⌜he has given⌝ us understanding so that ⌜we will know⌝ him who is true ⌜ ⌝—and we are in that one who is true, in his Son Jesus Christ ⌜ ⌝. He is the true God and ⌜eternal life⌝.

John has written of the common knowledge shared by believers using "we know" language previously (3:2, 14; see exegesis of 3:2 and table in the exegesis of 2:20–21). Many other linguistic features of 5:18 occur earlier in the letter, too: being born of God (2:29; 3:9; 4:7; 5:1, 4), ἐκ τοῦ θεοῦ (*ek tou theou*, of God; 4:1), ἁμαρτάνω (*hamartanō*, to sin; 1:10; 2:1 [2x]; 3:6 [2x], 8, 9; 5:16 [2x]), and Christians not sinning (3:6, 9).

In 5:18, then, John draws heavily on truths he has already stated (cf. Painter 2002: 321–22). He begins by reassuring readers who may have been nonplussed by his counsel regarding sin and death in previous verses. If they are born of

God, they do not sin—that is, they do not persist in the sorts of sin that John writes this epistle to decry and correct. Deadly sins on their part are of no concern (cf. Bede in Bray 2000: 228).[1]

Why? Their assurance is christologically founded. "The one born of God" comes to their aid.[2] By now such a phrase is shorthand for the numerous ministries performed for believers by Jesus: coming to bring eternal life (1:2), cleansing from sin (1:7), interceding in the Father's presence (2:1), dying a propitiatory death (2:2), confirming knowledge (2:20), destroying the devil's works (3:8), teaching believers the meaning of love (3:16)—a complete list would be a summary of the whole of 1 John to this point. In the first two clauses of 5:18, John brings home that faithful readers need not be anxious despite the dire warnings implicit in previous verses.

Specifically, the Son "keeps" (τηρεῖ, *tērei*) the believer. Forms of the verb τηρέω (*tēreō*, to keep) have occurred six times previously in 1 John, but always to denote keeping commandments or Jesus's word. This is also the usage of the word that predominates among its eighteen occurrences in John's Gospel. But in John 17:11 Jesus prays, "Holy Father, keep [τήρησον, *tērēson*] them by the power of your name." Earlier in John, Jesus had described himself as the Good Shepherd who protects his sheep, even laying down his life for them (10:7–18). Jesus summarized, "I give them eternal life, and they shall never perish; no one can snatch them out of my hand. My Father, who has given them to me, is greater than all; no one can snatch them out of my Father's hand" (10:28–29 NIV). In 1 John 5:18, John draws on this image of Christ protecting and preserving the life and soul of the one who trusts in him because this one has been born of God (cf. 5:1; Jude 1).

Yet this is no Pollyannaish assurance. The devil dogs the steps of the follower of Christ, just as the wolf sought to scatter the flock under the Good Shepherd (John 10; cf. Matt. 7:15; Acts 20:29). First John 5:18 names the enemy and meets his threat head on: "the evil one does not touch" Christ's followers ("touch" is a euphemism; cf. Stott 1988: 195).[3] He had no hold on the Son (John 14:30) and so cannot bring down and destroy his followers. This is akin to Paul's affirmation that nothing can separate the believer from God's love in Christ Jesus (Rom. 8:35–39). There is no illusion of discipleship being free of danger; the Johannine

1. A broader interpretation is possible: "Because they are born of God, believers are characterized not by sin and death but by truth and life" (Thompson 1992: 146). This would be to understand John as speaking proverbially (cf. Akin 2001: 211: John gives "a general rule") rather than apodictically.

2. On another translation based on a slightly different text, it is the born-of-God believer who "keeps himself." This seems less likely contextually (cf. Schlatter 1950: 110; Marshall 1978: 252; Strecker 1996: 208–9; Rensberger 1997: 142; Painter 2002: 324; otherwise Calvin 1988: 312 [whose text-critical knowledge here was lacking]; Holtzmann 1908: 359–60; Thompson 1992: 146–47n). On the textual question, see additional notes on 5:18.

3. Cf. Calvin 1988: 312: Satan not "touching" believers "refers to a deadly wound. For the children of God do not remain untouched by the wounds of Satan, but ward off his blows with the shield of faith, so that they do not penetrate into their hearts. Therefore spiritual life is never extinguished in them."

Jesus warns of bitter persecution (John 16:1–4). He knew the dangers to which his followers would be exposed and prayed for their preservation: "My prayer is not that you take them out of the world but that you protect [τηρήσῃς, *tērēsēs*] them from the evil one" (17:15 NIV). The "evil one" (ὁ πονηρός, *ho ponēros*) of 17:15 is linguistically identical to "the evil one" of 1 John 5:18, whom John has also mentioned in 2:13–14 (cf. the reference to "the devil" at 3:8, 10). But since the Son bestows life (5:12), even the worst ravages of "the evil one" must prove short-lived. His malevolent touch will be no more lasting than the blow that sent "the one born of God" from the cross to a tomb that was shortly emptied. John can offer the assurance of Jesus's aid because Christ has himself blazed the trail leading from endangerment to deliverance.

The second "we know" statement (5:19) begins by echoing 5:18a, only in different words. Instead of "born of God" believers simply "are of God." They are his creation, his re-creation in Christ (the connotation of "born of God"), and therefore his eternal possession. Schlatter (2005: 402) writes of the NT-era believer, "The person who recognized himself as the work and possession of God always lived in hope." John does not speak of hope explicitly (but see 3:3), but the assurance of the knowledge of being God's possession in a world of sin, the devil, and death is tantamount to it.

In contrast to believers, "the whole world[4] languishes under the evil one." "Languishes" translates κεῖται (*keitai*). The word means simply "to lie," as when Jesus "was lying" in a manger (Luke 2:12), but it can also have the sense to be "destined" for something (2:34; Phil. 1:16; 1 Thess. 3:3). In 1 John 5:19 it seems to carry the connotation of languishing—the world is lying in a dispirited state and lacks the vitality that it might be expected to show. And no wonder, for apart from those who are "of God," "the world" lacks eternal life. The same evil one who cannot touch the believer owns the world (cf. Gal. 1:4; Eph. 5:16), even if his dominion is fleeting and in any case limited by the Son's sovereignty (cf. 1 John 5:18). So even though John's statement translated literally ("the whole world lies in the evil one") and removed from its context is daunting[5] and depressing, when set against the backdrop of God's ownership of his people and their settled understanding of their status, John's allusion to this evil figure is transformed to good news. John's readers can rejoice in the woe from which they are delivered and the fellowship to which they have been called (cf. 1:3–4).[6] "By God acting on us in his fatherly capacity and,

4. John uses κόσμος in 2:2, 15 (3x), 16 (2x), 17; 3:1, 13, 17; 4:1, 3, 4, 5 (3x), 9, 14, 17; 5:4 (2x), 5, 19. Patristic interpreters like Clement of Alexandria, Didymus, Bede, and Isho'dad of Merv (see Bray 2000: 228) stressed that "world" means only worldly and evil people. It is better to take note of John's "already/not yet" outlook—Christ's victory is already assured but is not yet fully manifest—and leave room for ravages of the world to affect even Christians.

5. Calvin 1988: 313 focuses on the need to take extreme measures against the world: "Since corruption fills all nature, believers should study self-denial."

6. Luther's almost paranoid explanation (1967: 326) of this verse is to be rejected. He believed that the text was instructing Christians to "trust no one" and to treat all unbelieving people as ingrates and enemies.

by his Spirit, making his Word the basis of our lives, we gain freedom from dependence on that which is of Satan" (Schlatter 2005: 543).

The third "we know" statement (5:20) is summative, as δέ (*de*, but) indicates (see first additional note on 5:20 on whether δέ should actually be καί). Despite the evil one's sway, John issues a concluding threefold reminder. This is, as it turns out, the final indicative declaration of the epistle. He and his readers share certainty regarding three matters.

First, "the Son of God has come" (5:20a; cf. John 8:42; on "Son of God," see exegesis of 3:7–8). Modern translations are unanimous, it seems, in rendering the present tense ἥκει (*hēkei*, he has come) as a perfect (so also Schnackenburg 1992: 261–62; Painter 2002: 325). Whatever the nuance of the verbal aspect, John's point is that the incarnation is not at issue in the community he addresses (cf. Strecker 1996: 209). From the Son's coming flow all of the good things the epistle affirms. Moreover, due to his coming, followers can anticipate his return (cf. 2:28; 3:2). This will mean vindication for them and judgment for the gospel's detractors. As John closes his epistle, it is fitting that he remind them of the basis for the big picture dominating the landscape of the Johannine worldview: the appearance of the invisible God in human form and history.

Second, this Son of God "has given [δέδωκεν, *dedōken*] us understanding so that we will know him who is true" (5:20b). "Even at the end of his letter, John never stops insisting on the need for right doctrine" (Andreas in Bray 2000: 229). This is far from all that God has given Christ's followers, according to 1 John:

1 John	Form of δίδωμι (*didōmi*, to give)	Giver	Object given
3:1	δέδωκεν (perfect)	Father	love
3:23	ἔδωκεν (aorist)	Jesus	love commandment
3:24	ἔδωκεν (aorist)	Son	Spirit
4:13	δέδωκεν (perfect)	God	Spirit
5:11	ἔδωκεν (aorist)	God	eternal life
5:16	δώσει (future)	God	life

Third, yet none of these divinely granted favors is of much use without a kind and degree of awareness that would facilitate reception of them. Therefore in addition to these gifts, 5:20b adds "understanding" (διάνοια, *dianoia*). The word occurs some dozen times in the NT, as in Gospel references to loving God with all one's "mind" or "understanding" (Matt. 22:37; Mark 12:30; Luke 10:27). It is the faculty of rational cognition or the data grasped by that faculty.[7] The same word is used in Jeremiah's celebrated new-covenant prophecy (Jer. 31:31–34 [38:31–34 LXX]) and cited by Hebrews twice: "I will

7. Luther 1967: 327 goes astray in seeing διάνοια as the Holy Spirit, though the Spirit no doubt operates upon it.

put my laws in their minds [διάνοιαν] and write them on their hearts" (Heb. 8:10 NIV; cf. 10:16). Peter calls on readers to "gird up the loins of [their] minds [διάνοιας]" (1 Pet. 1:13). It is probably both unfruitful and unwise to seek to nail down some nuance of διάνοια too tightly, since this is the NT's only Johannine occurrence; contextually its significance lies in its function: to enable the knowledge of God and understanding of the world,[8] of which people in general are at least ignorant and more likely willfully blind. (On knowing God in 1 John, see exegesis of 2:1a and 2:3.)

The action denoted by the verb γινώσκομεν (*ginōskomen*, we will know)[9] has a relational focus (which is by no means to deny John's repeated stress on factual and empirical components in saving Christian confession: "faith" is very much intertwined with "knowledge"). It "describes not only a theoretical belief that something is true but a being involved with something" (Strecker 1996: 40) or, better, "someone." Forms of γινώσκω (*ginōskō*, to know) occur twenty-five times in 1 John—once every four verses on average—and point to a major theme of the epistle. The settled conviction that John commends in 5:18–20's threefold "we know" grows out of an existential, personal, interactive relationship.

The God who is known, whether as Father or Son, is described as the "true" one (ἀληθινόν, *alēthinon*; see third additional note on 2:8). The adjective suffix -ινος (*-inos*) tends to convey the sense of being "made of." It is fair to say that in John's usage this adjective most frequently points to an object or person who is "made of" the divine nature[10]—divinity or a divine attribute is in some sense inherent to its/his character: the true light coming into the world (John 1:9; cf. 1 John 2:8), the true bread from heaven (John 6:32), the true heavenly Father (7:28; 17:3; cf. Rev. 6:10) and his true ways (Rev. 15:3), Jesus's true judgments (John 8:16) as well as the true judgments of the Father (Rev. 16:7; 19:2), Jesus as the true vine (John 15:1), Jesus himself as "true" (Rev. 3:7; 19:11), God's true words (19:9; 21:5; 22:6). In other NT writers, God is living and "true" (1 Thess. 1:9), and "true/real" is the heavenly sanctuary into which the Son enters "now to appear for us in God's presence" (Heb. 9:24; cf. 8:2). There is perhaps no loftier modifier for John to use as a substantive for the Son than ἀληθινός, which occurs three ponderous times in 1 John 5:20.

Not only does John commend knowledge of the Son (or of God—there is a fluid boundary between the two in 5:20): he also declares that believers are "in" this same figure who is "true." The world is "in" the evil one, but believers are "in" the one for whom any adjective, even "true," is an inadequate

8. Cf. Westcott 1883: 196: the incarnation "vitally welcomed carries with it the power of believing in and seeing little by little the divine purpose of life under the perplexing riddles of phenomena."

9. I read the variant, which is indicative, rather than the (grammatically correct) subjunctive. See fourth additional note on 5:20; also Caragounis 2006: 192n192.

10. Sloyan 1995: 59: "This is the adjective favored by [the Gospel of John] to convey what is real or genuine because divine." Turner 1963: 13 notes that the construction points to "a quality *par excellence*."

approximation. The mutual indwelling of believers in the Son or the Father or vice versa has been a frequent theme of the epistle wherever there is talk of "abiding" (cf. Kruse 2000: 196–97). This positioning of believers begs comparison with Paul's notion of being "in" Christ.

John adds an appositional clause: "in his Son Jesus Christ." Linguistically this is superfluous. "The Son of God" appears a scant few clauses earlier. But the end of the epistle is at hand. John may be striving for effect that is elegant and doxological in substance if not in literary form (Westcott 1883: 193 speaks of the "rhythmic form" of the passage). This is confirmed by the second sentence of 5:20: "He is the true God and eternal life." What higher commendation is possible? He is the ultimate with respect to both who he is (God, though in Johannine theology not God the Father) and what he confers (eternal life). While translations have often rendered the near demonstrative adjective οὗτος (*houtos*, this one [masculine]) as the impersonal "this" (KJV, RSV, TEV, JB, NEB), there is a more recent trend to translate it as "he" (NRSV, NIV/TNIV, NLT, HCSB, ESV). Justification may be drawn from numerous Johannine passages where "he" is as defensible a rendering as "this" or "this one" (e.g., John 1:2, 7, 30, 33, 34; 3:2, 26; 4:47; 6:46, 71). Wallace (1996: 327) rightly concludes that "there are no grammatical reasons for denying" that John here calls Jesus "the true God."[11] John calls Jesus God "without ifs or ands" (Sloyan 1995: 59). Schnackenburg (1992: 262) concurs: "Therefore there is no longer any doubt" that here John "refers to Jesus Christ."

Apart from the postscript of 5:21, 1 John ends with the words "eternal life." This serves as a fitting bookend to an epistle whose opening two verses feature three mentions of this life. Like several other expressions in 5:20—"we know," "Son of God," "Jesus Christ," "true"—"eternal life" serves to confirm earlier emphases (cf. Rensberger 1997: 145) and leave readers finally oriented in the direction to which the epistle's opening lines first pointed them: toward eternity, toward God, toward the incarnation, toward the Son, toward witness, toward eternal life.

Additional Notes

5:18. The anomalous reading of 33 that the one born of God does not sin but "was born [of God]. And the one born of . . ." (ἐγεννήθη· ὁ δὲ γεννήθεις ἐκ, *egennēthē; ho de gennētheis ek*) should be set aside on external grounds. Three minuscules and a smattering of versions change ὁ γεννηθεὶς ἐκ to ἡ γέννησις (*hē gennēsis*, the birth). This would yield "but the birth of God keeps him." It would take stronger external evidence than is found here to sustain this convenient proof text for later church teaching on the incarnation and the nature of Christ. Origen read the perfect ὁ γεγεννημένος instead of the aorist ὁ γεννηθείς. This conforms the latter half of the verse to the former, which also contains ὁ γεγεννημένος. Then Origen reads ἑαυτόν instead of αὐτόν later in the verse (see

11. So also Marshall 1978: 254n47; D. Smith 1991: 137; Burge 1996: 218; Strecker 1996: 211–12. Against this, see Holtzmann 1908: 361 (who writes in a setting where newer translations in Germany were rejecting the notion that 5:20 predicates full divinity of Christ); Turner 1963: 44; Loader 1992: 79; Rensberger 1997: 144; Painter 2002: 326–27.

next additional note). This yields the meaning "but the one begotten of God keeps himself." Origen's reading is too thinly attested to be accepted.

5:18. Important witnesses (including ℵ, the corrector of A, P, 𝔐, and 33) read ἑαυτόν (himself) instead of αὐτόν (him or himself [if a rough breathing mark is assumed: αὑτόν; cf. Moule 1994: 207]). Interpreters who think the second half of the verse refers to Christ choose the former, in which case the believer born of God keeps "himself." Those viewing ὁ γεννηθεὶς ἐκ τοῦ θεοῦ as a reference to Christ read αὐτόν—Christ keeps "him," meaning the believer. External evidence is not decisive either way. See exegesis of 5:18.

5:20. The first two words of the verse are disputed: should they be καὶ οἴδαμεν (but we know; supported by two uncials and several minuscules), simply οἴδαμεν (favored by a few, mainly late manuscripts), or οἴδαμεν δέ (and/but we know; ℵ, B, 𝔐, and one version)? The last reading has the best external support, but the meaning is very nearly identical with the first option.

5:20. Some manuscripts in the Latin tradition insert the words "and took on flesh for our sake and suffered and rose from death. He raised us." This is interesting commentary but can make little claim to have come from John's pen.

5:20. Instead of the perfect δέδωκεν, three uncials and a handful of minuscules read the aorist ἔδωκεν. External evidence supports the NA[27] reading, although the meaning is not greatly affected either way.

5:20. An impressive array of witnesses—including ℵ, A, B*, and other uncials as well as minuscules—read the indicative γινώσκομεν instead of NA[27]'s subjunctive γινώσκωμεν, which apart from 𝔐 has marginal support. Not only is NA[27]'s choice inferior with regard to external evidence; it is also the easier reading, for ἵνα plus a subjunctive is clearly proper grammar, while ἵνα with an indicative following "must be regarded as a corruption" (Schnackenburg 1992: 262n196). "Corruption" may be an overstatement: John used an indicative verb after ἵνα just a few verses back (cf. 5:15: ἐὰν οἴδαμεν), and Zerwick 1994: §336 lists numerous "analogous . . . Hellenistic anomalies" (see also Turner 1963: 115–16). It is hard to avoid the impression that ἵνα γινώσκομεν (indicative) is what John did indeed write or dictate (so Marshall 1978: 253n44; Painter 2002: 321). Westcott 1883: 196 notes that many manuscripts attest the same construction in Jesus's parallel words in John 17:3: ἵνα γινώσκουσιν (indicative) instead of NA[27]'s ἵνα γινώσκωσιν (subjunctive).

5:20. Two uncials, several minuscules, and a few versions add θεόν. This seems to be a scribal move to make explicit that τὸν ἀληθινόν is God, perhaps under the influence of John 17:3 (τὸν μόνον ἀληθινὸν θεόν).

5:20. Harnack's conjecture that ὄντες should be added is without manuscript support. In addition, it is unnecessary to make sense of the passage. It should therefore be set aside.

5:20. Instead of concluding the verse with ζωὴ αἰώνιος, a few late uncials and minuscules insert articles to yield ἡ ζωὴ ἡ αἰώνιος. External support is weak, and the reading is easier because the articular expression fits well with οὗτος and ὁ ἀληθινὸς θεός earlier in the verse. It is therefore rightly rejected by NA[27]. Scribes may also have had in mind the description of Jesus as τὴν ζωὴν τὴν αἰώνιον of 1:2, one of only two places in the whole NT where articular ζωή is followed by articular αἰώνιον (the other is 2:25). The reading of Ψ, ζωὴν αἰώνιον παρέχων (bringing about eternal life), seems to be a scribe's attempt to lend a little elegance to John's laconic parataxis.

C. Final Pastoral Appeal (5:21)

From one angle this verse is puzzling. The mention of "idols" is abrupt. This brusque effect is compounded by the absence of any formal doxology or concluding farewell (cf. 2 John 13; 3 John 15 [14b NIV]). Yet NT epistles frequently sound analogous notes of concern and admonition in at least their penultimate lines (Rom. 16:17–20; 1 Cor. 16:13–14; 2 Cor. 13:5, 10; Gal. 6:17; Eph. 6:10–20; Phil. 3:1–2; Col. 4:5; 1 Thess. 5:22; 2 Thess. 3:6–15; 1 Tim. 5:20; Titus 3; Philem. 21; Heb. 13:9, 22; James 5; 1 Pet. 5:8; 2 Pet. 3:17; 2 John 10–11; 3 John 11; Jude 17–23). The "he who has an ear" warnings near the end of the seven letters to the churches of Rev. 1–3 are similar in effect. The Letter of Jeremiah 6:73 in the OT Apocrypha ends with no less of a sudden jolt: "Better therefore is a just man who has no idols, for he will be far from reproach" (RSV). The intended beneficial effect of the whole of 1 John could be swept away if readers are not alert to dangers and diligent to counteract them. These last six words (in Greek) are evidently John's way of rallying them to a proactive appropriation of his message.

Exegesis and Exposition

21Little children, keep ⌜yourselves⌝ from idols. ⌜ ⌝

For the seventh and last time in this epistle, John calls his readers τεκνία (*teknia*, little children; elsewhere 2:1, 12, 28; 3:7, 18; 4:4; see exegesis of 2:12–13). Along with ἀγαπητοί (*agapētoi*, beloved), which occurs six times in 1 John (see exegesis of 2:7), this is a preferred term of endearment. While the epistle lacks a formal concluding greeting, this affectionate noun of direct address does lend a personal touch (cf. Jesus's use of τεκνία in John 13:33). The readers share with John the status of being "children of God" (3:1–2; cf. 3:10; 5:2), since they are all "born of God" (2:29; 3:9; 4:7; 5:1, 4, 18). As their spiritual adviser, if not father, it is appropriate for John to employ a term that is evocative of both his leadership role and the divine parentage and resultant sibling ties shared by readers and writer (cf. Balla 2006: 224). It is possible that John here takes up the pen himself to write a final line after scribal assistance in the rest of the letter (cf. Ellis 2000: 220).

No unusual importance attaches to the imperative translated "keep" (φυλάξετε, *phylaxete*).[1] It is synonymous with τηρέω (*tēreō*, to keep), which appears more frequently in the NT. Either verb can be used with the preposi-

1. Painter 2002: 327 believes that the aorist "suggests a response to the present crisis rather than an ongoing general response."

tion ἀπό (*apo*, from).[2] The interpretative challenge of the verse is posed by mention of "idols" (εἰδώλων, *eidōlōn*). In one sense the meaning is clear. The word is used in the NT to refer to the golden calf to which Israel made sacrifice (Acts 7:41) and more broadly to objects made of wood or stone or metal representing the deities of classical antiquity (15:20; Rom. 2:22; 1 Cor. 8:4, 7; 10:19; 12:2; 1 Thess. 1:9; Rev. 9:20). The gospel demanded that believers make a break with such key components of pagan devotion.

If John is addressing people who have come to Christ from backgrounds of idolatry, perhaps in western Asia Minor and the Ephesus area as tradition maintains,[3] then John uses that background as a foil. "Idols" become for John a central symbol to highlight the commitment that believers owe, not to images of whatever sort, physical or mental or both, but to the doctrine, ethics, and devotion that only the Son of God reveals and defines. Calvin (1988: 315) grasps this thrust: "Godliness is corrupted whenever a corporeal figure is ascribed to God, or whenever statues and pictures are set up for worship." He continues: "Let us therefore remember that we should be so careful to remain in the spiritual worship of God as to banish far from us everything that may turn us aside to gross and carnal superstitions." Calvin's words are directed against the excesses he perceived in Roman Catholic doctrine and practice of his day, but every age can likely find analogous applications.[4]

The word "idol" appears ninety-one times in the LXX, often with ἀπό, which probably reflects Semitic influence (Painter 2002: 327). An idol is what God's people must not worship, according to the second commandment of the Decalogue (Exod. 20:4). There are dozens of references to idols that God's people toyed with or were commanded to abhor. But a survey of the references suggests that Zech. 13:2 may deserve particular attention: "'On that day, I will banish the names of the idols [εἰδώλων] from the land, and they will be remembered no more,' declares the LORD Almighty. 'I will remove both the [false] prophets and the spirit of impurity from the land'" (NIV).

2. Τηρέω + ἀπό occurs in James 1:27, φυλάσσω + ἀπό in Luke 12:15 and 2 Thess. 3:3; cf. Testament of Reuben 4.8. Yet it may be significant that τηρέω + ἀπό meaning "to keep, abstain from, avoid" occurs in the LXX only once (Prov. 7:5), while φυλάσσω + ἀπό bearing the same sense is found numerous times, including passages that warn against contact with defiling, unholy, or dangerous objects or people: Deut. 23:9 (23:10 LXX; impure things); Josh. 6:18 (things devoted to the ban); 1 Sam. 21:4 (21:5 LXX; sexual relations with women); Pss. 18:23 (17:24 LXX; lawlessness, ἀνομία]); 121:7 (120:7 LXX; evil, harm); 141:9 (140:9 LXX; snares of enemies); Sir. 4:20 (evil); 12:11 (a deceptive enemy); 22:13 (a foolish man); Ezek. 33:8 (destructive ways). In the LXX and NT, φυλάσσω + ἀπό seems to be the default idiom for issuing the kind of warning found in 1 John 5:21.

3. Cf. Didymus (in Bray 2000: 229): "There must have been many in that assembly who were former idolaters, and he adds this caution for their benefit." So also Burge 1996: 218 and Painter 2002: 330. Luther 1967: 327 suggests that because of persecution, believers needed encouragement not to return to old ways.

4. Neander, in a mid-19th-century Germany enamored of Idealism and Romanticism, wrote: "Specially appropriate is the application to our own age, whose ruling tendency is deification of Self and deification of the World; an age of conscious apostacy from the only true God" (1852: 319).

Four reasons may be advanced why John's warning in 5:21 can plausibly be tied to Zechariah's prophecy concerning idols. First, John clearly sees himself and his readers as inhabiting the eschatological day of which Zechariah speaks. The Son of God has come, and believers now await only his reappearing before the coming final age. This is seen, second, by the Gospel of John's citation of Zech. 12:10 and probable allusion to 13:7.[5] For John, the coming of Jesus, right down to the spear in his side as he hung from the cross, is specifically foretold in this extended passage (John 19:37). Third, Zechariah says that the coming of this messianic figure will result in removal of "[false] prophets and the spirit of impurity from the land" (Zech. 13:2). Treacherous spirits and the "prophets" through which they would have spoken were clearly issues that John needed to address (1 John 4:1–6). Every reference to aberrant doctrine, ethics, or devotion in this epistle qualifies as "impurity." Fourth, Zechariah like all OT prophets is moved by a vision of God's faithfulness and radiant purity. First John has from the beginning been concerned to set forth and extend a true conception of God (Hilary of Arles in Bray 2000: 229; Holtzmann 1908: 361, calling attention to 1 John 1:5).

Other theories abound for why John ends on what feels to current readers as a peculiar note.[6] It is impossible to know for certain that John had the Zechariah passage in mind. But what it foretells (if we admit the possibility of predictive prophecy in the Bible) does appear to find a measure of fulfillment in Jesus's coming and saving work. It is hard to deny that 5:21 admits of a reading taking Zechariah as relevant background and encouraging believers to work at steering clear of the idols that were ubiquitous fixtures in their culture and the false prophets, the spirits that animated them, and their combined desolating effects. It may be worth recalling that according to Acts 19:18–19, believers in Ephesus clung to their occult paraphernalia for some time following their entrance into the church. Much of 1 Corinthians is taken up by concerns about idols. The Jerusalem Council likewise found it necessary to broach the topic (Acts 15:20, 29; 21:25).

5. Zech. 12:10: "They will look on me, the one they have pierced"; cf. John 19:37: "And, as another scripture says, 'They will look on the one they have pierced.'" Zech. 13:7: "'Awake, O sword, against my shepherd, against the man who is close to me!' declares the Lord Almighty. 'Strike the shepherd, and the sheep will be scattered'"; cf. John 16:32: "But a time is coming, and has come, when you will be scattered, each to his own home. You will leave me all alone." (All quotations from the NIV.)

6. Holtzmann 1908: 361 suggests gnosticism as a background. He also suggests that mention of idols might have been precipitated by 5:20's focus on the "true" God. Marshall 1978: 255 points to the possibility that John had in mind false conceptions of God. Thompson 1992: 148 writes: "The idols here are not pagan deities or images of stone or wood. An idol is a false picture of God." Or, as in many Dead Sea Scrolls, idolatry may here be simply a synonym for sin (Sloyan 1995: 59). But this would be to end on a flatly moralistic note inconsistent with the rest of the epistle. Kruse 2000: 202, drawing on R. Brown, points out that there are nearly a dozen possible explanations of what John means by idols. No single proposal is likely to command universal assent.

Positively, 1 John 5:21 clears the ground to implement the message of 1 John in a robust way (cf. Strecker 1996: 214). "Reject the false and embrace the real" (Akin 2001: 215). Undistracted and unencumbered by the Christ-substitutes that for so long literally bedeviled God's people, believers are now freed to walk in the truth: the light, the faith, the love, and the eternal life won for them by the Son of God.

Additional Notes

5:21. NA[27] reads ἑαυτά, which agrees in gender (neuter) with τεκνία earlier in the verse. Some manuscripts introduce a *constructio ad sensum* by reading the masculine (and therefore more overtly personal) ἑαυτούς. The neuter is preferable on both external grounds and as the harder reading.

5:21. External support for the omission of ἀμήν is decisive. If it were original, there is no accounting for its uniform absence among earlier copies in the tradition.

2 John

Introduction to 2 John and 3 John

Quite apart from canonical placement and John's name in the title of Greek manuscripts, 2 John and 3 John read enough like 1 John in vocabulary and diction that common authorship is a reasonable assumption on which to proceed (R. Brown 1982: 755–56; 1997: 395; Painter 2002: 336; Thielman 2005: 536n1; Witherington 2006: 396, 564).[1] L. Johnson (1999: 560–61) suggests that 2 John and 3 John were originally preserved because they were part of a single three-letter shipment containing all three Johannine Letters. He proposes that 3 John was a recommendation letter to Gaius, commending the courier of the shipment, Demetrius (3 John 12). Second John was to be read aloud to Gaius's church. First John, in Johnson's view, was a hortatory homily and "not really a letter at all" (1999: 562). This is all debatable, but the theory of a single packet for the three documents (arguably all letters) simplifies the circumstances of their origin and distribution. It is no less likely, and less speculative, than many other theories of the composition and audiences of the letters. It is a plausible scenario that will be loosely assumed below.

The author of 2 John and 3 John calls himself "the Elder" (2 John 1; 3 John 1). In NT times and into the postapostolic era, the word "elders" (πρεσβύτεροι, *presbyteroi*) could refer to the pastoral leaders of local congregations. They appear by this title first in Acts 11:30, which speaks of church leaders (pastors) in Jerusalem in the mid-40s (for chronology, see Carson and Moo 2005: 369; the year is given as 44 in Schnabel 2004: 2.1019–20). Paul and Barnabas appointed elders as overseers and ministers in the churches they planted in the next few years (Acts 14:23). Elders presided at the Jerusalem Council in approximately 49 alongside the apostles (15:2, 4, 6, 22, 23; 16:4). Nearly a decade later Paul addressed the elders, apparently the pastors of churches at and probably around Ephesus (20:17). Elders at Jerusalem are alongside head

1. For discussion of scholarship on 2 John, see "Introduction to the Johannine Letters." For my conclusion that the author of 1 John was John son of Zebedee, Jesus's disciple, whose writing activity may be placed in the area of Ephesus in the final decades of the first century and perhaps as late as approximately 100, see "Setting and Date." For thoughts on the message of 2 John and 3 John taken together with 1 John, see "The Significance of John's Letters."

elder James (who elsewhere is called an apostle; Gal. 1:19) when Paul reports back to the church at the end of the third missionary journey (Acts 21:18). Unless Luke is guilty of anachronism in all this, the evidence shows that the title "elder" for pastoral leaders at Ephesus had been in use for twenty to forty years by the time 2 John and 3 John were written and was widely employed elsewhere in the early church, particularly around Jerusalem but also in distant areas like Ephesus.[2]

Peter, addressing churches around Ephesus ("Asia") as well as congregations in numerous other areas (Pontus, Galatia, Cappadocia, Bithynia; 1 Pet. 1:1), calls himself a "fellow elder" (5:1: συμπρεσβύτερος, *sympresbyteros*) alongside other "elders" (πρεσβύτεροι). This indicates not only the widespread geographical usage of the term but also the fluid relation between *apostles* like Peter and John and perhaps James, who were in a sense the church's foundation, and the *pastors* of the early Christian decades, the local field officers as it were. People called "apostles" (James, Peter, John) also served in pastoral capacities. While Paul is never called an "elder," his pastoral identity and role are undeniable (P. Beasley-Murray, *DPL* 654–58; Schreiner 2001: 38; for Schreiner, however, Paul's missionary identity predominates). He understands himself as a διάκονος (*diakonos*, servant, minister), a term he also applies to Timothy, who pastors at Ephesus (1 Tim. 4:6; cf. 1 Thess. 3:2).

Given this usage, and the relative literary homogeneity of 1–3 John, it seems reasonable to view the author of all three letters as one person, who in calling himself "the elder" in 2–3 John is simply affirming his pastoral self-understanding and probably public identity, as Peter does in 1 Pet. 5:1 (cf. Akin 2001: 219). This does not somehow disqualify either Peter or John from being identified as Jesus's disciples and apostles (cf. Holtzmann 1908: 364). John's pastoral style and concerns are evident throughout 1 John (see "The Significance of John's Letters" in the introduction to 1 John). John called himself "the elder" in 2–3 John because that is, in large measure, what he was and how he understood himself at the time of writing and in that locale (Ephesus?). We do not know why he did not call himself "the elder" or why he did not name himself explicitly in 1 John, where the familiar tone and numerous first-person verbs nevertheless suggest that he was known to his readers. Perhaps John intended for 1 John to be circulated beyond the single church to which it was first sent, the "elect lady" of 2 John. He was not "the pastor" to those other churches, so he did not identify himself by that term in the document he composed for wider distribution.

Eusebius, who is rightly credited with discovering an "Elder John" in addition to the apostle by that name in the writings of Papias (see pp. 14–15 in

2. Painter 2002: 339 discounts all the Acts parallels, observing: "Acts refers to elders, but to no singular Elder (*the* Elder)." Besides being an argument from silence, this misses the point that John the apostle may not have called himself "the Elder" until circumstances took him to Ephesus, where he assumed a new pastoral charge. We cannot demand of Acts, which covers 30–62, precisely the same linguistic usage that appears to have emerged in connection with John in subsequent years. On the origin and rise of the office of elder/pastor, with stress on its roots in Judaism, see Beckwith 2003.

the introduction),[3] knows full well that in the early generations of the church an apostle could also be called an elder. Papias, whom Eusebius quotes in *Eccl. Hist.* 3.39.3–4, uses the term "elder" to designate Jesus's first followers, including Andrew, Peter, Philip, Thomas, James, and John—all members of the apostolic circle. There is no compelling exegetical reason to go along with the spin Eusebius tries to put on this, making the "elders" people different from the apostles; he betrays his own argument by later equating the elders and apostles (3.39.4). In Eusebius's account, Papias then speaks of subsequent elders like Aristion and John, who are still alive and speaking (λέγουσιν, *legousin*). But as already explained, Eusebius, like others following Origen's amillenarian lead, needed to find a John of early times to whom to attribute the putatively millenarian book of Revelation. Whereas Dionysius seized on the language of Revelation to do this, Eusebius stretched the language of Papias.

Bray (2000: xx) perceptively observes that things have not progressed too far beyond all this in contemporary studies: "Literary considerations" like those adduced by Dionysius and Eusebius "are still the strongest arguments for those who deny the traditional ascriptions of authorship" to 2–3 John, while "those who defend" their Johannine origin "still use the historical argument that there is no compelling alternative explanation that obliges us to reject the tradition." The tradition—which is to say, the historical evidence, as opposed to literary theorizing—weighs heavier on the side of attributing 2–3 John to John, the author of 1 John and of the Fourth Gospel.

Next to 3 John, 2 John is the shortest book in the NT. Travelers sometimes joke about driving through a town so small that they missed it because they blinked. The reader of the Catholic Epistles can easily turn from the Petrine Epistles and 1 John to Jude and Revelation without even noticing 2 John, which fills one page plus eight lines in the compact format of NA[27]. What is remarkable is how much ground is covered, given the letter's terseness. As to the number of words, one can ask why the author bothered to write at all. But as to weight of words, one wishes the author had lingered longer over, expanded upon, and fleshed out virtually every clause. Reading 2 John is not simply like hearing one side of a phone conversation: it is like hearing one side of a phone conversation that is bleeding in and out of your phone from the cellular transmission of someone else. We are often not quite sure of the

3. Dionysius of Alexander (cited in Eusebius, *Eccl. Hist.* 7.24.7; 7.25.16) proposes that some other John wrote Revelation. But he never calls this other John an "elder"—that connection remained for Eusebius to propose. Nor does Dionysius give any serious historical evidence for the existence of this John; his argument is based on Revelation's language, which is somewhat different (not drastically, given Revelation's genre and subject matter) from John's other writings. His evidential warrant is hearsay: he "thinks" some other John did exist, since "they say" that "there are said to be" two tombs at Ephesus, each of which is called John's. This speculation from ca. 250 is tenuous to say the least. It is best viewed as a desperate expedient to find someone ancient to whom to attribute Revelation, a millenarian-sounding treatise for which the Alexandrian wing of the church was by that time losing its appetite as far as its chiliastic overtones were concerned.

one side we can hear, let alone the other side of which we can detect virtually nothing with certainty.

What we can detect is a pastoral writer effusive in his affection yet also in his concern for his readers. Affection comes to the fore in verbs or nouns for "love" (four occurrences in the first six verses). Concern is reflected in the fivefold reference to truth in the opening four verses. When seen in the light of subsequent references to false teachings and teachers, this signals the writer's apprehension that the church he addresses is in danger of going significantly astray. He will be there soon, so there is no need to write at length (2 John 12). But there is need to write. Things can go downhill fast in congregational life once deterioration sets in. Hence, he composes 2 John, which unlike 1 John is unmistakably epistolary in genre based on its prominent formal aspects: greetings, well-wishes, body, and closing (see R. Brown 1982: 788–95). The communiqué can be outlined as follows:

I. Greeting: John's love in truth (1–3)
II. John's joy yet concern (4–8)
III. John's warning (9–11)
IV. John's farewell (12–13)

I. Greeting: John's Love in Truth (1–3)

The preponderance of love language noted in 1 John, and dominant too in John's Gospel when compared with the Synoptics, strikes the reader from the very first verse of 2 John. But so does a conundrum, from today's standpoint: who is this "elect lady" (KJV, ESV, NRSV), "lady/Lady chosen by God" (TNIV, NEB), "very special woman" (CEV), or "dear Lady" (TEV)? "She" presumably knew, but interpreters today are less certain. Moreover, she is spoken of as having children; is this literal or metaphorical? (For succinct airing of the issues, see Akin 2001: 220n4.) Beyond such questions, what emerges is an author voicing ardent affection and at the same time zeal for truth. "Even in wishing them blessing, he cites the two great components truth and love, which together are the sign of genuinely constituted Christian existence" (Schlatter 1950: 115). This is truth within a particular framework: several key terms like "grace," "mercy," and "peace," in conjunction with reference to God the Father and Jesus Christ, point to a strong theological consciousness. Both as a human being with affections and a pastoral guardian with convictions, the author has thoughts and sentiments too urgent, in view of circumstances largely invisible to us, not to send in advance of a coming personal visit.

Exegesis and Exposition

⌜Second John⌝

1 The elder, [writing] to an elect assembly and to its children, whom I love in truth—
and not I alone but also all who have come to know the truth. 2 ⌜For the truth⌝ ⌜abiding⌝
among ⌜us⌝ will also be with ⌜us⌝ forever. 3 Grace, ⌜mercy⌝, peace ⌜will be with us⌝, from
God the Father and ⌜from⌝ Jesus Christ ⌜the Son of the Father⌝, in truth and love.

"The elder," as explained above, can be taken to be the John who wrote 1 John and for that matter the Fourth Gospel. Sloyan (1995: 61) notes the similarity of situation assumed by 1–3 John plus indications of "a community well familiar with John's Gospel." But John writes here in an overtly pastoral role, "elder" being an early church term for local congregational overseer. That he writes from the location of a "sister church" is clear from 2 John 13.

But to whom is he writing? Is ἐκλεκτῇ κυρίᾳ (*eklektē kyria*, chosen lady) the proper name of a lady ("Kyria"), with "chosen" as a modifier? (R. Brown 1982: 653 points out that "Eklecta" is unattested as a name at this time.) This view goes back to Clement of Alexandria's *Adumbrations* 4 (Bray 2000: 231) and is also reflected in a Syriac version (Westcott 1883: 224). Among commentators,

Alexander (1901: 283–86) takes this position, with great imaginative powers sketching her as a lonely but noble widow of heroic stature. Marshall (1978: 60n5) cites some older scholars who follow suit. A parallel might be Rom. 16:13, where Paul writes, "Greet Rufus, the chosen [τὸν ἐκλεκτόν, *ton eklekton*] in the Lord." Since 2 John lacks the definite article before "chosen," however, Rom. 16:13 is not a good parallel (Painter 2002: 340 and many others).

If neither ἐκλεκτῇ nor κυρίᾳ is apt to be a personal name, the possibility raised and rightly rejected by Loader (1992: 84–85) that this refers to a prominent Christian sister is unlikely. Apart from the unsuitedness of either of the words for this purpose, the discourse in the epistle shifts so frequently to second-person plural that most likely a group, not an individual, is being addressed.

More likely the words simply refer to a congregation. "It is now generally agreed that this title refers to a sister church" (Culpepper 1998: 276; cf. R. Brown 1982: 654–55; O'Day 1992: 375; Witherington 2006: 563–64).[1] Thompson (1992: 151) points out that the people of God, whether Israel or the church, are frequently referred to in Scripture as a woman or bride, whether of God or of Christ (Isa. 54:1, 6, 13; Jer. 6:2; 31:21, 32; John 3:29; Gal. 4:25–26; Eph. 5:22; Rev. 18–19). First Peter refers to "elect" (ἐκλεκτοῖς, *eklektois*) sojourners (1:1) as the author writes from a "co-elect" (συνεκλεκτή, *syneklektē*) congregation in "Babylon"—likely Rome (5:13)—showing that ἐκλεκτή can denote a local church (R. Brown 1982: 655). The Greek word κυρία (*kyria*, lady) could also refer to a unit of civic organization comprised of multiple assemblies (ἐκκλησίαι, *ekklēsiai*, the plural form of the word often translated "church" in the NT).[2] With κυρία John may be using not a metaphorical but an actual word for a local congregation that is not attested elsewhere in early Christian writings. In any case we have here simply a "chosen congregation."

The "children" (τέκνα, *tekna*) of the group (see also 2 John 4, 13; 3 John 4) would be the church members. In 1 John the term is always used to refer to "children of God" (3:1, 2, 10; 5:2). First John addresses readers as "children" seven times (2:1, 12, 28; 3:7, 18; 4:4; 5:21), using, however, not τέκνα (from τέκνον) but τεκνίον (*teknion*, little child; see exegesis of 1 John 2:1a).

John immediately affirms his love for his readers, in a rhetorical flourish that is at once awkward and elegant. It is elegant in that "love" and "truth" stand at the head of John's statement ("whom I love in truth," a phrase artfully unpacked in Akin 2001: 220–21), while the same words in reverse order stand at the end of the section (2 John 3: "in truth and love"). There is perhaps also a certain elegance in the loftiness of rhetoric throughout this section, framed by "love" fore and aft, dotted with "truth" (four times in three verses), and reinforced midway through with the "grace, mercy, peace" of a classic Christian

1. A rare recent writer arguing that 2 John is written to an individual woman is Callahan 2005: 2, 11. But he gives no reason other than that women of the Order of the Eastern Star, part of the Prince Hall order of Masons, favor this view.

2. Strecker and Schnelle 1996: 2.1442 call attention to passages from Aristotle and Aristophanes. Cf. Sloyan 1995: 62–63; other references in Strecker 1996: 221.

greeting. At the same time a certain awkwardness inheres—just what is "truth" in each of these four occurrences? And why the slightly peculiar word order: τὴν ἀλήθειαν τὴν μένουσαν ἐν ἡμῖν καὶ μεθ' ἡμῶν ἔσται (*tēn alētheian tēn menousan en hēmin kai meth' hēmōn estai*, the truth abiding among us also with us will be)?[3] And why the future indicative ἔσται in the greeting instead of the implied subjunctive of εἰμί (*eimi*, to be) common in Paul (e.g., Rom. 1:7; 1 Cor. 1:3; 2 Cor. 1:2; Phil. 1:2) or the optative of πληθύνω (*plēthynō*, to increase) found in Peter's greetings (1 Pet. 1:2; 2 Pet. 1:2)? The same combination of sublime reference and slightly peculiar diction that 1 John features is also present in 2 John's opening lines.

John loves his readers, at any rate, "in truth" (2 John 1). This could simply mean "really" or "truly" (cf. Turner 1963: 178, who also cites Zerwick's suggestion that articular "truth" refers specifically to Christ). Or it could mean "according to the demands of revealed truth" (Zerwick 1993: 734). R. Brown (1982: 655–56) speaks of "a major discussion" surrounding this question and concludes that to love "in truth" refers to "a love based on a revelation of God in Jesus Christ who is the truth." John is not alone in this sentiment. "All who know the truth" (= know Christ?) join him. This likely refers first to fellow believers[4] from whose midst John writes and then by extension to "all" those in the early Christian movement that by this time had spread across much of the Roman Empire and beyond. John's is not a lone voice, and by stating this he amplifies the weight of the epistle's counsel.

His assurance packs punch because the truth presently "abiding" with them is not just for the present time but for all eternity. We should pause here to entertain Pilate's question, "What is truth?" (John 18:38). The Johannine Epistles contain numerous references to ἀλήθεια (*alētheia*, truth), ἀληθής (*alēthēs*, true), and ἀληθινός (*alēthinos*, true) and the reality underlying these terms (1 John 1:6, 8; 2:4, 8, 21 [2x]; 3:18, 19; 4:6; 5:6; 2 John 1 [2x], 2, 3, 4; 3 John 1, 3 [2x], 4, 8, 12). No single definition explains every occurrence. The references (all of which have correlates in John's Gospel) seem to fit into the following categories:

1. Truth is possessed and imparted by the Holy Spirit (1 John 2:20), who is truth (4:6; 5:6; 3 John 12; cf. John 14:17; 15:26; 16:13a).
2. Truth refers to the ethical standards that God has established for his people as expressed in his commandments (1 John 1:6; 2:21a; 3:18; 2 John 4; 3 John 3b, 4; cf. "doing the truth" in John 3:21; also 8:32; 14:15, 23; 15:10, 14).

3. Zerwick 1994: §375 calls attention to the repeated use of an analogous construction in Revelation. BDF §442.6 sees the joining of this clause with the next using καί as "Hebraizing (and slovenly vernacular)." See also BDF §468.3.

4. The perfect participle οἱ ἐγνωκότες (*hoi egnōkotes*, those who know) may describe the settled conviction of those who have embraced the gospel message that John explicates in 1 John. For a lengthy excursus, see Strecker 1996: 222–26.

3. Truth is God's revealed and personal sanctifying presence that gives the believer the capacity to reflect God's character traits, like love and aversion to sin (1 John 1:8; 2:4, 21b; cf. John 1:14, 17; 4:23–24; 8:32; 16:7; 17:17a, 19).
4. Truth refers to the quality of conformity to the way things are in God's omniscient wisdom (1 John 2:8; cf. John 5:33; 8:40, 44a, 45, 46).
5. Truth refers to the gospel of Jesus Christ, its implications, and the sphere of eternal life into which the gospel ushers those who embrace it (1 John 3:19; 2 John 1b, 2, 3; 3 John 1, 8; cf. John 14:6; 16:13b; 17:17b; 18:37a).

If this breakdown holds true, then the opening verses of 2 John extend to readers the assurance that the truth to which they have entrusted their souls by believing the gospel message is as alive, stable, and enduring as Christ himself, who is the truth (cf. John 14:6).[5] John's use of ἔσται to confirm this assurance in 2 John 2 is followed immediately by the same word beginning 2 John 3, the center of John's formal greeting.

He does not express a wish for the readers, as is typical for Paul (usually "grace and peace to you"), but rather uses a future indicative to state what will surely be: "Grace, mercy, peace will be with us." Since "truth" in 2 John 2 abides and "will be" eternally with readers, it is reasonable to see "grace, mercy, peace," which also "will be with" them, as to some extent unpacking what John means by "truth." While the triad may be somewhat conventional (1 Tim. 1:2; 2 Tim. 1:2; cf. Jude 2), none of the three terms is common in John's Letters. "Grace" (χάρις, *charis*) is found elsewhere in the Johannine corpus only in John 1:14, 16 (2x), 17 and at the beginning and end of Revelation (1:4; 22:21). "Mercy" (ἔλεος, *eleos*) occurs only here in that corpus. "Peace" (εἰρήνη, *eirēnē*) is almost as rare, occurring only in Jesus's last words to the Eleven (John 14:27 [2x]; 16:33), in a greeting from the resurrected Christ ("peace to you"; 20:19, 21, 26), in a greeting from John on Patmos (Rev. 1:4), in a description of the red horse of the tribulation (6:4), and in a closing blessing on Gaius (3 John 15 [14b NIV]). We may take the words as pointing to God's unmerited favor to his people, his willingness to pardon their sin, and his abiding hand of blessing, each long-revered aspects of God's covenant love (cf. Num. 14:18; Isa. 26:3). Akin (2001: 222) finds the word order significant: "God's grace is always prior. Mercy and peace flow from it."[6]

5. Rensberger 2001: 110 reduces truth mainly to "the particular understanding of Jesus held by the elder and his party." This makes sense if one sees in 2 John primarily a revelation of internecine partisanship.

6. Rensberger 2001: 109 views this as "a standard phrase in early Christian letters, so there is no point in trying to work out distinct meanings for each of the terms." This overlooks John's nonstandard use of these terms (pointed out by Kruse 2000: 206; also Strecker 1996: 227). It is possible that John viewed God's "grace, mercy, and peace" with actual relish rather than ennui, making this not a boring set phrase but a fresh expression of personal conviction and apostolic creativity.

John points to the origin of this threefold favorable regard: it is "from God the Father and from Jesus Christ the Son of the Father" (2 John 3). The gospel message, believed, mediates eternal heavenly favor from the same OT God appealed to in John's Gospel and 1 John. The theocentric and christocentric focus of 1 John continues here. For that reason we may see the Holy Spirit, prominent in John, as implicitly present, too. John is Trinitarian but not pedantically so, particularly when the Spirit's task is to point to the Son and Father (John 16:14–15). "In truth and love" reflects John's conviction that there is a theological norm ("truth") grounded in God's wisdom suffused with an agapic quality ("love") innate to God's being (1 John 4:8). The truth and love of Father and Son establish a framework within which, John is certain, God's grace, mercy, and peace will be at work among Christ's followers. On this basis it is understandable that John moves next to expressing joy—tinged, however, with apprehension.

Additional Notes

Title/Superscription. Most manuscripts carry the title "John's Second Epistle," with K and minuscule 614 adding "Catholic." But most manuscripts are of late vintage. The reading of 049 can be set aside as otherwise unattested: "Second Epistle of the Same [John]." Almost as rare is the title found in uncial L: "Second Epistle of the Holy Apostle John the Theologian." NA[27] opts for the shorter reading ΙΩΑΝΝΟΥ Β΄ (*iōannou b΄*, Second John), though of the four witnesses listed, all uncials, only 048 contains exactly this reading.

2. A scant half dozen minuscules along with a sparse selection of versions and Cassiodorus follow Ψ in omitting the prepositional phrase διὰ τὴν ἀλήθειαν. This is weak external evidence. The error could be due to homoioteleuton. Or a scribe may have felt that the phrase was repetitious and was there due to an earlier scribal error, in which case leaving it out would have been a slight improvement.

2. While NA[27] has the truth "abiding" (μένουσαν, *menousan*) in the readers, two uncials (A, 048) read ἐνοικοῦσαν (*enoikousan*, dwelling). This is unconvincing external evidence, and forms of the verb ἐνοικέω (*enoikeō*, to dwell) are otherwise limited to Paul in NT writings (Rom. 8:11; 2 Cor. 6:16; Col. 3:16; 2 Tim. 1:5, 14). A few minuscules and the Coptic version read οὖσαν, but like another variant, which omits μένουσαν altogether, this is no real challenge to the preponderance and likelihood of the NA[27] reading.

2. Instead of the truth dwelling "among us" (ἐν ἡμῖν), a few manuscripts (including P and 81) read "among you." This is an example of insignificant confusion between the first-person and second-person plural forms of the personal pronoun.

2. Minuscule 81 and a Vulgate manuscript read "with you" (μεθ' ὑμῶν) instead of NA[27]'s "with us." This is an obvious scribal miscue.

3. Confusion between forms of ἡμεῖς and ὑμεῖς explains why two minuscules and a smattering of versions read "will be with you" instead of "will be with us." Minuscule 81 leads the way in opting for the second-person form throughout this section (see two previous additional notes). Following 81 are a few Latin and Bohairic Coptic witnesses. But the second-person version is no more likely to be original than the complete omission of "will be with us" (μεθ' ἡμῶν ἔσται) from Codex A, several minuscules, and the Harklean Syriac. External evidence starting with ℵ and B points clearly to "with us."

3. For the few manuscripts (including 630 and 1505) that omit "will be with us," the first word of 2 John 3 becomes χάρις. These witnesses compensate for the omission by inserting ὑμῖν καί after "grace," so that John writes, "Grace to you and." This is a fine Pauline greeting but not the prose of the Elder.

3. Witnesses offer several possibilities after χάρις ἔλεος εἰρήνη: (1) "From God the Father and from the Lord Christ" (παρὰ κυρίου χριστοῦ). The evidence here, including 𝔐 and the second corrector of א, looks late and secondary. (2) "From God the Father and the Lord Christ" (omitting παρά before κυρίου). The only weighty witness for this rare reading is א*. This is too slender to be likely. (3) "From God the Father and from Christ." This has extremely weak support among the witnesses. (4) "From God the Father and from Jesus Christ" (παρὰ ἰησοῦ χριστοῦ). The support of uncials including A and B along with key minuscules leads NA[27] to select this last option, which may best explain the other readings, although the decision can hardly be definitive given the evidence.

3. The word order of NA[27]'s τοῦ υἱοῦ τοῦ πατρός is slightly different in a couple of very insignificant manuscript groups. Ψ and a very few minuscules omit the first τοῦ from the phrase. One minuscule (945) and Cassiodorus omit τοῦ πατρός. Another minuscule (1881) replaces πατρός with θεός to yield τοῦ υἱοῦ τοῦ θεοῦ. NA[27] has the preponderance of manuscript evidence on its side.

I. Greeting: John's Love in Truth (1–3)
➤ II. John's Joy yet Concern (4–8)
III. John's Warning (9–11)
IV. John's Farewell (12–13)

II. John's Joy yet Concern (4–8)

In dense formulations highly reminiscent of 1 John (Holtzmann 1908: 365), this section articulates John's joy that his readers are living in obedience to God. But beyond the joy lies a concern, first, that their good beginning extend in breadth and intensity. The claim and work of the gospel in believers' lives does not permit complacency, stagnation, and self-satisfaction. Rather, just as Paul commended the Thessalonians' active faith and love, yet goaded them to excel still more (1 Thess. 1:3; 4:1, 10), so John commends his readers' progress to date, yet underscores the imperative to continue forging onward.

A second area of concern relates to false doctrine and its purveyors. Just as many antichrists and false prophets have gone forth (cf. 1 John 2:18; 4:1), so have many deceivers. John exhorts readers that they have all come too far to throw away their reward now. The problem seems to be that an entailment of the false doctrine has been relational and ethical lapse.

Exegesis and Exposition

[4]I rejoiced exceedingly that I came across some of your children walking in the
truth, just as ⸢we received⸣ commandment from the Father. [5]And now I request you, as
the church, that we love one another—not as ⸢writing a new commandment to you⸣,
just the one we had from the outset. [6]And here is what I mean by love: that we live in
keeping with his commandments. And here ⸢is what I mean by commandment⸣: ⸢ ⸣
just as you heard from the start, ⸢that⸣ you live by it. [7]For many deceivers ⸢have gone
out⸣ into the world. They do not confess Jesus Christ as coming in the flesh. This is
the deceiver and ⸢the⸣ antichrist. [8]Watch yourselves so that you do not ⸢lose⸣ what
⸢we have worked for⸣ but ⸢may receive⸣ a full reward.

John states (2 John 4) that he rejoiced[1] λίαν (*lian*, exceedingly). The word is not common in the NT (twelve times) and occurs elsewhere in John's writings only at 3 John 3.[2] John must have been truly pleased. Jesus is depicted as having "rejoiced" at the opportunity for glorifying God occasioned by Lazarus's death (John 11:15), the only first-person use of χαίρω (*chairō*, to rejoice) in the Gospels. Paul expresses his personal joy using this expression in some eight different passages (Rom. 16:19; 1 Cor. 16:17; 2 Cor. 7:9, 16; Phil. 1:18; 2:17;

1. On the passive form ἐχάρην (*echarēn*, I rejoiced) being used with middle force, see Caragounis 2006: 153.

2. Λίαν is, however, frequent in the apostolic fathers (over three dozen occurrences), especially in the Shepherd of Hermas.

4:10; Col. 1:24). It could be that John's intense happiness helped precipitate the penning of this note.

But this is joy for a particular reason. John encountered (εὕρηκα, *heurēka*) people affiliated with the congregation to which he writes ("some of your children"; on "children" in the sense of church members or children of God, see exegesis of 2 John 1–3). In the same way that Chloe's people relayed information to Paul (1 Cor. 1:11), these individuals may have informed John of conditions in their congregation requiring apostolic attention. The respective constructions are similar: in both cases a prepositional phrase functions as a noun (3 John 4: ἐκ τῶν τέκνων σου, *ek tōn teknōn sou*, [some] of your children;[3] 1 Cor. 1:11: ὑπὸ τῶν χλόης, *hypo tōn chloēs*, [some] from Chloe). What cheered John about these individuals was their circumspect lives: they were "walking in the truth," the fourth and final mention of truth in this epistle (see exegesis of 2 John 1–3). "The phrase reveals an author whose idioms are influenced by Semitic language" (Painter 2002: 346). In the same way that David told God, "I walked before you in truth and with a full [= perfect] heart" (περιεπάτησα ἐνώπιόν σου ἐν ἀληθείᾳ καὶ ἐν καρδίᾳ πλήρει, *periepatēsa enōpion sou en alētheia kai en kardia plērei*; 2 Kings 20:3), John credits these believers with walking in an exemplary manner (for this metaphor, see exegesis of 1 John 1:6–7; 2:6, 11; for parallels in Jewish literature, see R. Brown 1982: 662). It is unfounded to infer from this that "the truth is not something one knows; it is something one does" (Callahan 2005: 11), since John has just stressed knowledge of the truth (2 John 1) and the abiding presence of the truth in and among believers (2 John 2). Rightly stressing the conjunction of "doctrine and duty, creed and conduct" is Akin (2001: 225).

John's personal joy is more than a matter of personal preference: they are walking "just as we received commandment from the Father." This probably means that they were living in compliance with divine commands in general, a concern much in evidence in 1 John (see exegesis of 1 John 2:3). Since commandments "from the Father" in John's Gospel are divine ordinances received and passed along by Jesus (e.g., 10:18; 12:49; 14:31), this is indirect evidence of John's belief in the Son's divinity.

In 2 John 5 John shifts from the sterling example of the people he has encountered to their home congregation, John's addressees. The opening words καὶ νῦν (*kai nyn*, and now) take the situation of 2 John 4 and make it the basis for exhortation: John requests "that we love one another." There are several notable ecclesial dimensions latent in this plea. First, this is a request, not a decree. Paul uses a similar mode of address with the same Greek verb ἐρωτάω (*erōtaō*, to request) in Phil. 4:3; 1 Thess. 4:1; 5:12; 2 Thess. 2:1. The leadership being exercised here is consensual.[4] Second, John addresses them as a single

3. Turner 1963: 209 notes that this use of ἐκ is rare in Classical Greek but common in the LXX.

4. Akin 2001: 218 thinks John's request comes with "an imperatival force" due to its proximity to the repeated use of "command" nearby in the discourse.

unit, σέ (*se*, you [singular]). This is reminiscent of Paul viewing large numbers of individual Christians as nevertheless a single body (e.g., 1 Cor. 12). The church having many members is nonetheless one. Third, John calls readers κυρία (*kyria*, lady; cf. the exegesis of 2 John 1–3), a respectful term continuing the idea of corporate identity and perhaps by virtue of its feminine gender evoking associations with other feminine words for "church" (e.g., ἐκκλησία [*ekklēsia*, church]; also νύμφη [*nymphē*, bride] in Rev. 21:2, 9; 22:17]). It is difficult to translate to sensible effect; I have rendered it "as the church" (set off by commas to preserve a vocative feel by making the phrase appositional to "you") to avoid the awkward sound of lexical glosses like "lady" or "mistress" and to reflect John's apparent vision here of all his readers constituting a single ecclesial entity. "As the church" is not an ideal translation, but a direct equivalent in English is elusive—"folks," for example, is too quaint, and "people" carries pejorative overtones. Fourth, the elder addresses them in a pastoral mode with a de facto hortatory subjunctive: let us "love one another." He does not launch an imperative in their direction[5] but includes himself in the call to renewed interpersonal devotion. This is collegial or familial (cf. Painter 2002: 348) rather than bureaucratic appeal. "He writes with authority and yet with a father's warmth" (Schnackenburg 1992: 276).

Sandwiched between 2 John 5's opening address and its concluding exhortation is a parenthesis of definition. It is not as if[6] John is writing a "new commandment" (see exegesis of 1 John 2:7–8); he is rather calling to mind one of the rudiments of living out eternal life in the community Christ founded, of which John was part (hence he speaks of the command "we had from the outset"—John was there; see Schnackenburg 1992: 282). Accordingly his readers are to love each other too. Of course this was a leading motif of Jesus's final discourse in John's Gospel (13:34). It is hard to say whether John mentions this because the members he had encountered (2 John 4) were so loving that they prompted John to use their high achievement to rally their home congregation or whether they were perhaps zealous for truth and confessional fidelity in various ways but left something to be desired in their relational focus. In the latter case John has diagnosed from the traveling members a deficiency that the home congregation needs to correct, particularly at a juncture (2 John 7) where doctrinal error threatens spiritual and ethical integrity.

Second John 5 speaks of commandment and love, in that order; 2 John 6 completes a chiasm by touching on each in the opposite sequence. "And here is what I mean by love" in my translation interprets the bare καὶ αὕτη ἐστὶν ἡ ἀγάπη (*kai hautē estin hē agapē*, lit., and this is love) as underscoring not some abstract concept but the love called for in 2 John 5. The clause thus forms a bridge from the exhortation to love (expressed with ἵνα + subjunctive) at the

5. On the frequent and effective "mitigation" of imperatives in John's Letters, see Culy 2004: xviii–xx.

6. The construction using οὐχ ὡς (*ouch hōs*, not as) here "gives the subjective motivation of the subject of the discourse" (BDF §425.3).

end of 2 John 5 to the corresponding exhortation (also a clause with ἵνα + subjunctive) to "live [lit., walk] in keeping with his commandments" in 2 John 6. (For the use of ἵνα here, see Turner 1963: 139.)

The plural "commandments" is significant. It points beyond any single directive—the love command, for example—and rules out a reductionist understanding of John's counsel, as if his concern were merely to incite human concern and compassion. He is not speaking merely of the love command (the view of most commentators; but see Schlatter 1950: 115–16).[7] We saw throughout 1 John that John is consistently, one might even say incessantly, engaged in calling believers to full-orbed confessional (doctrinal), behavioral (ethical), and relational (devotional) integrity before God. His readers are not free to pick the aspect they like best and collapse the whole gospel into it.

John completes the chiasm that spans 2 John 5–6 with the words "this is the commandment" (αὕτη ἡ ἐντολή ἐστιν, *hautē hē entolē estin*).[8] It would be possible to try to understand a reference to the love command, but there is a stronger case to be made for a different twist. Here John wishes not to underscore *which* commandment is primal and foremost but *that* the command structure of Christian experience is nonnegotiable. As articular "love" earlier in the verse was not "the love," so here John is not speaking of "the commandment"; he is rather using the article to connote a quality associated with ἐντολή of which his readers need to be reminded. Gospel-minded readers had heard "from the start" of their life of faith in Christ that discipleship involves obedience to revealed truths. Both repentance of sin and faith in Christ involve deference to counterintuitive claims with heavenly rootage but human conveyance (which is not to discount the Holy Spirit but to concede that he uses means). Absent this orientation, the Christian faith portrayed in the NT would never have arisen. In 2 John 6, John underscores that by "commandment," he means, among other things, "live by it." *Do* what God, Christ, and the faith that they engender stipulate! "By it" enjoys emphatic placement in Greek. Parameters revealed by God by and through Christ (and means endorsed by Christ, like the OT Scriptures and leading luminaries of the divine economy, whether OT prophets or NT apostles) are to be hallowed in practical living. Once again John uses a form of περιπατέω (*peripateō*, to walk) to make his point. But whereas 2 John 5 addressed readers as "you" singular, 2 John 6 terminates with "live by it" in the plural. John's counsel applies to the group as a whole and to every single one of its members.

7. See also Holtzmann 1908: 366, who perceptively notes, "The only way this constitutes a sequence of thought is if we distinguish the single ἐντολή, the love command, from the ἐντολαί, the individual directives by which love must validate itself as it complies with them." Most commentators fail to make this distinction and thereby force John into tautology.

8. There is a microchiasm in 2 John 6: walk-commandment-commandment-walk. Gifted, practiced, and effective pastoral teachers learn to speak succinctly and aptly to the situation (as Jesus's discourses and Paul's Letters confirm); this phenomenon may be on display in these verses.

Second John 7–8 is the core of the epistle and probably reveals the immediate occasion for writing. Once John arrives there to visit, as he hopes (2 John 12; cf. 3 John 14 [14a NIV]), he can stabilize matters in person. For now, there is trouble afoot that John feels calls for his clear identification and opposition.

Second John 7 serves to identify John's concern. The initial ὅτι (*hoti*, for) indicates a connection between 2 John 7 and the preceding discourse (R. Brown 1982: 668). John's readers must remain steadfast in love and God's commands (2 John 5–6) "for [ὅτι] many deceivers have gone out into the world." The adjective πλάνος (*planos*, deceitful) occurs only five times in the NT, and two of them are in this verse.[9] The sad and sometimes sinister fact of deception in the ranks of believers was a prominent feature of 1 John: the verb πλανάω (*planaō*, to wander) occurs at 1:8; 2:26; 3:7; and a cognate noun form πλάνη (*planē*, wandering, deception) appears at 4:6.

The threat posed by the deceivers is toxic because an evidently central conviction that they profess runs counter to a foundational Christian claim: the incarnation. They are not confessing, which is to say they deny, "Jesus Christ as coming[10] in the flesh" (see exegesis of 1 John 4:2–3).[11] The anarthrous participle ἐρχόμενον (*erchomenon*, coming) is not adverbial but attributive (BDF §412.4), though it also does supplement the verbal action implied in the participle ὁμολογοῦντες (*homologountes*, confessing; BDF §416.3; on the verb ὁμολογέω [*homologeō*, to confess], see exegesis of 1 John 1:9). The participle translated "coming" is present tense and is a case of "indirect discourse after a verb of . . . communication," namely, confessing (Wallace 1996: 645–46). As Wallace points out, the clause can be rendered "coming in the flesh," "to have come in the flesh," or "has come in the flesh." The semantics of the present participle of ἔρχομαι (*erchomai*, to come) are sufficiently elastic to allow application to past activities (e.g., Luke 16:21; 23:26 [Simon was not "coming" but was already there when they loaded Jesus's cross on him]; John 1:9). Martha described Jesus as "coming" (present participle) even after he had been on earth about thirty years (11:27). Moreover, Jesus is called "the Coming One" or is referred to so often as "coming" in the NT that it may be regarded as a virtually titular descriptor. To confess Jesus as "coming" is to represent him as he was, is, and will be (Heb. 10:37; Rev. 1:4).[12] Not to confess him as "coming" is to misrepresent him. That is the problem that John addresses. There is, therefore, no definite demonstrable distinction between the

9. In Matt. 27:63 Jesus is called a deceiver. In 2 Cor. 6:8 Paul recounts how apostles are regarded as "deceivers" despite being men of integrity. These are both substantival uses as in 2 John 7. In 1 Tim. 4:1 Paul uses the adjectival form to speak of "deceitful spirits."

10. Note Cuadrado's massive 1993 study devoted to "the Coming One," helpfully reviewed by Silva 1995, to whom I am grateful for these references.

11. There is no compelling case for the view that by this expression John means "Jesus Christ in one's own flesh, that is, in one's own sanctified carnality" (Callahan 2005: 12).

12. As Akin 2001: 229 rightly notes, John is emphasizing "the abiding reality of the incarnation." See also Thompson 1992: 154–55n7. Strecker 1996: 233 thinks the participle "has either a present or a future meaning." But see Schnackenburg 1992: 284.

"coming" here and the "coming" or "having come" of 1 John 4:2, where the perfect participle is used (cf. Holtzmann 1908: 366).[13]

While John represents these "deceivers" as numerous, in the second half of 2 John 7 he speaks of any given one of them generically, using the near demonstrative οὗτος (*houtos*, this one, he). The sense is that "such a person" (Wallace 1996: 332) who joins ranks with the deceivers is "the deceiver and the antichrist." The articles in front of "deceiver" (ὁ πλάνος, *ho planos*) and "antichrist" (ὁ ἀντίχριστος, *ho antichristos*) should be seen as marking out a certain category of persons (Wallace 1996: 227–30). This is a common Johannine usage (1 John 2:23; 3:6; Rev. 2:11) and will recur in 2 John 9. Someone making such misrepresentations of Christ[14] belongs to the category of deceptive individuals and indeed "antichrists," who abound, as 1 John repeatedly affirmed (on "antichrist[s]," see exegesis of 1 John 2:18, 22; 4:2–3).

John does not single out these persons for political, personal, or arbitrary reasons but because he is concerned for the joy, truth, and love that are features of this epistle from its opening to its closing lines. To have these graces, a certain kind of Christ must be confessed. Otherwise the love of God he mediates and the commandments that steer and regulate recipients of that love are in jeopardy (Sloyan 1995: 65–66), as 2 John 5–6 seen in the light of 2 John 9 indicates. A nonincarnate Christ is not the true Christ. Anything short of the true Christ will not be able to deliver on the gospel's promises either in this life or the next. Thompson's defense (1992: 156) of John against the charge of intolerance is apt.

The grave threat posed by deceivers leads John, it seems, to use one of only two explicit imperatives in this letter (the other is in 2 John 10). Considering how many issues and concerns John pushes, his use of the command form is relatively rare (only ten in all of 1 John [see table in the exegesis of 1 John 2:15a]; only two in 3 John, one of them purely formal [3 John 14 (14a NIV)]). But in 2 John 8 he warns readers, "Watch yourselves." The pronoun is reflexive ("yourselves"), not reciprocal ("one another"), but the sense is surely not purely everyone-for-themselves: there needs to be comprehensive awareness within each person and among all persons. "Watch" translates the imperative βλέπετε (*blepete*). Jesus used the same word to warn of deceivers (Matt. 24:4; Mark 13:5; Luke 21:8) and in Mark 13:9 even used the very expression βλέπετε ἑαυτούς (watch yourselves) found in 2 John 8. Paul frequently used βλέπετε to admonish or call for awakening (Acts 13:40; 1 Cor. 8:9; Gal. 5:15; Eph. 5:15; Phil. 3:2 [3x]; Col. 2:8), and so did the writer of Hebrews (3:12; 12:25). To that extent there is nothing singular about John's call to vigilance and caution.

13. It is therefore unnecessary to posit here a reference to a future coming, as does Loader 1992: 92–93; cf. already Oecumenius (in Bray 2000: 236). This is not to deny the relevance of this doctrine to the future; see Schlatter 1950: 116–17.

14. Cf. Strecker 1996: 241: "Ἀντίχριστος appears as leading the community astray through false teaching, specifically a false christology."

What distinguishes John's command are the consequences, good or bad, that he projects. On the good side is a "full reward."[15] "Reward" (μισθός, *misthos*) is the blessing that believers will receive in the age to come in the wake of confessing and following Christ in this life (cf. Strecker 1996: 241–42). Loader (1992: 94) rightly notes, "The thought should not be confused with attempts to gain justification by works." Since μισθός occurs over two dozen times in the NT, often on Jesus's lips, it will be helpful to characterize usage graphically:

Text	Good Work	Eschatological Reward
Matt. 5:12	enduring slander and persecution for Jesus's sake	"reward is great in heaven"
Matt. 10:41 (2x)	receiving a prophet or a righteous person in the name of a prophet or righteous person	"a prophet's reward," "a righteous person's reward"
Matt. 10:42	giving a cup of cold water to little ones in the name of a disciple	"he shall not lose his reward"
Mark 9:41	giving others a cup of water to drink because you bear Christ's name	"he shall not lose his reward"
Luke 6:23	enduring hatred, exclusion, reviling "on account of the Son of Man"	"your reward is great in heaven"
Luke 6:35	loving enemies, doing good, lending while expecting nothing in return	"your reward will be great, and you will be sons of the Most High"
John 4:36	reaping the fields that are white unto harvest	"wages," "fruit for eternal life"
1 Cor. 3:8	planting and watering (like Apollos and Paul did)	"his wages according to his labor"
1 Cor. 3:14	work built on the foundation of Christ	"he will receive a reward"
1 Cor. 9:17–18	preaching the gospel for the gospel's sake	the reward of presenting "the gospel free of charge"
Rev. 11:18	fearing God's name	reward for God's servants, "the prophets and saints, both small and great"
Rev. 22:12	what every person has done	the recompense that Christ brings when he returns, "to repay everyone for what he has done"

While it is of course impossible to determine for certain the exact relation between John's rallying words in 2 John 8 and the convictions expressed in the passages above, it can hardly be denied that there was in the early church a dominical and apostolic tradition that Christian beliefs and behavior carried

15. In Ruth 2:12 Boaz wishes Ruth ὁ μισθός σου πλήρης παρὰ κυρίου θεοῦ Ισραηλ (*ho misthos sou plērēs para kyriou theou Israēl*, your full reward from the Lord God of Israel). The notion of God gracing his people with transcendent favor was already ancient in John's day. Cf. Schnackenburg 1992: 285.

with them the promise of eternal benefit. At the same time, sub-Christian beliefs and behavior would have disastrous results, as the following table demonstrates:

Text	Evil Work	Eschatological Reward
Matt. 5:46	loving only those who love you	none (implied)
Matt. 6:1	practicing piety to be seen by others	none
Matt. 6:2	giving alms for public show	none; they have their reward of being seen by other people in this life and age
Matt. 6:5	praying for public recognition	(ditto)
Matt. 6:16	fasting to be seen by others	(ditto)
Acts 1:18	Judas's purchase of a field with the "reward" of betraying Christ	perdition (implied)
2 Pet. 2:13, 15	unrighteous acts; doing wrong for personal benefit like Balaam did	divine rebuke and woe
Jude 11	walking in Cain's way, abandoning themselves to Balaam's error for the sake of "reward," perishing in Korah's rebellion	severe divine displeasure

John's warning in 2 John 8 is likely conditioned by the convictions reflected in both lists above; for lives that are gospel-compliant, there are eschatological incentives, in addition to the daily gratification of things like love, truth, joy, peace, mercy, and fellowship already mentioned in 2 John (and 1 John). A life lived in harmony with God's commands brings weighty daily benefit. But John's vision extends beyond this life and age (contra Painter 2002: 353). He calls believers to a consciousness and practical responsiveness that will position them to receive back (on ἀπολαμβάνω [*apolambanō*, to receive back], see Caragounis 2006: 280) eternal reward in the wake of their devotion to Christ rather than its opposite, each reflected in the tables above.

Eschatological reward is something for which, John says, "we have worked" (εἰργασάμεθα, *eirgasametha*).[16] The verb ἐργάζομαι (*ergazomai*) frequently denotes the performing or accomplishing of works that meet God's approval (e.g., Matt. 26:10 and parallels; Acts 10:35; Rom. 2:10; 1 Cor. 16:10; Gal. 6:10; Col. 3:23; Heb. 11:33; 3 John 5). Jesus as presented in John's Gospel is particularly fond of this word as denoting good and godly actions (John 5:17 [2x]; 6:27; 9:4 [2x]). The cognate noun ἔργον (*ergon*, work) is used by Jesus to answer the question of what people should do in order to perform (ἐργάζομαι) "the works of God" (6:28). Jesus's answer is that they should believe in the one

16. Moulton 1908: 116 sees here emphasis "on the *activity* rather than on its product" (emphasis original). If true, this could argue against the translation "we have worked for" and suggest "we worked for" instead. But it is hard to separate between activity and product in this particular discourse, particularly where the activity of work is joined explicitly to the result of receiving recompense.

whom God has sent. In Johannine teaching, faith and works are not exclusive of each other but rather mutually conditioning.

The poignancy of John calling readers not to throw away what they all, John included (cf. Culy 2004: 149), have worked for should not be missed. Loader (1992: 94) rightly calls attention to the partnership dimension of John's appeal. Christian confession in this setting was not an easy thing. John had seen his coworkers James and Peter martyred in years past. Neither the Roman world with its pagan religions and occasional imperial opposition nor the Jewish milieu in which the early church was rooted made the rise and growth of apostolic Christianity easy. Nor is there reason to suppose that John's readers knew only success and ease in their walk of discipleship. On the contrary, all three of John's Letters testify to the existence of imposing challenges. These are sufficiently formidable for John to devote the next three verses to describe and counteract what will otherwise result in the loss of both temporal and eternal divine reward.

Additional Notes

4. Did John write "just as we received" (ἐλάβομεν), as NA[27] reads, or "just as they [*or possibly* I] received" (ἔλαβον), as one finds in a couple of Greek witnesses, including ℵ? Too many and various witnesses support the former for the latter to be regarded as original.

5. The words καινὴν γράφων σοι appear in three different configurations. The NA[27] reading is backed by five uncials (among them ℵ and A), important minuscules, and the Vulgate. NA[25] followed uncials B and P, plus 𝔐, in reading γράφων σοι καινήν. This is weighty evidence; the NA[27] reading is not indisputable. Less plausible is a different phrasing found in Ψ, some minuscules, and some Latin witnesses: a commandment that is "new I write to you" (καινὴν γράφω σοι). The weak support of this third option leaves the field open for debate between the first two.

6. The word order ἡ ἐντολή ἐστιν is supported by five uncials, among them A and B. Codex P and 𝔐 support ἐστὶν ἡ ἐντολή, which may be less awkward word order in Greek, where subjects often follow verbs. But that is weak external evidence. A third possibility, ἐστὶν ἡ ἐντολή αὐτοῦ, echoes Jesus's words in John 15:12 directly (αὕτη ἐστὶν ἡ ἐντολὴ ἡ ἐμή), but this fact, combined with a slender range of support (just ℵ and 1846 and a few others), makes the reading slightly less likely.

6. ℵ and A join two other uncials, some minuscules, and some versions in inserting ἵνα after ἐστιν. The conjunction would make for improved literary flow, and for that reason its absence makes for a harder reading. That fact, plus the relatively poor external support, speak in favor of the NA[27] decision.

6. Uncial K, noteworthy minuscules, Vulgate, and the Coptic version omit ἵνα after ἀρχῆς. In its favor are superior external attestation and its omission being considered a stylistic improvement. The harder reading rightly gets the nod here.

7. Instead of many antichrists having gone out (ἐξῆλθον) into the world, as NA[27] reads (supported by 𝔓[74], ℵ, A, B, and numerous other witnesses), two uncials (P, 049) along with 𝔐 and the Bohairic read εἰσῆλθον (came into). The superior external support for ἐξῆλθον is decisive.

7. The definite article ὁ before ἀντίχριστος is not necessarily required (cf. 1 John 2:18) and is in fact not found in ℵ and some half dozen minuscules. But the weight of manuscript evidence is for the inclusion.

8. NA[27]'s second-person plural ἀπολέσητε (lose, from ἀπόλλυμι) is replaced with a first-person plural form by uncial P and 𝔐, with a corresponding change from the second-person plural ἀπολάβητε to the first-person plural ἀπολάβωμεν in the last word of the verse in the same manuscripts. NA[27] reasonably opts for the second-person plural, supported by the original hand of ℵ in addition to uncials A, B, and others, plus various minuscules and versions. (One of the minuscules, 33, has the imperative ἀπολάβετε instead of the subjunctive ἀπολάβητε, but this still amounts to support for the second-person form.)

8. NA[27]'s first-person plural εἰργασάμεθα (first aorist middle indicative of ἐργάζομαι) has in its favor the corrector of B plus P, 𝔐, and versional support. Nearly equally impressive, however, is evidence for the second-person plural form εἰργάσασθε (ℵ, A, two other uncials, important minuscules, noteworthy versions). The evidence for either reading is strong.

III. John's Warning (9–11)

Second John 9–11 forms a new paragraph in NA[27] but is in full continuity with 2 John 4–8. The problem is the lure of deceivers (who are not gnostics; see Strecker 1996: 243; Painter 2002: 350), and the challenge is to remain proactive in daily Christian living without succumbing to misdirection. John responds by contrasting two approaches to the "teaching" (διδαχή, *didachē*) that was the common possession of the Christian communities he recognized (2 John 9). Since there is dissent, divergence, and apparently aggressive evangelization by members of rival groups, whose members are apparently not honoring the apostolic "teaching," John gives practical counsel regarding how to handle their overtures (2 John 10). The section concludes with John explaining why the act of greeting these rivals, something seemingly commended by Christ (by reasonable inference from Matt. 5:44, 47), is actually an unwise and diabolical act.

Exegesis and Exposition

9Everyone who ⸢innovates⸣ and does not abide in the ⸢teaching⸣ of Christ does not have God. The one who abides in the teaching ⸢ ⸣, this person has both the ⸢Father and the Son⸣. 10If someone comes to you and does not bear this teaching, do not receive him into your home, and do not exchange [Christian] greetings with him. 11For whoever ⸢bids him⸣ greetings shares in his evil deeds. ⸢ ⸣

John continues to enlarge on the problem of deceivers (2 John 7) with their aberrant confession—persons who amount to antichrists. Their error was not that they entertained new thoughts and formulations but that their proposals violated what God has already revealed and established (cf. 1 John 1:1–3). Their mischief could rob God's people of their reward (2 John 8), which is to say the integrity of their belief and behavior, which would have both immediate and eternal consequences. John takes critical steps to frustrate this unfolding development.

First, he provides an instructive contrast. On the one hand is the person who, if we simply follow the etymology of the components of the word, "goes ahead" or "leads forward." The verb προάγω (*proagō*) occurs about twenty times in the NT, but this is the only place where it is used with the particular nuance found here. Clues for an apt translation come from the next clause, the second half of John's instructive contrast: "And does not abide in the teaching [διδαχή, *didachē*] of Christ" (cf. Schnackenburg 1992: 286n79). From the beginning to the end of Jesus's ministry, people were amazed at his "teaching" (Mark 1:22; Matt. 22:33). Jesus was conscious of having a distinctive teaching (John 7:16–17) and was interrogated regarding it by the Sanhedrin at his trial (18:19). The gospel spreads in Acts in conjunction with a teaching about Christ (2:42; 5:28; 13:12; 17:19), which in some form at least becomes established in various early churches (Rom. 6:17; 16:17; 2 Tim. 4:2; Titus 1:9). The NT epistles as a body may be regarded as the apostolic "teaching" regarding Christ. Ridderbos (1988) makes the case that this teaching and the writings that contain it were commissioned by Jesus, particularly as reflected in John 14–17.

Whether we understand this as the teaching that Christ gave (subjective genitive) or the teaching about Christ conveyed by John and others (objective genitive) makes little difference if we understand John to have been a personal follower of Jesus (for full airing of possibilities, see R. Brown 1982: 674–75). Either way, to "go ahead" (Loader 1992: 95 suggests "go beyond") means to represent Christ in ways that are inconsistent and irreconcilable with established apostolic recollections that crystallized in Christian congregations over a period of a half century or so. What Christ taught and what he taught his followers to teach are matters John is competent to adjudicate. Here he does so, first by warning against bogus spokespersons who are arising. I chose to translate "innovates," in the sense of presenting something different, faithlessly novel, and supplanting what was former, established, and valid. There is an obvious danger if Jesus commissioned his followers to "teach all the things that I have commanded you" (Matt. 28:20), and then people come along who fail by this measure. At least there is danger if Christian practice and experience are to be rooted in particular forms of doctrine, particularly doctrines about Christ (see 2 John 7). For John they certainly are. (On "innovating" currently, see the excursus at the end of this section.)

John is concerned about gratuitous innovation because the person who departs from what was initially received "does not have [ἔχει, *echei*] God." This is perhaps not far removed from what Paul diagnosed at Corinth where people were said to "have [ἔχουσιν, *echousin*] ignorance of God" (1 Cor. 15:34). John claims that Jesus called the highest-honed religious leaders of his day liars and sons of the devil (John 8:44). God was far from them despite appearances and their claims to didactic authority.

The notion of "having" God cropped up in 1 John 2:23, where "having" Son and Father was referred to (see exegesis of 1 John 5:10–12). While it may sound generically Johannine, the locution is actually rare in John's corpus. It appears nowhere else in his epistles. In John's Gospel, we read only of Jesus's detractors claiming to "have one Father, God" (8:41). Yet the concept is probably not very obscure: to have God may be understood as standing in the saving relationship to him that Christ mediated by his appearing, death, and resurrection.[1] This relationship is entered into by faith or personal trust.

1. Cf. R. Brown 1982: 675: "'To have God' echoes covenantal language and involves a living relationship based on having God's own life, which is possible only through Jesus."

Much of John's Gospel (programmatically 3:16) and all of 1 John serve to describe what this means, how it came to be preached, and how it ought to be lived out by those who have received authorization to be children of God (John 1:12). The second half of John's instructive contrast summarizes: "The one who abides in the teaching, this person has both the Father and the Son" (2 John 9). In John's outlook no higher commendation can be imagined, since to have this possession is actually a sign of having been possessed by God—or "born of God" (John 1:13). First John 2:24 made it clear that to abide by what Christ's followers "heard from the beginning" (= "the teaching of Christ") would be to "abide in both the Son and the Father." Second John 9 enjoins this by favorable description. "The call and posture of the true disciple is to follow his Lord. It is the Lord's role to lead; the disciple in contrast defers to him, complies with his instruction, clings to his word, and makes the way of the Master his own" (Schlatter 1950: 118).

Faced with the possibility of usurpers of apostolic doctrine, in 2 John 10 John issues a policy statement (cf. Painter 2002: 354–55; Moulton 1908: 125 observes that the present imperatives in this verse have iterative force). "If someone comes to you and does not bear this teaching" envisions an ecclesial challenge (cf. 2 Cor. 11:4). John is not talking about personal friends, exchange students from another country and perhaps of other faiths, international students at the local university to which your church is trying to reach out, or non-Christian family members. This verse has generated untold angst (expressed perhaps independently of 2 John already in antiquity; see Did. 11.1–2) in the form of misguided conviction regarding the propriety of showing hospitality to non-Christians.[2] That is not John's subject here.

When he writes "do not receive him into your home, and do not exchange [Christian] greetings with him," he has in mind aiding and abetting people who are undercutting apostolic doctrine and leadership as represented by John. Such figures are evidently seeking entrance into already established church circles, and even personal residences, to convince the unwary of new and different teaching about Christ and salvation. An analogy today would be Jehovah's Witness, Mormon, or other missionaries who seek to spread quasi-Christian views. While there is no call to be uncivil to them, to receive them in the sense of endorsing their teaching, giving them financial support, and offering them personal encouragement makes no sense when their teaching clearly rejects historic Christianity. In John's house-church setting, to receive opponents of Christian belief into your home meant granting to them and their doctrine the honor and respect that are due only to true Christian faith and practice (Rensberger 2001: 114–15). John's point is that they stand for something else. What they stand for calls for different treatment. It is entirely consistent, on the other hand, when he commends support for traveling Christian workers who are faithful to "the name" and "fellow workers for the truth" (3 John 5–8).

2. See Akin 2001: 271–72 for counsel on applying John's teaching today. For a summary of Mediterranean customs of hospitality, see Kruse 2000: 215–16.

John is calling, in a sense, for an expression of ecclesial identity that follows logically from what Paul taught (1 Cor. 5:9–13; 2 Cor. 6:14–7:1; 2 Thess. 3:6–15; Titus 3:10–11).[3] He insists that flagrant opponents of the gospel who arise inside the church be graciously but firmly disbarred from normal involvement until they make a turnaround. How much more reasonable and necessary is it to prevent wolves presently on the outside from exercising their predatory wiles inside the οἰκία (*oikia*, household) of the faithful?

As for not greeting such figures, John is not talking about a casual hello on the street. He rather has in mind something like the "greetings" of Christian epistles, often marked by use of the word ἀσπάζομαι (*aspazomai*, to greet) and sometimes combined with a kiss (Luke 7:45; Rom. 16:16; 1 Cor. 16:20; 2 Cor. 13:12; 1 Thess. 5:26; 1 Pet. 5:14), which express mutual acceptance and affection on the basis of shared conviction regarding and commitment to the apostolic Christ. "Christian greetings generally carried a recognition of the true Christian standing of those being greeted" (Kruse 2000: 214; cf. Schnackenburg 1992: 287). Where that Christ has been redefined in the ways that John indicates, such greetings are clearly out of place, not out of animosity but out of honesty and respect for what the outsiders have opted to stand for—which is something different than John upheld and instilled among the congregations he addresses

Second John 11 gives a concise rationale. Church reception and mutual Christian greetings are disallowed, "for whoever bids him greetings shares in his evil deeds." Paul issued a similar warning to Timothy (1 Tim. 5:22; for a Latin parallel, see Plautus, *Trinummus* 2.2.281–84, cited in Strecker and Schnelle 1996: 2.1443). "Shares" translates a form of the Greek verb κοινωνέω (*koinōneō*). In several NT passages this verb denotes the sharing among believers of Christian faith's highest privileges: meeting the needs of the saints (Rom. 12:13), the spiritual blessing given to the Jews and extended in the gospel to gentiles (15:27), the good things that those taught are to share with their Christian catechists (Gal. 6:6), financial support for ministry and survival of imprisonment (Phil. 4:15), and the sufferings of Christ (1 Pet. 4:13). These are the kinds of things that believers are called to further and hold in common. Giving ecclesial support to the "evil deeds" of those who deny Christian doctrine and thereby promote sub-Christian practice is understandably not on this list.

Additional Notes

9. Instead of "everyone who goes ahead [i.e., erroneously innovates]" (προάγων) as found in NA[27] (backed by ℵ, A, B, 0232, and versions), two later uncials and a host of minuscules along with the Syriac read παραβαίνων, a familiar term for "transgresses" or "transgressor." The less common, better attested προάγων is to be preferred.

3. Cf. Hilary of Arles in Bray 2000: 237: "Here you see an example of excommunication in the New Testament, both from table fellowship at home and from table fellowship in church." But Schnackenburg 1992: 288 thinks this goes too far.

9. It is little more than a curiosity that minuscule 33 (not "the minuscules," as claimed by Callahan 2005: 12) replaces διδαχῇ with ἀγάπῃ. This is reminiscent of 1 John 4:16, which speaks of abiding in love, but it has no serious claim to be original. Callahan's defense of this reading seems rooted in an animus against doctrine.

9. Inferior support exists for the insertion of τοῦ χριστοῦ (P, 𝔐, some versions, Augustine) or αὐτοῦ (some Latin and Syriac versions, Lucifer). Evidence for an unmodified ἐν τῇ διδαχῇ (א, A, B, Ψ, important minuscules, various versions, the Didache) is overwhelming.

9. The order of the words πατέρα καὶ τὸν υἱόν is changed to υἱόν καὶ τὸν πατέρα in A, noteworthy minuscules, and some Latin versions. The former reading is more likely, but the meaning is the same in either case.

11. NA[27]'s ὁ λέγων γὰρ αὐτῷ becomes ὁ γὰρ λέγων in two uncials (K, 049), one minuscule, and the Latin translation of Clement of Alexandria. The dearth of Greek witnesses is fatal to the viability of the (normally preferable) shorter reading.

11. There is no Greek evidence for the insertion at the end of 11 in some Latin manuscripts: "Look! I have foretold [it] to you lest you be confused [*or* condemned] on the Day of the Lord" (R. Brown 1982: 677). The addition may have the effect of heightening the fear factor (by bringing in the specter of eschatological judgment) in readers who otherwise might be tempted to take the dire warning of this passage too lightly.

Excursus: The Warning against ὁ Προάγων

What did John mean when he warned against ὁ προάγων (*ho proagōn*, the one who goes ahead/innovates)? And what constitutes "innovating" today? A primarily historical and linguistic commentary is not the place to explore that fully, but a few pointers may be ventured.

First, any current manifestations are not a new development, since John warns of it not only here but through all of 1 John (as do most other authors of NT epistles in one form or another). And in fact Jesus's own ministry, if the Gospels may be trusted, was beset by rival teachers who arrived at very different religious syntheses—and in that sense innovated—compared with the vision presented by Jesus. Innovation is not a distinctly modern or post-modern phenomenon. To spot it today, we had better have a keen eye for its primal roots (for keen insight here, see Sloyan 1995: 67). Rensberger (2001: 113–14) lays out the issues well:

> One of the most difficult things about Christianity, which began as a movement of newness, . . . is to find ways of preserving new insights once they have become traditional. How can our religion manage to preserve the freshness and distinctiveness of its beliefs and way of life, without either falling apart into fads and meaningless innovations or falling back into cultural traditionalism and falling down into a close-minded and narrow dogmatism?

Second, even a cursory glance at church history discloses the ongoing challenge of keeping Christian confession, institutional existence, and personal religion within recognizably traditional bounds. Even the best attempts do not seem always to have met success.

Third, many will see fateful innovation in the Reformation, whether by Protestants in formalizing a permanent breakaway from the seemingly eternalized Roman hierarchy or by Catholics in the crystallizing of a form of doctrine (epitomized by Trent) that former Catholics like Luther and Calvin felt subordinated Scripture and soteriology to hierarchical fiat, with disastrous consequences.

Fourth, pietists like Francke and Spener innovated, some feel, when they challenged Protestant Orthodoxy with less formal, ostensibly more biblical expressions of Christian faith and practice. It is hard to gainsay that they got much right, but later generations seem to have left the rails in important ways, as the staunch confessionalist Hofmann (1886: 3–4) points out:

> As Reformation scholars turned to Scripture to refute the dominant doctrine [of the Roman Catholic Church], so Pietism used Scripture to refute [Protestant] Scholastic formulations of church doctrine. Pietism did not dispute the content of that doctrine, but it contrasted its man-made complexity with the simplicity of Scripture. But from Pietism came no alternative formulation of theology. It did not go beyond saddling theology with an inappropriate fixation with personal godliness. What Pietism accomplished was twofold. First, it broke the power of the reigning Scholastic system of doctrine. Second, it prepared the way for those who would soon raise their objections to the content of Protestant teaching, adducing Scripture in their effort. Central in this movement was Semler.

Fifth, mention of Johann Semler (1725–91), important in arguing against the authority of the canon, in this connection conjures up the image of F. D. E. Schleiermacher (1768–1834), who forsaking the faith of his (pietist) ancestral home came to be celebrated as the father of theological liberalism. By intention and design, he along with a growing host of churchmen and academic leaders pioneered an approach to Christian faith that constituted innovation in no uncertain terms. This eventuated in a mainline Protestant establishment that by the mid-twentieth century dominated European and North American academic and ecclesial centers of theological research and training. Distinctive to it from a church historical standpoint was the rejection of virtually all doctrines formerly held to be central to the Christian faith, Christology foremost among them. Forget about Christ; even Jesus was lost, and three waves of quests have yet to find him to the satisfaction of critical consensus.

So where is innovation today? It depends on how one defines any surviving viable theological center. In the judgment of many, the pluralism of Western intelligentsia relegates all religions to the status of mere subjective preference. Mainline Protestant thought continues its somewhat erratic and currently declining career, having baptized the post-Christian social order of abortion on demand and fighting hard now for full ecclesial affirmation of homosexual union for members and clergy alike. A resurgence of evangelical faith and practice gained center stage in North America by the end of the twentieth century, by which time a much larger and more robust renewal of generally bibliocentric Christian faith, much of it charismatic, was attracting tens of millions of new adherents in South America, Africa, and Asia. From an evangelical standpoint, the fading Protestant mainline was often a good example of what 2 John 9 warns against.

But in the twenty-first century's opening years, individuals and communities associated with evangelical faith and practice have themselves made news with doctrinal and ethical shifts (and lurid escapades) that many feel are reminiscent of the mainline a century or so ago. History may be repeating itself in an unexpected and ironic way. And it is too early to conclude that the millions being swept into spiritual movements of the majority world will succeed in establishing a society-transforming, Christian institutional presence capable of withstanding the stern tests of time, adversity, and the judgment of generations yet unborn.

Perhaps the lesson to take from John's warning about "the one who innovates" is no more profound than Bengel's dictum: "Apply yourself totally to the text; apply the text totally to yourself." Or Paul's counsel: "Let him who thinks he stands take heed lest he fall" (1 Cor. 10:12 NASB). Or Jesus's teaching to remove the beam before worrying about someone else's mote (Matt. 7:5 KJV). Doubtless there is still today unwise and destructive divergence from biblical and historic Christian faith and practice to be observed in many quarters. But it also happened right under John's nose, within living memory of Christ's coming. It is unlikely that we have to look far beyond our own circles, if indeed our own souls are spared, to spot analogies today.

The challenge, then, is to follow John's apostolic lead of discerning decline, of admonishing and encouraging and serving the faithful, and of continually recovering ("abiding in") the truth, faith, love, mercy, peace, grace, and full range of other benefits—and commands—mediated by God's Word in Christ. For John's thrust here in 2 John, as in 1 John, is clear: "Whoever chooses a different way than Jesus's words show to the church separates himself not only from Christ but also at the same time from God" (Schlatter 1950: 118).

IV. John's Farewell (12–13)

Proportional to such a brief epistle, John finishes with a brief ending. Ellis (2000: 220) suggests that scribal assistance can be inferred up to this point in the epistle; now John takes up the pen himself. He alludes to how much more he has to convey (Loader 1992: 97 sees a parallel with John 21:25) and to his hope to be with them soon in person to convey it. He also states one of the motivations driving him to see them: the enhancement of their mutual joy. Such joy is in part a harbinger "of the messianic age" (Strecker 1996: 250). He concludes by conveying the greetings of the congregation, whether sole or combined, from the midst of which he writes.

Exegesis and Exposition

12⌜Having⌝ a great deal ⌜to write⌝ to you, I did not wish [to try to say it all] using
paper and ink. ⌜But I hope to be⌝ with you and to speak face to face so that ⌜your joy
will find full expression⌝. 13The children of your ⌜elect⌝ sister greet you. ⌜ ⌝

Second John 12 parallels closely 3 John 13–14 (13–14a NIV). The only real difference is that 2 John makes mention of fulfilling everyone's joy (Schnackenburg 1992: 289 thinks "the author is only referring to himself"; cf. 1 John 1:4), while this is lacking in 3 John. Side-by-side comparison furnishes a useful look at how language functions, with much the same thing being said by means of different linguistic forms. Yet there are different nuances, most due to 2 John being written to a group and 3 John being written to an individual personal acquaintance.

Both verses begin with how much John has to say:

2 John 12	πολλὰ	ἔχων	ὑμῖν	γράφειν
	much	having	to you (plural)	to write
3 John 13	πολλὰ	εἶχον	γράψαι	σοι
	much	I had	to write	to you (sing.)

Second John 12 uses a participle + infinitive construction, both forms in the present tense, which depicts the dynamic of the situation as John purposed ("did not want" in the next clause is aorist) to write or dictate. Third John 13 uses an imperfect + aorist infinitive. The effect is slightly different: the attention of the reader is drawn to sense with John how he has to cut short his remarks at the time of writing ("do not want" in the next clause is present). Third John 13 may be slightly less formal and in that sense more apt as a letter to an individual.

The lack of adversative conjunction in 2 John 12 indicates that the previous participle ἔχων is concessive ("*though* having"):

2 John 12	οὐκ ἐβουλήθην	διὰ χάρτου καὶ μέλανος	
	I did not want	through paper [papyrus] and ink	
3 John 13	ἀλλ' οὐ θέλω	διὰ μέλανος καὶ καλάμου	σοι γράφειν
	but I do not want	through ink and pen	to you to write

The verbs βούλομαι (*boulomai*) and θέλω (*thelō*) are synonyms. John speaks of "paper and ink" in 2 John 12, "ink and pen" in 3 John 13. Second John 12 is more elliptical: John leaves unstated what he did not want to do (try to express everything in writing). Third John 13 completes the thought with a present tense verb + present infinitive, analogous to the present participle + present infinitive of the same verb in 2 John 12.

Ἀλλά and δέ are synonymous adversative conjunctions here:

2 John 12	ἀλλὰ ἐλπίζω γενέσθαι πρὸς ὑμᾶς	καὶ στόμα πρὸς στόμα λαλῆσαι
	but I hope to be with you	and face to face[1] to speak
3 John 14 (14a NIV)	ἐλπίζω δὲ εὐθέως σε ἰδεῖν	καὶ στόμα πρὸς στόμα λαλήσομεν
	but I hope soon you to see	and face to face we will speak

Second John 12's "I hope to be with you," using the prepositional phrase, may be a little more formal than "I hope to see you soon," more appropriate in addressing an individual. The same is true for the second clause: "hope . . . to speak [λαλῆσαι]" is a little less personal than "hope to see you, and . . . we will speak [λαλήσομεν]." Both verses imply that John looks forward not only to speaking with them but also hearing from them, for their maximal appropriation of the apostolic word (Schlatter 1950: 120).

The comparisons above show that John wraps up both letters in straightforward fashion. He hopes to be there soon and can then enlarge on what his letters could only barely broach (Schnackenburg 1992: 288 thinks the issues in 2 John may have been politically and personally sensitive). Second John does, however, conclude on a pair of distinctive notes.

First, he hopes to come "so that your joy will find full expression" (ἵνα ἡ χαρὰ ὑμῶν πεπληρωμένη ᾖ, *hina hē chara hymōn peplērōmenē ē*). First John opens on this note (1:4). Jesus spoke repeatedly of the joy that he wished to generate among his disciples (John 15:11; 16:20, 22, 24; 17:13). John has already expressed the delight he enjoyed when he saw the upright lives of members of the congregation to whom 2 John is addressed (2 John 4). John's religion is not

1. Literally, "mouth to mouth," but in English that sounds like resuscitation. And the English idiom "nose to nose" implies confrontation. John is using metonymy, "in which one thing" (in this case physical proximity that will make verbal communication possible) "is designated by the mention of something associated with it" (in this case a body part central to conversation; Demoss 2001: 84).

ascetic self-denial. He anticipates and in a small way legitimates the answer to the first question of the Westminster Catechism (emphasis added):

> Q. What is the chief end of man?
> A. The chief end of man is to glorify God and *to enjoy him* forever.

John, however, underscores what the catechism does not: Christian joy in God, while given by and suffused with God, has its correlate in the joyous sentiments that God's people share with one another (cf. Loader 1992: 97: "This is also part of the reward on earth"). John may be "the old man" (the ill-fitting translation of 2 John 1 and 3 John 1 in Witherington 2006: 564, 584), but far from sounding bitter and isolationist, he retains the will and energy to delight in the prospect of people experiencing ebullience in their relationship with God.

Second, the epistle's closing words, "The children of your elect sister greet you," point to John's ecclesial setting. Despite his senior and supervisory status, he writes as a fellow member of the body of Christ that he oversees.

Moreover, the ecclesial bodies connected by his epistle are "family"—members are "children," and a fellow church can be viewed corporately as a "sister." This follows logically and theologically from their mutual recognition of God as "Father" (2 John 3 [2x], 4, 9; see also 1 John 1:2, 3; 2:1, 13, 15, 16, 22, 23, 24; 3:1; 4:14). In addition, they are children of the Father by virtue of being "elect" (2 John 1). God has willed them to know a spiritual rebirth, a birth from above (cf. John 1:13). This fact leads naturally to a final feature of this verse.

John notes that the believers ("children") from whose midst he writes "greet" the congregation who will receive this epistle. "Greet" translates ἀσπάζεται (*aspazetai*),[2] a word denoting action that was often accompanied by a (holy) kiss (Rom. 16:16; 1 Cor. 16:20; 2 Cor. 13:12; 1 Thess. 5:26; 1 Pet. 5:14) and connoting affection even when the kiss was not mentioned. It is fitting that the final words of 2 John are redolent of the love that pervades the Johannine corpus and that marks the character of the God and Christ John serves.

Additional Notes

12. Did the Elder write, "I have [ἔχω] many things to write" or "having [ἔχων] many things to write"? The former reading is support by ℵ* and A* and minuscule 323. Such sparse attestation is why the latter is chosen by NA[27].

12. A half dozen or fewer witnesses (most notably A) read the aorist infinitive γράψαι. But the preponderance of evidence, in quality and quantity, is behind the present infinitive γράφειν.

12. For NA[27]'s ἀλλὰ ἐλπίζω γενέσθαι, supported by ℵ, B, Ψ, and other witnesses, there are two other readings. Codex A, significant minuscules, and the Vulgate read ἐλπίζω γὰρ γενέσθαι. This appears

2. Ἀσπάζεται is a singular verb, following the general rule governing neuter plural subjects (in this case τέκνα, *tekna*, children; BDF §133).

to be a stylistic improvement that at most offers a slightly different discourse nuance. The second option is ἀλλὰ ἐλπίζω ἐλθεῖν (P, 𝔐, some versional support). The NA[27] choice is defensible but probably not beyond question. Meaning will not be greatly affected whichever reading is chosen.

12. There are three options for what follows the joy of which John speaks:

1. NA[27] opts for ἡμῶν πεπληρωμένη ᾖ (our [joy] may be full). This is basically supported by the original hand of ℵ and some Vulgate manuscripts—not a wide range of witnesses.
2. Numerous Greek manuscripts, including P, Ψ, and 𝔐, have a different word order: ἡμῶν ᾖ πεπληρωμένη. This word order fits perfectly with two identical NT passages (John 16:24 and 1 John 1:4). This is an easier reading (in the sense that it harmonizes) than the harder reading represented by ℵ.
3. A sizable selection of Greek witnesses, with support from Latin versions, reads ὑμῶν ᾖ πεπληρωμένη: that "your [joy] may be full." Among these are uncials A and B, with the important difference that while B reads ὑμῶν with others in this grouping, it also supports the word order found in ℵ.

In the end, it appears that NA[27] has chosen the harder word order based on the confluence of ℵ, B, and some other support. They have chosen ἡμῶν (against A and B), a decision for which evidence either way seems evenly balanced. My translation decides against NA[27] on the basis of strong external support and the likelihood that John's desire is primarily for his readers' joy. Note the strong arguments to this effect in Caragounis 2006: 532–33.

13. A handful of witnesses, among them minuscule 307, read ἐκκλησίας instead of ἐκλεκτῆς. The poor quality of this very small number rules out the viability of the easier reading (easier because in extant literature "sister church [ἐκκλησία]" is a much commoner NT designation than "elect [ἐκλεκτή] sister").

13. NA[27] follows a respectable range of Greek witnesses, headed up by ℵ, A, B, P, Ψ, and others, including Latin and Coptic versions, in ending the epistle with the word ἐκλεκτῆς. A few minuscules, some Syriac versions, and some Vulgate manuscripts add ἡ χάρις μετὰ σοῦ. ἀμήν. Other Vulgate manuscripts and the numerous Greek manuscripts denoted by 𝔐 follow ἐκλεκτῆς simply with ἀμήν. The NA[27] reading has the weight of external evidence behind it, in addition to the principle of the shorter reading.

3 John

Introduction to 3 John

The shortest book in the NT, 3 John addresses a certain "Gaius," about whom nothing else is known (C. M. Kerr, *ISBE* 2:1154; J. Gillman, *ABD* 2:869; Schnackenburg 1992: 290).[1] It was a common name. He is not likely to have been the Gaius baptized by Paul at Corinth (1 Cor. 1:14), who is perhaps also mentioned in Rom. 16:23 as Paul's host while he wrote Romans. Nor can he with any confidence be equated with the Macedonian Gaius who accompanied Paul on the third missionary journey (Acts 19:29) or Gaius of Derbe (20:4). What is definite is only that he is a dear friend of John, who repeatedly addresses him as "Beloved" (ἀγαπητέ, *agapēte*; 3 John 2, 5, 11). The two men enjoyed a warm relationship, mutually bound by Christian love (3 John 1, 6). John's traditional reputation as the apostle of love is not only a function of his abundant agapic God-talk. John and Gaius are also bound by the truth (3 John 1, 3, 4, 8, 12)—as well as the ecclesial politics that 3 John reflects, as the exegesis will show.

The language of 3 John suggests that it is in part a letter of commendation for Demetrius (3 John 12), who is apparently the courier of it along with 2 John (and perhaps 1 John too, if L. Johnson 1999: 560–61 is correct; see "Introduction to 2 John and 3 John"). Demetrius would have arrived with a packet of at least two epistles and handed them to Gaius, who must have had a position of leadership in the "elect lady" church (2 John 1, 5). Perhaps he was a pastor under John's oversight (Schnackenburg 1992: 290 terms him "a friendly member of the laity") or serving parallel to John in the same region. Reading 3 John, Gaius would have understood John's words "I have written something to the church" (3 John 9) to refer to 2 John. Third John warns Gaius in advance of another church figure, Diotrephes, who opposes John (3 John 10) and who may therefore make trouble when 2 John is read. If he does, Gaius should take heart and stand his ground (3 John 11), for John will come in due course to sort things out (3 John 10, 14 [14a NIV]).

The book can be outlined as follows:

I. Greeting to Gaius (1–4)
II. Commendation of Gaius (5–8)

1. For discussion of scholarship on 3 John, see "Introduction to the Johannine Letters." For my conclusion that the author of 1 John was John son of Zebedee, Jesus's disciple, whose writing activity may be placed in the area of Ephesus in the final decades of the first century and perhaps as late as approximately 100, see "Setting and Date." For thoughts on the message of 2 John and 3 John taken together with 1 John, see "The Significance of John's Letters." For additional introductory comments on 3 John, see "Introduction to 2 John and 3 John."

III. Dealing with Diotrephes (9–10)
IV. Concluding counsel and commendation (11–12)
V. Farewell (13–15 [13–14b NIV])

This is a letter with which seasoned ministers should resonate. There are no frills. There is no explicit reference to Jesus or Christ or the Spirit. There did not need to be. The reality, identity, and expectations of the God they both serve (but who is mentioned explicitly in only 3 John 6, 11) is not at issue. This is a brisk note of encouragement to a trusted and well-grounded colleague, not a letter of formal instruction, diplomatic appeal, or christological testimony.

After a greeting (3 John 1–4) John commends Gaius (3 John 5–8), warns regarding Diotrephes (3 John 9–10), gives concluding counsel and commendation of Demetrius (3 John 11–12), and bids farewell (3 John 13–15 [13–14b NIV]). It is all very straightforward, a slice of a day in the life of two ministerial colleagues dealing with typical issues of their age. It will be seen that in some ways not a lot has changed in the intervening centuries.

➤ I. Greeting to Gaius (1–4)
II. Commendation of Gaius (5–8)
III. Dealing with Diotrephes (9–10)
IV. Concluding Counsel and Commendation (11–12)
V. Farewell (13–15 [13–14b NIV])

I. Greeting to Gaius (1–4)

The opening words of 3 John echo those of 2 John, except that here John addresses one person and not a congregation. Common Johannine locutions predominate, particularly "love" and "truth." Yet there are anomalies, too: John's wish for Gaius's good health (3 John 2) prefaced by περὶ πάντων (*peri pantōn*, concerning all things) appears to be otherwise unattested in ancient Greek literature (BDF §229.2). The normal usage is πρὸ πάντων (*pro pantōn*, before all things). The elder, clearly a person in a position of oversight (Ellis 2000: 203), "rejoices" (3 John 3), as he did in 2 John 4, because of people "walking in the truth," whether Gaius (3 John 3) or the elder's "children" more generally (3 John 4). John does not generate verbiage but tersely expresses his current state of mind and his best wishes for "beloved" Gaius. All of this sets the stage for the compressed series of remarks that follow.

Exegesis and Exposition

⌜ ⌝

1 The elder, [writing] to beloved Gaius, whom I love in truth. 2 Beloved, ⌜in all respects⌝
I wish for you to prosper and be healthy, just as your life is going well. 3 ⌜For⌝ I rejoiced
greatly when brethren came and ⌜testified⌝ of your integrity, how you walk in truth.
4 ⌜I have no joy⌝ ⌜greater than⌝ to hear about my children that they are walking in
⌜the⌝ truth.

While the words of 3 John 1 are simple and direct, in their way they are rare. John uses the first-person singular of ἀγαπάω (*agapaō*, to love), one of only five times this form appears in the NT (also John 14:31; 2 Cor. 11:11; 1 John 4:20; 2 John 1; only 2 John 1 and 3 John 1 add the [possibly emphatic; see Wallace 1996: 323] personal pronoun ἐγώ [*egō*, I]). It occurs only once in the apostolic fathers, when Ignatius says, "I strongly desire [ἀγαπῶ] to suffer" (*Trall.* 4.2). While the expressed sentiment of love is ubiquitous in NT letters, such direct personal address by one individual to another is not. This need not mean that John and Gaius had a unique relationship, but it does imply that they enjoyed close and warm ties.

Less uncommon is John's use of the singular adjective ἀγαπητός (*agapētos*, beloved) to describe another person (on the use of the plural by John as a term of affection for the recipients of 1 John, see exegesis of 1 John 2:7; elsewhere, 3:2, 21; 4:1, 7, 11). Paul uses this word to express his affection for Timothy (1 Cor. 4:17; 2 Tim. 1:2). He also applies the word to Tychicus (Eph. 6:21; Col.

4:7), Epaphras (Col. 1:7), Onesimus (4:9), Luke (4:14), and Philemon (Philem. 1, 16). Peter uses it to refer to Paul (2 Pet. 3:15). Ignatius asks Polycarp to appoint someone who is "especially dear" (ἀγαπητὸν λίαν, *agapēton lian*) to carry a message to the church in Syria (*Pol.* 7.2). Ignatius also refers to Attalus as "my beloved" or "my dear friend" (ἀγαπητόν μου, *agapēton mou*; *Pol.* 8.2). My translation prefers "beloved" to "dear friend" for reasons detailed in the exegesis of 1 John 2:7. "Friend" falls short of the connotation of the Greek word used by John in this setting.

While it is possible to understand John's usage as stereotypical or hackneyed, a phone call I received while writing these lines suggests another possibility. A Sudanese Christian friend called from near Darfur, exhausting dwindling cell-phone minutes and batteries. It was 3:30 AM in Sudan. He was sleepless because of the human carnage he had witnessed—and, he said, because of the palpable hatred observable at every turn. "Only God's love," he lamented in his Arabic-tinged English, "can make a real difference here. And it is hardly to be found."

Though John was not writing from an exactly analogous war zone, conflict is clearly in the air in all three Johannine Letters. John's simple diction could in part be due to the severity of circumstances forcing his thought back to theological fundamentals, the most basic of which, in John's view of God, is love (1 John 4:8). In a dire hour of darkness, a person whose only hope is God's love may quite honestly and without affect express that love cleanly and directly by reaching out to a fellow Christian minister. Historical evidence cannot confirm that something like this animates John. But neither can it rule it out.

It is both Hellenistic letter convention (cf. BDF §392.1c) and basic human decency for John to move next, in 3 John 2, to good wishes for Gaius's health. Some form of remembrance (common in Paul's Letters) or a health wish was common after the opening lines of secular letters of the era, but 3 John "gives the best and only clear example" of such an opening in a NT epistle (R. Brown 1982: 790). Papyrus Oxyrhynchus 292 (ca. AD 25) records Theon writing to Tyrannos, "Before all else you have my good wishes for unbroken health and prosperity." A second-century letter states, "Before all else I pray you are in good health" (for both examples, see Elwell and Yarbrough 1998: 194). Given the brief life spans and marginal medical care of antiquity, this would always be a point well taken.

Third John 2 opens with a vocative form of the adjective "beloved," a word discussed in the previous verse. Only here (and in 3 John 5, 11) does this singular form appear in all the NT. John prays or wishes (either translation is possible)[1] that "in all respects" (περὶ πάντων, *peri pantōn*, lit., concerning all things) things will go well for Gaius and that he will be enjoy good health. "Go well" or "prosper" translates the infinitive form of εὐοδόω (*euodoō*), a

1. Εὔχομαι (*euchomai*) probably means "to pray" in Acts 26:29; 2 Cor. 13:7, 9; James 5:16. It may connote "to wish" in Acts 27:29; Rom. 9:3; and here. These are all the NT uses of the word.

word that occurs elsewhere in the NT only at Rom. 1:10 and 1 Cor. 16:2 (for LXX uses, see, e.g., Josh. 1:8; Judg. 18:5; 1 Chron. 13:2; 2 Chron. 7:11; 13:12; Tob. 4:6). The word connotes succeeding or attaining a given aim and does not necessarily refer to material or financial windfall.

As John writes, he knows and assumes that things go well for Gaius in terms of his life (ψυχή, *psychē*, but probably not "soul" in contradistinction to body here)[2] generally. But as far back as Jesus giving the Lord's Prayer, John would have learned not to take the future for granted. So he registers solicitude for Gaius's continued daily well-being at the letter's outset.

Landrus (2002) explores the history of interpretation of this verse. From various angles going back at least to Tertullian, interpreters always tended to stress John's concern for Gaius's overall welfare and especially his spiritual well-being. But beginning with Oral Roberts in 1947, 3 John 2 has been interpreted by some to say "something truly different" (Landrus 2002: 81). Followed by Kenneth Hagin and others, Roberts takes "the greeting of Third John . . . to secure the promise of physical, financial and spiritual prosperity for all believers" (Landrus 2002: 82). While it is possible to mount a defense of this approach (as Roberts 2002: 96–97 attempts; but see McConnell 1988), if Jesus came proclaiming a gospel of material prosperity, it is otherwise absent from the Johannine corpus. For that reason, and particularly in the current era of persecution of Christians on such a wide and ferocious scale going back to the early twentieth century, most careful "interpreters could not . . . responsibly encourage anyone today to anchor an exposition of God's intent for his people to prosper on 3 Jn 2" (Roberts 2002: 96). This is of course not to deny that it is within God's ability, and frequently his will, to bless his people materially in all kinds of ways.

John alludes to what may have helped trigger the writing of this letter. Corresponding almost exactly to 2 John 4, which speaks of John "rejoicing exceedingly" (ἐχάρην . . . λίαν, *echarēn . . . lian*) when he encountered members of Gaius's church "walking in the truth," John writes in 3 John 3, "For I rejoiced exceedingly" (ἐχάρην γὰρ λίαν, *echarēn gar lian*) due to contact with certain faithful believers who brought him word of Gaius. The present participles of this genitive absolute construction (ἐρχομένων [*erchomenōn*, coming] and μαρτυρούντων [*martyrountōn*, testifying]) could be causal or temporal; my translation opts for a temporal understanding ("when"). When "brothers" (ἀδελφῶν, *adelphōn*)—the masculine plural is inclusive, so "brethren" is used in my translation—arrived at John's locale, they bore witness to Gaius's truth (lit., "to your truth"; see exegesis of 2 John 1–3). This can reasonably be taken to refer to Gaius's personal appropriation of the ethical standards that faith in God and his word brings with it and has been rendered "integrity" in my translation. Consistent with this, John adds "how[3] you walk in truth," an

2. Ψυχή should rather be understood to refer to "the whole person in the totality of his or her being" (Schnackenburg 1992: 292).

3. This is one possible understanding of καθώς (cf. Acts 15:14). It is possible to understand this as connoting indirect discourse; cf. BDF §453.2.

expression describing Gaius's mode of practical living (on "walking in truth," see exegesis of 2 John 4–8). Third John 3 serves, then, to underscore why (cf. γάρ [*gar*, for] at the beginning of the verse) John expresses the well-wishes of 3 John 2: the arrival of brethren vouching for Gaius's exemplary steadfastness rekindles John's zeal for his colleague's welfare.

Third John 4 elaborates on John's joy. First, he says it is incomparable. The word order in the first clause is awkward, probably for emphasis, and the grammar is surprising, with John writing literally "greater than *these* I do not have joy" (emphasis added). The italicized "these" (τούτων, *toutōn*) was felt to be problematic[4] by copyists, who tried to improve either on it or the preceding comparative adjective μειζοτέραν (*meizoteran*, greater)[5] (see first two additional notes on 3 John 4). John could be referring back to "these [joys]" brought to him by the brethren in 3 John 3. Or he could be referring forward to the joys spoken of in the latter half of 3 John 4. It is not conducive to clarity to translate the clause exactly anyway, so the matter is of mainly text-critical interest.

Second, John states the basis of his joy: he hears (see Turner 1963: 161) that Gaius can be numbered among a broader group of his[6] parishioners (and, given his reference to "children," possibly converts) who "are walking in the truth," almost exactly as Gaius was said to be in 3 John 3. The difference is that in 3 John 3, Gaius walks "in truth," while John's children in 3 John 4 walk "in the truth." The variation (contested in the manuscript tradition; see fourth additional note on 3 John 4) could be stylistic, to avoid repetition. Or the added "the" in 3 John 4 could be anaphoric (Wallace 1996: 217–20), pointing back to the truth in which Gaius likewise walked.

In either case, John exults in the report he has received (or heard) that[7] Gaius has shown himself to rank among Christians whom John has somehow encouraged in the past (his "children"; cf. 1 John 3:1, 2, 10; 5:2; 2 John 1, 4, 13) by living uprightly and consistent with his confession of faith in Christ. In the next few verses, John will elaborate on what Gaius has done to elicit such praise.

Additional Notes

Title/Superscription. No Greek manuscript bears precisely the title shown in NA[27]. א, A, and B come closest, though each diverges in minor ways (detailed on NA[27], p. 745). Other readings, most with slight variations in some manuscripts, are "John's Third Epistle," "The Third Epistle of the Holy Apostle John," "Saint John's Third Catholic Epistle," and "The Epistle of John to Gaius." What no manuscripts appear to question is that John is the author.

4. Wallace 1996: 332 discusses this as a possible *constructio ad sensum*.

5. Μειζοτέραν is a double comparative; see Moulton 1908: 236, Turner 1963: 29; Wallace 1996: 302n23.

6. John's "my" could be reflexive: "my *own* children" (cf. Turner 1963: 191). The pronoun "strengthens his close relationship to them" (Schnackenburg 1992: 293).

7. Ἵνα (*hina*) is appositional; see Wallace 1996: 476. The great joy expressed in 2 John 4a is equivalent to what John hears about in 2 John 4b.

2. German theologian Johannes Fischer, or Piscator (1546–1625), conjectured that instead of περὶ πάντων the original reading may have been πρὸ πάντων. The conjectured reading has a parallel in an ancient papyrus (Papyrus Oxyrhynchus 292.11–12; cf. Strecker 1996: 256n6), but few if any scholars argue that it was in the original document.

3. One uncial (א), some half dozen minuscules, and both Latin and Coptic witnesses attest to omission of γάρ. This is too weak to demonstrate that the original did not contain it. Scribes omitting it may possibly have been conforming this verse to the γάρ-less parallel in 2 John 4.

3. Instead of the final participle in the genitive absolute construction ἐρχομένων ἀδελφῶν καὶ μαρτυρούντων, Codex B reads μαρτυροῦν. The reading of a single manuscript is seldom likely to contain the original reading. The shortened form may have been felt to be a little less awkward than the lengthy absolute clause.

4. Three minuscules prefer the form μείζονα rather than NA[27]'s μειζοτέραν. The latter form, with its -τερος comparative suffix, was by the NT period supplanting the former form, which was already comparative (of μέγας). There was a "gradual disappearance of feeling" for the shorter comparative form, giving rise to the longer one (BDAG 623; Mounce 1994: 221n2; Wallace 1995: 302n23 calls this a "double comparative"). The suffixed hapax legomenon is undoubtedly original, not least on overwhelming external grounds.

4. Instead of NA[27]'s μειζοτέραν τούτων, three minuscules read μειζότερον ταύτης, and several others read μειζοτέραν ταύτης. NA[27] is justified both on external evidence grounds and by virtue of the principle of the harder reading (the singular ταύτης could be felt to make better sense than the plural τούτων, which is usually accorded a singular sense in English translations; see Wallace 1995: 332–33).

4. The words οὐκ ἔχω χαράν are found in a different order (χαρὰν οὐκ ἔχω) in Codex C and a half dozen minuscules. This is weak external attestation. Stronger is B and (with word order changes) two minuscules along with Latin and Bohairic versions, which read οὐκ ἔχω χάριν. This has John speaking of gratitude (χάριν) rather than joy (χαράν). None of the variants affects the sense of the passage in a fundamental way.

4. An impressive array of witnesses omits the article in the phrase ἐν τῇ ἀληθείᾳ: א, C[2], P, Ψ, 𝔐, and others. A far smaller number of manuscripts (A, B, C*, 33, 81[vid], and a few others) contain the article. It is not easy to see a clear justification for NA[27]'s decision on external grounds alone. Internally, the anarthrous construction occurs nine other times in the NT (Matt. 22:16; John 17:19; 2 Cor. 7:14; Eph. 6:14; Col. 1:6; 2 John 1, 3, 4; 3 John 1). The articular ἐν τῇ ἀληθείᾳ occurs elsewhere only at John 8:44; 16:13; 17:17. This could make it seem to be the harder reading in terms of 3 John.

I. Greeting to Gaius (1–4)
➤ II. Commendation of Gaius (5–8)
III. Dealing with Diotrephes (9–10)
IV. Concluding Counsel and Commendation (11–12)
V. Farewell (13–15 [13–14b NIV])

II. Commendation of Gaius (5–8)

It now becomes clear why John is pleased with Gaius. He has encouraged, and probably even furnished aid to, individuals who appear to be traveling ministers of some kind, whether itinerant preachers or missionaries (so, e.g., Schnabel 2004: 2.1514) or even what we might term church planters. Despite their status as strangers (3 John 5) initially, Gaius has assisted them (3 John 6), and it is important that he did so, because they were not receiving help from non-Christian quarters (3 John 7). This leads John to make a general statement about the importance of standing behind such traveling servants of the gospel (3 John 8). "The Christian spirit of mutual love and missionary zeal bursts the constricting fetters of ecclesiastical parochialism" (Schnackenburg 1992: 294).

Exegesis and Exposition

5Beloved, you are acting faithfully regarding ⌜whatever you provide⌝ for these
brethren—and ⌜this⌝ despite their being strangers—6⌜who⌝ testified to your ⌜ ⌝ love
before the whole church. ⌜You will do well by sending them on their way with all they
need⌝, worthily of what God expects. 7For they went out on behalf of ⌜the⌝ name,
receiving nothing from ⌜nonbelievers⌝. 8So we ought ⌜to accommodate⌝ such persons,
in order that we might be coworkers ⌜in the truth⌝.

John begins 3 John 5 with a reiteration of affectionate address: "beloved" (ἀγαπατέ, *agapēte*; see exegesis of 3 John 1–4; cf. 3 John 11). This tone of camaraderie is a major component in the coherence of the entire epistle. By starting the clause with "faithfully" (πιστόν, *piston*),[1] John underscores the virtue of Gaius's action, which relates to the traveling Christian workers already mentioned in 3 John 3. John acknowledges that Gaius has been providing them something, though ὃ ἐάν (*ho ean*) leaves this rather indefinite (on interchange of ἄν and ἐάν, see BDF §107). Gaius undoubtedly understood. The neuter singular accusative ὅ fronts a clause that can be understood as an accusative of respect, reflected by "regarding" in my translation. John is working or providing (ἐργάσῃ, *ergasē*)[2] "for" (εἰς, *eis*) the traveling workers (for an analogous use of a form of ἐργάζομαι [*ergazomai*, to work], see Mark 14:6). John will shortly underscore (3 John 8) why this sort of involvement is so desirable and critical.

1. Πιστόν is an adverbial accusative; see Wallace 1996: 200 with note 87; BDF §160.

2. Ἐργάσῃ is a constative aorist, surveying "in perspective the continuous labour which is so often expressed by ἐργάζεσθαι" (Moulton 1908: 116).

An element in Gaius's labor is particularly exemplary. John writes καὶ τοῦτο ξένους (*kai touto xenous*, lit., and this strangers). Τοῦτο must refer to the good work in which Gaius is involved. And the function of ξένους is less ambiguous in English than in Greek, because its grammatical form links it with εἰς several words earlier. Ξένους stands in apposition to ἀδελφούς (*adelphous*, brethren).[3] The traveling workers whom Gaius has faithfully served were not old friends or even acquaintances: they were just ministers passing that way—mere "strangers" to Gaius. This is the same word used by Jesus in the Olivet Discourse when he said, "I was a stranger and you welcomed me" (Matt. 25:35; cf. 25:38, 43, 44). This is, apparently, exactly what Gaius did. In the early church not just any old touring religious workers were to be welcomed; some were treacherous (e.g., Matt. 23:15; 2 Cor. 11:4; 2 Pet. 2:1; Jude 4). But Gaius must have exercised discernment in realizing that these persons were not false and then extended hospitality by taking practical measures to support their labor and indeed their lives.

These workers, now strangers no longer, were sent on their way by Gaius and encountered John (2 John 4). In 3 John 6 John relates that they testified to Gaius's love "before the[4] whole church" (ἐνώπιον ἐκκλησίας, *enōpion ekklēsias*), apparently the church where John was resident or at least present. The word "whole" has been added to my translation to convey the sense of complete open disclosure implied both by the main verb "testified" and by the improper preposition ἐνώπιον, which can carry the idea of "right in front of." What Gaius did for them, perhaps discreetly (Matt. 6:2–4; Luke 8:17; 12:2–3), was brought to light. Specifically, Gaius's "love" was seen. This is a reminder of the three-dimensional viewpoint that permeates John's Letters, with primary truths of the faith possessing doctrinal, ethical, and relational aspects (see exegesis of 1 John 2:1a). In 3 John 6, Gaius's ἀγάπη is clearly not just a doctrinal affirmation; it is also a felt (emotional) conviction that has resulted in ethical action by Gaius in the form of tangible support for these individuals. Gaius has effectively embodied the teaching of his colleague or mentor John (1 John 3:17–18).

John next writes that Gaius "will do well by sending them on their way with all they need." "You will do well" translates καλῶς ποιήσεις (*kalōs poiēseis*), which according to Moulton (1908: 228) "is the normal way of saying 'please' in the papyri, and is classical." In any case it is clear that this is not a prediction but a gentle directive (cf. Schnackenburg 1992: 294n117: "the rule for behavior generally"; Culy 2004: 161 speaks of a "mitigated exhortation"). John could be implying that they will eventually loop back around to Gaius's church, and at that point Gaius should be ready to provision them once more. Or the relative pronoun οὕς (*hous*, whom) that begins the clause could be generic (cf.

3. Wallace 1996: 281 suggests that ξένους is a subgroup of ἀδελφούς. It seems more likely that all of the brethren were strangers—at least there is no textual clue that only some were.

4. The definite article is often omitted with common nouns when a definite sense is required (Turner 1963: 174–76). Cf. the use of ἐκκλησία in 1 Cor. 14:4.

Wallace 1996: 344). John could be starting to broaden the discourse already at this point (he certainly does so in 3 John 8) by referring to "these sorts of persons," individuals who labor loyally but itinerantly. In that case John is saying that in the future, too, when people like this appear on the church's doorstep, Gaius should be prepared to be as helpful as he was with this group in the past.

"By sending . . . on their way with all they need" is an admittedly expansive translation of a form of προπέμπω (*propempō*, to send forth). The aorist participle προπέμψας (*propempsas*, sending) is taken here as instrumental. The word can mean just "to escort" (Acts 20:38; 21:5). But it can have a more specific connotation "to send forth" with appropriate support (15:3) and even provisions (Rom. 15:24; 1 Cor. 16:6, 11; 2 Cor. 1:16; Titus 3:13). It carries the latter sense here. Workers are worthy of their wages (Matt. 10:10; Luke 10:7; 1 Tim. 5:18; cf. 1 Cor. 9:7, 14). Paul blessed the Philippians for their support (Phil. 4:14–19). These "strangers" were doing the Lord's work, and in this they merited assistance from God's people. John spells this out by adding the adverbial clause ἀξίως τοῦ θεοῦ (*axiōs tou theou*, worthily of God). This does not mean "worthily of [the support] God [needs]," for God needs no support (Job 35:7; 41:11 [41:3 MT]; Ps. 50:10; Hag. 2:8; Rom. 11:35). It rather means, as my translation puts it, "worthily of what God expects."[5] Part of the fabric of fellowship in the gospel is coworkers (in this case Gaius) stepping up and executing so that ministry opportunities are met and others (in this case John) are gratified and encouraged. In one sense it is this dynamic on which the whole epistle turns.

In 3 John 7 John specifies why (cf. γάρ, *gar*, for) these traveling workers, or such workers generally, are worthy of aid. First, their motivation is right. It is "on behalf of the name." The absolute use of "name" is found also at Acts 5:41, where it seems to refer most immediately to Jesus. The other comparable NT passage is Phil. 2:9, "the name above every [other] name." Here "the name" implicates so completely and perfectly both Jesus in his earthly divine self-disclosure and "the one Lord, Yahweh" (cf. Silva 2005: 112) that it is hardly possible to disentangle the two (though Silva 2005: 112n33 makes it clear that he does not think that "name" in Phil. 2:9–10 "is a direct reference to Yahweh"). This is perhaps also the case in 3 John 7. The traveling workers "went out" (ἐξῆλθον, *exēlthon*) for the sake of Jesus Christ and God, not for their own sake. Like Paul in a setting that was likewise less than optimal (Phil. 1:18), John rejoices that God's interests as represented in his Son are being advanced.

Another relevant passage here is surely John 17:11–12. Jesus prays to the Father regarding his followers being "kept" (both by the Father and by Jesus himself) "in your name that you gave me." The exact wording (ἐν τῷ ὀνόματί

5. Or possibly "worthily of [what servants of] God [require]." See comparable uses of ἀξίως at Phil. 1:27 ("worthily of the gospel of Christ"); Col. 1:10 ("worthily of the Lord"); and 1 Thess. 2:12 ("worthily of God").

σου ᾧ δέδωκάς μοι, *en tō onomati sou hō dedōkas moi*) occurs twice. There is a twofold conflation here: the "keeping" function of both Father and Son, and the "name" of the Father that Jesus says the Father "gave" to him. Both work and person of Father and Son are so thoroughly blurred as to be indistinguishable. Applied to 3 John 7, the inference would be that "the name" could have either God or Christ in mind, but in either case use of the one fully includes rather than excludes the identity and supporting activity of the other.

A second pointer to the praiseworthy theocentricity or Christocentricity of these workers is their resolve to "receive nothing" from people whom John terms τῶν ἐθνικῶν (*tōn ethnikōn*). This word is not, as some translations seem to imply, a form of ἔθνος (*ethnos*, nation, people, gentile), but rather a substantival use of the adjective ἐθνικός (*ethnikos*; elsewhere in the NT only at Matt. 5:47; 6:7; 18:17). BDAG 276 defines it as "pert[aining] to nationhood foreign to a specific national group, w[ith] focus on morality or belief, *unbelieving, worldly, polytheistic*" (emphasis original). Translators have opted here for "the Gentiles" (KJV, ESV), "the heathen" (RSV), "pagans" or "the pagans" (NIV/TNIV, HCSB, JB, NEB), "those who are not Christians" (LB, NLT), "anyone who wasn't a follower" (CEV), "non-believers" (NRSV), and "unbelievers" (TEV).

John may take the same tack here as he does in his Gospel, where the word "Jews" is used dozens of times to refer to a certain subset of Jewish individuals—particularly the Jerusalem hierarchy who rejected John's baptism and Jesus's messiahship—in a larger setting where nearly everyone is Jewish. In 3 John 7, John may be using τῶν ἐθνικῶν in a largely non-Jewish social setting (the Roman province of Asia) where the traveling workers themselves would formerly have been "unbelieving, worldly, polytheistic," just like the bulk of the populace. Now, however, they have believed in and proclaim Christ. They are gospel insiders, while most around them are not. Since what separates the two parties is confession of faith in Christ, "nonbelievers" seems to capture the biggest share of what John is getting at by referring to τῶν ἐθνικῶν. In a sea of humanity whom Paul some years earlier had described as "separated from Christ, alienated from Israel and strangers to the covenants of promise, having no hope and without God in the world" (Eph. 2:12), these workers ply their calling in reliance on the true God revealed in Jesus Christ alone. Anyone today who has witnessed analogous heroism on the parts of, say, Muslim converts in Islamic countries seeking to bear Christian witness without social compromise can appreciate John's commendation of these gritty gospel servants. Paul's insistence on working for his own upkeep, refusing to receive aid from most churches he planted and served (1 Cor. 4:12; 9:12; 1 Thess. 2:9), points to analogous if not even more rigorous scruples. Jesus sent out his own disciples with the expectation that God would provide their needs through local resources they would encounter (Matt. 10:1–40; Mark 6:7–13, 30; Luke 9:1–6, 10; 10:1–20; cf. Gehring 2004: 48–53, 282–83).

John rounds off this segment of the letter with a summary statement. Using the only οὖν (*oun*, therefore) in the Johannine Epistles,[6] he states, "We ought to support such persons." He refers to them as τοὺς τοιούτους (*tous toioutous*). This expression can be used to "individualiz[e] a class" of persons (Turner 1963: 193–94), the class here being the sort of people who have gone on the road, so to speak, with the gospel tidings. John confirms that "we," believers in those surroundings generally, should follow Gaius's lead. The verb "ought" (ὀφείλω, *opheilō*) is unremarkable and not frequent either in the Fourth Gospel (John 13:14; 19:7) or in John's other letters (1 John 2:6; 3:16; 4:11). It is paired with an equally prosaic infinitive ὑπολαμβάνειν (*hypolambanein*), which carries here the meaning either "receive as a guest" or "support" (Schnackenburg 1992: 296n123). My translation uses "accommodate," which is broad enough to support both ideas. John's statement is too laconic to determine any very subtle nuance in the statement. Clearly, on a broad basis he is expressing affirmation of what Gaius in particular has done.

But John goes on to give a reason why such support is a worthy goal: "in order that we[7] might be coworkers in the truth." Συνεργοί (*synergoi*) is used elsewhere in the NT only by Paul about his coworkers:

Rom. 16:3	Prisca, Aquila
Rom. 16:9	Urbanus
Rom. 16:21	Timothy
1 Cor. 3:9	Apollos
2 Cor. 1:24	the Corinthians
2 Cor. 8:23	Titus
Phil. 2:25	Epaphroditus
Phil. 4:3	Clement and others
Col. 4:11	Aristarchus, Mark, Justus
1 Thess. 3:2	Timothy
Philem. 1	Philemon
Philem. 24	Mark, Aristarchus, Demas, Luke

This list suggests that "coworkers" is not a formal category, since not everyone with whom Paul labors is given this name. Silas is missing, for example. And if the Corinthians are Paul's coworkers (2 Cor. 1:24), surely other congregations on whose behalf he labored are, too. The list is, however, a helpful reminder of the high privilege of participation in the apostolic mission. The achievement of Paul and these helpers was epochal. It was foundational to the establishment of Christianity in the Roman world and beyond. John represents another wing of that thrust—but one that is closely related, especially if John

6. This seems surprising given that the word occurs close to two hundred times in John's Gospel. On the other hand, the same word occurs nearly fifty times in Romans, or about three times per chapter—but much less frequently in other Pauline writings (on average about once per chapter, in a few books much less). Cf. BDF §451.1.

7. This pronoun is inclusive we or literary plural; see Wallace 1996: 398.

ministers around Ephesus, for that was an area of strong Pauline influence in previous decades. Like Paul, John sees the virtue of having an integral part in God's present ongoing work in the world through the gospel (on the common elements between Paul and John along with John's independence from Paul, see Schlatter 1999: 178–84). Support of Gaius's traveling workers, and others like them, is one way to join the ranks of illustrious brethren like those named above and so express love for God.

The virtue of coworker status stands, however, in direct correlation to the quality of the work that is performed. John commends being coworkers "in the truth." It could also be rendered "for the sake of the truth" (dative of advantage).[8] The net outcome is not vastly different. Central in either case is the integrity—the truth—of the message represented by those whom John, Gaius, and their churches support (although Turner 1963: 178 thinks it refers directly to Christ). Truth (see exegesis of 2 John 1–3) is prominent in all three Johannine Letters (nine times in 1 John, five times in 2 John, six times in 3 John) as well as in John's Gospel, where it appears nearly as frequently as in the other Gospels and Paul's *Hauptbriefe* (Romans, 1–2 Corinthians, Galatians) combined, for example. In John's Letters we may think of truth in terms of the sum of the teaching, the ethics, and the love that Christ has brought into the world and that humans are called on to receive and then live out. While truth may be imperiled by the trends of this age (Carson 1996b) and scarce even in churches that are supposed to uphold it (Wells 1994; 2005), this is not a new development: "Truth is lacking, and he who departs from evil makes himself a prey" (Isa. 59:15). In every age there is need for reappropriation of the verities that constitute John's truth. In 3 John 8 John reminds Gaius of the high calling of being coworkers in this critical ongoing enterprise.

Additional Notes

5. For NA[27]'s ἐὰν ἐργάσῃ (aorist subjunctive verb), there is another option: ἐὰν ἐργάζῃ (present subjunctive). The latter reading's best support comes from uncials A and Ψ, but this is too thin to overturn the better support for the aorist. At this temporal distance it is hard to be sure of the difference in meaning between aorist and present in this instance. Minuscule 630 offers the slightly different ὃ ἄν (not attested elsewhere in the NT) instead of ὃ ἐάν (sixteen times elsewhere in the NT).

5. For NA[27]'s καὶ τοῦτο ξένους, P and 𝔐 read an explicit prepositional phrase: καὶ εἰς τοὺς ξένους. This is an easier reading and with dubious external support deserves to be rejected. A couple of minuscules read simply καὶ τοὺς ξένους, understanding εἰς from the previous line. This too is obviously secondary. The NA[27] reading is supported by six uncials (among them ℵ, A, and B), important minuscules, and important versions.

6. The initial nominative plural relative pronoun οἵ is replaced by the neuter single ὅ in two manuscripts (K, 630). This yields a tolerable sense but can make no claim to be original.

8. Wallace 1996: 160 identifies this as a dative of association: "with." I interpret it more along the lines of a dative of sphere (Wallace 1996: 153–54).

6. Instead of testimony to Gaius's love alone (σου τῇ ἀγάπῃ), a few minuscules and a Syriac version add "truth": σου τῇ ἀληθείᾳ καὶ ἀγάπῃ. This nicely restates a theme touched on in earlier verses but is clearly a scribal addition: all you need is love.

6. Uncial C and the Clementine Vulgate attest an aorist participle of ποιέω + future indicative of προπέμπω instead of NA[27]'s future indicative + aorist participle: ποιήσεις προπέμψας. The variant is rightly rejected.

7. A range of relatively unimpressive witnesses makes "his" (αὐτοῦ) name in whom some go out rather than simply "the name" as found in NA[27]. The shorter reading is preferable here.

7. P, 𝔐, and the Vulgate attest to the more common ἐθνῶν (over 160 times in NT) rather than a word occurring only four times. But the rarer form may be regarded as harder, and combined with superior external support (including א, A, B, important minuscules, and Jerome), the NA[27] choice is highly defensible.

8. Instead of "receiving" in the sense of "supporting" those who go out (ὑπολαμβάνειν; five times in the NT) as in NA[27] (following א, A, B, C*, and a half dozen other witnesses), later witnesses (C^2, P, 𝔐) use the marginally more common ἀπολαμβάνειν (welcome). The difference, while nuanced, is of some import, and the NA[27] reading has stronger external support.

8. Did John commend being coworkers τῇ ἀληθείᾳ (NA[27])? Or did he write the genitive τῆς ἀληθείας? The latter reading has weak support from some half dozen minuscules and Latin witnesses. The former reading is most likely original. Somewhat stronger (א*, A) is evidence for the reading τη ἐκκλησίᾳ. But this is too weak to outweigh the preponderance of witnesses. The word "church" may have suggested itself to scribes because it is used three times elsewhere in 3 John (6, 9, 10), though nowhere else in John's Epistles. Its presence in 3 John 8 could be due to homoioteleuton.

III. Dealing with Diotrephes (9–10)

Third John 9–10 marks a critical point in the epistle. It will become clear that John foresees a problem in the reception of the letter he wrote "to the church" (3 John 9). This most likely refers to 2 John (Gehring 2004: 282; but cf. Schnackenburg 1992: 296; the matter is disputed among commentators). John knows that someone named Diotrephes may dispute what John has written there. Diotrephes may lead the church astray by encouraging it to defy John's leadership. John needs to brace Gaius for this somewhat ugly contingency. In 3 John 9–10 he undertakes this delicate task.

Exegesis and Exposition

9 ⌜I wrote something⌝ to the church. But that status-loving Diotrephes does not acknowledge us. 10 Because of this, if I come, I will call attention to his dealings, undercutting ⌜ ⌝ us with his destructive talk. And as if that were not enough, he does not acknowledge the brethren, and he wrongly obstructs those who ⌜wish to⌝ and seeks to expel them ⌜from⌝ the congregation.

In 3 John 9 John points Gaius to 2 John, the "something" that John "wrote [epistolary aorist] to the church." He knows that at least parts of it will be disputed when it is read. John surmises that a church member and possibly leader named Diotrephes, obviously known to Gaius, will be at the center of the controversy.

Informing John's assessment of Diotrephes could be a well-known leadership principle of Jesus: "Whoever wishes to be first among you, that person is to be your servant" (Matt. 20:27). This teaching may have stuck in John's memory because his selfish ambition (or perhaps that of his mother; 20:20–21) called it forth. Perhaps this is part of the explanation for John styling himself "elder" rather than apostle (2 John 1; 3 John 1). He is not flaunting his apostolic privilege but serving as a pastoral leader alongside others (cf. 1 Pet. 5:1).

In contrast to Jesus's ethic of servanthood and self-abnegation, Diotrephes is characterized as ὁ φιλοπρωτεύων (*ho philoprōteuōn*, the one who loves being first). In theory this could be an unfair assessment, but we have no way to confirm that. Unless John is being gratuitously critical, he has reason to think that things he writes in 2 John will not meet with Diotrephes' approval. If that is the case, he may deserve this gentle censure, since there is nothing particularly objectionable in 2 John for someone of Christian conviction. Or possibly this is a personality clash: John just rubs Diotrephes the wrong way for some reason. That still hardly justifies the behavior that John describes.

The verb φιλοπρωτεύω (*philoprōteuō*, to love to be first) occurs nowhere else in the NT. Usage elsewhere permits little more to be said than that it can connote a penchant for controlling others (BDAG 1058; cf. LSJ 1939). It is possible that Diotrephes fits the description of a person who likes to innovate to the detriment of apostolic διδαχή (*didachē*, teaching) about Christ (2 John 9). Or perhaps Diotrephes simply left the door open wider to those advancing subversive views than he should have (2 John 10). Little here can be determined with certainty. Gehring (2004: 281) notes, "To this day, scholars have not come to a consensus on the reason for the dispute" between Diotrephes and John. Hill (2004: 99) sees a possible allusion to this passage in Irenaeus (*Ag. Her.* 4.26.3), who speaks of those "believed to be presbyters" but who serve themselves, do not fear God, and "conduct themselves with contempt toward others," being "puffed up with the pride of holding the chief seat, and work evil deeds in secret."

John's wording can be taken in the sense that Diotrephes loves to lord it over others in the church (αὐτῶν [*autōn*, them] is a genitive of subordination; cf. Wallace 1996: 103). In this case the pronoun αὐτῶν goes with the participle. Or John could be writing "their Diotrephes," that is, the Diotrephes who belongs to that congregation. My translation, "that status-loving Diotrephes," hovers between both ideas, with the word "that" serving to locate him in "the church" just mentioned, and "status-loving" (a slightly extended but reasonable translation of φιλοπρωτεύων) making it clear that he seeks priority over other church members.

Either way, the challenge that Diotrephes poses is that he "does not acknowledge us." "Us" (ἡμᾶς, *hēmas*) could be an editorial plural meaning John, or it could carry the inclusive sense and refer to John and Gaius and by extension to others who affirm what 2 John sets forth. The negated verb translated "does not acknowledge" (ἐπιδέχομαι, *epidechomai*) should be understood in its most basic sense: "to accept or receive." A letter written by the apostle John merits respect. John has reason to think that Diotrephes will withhold this when the letter's contents are revealed to the church. So he places Gaius on notice.

Because of all this (διὰ τοῦτο, *dia touto*), John states (3 John 10) what he plans to do about it if he is able to visit as he hopes (3 John 14 [14a NIV]). First, he is going to call Diotrephes out. The verb ὑπομνήσω (*hypomnēsō*) here means call attention to. When used transitively, its direct object is in the accusative case (e.g., John 14:26; 2 Tim. 2:14; Titus 3:1; Jude 5). In 3 John 10 the whole phrase "his deeds that he is doing" (αὐτοῦ τὰ ἔργα ἃ ποιεῖ, *autou ta erga ha poiei*) functions as a direct object. I translated this simply as "his dealings." John qualifies these dealings with words that could be rendered literally "with evil words maligning us" (λόγοις πονηροῖς φλυαρῶν ἡμᾶς, *logois ponērois phlyarōn hēmas*). I translated the phrase as "undercutting us with his destructive talk." The verb φλυαρέω (*phlyareō*, to prattle, talk nonsense, charge unjustly) is used nowhere else in the NT, though the noun cognate is found at 1 Tim. 5:13.

The picture that emerges is not one of John picking a fight with Diotrephes. It is rather a case of Diotrephes having already thrown down a gauntlet of defiance when it comes either to the fairly generic and mundane Christian teaching and counsel that 2 John contains or to the person of John behind that teaching and counsel. Perhaps John is aware of this via prior contact with Gaius. Or perhaps the traveling workers have informed John of the Diotrephes problem, for the remainder of the verse appears to bring them into the picture once more.

The latter half of 3 John 10 states that Diotrephes is not content (μὴ ἀρκούμενος, *mē arkoumenos*) simply to oppose John or things he stands for. He is out of line for additional reasons (ἐπὶ τούτοις, *epi toutois*) as well. I translated this whole clause *ad sensum*: "And as if that were not enough," showing Diotrephes' discontent and referring to the occurrences of his multiple past errant conduct. So where has Diotrephes gone wrong, in John's estimation?

John prefaces his statement with the negative correlative οὔτε (*oute*, neither), which works in tandem with the following καί (*kai*, here carrying the unusual connotation "nor"; cf. BDF §445.3). First, "he does not acknowledge the brethren." "Acknowledge" translates the same verb (ἐπιδέχεται, *epidechetai*) that appeared in 3 John 9: "Diotrephes does not acknowledge us."[1] At least Diotrephes is consistent. He gives short shrift to John, and he treats "the brethren" whom John endorses the same way. "Brethren" here is most naturally taken as the "brethren" mentioned earlier (3 John 3, 5), who are likely among those extolled in 2 John 4. Gaius and others have given assistance to these traveling workers whose praises John has just sung (3 John 7–8). Diotrephes does not. Yet that is not all.

Second, he hinders (κωλύει, *kōlyei*) those who want to assist the traveling workers. It would be going too far to call the root word κωλύω a technical term per se, but it is striking how frequently it is used in the NT to connote the wrongful obstruction of the progress of something that ought not be opposed:

Text	Distinctive Use of Κωλύω (to Hinder)
Matt. 19:14; Mark 10:14; Luke 18:16	disciples *keeping* children *from* coming to Jesus
Mark 9:38–39; Luke 9:49–50	John and others trying to *keep* people who are not Jesus's disciples *from* casting out demons
Luke 6:29	a disciple *hindering* the one who demands his cloak from taking his tunic too
Luke 11:52	lawyers who take away "the key of knowledge" and *hinder* people from gaining it
Luke 23:2	Jesus allegedly *hindering* Jews from paying tax to Rome

Continued

1. Cf. Gehring 2004: 282n305: "More and more scholars advocate the same translation of ἐπιδέχεσθαι for both 2 John 9 and 3 John 10," though Gehring prefers "receive."

Text	Distinctive Use of Κωλύω (to Hinder)
Acts 10:47; 11:17	Peter or others possibly *standing in the way of* Cornelius and his friends' baptism
Acts 24:23	Paul's friends being *hindered* from rendering him aid
Rom. 1:13	Paul being *hindered* from travel to Rome
1 Cor. 14:39	Corinthians *restraining* others from tongues
1 Thess. 2:16	Judean Jews *preventing* Paul from preaching to gentiles
1 Tim. 4:3	extremists *hindering* lawful Christian marriage

While there are examples of κωλύω used in neutral or favorable semantic situations (Acts 8:36; 16:6; 27:43; Heb. 7:23; 2 Pet. 2:16), 3 John 10 conforms to the more dominant pattern of something desirable being thwarted. For that reason I translated that Gaius "wrongly obstructs" those who "wish to" (τοὺς βουλομένους, *tous boulomenous*) aid the traveling workers.

For Diotrephes, one excess leads to another. He not only wrongly obstructs: he also expels (ἐκβάλλει, *ekballei*)[2] fellow church members who do not toe the line he has drawn. This could refer to actual and successful excommunication, but in that case it is hard to see how Gaius, who is clearly on John's side, could still be in the congregation. And it would also suggest that 2 John should have been written to the group that is outside Diotrephes' congregation, since he has expelled them. This problem could be solved by conjecturing that Diotrephes had succeeded in throwing out only some. Or it could be solved by understanding the verb "expel" as conative, in which case John is saying that Diotrephes "seeks to expel" those sympathetic to the traveling workers. He applies pressure in this direction but does not necessarily succeed to the degree he would like (but see Culy 2004: 165). When John comes, he will address this. Until that time, Gaius in 3 John 9–10 now has an apostolic assessment of the problem that can help sustain his morale and integrity of leadership in the interim.

Additional Notes

9. There are four possibilities for the opening of 3 John 9:

ἔγραψα	C, P, Ψ, 𝔐
ἔγραψα ἄν (323 and a few others read ἄν τι)	א[2], seven minuscules, Latin, Syriac
ἔγραψάς τι	B, Coptic
ἔγραψά τι	NA[27], supported by א*, A, 048[vid], a few minuscules, some Bohairic manuscripts

2. In John 9:34–35 ἐκβάλλω is used to describe the man born blind (but healed) being excluded from the synagogue. More commonly in John, a form of the adjective ἀποσυνάγωγος (*aposynagōgos*, expelled from a synagogue) is used (John 9:22; 12:42; 16:2).

The second and third options are unworkable due to weak external support; the fourth reading best explains the existence of the others.

10. Following the participle φλυαρῶν, uncial C and the Vulgate attest to εἰς before the pronoun ἡμᾶς. This weak external support marks the insertion as secondary.

10. Those who are "willing" (τοὺς βουλομένους) to welcome the itinerant brethren are styled simply "those who welcome" (τοὺς ἐπιδεχομένους) in Codex C, some minuscules, and various versions. This slightly easier reading is rightly rejected.

10. The first word of the prepositional phrase ἐκ τῆς ἐκκλησίας is omitted by ℵ, 049, and some minuscules. It is not needed since it is implicit in the main verb of the clause (ἐκβάλλει) and may have been omitted by some scribes for that reason.

IV. Concluding Counsel and Commendation (11–12)

In 3 John 11–12 John angles toward his closing. He first deems it wise to admonish Gaius, which he does by calling him to a robust orthopraxy (right practice) rooted in an equally robust orthodoxy (right belief), one in which the practitioner is from God and has seen God, so to speak (3 John 11). He then commends Demetrius, piling up evidences from three quarters that this individual, probably the courier of 2 John and 3 John, is trustworthy (3 John 12). John sees fit to vouch not only for Demetrius's veracity but also for his own.

Exegesis and Exposition

[11]Beloved, do not imitate what is evil but what is good. The one who does good is of God. ⌜The one who does evil⌝ has not seen God. [12]Demetrius is endorsed by everyone and by the ⌜truth⌝ itself. And we, too, vouch for him, and ⌜you know⌝ that our testimony is true.

Third John 11 begins with John's third "Beloved," a term of endearment found in the singular elsewhere in the NT only in 3 John 2, 5. Using one of only two imperatives in the whole epistle (the other is "greet" in 3 John 15 [14b NIV]), John warns Gaius not to "imitate" (μιμοῦ, *mimou*) what is bad or evil. The verb μιμέομαι (*mimeomai*) occurs only three other times in the NT. In 2 Thess. 3:7, 9 it is used positively of people imitating Paul. Hebrews 13:7 commends imitating the faith of upstanding Christian leaders. There is a place, certainly, for the imitation of others in the Christian life. But John may have Diotrephes' dealings in mind when he tells Gaius not to imitate τὸ κακόν (*to kakon*, the bad or evil thing), a term often used to denote the opposite of what is good (Rom. 3:8; 7:19, 21; 12:21 [2x]; 13:3; 16:19; Heb. 5:14; 1 Pet. 3:11). It is used this way here, with John contrasting "the evil" that Gaius must not emulate with "the good" (τὸ ἀγαθόν, *to agathon*) that he should. This could just be stock paraenesis, like the parents of a teenager blurting "Be careful!" as their child takes off in the family car. That John uses "imitate" rather than simply telling Gaius to "Be good!" suggests that the warning is actually crafted to fit Gaius's exact situation, one in which pressures (including Diotrephes' own force of personality or church influence) might tempt him to weaken his loyalty to convictions he shares with John.

John next gives a twofold reason why Gaius should imitate "what is good." First, it is a character trait of the person who is "of God" (see exegesis of 1 John

4:1). Doing good flows naturally from the person born of God, just as doing evil is a calling card of "children of the devil" (3:10). The verb that John uses in 3 John 11 (ἀγαθοποιέω, *agathopoieō*, to do good) appears elsewhere in the NT only on Jesus's lips in the Gospels (Mark 3:4 [variant reading]; Luke 6:9, 33 [2x], 35) and repeatedly in the central section of 1 Peter (2:15, 20; 3:6, 17, along with the cognate noun ἀγαθοποιΐα [*agathopoiia*, doing good] in 4:19 and the cognate adjective ἀγαθοποιός [*agathopoios*, doing good] in 2:14). The comportment that John calls for from Gaius is not an anomaly in dominical and apostolic paraenesis.

John concludes his counsel for Gaius with the observation that "the one who does evil has not seen God." Not seeing God is paired with not knowing God in 1 John 3:6; the two expressions are essentially synonymous (see also 4:20). Very much like words for "doing good" listed in the previous paragraph, the "doing evil" terms in the NT (κακοποιέω [*kakopoieō*, to do evil] in Mark 3:4; Luke 6:9; 1 Pet. 3:17; and κακοποιός [*kakopoios*, evildoing] in 1 Pet. 2:12, 14; 4:15) occur only on Jesus's lips and in 1 Peter. John's usage could possibly be a vestige of time spent with the Lord and of his decades of colabor with Peter in Jerusalem. In any case it is a stern note on which to end his admonition to Gaius. It may also be an indirect indictment of Diotrephes, indicating his distance from real knowledge of the God in whose name he presumably exercises his excommunicative zeal.

Third John 12 shifts from counsel to commendation. The sudden mention of Demetrius (a common name) implies that he is known to Gaius, if for no other reason than that he is delivering 3 John into Gaius's possession. In that sense he needs no introduction. But he apparently does need certification of sorts. If Demetrius is indeed completely reliable, as John now seeks to demonstrate, there is no ground for fearing that he is somehow delivering a spurious letter (cf. 2 Thess. 2:2). Richards (2004: 207–9) argues that letter carriers often played an active role in interpreting and explaining Paul's Letters. If Demetrius serves John in this way, it is all the more important that Gaius be given reasons inducing him to listen to him.

John appeals to a threefold testimony on Demetrius's behalf. First, he is "endorsed by[1] everyone." The simple perfect passive verb (Wallace 1996: 440) translated "endorsed" (μεμαρτύρηται, *memartyrētai*) can carry the sense of being approved, well spoken of (Acts 6:3 [seven men chosen for service]; 10:22 [Cornelius]; 16:2 [Timothy]; 22:12 [Ananias]; Heb. 11:2, 4, 5, 39 [OT luminaries]). Demetrius has the approbation of "all" those, presumably in John's immediate setting, from whose midst he was selected to serve as courier.

Second, he is commended by "the truth itself" (for this use of a form of αὐτός [*autos*, himself], see Wallace 1996: 349). This makes most sense as an allusion either to the true gospel message, which Demetrius faithfully affirms and represents, or to deity (i.e., God or Christ [so Turner 1963: 178]), whom Demetrius faithfully venerates, leading John to believe that the deity is, in turn, fully supportive of Demetrius.

1. Ὑπό indicates personal agency; see Wallace 1996: 433.

Third, he is commended by the "we" implied in the verb μαρτυροῦμεν (*martyroumen*, we vouch for). This is likely an editorial plural referring to John. In language reminiscent of John 19:35 (where John witnesses Jesus's crucifixion), John reminds Gaius of the veracity of John's apostolic endorsement. The language also recalls 21:24, where "the disciple [John] who testifies" presents a "testimony that is true." While for the most part any ecclesial authority possessed by the author of 3 John is so understated as to be virtually invisible, the last words of 3 John 12 may be the one place where the author pulls rank on Gaius. Even here, however, it is not for John's own sake, but for the sake of Gaius's steadfastness and his opposition, if need be, to Diotrephes. If Gaius were for some reason to allow Demetrius to be impugned, the redemptive force of both 2 John and 3 John would be lost. In 3 John 12 John invokes his own name, historical reputation, and testimony to head off this contingency before it can arise.

Additional Notes

11. A few witnesses (one uncial, a few minuscules, a few versions) insert a connective (δέ). This makes explicit the adversative relation that is easily inferred between this proposition and the preceding one. But with such weak support, it is bound to be a stylistic improvement not original to the document.

12. Who or what testifies regarding Demetrius? Is this testimony from the church (ἐκκλησίας), as in what appears to be the original hands of 𝔓[74] and Codex A? Is it from the church and the truth, as in Codex C and fringe Syriac witnesses? Or is it, as NA[27] reads, from the truth (ὑπὸ . . . τῆς ἀληθείας)? This last reading has overwhelming support, including both ℵ and B and 𝔐, a strong combination when they all concur.

12. The text tradition poses another question: who is said to "know" that the Presbyter's testimony is true? P, 𝔐, and two versions say οἴδατε. Even weaker is the evidence for οἴδαμεν: a couple of minuscules and a version. Overwhelming, by comparison, is the choice of οἶδας by the editors of NA[27]. This also comports with the second-person singular verbs that dominate the discourse elsewhere (3 John 3, 5, 6, 11, 14 [14a NIV]). There do not appear to be any second-person plural verbs in the epistle, though there were thirty-nine in 1 John and seven in 2 John—occurrences that may have lulled scribes into placing one here.

I. Greeting to Gaius (1–4)
II. Commendation of Gaius (5–8)
III. Dealing with Diotrephes (9–10)
IV. Concluding Counsel and Commendation (11–12)
➤ V. Farewell (13–15 [13–14b NIV])

V. Farewell (13–15 [13–14b NIV])

The last three verses of 3 John perform the single function of bidding adieu until a likely visit in the near future. As part of this, John ventures, in 3 John 15 (14b NIV),[1] a more personalized and less perfunctory ending than he manages in either 1 John or 2 John. John is nevertheless terse. The brevity "is consistent with the distinctly private character of the letter" (Schnackenburg 1992: 301).

Exegesis and Exposition

[13]I had many things ⌜to write to you⌝. But ⌜I did not wish⌝ ⌜to write you⌝ with ink and pen. [14[14a]]Rather, I hope ⌜to see you⌝ very soon. Then ⌜we will converse personally⌝. [15[14b]]Peace to you. The ⌜friends⌝ greet you. ⌜Greet⌝ the ⌜friends⌝ by name. ⌜ ⌝

Most of the grammatical, syntactical, and translational issues of 3 John 13–14 (13–14a NIV) have been dealt with in the detailed clause-by-clause comparison in the exegesis of 2 John 12–13. Here it need only be reiterated that with these two verses, John voices the frustration, perhaps felt also by Gaius, that he has been so laconic. (Ellis 2000: 220 suggests that John's closing greetings imply scribal assistance up to this point in the epistle.) He compensates for this by admitting how little he has communicated, compared with what ought to be said, and by justifying the brevity by pointing to the inherently limited nature of written communication ("ink and pen"). He also justifies it by projecting an imminent visit. This stands in some tension with the "if I come" remark in 3 John 10. But in concluding, John hopes for the best. When they can actually sit down face to face, the "many things" (3 John 13) that John wanted to say but declined to broach in the tiny epistles of 2 John and 3 John can receive the fuller airing they deserve.

To conclude his letter to Gaius, in 3 John 15 (14b NIV) John first wishes him "peace" (εἰρήνη, *eirēnē*; on the verbless construction, see Turner 1963: 304). This word is almost absent from John's Letters, appearing there otherwise only in 2 John 3 (see exegesis of 2 John 1–3 on other uses in John, Revelation, and the OT). John wishes for Gaius God's covenant blessing, protection, and provision in all its fullness. Given the troubled situation that 2 John and 3 John envisage, he is going to need it. To wish "peace" in an epistle's last verse is

1. Third John 14 and 3 John 15 are combined into a single verse (3 John 14) by the KJV, NASB, NEB, and NIV/TNIV. CEV, ESV, JB, LB, NLT, NRSV, RSV, and TEV follow NA^{27} in numbering two verses here. Throughout my commentary I refer to these verses as 3 John 14 (14a NIV) and 3 John 15 (14b NIV).

unusual even in the NT (contra Loader 1992: 101). The far more common parting blessing is χάρις (*charis*, grace).

As the apostle of love, John is also a broker of fellowship, and the two last sentences of 3 John remind of this. He lets Gaius know that "the friends" (οἱ[2] φίλοι, *hoi philoi*), or John's fellow believers in the place from which he writes, convey their greetings (on the ancient Christian practice of "greeting," see exegesis of 2 John 9–13). In these verses, however, John does not speak of "friends." This term is never found in Paul. It is also absent from other Johannine Letters. It is absent likewise from the other Catholic Letters apart from two occurrences in James (2:23; 4:4). But in John's Gospel, Jesus terms Lazarus a friend (11:11). And in a brief but notable flourish in Jesus's final passion discourse, he calls the Eleven "friends" (15:14–15). There he reminds the disciples that laying down one's life "for his friends" (ὑπὲρ τῶν φίλων αὐτοῦ, *hyper tōn philōn autou*) is the mark of the love that he commands his disciples to show to each other: they are to love as Jesus loved them (15:12). John's last words to Gaius show that this vision did not die with Jesus. Geopolitical tensions of the twenty-first century underscore that such love is not the staple of other religions or an ideal of societies, to the extent that it tends to be in Christian churches and the societies that they have been successful in impacting. Disciples who live in Christ's love join with John in conveying loving greetings to Gaius.

In the last sentence of 3 John, Gaius is asked to move beyond soaking up this warm greeting solely for himself. He is rather to "greet the friends by name" (on the distributive use of κατά, *kata*, see BDAG 512). The ESV fittingly translates, "Greet the friends, every one of them." As a congregational leader, it is his high privilege to convey the Christian love of John and others to the individual members of his own local body of believers, Diotrephes' anticipated antagonism notwithstanding.

Thus the epistle ends with the image of Gaius greeting each sheep of the flock one by one, despite divisions that may be present. A blanket and impersonal communiqué will not do, much less silent neglect or indifference. Nor would greetings reflecting partisan favoritism—some but not others—suffice (in John 13 Jesus washes Judas's feet, too). Jesus commended the shepherd who "calls his own sheep by name" (10:3). John's words impel Gaius to walk in Jesus's pastoral footprints. This will express the "love in truth" to fellow believers that John with this letter has shown to Gaius (3 John 1).

Additional Notes

13. Uncial P and 𝔐 read the present infinitive γράφειν alone where NA[27] reads the aorist infinitive plus a pronoun: γράψαι σοι. The strong external support leaves little doubt that the latter is original.

13. Instead of NA[27]'s slightly harsh οὐ θέλω, Codex A and the Vulgate read οὐκ ἐβουλήθην. The latter reading is by comparison poorly attested, while the earlier is harder because of the shift in tense from the word to which it is syntactically parallel (εἶχον). The NA[27] reading is to be preferred.

2. On this use of the article, see Wallace 1996: 225.

13. The closing two words of 3 John 13 are disputed. Are they σοι γράφειν (NA[27], following ℵ, B, C, and a few other witnesses)? Or did John write these words but reverse their order (A, three other uncials, many minuscules)? Or, with P and 𝔐, did John use the aorist infinitive and write σοι γράψαι? Evidence seems to point to one of the first two options. But the meaning is nearly the same whichever option is chosen.

14 (14a NIV). The word order σε ἰδεῖν is disputed. ℵ, P, Ψ, and 𝔐 reverse that order. NA[27] is supported by A, B, C, 048[vid], and over a half dozen minuscules. Respectable evidence is not lacking for either reading.

14 (14a NIV). Instead of the future active λαλήσομεν, a few Greek witnesses (among them K, 049, 0251) opt for the hortatory subjunctive λαλήσωμεν, and a very small number reads the aorist infinitive λαλῆσαι. Evidence for the first variant is weak and for the second is almost nonexistent. The second reading looks like an attempt to make this verse parallel 2 John 12—the only place in all John's writing where the infinitive of λαλέω definitely appears.

15 (14b NIV). Ἀδελφοί replaces φίλοι in A, 33, and 81*. This is not strong support. The Johannine Jesus calls his followers φίλοι three times in John 15:13–15.

15 (14b NIV). ℵ and a few other manuscripts have the aorist middle imperative ἄσπασαι (a form that occurs in the NT only at 2 Tim. 4:19 and Titus 3:15). It is clearly not original here; but see BDF §337.4.

15 (14b NIV). Instead of φίλους, a few minuscules and two versions read ἀδελφούς. Such thin external evidence is unlikely to preserve the original reading.

15 (14b NIV). Only a few witnesses support a concluding and ceremonial ἀμήν, among them the single uncial L, a few minuscules, and some Vulgate manuscripts. The addition is not from the original author's hand.

Works Cited

Abbott, E. A.

1906 *Johannine Grammar*. London: Black.

ABD *The Anchor Bible Dictionary*. Edited by D. N. Freedman et al. 6 vols. New York: Doubleday, 1992.

Akin, D. L.

2001 *1, 2, 3 John*. New American Commentary 38. Nashville: Broadman & Holman.

Aland, B., et al. (eds.)

2003a *Novum Testamentum Graecum Editio Critica Maior*, vol. 4: *Catholic Letters*, part 1: *Text*, installment 3: *The First Letter of John*. Stuttgart: Deutsche Bibelgesellschaft.

2003b *Novum Testamentum Graecum Editio Critica Maior*, vol. 4: *Catholic Letters*, part 2: *Supplementary Material*, installment 3: *The First Letter of John*. Stuttgart: Deutsche Bibelgesellschaft.

2005a *Novum Testamentum Graecum Editio Critica Maior*, vol. 4: *Catholic Letters*, part 1: *Text*, installment 4: *The Second and Third Letter of John*. Stuttgart: Deutsche Bibelgesellschaft.

2005b *Novum Testamentum Graecum Editio Critica Maior*, vol. 4: *Catholic Letters*, part 2: *Supplementary Material*, installment 4: *The Second and Third Letter of John*. Stuttgart: Deutsche Bibelgesellschaft.

Aland, K., and B. Aland

1987 *The Text of the New Testament*. Translated by E. F. Rhodes. Grand Rapids: Eerdmans.

Alexander, W.

1901 *The Epistles of St. John*. New York: Armstrong.

Alsup, J. E.

1996 "Expiation." Pp. 319–20 in *The HarperCollins Bible Dictionary*. Edited by P. Achtemeier. San Francisco: HarperCollins.

Ambrose, S.

1997 *Citizen Soldiers*. New York: Simon & Schuster.

Anderson, J.

1990 "Cultural Assumptions behind the First Epistle of John." *Notes on Translation* 4:39–44.

Antoniotti, L.-M.

1988 "Structure littéraire et sens de la première épître de Jean." *Revue thomiste* 88:5–35.

Aulén, G.

1960 *The Faith of the Christian Church*. Translated by E. H. Wahlstrom. Philadelphia: Fortress.

Baird, W.

1992 *History of New Testament Research*, vol. 1: From *Deism to Tübingen*. Minneapolis: Fortress.

Balla, P.

2006 *The Child-Parent Relationship in the New Testament and Its Environment.* Peabody, MA: Hendrickson.

Barmash, P.

2005 *Homicide in the Biblical World.* New York: Cambridge University Press.

Baron-Cohen, S.

2003 *The Essential Difference: The Truth about the Male and Female Brain.* New York: Basic Books.

Barrosse, T.

1957 "The Relationship of Love to Faith in St. John." *Theological Studies* 18:538–59.

Bauckham, R.

2003 "The Eyewitnesses and the Gospel Traditions." *Journal for the Study of the Historical Jesus* 1:28–60.

2006 *Jesus and the Eyewitnesses: The Gospels as Eyewitness Testimony.* Grand Rapids: Eerdmans.

Bauckham, R. (ed.)

1998 *The Gospels for All Christians: Rethinking the Gospel Audiences.* Grand Rapids: Eerdmans.

Baum, A.

2001 *Pseudepigraphie und literarische Fälschung im frühen Christentum: Mit ausgewählten Quellentexten samt deutscher Übersetzung.* Wissenschaftliche Untersuchungen zum Neuen Testament 2/138. Tübingen: Mohr Siebeck.

Bayinsana, E.

1996 "Christ as Reconciler in Pauline Theology and in Contemporary Rwanda." *African Journal of Evangelical Theology* 15:19–28.

Baylis, C.

1992 "The Meaning of Walking 'in the Darkness' (1 John 1:6)." *Bibliotheca Sacra* 149:214–22.

BDAG *A Greek-English Lexicon of the New Testament and Other Early Christian Literature.* By W. Bauer, F. W. Danker, W. F. Arndt, and F. W. Gingrich. 3rd edition. Chicago: University of Chicago Press, 2000.

BDB *A Hebrew and English Lexicon of the Old Testament.* Edited by F. Brown, S. R. Driver, and C. A. Briggs. Oxford: Oxford University Press, 1966.

BDF *A Greek Grammar of the New Testament and Other Early Christian Literature.* By F. Blass, A. Debrunner, and R. W. Funk. Chicago: University of Chicago Press, 1961.

Beale, G.

2004 *The Temple and the Church's Mission: A Biblical Theology of the Dwelling Place of God.* New Studies in Biblical Theology 17. Leicester, UK: Apollos/ Downers Grove, IL: InterVarsity.

Beckwith, R.

2003 *Elders in Every City: The Origin and Role of the Ordained Ministry.* Carlisle, UK: Paternoster.

Bell, A., Jr.

1994 *A Guide to the New Testament World.* Scottdale, PA: Herald.

1998 *Exploring the New Testament World.* Nashville: Nelson.

Black, C.

2000 "Short Shrift Made Once More." *Theology Today* 57:386–94.

Black, D. A.

1992 "An Overlooked Stylistic Argument in Favor of πάντα in 1 John 2:20." *Filología neotestamentaria* 5:205–8.

Blocher, H.

2004 "Biblical Metaphors and the Doctrine of the Atonement." *Journal of the Evangelical Theological Society* 47:629–45.

Bloesch, D.

1978 *Essentials of Evangelical Theology,* vol. 1: *God, Authority, and Salvation.* San Francisco: Harper & Row.

Blomberg, C.

2001 *The Historical Reliability of John's Gospel: Issues and Commentary.* Downers Grove, IL: InterVarsity.

Bockmuehl, M.

1990 *Revelation and Mystery in Ancient Judaism and Pauline Christianity.* Wissenschaftliche Untersuchungen zum Neuen Testament 2/36. Tübingen: Mohr.

1994 *This Jesus: Martyr, Lord, Messiah.* Edinburgh: T&T Clark.

2006 *Seeing the Word: Refocusing New Testament Study.* Grand Rapids: Baker Academic.

Bonhoeffer, D.

1954 *Life Together.* Translated by J. W. Doberstein. San Francisco: Harper & Row.

Braswell, G. W., Jr.

1996 *Islam: Its Prophet, Peoples, Politics, and Power.* Nashville: Broadman & Holman.

Bray, G. (ed.)

2000 *James, 1–2 Peter, 1–3 John.* Ancient Christian Commentary on Scripture: New Testament 11. Downers Grove, IL: InterVarsity.

Brown, C.

1989 *Jesus in European Protestant Thought, 1778–1860.* Reprinted Grand Rapids: Baker Academic.

Brown, R. E.

1966 *The Gospel according to John*, vol. 1. Anchor Bible 29. Garden City, NY: Doubleday.

1982 *The Epistles of John.* Anchor Bible 30. Garden City, NY: Doubleday.

1997 *An Introduction to the New Testament.* Anchor Bible Reference Library. New York: Doubleday.

Brown, T. G.

2003 *Spirit in the Writings of John: Johannine Pneumatology in Social-Scientific Perspective.* Journal for the Study of the New Testament Supplement 253. New York: T&T Clark.

Bruce, F. F.

1970 *The Epistles of John.* London: Pickering & Inglis/Old Tappan, NJ: Revell.

Bruns, J. E.

1967 "A Note on John 16:33 and 1 John 2:13–14." *Journal of Biblical Literature* 86:451–53.

Bullock, A.

1993 *Hitler and Stalin: Parallel Lives.* London: HarperCollins.

Bultmann, R.

1973 *The Johannine Epistles.* Translated by R. P. O'Hara. Edited by R. W. Funk. Hermeneia. Philadelphia: Fortress.

Burge, G. M.

1996 *The Letters of John.* NIV Application Commentary. Grand Rapids: Zondervan.

Calhoun, D. B.

1994 *Princeton Seminary*, vol. 1: *Faith and Learning, 1812–1868.* Edinburgh, UK/ Carlisle, PA: Banner of Truth.

Callahan, A. D.

2005 *A Love Supreme: A History of the Johannine Tradition.* Minneapolis: Fortress.

Calvin, J.

1960 *Institutes of the Christian Religion.* 2 vols. Edited by J. T. McNeill. Translated by F. L. Battles. Library of Christian Classics 20–21. Philadelphia: Westminster.

1988 *The Gospel according to St. John 11–21 and the First Epistle of John.* Translated by T. H. L. Parker. Grand Rapids: Eerdmans.

Candlish, R.

1866 *A Commentary on 1 John.* Reprinted Carlisle, PA: Banner of Truth, 1973.

Caner, E. M., and E. F. Caner

2002 *Unveiling Islam.* Grand Rapids: Kregel.

Caragounis, C. C.

2006 *The Development of Greek and the New Testament: Morphology, Syntax, Phonology, and Textual Transmission.* Grand Rapids: Baker Academic.

Carson, D. A.

1996a *Exegetical Fallacies.* 2nd edition. Grand Rapids: Baker Academic.

1996b *The Gagging of God.* Grand Rapids: Zondervan.

2000 "The Johannine Writings." Pp. 132–36 in *New Dictionary of Biblical Theology.* Edited by T. D. Alexander and B. S. Rosner. Leicester, UK: Inter-Varsity/ Downers Grove, IL: InterVarsity.

2002 *Love in Hard Places.* Wheaton: Crossway.

Carson, D. A., and D. Moo

2005 *An Introduction to the New Testament.* 2nd edition. Grand Rapids: Zondervan.

Cassirer, H. W.

1989 *God's New Covenant: A New Translation.* Grand Rapids: Eerdmans.

CCC *Catechism of the Catholic Church.* Liguori, MO: Liguori, 1994.

Cernuda, A. V.

1977 "La filiación divina según *kai* en 1 Jn 2,29 y 3,1." *Estudios bíblicos* 36:85–90.

Chapman, J.

1911 *John the Presbyter and the Fourth Gospel.* Oxford: Clarendon.

Charry, E.

1994 "Biblical Preaching as a Subversive and Public-Spirited Activity." *Sewanee Theological Review* 38:39–53.

Clavier, H.

1968 "Notes sur un mot-clef du johannisme et de la sotériologie biblique: *hilasmos.*" *Novum Testamentum* 10:287–304.

Collins, F.

2006 *The Language of God.* New York: Free Press.

Conybeare, F. C., and S. G. Stock

1905 *Grammar of Septuagint Greek.* Reprinted Peabody, MA: Hendrickson, 1988.

Cooper, E. J.
1972 "The Consciousness of Sin in 1 John." *Laval théologique et philosophique* 28:237–48.

Cotton, J.
1962 *An Exposition of First John.* Reprinted Evansville, IN: Sovereign Grace.

Cross, F. L.
1960 *The Early Christian Fathers.* London: Duckworth.

Cuadrado, J. F.
1993 *"El Viniente": Estudio exegético y teológico del verbo ἔρχεσθαι en la literatura joánica.* Monografías de la Revista Mayéutica 1. Marcilla (Navarra, Spain): Centro Filosófico-Teológico.

Culpepper, R. A.
1998 *The Gospel and Letters of John.* Nashville: Abingdon.

Culy, M.
2004 *1, 2, 3 John: A Handbook on the Greek Text.* Waco: Baylor University.

Cummins, S. A.
2004 "The Theological Interpretation of Scripture: Recent Contributions by Stephen E. Fowl, Christopher R. Seitz, and Francis Watson." *Currents in Biblical Research* 2:179–96.

Curtis, E. M.
1992 "The First Person Plural in 1 John 2:18–27." *Evangelical Journal* 10:27–36.

Darby, J. N.
1907 *Nine Lectures on the First Epistle of John.* 7th edition. London: Rouse.

Dawes, G.
1999 *The Historical Jesus Quest: Landmarks in the Search for the Jesus of History.* Louisville: Westminster.

Deissmann, A.
1911 *Light from the Ancient East.* Translated by L. R. M. Strachan. London: Hodder & Stoughton.

Demarest, B. A.
1984 "Amyraldianism" and "Amyraut, Moise (1596–1664)." Pp. 41–42 in *Evangelical Dictionary of Theology.* Edited by W. Elwell. Grand Rapids: Baker Academic.

Demoss, M. S.
2001 *Pocket Dictionary for the Study of New Testament Greek.* Downers Grove, IL: InterVarsity.

Dobson, J. H.
1971 "Emphatic Personal Pronouns in the New Testament." *Bible Translator* 22/2:58–60.

Dodd, C. H.
1937 *The First Epistle of John and the Fourth Gospel.* Manchester, UK: Manchester University Press.
1946 *The Johannine Epistles.* London: Hodder & Stoughton.

DPL *Dictionary of Paul and His Letters.* Edited by G. F. Hawthorne and R. P. Martin. Downers Grove, IL: InterVarsity, 1993.

Dryden, J. D.
1998 "The Sense of σπέρμα in 1 John 3:9 in Light of Lexical Evidence." *Filología neotestamentaria* 11:85–100.

Edwards, R.
1996 *The Johannine Epistles.* Sheffield, UK: Sheffield Academic Press.

Ehrman, B.
1993 *The Orthodox Corruption of Scripture.* New York: Oxford University Press.
1997 *The New Testament: A Historical Introduction to the Early Christian Writings.* New York: Oxford University Press.
2004 *The New Testament: A Historical Introduction to the Early Christian Writings.* 3rd edition. New York: Oxford University Press.
2005 *Misquoting Jesus: The Story behind Who Changed the Bible and Why.* San Francisco: Harper.

Elliott, M.
2005 *Faithful Feelings: Emotion in the New Testament.* Leicester, UK: Inter-Varsity.

Ellis, E.
1999 *The Making of the New Testament Documents.* Leiden: Brill.
2000 *Christ and the Future in New Testament History.* Leiden: Brill.
2002 "God's Sovereign Grace in Salvation and the Nature of Man's Free Will." *Southwestern Journal of Theology* 44/3:28–43.

Elwell, W. (ed.)
1991 *Topical Analysis of the Bible.* Grand Rapids: Baker Academic.

Elwell, W., and R. W. Yarbrough
1998 *Readings from the First-Century World.* Grand Rapids: Baker Academic.

Ericson, M.
2003 "Evangelical Scholarship in the Twenty-First Century." *Journal of the Evangelical Theological Society* 46:5–27.

Feldman, L., and M. Reinhold (eds.)
1996 *Jewish Life and Thought among Greeks and Barbarians*. Minneapolis: Fortress.

Ferguson, E.
1987 *Backgrounds of Early Christianity*. Grand Rapids: Eerdmans.

Ferraro, G.
1988 "Il tema della gioia nella lettere giovannee." *Revista bíblica* 36:439–61.

Finegan, J.
1989 *Myth and Mystery*. Grand Rapids: Baker Academic.

Funk, R. W.
1996 *Honest to Jesus*. San Francisco: Harper Collins.

Gehring, R.
2004 *House Church and Mission: The Importance of Household Structures in Early Christianity*. Peabody, MA: Hendrickson.

Gilkey, L.
1961 "Cosmology, Ontology, and the Travail of Biblical Language." *Journal of Religion* 41:194–205.

Goodspeed, E. J. (ed.)
1960 *Index patristicus*. Corrected edition. Naperville, IL: Allenson.

Grant, R.
1974 "Papias in Eusebius' Church History." Pp. 209–13 in *Mélanges d'histoire des religions*. Paris: Presses Universitaires de France.
1980 *Eusebius as Church Historian*. Oxford: Clarendon.

Grant, R., and D. Tracy
1984 *A Short History of the Interpretation of the Bible*. 2nd edition. Minneapolis: Fortress.

Greenlee, J.
2000 "1 John 3:2: 'If It/He Is Manifested.'" *Notes on Translation* 14:47–48.

Griffith, T.
2002 *Keep Yourselves from Idols: A New Look at 1 John*. Journal for the Study of the New Testament Supplement 233. Sheffield, UK: Sheffield Academic Press.

Gryclewicz, F.
1958 "Prolog ewangelii listu sw. Jana." *Ruch biblijny i liturgiczny* 11:15–22.

Guthrie, D.
1981 *New Testament Theology*. Leicester, UK: Inter-Varsity/Downers Grove, IL: InterVarsity.

Hadas, M. (ed.)
1961 *Essential Works of Stoicism*. New York: Bantam.

Hagenbach, K.
1862 *A Text-Book of the History of Doctrines*, vol. 2. Translated by H. B. Smith. New York: Sheldon.

Hamilton, J., Jr.
2003 "Old Covenant Believers and the Indwelling Spirit: A Survey of the Spectrum of Opinion." *Trinity Journal* n.s. 24:37–54.

Harnack, A. von
1886 *Lehrbuch der Dogmengeschichte*, vol. 1: *Die Entstehung des kirklichen Dogmas*. Freiburg i. B.: Mohr.
1904 *What Is Christianity?* Translated by T. B. Saunders. 3rd revised edition. London: Williams & Norgate.

Harris, H.
1975 *The Tübingen School*. Oxford: Clarendon.

Harvey, W.
1857 *Sancti Irenaei*, vol. 2. Cambridge: Typis Adademicus.

Hass, C., M. de Jonge, and J. L. Swellengrebel
1972 *A Handbook on the Letters of John*. New York: United Bible Societies.

Hatina, T.
1999 "The Perfect Tense-Form in Colossians: Verbal Aspect, Temporality, and the Challenge of Translation." Pp. 224–52 in *Translating the Bible: Problems and Prospects*. Edited by S. E. Porter and R. S. Hess. Sheffield, UK: Sheffield Academic Press.

Haupt, E.
1879 *The First Epistle of St. John: A Contribution to Biblical Theology*. Translated by W. B. Pope. Edinburgh: T&T Clark.

Hawthorne, G. F.
1991 *The Presence and the Power*. Waco: Word.

Hays, R.
1996 *The Moral Vision of the New Testament*. San Francisco: HarperCollins.

Heckel, T. K.
2004 "Die Historisierung der johanneischen Theologie im Ersten Johannesbrief." *New Testament Studies* 50:425–43.
2005 Review of C. Hill, *The Johannine Corpus in the Early Church*. *Theologische Literaturzeitung* 130:1321–23.

Helm, R.
1913 *Eusebius Werke*, vol. 7: *Die Chronik des Hieronymus: Hieronymi Chronicon*, part 1: *Text*. Leipzig: Hinrichs.

Henderson, D. W.
1998 *Culture Shift: Communicating God's Truth to Our Changing World*. Grand Rapids: Baker Books.

Henry, M.
ca. 1710 *Matthew Henry's Commentary on the Whole Bible*, vol. 6. Reprinted Old Tappan, NJ: Revell.

Henžel, J.
2003 "When Conversion Is Joy and Death Victory: Historical Foundations of the Doctrine of Perseverance." *Tyndale Bulletin* 54/2:123–48.

Hiebert, D. E.
1988 "An Expositional Study of 1 John," part 2: "An Exposition of 1 John 1:5–2:6." *Bibliotheca sacra* 145:329–42.
1991 *The Epistles of John: An Expositional Commentary*. Greenville, SC: Bob Jones University Press.

Hill, C. E.
2004 *The Johannine Corpus in the Early Church*. Oxford: Oxford University Press.

Hodges, Z. C.
1972 "Fellowship and Confession in 1 John 1:5–10." *Bibliotheca sacra* 129:48–60.

Hoffman, T. A.
1978 "1 John and the Qumran Scrolls." *Biblical Theology Bulletin* 8:117–25.

Hoffmann, R. J.
1987 *Celsus on the True Doctrine: A Discourse against the Christians*. New York: Oxford University Press.
2002 "Love for Love: Conceptual Unity and Idiomatic Difference in the Johannine Tradition." *Theological Review—Near East School of Theology* 23/2:67–94.

Hofmann, J. C. K.
1886 *Die heilige Schrift neuen Testaments zusammenhängend untersucht*, vol. 11: *Biblische Theologie des neuen Testaments*. Compiled by W. Volck. Nördlingen: Beck.

Holladay, C.
2005 *A Critical Introduction to the New Testament: Interpreting the Message and Meaning of Jesus Christ*. Nashville: Abingdon.

Holman, C. H.
1977 *A Handbook to Literature*. 3rd edition. Indianapolis: Odyssey.

Holmes, M. W.
1997 "Ignatius of Antioch." Pp. 530–33 in *Dictionary of the Later New Testament and Its Developments*. Edited by R. P. Martin and P. H. Davids. Downers Grove, IL: InterVarsity.
1999 *The Apostolic Fathers: Greek Texts and English Translations*. Grand Rapids: Baker Academic.

Holtzmann, H. J.
1908 *Briefe und Offenbarung des Johannes*. 3rd edition. Hand-Commentar zum Neuen Testament 4.2. Edited by W. Bauer. Tübingen: Mohr.

Horst, P. W. van der
1972 "A Wordplay in 1 Joh 4:12?" *Zeitschrift für die neutestamentliche Wissenschaft* 63/3–4:280–82.

Houlden, J. L.
1982 "Salvation Proclaimed, II: 1 John 1:5–2:6: Belief and Growth." *Expository Times* 93:132–36.

Hultgren, A.
1994 *The Rise of Normative Christianity*. Minneapolis: Fortress.

Hunter, W. B.
1986 *The God Who Hears*. Downers Grove, IL: InterVarsity.

ISBE *The International Standard Bible Encyclopedia*. Edited by J. Orr. Chicago: Howard-Severance, 1925.

Jellicoe, S.
1968 *The Septuagint and Modern Study*. Oxford: Oxford University Press. Reprinted Winona Lake, IN: Eisenbrauns, 1993.

Jenkins, P.
2002 *The Next Christendom: The Coming of Global Christianity*. Oxford: Oxford University Press.
2006 "Believing in the Global South." *First Things* 168:12–18.

Jenks, G. C.
1991 *The Origins and Early Development of the Antichrist Myth*. Berlin: de Gruyter.

Johnson, L. T.
1999 *The Writings of the New Testament: An Interpretation*. Revised edition. Minneapolis: Fortress.

Johnson, P. E.
1995 *Reason in the Balance: The Case against Naturalism in Science, Law, and Education*. Downers Grove, IL: InterVarsity.

Jomier, J.
2002 *The Bible and the Qur'an*. San Francisco: Ignatius.

Jonge, H. J. de
1980 "Erasmus and the Comma Johanneum." *Ephemerides theologicae lovanienses* 56:381–89.

Keener, C.
2003 *The Gospel of John: A Commentary*. 2 vols. Peabody, MA: Hendrickson.

Kim, J.
2001–5 "The Concept of Atonement in Hellenistic Thought and 1 John." *Journal of Greco-Roman Christianity and Judaism* 2:100–116.

Klauck, H.-J.
1989 "In der Welt—aus der Welt (1 Joh 2,15–17): Beobachtungen zur Ambivalenz des johanneischen Kosmosbegriffs." *Franziskanische Studien* 71:58–68.
1990 "Zur rhetorischen Analyse der Johannesbriefe." *Zeitschrift für die neutestamentliche Wissenschaft* 81:205–24.
1991 *Die Johannesbriefe*. Darmstadt: Wissenschaftliche Buchgesellschaft.
1998 *Das antike Briefliterature und das Neue Testament*. Paderborn: Schöningh.

Klein, G.
1971 "'Das wahre Licht scheint schon': Beobachtungen zur Zeit- und Geschichtserfahrung einer urchristlichen Schule." *Zeitschrift für Theologie und Kirche* 68:261–326.

Köstenberger, A. J.
2004 *John*. Baker Exegetical Commentary on the New Testament. Grand Rapids: Baker Academic.

Kotzé, P. P.
1979 "The Meaning of 1 John 3:9 with Reference to 1 John 1:8 and 10." *Neotestamentica* 13:68–83.

Kruse, C. G.
2000 *The Letters of John*. Pillar New Testament Commentary. Grand Rapids: Eerdmans/Leicester, UK: Apollos.
2003a *John*. Tyndale New Testament Commentaries. Grand Rapids: Eerdmans.
2003b "Sin and Perfection in 1 John." *Australian Biblical Review* 51:60–70.

Landrus, H. L.
2002 "Hearing 3 John 2 in the Voices of History." *Journal of Pentecostal Theology* 11:70–88.

La Potterie, I. de
1959 "L'onction du chrétien par la foi." *Biblica* 40:12–69.

Law, R. L.
1909 *The Tests of Life: A Study of the First Epistle of St. John*. Edinburgh: T&T Clark.

Lawlor, H. J.
1922 "Eusebius on Papias." *Hermathena* 43:167–222.

Lawlor, H. J., and J. E. L. Oulten
1954 *Eusebius, Bishop of Caesarea: The Ecclesiastical History and the Martyrs of Palestine*. 2 vols. London: SPCK.

Lazure, N.
1969 "La convoitise de la chair en 1 Jean, ii,16." *Revue biblique* 76:161–205.

LEH *Greek-English Lexicon of the Septuagint*. Edited by J. Lust, E. Eynikel, and K. Hauspie. Revised edition. Stuttgart: Deutsche Bibelgesellschaft, 2003.

Lietaert Peerbolte, L. J.
1996 *The Antecedents of the Antichrist: A Traditio-Historical Study of the Earliest Christian Views on Eschatological Opponents*. Leiden: Brill.

Lieu, J. M.
1988 "Blindness in the Johannine Tradition." *New Testament Studies* 34:83–95.
1991 *The Theology of the Johannine Epistles*. Cambridge: Cambridge University Press.
1993 "What Was from the Beginning: Scripture and Tradition in the Johannine Epistles." *New Testament Studies* 39:458–77.
2005 "How John Writes." Pp. 171–83 in *The Written Gospel*. Edited by M. Bockmuehl and D. Hagner. Cambridge: Cambridge University Press.

Lightfoot, J. B.
1891 *The Apostolic Fathers*. London/New York: Macmillan.

Lillie, W.
1967 "'We' Inclusive and Exclusive in the New Testament." *Expository Times* 78:119–20.

Lincoln, A. T.
2002 "The Beloved Disciple as Eyewitness and the Fourth Gospel as Witness." *Journal for the Study of the New Testament* 85:3–26.

Lloyd-Jones, D. M.
1993 *Fellowship with God*. Wheaton, IL: Crossway.

LN — *Greek-English Lexicon of the New Testament Based on Semantic Domains.* Edited by J. P. Louw and E. A. Nida. 2 vols. 2nd edition. New York: United Bible Societies, 1988–89.

Loader, W.

1992 — *The Johannine Epistles.* London: Epworth.

Lorein, G. W.

2003 — *The Antichrist Theme in the Intertestamental Period.* London: T&T Clark.

Louw, J. P.

1975 — "Verbal Aspect in the First Letter of John." *Neotestamentica* 9:98–104.

LSJ — *A Greek-English Lexicon.* Compiled by H. G. Liddell and R. Scott. Revised by H. S. Jones. 9th edition. Oxford: Oxford University Press, 1968.

Luther, M.

1967 — "Lectures on the First Epistle of St. John." Translated by W. A. Hansen. Pp. 219–327 in *Luther's Works,* vol. 30: *The Catholic Epistles.* Edited by J. Pelikan and W. A. Hansen. St. Louis: Concordia.

Lyonnet, S.

1957 — "De natura peccati quid doceat Novum Testamentum—de scriptis Ioanneis." *Verbum domini* 35:271–78.

Maier, G.

1994 — *Biblical Hermeneutics.* Translated by R. W. Yarbrough. Wheaton: Crossway.

Maki, S. L.

1999 — "The Limits of a Limitless Science." *Asbury Theological Journal* 54:23–39.

Malatesta, E.

1978 — *Interiority and Covenant: An Exegetical Study of* εἶναι ἐν *and* μένειν ἐν *in the First Letter of Saint John.* Rome: Pontifical Biblical Institute Press.

Manns, F.

1988 — "'Le péché, c'est Bélial': 1 Jn: 3,4 à la lumière du judaïsme." *Revue des sciences religieuses* 62:1–9.

Marshall, I. H.

1978 — *The Epistles of John.* New International Commentary on the New Testament. Grand Rapids: Eerdmans.

2004 — *New Testament Theology: Many Witnesses, One Gospel.* Downers Grove, IL: InterVarsity.

Martino, C.

1979 — "La riconciliazione in 1 Gv 1,9." *Antonianum* 54:163–224.

Matera, F.

2007 — *New Testament Theology: Exploring Diversity and Unity.* Louisville: Westminster John Knox.

Maynard, M.

1995 — *A History of the Debate over 1 John 5,7–8: A Tracing of the Longevity of the Comma Johanneum, with Evaluations of Arguments against Its Authenticity.* Tempe, AZ: Comma.

McConnell, D.

1988 — *A Different Gospel.* Peabody, MA: Hendrickson.

McGrath, A.

1988 — *The Mystery of the Cross.* Grand Rapids: Zondervan.

McLeish, K. (ed.)

1995 — *Key Ideas in Human Thought.* Rocklin, CA: Prima.

Metzger, B. M.

1992 — *The Text of the New Testament: Its Transmission, Corruption, and Restoration.* New York: Oxford University Press.

1994 — *A Textual Commentary on the Greek New Testament.* 2nd edition. London: United Bible Societies.

Mian, F.

1988 — "Due note alla prima epistola di Giovanni." *Bibliotheca orientalis* 30:35–37.

MM — *The Vocabulary of the Greek Testament: Illustrated from the Papyri and Other Non-literary Sources.* By J. H. Moulton and G. Milligan. 1930. Reprinted Grand Rapids: Eerdmans, 1980.

Morris, L.

1969 — *Studies in the Fourth Gospel.* Grand Rapids: Eerdmans.

1979 — "Antichrist." Pp. 39–40 in *The New Bible Dictionary.* Edited by J. D. Douglas. Grand Rapids: Eerdmans.

Moule, C. F. D.

1994 — *An Idiom-Book of New Testament Greek.* 2nd edition. Cambridge: Cambridge University Press.

Moulton, J. H.

1908 — *A Grammar of New Testament Greek,* vol. 1: *Prolegomena.* 3rd edition. Edinburgh: T&T Clark.

Mounce, W.

1994 — *The Morphology of Biblical Greek.* Grand Rapids: Zondervan.

Murray, I.

1995 *Spurgeon v. Hyper-Calvinism: The Battle for Gospel Preaching*. Edinburgh: Banner of Truth.

NA[25] *Novum Testamentum Graece*. Edited by E. Nestle, E. Nestle, and K. Aland. 25th revised edition. Stuttgart: Württembergische Bibelanstalt, 1963.

NA[27] *Novum Testamentum Graece*. Edited by [E. Nestle and E. Nestle], B. Aland, K. Aland, J. Karavidopoulos, C. M. Martini, and B. M. Metzger. 27th revised edition. Stuttgart: Deutsche Bibelgesellschaft, 1993.

Nauck, W.

1957 *Die Tradition und der Charakter des ersten Johannesbriefes*. Wissenschaftliche Untersuchungen zum Neuen Testament 3. Tübingen: Mohr.

Neander, A.

1852 *The First Epistle of John, Practically Explained*. Translated by H. C. Conant. New York: Colby.

Neuer, W.

1995 *Adolf Schlatter: A Biography of Germany's Premier Biblical Theologian*. Translated by R. W. Yarbrough. Grand Rapids: Baker Academic.

Neufeld, D.

1994 *Reconceiving Texts as Speech Acts: An Analysis of 1 John*. Leiden: Brill.

NIDNTT *The New International Dictionary of New Testament Theology*. Edited by L. Coenen, E. Beyreuther, and H. Bietenhard. English translation edited by C. Brown. 3 vols. Grand Rapids: Zondervan, 1975–78.

NIDOTTE *New International Dictionary of Old Testament Theology and Exegesis*. Edited by W. A. VanGemeren. 5 vols. Grand Rapids: Zondervan, 1997.

Noack, B.

1960 "On 1 John 2:12–14." *New Testament Studies* 6:236–41.

O'Day, G.

1992 "1, 2, and 3 John." Pp. 374–75 in *The Women's Bible Commentary*. Edited by C. Newsom and S. Ringe. London: SPCK/ Louisville: Westminster John Knox.

Oden, T. C.

2003 *The Rebirth of Orthodoxy: Signs of New Life in Christianity*. San Francisco: HarperCollins.

Orr, J. E.

1971 *Campus Aflame: Dynamic of Student Religious Revolution*. Glendale, CA: Regal.

OTP *The Old Testament Pseudepigrapha*. Edited by J. H. Charlesworth. 2 vols. Garden City, NY: Doubleday, 1983–85.

Painter, J.

2002 *1, 2, and 3 John*. Sacra pagina 18. Collegeville, MN: Liturgical Press.

Panikulam, G.

1994 *Koinonia in the New Testament: A Dynamic Expression of Christian Life*. Rome: Pontifical Biblical Institute Press.

Patrick, J.

2004 "Insights from Cicero on Paul's Reasoning in 1 Corinthians 12–14: Love Sandwich or Five Course Meal?" *Tyndale Bulletin* 55/1:43–64.

Pendrick, G.

1995 "Μονογενής." *New Testament Studies* 41:587–600.

Perkins, P.

2004 "Preserving the Testimony in the Johannine Churches." *Bible Today* 42:19–23.

Persson, A.

1990 "Some Exegetical Problems in 1 John." *Notes on Translation* 4:18–26.

Peterson, R., and M. Williams

2004 *Why I Am Not an Arminian*. Downers Grove, IL: InterVarsity.

Pfeiffer, R. H.

1951 "Facts and Faith in Biblical History." *Journal of Biblical Literature* 70:1–14.

Pilch, J., and B. Malina (eds.)

1998 *Handbook of Biblical Social Values*. Peabody, MA: Hendrickson.

Porter, S. E.

1989 *Verbal Aspect in the Greek New Testament, with Reference to Tense and Mood*. New York: Peter Lang.

1999 "The Contemporary English Version and the Ideology of Translation." Pp. 18–45 in *Translating the Bible: Problems and Prospects*. Edited by S. E. Porter and R. S. Hess. Sheffield, UK: Sheffield Academic Press.

Preuschen, E.

1963 *Griechisch-deutsches Taschenwörterbuch zum Neuen Testament*. 5th edition. Berlin: Töpelmann.

Pryor, J.

1992 *John: Evangelist of the Covenant People: The Narrative and Themes of the Fourth Gospel*. Downers Grove, IL: InterVarsity.

Reim, G.

2005 "Die Sondersprache des Evangelisten Johannes—oder: Warum spricht er so, wie er spricht?" *Biblische Zeitschrift* 49:93–102.

Reinach, S.

1930 *Orpheus: A History of Religions*. Translated by F. Simmonds. New York: Liveright.

Rensberger, D.

1997 *1 John, 2 John, 3 John*. Abingdon New Testament Commentaries. Nashville: Abingdon.

2001 *The Epistles of John*. Louisville: Westminster John Knox.

Richards, E. R.

2004 *Paul and First-Century Letter Writing*. Downers Grove, IL: InterVarsity.

Ridderbos, H. N.

1988 *Redemptive History and the New Testament Scriptures*. Translated by H. De Jongste. Revised by R. B. Gaffin Jr. Phillipsburg, NJ: Presbyterian & Reformed.

1997 *The Gospel of John: A Theological Commentary*. Translated by J. Vriend. Grand Rapids: Eerdmans.

Ritchie, M. A.

1996 *Spirit of the Rainforest: A Yanomamö Shaman's Story*. Chicago: Island Lake.

Roberts, M.

2002 "A Hermeneutic of Charity: Response to Heather Landrus." *Journal of Pentecostal Theology* 11:89–97.

Robinson, J. A. T.

1985 *The Priority of John*. Edited by J. F. Coakley. London: SCM.

Rothenberg, F. S.

1965 *Theologische Fremdwörter*. Wuppertal: Brockhaus.

Rusam, D.

1993 *Die Gemeinschaft der Kinder Gottes: Das Motiv der Gotteskindschaft und die Gemeinden der johanneischen Briefe*. Beiträge zur Wissenschaft vom Alten und Neuen Testament 7/13. Berlin: Kohlhammer.

Rutgers, L. V.

1998 "Roman Policy toward the Jews: Expulsions from the City of Rome during the First Century C.E." Pp. 93–116 in *Judaism and Christianity in First-Century Rome*. Edited by K. P. Donfried and P. Richardson. Grand Rapids: Eerdmans.

Schlatter, A.

1927 *Die Gründe der christlichen Gewißheit: Das Gebet*. Stuttgart: Calwer.

1950 *Die Briefe und die Offenbarung des Johannes*. Erläuterungen zum Neuen Testament 10. Stuttgart: Calwer.

1999 *The Theology of the Apostles*. Translated by A. J. Köstenberger. Grand Rapids: Baker Academic.

2005 *Do We Know Jesus?* Translated by A. J. Köstenberger and R. W. Yarbrough. Grand Rapids: Kregel.

Schmid, H.

2002 *Gegner im 1. Johannesbrief? Zu Konstruktion und Selbstreferenz im johanneischen Sinnsystem*. Stuttgart: Kohlhammer.

Schmithals, W.

1992 *Johannesevangelium and Johannesbriefe: Forschungsgeschichte und Analyse*. Berlin: de Gruyter.

Schnabel, E.

2004 *Early Christian Mission*. 2 vols. Downers Grove, IL: InterVarsity/Leicester, UK: Apollos.

Schnackenburg, R.

1992 *The Johannine Epistles: Introduction and Commentary*. Translated by R. Fuller and I. Fuller. New York: Crossroad.

Schnelle, U.

1998 *The History and Theology of the New Testament Writings*. Translated by M. E. Boring. Minneapolis: Fortress.

Scholtissek, K.

2004 "Die Relecture des Johannesevangeliums im ersten Johannesbrief." *Bibel und Kirche* 59:152–56.

Schreiner, T.

2001 *Paul, Apostle of God's Glory: A Pauline Theology*. Downers Grove, IL: InterVarsity/Leicester, UK: Apollos.

Schweizer, E.

1957 "Die hellenistische Komponente im neutestamentlichen *sarx*-Begriff." *Zeitschrift für die neutestamentlichen Wissenschaft* 48:237–53.

1966 "Zum religionsgeschichtlichen Hintergrund der 'Sendungsformel' Gal 4:4f., Rm 8:3f., John 3:16f., I Joh 4:9." *Zeitschrift für die neutestamentliche Wissenschaft* 57/3–4:199–210.

1989 *Theologische Einleitung in das Neue Testament*. Göttingen: Vandenhoeck & Ruprecht.

Segalla, G.

1981 "L'impeccabilità del credente in *1 Giov.* 2,29–3,10 alla luce dell'analisi strutturale." *Rivista biblica* 29/3–4:331–41.

1993 "*Holos ho kosmos* come figura dell'umanità salvata da Gesú nella 1 Gv 2,2b." *Studia patavina* 40:377–85.

Shiflett, D.

2005 *Exodus: Why Americans Are Fleeing Liberal Churches for Conservative Christianity*. New York: Sentinel.

SHNT *Scholia Hellenistica im Novum Testamentum*. London: Pickering, 1848.

Silva, M.

1995 Review of J. F. Cuadrado, *"El Viniente": Estudio exegético y teológico del vero* ἔρχεσθαι *en la literatura joánica*. *Novum Testamentum* 37:303–5.

2005 *Philippians*. 2nd edition. Baker Exegetical Commentary on the New Testament. Grand Rapids: Baker Academic.

Sloyan, G. S.

1995 *Walking in the Truth: Perseverers and Deserters: The First, Second, and Third Letters of John*. Valley Forge, PA: Trinity.

Smalley, S. S.

1978 *John: Evangelist and Interpreter*. Exeter, UK: Paternoster.

1984 *1, 2, 3 John*. Word Biblical Commentary 51. Waco: Word.

2007 *1, 2, 3, John*. Revised edition. Word Biblical Commentary 51. Nashville: Nelson.

Smith, D. M.

1991 *First, Second, and Third John*. Louisville: John Knox.

Smith, H.

2005 "Reasons for Joy." *Christian Century* 122/20 (October 4):10–11.

Soulen, R. N.

1981 *Handbook of Biblical Criticism*. 2nd edition. Atlanta: John Knox.

Soulen, R. N., and R. K. Soulen

2001 *Handbook of Biblical Criticism*. 3rd edition. Louisville: Westminster John Knox.

Spicq, C.

1958 "Notes d'exégèse johannique: La charité est amour manifeste." *Revue biblique* 65:358–70.

Stark, R.

1997 *The Rise of Christianity: How the Obscure, Marginal Jesus Movement Became the Dominant Religious Force in the Western World in a Few Centuries*. San Francisco: HarperCollins.

Stott, J. R. W.

1964 *The Epistles of John: An Introduction and Commentary*. Tyndale New Testament Commentaries 19. Grand Rapids: Eerdmans.

1988 *The Epistles of John*. Leicester, UK: InterVarsity/Grand Rapids: Eerdmans.

Stowers, S. K.

1986 *Letter Writing in Greco-Roman Antiquity*. Library of Early Christianity 5. Philadelphia: Westminster.

Strauss, D. F.

1972 *The Life of Jesus Critically Examined*. Edited by P. C. Hodgson. Translated by G. Eliot. Philadelphia: Fortress.

Strecker, G.

1996 *The Johannine Letters: A Commentary on 1, 2, and 3 John*. Translated by L. M. Maloney. Edited by H. W. Attridge. Hermeneia. Minneapolis: Fortress.

Strecker, G., and U. Schnelle (eds.)

1996 *Neuer Wettstein*, vol. 2. Berlin: de Gruyter.

Swadling, H. C.

1982 "Sin and Sinlessness in 1 John." *Scottish Journal of Theology* 35:205–11.

Tan, R. K. J.

2002 "Should We Pray for Straying Brethren? John's Confidence in 1 John 5:16–17." *Journal of the Evangelical Theological Society* 45:599–609.

TDNT *Theological Dictionary of the New Testament*. Edited by G. Kittel and G. Friedrich. Translated and edited by G. W. Bromiley. 10 vols. Grand Rapids: Eerdmans, 1964–76.

Thatcher, T.

2001 "'Water and Blood' in AntiChrist Christianity (1 John 5:6)." *Stone-Campbell Journal* 4:235–48.

Thielman, F.

2005 *Theology of the New Testament: A Canonical and Synthetic Approach*. Grand Rapids: Zondervan.

Thompson, M. M.

1992 *1–3 John*. IVP New Testament Commentary. Downers Grove, IL: InterVarsity.

Thornton, T. C. G.

1968 "Propitiation or Expiation? *Hilastērion* and *Hilasmos* in Romans and 1 John." *Expository Times* 80:53–55.

Thrall, M.

1962 *Greek Particles in the New Testament*. Grand Rapids: Eerdmans.

Thüsing, W.
1965 "Die johanneische Theologie als Verkündigung der Grösse Gottes." *Trier theologische Zeitschrift* 74:321–31.

Tiemeyer, L.-S.
2006 "God's Hidden Compassion." *Tyndale Bulletin* 57:191–213.

Trebilco, P.
2004 *The Early Christians in Ephesus from Paul to Ignatius*. Wissenschaftliche Untersuchungen zum Neuen Testament 166. Tübingen: Mohr Siebeck.

Trueman, C.
2005 "Sherlock Holmes and the Curious Case of the Missing Book." *Themelios* 30/3:1–5.

Turner, N.
1963 *A Grammar of New Testament Greek*, vol. 3: *Syntax*. Edinburgh: T&T Clark.

Turretin, F.
1992–97 *Institutes of Elenctic Theology*. 3 vols. Translated by G. M. Giger. Edited by J. T. Dennison Jr. Phillipsburg, NJ: P&R.

TWOT *Theological Wordbook of the Old Testament*. Edited by R. L. Harris. 2 vols. Chicago: Moody, 1980.

UBS[4] *The Greek New Testament*. Edited by B. Aland, K. Aland, J. Karavidopoulos, C. M. Martini, and B. M. Metzger. 4th revised edition. Stuttgart: Deutsche Bibelgesellschaft/United Bible Societies, 1993.

Uebele, W.
2001 *"Viele Verführer sind in die Welt ausgegangen": Die Gegner in den Briefen des Ignatius von Antiochien und in den Johannesbriefen*. Beiträge zur Wissenschaft vom Alten und Neuen Testament 8/11. Stuttgart: Kohlhammer.

Vanhoozer, K. J.
1998 *Is There a Meaning in This Text? The Bible, the Reader, and the Morality of Literary Knowledge*. Grand Rapids: Zondervan.

Vanhoozer, K. J., et al. (eds.)
2005 *Dictionary for Theological Interpretation of the Bible*. Grand Rapids: Baker Academic.

Vermes, G.
1997 *The Complete Dead Sea Scrolls in English*. New York: Lane/Penguin.

Wahlde, U. C. von
1990 *The Johannine Commandments: 1 John and the Struggle for the Johannine Tradition*. New York: Paulist.

2002 "The Stereotyped Structure and the Puzzling Pronouns of 1 John 2:28–3:10." *Catholic Biblical Quarterly* 64:319–38.

Wallace, D. B.
1996 *Greek Grammar beyond the Basics: An Exegetical Syntax of the New Testament*. Grand Rapids: Zondervan.

2006 "The Gospel according to Bart: A Review Article of *Misquoting Jesus* by Bart Ehrman." *Journal of the Evangelical Theological Society* 49:327–49.

Warfield, B. B.
1932 "The Spirit of God in the Old Testament." Pp. 101–29 in *The Collected Works of Benjamin B. Warfield*, vol. 3: *Biblical Doctrines*. New York: Oxford University Press.

Warner, R. (trans.)
1972 *Fall of the Roman Republic*. By Plutarch. New York: Penguin.

Washburn, D. L.
1990 "Third Class Conditions in First John." *Grace Theological Journal* 11:221–28.

Watson, D. F.
1989 "1 John 2.12–14 as Distributio, Conduplicatio, and Expolitio: A Rhetorical Understanding." *Journal for the Study of the New Testament* 35:97–110.

Weiss, B.
1887–88 *A Manual of Introduction to the New Testament*. Translated by A. J. K. Davidson. 2 vols. London: Hodder & Stoughton.

Wells, D.
1994 *No Place for Truth; or, Whatever Happened to Evangelical Theology?* Grand Rapids: Eerdmans.

2005 *Above All Earthly Pow'rs: Christ in a Postmodern World*. Grand Rapids: Eerdmans.

Wenham, J.
1994 *Christ and the Bible*. 3rd edition. Grand Rapids: Baker Academic.

Wennemer, K.
1960 "Der Christ und die Sünde nach der Lehre des ersten Johannesbriefes." *Geist und Leben* 33:370–76.

Westcott, B. F.
1881 *The Gospel according to St. John: The Authorized Version with Introduction and Notes*. London: Murray. Reprinted Grand Rapids: Eerdmans, 1978.

1883 *The Epistles of St. John: The Greek Text with Notes and Essays*. Reprinted Grand Rapids: Eerdmans, 1966.

1888 *An Introduction to the Study of the Gospels*. 7th edition. London: Macmillan.

1908 *The Gospel according to St. John: The Greek text with Introduction and Notes*. 2 vols. London: Murray.

Wilder, T. L.

2004 *Pseudonymity, the New Testament, and Deception: An Inquiry into Intention and Reception*. Lanham, MD: University Press of America.

Winter, E. F. (trans. and ed.)

1966 *Erasmus-Luther: Discourse on Free Will*. New York: Ungar.

Witherington, B., III

2006 *Letters and Homilies for Hellenized Christians*, vol. 1: *A Socio-Rhetorical Commentary on Titus, 1–2 Timothy, and 1–3 John*. Downers Grove, IL: IVP Academic/Nottingham: Apollos.

Wrede, W.

1907 "Charakter und Tendenz des Johannesevangeliums." Pp. 178–231 in Wrede's *Vorträge und Studien*. Tübingen: Mohr.

Wylen, S. M.

1996 *The Jews in the Time of Jesus*. New York: Paulist.

Yarbrough, R. W.

1983 "The Date of Papias: A Reassessment." *Journal of the Evangelical Theological Society* 26:181–91.

1995 "Divine Election in the Gospel of John." Vol. 1 / pp. 47–62 in *The Grace of God and the Bondage of the Will*. Edited by T. Schreiner and B. Ware. Grand Rapids: Baker Academic.

1996 "Eternal, Eternity." Pp. 209–12 in *Evangelical Dictionary of Biblical Theology*. Edited by Walter Elwell. Grand Rapids: Baker Academic.

2002 "1 John," "2 John," "3 John." Vol. 4 / pp. 176–227 in *Zondervan Illustrated Bible Backgrounds Commentary*. Edited by C. E. Arnold. Grand Rapids: Zondervan.

2004a "Jesus' Teaching on Hell." Pp. 67–90 in *Hell under Fire*. Edited by C. Morgan and R. Peterson. Grand Rapids: Zondervan.

2004b *The Salvation Historical Fallacy? Reassessing the History of New Testament Theology*. Leiden: Deo.

Yarid, J. R.

2003 "Reflections on the Upper Room Discourse in 1 John." *Bibliotheca sacra* 160:65–76.

Yonge, C. D. (trans.)

1993 *The Works of Philo*. Peabody, MA: Hendrickson.

Zerwick, M.

1993 *A Grammatical Analysis of the Greek New Testament*. 4th edition. Translated by M. Grosvenor. Rome: Pontifical Biblical Institute Press.

1994 *Biblical Greek Illustrated by Examples*. Translated by J. Smith. Scripta Pontificii Instituti Biblici 114. Rome: Pontifical Biblical Institute Press.

Index of Subjects

Index of Authors

Index of Greek Words

Index of Scripture and Other Ancient Writings

Old Testament

Joshua

Judges

Ruth

1 Samuel

2 Samuel

1 Kings

2 Kings

1 Chronicles

2 Chronicles

Ezra

Nehemiah

Esther

Job

Psalms

Proverbs

New Testament

Mark

Acts

Romans

1 Corinthians

2 Corinthians

1 Timothy

2 Timothy

Titus

Philemon

Hebrews

James

1 Peter

2 Peter

1 John

2 John

Old Testament Apocrypha

1 Esdras

Judith

1 Maccabees

2 Maccabees

3 Maccabees

4 Maccabees

Sirach

Tobit

Wisdom of Solomon

Old Testament Pseudepigrapha

Apocalypse of Abraham

Apocalypse of Moses

1 Enoch

2 Enoch

Jubilees

Letter of Aristeas

Odes of Solomon

Psalms of Solomon

Testament of Benjamin

Testament of Gad

Church Fathers

Miscellaneous